# A FIRST-YEAR COURSE IN CRIMINAL LAW: TRIALS, APPEALS, THEORIES

## Third Edition

*MPC mental states*
- Purposefully
- Knowingly
- Recklessly — Texting while driving after knowing it was a substantial and unjustifiable risk
- Negligence

**EDITORIAL ADVISORS**

**Rachel E. Barkow**
Segal Family Professor of Regulatory Law and Policy
Faculty Director, Center on the Administration of Criminal Law
New York University School of Law

**Erwin Chemerinsky**
Dean and Jesse H. Choper Distinguished Professor of Law
University of California, Berkeley School of Law

**Richard A. Epstein**
Laurence A. Tisch Professor of Law
New York University School of Law
Peter and Kirsten Bedford Senior Fellow
The Hoover Institution
Senior Lecturer in Law
The University of Chicago

**Ronald J. Gilson**
Charles J. Meyers Professor of Law and Business
Stanford University
Marc and Eva Stern Professor of Law and Business
Columbia Law School

**James E. Krier**
Earl Warren DeLano Professor of Law
The University of Michigan Law School

**Tracey L. Meares**
Walton Hale Hamilton Professor of Law
Director, The Justice Collaboratory
Yale Law School

**Richard K. Neumann, Jr.**
Alexander Bickel Professor of Law
Maurice A. Deane School of Law at Hofstra University

**Robert H. Sitkoff**
John L. Gray Professor of Law
Harvard Law School

**David Alan Sklansky**
Stanley Morrison Professor of Law
Faculty Co-Director, Stanford Criminal Justice Center
Stanford Law School

ASPEN SELECT SERIES

# A FIRST-YEAR COURSE IN CRIMINAL LAW: TRIALS, APPEALS, THEORIES

Third Edition

Daniel B. Yeager
Earl Warren Professor of Law
California Western

Wolters Kluwer

Copyright © 2019 CCH Incorporated. All Rights Reserved.

Published by Wolters Kluwer in New York.

Wolters Kluwer Legal & Regulatory U.S. serves customers worldwide with CCH, Aspen Publishers, and Kluwer Law International products. (www.WKLegaledu.com)

No part of this publication may be reproduced or transmitted in any form or by any means, electronic or mechanical, including photocopy, recording, or utilized by any information storage or retrieval system, without written permission from the publisher. For information about permissions or to request permissions online, visit us at www.WKLegaledu.com, or a written request may be faxed to our permissions department at 212-771-0803.

To contact Customer Service, e-mail customer.service@wolterskluwer.com,
call 1-800-234-1660, fax 1-800-901-9075, or mail correspondence to:

> Wolters Kluwer
> Attn: Order Department
> PO Box 990
> Frederick, MD 21705

Printed in the United States of America.

1 2 3 4 5 6 7 8 9 0

ISBN: 978-1-5438-0323-5

Library of Congress Cataloging-in-Publication Data

Names: Yeager, Daniel Brian, author.
Title: A first-year course in criminal law : trials, appeals, theories / Daniel B. Yeager, Earl Warren Professor of Law, California Western.
Description: Third edition. | New York : Wolters Kluwer, [2018] | Series: Aspen select series | Includes bibliographical references and index.
Identifiers: LCCN 2018032857 | ISBN 9781543803235
Subjects: LCSH: Criminal law--United States. | Torts--Untied States. | Criminal law--Study and teaching--United States.
Classification: LCC KF9219 .Y43 2018 | DDC 345.73--dc23
LC record available at https://lccn.loc.gov/2018032857

## About Wolters Kluwer Legal & Regulatory U.S.

Wolters Kluwer Legal & Regulatory U.S. delivers expert content and solutions in the areas of law, corporate compliance, health compliance, reimbursement, and legal education. Its practical solutions help customers successfully navigate the demands of a changing environment to drive their daily activities, enhance decision quality and inspire confident outcomes.

Serving customers worldwide, its legal and regulatory portfolio includes products under the Aspen Publishers, CCH Incorporated, Kluwer Law International, ftwilliam.com and MediRegs names. They are regarded as exceptional and trusted resources for general legal and practice-specific knowledge, compliance and risk management, dynamic workflow solutions, and expert commentary.

*To my wife and kids, whom I love more than life*

# TABLE OF CONTENTS

*Preface* — xiii
*Acknowledgments* — xxii
*Notes on Editing* — xxiii
*Introduction* — xxiv

## CHAPTER 1

### THE NEGLIGENCE-RECKLESSNESS DISTINCTION — 1

A. Action v. Nonaction — 1
    *People v. Emil Decina* — 3
    Questions on *Decina* — 14
    Notes on *Decina* — 18
B. Action v. Inaction: The Law of Omissions — 27
    *Robert L. Flippo, Jr., and Robert M. Flippo v. State* — 34
    Questions on *Flippo* — 38
    Notes on *Flippo* — 41

## CHAPTER 2

### THE RECKLESS-INTENTIONAL DISTINCTION — 47

A. Second-Degree Murder and Involuntary Manslaughter — 47
    *People v. Robert Lee Watson* — 52
    Questions on *Watson* — 64
    Notes on *Watson* — 66
B. Specific and General Intent — 73
    *People v. Stephen Martin Whitfield* — 76
    Questions on *Whitfield* — 97
    Notes on *Whitfield* — 100

## CHAPTER 3
## ANGER AND FEAR AS EXTENUATION — 109

| | | |
|---|---|---|
| A. | Anger as Partial Defense: Provocation/Heat of Passion | 109 |
| | *Dennis R. Greene Sr. v. Commonwealth* | 111 |
| | Questions on *Greene* | 118 |
| | Notes on *Greene* | 121 |
| | *People v. Clyde Richard Spurlin* | 137 |
| | Questions on *Spurlin* | 145 |
| | Notes on *Spurlin* | 149 |
| B. | Fear as Complete Justification: Perfect Self-Defense | 159 |
| | *People v. Bernhard Goetz* | 163 |
| | Questions on *Goetz* | 178 |
| | Notes on *Goetz* | 180 |
| C. | Fear as Partial Excuse: Imperfect Self-Defense | 183 |
| | *People v. Charles Elmore* | 186 |
| | Questions on *Elmore* | 198 |
| | Notes on *Elmore* | 199 |

## CHAPTER 4
## INCHOATE CRIMINALITY AS PARTIAL EXCUSE — 207

| | | |
|---|---|---|
| A. | The *Mens Rea* of Attempt | 207 |
| | *People v. Jackey Lee Bond* | 211 |
| | Questions on *Bond* | 218 |
| | Notes on *Bond* | 223 |
| B. | Inculpatory Mistakes: Impossible Attempts | 228 |
| | *People v. Melvin Dlugash* | 239 |
| | Questions on *Dlugash* | 250 |
| | Notes on *Dlugash* | 252 |
| C. | Solicitation and Its Relation to Attempt | 253 |
| | *Superior Court v. Ronald Decker* | 255 |
| | Questions on *Decker* | 267 |
| | Notes on *Decker* | 269 |

| | | | |
|---|---|---|---|
| D. | Conspiracy | | 277 |
| | *People v. Gregory Fred Zielesch* | | 280 |
| | Questions on *Zielesch* | | 289 |
| | Notes on *Zielesch* | | 292 |
| E. | Complicity | | 295 |
| | 1. Positive Association with the Venture | | 295 |
| | *United States v. Clayton Fountain, Thomas E. Silverstein, and Randy K. Gometz* | | 304 |
| | Questions on *Fountain* | | 307 |
| | Notes on *Fountain* | | 309 |
| | 2. Departures from the Common Scheme | | 313 |
| | *People v. Richard D. Prettyman* | | 314 |
| | Questions on *Prettyman* | | 330 |
| | Notes on *Prettyman* | | 333 |
| | 3. Transferability of Defenses from Principal to Accomplice | | 334 |
| | *People v. Ejaan Dupree McCoy* | | 335 |
| | Questions on *McCoy* | | 343 |
| | Notes on *McCoy* | | 346 |

# CHAPTER 5

## FELONY MURDER — 349

| | | | |
|---|---|---|---|
| A. | The Criteria of Felony Murder | | 349 |
| | 1. Malice or No Malice? | | 349 |
| | 2. Inherently Dangerous Felonies | | 350 |
| | 3. A Non-Assaultive Element: Merger | | 352 |
| B. | Principal and Accomplice Liability in Felony Murder | | 356 |
| | *People v. Jonathan Earl Stamp, Michael John Koory, and Billy Dean Lehman* | | 357 |
| | Questions on *Stamp* | | 362 |
| | Notes on *Stamp* | | 364 |
| C. | Provocative-Act Murder: A Tract on Causation | | 378 |
| | *People v. Israel Cervantes* | | 379 |
| | Questions on *Cervantes* | | 391 |
| | Notes on *Cervantes* | | 393 |

## CHAPTER 6

## TYING IT ALL TOGETHER: THE CASE OF THEFT     405

| | | |
|---|---|---|
| A. | Overview | 405 |
| B. | Larceny | 407 |
| C. | Embezzlement | 408 |
| D. | Larceny by Trick | 411 |
| E. | Fraud (False Pretenses) | 413 |
| | *People v. Kenneth D. Davis* | 417 |
| | Questions on *Davis* | 430 |
| | Notes on *Davis* | 435 |

| | |
|---|---|
| *Table of Cases* | 442 |
| *Table of Statutes* | 454 |
| *Table of Secondary Authorities* | 458 |
| *Index* | 463 |

# PREFACE

Twenty-five years into full-time teaching, I wrote a casebook. The occasion was my finally acknowledging that my non-trivial differences with the prominent text I had been using since 1991 began to place a sort of drag on my teaching. That I seemed constantly to be cutting against the book frustrated my students more than a little as I attempted to locate the editors' methods within my own way of thinking, writing, and talking about criminal law. My intended audience was and remains primarily first-year law students, whose professors would adopt this book for their required, one-semester course on criminal law. A secondary audience is undergraduates in pre-law programs, where criminology, sociology, or political science courses address substantive criminal law. Below I elaborate the three areas in which this casebook departs from typical casebook conventions: its structure; the way in which cases are presented; and the function and focus of questions and note materials. Thereafter, I set out the conceit of the second and now third editions.

## 1. STRUCTURE: THE INTERNAL RELATION OF ACCUSATIONS AND DEFENSES

The basic convention of casebooks in criminal law is to warm up with chapters on courts, justifications of punishment, proof beyond a reasonable doubt, legality, prosecutorial discretion, and other topics that are both relevant and of personal interest to the editors. After that, there is a striking sameness to the structure of criminal law casebooks, which tend to stick to the following order: 1) the general part of criminal law: action, nonaction, and inaction, followed by sections on *mens rea;* 2) the special part of criminal law: grave crimes (murder, manslaughter, rape); 3) more on the general part of criminal law: causation, attempt, group criminality, justifications, and excuses; and 4) more on the special part of criminal law in the form of a smattering of other crimes. This is the setup not only of, for example, *Kadish and Schulhofer*, but a dozen other major-press offerings that have fashioned themselves after that leading text.

The basic convention gets off to a confusing start by indicating that the early sections on the voluntary-act requirement, omissions, and *mens rea* are somehow distinct from the later sections on justifications (self-defense, necessity) and excuse (intoxication, insanity, duress). But they are not; nonaction, inaction, and lack of *mens rea are* excuses. Thus it is never made apparent just how the beginning and ending sections of the leading texts from the major presses relate either to each other or to the rest of the material within the texts themselves.

To correct what I take to be a structural problem with the basic convention, I avoid any indication that the inculpatory and exculpatory aspects of criminal law are distinct. Rather than treat crimes and defenses as "tubs on their own bottoms" (as Duncan Kennedy might put it), I present the defenses *within* the crimes. In other words, the book is structured to bring out that crime occurs only in the absence of fully or partially successful exculpatory pleas. Indeed, the book is built largely upon the law of homicide, which brings out the various exculpatory pleas as part of, rather than apart from, what counts as a homicide. Although homicide is the crime that organizes the book, the elements and scope of other crimes are presented within the law of homicide. For example, comprehension of assault, burglary, arson, kidnapping, mayhem, robbery, and rape is crucial to the cases I use to present the law of felony murder. Those crimes are analyzed in the cases, questions, and notes sufficiently to provide students with competency in the grammar of those crimes. If as the course nears its end any doubt about the efficacy of such an emphasis remains, the final chapter poses a chance to map those skills acquired in such a close study of homicide onto the law of theft, an exercise that will as a by-product provide a high payoff in preparation for the Bar exam of any state.

To illustrate what I mean when I say I present defenses *within* crimes, the first two cases herein do bring out the defenses of nonaction and inaction (and the narrow exceptions to those defenses); not, however, in a way that divorces the notions of nonaction and inaction from the specific criminal accusations in which their meaning is raised. The basic convention is to present human action as an *introductory* matter: an essential element of crime that operates in all cases except those where liability is based on an omission, that is, where one can be held responsible for doing nothing. The basic convention is to convey the central concepts of the general part of criminal law with no attempt at thematic unity. *Kadish & Schulhofer*, for example, relies on statutes criminalizing, *inter alia*, public drunkenness, child abuse, eloping, and malicious destruction of property as the vehicles for expressing the concepts of action, inaction, and *mens rea*. One gets the impression from this assortment of criminal prohibitions that the crimes are both separate from and subordinate to the generalized concepts on which they depend.

My approach, contrariwise, confronts the notions of action, inaction, and *mens rea* as aspects of negligent homicide, manslaughter, or murder. Whether an accused has done something or can be held responsible for doing nothing are questions that arise within, not apart from, crime. Put slightly differently, the notions of action and inaction are both inculpatory and exculpatory and have no real point in criminal law apart from cases in which there is some question about whether an action really did occur (or whether a duty-based omission can, on those facts, substitute for action). Moreover, by tying the different concepts that make up the general part of criminal law to modes of homicide rather than to a hodgepodge of unrelated crimes (that are then promptly dropped from further discussion within the text), the internal relation of the general part of criminal law to the special part can be more successfully conveyed to students.

As this casebook progresses through the law of homicide, it progresses through the defenses that determine whether a homicide, or what type of homicide, has been committed. On the one hand, this casebook is ordered to allow students to absorb the elements or grammar of negligent homicide, involuntary manslaughter, implied-malice murder, express-malice murder, premeditated and deliberate murder, provoked killings, and killings done in both imperfect and perfect self-defense. On the other hand, those modes of homicide make no doctrinal sense apart from the role that actions and intentions play in criminal responsibility. The law of homicide *is* the law of *mens rea;* they are not two separate spheres of doctrine that could somehow be studied in isolation. Accordingly, throughout the homicide materials are sustained analyses of accident and mistake, which account for the bulk of exculpatory pleas proffered by accused killers who bring about harm unintentionally. Intentional harm, too, is illuminated by a study of homicide, as is harm that is neither intentional nor quite unintentional—that is, harm brought about by what lawyers call "recklessness."

## 2. CASES: DOING AWAY WITH STICK-FIGURE ACCOUNTS OF FACTS

The basic convention of all casebooks—not just casebooks in criminal law—is to present heavily edited appellate opinions from all over the place, followed by note material that poses more questions and, in turn, alludes to more appellate opinions from all over the place. The typical rhythm or balance of the books is, for each segment of material, to put in three or four opinions of two or three pages each, followed by blurbs on about double that number of cases in notes and questions. Due to a widespread habit of over-editing, the cases feature stick-figure accounts of the facts, followed by (also edited) statements of the controlling legal rules at stake, which are then applied to the facts to produce a ruling. The notes and questions tend to present contrary rulings with no explanations, statutes whose relation to the case in question goes unexplained, and a series of new questions (to which no answers are provided in the cases or notes), some implied by the case and some entirely peripheral. Not infrequently, the questions will change a single fact from the case, ask what outcome should obtain, and then cite a case, again without elaborating. Interspersed is a dose of the musings of this or that professor, whose attempts to summarize a complex area of law are usually reduced to a few sentences. These grenades are continually lobbed over the wall throughout the text.

After reading over-edited cases and lengthy note materials, students are often in a fog as to what exactly they have just learned. Are they to take from their readings that statutes are so textually open that just about any interpretation is plausible? Or is the message that the law is all over the lot and, as a result, students must memorize a half-dozen approaches to each issue with which they are presented? Whether a case or statute is representative in any sense is rarely stated. Instead, the intention of the editors seems to be to get as many plausible positions shoe-horned into the cases and notes as possible.

To correct this difficulty with the way cases are selected and presented, this book relies on full-text opinions (though I have redacted some digressions and dissents whose ramblings stymie the momentum of the case) preceded by an introductory summary of the law that the case will address. In the selection of cases, my strong preference is for courts that attempt to reconcile their opinions with a view of criminal law that is thematically unified, respectful of the history of legislative and common-law development of the doctrine in question, yet open to reconsideration and refinement. By presenting the whole case as opposed to a bare-bones version, in-class study of the case can be much more sensitive to facts, which, when unedited, are both lengthier and harder to decode than ready-made versions, which do far too much of the students' own dirty work for them. Because we have only one case to master per session, however, the extra time spent in class on facts is available. As for the payoff of more facts, to my mind it is only a full factual account that makes agreement *or* disagreement with an opinion possible. With stick-figure accounts of facts, neither praise nor criticism of the opinion seems in order. Indeed, on stick-figure facts, conventional texts emit a vibe more consistent with a hornbook than a casebook: rules get stated, but not applied in a specific context in which their application can be fully appreciated.

Another payoff of full-text opinions results from including issues that may be peripheral to the narrow question meant to be isolated for study. That way, students come to see how appellate litigation features multiple issues to be integrated, prioritized, and juggled within a single discussion. For example, cases herein do often feature, as they must, challenges to the factual sufficiency of the evidence and challenges to a trial judge's choice and phrasing of jury instructions. But in addition to those essential bases of criminal appeals, cases herein include challenges to the admissibility of evidence (based on, e.g., unduly prejudicial content, physician-patient or spousal privilege, or a confession coerced from defendant by police), claims of perjury on the part of a prosecution witness, or alternative theories of liability that were covered earlier in the course or have yet to be covered. This way, students learn the whole case, not just a boiled-down version, while benefitting at once from review of familiar material and sneak peeks at future material that can be made easier by repeated passes at the same ideas, though with different levels of intensity.

Finally, full-text opinions confront standards of review in ways that heavily edited opinions slough off. For instance, when reviewing a trial court's ruling on probable cause to charge a defendant, or the factual sufficiency of a jury verdict, appellate opinions sometimes devote significant energy to evaluating not merely whether the ruling below was erroneous, but whether it was *plainly* erroneous. Indeed, much disagreement in cases that generate separate opinions is not merely about whether the jury was right or wrong, but about whether the jury, if wrong, was nonetheless rational in its application of the facts to the instructions. As crucial as standards of review are to appellate litigation, their importance is easily diminished by over-edited opinions.

## 3. CASEBOOK AS TEACHING TOOL: QUESTIONS AND NOTES

One frustration in teaching any audience is the gap between the intended and actual progress made by the class. Too often the discussion bogs down at levels that are below the professor's expectations, which, as a result, are adjusted downward. But in some instances, the under-performance of the class owes to the students' difficulties in anticipating or preparing for the more difficult content. And it's not their fault: too often that more difficult content is just adumbrated in the cases, questions, and notes (in a way I referred to in Part 2 above as lobbing grenades over the wall).

### A. Questions: Raising the Bar by Scripting Class Dialogue

Once the facts, procedural history, and disposition of the case are brought out in dialogue with students, I pose the questions that follow each case to the students in the order in which they appear in the text. This takes away, favorably in my view, much of the mystery of class discussion, which is more likely to flourish when the students have prepared their answers to the questions. If the questions are sensibly ordered and pitched at the right level of specificity and sophistication, discussions will elevate rather than leave students, who otherwise may feel that the questions come from out of nowhere, to attempt to decode the questions on the fly.

The answers to most of the questions are in the cases. The process of extracting that information will in the end make the students better and closer readers; so too will the students begin to pick up on the sorts of questions that *count* in close readings of cases. By design, some of the questions are real softballs, lobbed in to highlight key information and also to provide some momentum in the question–answer dialogue, which will inevitably snag at least a little on some of the harder questions. The answers to the harder questions are not in the cases, or not in them in the same literal way. Those harder questions require a different sort of effort, which repays not just an attentive reading of the cases, but in addition, careful thought about the question plus absorption of the introductory materials preceding the cases and notes that follow.

**B. Notes: Elaborating, Not Repudiating, the Cases and Questions**

Following each set of questions is a set of notes that provide information and explanations of the doctrinal implications of the cases. In addition, the notes put into context the legal maneuverings and procedural niceties with which students are likely to be unfamiliar. These notes provide, little by little, a sufficiently detailed depiction of police investigation, charges, pre-trial motions, verdicts, judgments, post-trial motions, sentencing, and appeals. That way the cases can make sense procedurally in their live adversarial context rather than function simply as hornbook proclamations about legal rules. More specifically, the book contains sufficiently complete discourses on procedural matters such as: charging (probable cause, complaints, informations, preliminary hearings, grand juries), pre-trial motions, Double Jeopardy and other doctrines of past adjudication (as in issue preclusion), rights to counsel and trial by jury, trial courts' sua sponte obligations, interlocutory appeals, general v. special verdicts, a range of sentencing matters (determinate v. indeterminate, concurrent v. consecutive, executed v. suspended, first-offender v. recidivist, incarcerative v. probationary, probation v. parole, proportionality), harmless error, burdens of proof (including presumptions), direct appellate v. collateral attacks on convictions or sentences (and, accordingly, the operation of discretionary review and removal jurisdiction) to name just a few. Indeed, I try to take nothing for granted regarding what is being taught or absorbed in other classrooms: there are notes elaborating, for example, the meaning and operation of case captions, differences between civil and criminal litigation, and the functions of trial judges and magistrates.

Rather than blurbs taken from dozens of cases, statutes, and academic commentary, the notes usually include a detailed version of just one pertinent case (sometimes more), the function of which is always set forth. As for statutes, they are included or embellished in the notes only when they add something to the cases themselves, which may or may not include statutory texts. For example, a case may set forth a relevant statute, but if the statute is terse, or makes no mention of punishment, then jury instructions or additional statutory material will appear in the notes. Frequently California decisions, for example, allude to the Model Penal Code (though California law is based on its own 1872 Penal Code), as do New York decisions, given that the revised New York Penal Code of 1967 was a reaction to the first official draft of the Model Penal Code. But I do not reproduce every Model Penal Code provision in the notes or elsewhere. Because there is no payoff for saddling students with the responsibility of absorbing superfluous data, I present only those Model Penal Code provisions whose take on the law diverges in a remarkable way from the approach presented in the principal case at hand. In place of gobs of academic commentary, the secondary materials I provide in my notes tend to be immediately pertinent to the cases after which they appear. They contain, for example, excerpts from the trial transcript and intermediate appellate court ruling (in cases that are in the state's high court), plus subsequent legislative and precedential history of the case if the ruling is reversed or modified. And of course there is gossip about the litigants, whose post-ruling predicaments are always of interest to the students.

This book is considerably shorter than the conventional books in introductory criminal law, which are more than twice its length and, as such, impose more than twice the reading load that can be accomplished in a 14-week, three-credit course. The excess bulk of those texts leads to teacher's manuals that propose a series of alternative syllabi, each omitting more than half the book's content from the plan. While that sort of cover-all-bases approach is popular, it does betray a lack of thematic unity to the books. In place of unity is a flexibility sufficient to accommodate the intentions, preferences, and limitations of whoever is teaching from the book. This book, on the other hand, proposes just one structure, and is meant to be read in its entirety in a series of 15-ish-page assignments.

## 4. THE CONCEIT OF THE SECOND AND THIRD EDITIONS

Teaching from the first edition for five semesters brought out the following correctible shortcomings: First, introductions to each chapter and sub-section needed more patient explication, both generalized and detailed. Second, some questions and notes needed editing/re-ordering to improve flow and avoid unintended redundancies. Third, when thematic redundancies *were* intentional, a lack of internal cross-referencing impeded students from the benefits of being alerted to the fact that topics *are* recurring. Fourth, that part of Chapter 3 on the role of fear in homicide cases needed reduced reliance on a lengthy disquisition on deadly force in the context of policing, and increased emphasis, through a full-text opinion, on the function of mental illness. Lastly, because legal argument, unlike philosophy, is a series of assertions followed up by supporting authority, too infrequently were those authorities made explicit through searchable citations. Some 10% longer as a result, the second edition manifested an earnest effort to rectify all five of the above-mentioned shortcomings of the first edition.

This third edition reveals another stab at editing my introductory explanations, questions, and notes (including both the addition and redaction of some note cases), plus an elaborated index, while correcting technical errors of prior editions and accounting for intervening changes in the law.

I am grateful for the excellent research assistance of Jenna Gamble, who worked on the first edition, Catherine Mineo and Vincent Salminen, who worked on the second, and Hana Maazaoui-Willard, who worked on the third.

DBY
May 1, 2018
San Diego, CA

## Textbook Resources

The companion website for *Criminal Law: Homicide and Exculpation*, available at www.aspenlawschool.com/books/yeager_crimlaw, includes additional resources for instructors.

# ACKNOWLEDGMENTS

Permission to reprint excerpts from the following works is gratefully acknowledged:

J.L. Austin, *A Plea for Excuses: The Presidential Address*, Proceedings of the Aristotelian Society, New Series, Vol. 57 (1956–1957), pp. 1-30 (Blackwell Publishing on behalf of The Aristotelian Society). Reprinted by courtesy of the Editor of the Aristotelian Society: © 1956.

J.L. Austin, Sense and Sensibilia (G.J. Warnock, ed.), (Oxford University Press, 1962). By permission of Oxford University Press.

J.L. Austin, *Three Ways of Spilling Ink*, The Philosophical Review, Vol. 75, No. 4 (1966), pp. 427-440. Reprinted by permission of Duke University.

Thomas E. Baker, *Preview of United States Supreme Court Cases* 475-85 ©2004. Published in Preview, 2004, by the American Bar Association. Reproduced with permission. All rights reserved. This information or any portion thereof may not be copied or disseminated in any form or by any means or stored in an electronic database or retrieval system without the express written consent of the American Bar Association or the copyright holder.

R.A. Duff, *Criminal Attempts* (Oxford University Press, 1997). By permission of Oxford University Press.

H.L.A. Hart, Punishment and Responsibility (Oxford University Press, 1968). By permission of Oxford University Press. Reprinted from *The Jubliee Lectures of the Faculty of Law, University of Sheffield (1960)* (O.R. Marshall, ed.), by permission of the publishers Stevens and Sons and Tamara Hervey, successor to The University of Sheffield and the Dean of the Faculty of Law.

# NOTES ON EDITING CASES

The cases herein indicate redacted material by ellipses, except for the redaction of supporting authorities and footnotes, which are not indicated. My additions to the text of cases are bracketed. Footnotes that are retained within the text of cases retain their original numbering. Editor's footnotes appear outside the cases and are lettered (not numbered), starting anew with each chapter. Citations have been conformed to a hybrid of the Bluebook and California Style Manual; parallel cites are redacted. I have taken the liberty to spell out rather than abbreviate the names of scholarly journals as well as any other references not easily ascertained when in a shortened form. References to the California Penal Code and California Jury Instructions (Criminal) are to the West imprint, specified by year of publication when relevant. References to the Model Penal Code and Commentaries are to the 1985 Official Draft unless otherwise noted.

# INTRODUCTION

This book attempts to summarize both the general and special parts of criminal law as illustrated in appellate cases primarily involving homicide and theft, and other crimes secondarily.

The general part of criminal law is that part of criminal law which is common to, or part of, all criminal cases. For example, that harm caused accidentally or mistakenly is for the most part *not* the concern of criminal law, but that harm caused intentionally or knowingly *is* the concern of criminal law, is a notion belonging to the general part of criminal law. Likewise does it belong to the general part of criminal law that crime can on the one hand be attempted, helped, or the target of a conspiracy, or, on the other hand, be defended as justified, excused, or a combination of the two. The special part of criminal law, contrariwise, is concerned with specific crimes such as murder, theft, rape, and the like. This book presents cases, statutes, and jury instructions within the general and special parts of criminal law, the enforcement of which is meant to protect persons and their property from unwelcomed aggressions by, among others, muggers, thieves, and rapists.

Cases are the primary source of law not just in law school, but in law, period. Basic civics tells us that legislatures make laws and courts interpret them. But statutes are drafted at too high a level of generality or abstraction to serve alone as authoritative pronouncements of law except in the easier cases that arise, where the facts at issue pose no interpretive difficulties. For example, it is easy to say that a murder occurs when a contract-killing is videotaped and confessed to by a mentally competent defendant in an un-coerced interrogation. But it is not so easy when defendant insists, with good but not overwhelming cause, that the killing was accidental, provoked, or in self-defense.

As many as 95% of all criminal charges are settled without trial. *See* Stephanos Bibas, *Regulating the Plea-Bargaining Market: From Caveat Emptor to Consumer Protection*, 99 California Law Review 1117, 1138 (2011). Most cases that *are* tried are difficult because they present facts at the borders of the statutes that regulate the disputes. If the facts did not pose a close call, they likely would be settled, that is, resolved by plea bargain. When the applicability or meaning of a statute in a dispute poses a close call, a court must interpret the statute to determine its applicability or meaning. Once a court interprets a statute, the court's ruling becomes precedent that will bind other courts in identical or sufficiently similar factual circumstances so long as 1) the court's ruling is explained in a written opinion; 2) the other courts are in the same jurisdiction as the court issuing the ruling; and 3) no other court of the same or higher authority in a controlling jurisdiction issues a contrary written ruling.

The cases herein are appellate opinions from the state courts of Arkansas, California, Illinois, Kentucky, and New York, plus one federal case, that being brought by a prisoner seeking to upset his conviction for having murdered, among others, a guard in a federal penitentiary. Although there is a federal criminal code in addition to the criminal codes of each state, the protection of persons and their property from criminal aggressions has long been the province of states, though this is less true today than it was a half-century ago.

Not only are most criminal-law interpretations performed by state courts, not federal courts, but most *binding* criminal-law interpretations are performed by appellate courts, not trial courts. This is because unlike appellate courts, trial-court rulings bind only the parties, not other litigants or courts at any level. As a consequence, state trial courts tend not to explicate their opinions. They announce a disposition, outcome, or what lawyers call a "holding" of the dispute; that is, they *decide* cases, but rarely do they even cite, let alone explain, the relevant legal rules that support their holdings. In other words, a trial-court judgment, whether civil or criminal, is announced but rarely justified. Instead, they are typically terse, unelaborated holdings, e.g., "defendant is liable for medical malpractice and must pay plaintiff $1,000,000 in general and special damages," or "defendant is guilty of petty theft and subject to supervised release for a term of three years."

From such trial-court judgments the losing party often appeals. In a civil case, the decision to appeal is based largely on economics. A party who loses a civil trial asks: what are my odds of winning the appeal? How much will the appeal cost me if I win? How much if I lose? Will my attorney's fees squander the anticipated gains of my victory (or can I charge my attorney's fees to the other side)? Can I end up responsible for the other side's attorney's fees if I lose on appeal? Apart from economic costs, if I lose, will the time and annoyance of the appeal only make matters worse? Or maybe matters will be made worse even if I *win* my appeal. For example, suppose I succeed in getting the damages judgment against me vacated, and in my retrial of identical facts, a second jury awards the plaintiff even more money than the first jury did. Maybe I should just cut my losses and let it go.

In a criminal case, oppositely, the Federal Constitution places two quite different pressures on the decision to appeal that are not present in civil cases: first, for the defendant who is convicted at trial, Supreme Court interpretations of the due process and equal protection clauses state that there are no costs to an appeal (*an appeal, not numerous appeals*) to defendants who cannot afford to pay for filing fees, trial transcripts, and an appellate lawyer to research, brief, and argue the appeal. Each of these tools is provided to indigent appellants at the State's expense. Thus, it is not surprising that convicted defendants—most of whom are indigent—customarily take advantage of subsidized appellate litigation without the cost-benefit analyses that civil litigants engage in, as detailed above. Second, the prosecution's opportunities to appeal are severely limited by the constitutional ban on Double Jeopardy, that is, the guarantee against multiple trials or punishments for the same offense. Unlike indigent criminal defendants, the State is unconstrained by the costs of appeal since taxpayers pay the tab. But the State cannot appeal an acquittal if the remedy sought by a successful appeal will require that the acquitted defendant be retried for the same offense—this time free of the error that provided the basis of the prosecution's appeal in the first place.

Three of our principal cases are prosecution appeals brought pre-trial to reinstate dismissed charges. The remainder of our principal cases are appeals brought by indigent defendants dissatisfied with their convictions and sentences. Despite my inclusion of principal cases from other states, the book emphasizes California cases without at all dedicating itself to the mastery of the laws of any single jurisdiction. It just so happens that because California has both a very large population and impressively high crime rates in some areas, appellate litigation abounds, which means a lot of law is made here. In addition, the principles of California criminal law are very closely aligned with the multistate portion of most state licensing exams. And, most importantly, decisions of the California Supreme Court, more than any other court apart from the New York Court of Appeals (the next-best represented court in this casebook) attempt in earnest to locate their rulings within a significant precedential history. Those decisions certainly can be praised and blamed, but not for saying too little or failing to engage the real issues.

Every criminal case involves the interpretation of a statute. In most cases, the pertinent language of the statute is presented in the case. Still, there is a small collection of stand-alone statutes in the questions and notes of this book. I include them because they are important and, for one reason or another, the text of the statute is not presented in the case to which they relate. This small collection of statutes is from the various criminal codes that can be fairly labeled versions of the Pennsylvania Criminal Code of 1794, the California Penal Code of 1872, and the Model Penal Code. The Model Penal Code is an important piece of sample or idealized legislation finalized by the American Law Institute in 1962, since adopted in various iterations by some two-thirds of the United States.

So too have I included examples from the Federal Criminal Code, which has inexorably expanded since the federal government's interest in crime control has itself inexorably expanded since the Crimes Act of 1790, when federal crime was a very narrow notion. The Framers of the Constitution had empowered Congress to crack down on very few activities: counterfeiting, piracy, offenses against the law of nations, and treason, to which the Crimes Act of 1790 added a few common-law crimes, like larceny and murder, if committed on a federal enclave. But the ordinary robbery, larceny, or homicide was the sole province of the states. Even today, crime control is largely the business of localities, who employ 765,000 sworn personnel authorized to make arrests and carry guns, compared with 120,000 in the federal government, whose impact is felt mainly in enforcing drug and immigration laws. Indeed, today nearly half of federal law enforcers work for the Department of Homeland Security.

Because criminal statutes, state or federal, are drafted in a way that leaves their meaning somewhat open, at the close of evidence in criminal cases, lawyers suggest instructions to judges to pass on to jurors, whose task is to apply those statutes, the meaning of which is at times too open to pin down. Jury instructions are worded in a systematic or elemental way so that the sometimes slippery legal language of the pertinent statutes they address can be broken down for jurors. After a while, an instruction can work its way into a pattern jury instruction book, which reflects years, sometimes decades, of lawyers and judges refining what they take to be the most accurate statement of the scope and meaning of a statute. Those instructions are sometimes challenged by parties who contend that the instruction misrepresents the statute. When an appellate court upholds an instruction as an accurate statement of the statute, the appellate opinion so holding gives the instruction the precedential force of law. With that in mind, our book contains pattern jury instructions whenever our understanding of a crime or defense would profit from attention to what lawyers call "black letter law," that is, elementized attempts at making application of the open wordings of statutes as mechanistic as possible. Unlike the appellate opinions and statutes we will study, the pattern jury instructions enclosed herein are meant to boil down legal rules in a way that is comparatively unencumbered by legalese.

# CHAPTER 1

## The Negligence-Recklessness Distinction

### A. ACTION V. NONACTION

If criminal law regulates untoward action that causes or threatens unwelcomed harm, then it may repay our efforts to meditate on what, exactly, an action is.

It makes good sense that the law requires that criminals actually *do* something before we call them "criminals." The requirement that criminality entails action is almost without exception: only in the rarest circumstances is someone punished for doing absolutely nothing, as where parents neglect rather than nourish their child or a lifeguard refuses to save a drowning swimmer. In fact, the requirement of untoward human action is so embedded in the notion of criminal liability that asking whether what someone has done is an action is a question that arises sparingly in criminal litigation.

More typically, when victims get strangled, raped, kidnapped, or robbed, there is no question about whether what the murderer, rapist, kidnapper, or thief has done counts as an action. Rather, questions arise about the extent of what was done, the way in which it was done, and whether the actor knew that what he was doing was likely to end up causing harm to another. In those cases there is typically no occasion to confront the question, "what is an action?" Understandably, the question arises only when what happened *merely* happened, but was not *quite* done, performed, or committed as an upshot or consequence of human action as we understand it.

The idea that action is essential to responsibility is itself straightforward enough; an unconscious person is not responsible for what he or she does since the notion of "doing" in such cases is itself all out of joint. What is far from straightforward, however, is identifying the conditions of nonactions, that is, when what someone has done was not really *done* at all, but is more like an earthquake or other happening or occurrence than it is like an action. Asking "was that an action?" can lead, at least for some, to the question, "what is an action?"

So what *is* an action? If the question is put to us, it may be the sort of term of that is best defined negatively, by identifying the conditions that negate action, e.g., unconsciousness and the like. But there is also a positive sense to the term or concept of action—a sort of future-looking term usually coupled with an infinitive, as in, "I intend to do *X*." It may be most helpful, I suspect, to recognize that all actions have intentions. It is this idea of knowing what you are doing—of having a plan (though nothing so concrete as a plan, necessarily)—that characterizes all human action. While sometimes the plan or intention misfires, such as when you mean to bring about one result (say, throw a ball to a friend while playing catch) and another occurs (say, you accidentally throw the ball through a neighbor's window), that at least something was intended and done is a prerequisite of human action.

Accordingly, criminal law's so-called voluntary-act requirement may itself be a little misleading because it fails to suggest just how narrow the circumstances are in which actions may somehow be involuntary. For example, robbery victims involuntarily give over their property to their robbers. In such cases, it would make no sense to say that robbery victims do so either intentionally or voluntarily; the constraint placed on their will makes their surrendering their property rational, but neither intentional nor voluntary. Yet there is action in such cases. Unlike unconscious agents, robbery victims know what they are doing, yet they are acting under duress. Their parting with their property against their will is an action that is coerced, not a mere happening or occurrence.

It is important to distinguish coerced or involuntary action from nonaction that involves involuntary *movements*, not actions. A close consideration of *People v. Decina*, 2 N.Y.2d 133 (1956) should facilitate our making such judgments. There, defendant was convicted of four counts of homicide arising out of a traffic mishap, but defended that he did not "do" it; that, while he did run over four pedestrians, he did so while he was unconscious due to the onset of an epileptic seizure. In reading the case, consider both whether Decina engaged in action as we know it, and the extent to which the answer to that question determines whether he should remain on the hook for what happened.

# COURT OF APPEALS OF NEW YORK
*THE PEOPLE OF THE STATE OF NEW YORK, APPELLANT-RESPONDENT*
*V.*
*EMIL DECINA, RESPONDENT-APPELLANT*
NOV. 29, 1956

FROESSEL, Judge

At about 3:30 p. m. on March 14, 1955, defendant was driving in a northerly direction on Delaware Avenue in Buffalo. The portion of Delaware Avenue here involved is 60 feet wide. At a point south of an overhead viaduct of the Erie Railroad, defendant's car swerved to the left, across the center line in the street, so that it was completely in the south lane, traveling 35 to 40 miles per hour.

It then veered sharply to the right, crossing Delaware Avenue and mounting the easterly curb at a point beneath the viaduct and continued thereafter at a speed estimated to have been about 50 or 60 miles per hour or more. During this latter swerve, a pedestrian testified that he saw defendant's hand above his head; another witness said he saw defendant's left arm bent over the wheel, and his right hand extended towards the right door.

A group of six schoolgirls were walking north on the easterly sidewalk of Delaware Avenue, two in front and four slightly in the rear, when defendant's car struck them from behind. One of the girls escaped injury by jumping against the wall of the viaduct. The bodies of the children struck were propelled northward onto the street and the lawn in front of a coal company, located to the north of the Erie viaduct on Delaware Avenue. Three of the children, 6 to 12 years old, were found dead on arrival by the medical examiner, and a fourth child, 7 years old, died in a hospital two days later as a result of injuries sustained in the accident.

After striking the children, defendant's car continued on the easterly sidewalk, and then swerved back onto Delaware Avenue once more. It continued in a northerly direction, passing under a second viaduct before it again veered to the right and remounted the easterly curb, striking and breaking a metal lamppost. With its horn blowing steadily apparently because defendant was stooped over the steering wheel, the car proceeded on the sidewalk until it finally crashed through a brick wall of a grocery store, injuring at least one customer and causing considerable property damage.

When the car came to a halt in the store, with its horn still blowing, several fires had been ignited. Defendant was stooped over in the car and was bobbing a little. To one witness he appeared dazed, to another unconscious, lying back with his hands off the wheel. Various people present shouted to defendant to turn off the ignition of his car, and "within a matter of seconds the horn stopped blowing and the car did shut off."

Defendant was pulled out of the car by bystanders and laid down on the sidewalk. To a policeman who came on the scene he appeared "injured, dazed"; another witness said "he looked as though he was knocked out, and his arm seemed to be bleeding." An injured customer in the store, after receiving first aid, pressed defendant for an explanation of the accident and he told her: "I blacked out from the bridge."

When police arrived, defendant attempted to rise, staggered and appeared dazed and unsteady. When informed that he was under arrest, and would have to accompany the police to the station house, he resisted and, when he tried to get away, was handcuffed. The foregoing evidence was adduced by the People, and is virtually undisputed. Defendant did not take the stand nor did he produce any witnesses.

From the police station defendant was taken to the E. J. Meyer Memorial Hospital, a county institution, arriving at 5:30 p.m. The two policemen who brought defendant to the hospital instructed a police guard stationed there to guard defendant, and to allow no one to enter his room. A pink slip was brought to the hospital along with defendant, which read:

> Buffalo Police Department, Inter-Departmental Correspondence. To Superintendent of Meyer Memorial Hospital, from Raymond, J. Smith, Captain, Precinct 17. Subject, Re: One Emil A. Decina. Sir: We are forwarding one Emil A. Decina, age 33, of 87 Sidney Street, to your hospital for examination on the recommendation of District Attorney John Dwyer and Commissioner Joseph A. De Cillis. Mr. Decina was involved in a fatal accident at 2635 Delaware Avenue at 3:40 p.m. this date. There were three fatalities, and possibly four. A charge will be placed against Mr. Decina after the investigation has been completed.

On the evening of that day, after an intern had visited and treated defendant and given orders for therapy, Dr. Wechter, a resident physician in the hospital and a member of its staff, came to his room. The guard remained, according to his own testimony, in the doorway of the room; according to Dr. Wechter, the guard remained outside, 6 or 7 feet away. He observed both Dr. Wechter and defendant on the bed, and he stated that he heard the entire conversation between them, although he did not testify as to its content. Before Dr. Wechter saw defendant, he read the hospital admission record, and had either seen or committed to him the contents of the pink slip. While he talked with defendant, another physician came in and left.

After giving some additional brief testimony, but before he was permitted to relate a conversation he had with defendant which was contained in the hospital notes, defense counsel was permitted with some restriction to cross-examine the doctor. During that cross-examination, the doctor testified that he saw defendant in his professional capacity as a doctor, but that he did not see him for purposes of treatment. However, it was shown that at a former trial he stated that the information he obtained was pursuant to his duties as a physician; the purpose of his examination was to diagnose defendant's condition; he questioned defendant for the purpose of treatment, among other things; and that in the hospital they treat any patient that comes in.

He further testified at this trial that ordinarily the resident on the floor is in charge of the floor; that defendant was treated by more than one doctor; and that he took the medical history. At the previous trial, when he was asked whether he represented the police and the district attorney, he replied: "I don't know. I just [saw] him as a patient coming into the hospital." He now stated that he saw defendant as part of his routine duties at the hospital; that he would say that defendant "was a patient"; that he was not retained as an expert by the district attorney or the Police Department, and was paid nothing to examine defendant; that his examination was solely in the course of his duties as a resident physician on the staff of the hospital; and that, whether or not he had a slip from the police, so long as that man was on his floor as a patient, he would have examined him.

He also stated he never told defendant that he had any pink slip, or that he was examining him for the district attorney or the Police Department, or that defendant was under no duty to talk, or that anything he said might be used against him at a later trial. He further testified that he was a doctor at the hospital at which defendant was a patient; that he personally wrote items in the hospital record after his conversations with defendant; that he saw defendant three times; that he was asked by the district attorney to submit a voucher for consideration by the comptroller's office, but that was not done until after the first trial. He also stated at this trial that the discharge summary was made out by him, and that of the four sheets of progress notes, at least the first two sheets were in his handwriting.

The direct examination was then continued, the doctor being permitted to state the conversation with defendant over objection and exception. He asked defendant how he felt and what had happened. Defendant, who still felt a little dizzy or blurry, said that as he was driving he noticed a jerking of his right hand, which warned him that he might develop a convulsion, and that as he tried to steer the car over to the curb he felt himself becoming unconscious, and he thought he had a convulsion. He was aware that children were in front of his car, but did not know whether he had struck them.

Defendant then proceeded to relate to Dr. Wechter his past medical history, namely, that at the age of 7 he was struck by an auto and suffered a marked loss of hearing. In 1946 he was treated in this same hospital for an illness during which he had some convulsions. Several burr holes were made in his skull and a brain abscess was drained. Following this operation defendant had no convulsions from 1946 through 1950. In 1950 he had four convulsions, caused by scar tissue on the brain. From 1950 to 1954 he experienced about 10 or 20 seizures a year, in which his right hand would jump although he remained fully conscious. In 1954, he had 4 or 5 generalized seizures with loss of consciousness, the last being in September 1954, a few months before the accident. Thereafter he had more hospitalization, a spinal tap, consultation with a neurologist, and took medication daily to help prevent seizures.

On the basis of this medical history, Dr. Wechter made a diagnosis of Jacksonian epilepsy, and was of the opinion that defendant had a seizure at the time of the accident. Other members of the hospital staff performed blood tests and took an electroencephalogram during defendant's three-day stay there. The testimony of Dr. Wechter is the only testimony before the trial court showing that defendant had epilepsy, suffered an attack at the time of the accident, and had knowledge of his susceptibility to such attacks.

*initial verdict*

Defendant was indicted and charged with violating §1053-a of the Penal Law. Following his conviction, after a demurrer to the indictment was overruled, the Appellate Division, while holding that the demurrer was properly overruled, reversed on the law, the facts having been "examined" and found "sufficient." It granted a new trial upon the ground that the "transactions between the defendant and Dr. Wechter were between physician and patient for the purpose of treatment and that treatment was accomplished," and that evidence thereof should not have been admitted. From its determination both parties have appealed.

We turn first to the subject of defendant's cross-appeal, namely, that his demurrer should have been sustained, since the indictment here does not charge a crime. The indictment states essentially that defendant, knowing "that he was subject to epileptic attacks or other disorder rendering him likely to lose consciousness for a considerable period of time," was culpably negligent "in that he consciously undertook to and did operate his Buick sedan on a public highway" and "while so doing" suffered such an attack which caused said automobile "to travel at a fast and reckless rate of speed, jumping the curb and driving over the sidewalk," causing the death of 4 persons. In our opinion, this clearly states a violation of §1053-a of the Penal Law. The statute does not require that a defendant must deliberately intend to kill a human being, for that would be murder. Nor does the statute require that he knowingly and consciously follow the precise path that leads to death and destruction. It is sufficient, we have said, when his conduct manifests a "disregard of the consequences which may ensue from the act, and indifference to the rights of others." No clearer definition, applicable to the hundreds of varying circumstances that may arise, can be given. Under a given state of facts, whether negligence is culpable is a question of law. *People v. Angelo*, 246 N.Y. 451, 457 (1927).

Assuming the truth of the indictment, as we must on a demurrer, this defendant knew he was subject to epileptic attacks and seizures that might strike at any time. He also knew that a moving motor vehicle uncontrolled on public highway is a highly dangerous instrumentality capable of unrestrained destruction. With this knowledge, and without anyone accompanying him, he deliberately took a chance by making a conscious choice of a course of action, in disregard of the consequences which he knew might follow from his conscious act, and which in this case did ensue. How can we say as a matter of law that this did not amount to culpable negligence within the meaning of §1053-a?

To hold otherwise would be to say that a man may freely indulge himself in liquor in the same hope that it will not affect his driving, and if it later develops that ensuing intoxication causes dangerous and reckless driving resulting in death, his unconsciousness or involuntariness at that time would relieve him from prosecution under the statute. His awareness of a condition which he knows may produce such consequences as here, and his disregard of the consequences, renders him liable for culpable negligence, as the courts below have properly held. To have a sudden sleeping spell, an unexpected heart or other disabling attack, without any prior knowledge or warning thereof, is an altogether different situation, and there is simply no basis for comparing such cases with the flagrant disregard manifested here.

It is suggested in the dissenting opinion that a new approach to licensing would prevent such disastrous consequences upon our public highways. But the mere possession of a driver's license is no defense to a prosecution under §1053-a; nor does it assure continued ability to drive during the period of the license. Section 1053-a places a personal responsibility on each driver of a vehicle whether licensed or not and not upon a licensing agency. Accordingly, the Appellate Division properly sustained the lower court's order overruling the demurrer.

The appeal by the People challenges the determination of the Appellate Division that the testimony of Dr. Wechter was improperly admitted in contravention of §352 of the Civil Practice Act, which states that a physician "shall not be allowed to disclose any information which he acquired in attending a patient in a professional capacity, and which was necessary to enable him to act in that capacity." Two questions are raised by the People's appeal. The first is whether a physician-patient relationship existed between Dr. Wechter and defendant, and, if so, whether the communications made by defendant to him were necessary for the doctor to act in his professional capacity. The second is whether the presence of the police guard in the doorway of the room destroys any privilege arising under §352 and permits the doctor to testify. Defendant, as the party asserting the privilege, bears the burden of showing its application in the present case. He claims to have sustained the burden on the basis of [the People's] own evidence previously outlined.

[The People] contend that no professional relationship arose because the doctor was sent by the district attorney to examine, not treat, the defendant, and in fact he did not treat him. The cases upon which [the People] rely are readily distinguishable from the one now before us. In *People v. Schuyler*, 106 N.Y. 298 (1887), for example, a jail physician was allowed to testify, over an objection based on the predecessor statute to §352 of the Civil Practice Act, to his observations of the prisoner's mental condition. There was no evidence that the prisoner was ill, or that he was attended by, treated, or required any treatment by said jail physician while in custody.

In *People v. Koerner*, 154 N.Y. 355, 365-66 (1897), testimony of physicians was admitted, but in each case the defendant was explicitly informed that the physician was not acting in his capacity as a doctor. There are additional instances where the testimony of physicians who held examinations in jails was admitted, since no evidence was adduced from which it might be found that the defendants could reasonably have regarded the physician as acting in a professional capacity towards them.

[The People] further contend that there can be no finding of physician-patient relation in this case because there is no evidence that Dr. Wechter actually treated defendant. But the cases relied on by [the People] properly hold that where a physician does treat a person, regardless of whether it is at his request, or with his consent, the relation arises, but they do not hold the converse. In determining whether information necessary for treatment is privileged, the question as to whether actual treatment is undertaken is not decisive.

Although Dr. Wechter testified that he personally did not treat defendant, he admitted that other doctors and interns in the hospital did treat him for Jacksonian epilepsy. He himself made that diagnosis. To say that where there is division of duties among the staff, the relation of physician and patient does not arise with regard to those members of the staff who do not actually treat the patient is unsound. It would place upon §352 strictures that are opposed to our oft-expressed view that the statute is to be liberally construed.

It is apparent that the information here given by the defendant was necessary for his treatment. Those cases allowing disclosure by physicians of information related to them by their patients deal with such nonprofessional matters as details of an accident entirely unrelated to treatment, or facts such as a layman might observe. Evidence of a prior medical history of a disease for which defendant was treated cannot be said to be information unnecessary for treatment. The communication is therefore within the conditions set forth in §352.

The second question will now be dealt with. The problem here is what effect, if any, the presence of the police guard, pursuant to the orders of the district attorney, in or about the doorway of the hospital room, where he could overhear the conversation between Dr. Wechter and defendant, has upon the privilege under §352. That section does not require that a communication be confidential or confidentially given in order to be privileged. So we turn to the cases.... Faced with the problem of the effect on the privilege of the presence of third persons, our Appellate Divisions found authority for holding the testimony of the physicians privileged. In *Denaro v. Prudential Ins. Co.*, 154 A.D. 840, 843 (N.Y. 1913), a patient was examined by a doctor "in the presence of (his) father or others near," and it was held that the physician could not testify; the persons present may testify, but the physician is bound by the rule. *Hobbs v. Hullman*, 183 A.D. 743 (N.Y. 1918) decided that where a conversation was had between a physician and a patient in the presence of a nurse, who was neither a professional nor a registered nurse, the doctor's testimony was inadmissible. A third case, *Sparer v. Travelers Ins. Co.*, 173 N.Y.S. 673, 675 (App. Div. 1919), reached the same conclusion; it did not allow the testimony of a physician as to the details of an operation he performed to be received in evidence, although a medical student was present during its performance. And now the fourth department in the case at bar has impliedly held likewise in the case of a police guard. The present case falls clearly within the scope of these decisions. If anything, it presents an even stronger situation, for the guard's presence was ordered by command of the public authorities.

An opposite result is not indicated by those cases dealing with the effect of the presence of a third person upon the attorney-client privilege under §353 of the Civil Practice Act. Under §353, relating to attorneys, the privilege extends only to "a communication, made by his client to him." Under §352 relating to physicians, however, the privilege extends to "any information which he acquired in attending a patient"; since such information may be acquired from third persons and third persons who have some definite relationship to the patient are often present, the situation is not analogous to an attorney-client relationship.

Whether or not this distinction accounts for the fact that in attorney-client cases it has been held that the presence of a third person destroys the privilege, the cases suggest that even here there are exceptions. So, if the communication was intended to be confidential, the fact that it may have been overheard by a third person does not necessarily destroy the privilege, see *People v. Cooper*, 307 N.Y. 253, 259 n.3 (1954).

The true test appears to be whether in the light of the surrounding circumstances, and particularly the occasion for the presence of the third person, the communication was intended to be confidential and complied with the other provisions of the statute. Applying this test, we hold that under §352, and the cases construing it, the communication by defendant to Dr. Wechter was privileged, and admission of it by the trial court was error, as correctly stated by the Appellate Division.

Defendant raises the subsidiary question that the hospital record was improperly received in evidence before the Grand Jury, and the indictment should, therefore, be dismissed. But he made no motion for inspection of the minutes of the Grand Jury. We do not know what evidence was adduced there, for the Grand Jury minutes are not a part of this record. Even if we assume that the hospital record was improperly before the Grand Jury, we have no way of knowing what other evidence may have been adduced and formed a sufficient basis for the indictment. There is a presumption that an indictment is based on legally sufficient evidence. We cannot here rule on the legal sufficiency of evidence before the Grand Jury without knowing what that evidence is. Defendant should have taken appropriate steps below and made a record so as to be in a position properly to raise the question on appeal.

The order of the Appellate Division is affirmed. [Ruling]

DESMOND, Judge (concurring in part and dissenting in part).

I agree that the judgment of conviction cannot stand but I think the indictment should be dismissed because it alleges no crime. Defendant's demurrer should have been sustained.

The indictment charges that defendant, knowing that "he was subject to epileptic attacks or other disorder rendering him likely to lose consciousness," suffered "an attack and loss of consciousness which caused the said automobile operated by the said defendant to travel at a fast and reckless rate of speed" and to jump a curb and run onto the sidewalk "thereby striking and causing the death" of 4 children. Horrible as this occurrence was and whatever necessity it may show for new licensing and driving laws, this indictment charges no crime known to the New York statutes. Our duty is to dismiss it.

Section 1053-a of the Penal Law describes the crime of "criminal negligence in the operation of a vehicle resulting in death." Declared to be guilty of that crime is "a person who operates or drives any vehicle of any kind in a reckless or culpably negligent manner, whereby a human being is killed." The essentials of the crime are, therefore, first, vehicle operation in a culpably negligent manner, and, second, the resulting death of a person. This indictment asserts that defendant violated §1053-a, but it then proceeds in the language quoted in the next-above paragraph of this opinion to describe the way in which defendant is supposed to have offended against that statute. That descriptive matter shows that defendant did not violate §1053-a. No operation of an automobile in a reckless manner is charged against defendant. The excessive speed of the car and its jumping the curb were "caused," says the indictment itself, by defendant's prior "attack and loss of consciousness."

Therefore, what defendant is accused of is not reckless or culpably negligent driving, which necessarily connotes and involves consciousness and volition. The fatal assault by this car was after and because of defendant's failure of consciousness. To say that one drove a car in a reckless manner in that his unconscious condition caused the car to travel recklessly is to make two mutually contradictory assertions. One cannot be "reckless" while unconscious. One cannot while unconscious "operate" a car in a culpably negligent manner or in any other "manner." The statute makes criminal a particular kind of knowing, voluntary, immediate operation. It does not touch at all the involuntary presence of an unconscious person at the wheel of an uncontrolled vehicle. To negate the application of §1053-a to these alleged facts we do not even have to resort to the rule that all criminal statutes are strictly construed in favor of the citizen and that no act or omission is criminal unless specifically so labeled by a clearly worded statute. Section 1053-a has the same meaning: penalization of conscious operation of a vehicle in a culpably negligent manner. It is significant that until this case no attempt was ever made to penalize, either under §1053-a or as manslaughter, the wrong done by one whose foreseeable blackout while driving had consequences fatal to another person.

Section 1053-a was passed to give a new label to, and to fix a lesser punishment for, the culpably negligent driving which had formerly been prosecuted under §1052 of the Penal Law defining manslaughter in the second degree. It had been found difficult to get manslaughter convictions against death-dealing motorists. But neither statute has ever been thought until now to make it a crime to drive a car when one is subject to attacks or seizures incident to epilepsy and other diseases and conditions.

Now let us test by its consequences this new construction of §1053-a. Numerous are the diseases and other conditions of a human being which make it possible or even likely that the afflicted person will lose control of his automobile. Epilepsy, coronary involvements, circulatory diseases, nephritis, uremic poisoning, diabetes, Meniere's syndrome, a tendency to fits of sneezing, locking of the knee, muscular contractions, any of these common conditions may cause loss of control of a vehicle for a period long enough to cause a fatal accident. An automobile traveling at only 30 miles an hour goes 44 feet in a second. Just what is the court holding here? No less than this: that a driver whose brief blackout lets his car run amuck and kill another has killed that other by reckless driving. But any such "recklessness" consists necessarily not of the erratic behavior of the automobile while its driver is unconscious, but of his driving at all when he knew he was subject to such attacks. Thus, it must be that such a blackout-prone driver is guilty of reckless driving whenever and as soon as he steps into the driver's seat of a vehicle. Every time he drives, accident or no accident, he is subject to criminal prosecution for reckless driving or to revocation of his operator's license. And how many of this State's 5,000,000 licensed operators are subject to such penalties for merely driving the cars they are licensed to drive? No one knows how many citizens or how many or what kind of physical conditions will be gathered in under this practically limitless coverage of §1053-a of the Penal Law. It is no answer that prosecutors and juries will be reasonable or compassionate. A criminal statute whose reach is so unpredictable violates constitutional rights, as we shall now show.

When §1053-a was new it was assailed as unconstitutional on the ground that the language "operates or drives any vehicle of any kind in a reckless or culpably negligent manner" was too indefinite since a driver could only guess as to what acts or omissions were meant. Reckless driving and culpable negligence have been judicially defined in manslaughter cases as meaning the operation of an automobile in such a way as to show a disregard of the consequences. *See People v. Angelo*, 246 N.Y. 451 (1927). The manner in which a car is driven may be investigated by a jury to see whether the manner shows a reckless disregard of consequences. But giving §1053-a the new meaning assigned to it permits punishment of one who did not drive in any forbidden manner but should not have driven at all, according to the present theory. No motorist suffering from any serious malady or infirmity can with impunity drive any automobile at any time or place, since no one can know what physical conditions make it "reckless" or "culpably negligent" to drive an automobile. Such a construction of a criminal statute offends against due process and against justice and fairness. The courts are bound to reject such conclusions when, as here, it is clearly possible to ascribe a different but reasonable meaning.

A whole new approach may be necessary to the problem of issuing or refusing drivers' licenses to epileptics and persons similarly afflicted. But the absence of adequate licensing controls cannot be supplied by criminal prosecutions of drivers who have violated neither the language nor the intent of any criminal law. Entirely without pertinence here is any consideration of driving while intoxicated or while sleepy, since those are conditions presently known to the driver, not mere future possibilities or probabilities.

The demurrer should be sustained and the indictment dismissed.

CONWAY, C.J., DYE and BURKE, JJ., concur with FROESSEL, J.; FULD and VAN VOORHIS, JJ., concur with DESMOND, J.

## QUESTIONS ON *DECINA*

**1. Involuntary action v. nonaction.** After the onset of his seizure, did Decina perform involuntary *movements* (happenings or occurrences) or involuntary *actions*?

In answering, please remember to ask:

**a.** Did the movements have any intention whatsoever? If so, then they are actions.

**b.** Did the movements lack any intention whatsoever because they were coerced or performed under duress? If so, then they are involuntary actions.

**c.** Did the movements lack any intention whatsoever, but were not coerced or performed under duress? If so, then they are nonactions (they are mere movements, happenings, occurrences) not actions, involuntary or voluntary.

**2. Involuntary action v. unintentional action.** Robbery victims give over their property to robbers neither intentionally nor voluntarily. Rather, they give it over involuntarily. Would it make sense to say that robbery victims give over their property unintentionally?

**3. Medical history and criminal proceedings.** Dr. Wechter examined Decina at E.J. Meyer Memorial Hospital in Buffalo. At trial, over Decina's objection, the history of seizures of varying severity that Decina had described to Dr. Wechter was brought out in the prosecution's direct examination of Dr. Wechter.

    **a.** What is a direct examination? Direct as opposed to what, indirect?

    **b.** Is Decina's medical history even relevant?

    **c.** Did Decina complain about any *pre*-trial use of his medical history? If so, to what end?

    **d.** The New York Court of Appeals ruled that the trial judge should not have allowed Dr. Wechter's testimony into evidence. On what ground?

**4. Eavesdropping.** The police guard outside Decina's hospital room overheard Decina's conversation with Dr. Wechter, but did not testify at trial as to the content of that conversation.

    **a.** Could the guard lawfully have so testified?

    **b.** What case does the majority cite as an answer to question 4a?

    **c.** Is there any support for the proposition that the majority's ruling on the admissibility of Dr. Wechter's testimony might have been different had Wechter been Decina's attorney instead of his physician?

**5. Elements of offense.** Decina was charged with four counts of violating New York Penal Law §1053-a. The Court of Appeals tells us that "[t]he statute does not require that a defendant must deliberately intend to kill a human being, for that would be murder. Nor does the statute require that he knowingly and consciously follow the precise path that leads to death and destruction." What, then, does it require?

**6. Guilty of unconsciousness.** Judge Froessel's opinion for the court likens Decina's history of seizures to voluntary intoxication, while distinguishing both conditions from "a sudden sleeping spell, an unexpected heart or other disabling attack, without any prior knowledge or warning thereof...."

**a.** What distinction is Froessel making there?

**b.** Does that distinction have any bearing on whether Decina committed culpably negligent homicide?

**c.** In concluding that Decina's motion to dismiss the charges against him should have been granted, Judge Desmond distinguishes "[e]pilepsy, coronary involvements, circulatory diseases, nephritis, uremic poisoning, diabetes, Meniere's syndrome, a tendency to fits of sneezing, locking of the knee, [and] muscular contractions" from "driving while intoxicated or while sleepy." About what, if anything, do Froessel and Desmond agree?

**7. Reckless while unconscious.** In his separate opinion, Judge Desmond insists that Decina committed no act of culpably negligent driving causing death. What is Desmond's point, exactly?

**8. Prior knowledge and probabilities.** At the close of the majority's recounting of the prosecution's direct examination of Dr. Wechter, we learn that after September 1954, Decina "had more hospitalization, a spinal tap, consultation with a neurologist, and took medication daily to help prevent seizures."

Notably omitted from the majority's account is the Appellate Division's remark that Decina "had had treatment; had seen a neurologist for a check-up two weeks prior to the accident in question, and had been taking medication to prevent the seizures." *People v. Decina*, 1 A.D.2d 592, 595 (N.Y. App. Div. 1956). Moreover, on March 16, 1955, the local *Binghampton Press* quoted the same-day edition of the *Buffalo Courier Express* reporting that family members said, due to "infrequent convulsions," Decina drove rarely; but after showing some improvement, had resumed driving just prior to the mishap.

Assume that Decina's medication reduced the likelihood of seizure to a level barely greater than that of non-epileptics. If he dutifully took his medicine, but still had a seizure that rendered him unconscious just before the impact, would he be in violation of Penal Law §1053-a?

**9. The grammar of "driving in his sleep."** If Decina was not acting—if, due to unconsciousness he was not (fully) driving the car when it struck the pedestrians—why would we say he was driving while unconscious? Likewise, if a bona-fide sleepwalker is not acting—if, due to unconsciousness, he is not (fully) walking—why do we call it "sleepwalking"? The cases in which we describe these happenings with action verbs are cases that really do look like ones where the agent did in fact act. H.L.A. Hart explains:

> The phrase 'sleep-walking' is alone sufficient to remind us that if the outward movements *appear* to be co-ordinated as they are in normal action, the fact that the subject is unconscious from whatever cause does not prevent us using an active verb to describe the case, though we would *qualify* it with the adverb 'unconsciously', or with the adverbial phrases 'in his sleep', 'in a state of automatism', etc. So in the case of 'driving' it would be natural, as a matter of English, to distinguish those cases where the movements of the body are wild or spasmodic or where the 'driver' simply slumps in his seat or collapses over the wheel, from cases where, though unconscious, he is *apparently* controlling the vehicle, changing gears, steering, braking, etc. In the latter case it might well be said that he drove the vehicle, changed gear, braked, etc. 'in his sleep' or 'in a state of automatism.' Such cases can certainly occur.

H.L.A. Hart, Punishment and Responsibility 109-10 (Oxford: 1968). In some cases, the nonaction is juxtaposed to the action it resembles in order to reveal something about it—that the nonaction has all the outward trappings of action—but really is just a mere happening or occurrence. No one would say that wild or spasmodic actions due to a seizure closely resemble a mode of driving, because the only feature they share with driving is that the subject is in a car. Where, however, the driver is handling the car in a way consonant with driving (seeing himself and being seen as driving), but is in actuality in a state of somnambulism, then our description is meant to note both the similarity to driving (he looks like he is driving) and what separates it from driving (but he is asleep).

Witnesses referred to the positions in which Decina's hands appeared as he crossed Delaware Avenue. According to their memory, after running over the four schoolchildren, Decina was stooped over behind the wheel (the horn blowing steadily), was bobbing a little, bleeding, and seemed knocked out.

What is the relevance of this testimony?

## NOTES ON *DECINA*

*1. Short-citing cases.* In criminal cases, the public is plaintiff, suing the wrongdoer on its own behalf, *not* on behalf of the victim or victims. As shorthand when referring to criminal cases, lawyers use just the name of the defendant throughout the case, even in so-called collateral attacks on the conviction through, for example, federal habeas corpus. Thus we refer to *People v. Decina* as *Decina*, since the shorthand "People" is too general (which people? People of where?). Should the case reach the U.S. Supreme Court, where the caption would substitute "New York" for "People" so the Court audience could tell from the caption where the case originated, lawyers would continue to short-cite the case simply as *Decina*. Short-cites are always italicized or underlined, depending on the citation form followed in the particular jurisdiction. Unlike citations to *Decina* the case, citations to Decina the person are not italicized or underlined.

*2. Amended elements of offense.* The elements of culpably negligent homicide are said to have been amended by New York's adoption of the Model Penal Code a decade after the state's high court ruling in *Decina*. The upshot of the amendment is to make proof easier for the prosecution. No longer is there a requirement that the fatal harm be the product of recklessness. Instead, defendant need only take an excessive risk that causes the prohibited harm, even *without* having considered the possibility that such a harm was in play. *Ketchum v. Ward*, 422 F.Supp. 934, 938 (W.D.N.Y. 1976), citing *People v. Buffington*, 304 N.Y.S.2d 746 (Supreme Court Monroe County 1969).

### 3. Impeachment of witnesses.

*a. Testilying.* To the Appellate Division, Dr. Wechter's testimony posed "whether the examination in question arose out of the relation of physician and patient and for the purpose of treatment or whether, as claimed by the People, the physician was acting solely as a representative of the prosecuting authorities." *People v. Decina*, 1 A.D.2d 592, 595-96 (N.Y. App. Div. 1956). The Court of Appeals cited a former trial where Wechter testified to questioning Decina as a patient, a story he changed at a second trial, where he testified to questioning Decina as a captive of the Buffalo Police Department.

Trial counsel at the second trial brought out Wechter's switcheroo, which couldn't have made the doctor look too good to jurors. Lying is to a point a mode of free speech protected by the First Amendment. An illustration is *United States v. Alvarez*, 132 S.Ct. 2537 (2012), ruling that Congress overstepped its bounds in its Stolen Valor Act, 18 U.S.C. §704 (2013), which criminalized fobbing oneself off as a decorated war hero. But that doesn't mean lying never has legal consequences. Indeed, there is no constitutional right to tell a lie on the witness stand. *United States v. Apfelbaum,* 100 S.Ct. 948, 950 (1980). Accordingly, in New York as elsewhere, trial counsel may "impeach" or discredit a witness's story by introducing a prior inconsistent statement made by that same witness under oath. Consolidated Laws of New York Annotated §60.35 (McKinney's 1970); Federal Rules of Evidence, rule 801(d)(1)(A).

*b. Refusing to testify.* The Court of Appeals said Decina "did not take the stand nor did he produce any witnesses." It was a motto of celebrated defense lawyer Melvin Belli (lawyer to, among others, Jack Ruby) that "[i]f the guy's guilty, you do not put him on [the stand]." Alan Dershowitz, Reversal of Fortune: Inside the von Bülow Case 204 (New York: Random House, 1986). Dershowitz elsewhere summed up: "One criminal lawyer I know, who charges $50,000 for a criminal trial, says that $45,000 is for advising the client at the close of the prosecution's case whether to take the witness stand." Alan Dershowitz, The Best Defense 95 (New York: Vintage Books, 1982).

Belli makes it sound simpler in the first quote than whomever Dershowitz is quoting in the second. While good witnesses can help their own cause by testifying, even bad witnesses can hurt their own cause by sitting mute, as is their right under *Griffin v. California,* 85 S.Ct. 1229 (1965). At Eddie Dean Griffin's trial for the December 1961 murder of Essie Mae Hodson, he did not testify, a fact from which both trial judge and prosecutor invited jurors to infer Griffin's guilt. After the jury convicted him, he was sentenced to death, a proceeding at which he did testify. The U.S. Supreme Court reversed Griffin's conviction on the ground that the judge and prosecutor, by commenting on his silence, burdened his Fifth Amendment privilege against compelled self-incrimination.

No doubt the costs of not testifying—for good witnesses *or* bad—are high. The prosecutor was ruled out of line for making this quip about Griffin's refusal to help jurors sort out unresolved facts: "These things he has not seen fit to take the stand and deny or explain. And in the whole world, if anybody would know, this defendant would know. Essie Mae is dead, she can't tell you her side of the story. The defendant won't." *Id*. at 1231. But even without the prosecutor's urging, jurors would have very likely felt the same way about Griffin's silence. While Casey Anthony famously and successfully sat mute in her 2011 murder trial, those sitting in judgment generally feel entitled to hear an accused's account, which they will accept or reject, but right or wrong, will punish an accused for withholding from them.

***c. Illegally obtained evidence.*** The value to the defense team of putting a credible and likeable witness on the stand explains why some police departments ignore the protocol of *Miranda v. Arizona*, 384 U.S. 436 (1966) and interrogate arrestees without first obtaining a waiver of their rights of silence and counsel. *Missouri v. Seibert*, 124 S.Ct. 2601, 2609 n.2 (2004). The purpose of such a move by police is to exploit the impeachment exception to the rule that unMirandized statements are inadmissible at trial. According to that exception, unMirandized statements are inadmissible *only* for the purpose of proving a defendant's guilt. They *are* admissible, however, to impeach defendants who take the stand and are led by their lawyers to deny the gist of the unMirandized statement/confession. *Kansas v. Ventris*, 129 S.Ct. 1841, 1846-47 (2009); *Harris v. New York*, 91 S.Ct. 643 (1971). That jurors figure out how to use confessions only to discredit witnesses and not to find them guilty is far-fetched. Consequently, by getting confessions without *Miranda* warnings, police make defendants choose between the risks of testifying (where otherwise inadmissible statements come in for impeachment purposes) and of remaining silent (a move likely to alienate jurors).

**4. *Civil suit.*** Both civil law and criminal law protect persons and their property: criminal law by punishing wrongdoers and civil law by compensating victims. Civil law also punishes wrongdoers in unusual cases in not-unlimited amounts for harms that are *not* brought about by accident. *See, e.g., Exxon Shipping Co. v. Baker*, 554 U.S. 471, 492-95, 512-15 (2008).

Now and then, both the prosecutor (who initiates the criminal case) and the victim-plaintiff (who initiates the civil case) seek to hold the wrongdoer responsible for the same act. For example, in the celebrated legal battles of former football star O.J. Simpson, the criminal case commenced in June 1994 when the prosecutor for Los Angeles County charged Simpson with murdering his ex-wife Nicole Brown and her friend, Ronald Goldman. Prior to the verdict in the criminal case, the civil (aka tort) case commenced when the victims' families sued Simpson to get compensation for lost happiness and lost income from the death of their loved ones, plus punitive damages to boot.

Simpson was acquitted in the criminal case in October 1995, despite a strong case against him. He was found liable in the civil case in February 1997 and ordered to pay $8.5M in compensatory damages to Goldman's parents, who were to split an additional $25M in punitive damages with Brown's children. The awards were upheld on Simpson's appeal in *Rufo v. Simpson*, 86 Cal.App.4th 573 (2001).

As is the case with countless civil judgments, Simpson's is unlikely to ever amount to a hill of beans. At the time of the tort, his net worth was $11M. That wealth is long gone, about half of it to his lawyers. His retirement pension from 11 years in the NFL is worth $25K/month for life, but is shielded by federal law from the reach of judgment creditors. His Miami home, encumbered by nearly $1M in debt to a lender, sold at auction in 2014 for $655K, just $100K over the price Simpson had paid in 2000. Goldman's mom (Sharon Rufo) is trying as we speak to sell her renewable $8.5M judgment (plus millions more in interest) in an online auction with a buy-it-now price of $1M and no minimum bid. Apart from the forced sale of some Simpson knick-knacks, the Goldmans did profit from the sale his 1968 Heisman Trophy ($230K) in 1999, and in 2007, a Florida bankruptcy trustee awarded them 90% of the rights to his book, *If I Did It: Confessions of the Killer* (Beaufort Books 2007).

*Decina*, too, involved a civil case that ran parallel to the criminal case. Jacob Azcanazy sued Decina (a riveter at the Bell Aircraft Corporation) on behalf of Azcanazy's seven-year-old daughter, Iris, one of Decina's four victims. Azcanazy's complaint prayed for $55,000 in damages (roughly $500,000 in 2017 dollars), alleging that Decina's negligence brought about the fatal curb-jumping incident from which Iris died two days later. Binghampton Press, Vol. 76-284, March 15, 1955 (Evening), at 1; North Tonawanda Evening News, March 29, 1955, at 7.

### 5. Criminal procedure.

*a. Composition of judicial panels.* Defendants who are convicted, be it by trial or guilty plea, have their challenges to their convictions or sentences heard by a three-judge appellate panel. When the case is unusually important, however, the appeal is entertained by all active, non-disqualified judges on a court as opposed to by a three-judge panel. Indeed, seven judges participated in the New York Court of Appeals' decision in *Decina*, three joining Judge Froessel to make a narrow 4–3 majority over Judge Desmond, whose opinion is joined by two other judges. The Northeastern Reporter breaks down the votes in the final lines of the decision.

*b. Standards for charging and convicting.* After discussing Dr. Wechter's testimony, the court states that Decina was "indicted and charged." Under New York law, misdemeanor crimes (crimes for which the maximum legislatively authorized punishment is one year's incarceration in a municipal jail) are prosecuted by probable-cause determinations made by prosecutors, who file charges in a document known as a complaint. Felonies (crimes for which the minimum legislatively authorized punishment is one year's incarceration in a state penitentiary) are prosecuted by probable-cause determinations made by a simple majority of a 23-person grand jury, charged in a document known as an indictment. A grand jury is convened for a month at a time by the prosecutor to investigate and charge crimes where there is probable cause of criminality: evidence strong enough to try the case, but not necessarily up to the proof beyond a reasonable doubt needed to obtain a conviction in a criminal trial. McKinney's New York Criminal Procedure Law §190.05, *et seq.*

*c. Procedural history of case.* In his separate opinion, Judge Desmond concurs in part and dissents in part. This outcome owes to the fact that the case involves the People's appeal *and* Decina's cross-appeal. Decina had moved pretrial, in a motion known as a "demurrer" (or denial), to have the charges dismissed on the ground that the facts did not make out a strong enough case of culpably negligent homicide to justify a trial on that charge. When the trial judge denied his motion, Decina was tried and convicted. Thereafter, he in effect renewed the failed demurrer by moving the trial court to "arrest" or vacate his judgment, again without success. From there, Decina appealed his conviction on three grounds: first, the trial judge erred in not granting his demurrer; second, the trial judge erred in not granting his motion to arrest judgment; and third, Dr. Wechter's testimony regarding his examination of Decina at the hospital should have been excluded from evidence at his trial.

The Appellate Division affirmed the trial judge's adverse rulings on the demurrer and the motion to arrest judgment, but reversed the conviction and ordered a new trial that was to be redone without any in-court reference to Dr. Wechter's examination of Decina. From that ruling both sides appealed to the New York Court of Appeals, which is the state court of last resort; in New York, the Supreme Court is just the trial court (which has its own intermediate appellate court), not the state high court.

While Judge Froessel's opinion for the high-court majority affirmed the Appellate Division's rulings, Judge Desmond concurred in the portion of the ruling affirming the Appellate Division's ruling that the trial judge erred in admitting Dr. Wechter's testimony, but dissented from the portion of the Appellate Division's ruling affirming the trial judge's denial of Decina's demurrer. (Desmond took no position on Decina's motion to arrest judgment). Under either account—Froessel's or Desmond's—Decina's conviction was tainted by the doctor's inadmissible testimony. Froessel ordered a new trial to that effect while Desmond would have dismissed the case altogether as improvidently charged in the first instance, quite apart from the trial judge's erroneous evidentiary ruling on Dr. Wechter's testimony.

**6. *It was no accident.*** The defense of nonaction is distinct from the defense of accident, though this distinction is not always clearly delineated. For example, in *Brown v. State*, 955 S.W.2d 276 (Tex. Crim. App. 1997), Brown appealed his conviction of murder on the ground that he did not knowingly kill the victim since the shooting was accidentally brought about when a third person bumped Brown from behind. Though in reversing Brown's conviction the court did not make the distinction obvious, Brown's claim on these facts is not, properly understood, that he shot the victim by accident, but rather, that he did not *shoot* him at all. Of course even this is a bit difficult to state; it would make sense here for Brown to say that the gun *discharged* by accident (though the accident was that of the person who bumped him), which is a quite different description of the action than to say that Brown *shot* the victim by accident.

The difference between these two descriptions—shooting and discharging—is that between an action or a doing on the one hand (a shooting) and a mere happening or occurrence on the other (a discharge). Accidents are the unforeseen results of actions, which in turn have intentions, without which there can be neither actions nor accidents. *See generally* Daniel Yeager, *What Is an Accident?*, 51 Criminal Law Bulletin 575 (2015).

Please note that the case is captioned *Brown v. State*. In Texas, defendants who appeal, just like civil plaintiffs who file lawsuits or any party who takes an appeal after losing a civil trial, occupy the left side of the caption. In other states, like California for example, the criminal defendant remains on the right side of the caption throughout the state-court litigation, even when the defendant is appealing an adverse trial- or appellate-court ruling.

### 7. Relation between ignored risk and materialized risk.

*a. Sleepwalking.* In *King v. Cogdon*, while dreaming that there were spiders on her daughter Patti's face, Ms. Cogdon went to Patti's room and slapped her face as if to brush the spiders off. Ms. Cogdon thereafter saw a doctor who gave her a sedative, but did not warn her of more serious issues associated with sleepwalking. That night Ms. Cogdon, again in her sleep, killed Patti with an axe. Although she had a known propensity to sleepwalk, the associated known risk (brushing "spiders" off her daughter's face) was not remotely close to what actually happened (brutally killing her daughter). In light of what Ms. Cogdon knew about her own propensities, by going to sleep in an unlocked room with Patti in the adjoining unlocked room, she, at best, consciously disregarded the risk that she would make an attempt to brush spiders off Patti's face. Ms. Cogdon was acquitted of homicide charges. *King v. Cogdon* (Victoria Supreme Court 1950) [unreported], *discussed in* Norval Morris, *Somnambulistic Homicide, Ghosts, Spiders, and North Koreans*, 5 Res Judicate 29 (1951).

Sleepwalking cases that attempt to make out a defense of unconsciousness are not as rare as one may think. Consider, for example, the case of Scott Falatar, a 43-year-old Motorola engineer who stabbed his wife of 20 years 44 times before holding her head under water in the family pool. Evidently, Falatar was trying to fix the pool's pump with a hunting knife when his wife interrupted the task. Taking pains to cover up a killing that dragged on for 45-50 minutes, Falatar changed his clothes and boots, which, along with the knife, he put in a plastic container, which he hid in the wheel-well of his car. Bolstered by testifying experts at his capital-murder trial, Falatar pleaded that the entire episode took place within a somnambulistic fugue state. After a Maricopa County jury rejected his plea, the trial judge spared him his life, consigning him instead to life without parole. *See* CNN.com 06/25/1999, CNN.com 05/08/1998; *see also* Eunice A. Eichelberger, Annotation, *Automatism or Unconsciousness as a Defense to a Criminal Charge*, 27 A.L.R.4th 1067 (1984) [collecting cases where somnambulism pleaded as a defense]; Adam Candeub, *Consciousness and Culpability*, 54 Alabama Law Review 113 (2002).

**b. *Shock-induced frenzy*.** On October 28, 1967, political activist Huey Newton fatally shot police officer John Frey in Oakland, California during a traffic stop. In a normal case, we can imagine a not-unlimited range of defenses that an accused who does not admit to the crime may raise: alibi (as in, "it wasn't me, it was someone else"); intoxication (as in, "I did it, but I was not my true self at the time"); accident (as in, "I did it, but the result was not what I intended to bring about"); mistake (as in, "I did it, but I saw things differently and took one thing for another"); self-defense (as in, "I did it, but I had no choice"); insanity (as in, "I did it, but lacked the capacity to respond to certain ethical arguments about 'the good'"); or provocation (a sort of hybrid of self-defense and insanity, as in, "the victim made me so mad I lost control and killed in a rage"). With the exception of the defense of alibi, in each of these instances the accused admits to having done what the accusation states—admits to *being* responsible for the harm in question—but denies that he or she should be *held* responsible.

In Newton's case, his account of the episode suggested that none of those defenses were specifically applicable. Instead, Newton had no recollection of the shooting whatsoever. He did recall the traffic stop (the lawfulness of which was not determined in his homicide case) and early aspects of its aftermath. But in describing his recollection of sensations consistent with his having been shot in the abdomen, he could recall no details of having shot Officer Frey or on how another officer on the scene, Herbert Heanes, had been shot, though non-fatally. Newton argued that if he did kill Officer Frey as the prosecutor charged, he must have been unconscious at the time.

In a ruling that Newton's lawyer inadvertently encouraged, the trial judge refused to instruct the jury on the defense of unconsciousness. Instead, the judge told the jury that, while there was insufficient evidence to suggest Newton's unconsciousness at the time that he was alleged to have shot Frey, there was sufficient evidence to suggest that Newton killed Frey in self-defense (which would fully justify the shooting and constitute no crime). In the alternative, jurors were told to consider whether Newton killed Frey while in an understandable rage brought on by provocative acts of Frey (which would partially justify the shooting and support a conviction not of murder, but of the less serious crime of voluntary manslaughter).

After the jury convicted Newton of the voluntary manslaughter of Frey and acquitted him of the nonfatal shooting of Heanes, Newton appealed. He argued that the trial judge erred by not instructing the jury on the defense of unconsciousness, which, if accepted, would negate Newton's responsibility for shooting Frey. The Court of Appeal agreed, vacating his conviction and releasing him, precluding any retrial on the ground that Newton had already served out a sentence for voluntary manslaughter by that point in the litigation. *People v. Newton*, 87 Cal.Rptr. 394 (1st Dist. Ct. App. 1970).

### 8. Additional authority.

*a. Cases.* Among other cases confronting the question of whether unconsciousness as a defense is precluded by pre-unconsciousness disregard of the risk of unconsciousness-based harms, notable is *People v. Holloway*, 164 Cal.App.4th 269 (2008). Holloway successfully appealed from his conviction of driving under the influence in a manner resulting in bodily injury to another. The Court of Appeal ruled that although Holloway knew taking prescription drugs could cause drowsiness and impair his driving, he did not necessarily know the drugs would cause him to unconsciously "drive" a car. Holloway caused two different wrecks when he plowed into oncoming traffic. Soon after the wrecks, three different prescription antidepressants were found in his blood. The labels of each bottle contained warnings about operating machinery and driving while drowsy, but none about blackouts and the threat of motor-activity while unconscious. Thus, the appellate court ruled that Holloway's jury should have received an instruction on unconsciousness due to involuntary intoxication.

The cases on point are not easy to reconcile. In *People v. Velez*, 175 Cal.App.3d 785 (1985), an appeal from Velez's conviction of assault with a deadly weapon, the appellate court affirmed, denying him an instruction on the defense of unconsciousness even though Velez became unconscious from voluntarily smoking a marijuana cigarette that he was unaware was laced with the hallucinogen PCP. Yet in *New Jersey v. Overton*, 815 A.2d 517 (N.J. App. Div. 2003), an appeal from Overton's conviction of child abuse and child endangerment, the court reversed his conviction. Specifically, the trial court had erred by not correcting the prosecutor's statement to the jury that it could find defendant guilty for going to bed naked in his unlocked bedroom with the children sleeping in the house, knowing he had a propensity to sleepwalk. It is safe to say, however, that reversal would have been improper had the evidence indicated a history on Overton's part that included child abuse.

**b. Statutes.** Unconsciousness-as-excuse, like other origins of nonaction, is typically codified in statutes (*e.g.*, California Penal Code §26, Ohio Revised Code §2901.21(D)(2), Model Penal Code §2.01) and in pattern jury instructions (*e.g.*, CALJIC Nos. 4.30-.31, 8.47).

## B. ACTION V. INACTION: THE LAW OF OMISSIONS

In 1983, six patrons of "Big Dan's," a New Bedford, Massachusetts bar, raped and sodomized a 22-year-old mother of two while patrons cheered. The victim had entered the bar, bought cigarettes, ordered a drink, and talked briefly with a woman she recognized and with her future assailants. She was then dragged kicking and screaming across the floor and thrown onto the pool table, where one attacker tried to pull her jeans off. After two others tried to force her to perform fellatio, two more raped her. "I could hear yelling, laughing, down near the end of the bar," she said. "My head was hanging off the edge of the pool table.... I was screaming, pleading, begging.... One man held my head and pulled my hair. The more I screamed, the harder he pulled...." Joyce Wadler, *Woman Leaves Seclusion to Tell Court of Assault, Cheering in Big Dan's Bar*, Wash. Post, Feb. 25, 1984, at A3. Finally, clothed only in a shirt and a shoe, she escaped, ran into the street, and flagged down a truck.

Although those who cheered on the assailants could have been prosecuted as accomplices, because no "special relationship" bound the victim and witnesses (except the unindicted bartender, who testified at trial), the bar full of bystanders violated no Massachusetts law, civil or criminal. In 1983, Massachusetts, like nearly all states, criminalized only those omissions that breached a legal duty to act. Legal duties to act arise out of 1) contract, 2) statute, 3) certain status relations (marriage, parent-child), or 4) the voluntary assumption of care of an imperiled person. Those special relationships alert both the bystander and the imperiled to the imperiled's right to that bystander's labor.

The law's idea of a special relationship is not, however, the one that may occur to a person on the street if asked whom one must aid. Service, employment, and economic relationships are special, while one's neighbor and the neighbor's baby, one's nephew, and even one's parent are strangers. If a relationship fits within this strained notion of special, the omitting party may, under some conditions, be criminally responsible for the resulting harm to the imperiled.

Under the majority approach, bystanders may be morally obligated to aid strangers, but the imperiled have no legal claim to that aid, absent a special relationship. A passerby need not warn a blind man of an open manhole, lift the head of a sleeping drunk from a puddle of water, throw a rope from a bridge to a drowning swimmer, or rescue (or report the discovery of) a child wandering lost in the woods. The law of omissions reflects that even if all men are brothers, they are not their brothers' keepers, not in the legal sense.

Seeing the majority approach as somehow having contributed to the New Bedford incident, in its aftermath, Massachusetts criminalized the failure of bystanders to report serious crimes. A minority of 10 states now mandates some sort of intervention on behalf of strangers in their true hour of need. The conceit of these Bad Samaritan laws (distinct from Good Samaritan laws, which insulate those who *do* help from paying damages in a civil suit if they botch the rescue), is that indifference to the suffering of others can be, under some conditions, legally inexcusable.

Under the minority approach, the imperiled may demand the aid of any bystander who knows of the imperiled's plight and can render aid without incurring risk. Only bystanders close enough temporally and spatially to the emergency are accountable for nonperformance. By requiring the distribution of positive good only when the bystander can bring about a substantial social benefit at a trivial personal cost, no substantial interest of the bystander is said to suffer.

Florida, Hawaii, Massachusetts, Minnesota, Ohio, Rhode Island, South Dakota, Vermont, Washington, and Wisconsin criminalize the refusal to engage in the easy rescue of another or to promptly report serious crimes of aggression. Superficially, the minority approach includes two types of Bad Samaritan laws. Under the first type (Minnesota, Vermont, Wisconsin), anyone who knowingly fails to undertake easy rescue is subject to prosecution.[a] Easy rescue neither endangers the bystander nor interferes with important duties the bystander owes others. Under the second type (Florida, Hawaii, Massachusetts, Ohio, Rhode Island, South Dakota, Washington), anyone who fails to report promptly that they have witnessed a serious crime is subject to prosecution.[b] Despite these superficial differences in statutory phrasing between the two types of Bad Samaritan laws, both ultimately require prompt reporting, not rescue.

While the easy-rescue laws of the first type (Minnesota, Vermont, Wisconsin) are phrased to require actual rescue or aid, none would require bystanders in the New Bedford rape to do much of anything, given the plausible risks of intervention on those facts. Though a collective effort would have stopped the attack, *no* law so requires. Indeed, Vermont's Bad Samaritan law—the only one that does not list summoning professional rescuers as a passable bystander course of conduct—"does not create a duty to intervene in a fight." *State v. Joyce*, 139 Vt. 638, 641 (1981). Like the other nine states taking the minority approach, Vermont's Bad Samaritan law demands from bystanders not heroics, but phoning police and, if called upon, testifying at trial.

By restricting mandatory intervention to calling professional State-actor rescuers, Bad Samaritan laws are contemporary versions of the dormant offense of misprision of felony: the concealment of a felony of which one knows, but did not commit or assist. The common-law elements are: 1) knowledge of the felony; 2) a reasonable opportunity to disclose the felony without harm; and 3)

---

[a] Minnesota Statutes Annotated §604A.01 (2001); Vermont Statutes Annotated tit. 12, §519 (1967); Wisconsin Statutes Annotated §940.34 (1995).

[b] Florida Statutes Annotated §794.027 (1997); Hawaii Revised Statutes §663-1.6 (1984); Massachusetts General Laws Annotated ch. 268, §40 (1983); Ohio Revised Code Annotated §2921.22 (2014); General Laws of Rhode Island, 1956, §11-56-1 (1984); South Dakota Codified Laws §22-11-12 (2013); Washington Revised Code Annotated §9.69.100 (1987).

failure to report the felony. Misprision of felony is widely condemned as a bogus mode of accessorial liability that threatens the Fifth Amendment guarantee against self-incrimination; it is, as a result, in a state of formal but not practical existence.

Whether misprision of felony was ever incorporated into the American common law is doubtful. Its unpopularity is traceable in part to Chief Justice John Marshall, who, in a throw-away line in a bankruptcy case, wrote: "It may be the duty of a citizen to accuse every offender and to proclaim every offence which comes to his knowledge; but the law which would punish him in every case for not performing this duty is too harsh for man." *Marbury v. Brooks*, 20 U.S. 556, 575-76 (1822). Indeed, no state court since 1878 has upheld a conviction for misprision of felony. (Federal misprision convictions under 18 U.S.C. §4 are not unheard of because they require active concealment, not just a failure to report).

Despite the wobbly status of misprision of felony, duty-to-report statutes have had a (limited) function when convicting a defendant for the unreported crime would be too harsh, or proof of a defendant's involvement in the unreported crime is weak. Despite the Fifth Amendment self-incrimination problems posed by a law that makes witnesses report crimes in which they themselves might have participated, duty-to-report laws have played a role in a smattering of plea negotiations. *See Percival v. People*, 2014 WL 3936333 (Virgin Islands 2014) at *2 n.4, citing Daniel B. Yeager, *A Radical Community of Aid: A Rejoinder to Opponents of Affirmative Duties to Help Strangers*, 71 Washington University Law Quarterly 1, 34 (1993). Still, the few precedents on point indicate that Bad Samaritan laws have been highly theatrical but legally insignificant legislative gestures. Even in the 10 states with Bad Samaritan laws, I have been able to find no appellate decision upholding a conviction on point.

As a result, we remain fully dependent on professional rescuers, bolstered by an uncertain contribution from volunteer do-gooders. But leaving rescue to the pros doesn't exactly mean they are on the hook for failing (or forgetting) to rescue us. Government's failure to rescue is not actionable under federal constitutional or state tort law, where the limitations on what count as special relationships present a barrier to civil litigants who claim that the inaction of police or fire personnel harmed them. To express gratitude toward those whose calling is to protect the public, courts have an even stingier view of special relationships than that which governs private actors.

For example, the California Supreme Court, in denying recovery to a personal-injury victim who could not pursue a civil action due to a botched police investigation, relied on the California Vehicle Code, which provides that highway patrol personnel may—not must—investigate accidents and aid stranded motorists. The dissent questioned the majority's reasoning, given that the victim's injuries and provisions in the Vehicle Code compelled the victim to remain on the scene, precluding private investigation on her part. California's high court recognized the counter-intuition of demanding nothing more from professionals than from amateurs:

> [Although] our tax dollars support police functions, it is settled that the [ordinary] rules concerning the duty—or lack thereof—to come to the aid of another are applicable to law enforcement personnel in carrying out routine traffic investigations .... No special relationship ... exist[s] between members of the California Highway Patrol and the motoring public ... or ... stranded motorists generally....

*Williams v. State of California*, 34 Cal.3d 18, 24 (1983). Acknowledging that officers' employment contracts seem to conflict with this notion of special relationships, the court cited the old saw that "the intended beneficiaries of any investigation that is undertaken are the People as prosecutors in criminal cases, not private plaintiffs in personal injury actions." *Id.* at 24 n.4

Similar examples are not hard to find. In *Warren v. District of Columbia*, 444 A.2d 1 (D.C. 1981), the D.C. Police Department repeatedly ignored the calls of two women who insisted that their downstairs neighbor was being burglarized, beaten, and raped. Officers' cursory drive-by and five-minute investigation permitted attacks not only on the neighbor, but also upon the reporting women in the apartment above. Prior to the rape, beating, and robbery of the two women who notified police, an officer had assured them that help was on the way, but failed to dispatch the call. Relying on their belief that the police officers were in the house, the two women yelled down to the victim below, inadvertently alerting the attacker to their presence. In denying recovery to all victims, the court noted "the fundamental principle that a government and its agents are under no general duty to provide public services, such as police protection, to any particular individual citizen." *Id.* at 3. The court cited cases involving the broken promises of police officers resulting in severe yet nonactionable harm to victims.

With professionals monopolizing the rescue business, and their failure to rescue anyone being only loosely actionable, Bad Samaritan laws operate as a flimsy add-on. We end up with volunteers, motivated solely by compassion, not fear of prosecution, to supplement an overburdened public rescue apparatus. But those in peril sometimes cannot await assistance from the designated social institutions. For example, while the critical period for resuscitation is two minutes, paid rescue personnel cannot reach heart-attack victims that quickly. Training the general population in resuscitation techniques would increase the likelihood that victims will have a heart attack near someone who can help. But there is a big difference between a population able to help and one willing to help.

Why those who see others in danger so often do nothing is unclear. In the case of witnesses to crimes, perceived danger and fear of retaliation account for some failures to intervene or notify authorities. In addition, because emergencies are for most of us exotic, a bystander's lack of opportunity for planning and rehearsal and the difficulty of quickly selecting the appropriate type of intervention may diminish assistance. Once the emergency does present itself, the presence of other bystanders reduces potential rescuers' individual sense of responsibility to the imperiled and increases the probability of free-riding. Each is lulled into a state of pluralistic ignorance, which induces multiple bystanders to interpret others' inaction as a sign of no danger. Despite the apparent incentive that risk-sharing would provide to potential co-rescuers, because of social inhibitions that arise in groups, we are more prone to respond to another's distress when we're alone than with other witnesses. Bystanders thus face a choice of nightmares: fail to intervene and experience the empathic distress of watching another human suffer, the guilt of failing to live up to a minimal level of decency, and the shame of having that failure witnessed by others; or, intervene and risk retaliation by an assailant, the derision of non-intervening bystanders, and the threat of being mistaken for the cause of the harm. Indeed, the victim may spurn, attack, or become dependent on the rescuer, while the legal system may enlist the rescuer as a witness subject to countless encounters with police, lawyers, and courts. The nightmare then may be most easily resolved by convincing oneself that the victim is not imperiled.

Anyone who would commit rape or any other violent crime might also injure an intermeddler. Because criminals pose danger not just to victims but to anyone who interferes, withholding aid is not necessarily indifference, let alone callousness. Criminals may be armed and vicious, undeterred both from crime and doing what it takes to get away with it. Despite the potential benefit to the victim, intervention may be too much to require when a criminal actor poses an immediate, quickly unfolding danger.

Contradictory norms further complicate bystander-imperiled encounters so as to produce inaction. Specifically, the norm to "mind one's own business" clashes with "do unto others." Even "do unto others" is not immune from criticism, perhaps because what is held out as compassion and altruism may just be masks for self-interest. The moral iffiness of whistle-blowing is manifest in *Roberts v. United States*, 445 U.S. 552 (1980), where a defendant appealed his drug sentence, which the trial court had increased when he refused to name his suppliers. Affirming his sentence, the Supreme Court condemned his contumacy as "antisocial." Justice Marshall dissented from the majority's conclusion that the defendant had a duty to inform on his suppliers, explaining:

> American society has always approved those who own up to their wrongdoing and vow to do better, just as it has admired those who come to the aid of the victims of criminal conduct. But our admiration of those who inform on others has never been as unambiguous as the majority suggests. The countervailing social values of loyalty and personal privacy have prevented us from imposing on the citizenry at large a duty to join in the business of crime detection. If the Court's view of social mores were accurate, it would be hard to understand how terms such as 'stool pigeon,' 'snitch,' 'squealer,' and 'tattletale' have come to be the common description of those who engage in such behavior.

*Id.* at 569-70 (Marshall, J., dissenting). Even relationships among doctors, lawyers, or police officers, who *are* guided by affirmative reporting requirements, carry pressures to cover for colleagues and not testify against them. Though the duty among strangers involves no affinity-based obstacles, a legal movement to convert private citizens into adjuncts to the police investigative function has never really gotten rolling.

Congress, for example, rejected the idea after mulling over the case of David Cash Jr., who, upon seeing friend Jeremy Strohmeyer violate and fatally strangle seven-year-old Sherrice Iverson in a casino bathroom, looked the other way, then kept mum until days later when security footage implicated the two 18-year-olds. See Ken Levy, *Killing, Letting Die, and the Case for Mildly Punishing Bad Samaritanism*, 44 Georgia Law Review 607, 623-28 & n.41 (2010). For his role, Strohmeyer got four life sentences in a segregated unit at Lovelock Correctional Center (Nevada); Cash got a nuclear engineering degree from University of California (Berkeley).

In our principal case on point on criminal omissions, *Flippo v. State*, 258 Ark. 233 (1975), the Supreme Court of Arkansas affirmed the manslaughter conviction of a hunter who told a severely injured man's father that the hunter would promptly get the injured man medical care; but the hunter then dilly-dallied around, his delay compounding the injured man's ultimately fatal plight. Our task in *Flippo* and similar cases that abide by the majority approach is to identify when we have stuck our necks out far enough to be legally punishable not for aggressing against others, but for ignoring them.

## SUPREME COURT OF ARKANSAS

### ROBERT L. FLIPPO, JR., AND ROBERT M. FLIPPO, APPELLANTS

### V.

### STATE OF ARKANSAS

### JUNE 2, 1975

HOLT, Justice

A jury found appellants guilty of involuntary manslaughter. The punishment of each was assessed at a one year suspended sentence in the State Department of Correction and fines of $100. The sole issue upon appeal is the sufficiency of the evidence to sustain the verdicts. Appellants recognize that in determining the sufficiency of the evidence, upon appellate review, it is only necessary to ascertain that evidence which is most favorable to the appellee and if any substantial evidence exists, then we must affirm. *Williams v. State*, 257 Ark. 8 (1974).

The appellants, Robert L. Flippo, Jr., and Robert M. Flippo, are respectively father and son. Late in the afternoon of the tragic occurrence, the father drove his son, Bobby, and the son's teenage friend, Terry Dunlap, to a clover field several miles from their home for the purpose of discovering deer tracks in preparation for the forthcoming hunting season. Among other weapons, Bobby, a college student, took a new .30.06 rifle with him. Mr. Flippo stopped the truck in the field and the two youths got out. Bobby took his rifle with him thinking he might see a deer. After walking about 150 yards, Bobby raised the rifle, which was equipped with a telescopic sight, and fired once, thinking he saw a deer. The weather conditions impaired visibility since it was overcast and approaching nightfall.

About a minute later, Bobby returned to the truck and expressed his belief that he had killed a deer, which he had heard "bay." Terry, however, said he heard three small-caliber rifle shots, which were later determined to be distress signals. After approximately ten minutes, Bobby convinced his father to return to the scene and search for the deer. Bobby and Terry found Roy Ralph Sharp approximately 140 yards from where Bobby fired his rifle in the direction of the victim. There was evidence that the victim was partially obscured by a tree with low branches from which the bullet ricocheted. The victim was conscious and asking for help. He was a "big man," weighing 225 pounds, and his left leg was "almost off at the hip." He had "drug" himself approximately twenty paces out of the woods. Bobby administered no first aid although there was evidence that he had won a "National 4-H Safetyman" award based upon his knowledge of "all aspects of safety." He and Terry ran to a nearby residence, which happened to be the residence of the victim's 72-year-old father. There they told Mr. Sharp that they had found a person who was wounded. The boys returned to the Flippo truck where they told Mr. Flippo about the accident. Bobby then told his father that Mr. Sharp was going to follow them back to the scene of the accident. When they arrived near the scene, Mr. Flippo and Bobby told Mr. Sharp that they were going to call an ambulance. Bobby gave Mr. Sharp directions as to the location of the victim. There was no offer of assistance to Mr. Sharp in removing the victim in one of the trucks for medical aid. After they had left, Mr. Sharp found the victim and then learned that he was his son. He asked his father to get assistance. Mr. Sharp told him "son, some folks have gone to call an ambulance. You lay right still and it will be here in just a few minutes."

The Flippos left and drove to the Flippo home which was twelve or fourteen miles away. Mr. Flippo, who was told by Terry that the victim's leg was nearly severed, drove past numerous houses, some of which had telephones, and a café, which was only 2.3 miles from the wounded man. The café was open and an outside public telephone was plainly visible. Mr. Flippo stopped once at a residence to use a phone at Bobby's suggestion and when the motor almost stopped, they continued on to the Flippo residence where they were certain there would not be a party line. "There was conversation about removing the rifle from the truck so nobody would know we had the rifle and was hunting out of season." At Mr. Flippo's direction, after reaching the residence, Bobby and Terry switched the high-powered rifle and another rifle from the truck to a shack for a shotgun, which was placed on the gun rack in the truck. Then, Mr. Flippo called an ambulance, which met him approximately 25 minutes later at the café, which he had passed en route to his residence. While Mr. Flippo waited at the restaurant for the ambulance, Terry and Bobby returned in the Flippo truck to the scene where they assisted Mr. Sharp in placing his son in the Sharp truck. A short distance down the road, they met the ambulance to which the victim was transferred. It appears Roy Sharp died either shortly before or after he was placed in the ambulance.

After giving up on the Flippos, Mr. Sharp left his son in the field and found someone at a nearby residence, who then had a neighbor call an ambulance. Mr. Sharp was only away from his son about four minutes. He further testified that from the time he found his son and Bobby and Terry returned, it was about forty minutes to an hour and fifteen minutes.

A pathologist testified that the victim bled to death, and it is possible that the victim "could have been saved" if he had been hospitalized while still conscious. He testified there were other things that could have possibly saved his life: i.e., "the quicker you get a person in the better their chances of living"; "if a shirt or anything had been put around the body, the thigh, above that point that would have stopped the bleeding." It was his opinion "that had proper treatment been initiated immediately at the site, he could have been saved."

Arkansas law defines involuntary manslaughter as: If the killing be in the commission of an unlawful act, without malice, and without the means calculated to produce death, or in the prosecution of a lawful act done without due caution and circumspection, it shall be manslaughter. Ark. Stat. Ann. §41-2209 (Repealed 1964). In *State v. Green*, 229 P.2d 318 (Wash. 1951), the court affirmed a manslaughter conviction where a hunter fired at what he thought was a bear. There the shooter was not sure of his target. The court held that the prosecution made a prima facie case of criminal responsibility from which the jury could find the appellant guilty. *See also Johnson v. Commonwealth*, 308 Ky. 709 (1948). In the case at bar, there is substantial evidence, when viewed most favorably to the appellee, from which the jury could find that Bobby, who was hunting out of season, was criminally negligent by acting without due caution and circumspection when he fired at an object he mistakenly believed to be a deer and then failed, as charged, to discharge his duty, as hereinafter discussed, to render aid.

A more difficult question is presented with respect to Mr. Flippo. He, as a parent, cannot be deemed an accessory after the fact in the circumstances here. Ark. Stat. Ann. §41-121 (Repealed 1964). The cases cited by appellee that appellant was an active participant in the tragic shooting are distinguishable. Those cases involve the owner of a car or truck who allows another to knowingly drive in a culpably negligent manner under the owner's direction and control. In this case, Bobby, a college student who is knowledgeable in gun safety, cannot be said to have been within his father's control. Neither did Mr. Flippo acquiesce in the culpable manner in which Bobby fired. Bobby was out of and away from the truck.

However, the State presented evidence to the jury that Mr. Flippo and his son had a duty to aid the wounded man, upon discovering him, and failed to do so, causing death. "For criminal liability to be based upon a failure to act it must be found that there was a duty to act—a legal duty and not simply a moral duty." Wayne R. LaFave & Austin W. Scott, Jr., Criminal Law 183 (1972). If the omission to act was intentional, but without the intention or expectation of fatality, the crime would be involuntary manslaughter because of criminal negligence. Perkins on Criminal Law 603 (2d ed. 1969). In *Jones v. United States*, 308 F.2d 307 (D.C. Cir. 1962), the court said:

> There are at least four situations in which the failure to act may constitute breach of a legal duty. One can be held criminally liable: first, where a statute imposes a duty to care for another; second, where one stands in a certain status relationship to another; third, where one has assumed a contractual duty to care for another; and fourth, where one has voluntarily assumed the care of another and so secluded the helpless person as to prevent others from rendering aid.

The case at bar presents a classic fact situation as to the latter situation mentioned above in *Jones v. United States*. Mr. Flippo assured the victim's elderly father that he would call for an ambulance. The father kept vigil and delayed seeking assistance in the belief assistance would be procured promptly by appellants. In the meantime the victim, known by the appellants to be seriously wounded, was bleeding to death, asking his father not to leave him after being assured assistance was forthcoming. During this time, Mr. Flippo drove twelve to fourteen miles to reach his residence although phones were in the vicinity of the shooting. A public phone, which the appellants passed, was 2.3 miles from the scene of the tragedy. Mr. Flippo was told that the victim's leg was "nearly blown off." Upon reaching his home he instructed the youths to place the rifles in a shack and substitute a shotgun and then used his phone to call an ambulance. According to Mr. Sharp, after waiting in vain for prompt assistance, within four minutes he was able to have someone at a nearby residence summon aid. There was medical evidence that if help had arrived sooner or if aid had been administered at the site by appellants, it was probable that the victim would have survived. The jury could infer that Mr. Flippo's delay caused the helpless victim to be secluded in the field awaiting the promised aid and prevented or hindered others from rendering timely aid. When we view the evidence most favorable to the appellee, as we must do on appeal, there is substantial evidence from which a jury could find appellants criminally negligent.

Affirmed.

BROWN and FOGLEMAN, JJ., dissent as to the affirmance with respect to Robert L. Flippo, Jr. [Mr. Flippo].

## QUESTIONS ON *FLIPPO*

**1. Elements of offense.**

**a.** What, elementally, is the relation between the involuntary manslaughter with which the Flippos were charged under Arkansas Statutes Annotated §41-2209 (Repealed 1964) and the negligently culpable homicide with which Decina was charged under New York Penal Law §1053-a?

**b.** The Arkansas Supreme Court had no trouble affirming son Bobby's conviction. After all, he shot a man, not quite sure what he was shooting at in the first place. The real rub in the case is the responsibility of Mr. Flippo (who happens to be Flippo junior). Evidently he was precluded from being held in the concealment of his son's crime. Ark. Stat. Ann. §41-121 (Repealed 1964). So too does the court doubt that Mr. Flippo somehow controlled, encouraged, or even acquiesced in his son's acts of recklessness, which, as a college student, Bobby was able to hatch all on his own. Instead, Mr. Flippo's conviction could stand, if at all, on a theory of omissions: that his duty-based failure to intervene on victim Roy Ralph Sharp's behalf recklessly contributed to Sharp's death.

Relying on Perkins's criminal law treatise—a book that attempts to summarize the law in various jurisdictions while noting and taking positions on unsettled questions—the *Flippo* majority quotes: "If the omission to act was intentional, but without the intention or expectation of fatality, the crime would be involuntary manslaughter because of criminal negligence." What does this require in terms of proof of Mr. Flippo's stance toward Roy Ralph Sharp?

> **(1)** That he meant for his delay to kill Sharp?
>
> **(2)** That he knew his delay would kill Sharp, but, hoping for the best, he delayed anyway?
>
> **(3)** That he suspected but not quite knew his delay would kill Sharp, but, hoping for the best, he delayed anyway?
>
> **(4)** That he had no idea that Sharp could die due to his (Mr. Flippo's) own delay, but he should have or could have known had he considered the matter?

**2. Standard of review.** The Arkansas Supreme Court announces at the outset "that in determining the sufficiency of the evidence, upon appellate review, it is only necessary to ascertain that evidence which is most favorable to [the State] and if any substantial evidence exists, then we must affirm." Another way of putting this is that reversal is proper only if "upon no hypothesis whatever is there sufficient substantial evidence to support the conclusion reached in the court below." *People v. Newland*, 15 Cal.2d 678, 681 (1940). A similar standard applies to all challenges to the sufficiency of evidence in federal cases, per *Jackson v. Virginia*, 443 U.S. 307 (1979). *Jackson* states that when a defendant claims on appeal that the facts were insufficient to support the conviction, with the evidence taken in the light most favorable to the government, only when no rational trier of fact could have found all the elements of the offense beyond a reasonable doubt is reversal justified. What does this mean, exactly?

    **a.** That the appellate court's hands are tied?

    **b.** That even if the jury was in error to convict, the conviction should be upheld anyway?

    **c.** That convictions are presumptively valid in the absence of plain error?

**3. Mistaking a man for a deer.** The state high court noted that Bobby, who was hunting out of season, "fired at an object he mistakenly believed to be a deer…." *Cf. State v. Green*, 229 P.2d 318 (Wash. 1951) [inexcusably taking a 15-year-old boy with a red hat for either a bear or a "three-point buck" at 102 feet], citing *State v. Newberg*, 278 P. 568 (Or. 1929) [inexcusably taking a man on horseback for a deer at 125 feet]. Strikingly absent is any explanation of *why* Bobby believed what he did: who would take a man for a deer at 140 yards, or at any distance for that matter? Where were the target's telltale antlers, tail, and spindly legs? Can we really take one thing for another "by mistake" if we are not even *trying* to get it right? See *infra* Chapter 3.C, note 2 on *Elmore*.

**4. Voluntary assumption of care.**

    **a. In *Flippo*.** The court insists that Mr. Flippo voluntarily assumed a sort of temporary responsibility for the well-being of Sharp and then failed to follow through. Did Mr. Flippo assume care of Sharp or did he refuse to assume care? Also, did he seclude Sharp? Or was he already secluded?

    **b. Elsewhere.** Compare *Flippo* with *People v. Oliver*, 258 Cal.Rptr. 138 (1st Dist. Ct. App. 1989), where defendant Carol Ann Oliver picked up the heavily intoxicated Carlos Cornejo in a bar in Pleasant Hill and drove him to her house, where she helped him shoot heroin, which caused him to overdose. Oliver returned to the bar and back home, where, with help from her daughter and her daughter's girlfriends, she dragged the unconscious Cornejo outside and placed him behind a storage shed where he would die later that night, to be found by Oliver early the next morning. The Court of Appeal upheld Oliver's conviction of involuntary manslaughter on a theory that

Oliver's breach of her duty to Cornejo contributed to his death. That is, Oliver's voluntary assumption of care for Cornejo prevented others from helping him. Had Oliver not neglected Cornejo once she found him unconscious, prompt medical attention would have saved his life. Because involuntary manslaughter entails recklessness, no conviction could lie without some awareness on Oliver's part of the threat that doing nothing posed to Cornejo's life.

Suppose that, without Oliver's knowledge, Cornejo shot the heroin while Oliver was in the bathroom, but the facts thereafter are identical to the facts of *Oliver*. Would that make a difference in your assessment of the propriety of a conviction of involuntary manslaughter on a theory of omissions?

**5. Counterfactuals.**

**a. When help wouldn't help.** A pathologist testified that timely medical care could have saved Sharp's life. But suppose the pathologist testified that timely care could *not* have saved Sharp. Would Mr. Flippo be off the hook completely and Bobby would take the rap alone?

**b. When help doesn't help.** Suppose now that, rather than take the detour they did, the Flippos had hurried in their truck to the very first house they saw and called an ambulance, which arrived without delay to provide care to Sharp, who died nonetheless.

**(1)** Would either Flippo remain on the hook for Sharp's death in such a case?

**(2)** Given that parent-child relations are "special," why wasn't Sharp's dad prosecuted for not saving his son's life?

# NOTES ON *FLIPPO*

### 1. Suspended sentences and judgments.

**a. Sentences.** Father and son each received one-year suspended sentences. To suspend the sentence of a convicted person, the trial judge must first pronounce a sentence of fine, imprisonment, or both, and then suspend rather than impose it. Suspended sentences come in two varieties. The first is an unconditional discharge of defendant's disabilities or penalties. An unconditionally suspended sentence ends the court's involvement, though the defendant's criminal conviction remains on the public record. The second is a conditionally suspended sentence, which withholds the penalty during the defendant's good behavior. For example, a person convicted of shoplifting for the first time might receive 30 days in jail as a penalty, with the imprisonment suspended on the condition that defendant commit no crimes for a year. Once the year passes without incident, the penalty is discharged. If, however, the defendant does offend within the year, the judge can revoke the suspension and impose the 30 days in jail. In this respect, a conditionally suspended sentence is like a sentence of probation except in that the court's probation department does not supervise the behavior of defendants under conditionally suspended sentences. *See, e.g.*, Colorado Revised Statutes Annotated §18-1.3-102 (West 2012).

In some jurisdictions, a postponement of sentencing is also considered a suspended sentence. A postponement of a criminal sentence means that the judge does not pronounce a penalty immediately after a conviction. Courts use postponements and conditionally suspended sentences to encourage convicted persons to stay out of trouble. Resolution of minor crimes in this way is common, particularly on behalf of convicted persons who have no criminal record. Given the widespread reality of overcrowding in jails, suspended sentences for petty crimes prevent further congestion.

**b. Judgments.** The Flippos suffered judgments of conviction; their jail terms were suspended. Not uncommon is suspension or deferral of the entry of judgment of conviction itself, again, reserved for minor offenses committed by criminal newbies. Though found technically guilty by trial or plea, no judgment is entered: the defendant is simply discharged while given a chance to lay low for a spell, burdened with community service or other minor disabilities (e.g., a low fine, anger management). Then the deferred judgment disappears, meaning it would be truthful to deny the conviction if asked. *See, e.g.*, 730 Illinois Compiled Statutes Annotated §5/5-6-1 (West's Smith-Hurd 2010); *People v. Johnson*, 174 Ill.App.3d 812, 813 (1988).

Unlike a deferred judgment, the fact of *arrest* may be erased only through an adjudicated expungement. See *Wakefield v. Department of State Police*, 994 N.E.2d 722 (Ill. App. Ct. 2013).

**2. Criminal procedure: straight to the high court.** Justice Holt wrote for the *Flippo* majority. Justices Brown and Fogelman dissented without opinion only as to the court's holding affirming the conviction of Mr. Flippo. The breakdown of the ruling is omitted (*Decina*, for example, broke down 4-3 in favor of affirming), nor are any other participating justices named, though the Arkansas Supreme Court has seven members.

Note that the court's opinion makes no reference to an intermediate ruling in the Arkansas Court of Appeals. Arkansas does allow for a limited number of trial-court judgments to bypass the Arkansas Court of Appeals and go straight to the Arkansas Supreme Court. *See* Arkansas Rules of Appellate Procedure (Criminal) 10 (2001) [death sentences]. *Flippo*, however, went straight from sentencing to the state supreme court for a quite different reason: when *Flippo* was decided in 1975, there was not yet an Arkansas Court of Appeals, which would be created in 1978 by Amendment 58 of the Arkansas Constitution, implemented in 1979 by Act 208 of the Arkansas General Assembly.

**3. Revised code clarifies elements.** References in the Arkansas Supreme Court's opinion to "criminal negligence," a lack of "malice," and an action performed "without due care and circumspection" do not provide much in the way of an answer to question 1 above. Clarification came soon after the *Flippo* Court's June 1975 ruling when, on January 1, 1976, the revised Arkansas Criminal Code, which replaced the state's 1947 Code with the Model Penal Code, became effective. *See* Arkansas Criminal Code, Act 1975, No. 928, §3 (Ark. Crim. Code §41-101, *et seq.* (1976)).

According to appellate rulings interpreting the revised Arkansas code, manslaughter (the Flippos' crime of conviction) requires that a killing be brought about by a defendant's *conscious awareness* of an excessive risk to life; negligent homicide—a less serious crime—requires only that the defendant take an excessive risk, not that he know it to be so. *Rollins v. State*, 302 S.W.3d 617, 618-20 (Ark. Ct. App. 2009), citing *Hoyle v. State*, 268 S.W.3d 313 (Ark. 2007); *see supra* Chapter 1.A, note 2 on *Decina*.

**4. Four bases of omissions liability.** Duty is the predicate of omissions liability. *See, e.g.,* Model Penal Code §2.01(3) ["Liability for the commission of an offense may not be based on an omission unaccompanied by action unless . . . a duty to perform the omitted act is otherwise imposed by law."]. Those duties arise out of:

*a. **Special relationships.*** Parent-child, husband-wife, and master-servant relationships, for example, give rise to legal duties to render aid. *See, e.g.*, Wayne R. LaFave & Austin W. Scott, Jr., Criminal Law §26, at 184 (1972); W. Page Keeton et al., Prosser and Keeton on the Law of Torts §56, at 373-85 (5th ed. 1984 & Supp. 1988); *Restatement (Second) of Torts* §§314A-317 (2d ed. 1965).

*b. **Contracts.*** *See* Arthur Leavens, *A Causation Approach to Criminal Omissions*, 76 California Law Review 547, 557-58 & nn.35-36 (1988); Paul H. Robinson, *Criminal Liability for Omissions: A Brief Summary and Critique of the Law in the United States*, 29 New York Law School Law Review 101, 115 (1984); *Jones v. United States*, 308 F.2d 307 (D.C. Cir. 1962) [trial court committed plain error by failing to instruct jury to decide whether long-term babysitter had contract-based legal duty to care for infant].

*c. **Statutes***. Statutes imposing criminal liability for inaction include: 50 U.S.C. app. §462 (1988) [failure to comply with provisions of Military Selective Service Act]; IRC §7203 (1988) [failure to file tax return, supply required information, or pay tax]; Tenn. Code Ann. §39-15-101 (1991) [nonsupport of minor child or disabled spouse or child]; Cal. Health & Safety Code §§3110, 3125, 3354 (West 1990) [failure to report communicable diseases]; Cal. Veh. Code §§20001-20004 (West 1971 & Supp. 1992) [hit-and-run/failure to stop at scene of accident].

In *Billingslea v. State*, 780 S.W.2d 271 (Tex. Crim. App. 1989) (en banc), a Texas court reversed the conviction of a man whose severe neglect of his 94-year-old mother led to her death. He was indicted under a statute that purported to criminalize omissions causing serious injury to elderly individuals. On appeal, however, the court held that the statute could not support a conviction because it was drafted too vaguely to create a legally enforceable statutory duty to care for her. Of the four bases of affirmative duties to act listed in this note, Texas expressly recognizes *only* statutory duties as the basis of criminal omissions. *Id.* at 275-77.

*d. **Voluntary assumption of care.*** This was the basis of Mr. Flippo's duty to the gunshot victim. *See also Restatement (Second) of Torts* §314A (2d ed. 1965) [special relationship exists between those who undertake to help another thus depriving others from doing the same]; *id.* §322 [duty to aid another harmed by actor's conduct]; *id.* §323 [negligent performance of undertaking to render services, whether gratuitously or for consideration]; *id.* §324 [duty of one who takes charge of another who is helpless].

**5. Non-enforcement of unpopular criminal laws.** The introduction to Chapter 1.B describes Bad Samaritan laws as having a "formal but not practical existence," rendering them no more than "highly theatrical but legally insignificant legislative gestures." Simply put, police and prosecutors largely ignore Bad Samaritan laws in the 10 states that have them, in part because strangers who want to stay out of the business (or suffering) of others hardly seem like criminals in the strict sense. Thus, it may be a relief that the substantial discretionary authority wielded by prosecutors and jurors prevents laws that seem susceptible to misapplication or abuse from culminating in unjust convictions.

    ***a. Regulating prosecutorial discretion.*** Prosecutors have discretion to file no charges at all, file charges less serious than the facts of the case suggest, divert cases for treatment rather than punishment, or dismiss cases for a range of reasons, none of which need be articulated. In fact, if for any reason a prosecutor refuses to prosecute *anyone*—even the most obviously guilty—there's nothing to be done short of the political rigmarole of having the noncompliant prosecutor removed from office. To illustrate, *Gomez v. Perez*, 93 S.Ct. 872 (1973) ruled that a Texas statute criminalizing nonpayment of child support applied as a constitutional matter of Equal Protection to children born out of wedlock. A few weeks later, *Linda R.S. v. Richard D.*, 93 S.Ct. 1146 (1973) ruled that the mother of a child born out of wedlock cannot affirmatively enjoin the prosecutor to enforce the child-support statute against the non-paying biological father. Instead, only the father of a child born *within* the marriage can, once threatened with prosecution, challenge the Texas law by complaining that similarly situated non-paying fathers—those of children born out of wedlock— are *not* being prosecuted.

    A technical way of saying this is that private persons have "no legally cognizable interest in the prosecution" of another. *In re McDonough*, 930 N.E.2d 1279, 1286 (Mass. 2010). A non-technical way of saying the same is that the only way to make prosecutors enforce the law is to have them removed from office for their failure to do so.

**b. Jury nullification.** Jurors have discretion to "nullify" the guilt of a defendant whom they know to have committed the crime. The constitutional ban on Double Jeopardy prevents retrial after a jury unanimously votes to acquit a defendant whose guilt they knowingly nullify or repudiate. A lone juror who chooses to ignore the law for any reason causes a mistrial for lack of unanimity. Mistrials, however, are no absolute bar to retrial. High court precedents hold that a "trial can be discontinued without barring a subsequent one for the same offense when particular circumstances . . . [such as a deadlocked jury] . . . manifest a necessity to declare a mistrial." *Blueford v. Arkansas*, 132 S.Ct. 2044, 2052-53 (2012). Only when the prosecution or the court stoops to "goading" the defendant into moving for a mistrial is retrial barred by Double Jeopardy. *Oregon v. Kennedy*, 102 S.Ct. 2083, 2088 (1982) [prosecutor calling defendant "a crook" *not* intended to goad defendant into moving for mistrial].

Though jurors have the (implicit) power to nullify or ignore the law, trial judges are precluded from (explicitly) telling them so. *State v. Maloney*, 490 A.2d 772, 775 (N.H. 1985) [nullifying law is juror's prerogative, not defendant's right]; *People v. Goetz*, 532 N.E.2d 1273, 1274 (N.Y. 1988) ["While there is nothing to prevent a petit jury from acquitting although finding that the prosecution has proven its case, this so-called 'mercy-dispensing power' ... is not a legally sanctioned function of the jury and should not be encouraged by the court"].

Courts do have devices for preventing and correcting misjudgments by jurors. For example, a directed verdict is when the trial judge orders judgment for defendant before the jury has found a verdict. If the trial judge orders judgment for defendant *after* the jury has found defendant guilty, the judge's ruling is known as a judgment notwithstanding the verdict (JNOV). Finally, appellate review is seen as a check on unjust convictions. Any error made by a jury not already corrected by the trial judge during trial or on post-trial motions can be corrected—*if* objected to below—when the defendant presents the error to a three-judge appellate panel. *Millar v. Berg*, 316 S.W.2d 499, 502 (Mo. 1958) ["[T]he proper way to preserve [claims] for appellate review is to file a motion for directed verdict at the close of all the evidence and to thereafter, in the event of an adverse verdict, assign as error the failure of the trial court to have directed such a verdict in a post-trial motion either for a new trial or to set aside a verdict and judgment and enter judgment for the opposite party"].

# CHAPTER 2

# The Reckless-Intentional Distinction

## A. SECOND-DEGREE MURDER AND INVOLUNTARY MANSLAUGHTER

Both *Flippo* and *Decina* are homicide cases in which defendants were convicted of unjustified killings. Flippo and Decina were charged with the same offense, though the offenses were differently labeled. Flippo was convicted of involuntary manslaughter and Decina was convicted of culpably negligent homicide. The Arkansas Supreme Court made a weak effort to state what sort of proof would support manslaughter convictions either on the part of Bobby Flippo (who shot Sharp) or Mr. Flippo (who neglected to get Sharp prompt care). As for *Decina*, the New York Court of Appeals referred to the element of "disregard of the consequences," but did not elaborate. Nonetheless, both statutes at issue required proof that defendants consciously disregarded a substantial and unjustifiable risk that what they were doing would cause another's death.

This phase of our course continues to elaborate the different modes of homicide and defenses that eliminate or mitigate criminal responsibility for homicide. Although different modes of homicide have different proof and sentences, those differences in proof on which those sentences rest can be difficult to make out. It is therefore helpful to compare the involuntary manslaughters of which the Flippos and Decina were convicted first with accidental homicides (which are often fully excused) and second with murders (which are severely punished).

The language of homicide, made up of terms such as malicious, premeditated, deliberate, intentional, willful, knowing, reckless, grossly negligent, and negligent, must be mastered to navigate the fine-grained distinctions between crimes. At the outset, one thorny issue in the law of homicide is the role of negligence. As you recall,

Decina was charged with the culpably negligent killing of four pedestrians. While ordinary (less than culpable) negligence is a term most relevant to tort law, less serious modes of criminal homicide also regulate ordinarily negligent conduct that causes death. Though some jurisdictions do not, the Model Penal Code recognizes negligent homicide, which criminalizes any killing committed in an unreasonable manner, that is, by taking risks that an ordinarily prudent person would not take (or, what is the same, by failing to take precautions that an ordinarily prudent person would take). *See* Model Penal Code §210.4. The test for what counts as negligent is objective. In other words, the test is not what risks the defendant *was* aware of; instead, the test is what risks the defendant *should have been* aware of.

When charged with negligent homicide, it is no defense for defendant to excuse the harm on grounds of accident. A negligently caused harm *is* an accident. Although negligently caused harms are by definition accidentally caused harms, the law of negligence familiar to any first-year student of torts deems those accidents inexcusable.

Laws punishing ordinary negligence (of which MPC §210.4 is an example) therefore recognize two types of accidents: negligent (inexcusable) and non-negligent (excusable). To *excuse* an action is not to call it right, permissible, or good (as we would a necessary, that is, *justified* action, as in one done in self-defense). *Excused* actions are wrong but forgivable (as in acts done by mistake, while intoxicated, under duress or, as here, non-negligently). While the negligent actor acts unreasonably, the non-negligent actor acts reasonably, but causes harm anyway. While the negligent actor causes foreseeable harm, the non-negligent actor causes unforeseeable harm. Harm is foreseeable if it is avoidable with ordinary precaution. Harm is unforeseeable if it is avoidable only with extraordinary precaution. That a given harm is either foreseeable or unforeseeable says nothing about what was actually foreseen by the actor; one who brings about harm by accident has not actually foreseen the harm that materialized. Instead, issues of foreseeability address only what should, could, or would have been foreseen with ordinary precaution. Negligent or not, reasonable or not, foreseeable or not—all are judgments we make to separate inexcusable from excusable accidents in a regime of ordinary civil (as opposed to culpable, criminal, gross) negligence.

Another way of saying this is that a negligently caused harm is unintentionally brought about. While all (non-coerced) actions have intentions, the consequences of our actions sometimes surpass our intentions. For example, when my grandfather clock stops working, I mean to repair it, but in attempting to do so, I aggravate the damage. Here the action is marked by the intention to repair the clock, but instead I end up ruining it by accident. Having an intention is related to the idea of knowing what you are doing. What you intend is what you mean to realize, it is your plan, what you are bent on, what you contemplate by the action. Whenever we do something, there are always other possible outcomes, impediments, actions of others, and various misfirings, some of which may occur to us, some of which may not. Those things that are outside our plans or intentions are therefore incidental to our plans or our intentions. An accidental harm occurs when an unforeseen incidental is brought about by our action, the intention of which departs from the harm in question. If we are playing a game of catch and I never consider that I may make an errant throw which may break a window, then the ultimate window breakage is accidental: an unforeseen incidental to my intention of playing catch. But not all incidentals are unforeseen.

> I realize that by insisting on payment of due debts I am going to 'ruin' my debtor—that is, he will be ruined as a consequence of being compelled to pay. I have absolutely no wish to ruin him, even wish not to: but maybe if I don't get payment both I and others are going to suffer severely; and very likely I think he has been faintly improvident. So I demand payment. He is ruined and, if you like, I ruined him. If this is said—I might resist and resent the imputation a bit—I think it must be admitted that I did ruin him deliberately; not, however, that I ruined him intentionally. At no time did I intend to ruin him; it was never part of my intention. (This, if it be admitted, is an especially interesting case: for plainly I am *not* here responsible for his ruin.)

J.L. Austin, *Three Ways of Spilling Ink, in* Philosophical Papers 278-79 (J.O. Urmson & G.J. Warnock eds.) (Oxford University Press 3d ed. 1979). This passage focuses on the relation of the debtor's ruin to the creditor's plan or intention of collecting a just debt. It would be an over-inclusive use of the word "accident" to characterize the ruin of the debtor as accidental. Thus it is crucial to this example that while the debtor's ruin was never what the creditor intended, this was no accident; that is, this was no unintentional ruining of the debtor either. Rather, the debtor's ruin here was neither intentional (since it was never in the creditor's plan) nor unintentional (since it was not an unforeseen consequence of the creditor's plan): the debtor's ruin was a foreseen incidental of the plan. In this way, the debtor's ruin is "not intentional"—neither intentional nor unintentional—a foreseen incidental of the collection of the debt.

Incidentals are consequences that were either foreseen (like the debtor's ruin here) or unforeseen (if, say, the creditor unexpectedly fell into a deep depression over having brought about the debtor's ruin by calling in the debt). *Any* consequence that is outside the plan is incidental to the intention. It is just that there are two types of incidentals: 1) those you anticipate before acting, that is, foreseen incidentals; and 2) those you do not anticipate before acting, that is, unforeseen incidentals. On our facts, the creditor's plan is to reclaim his money. He wishes things could be otherwise, but if he lets the debtor off the hook, "both [he] and others are going to suffer severely." The creditor has not called in the debt *for the purpose of* ruining the debtor. For the creditor, there is no choice. Plus, the "faintly improvident" debtor has brought it on himself in assuming the debt in the first place, perhaps with no plan or a poor plan for repaying it.

We can imagine facts where the creditor's plea that the debtor's ruin was incidental to the creditor's intention to reclaim his own money would leave us doubting the creditor's genuineness. For example, if the creditor had ample resources to wait for the debtor to execute a good-faith plan to cover the debt, the default on which was not faintly improvident, but rather, due to the debtor's sudden, grave illness. If the creditor in such a case still insisted on prompt payment, we would be skeptical about a plea that the debtor's ruin was incidental to the plan. There it should strike us that insisting on prompt payment smacks of an intention to ruin the debtor. Otherwise, why demand the debt *then*? There could still be innocent reasons for demanding the debt anyway, some with sound business justifications; but the point is that those reasons would need to be elaborated to avoid our getting the sense that the plan was to ruin the debtor. One cannot simply declare a consequence as incidental to the intention and make it so, not unless that declaration matches up with the facts available to us in the public observable world.

On the original set of facts posited above, it is given that the debtor's ruin was incidental to the creditor's plan of debt-collection. Still, we would not describe the debtor's ruin in that case as accidental. To do so would imply that the debtor's ruin came from out of nowhere, at least from the creditor's standpoint. For this creditor to enter a plea of accident would be a doomed attempt to evade responsibility since the creditor "realize[s] that by insisting on payment of due debts I am going to 'ruin' my debtor...." Once aware of this likely consequence, the creditor will not be heard to say that the debtor's ruin was "just an accident."

While it is tempting to say that all consequences that are incidental to one's intentions are accidents, to say so provides an over-inclusive domain for that plea. The foreseen incidental—what the law calls the "recklessly" caused harm—is, as accidents go, a bogus one. Foreseen incidentals may sometimes be excusable, as in cases where knowledge (that is, certainty) about a fact is an element of the offense or in cases where the harm in question must be intended. But foreseen incidentals are not accidents, whose domain is reserved for unforeseen incidentals. Non-bogus accidents are excusable because the actor did *not* "consciously disregard a substantial and unjustifiable risk" of harm.

The accusation in *Flippo*, that father and son committed involuntary manslaughter, required proof that Sharp's death was neither intentional nor unintentional, but rather, not intentional. Involuntary manslaughter requires proof that the victim's death was a foreseen incidental of the plan or intention. But what, exactly, are we to make of the crime of which Decina was convicted: "culpably negligent" homicide? Above I noted that ordinary, civil negligence is assessed by an objective test asking only whether defendant caused harm by taking an excessive risk. But by modifying the word "negligence" with the word "culpable," New York law identifies a special sense of *criminal* negligence that requires a subjective component that converts negligence into a term identical to recklessness. Unlike tort law, where negligent actions are customarily the basis of liability, thereby obligating defendant to *compensate* plaintiff for injuries caused by defendant, criminal law *punishes* defendants. Because punishment is viewed as an extraordinary remedy that stigmatizes, censors, and disgraces the defendant rather than merely transfer a portion of defendant's wealth to plaintiff (the upshot of tort remedies), the negligence that suffices for tort liability is rarely the basis of criminal liability. *But cf.* Model Penal Code §210.4 [negligent homicide based on civil negligence].

While civil negligence lies wherever defendant's excessive risk causes harm, criminal negligence lies only where defendant was aware of the excessive risk he was taking, but chose to run the risk anyway. This explains why Decina's responsibility for the deaths of the four pedestrians rests on the same standard of proof required in *Flippo* to support both Flippos' responsibility for Sharp's death. Risks that one should have considered, that is, risks that one was unreasonable not to have considered, are unforeseen incidentals and, as such, produce accidental or unintentional harm. As unforeseen incidentals, readily avoidable harms are brought about by ordinary civil negligence, not gross, culpable, or criminal negligence, which is reserved for recklessness, i.e., actually foreseen risks that materialize.

In our next principal case, *People v. Watson*, 637 P.2d 279 (Cal. 1981), defendant caused two deaths in a car crash in Redding, California that owed to his speeding, which in turn owed to his heavy intoxication. Under California law, there is a form of vehicular homicide that would impose liability for ordinary civil negligence. California Penal Code §192(c)(2). Therefore, if Watson's two victims were killed by a foreseeable accident, then that would be the most serious offense he committed. The prosecution's theory of the case, however, was that the deaths were neither accidental nor intentional; rather, the prosecution argued that the killings were not intentional. Accordingly, the issue for review was, as not-intentional killings go, whether Watson should have been charged with murder or the less-serious offense of vehicular manslaughter while intoxicated, which is an aggravated form of involuntary manslaughter. The primary purpose of our reading this case is to become familiar with how murder and manslaughter may be differentiated.

## SUPREME COURT OF CALIFORNIA

*THE PEOPLE, PLAINTIFF AND APPELLANT*
*V.*
*ROBERT LEE WATSON, DEFENDANT AND RESPONDENT*

NOV. 30, 1981

RICHARDSON, Justice

Defendant was charged with both second-degree murder and vehicular manslaughter. In this pretrial proceeding, he contends that the facts underlying the alleged offense disclose, at most, gross negligence punishable under the manslaughter statute. We have concluded, however, that the facts also support a finding of implied malice justifying the murder charge as well.

The circumstances of the offense, as elicited at the preliminary examination, are as follows: In the late night and early morning hours of January 2 and 3, 1979, defendant Robert Watson consumed large quantities of beer in a Redding bar. Approximately an hour and a half after leaving the bar, defendant drove through a red light on a Redding street and avoided a collision with another car only by skidding to a halt in the middle of the intersection. After this near collision, defendant drove away at high speed, approached another intersection and, although he again applied his brakes, struck a Toyota sedan. Three passengers in the Toyota were ejected from the vehicle and the driver and her six-year-old daughter were killed. Defendant left 112 feet of skid marks prior to impact, and another 180 feet of skid marks to the vehicle's point of rest.

The applicable speed limit at the accident scene was 35 miles per hour. Expert testimony based on the skid marks and other physical evidence estimated defendant's speed immediately prior to applying his brakes at 84 miles per hour. At point of impact, experts concluded that defendant's speed was approximately 70 miles per hour. Eyewitness Henke testified that defendant's car passed him "real fast" (estimated by Henke at 50 to 60 miles per hour) shortly before the collision. According to Henke, defendant swerved from the slow lane into the fast lane, suddenly braked and skidded into the intersection, and thereupon struck the other vehicle. Henke believed that the traffic light was green when defendant entered the intersection.

Defendant's blood alcohol content 30 minutes after the collision was .23 percent, more than twice that necessary to support a finding that he was legally intoxicated. The complaint charged defendant with two counts each of second-degree murder and vehicular manslaughter. At the preliminary examination, the magistrate found probable cause to charge defendant with vehicular manslaughter, but refused to hold him to answer the second-degree murder counts, concluding that the facts were insufficient to demonstrate the essential element of implied malice. Despite the magistrate's ruling, the People included in the information the two counts of second-degree murder that were rejected by the magistrate. Defendant's §995 motion to dismiss the murder counts was granted by the superior court, and the People appeal from the order of dismissal.

Based upon his review of the legislative history of the vehicular manslaughter statute, defendant claims that a murder charge is precluded. He asserts that the Legislature intended separately to classify and punish all vehicular homicide as manslaughter. We hold otherwise, concluding that nothing in the legislative history of this section suggests such an intent. Rather, we conclude that if the facts surrounding the offense support a finding of "implied malice," second-degree murder may be charged; if the facts demonstrate only "gross negligence," a vehicular-manslaughter charge may be sustained. Although the terms "gross negligence" and "implied malice" are similar in requiring an awareness of a risk of harm, the degrees of awareness differ. Because of that fact, the more specific vehicular-manslaughter statute does not preclude application of the more general murder statute. Finally, because the conduct of defendant in this case exhibited wantonness and a conscious disregard for life which would support a finding of implied malice, the order of dismissal must be reversed.

### 1. Application of Murder Statutes to Vehicular Homicides

Penal Code §187(a) provides: "Murder is the unlawful killing of a human being, or a fetus, with malice aforethought." Under §188, malice may be express or implied, and implied malice is present "when no considerable provocation appears, or when the circumstances attending the killing show an abandoned and malignant heart." Section 189 defines first-degree murder as murder committed by specified lethal means "or by any other kind of willful, deliberate, and premeditated killing," or a killing which is committed in the perpetration of enumerated felonies; all other kinds of murder are of the second degree.

Under §192, manslaughter is "the unlawful killing of a human being, without malice." One kind of manslaughter is defined in subdivision 3 of that section: "In the driving of a vehicle—in the commission of an unlawful act, not amounting to felony, with gross negligence; or in the commission of a lawful act which might produce death, in an unlawful manner, and with gross negligence."

Defendant reasons that the general murder statutes (§§187-189) are preempted by the more specific provisions applicable to vehicular homicides. §192(3)(a). In *In re Williamson*, 43 Cal.2d 651, 654 (1954), we said that: "Where the general statute standing alone would include the same matter as the special act, and thus conflict with it, the special act will be considered as an exception to the general statute whether it was passed before or after such general enactment." Defendant observes that the murder statutes deal generally with the unlawful killing of a human being, whereas the vehicular-manslaughter provision deals specifically with such killing while driving a vehicle. He therefore contends that the latter statute bars the application of the former under the *Williamson* rule.

The argument contains a flaw. We have held that the *Williamson* rule is applicable (1) when each element of the general statute corresponds to an element on the face of the special statute, or (2) when it appears from the statutory context that a violation of the special statute will necessarily or commonly result in a violation of the general statute. Neither of these two categories applies here. A prosecution for murder under §187 requires a finding of malice, while §192 defines manslaughter as a killing without malice. Moreover, in light of the malice requirement, a violation of the vehicular manslaughter statute would not necessarily or commonly result in a violation of the general murder statute. Thus, the *Williamson* rule is inapplicable. Nonetheless, defendant asserts that by charging him with second-degree murder based upon implied malice, the prosecution has charged him with an unintentional killing. He argues that because vehicular manslaughter also is an unintentional killing, the two crimes are coterminous, and that the more specific statute excludes the more general one.

This argument is not persuasive. The requisite culpability for the vehicular manslaughter charged here is gross negligence, which has been defined as the exercise of so slight a degree of care as to raise a presumption of conscious indifference to the consequences. On the other hand, malice may be implied when a person, knowing that his conduct endangers the life of another, nonetheless acts deliberately with conscious disregard for life. *Though these definitions bear a general similarity, they are not identical. Implied malice contemplates a subjective awareness of a higher degree of risk than does gross negligence*, and involves an element of wantonness which is absent in gross negligence. [Italics mine.]

Furthermore, we have applied different tests in determining the required mental states of gross negligence or malice. A finding of gross negligence is made by applying an objective test: if a reasonable person in defendant's position would have been aware of the risk involved, then defendant is presumed to have had such an awareness. However, a finding of implied malice depends upon a determination that the defendant actually appreciated the risk involved, i.e., a subjective standard.

In the present case, the prosecution will be required to show a higher degree of culpability in support of the second-degree murder charge than it will to establish vehicular manslaughter. Accordingly, because §187 and §192(3)(a) contemplate different kinds of culpability or criminal activity, the *Williamson* rule would not preclude a second-degree murder charge.

Defendant alternatively argues that if the Legislature clearly intends a special statute to apply to the exclusion of a more general statute, this intent must be given effect even if application of the *Williamson* rule would render both statutes applicable. Defendant contends that the Legislature enacted §192(3) with the specific intention of requiring prosecution of all vehicular homicides under that statute. Our own review of the legislative history, however, leads us to a contrary conclusion. Rather, §192(3)(a) was enacted to proscribe vehicular homicides which resulted from grossly negligent conduct, without precluding the possibility of a murder charge when the circumstances revealed more aggravated culpability.

In seeking the probable legislative intent behind §192(3), we examine its history. When the Penal Code was enacted in 1872, manslaughter was defined in §192 as an unlawful killing of a human being without malice, and was characterized as either voluntary or involuntary. A specific statute directed at vehicular homicides was enacted in 1935 as Vehicle Code §500. That section provided for imprisonment of one year in the county jail or three years in the state prison for deaths which occurred within one year as the proximate result of injuries caused by the negligent driving of a vehicle. In 1941, §500 was amended to elevate the standard of culpable conduct to a reckless disregard of, or willful indifference to, the safety of others. The amended statute specifically made the involuntary manslaughter statute inapplicable to vehicular homicides.

According to the People, because of the difficulty of proof, few convictions were obtained under this amended version of §500. Accordingly, in 1943 §500 was repealed, and §193 of the Penal Code was amended to provide a specific penalty for involuntary manslaughter resulting from driving. The ordinary term of imprisonment for manslaughter was not more than 10 years in state prison; however, amended §193 made involuntary vehicular manslaughter punishable by imprisonment in the county jail for not more than one year or in the state prison for not more than five years.

In 1945, subdivision 3 was added to §192 to provide a separate category for vehicular manslaughter in addition to the voluntary and involuntary categories. As previously noted, present §192(3)(a) describes as vehicular homicide the commission of an unlawful act, not amounting to a felony, with gross negligence, or the commission of a lawful act which might produce death, in an unlawful manner, and with gross negligence.

In sum, the requisite mental state for prosecution varied between the different versions of the vehicular manslaughter statute: the 1935 statute required mere negligence; the 1941 version referred to a willful indifference to, or a reckless disregard for, the safety of others (which, as the People note, required a showing that the defendant was subjectively aware of the risk involved); the present statute at issue here is directed at gross negligence. We stress, however, that the crime involved in each version was manslaughter, an offense which consistently has been defined as the unlawful killing of a human being without malice. Although the willful indifference standard in the 1941 version entailed the same element of subjective awareness that is present in implied malice, that standard was rejected by the Legislature soon after its enactment in favor of a gross-negligence standard. Thus, the Legislature specifically declined to include conduct of any greater culpability than gross negligence in the present vehicular manslaughter statute. Moreover, there is no indication that the Legislature intended the conduct of the culpable party in a vehicular homicide case automatically to be characterized as gross negligence in order to bring all vehicular homicides within the scope of §192(3)(a). Rather, when the conduct in question can be characterized as a wanton disregard for life, and the facts demonstrate a subjective awareness of the risk created, malice may be implied. In such cases, a murder charge is appropriate....

### 2. Probable Cause to Charge Second Degree Murder

Having determined that a defendant may be charged with second-degree murder upon facts which also would support a charge of vehicular manslaughter, we inquire whether the facts imply malice and therefore justify charging the greater offense, that is, whether there was probable cause to hold defendant to answer the second-degree murder charge. The magistrate and superior court concluded that no probable cause existed to support a charge of second-degree murder. This determination, based upon undisputed facts, constituted a legal conclusion subject to independent review on appeal. In such a case, our function is to determine whether a person of ordinary caution would be led to believe and conscientiously entertain a strong suspicion that defendant committed the crime charged.

We have said that second-degree murder based on implied malice has been committed when a person does "an act, the natural consequences of which are dangerous to life, which act was deliberately performed by a person who knows that his conduct endangers the life of another and who acts with conscious disregard for life." *People v. Phillips*, 64 Cal.2d 574, 587 (1966). Phrased differently, malice may be implied when defendant does an act with a high probability that it will result in death and does it with a base antisocial motive and a wanton disregard for human life.

Based upon our independent review of the record, we find a rational ground for concluding that defendant's conduct was sufficiently wanton to hold him on a second-degree murder charge. The facts on which we base this conclusion are as follows: Defendant had consumed enough alcohol to raise his blood-alcohol content to a level that would support a finding that he was legally intoxicated. He had driven his car to the establishment where he had been drinking, and he must have known that he would have to drive it later. It also may be presumed that defendant was aware of the hazards of driving while intoxicated. As we stated in *Taylor v. Superior Court*, 24 Cal.3d 890, 897 (1979): "One who willfully consumes alcoholic beverages to the point of intoxication, knowing that he thereafter must operate a motor vehicle, thereby combining sharply impaired physical and mental faculties with a vehicle capable of great force and speed, reasonably may be held to exhibit a conscious disregard of the safety of others." Defendant drove at highly excessive speeds through city streets, an act presenting a great risk of harm or death. Defendant nearly collided with a vehicle after running a red light; he avoided the accident only by skidding to a stop. He then resumed his excessive speed before colliding with the victims' car, and then belatedly again attempted to brake his car before the collision (as evidenced by the extensive skid marks before and after impact) suggesting an awareness of the great risk of harm which he had created. In combination, these facts support a conclusion that defendant acted wantonly and with a conscious disregard for human life.

We do not suggest that the foregoing facts conclusively demonstrate implied malice, or that the evidence necessarily is sufficient to convict defendant of second-degree murder. On the contrary, it may be difficult for the prosecution to carry its burden of establishing implied malice to the moral certainty necessary for a conviction. Moreover, we neither contemplate nor encourage the routine charging of second-degree murder in vehicular-homicide cases. We merely determine that the evidence before us is sufficient to uphold the second-degree murder counts in the information, and to permit the prosecution to prove, if it can, the elements of second-degree murder....

The judgment of dismissal is reversed.

TOBRINER, MOSK, NEWMAN and LACHS, JJ., concur.

BIRD, Chief Justice, dissenting.

Today, this court not only rewrites the law of implied malice, but makes it a virtual certainty that any individual who knowingly drives to a social outing, takes a few drinks, and while driving home is involved in an accident in which a death occurs, may be charged with murder in the second degree. In order to achieve this unusual result, the majority ignore facts and applies an improper legal standard to reverse the magistrate's refusal to hold respondent to answer and the superior court's grant of respondent's motion to dismiss the charge of murder under Penal Code §995.

The majority opinion ignores the following evidence which was presented at the preliminary hearing. The prosecutor called Paul Henke as an adverse witness. Henke testified that he was driving along Cypress Avenue when respondent sped by at 55 or 60 miles per hour. As respondent approached the intersection of Cypress and Athens, where the fatal accident occurred, the light was green. At the scene, Henke spoke to some officers, whom he identified at the trial. No one asked him to make a statement, and the officers merely told him to get out of the way. The next day, Henke called the police because he had heard a news report requesting that witnesses identify themselves. He informed them that he had been a witness. Henke did not know respondent before the accident and had not had any contact with him since.

The prosecutor argued before the magistrate that Henke had perjured himself and that he was hostile toward the police and the district attorney's office. The prosecutor called several officers who testified that they had not seen or spoken to Henke when they arrived at the scene. They testified that Henke may have arrived later. The prosecutor also contended that Henke's testimony could not be true and claimed it conflicted with expert testimony that respondent must have been speeding at 70 to 80 miles per hour on Cypress Avenue. Other expert testimony was presented concerning the timing of the traffic signal at the scene of the accident. However, the expert witness could not testify as to the color of the light at the time of the accident since he was not there. Apart from Henke, no witness testified about the color of the light.

The majority claim that they are only reviewing undisputed facts. But material facts—whether respondent drove down Cypress Avenue at 55 or 60 as opposed to 70 or 80 miles per hour, and whether he had a green light as he started into the intersection where the accident occurred—were disputed. The majority acknowledge Henke's testimony. However, in making the crucial determination as to whether there was probable cause to hold respondent to answer, they conveniently ignore Henke's testimony. The only way that they can ignore this testimony, which is in respondent's favor, is to first decide that Henke was not a credible witness. This is not an undisputed fact. It is a conclusion impermissibly drawn by the majority.

If the magistrate had held respondent to answer, the court could draw all legitimate inferences from the evidence which favored that action. Deference is given to a magistrate's finding of probable cause. The magistrate weighs the evidence, resolves any factual conflicts, and determines the credibility of the witnesses. The superior or appellate court may not substitute its judgment for that of the magistrate as it relates to conflicts in, or the weight of, the evidence. This rule is in accord with the general rule of appellate review that evidence adduced in the trial court is viewed on appeal in the light most favorable to the judgment entered below.

Here, the magistrate failed to find probable cause. Therefore, there is no legal or factual basis for this court to defer to the validity of the information. No deference can be given under these circumstances without directly interfering with the magistrate's power to weigh the evidence and decide disputed factual issues. Yet, that is what the majority have done. When a superior or appellate court reviews a magistrate's determination that probable cause did not exist, the court should resolve all conflicts and draw all reasonable inferences in favor of the judgment below.

In this case, any inferences drawn should be in favor of the magistrate's determination of lack of probable cause. These would include the facts that respondent had a green light on Cypress and that he was driving at 55 to 60 miles per hour. These inferences are reasonable. There was no evidence of fabrication or of a motive for Henke to fabricate. He did not know respondent. He had a reasonable explanation for waiting more than a day to give a statement to the police. The officers at the scene of the accident had told him to keep away.

At the preliminary hearing, the prosecution was required to present evidence of each element of a murder based on an implied-malice theory. As the majority recognize, those elements are that the accused, "knowing that his conduct endangered the life of another, nonetheless acted deliberately with conscious disregard for life." In other words, the accused must have (1) intended to commit an act likely to kill with (2) conscious disregard for life. The majority fails to demonstrate that the existence of either element can reasonably be inferred from the facts presented below.

Given Henke's testimony, it cannot be found that respondent committed an act likely to kill. The act of speeding through a green light at 55 or 60 miles per hour in a 35-mile-per-hour zone was dangerous, but was not an act likely to result in the death of another. It was 1 o'clock in the morning. The person whose car respondent nearly collided with testified that he saw no other cars around....

Respondent's acts were not comparable to those of the defendants in *People v. Fuller*, 86 Cal.App.3d 618 (1978), where the court observed in dicta that the defendants could be prosecuted for second-degree murder on an implied-malice theory. The defendants had fled from the police after being caught in an attempted auto burglary. They sped through the main thoroughfares of Fresno at 8:30 on a Sunday morning. They were driving on the wrong side of the road and cars had to swerve off the road to avoid them. They ran a red light, causing other cars to stop sharply in order to avoid collisions. They drove their car toward two police vehicles which were attempting to block them. The police were required to take defensive action to avoid a collision. The defendants ran a second red light, collided with another car, and killed its driver. Compare those facts with this case. Respondent drove down empty streets at 1 o'clock in the morning. There was no evidence that he ran a red light at the intersection where the accident occurred. His conduct was not like Fuller's whose acts were likely to result in the death of others.

The fact that respondent was under the influence of alcohol made his driving more dangerous. A high percentage of accidents is caused by such drivers. However, a rule should not be promulgated by this court that driving while under the influence of alcohol is sufficient to establish an act "likely to kill." Death or injury is not the probable result of driving while under the influence of alcohol. Thousands, perhaps hundreds of thousands, of Californians each week reach home without accident despite their driving intoxicated.

The majority also fail to demonstrate that it is reasonable to infer that respondent had a conscious disregard for life. Can a conscious disregard for life be established by the fact that several hours before the accident respondent drove his car to a bar? The majority hold as a matter of law that he "must have known" he would have to drive his car later and that he willfully drank alcohol until he was under its influence.

How does respondent's state of mind at the time he drove to the bar and began drinking justify an inference that he had a reckless state of mind at the time of the accident? This meager evidence does not justify the inference that by drinking alcohol he harbored a conscious disregard for life when he later drove his car. I submit that the majority's reasoning that such an inference may be drawn to support a finding of implied malice will be used to establish second-degree murder in every case in which a person drives a car to a bar, a friend's home, or a party, drinks alcohol so that he is under its influence, drives away and is involved in a fatal accident. Moreover, newly enacted legislation will make it easier than ever to establish implied malice. Under a bill recently signed by the Governor, the rebuttable presumption that a person is under the influence of alcohol if his blood alcohol content is 0.10 percent or more has been eliminated. Instead, the new statute makes it a crime to drive with a blood alcohol content of 0.10 percent or more. In effect, it creates a conclusive presumption that the driver is under the influence of alcohol. Under this conclusive presumption and the majority's erroneous expansion of the concept of implied malice, a person who had only a few drinks could readily find himself charged with and convicted of second-degree murder.

The majority's reasoning also perpetuates the fiction that when a person drinks socially, he willfully drinks to come under the influence of alcohol and with this knowledge drives home at a later time. This unfounded conclusion ignores social reality. "Typically (a person) sets out to drink without becoming intoxicated, and because alcohol distorts judgment, he overrates his capacity, and misjudges his driving ability after drinking too much." *Taylor, supra,* 24 Cal.3d at 908.

Clearly, evidence regarding respondent's drinking earlier in the evening bears little relevance to his state of mind at the time of the accident. The majority's reliance on evidence of respondent's presumed state of mind before he began driving violates the basic principle that a crime cannot be committed unless there is unity of act and intent.

The majority's errors are compounded by the fact that they improperly presume that respondent harbored a conscious disregard for life. Thus, they state that respondent "must have known" he would drive after drinking, and that it "may be presumed that he was aware of the hazards of driving while intoxicated." These presumptions improperly dilute the requirement that the prosecution must prove the accused's intent to commit an act likely to kill with conscious disregard for life. The majority point to respondent's drinking as evidence of the implied-malice element that he committed an act likely to kill. However, they ignore the fact that driving while under the influence may also show lack of a conscious appreciation of the risk of harm presented to others.

Finally, the majority distort the evidence and draw the wrong inference from the testimony presented at the preliminary examination that respondent put on his brakes just before the fatal accident. They infer that this shows that respondent knew of the risk he created to the lives of others [*or he worried about himself*]. However, the majority fail to draw the obvious inference that respondent consciously sought to *avoid* the risk of injuring or killing anyone. The latter inference tends to disprove the element required for implied malice that the act evidenced a conscious disregard for life.

The elements of implied malice have not been established. Speeding through a green light is not an act likely to kill. Nor was this act done intentionally with conscious disregard for life. The fact that respondent earlier that evening drove to a bar is of little probative value in determining his state of mind sometime later. The only evidence bearing significantly on respondent's state of mind was the fact that he was driving at a time when he was under the influence of alcohol. This fact tends to disprove the element of conscious disregard for life. To rule otherwise is to establish with one stroke of the pen a new crime of second-degree murder for anyone who is involved in an accident when driving a vehicle while under the influence of alcohol, where the accident results in the death of another.

The fact that the Legislature adopted a vehicular manslaughter statute (§192(3)) indicates that the Legislature intended that statute to cover these situations. I am certain the Legislature never foresaw that this court would expand the concept of implied malice so as to rewrite the law in this area. I cannot so lightly rewrite the Legislature's statutes nor so blithely ignore the pertinent facts to achieve a judicial result.

I respectfully dissent.

[The separate dissenting opinion of Justice IBANEZ is omitted].

## QUESTIONS ON *WATSON*

1. **Interlocutory appeal.** Was Watson tried and convicted? If so, of what offense or offenses? If not, from what does he appeal?

2. **Not all car "accidents" are accidents.** There is no evidence to suggest that the killings were intentional. Is there any evidence to suggest that they were unintentional, that is, accidental?

3. **Degrees of recklessness.** How does the majority characterize the difference between gross negligence (the crucial element in some vehicular and involuntary manslaughters) and implied malice (the crucial element in some second-degree murders)? Does one crime depend on an "objective" test and the other a "subjective" test?

4. **Elements of offenses.** Because defendants who go to trial do not confess to having intentionally or even recklessly killed someone, probability analysis plays an important role in separating intentional, not intentional, and unintentional killings from one another. Comparing the elements of implied-malice murder and involuntary (vehicular) manslaughter, Justice Richardson observes for the majority that "[t]hough these definitions bear a general similarity, they are not identical." How does he explain their differences?

**5. "Other minds": penetrating another's privacy.** Whether he is defending a manslaughter or murder charge, Watson is accused of killing two people while driving recklessly. A defendant who does not plead guilty to such charges bases his defense on either of two claims: 1) that the risks he took were not excessive, that is, that he was not driving that fast and did not run a red light at the intersection where the crash occurred; or 2) even if the risks he took were excessive, he was unaware of them at the time.

Again, defendants charged with crimes of recklessness rarely cop to consciously disregarding substantial and unjustifiable risks. Instead they plead, perhaps in good faith, that the risks that materialized never occurred to them at all. Given that a charge of murder requires proof that defendant knew that what he was doing was dangerous to life, Justice Richardson's opinion for the majority concluded that such knowledge can be said to reside in defendant's decision to go to a bar knowing both that he would become intoxicated and that he would later drive in an impaired condition. Indeed, that he slammed on his brakes twice before the fatal crash indicated to the majority that he knew his driving was putting the lives of others at risk; otherwise he would not have slammed on his brakes.

But what if Watson never thought about any of this? He was, after all, severely intoxicated. Or is general knowledge about risk, even if he did not consider it then and there, enough? Certainly one can know something without bearing it in mind at the time, right? (Otherwise there wouldn't be room for much). How are we to know what risks occurred to others before they went ahead with what they were doing?

**6. Standard of review.** Justice Richardson claims to be reviewing only undisputed facts. For this, Chief Justice Bird takes him to task. To begin with, Bird notes, witness-Henke's testimony is much more consistent with the rulings of the Superior Court and the magistrate than with the position taken by Justice Richardson's majority. In addition, just as a pre-trial judicial finding of probable cause should be reversed only if plainly erroneous (this was a principal point in the majority's ruling affirming the denial of Decina's demurrer to the indictment in Chapter 1.A, *supra*), so too should a pre-trial judicial finding that charges are *not* supported by probable cause be reversed only if plainly erroneous.

Did the California Supreme Court defer to the rulings below in Watson's favor? Or did it review those rulings *de novo*?

**7. Legislative history.** The vehicular manslaughter charge with which Watson's murder charge was being compared required proof of gross negligence. What sort of proof did the 1935 version of the law require?

## NOTES ON *WATSON*

***1. Criminal procedure: charging instruments.*** Justice Richardson notes that the People's *complaint* charged Watson with two counts of murder and two counts of manslaughter. Richardson adds that after Watson's preliminary hearing, the People's *information* made the same allegations. Like Decina's home state of New York, see *supra* Chapter 1.A, note 5b on *Decina*, Watson's home state of California commences misdemeanor prosecutions with the filing of a complaint. California Penal Code §740. Unlike New York, felony prosecutions in California do not typically commence by grand-jury indictment, though the procedure is still invoked from time to time at the prosecutor's discretion. E.g., *People v. Charles Manson et al.*, 132 Cal.Rptr. 265 (2d Dist. Ct. App. 1976). Instead of commencing felony prosecutions by grand-jury indictment, California relies heavily on a charging instrument known as an "information": an affidavit in which the prosecutor alleges the probable cause to support charges against defendant. California Penal Code §737. The time and expense to convene a grand jury to consider an indictment against a misdemeanant is justified only when the misdemeanor is appended to a felony charge. *People v. Lukenbill*, 234 Cal.App.3d Supp. 1 (1991).

After a felony complaint is filed, a preliminary hearing is held for the judge to assess whether there is probable cause to bind over any of the charges for trial. See California Penal Code §§859b, 871, 872. If the judge finds probable cause, the prosecutor files an information, which replaces the complaint as the charging instrument. California Penal Code §738. Again, to economize, a preliminary hearing is used to review only those misdemeanor complaints that are appended to a felony charge. California Penal Code §740; *Medellin v. Superior Court*, 166 Cal.App.3d 290 (1985).

Although the grand jury is considered a judicial body, *People v. Superior Court (1973 Grand Jury)*, 13 Cal.3d 430, 438 (1975), its proceedings are non-adversarial: no judge, no defense counsel, just a prosecutor, witnesses testifying under subpoena, and grand jurors.

Indeed, grand-jury proceedings are more inquisitorial than adversarial. For this reason, a battle was fought in the California courts over whether the adversarial, trial-like protocol of preliminary hearings (with a judge, evidentiary standards, right to counsel, compulsory process, and confrontation of adverse witnesses) is a constitutional prerequisite of charging. It is not. See California Constitution Art. 1, §14.1 (1990); *Bowens v. Superior Court*, 1 Cal.4th 36 (1991) (en banc); *cf. People v. McConnell*, 373 N.Y.S.2d 971, 975 (Supreme Court Queens County 1975) ["The weight of authority in both the federal and state courts appears to be uniform in holding that a defendant has no right under the United States Constitution ... to a preliminary hearing prior to indictment by a grand jury"].

**2. Interlocutory appeals.** Watson was charged with two counts of second-degree murder and two counts of vehicular manslaughter. At a pre-trial hearing, the magistrate found the murder counts unsupported by probable cause. From there, Watson's motion in the trial court to dismiss the murder counts was granted. From that ruling the prosecution appealed. After the Court of Appeal affirmed in *People v. Watson*, 108 Cal.App.3d 677 (1980), the California Supreme Court reversed, reinstating the murder counts in the opinion we just read.

[margin note: need malice]

Congress gives federal courts of appeals jurisdiction to hear challenges only from *final* judgments of district courts. 28 U.S.C. §1291. Otherwise, if every little pre-trial order were immediately appealable, the delays and disruptions of such "piecemeal litigation" would be intolerable. *United States v. FMC Corp.*, 84 S.Ct. 4, 7 (1963). Exempt from the final-judgment rule are "interlocutory" appeals (from the Greek "interlocutors," who participate in dialogue, the legal usage suggesting a sort of interruption). Interlocutory appeals involve a "small class of non-final orders which finally determine claims of right separable from, and collateral to, rights asserted in the action, too important to be denied review and too independent of the cause itself to require that appellate consideration be deferred until the whole case is adjudicated." *Cohen v. Beneficial Industrial Loan Corp.*, 69 S.Ct. 1221, 1225 (1949). Characteristic of an appealable order under *Cohen*'s "collateral order" doctrine is that if not reviewed before the proceedings terminate, it will never be meaningfully reviewed at all. *Mitchell v. Forsyth*, 105 S.Ct. 2806, 2814-15 (1985).

***a. Defense-side interlocutory appeals.*** Defendants who identify errors that are not vindicated pre-trial are largely relegated to post-conviction remedies. *United States v. Liotard,* 817 F.2d 1074, 1080 (3d Cir. 1987). This is true even for convictions based on evidence obtained by police in violation of the Fourth Amendment ban on unreasonable searches and seizures. *DiBella v. United States,* 82 S.Ct. 654 (1962). To illustrate, when federal agents got a search warrant for the blood and saliva of Jelanie Solomon—a convicted drug dealer whom agents suspected of killing a witness—Solomon tried to quash the warrant for lack of probable cause. *In re Solomon,* 465 F.3d 114, 122-23 (3d Cir. 2006). After the district court ruled against him, he appealed to the Third Circuit, which refused to review an order issuing a warrant in a case that was far from final. Because unreasonable searches and seizures occur on the street, not in the courtroom, Solomon would have to await his conviction to appeal the district court's denial of his motion to quash the warrant. *Ibid.* (Another way of saying this is the damage police inflict in executing the warrant will be water under the bridge by the time of trial, which itself would work no new Fourth Amendment wrong simply by entertaining the evidence).

Interlocutory appeals *shall* lie, however, for claims of excessive bail, *Stack v. Boyle,* 72 S.Ct. 1, 7 (1952), absolute immunity from damages suits, *Nixon v. Fitzgerald,* 102 S.Ct. 2690 (1982), or claims that a trial would violate Double Jeopardy, *Abney v. United States,* 97 S.Ct. 2034 (1977): all three of these claims are deemed separate from the merits of the underlying actions and incapable of being effectively vindicated post-trial.

**b. Prosecution-side interlocutory appeals.** In *Watson,* it was the prosecutor who took an interlocutory appeal from the trial court's dismissal of murder charges for lack of probable cause. Prosecution appeals from such pre-trial rulings are permitted so the People can get their theory of the appropriate charges before an appellate panel before such charges become barred by the constitutional ban on Double Jeopardy. The Double Jeopardy ban precludes multiple trials (following conviction, acquittal, or certain mistrials) or punishments for the same offense. U.S. Const. amend. V; *see North Carolina v. Pearce,* 89 S.Ct. 2072, 2076 (1969). Offenses are the same if they are too elementally similar to be treated differently. That is, two offenses are the same if one offense, call it the "greater" offense, cannot be committed without at once also committing another offense, call it the "lesser" offense. *Blockburger v. United States,* 52 S.Ct. 180, 182 (1932). In such cases, a defendant may not be convicted of both the greater and the lesser "included" offense, nor could he be retried—*at the prosecution's behest*—on either offense after trial on either offense, whether that first trial ends up in acquittal or conviction.

For example, assault and murder are the same offense in that murder elementally includes an assault (just as robbery is at times adjudged the same offense as both assault and larceny since assault and larceny are elements of robbery). *Cf. Downs v. State*, 962 So.2d 1255, 1260-62 (Miss. 2007). But while assault is a lesser-included offense of murder, assault with a deadly weapon is *not* a lesser-included offense of murder. Because use of a deadly weapon is not an element of murder, one may commit murder without at once also committing assault with a deadly weapon.

So too, involuntary manslaughter is a lesser-included offense of murder because murder requires malice (an intentional or extremely reckless killing) whereas manslaughter requires absence of malice (requiring instead a grossly negligent, that is, ordinarily reckless killing). Because one cannot commit an intentional or extremely reckless killing without at once also committing a grossly negligent/ordinarily reckless killing, the relation of murder to manslaughter is said to be one of greater to lesser offense.

If prosecution appeals of pre-trial rulings were *not* permitted, no appellate review of the prosecution's position would be available. Prosecution appeals are allowed whenever doing so would not violate Double Jeopardy. Because manslaughter is a lesser included of murder, then conviction or acquittal on manslaughter or murder would preclude retrial on either. That means if the prosecution appeal of the trial court's dismissal of Watson's murder counts had to await his trial and acquittal of manslaughter, the appellate court's only remedy would be to reinstate, and permit a trial on, the murder count. And that second trial would violate Double Jeopardy because once tried for manslaughter (considered the "same" offense as murder), no trial for murder can follow. If the trial court erred in dismissing the murder count for lack of probable cause, the prosecution deserves a chance to present such a claim to an appellate tribunal. Interlocutory appeal, which occurs before jeopardy attaches, provides that chance.

In *People v. Sanchez*, 24 Cal.4th 983 (2001), the California Supreme Court, over Justice Kennard's dissent, upheld defendant's conviction for second-degree murder *and* gross vehicular manslaughter while intoxicated, arising out of a single death in a traffic accident. The court reasoned that because driving and drunkenness are not elements of murder, gross vehicular manslaughter while intoxicated is *not* a lesser-included offense of murder.[a] As eccentric as it may sound, it would on the logic of *Sanchez* be perfectly lawful for Watson, once tried, to be convicted and sentenced on four counts of homicide arising out of two deaths. As *Sanchez* itself acknowledges, however (*id.* at 992), that eccentric outcome is blocked by California Penal Code §654(a), which states:

> An act or omission that is punishable in different ways by different provisions of law shall be punished under the provision that provides for the longest potential term of imprisonment, but in no case shall the act or omission be punished under more than one provision. An acquittal or conviction and sentence under any one bars a prosecution for the same act or omission under any other.

With section 654(a) capping punishment on Sanchez's homicide counts at one (not two), he got 15 years to life for second-degree murder, while sentencing on the manslaughter count was "stayed" (read, suspended, until completion of the murder term, when the stay would become permanent). *Sanchez* thus ends up a more technical than substantive ruling on the meaning and operation of "same offense" for purposes of Double Jeopardy. Watson could accordingly be *sentenced* under §654(a) for no more than two homicides, even if *convicted* of four.

Although DUI vehicular manslaughter is not considered a lesser included of murder, there is still a sound efficiency basis for a prosecution-side interlocutory appeal of the pretrial ruling dismissing the murder charges. *People v. Superior Court (Caudie),* 221 Cal.App.3d 1190, 1192-93 n.2 (1990) ["Interlocutory review is justified in the interest of avoiding multiple trials involving the same facts."].

Post-*Sanchez* rulings have addressed the fairness of pointing to two different modes of homicide for one killing to be used as two separate "strikes," that is, serious or violent felonies, for sentencing purposes under repeat-offender statutes. *In re Alejandro B.,* 186 Cal.Rptr.3d 763 (5th Dist. Ct. App. 2015); *People v. Vargas,* 174 Cal.Rptr.3d 277 (Cal. 2014).

---

[a] There is limited authority for the proposition that ordinary manslaughter, vehicular manslaughter, and gross vehicular manslaughter while intoxicated *are* all the same offense for purposes of Double Jeopardy. See 7 Texas Practice Series Criminal Forms and Trial Manual §52.1 (11th ed.).

**3. *Malice aforethought.*** The homicide laws of California, based as they are on the Pennsylvania Criminal Code of 1794, feature degreed murder. California has two degrees of murder, California Penal Code §189 (2012), while Pennsylvania has three. 18 Purdon's Pennsylvania Statutes and Consolidated Statutes §2502 (1978). In California, all murder, regardless of the degree, requires "malice aforethought." Malice is a broad term, encompassing killings that are done intentionally and killings that are done extremely recklessly. CALJIC Nos. 8.30 & 8.31. A killing that is done recklessly (that is, criminally, culpably, or grossly negligently), but not quite extremely recklessly, is involuntary manslaughter. CALJIC Nos. 8.45 & 8.46.

The Model Penal Code dispensed with the term "malice." Model Penal Code & Commentaries §2.10.2, at 13-21 (1980). Instead, under the Code, murder is a killing done "purposely," "knowingly," or "extremely recklessly." MPC §§2.02 & 2.10.2(1). Ordinarily reckless killings are manslaughter, *id.* at §210.3(1)(a), whereas ordinarily negligent killings are negligent homicide. *Id.* at §210.4(1). Non-negligent killings are non-criminal.

**4. *Sentencing.*** The stakes in distinguishing second-degree murder from involuntary manslaughter are high. Second-degree murder carries an incarcerative sentence of 15 years to life, California Penal Code §190(a), whereas involuntary manslaughter carries a "base" or presumptive incarcerative sentence of just three years. California Penal Code §193(b). Gross vehicular homicide while intoxicated was not a recognized offense until 1992. California Penal Code §191.5 [base term four years].

**5. *Conscious disregard for life*.**

*a. And intoxication.* In homicide cases involving defendant-motorists, absence of intoxication does not preclude a finding of implied malice. For instance, in *People v. Contreras,* 26 Cal.App.4th 944 (1994), an appeal from Heriberto Contreras's conviction of second-degree murder arising out of a car crash, the Court of Appeal affirmed the conviction on the ground that his driving record, prior accident, and obviously faulty brakes supported a finding of malice.

Citing *Contreras* with approval, a court of appeal upheld the second-degree-murder conviction of a sober Hal Lee Moore, who drove 70 mph in a 35-mph zone, crossed into opposing traffic, caused oncoming drivers to avoid him, ran a red light, and hit a car in the intersection without even attempting to brake. *People v. Moore*, 187 Cal.App.4th 937 (2010).

**b. Whose life?** In *Watson*, the court held that implied malice may be found when the facts establish a defendant's conscious disregard for life. In *People v. Albright*, 173 Cal.App.3d 883 (1985), defendant argued that implied malice requires awareness of life-threatening risk to the ultimate victim *specifically*, not to the lives of others generally. The court disagreed.

**6. Watson's trial and its aftermath.** On remand from the high court, Watson was convicted by a jury of two counts of second-degree murder on an information and jury instructions naming only murder, not manslaughter. His motion for a new trial on *Jackson v. Virginia* grounds was denied, but the trial court did reduce the murders to vehicular manslaughters, for which it sentenced Watson to two three-year terms to run concurrent. *See infra* Chapter 4.A, question 2 & note 6 on *Bond*. From that ruling both sides appealed, resolution of the prosecution's appeal rendering Watson's appeal moot.

The prosecution's appeal of the trial court's ruling modifying Watson's murder conviction offends no principle of Double Jeopardy because the prosecution, if successful, would not place Watson in new jeopardy on murder charges. Instead, a prosecution victory on appeal would mean a reinstatement—without trial—of the murder convictions. In other words, the reinstatement of Watson's murder convictions would be just the filing of a piece of paper, which in no way exposes him to the vexation and annoyance of a second trial, which is what Double Jeopardy bans.

Because the Court of Appeal sensed the trial court had modified the verdict based on non-evidence, the remand directed the trial court to order a new trial or justify the modified verdict with evidence on the record to support its finding of absence of malice on Watson's part. *People v. Watson*, 198 Cal.Rptr. 26 (3d Dist. Ct. App. 1983). On March 16, 1984, Shasta County Superior Court Judge W.H. Phelps granted Watson's motion for a new trial (Case. No. 62954/79F5). While a new trial held at defendant's request does *not* offend Double Jeopardy, Watson never was retried, at least according to the Shasta County Superior Court.

## B. SPECIFIC AND GENERAL INTENT

By now it should be clear that not all crimes require identical proof. Some very minor crimes, for example, require proof only that the act was committed; no room is given for excuses like accident, mistake, and intoxication. These are known as "strict liability" crimes. Minor traffic infractions fall into this class. *See, e.g., Peck v. Dunn*, 574 P.2d 367, 370 (Utah 1978). "I didn't know I was speeding," "my speedometer is broken," "everyone else was speeding too," or "I was late for work" are pleaded in vain as excuses for speeding. I say "in vain" because speeding statutes are not phrased in a way that allows for such excuses to mitigate or nullify liability. Speeding statutes regulate *all* speeding, not just intentional, knowing, reckless, or negligent speeding. It does not matter how much effort the speeding driver took to comply with the speed limit. It matters only that the speed limit was exceeded. These minor crimes are achieved when certain untoward results occur or are at least threatened (here, putting others at risk by driving too fast); such minor crimes make no mention in the text of the statute of the mindset, attitude, or intentions of defendant toward what he or she is doing. *E.g., State v. Kleppe*, 800 N.W.2d 311 (N.D. 2011) [hunting, taking, or possessing big game in North Dakota is an example of strict liability, punishable with no proof of fault]. If it sounds unfair, the justification is that the stakes are low: no incarceration or other severe stigmatizing that is normally part of criminal punishment attaches to the commission of minor strict-liability crimes.

Apart from strict-liability crimes, all offenses describe the requisite state of mind or *mens rea* that the prosecution must prove; or, where no subjective criminality is required, the offenses state that negligence will suffice as proof of guilt. Take, for example, murder, defined in California as the unlawful killing of a human being or viable fetus with malice aforethought. Murder has two elements: 1) killing a human or fetus without justification; and 2) malice aforethought. Assuming that defendant did in fact kill as required by the first element, he or she has committed murder if the killing was malicious. If the killing was intentional, then defendant has committed murder, given that an intentional killing is also a malicious killing. Likewise, if the killing was not intentional, but nonetheless extremely reckless, then that is an instance of murder. But, as killings that are not quite intentional go, a killing involving ordinary recklessness—but not extreme recklessness—is not murder. In other words, the notion of malice includes extremely reckless killings but excludes ordinarily reckless killings. And of course a killing that is in any sense accidental (negligent or not) is not murder.

To complicate things, California does not limit the terminology of murder and other homicide offenses to killings that are malicious (or not). It also separates killings into those done with specific intent and those done with general intent. Two distinct notions of specific intent pervade. The first is "vertical," which locates specific intent at the top of a hierarchy of fault: above knowledge, recklessness, and negligence. On this account, specific intent is that mode of action the Model Penal Code identifies with its notion of purpose. Under the vertical notion, an action is done with specific intent when the actor puts himself to the task, including the outcome, which is carried out or realized. The second notion of specific intent is "horizontal" or temporal, meaning that one act now, say, entering a building, is done with the specific intent of accomplishing some other act in the immediate future, say, stealing. Under the horizontal notion, that the unjustified entry is done with an eye toward the future act or consequence of stealing is what makes burglary a specific-intent crime. See William Roth, *General v. Specific Intent: A Time for Terminological Understanding in California*, 7 Pepperdine Law Review 67 (1979).

If specific-intent crimes contemplate some future act or consequence beyond the basic act that is being performed, the horizontal notion explains not just why burglary is a specific-intent crime, but theft, too. For example, larceny is a trespassory taking of property known to be that of another (now) with the specific intent to permanently deprive the rightful possessor (later). The horizontal notion works well with conspiracies, too, which are agreements between two or more persons (now) with the specific intent to commit a crime or crimes (later). And it works well enough, I suppose, with attempt crimes, which are direct but ineffectual acts performed (now) with the specific intent to succeed (later).

Assaultive offenses, however, have never quite fit this description, with the exception of premeditated and deliberate first-degree murder, where, having thought it through, one puts oneself to killing another, thus separating the intention from the action (or at least its outcome), albeit in an awkward way. This also explains why express malice second-degree murder is classified as a specific-intent crime: it is done now with an intention to cause the death of the victim (soon after). But crimes of recklessness simply do not fit the horizontal notion of specific intent in that they are not *directed* at all. Reckless actors are indifferent to results, not bent on them. Thus the list of crimes that qualify as specific intent includes: attempts, burglaries, conspiracies, solicitations, premeditated and deliberate and other expressly malicious murders, all types of theft (robbery, extortion, embezzlement, larceny, fraud), civil-rights offenses, and the underlying or trigger offenses within felony murder.

Like specific intent, general intent, too, was and remains a troubling notion for courts. According to the Model Penal Code's drafters, general intent "is present whenever there is specific intent, and also when the circumstances indicate that the offender, in the ordinary course of human experience, must have adverted to the prescribed criminal consequences as reasonably certain to result from his act or failure to act." MPC §2.02, at 230-31 n.3. This rolls into one the Code's formulations of purpose, knowledge, and recklessness. It is similar to what we have been equating with malice. To use a homely example, if I intend to throw a ball through my neighbor's window and do in fact break it, I break the window with specific intent; yet so too on those facts do I break the window with general intent. But suppose I throw the ball through the window trying to throw it *near* the window, while suspecting that I may not be able to quite pull it off, seeing the potential window breakage as in play the whole time. If breaking the window by playing catch in such close proximity is not intentional (neither intentional nor unintentional), then the foreseen incidental (breaking the window) is brought about with general intent. General-intent crimes have no future act or consequence contemplated; instead, there is no temporal division between the blunt, basic act and its consequences. Examples of general-intent crimes are arson, assault, kidnapping, rape, involuntary manslaughter, voluntary manslaughter, and second-degree implied-malice murder.

Whether charged with specific- or general-intent crimes, defendants try to excuse their actions by claiming accident, mistake, provocation, duress, insanity, or intoxication, or justify their actions by claiming self-defense. Intoxication is a tricky defense because it is not always clear whether it aggravates or mitigates the wrongfulness of an action. Indeed, intoxication was long seen as an additional charge that compounded wrongdoing, as in, "not only have you battered the tax-collector, but what makes matters worse, you're a drunk." *See Beverley's Case*, 76 English Reports 1118, 1123 (King's Bench 1603). It makes good sense, too: intentionally tying up your better judgment is an act of irresponsibility worth criticizing both on its own and in conjunction with the harmful acts you undertake while in that self-inflicted, impaired state. But by the 19th Century, a more compassionate approach to criminality insinuated itself into defining crimes and into sentencing offenders. That new approach was to treat the offender, not just the offense. Recognition of the limits that mental illness and intoxication place on responsibility led to recognition of insanity, diminished capacity, and intoxication as excuses defendants could raise to avoid or reduce responsibility in criminal cases.

That created problems as well. In a nutshell, alcohol causes violence. Thus the availability of intoxication as a defense to assaultive offenses paved the way for an undesirably high number of acquittals in assault cases where defendant's own actions not only put him in a position where he would be more prone to uncivilized acts, but put him in a position to excuse those acts as well. Presently, the law reflects the iffy state of the excuse of intoxication. *See Montana v. Egelhoff*, 116 S.Ct. 2013 (1996). The iffiness of intoxication-as-excuse explains in part the difficulties of the specific- and general-intent distinction as manifested in the following case, *People v. Whitfield*, 7 Cal.4th 437 (1994) (en banc).

## SUPREME COURT OF CALIFORNIA

### EN BANC

*THE PEOPLE, PLAINTIFF AND RESPONDENT*

*V.*

*STEPHEN MARTIN WHITFIELD, DEFENDANT AND APPELLANT*

### FEB. 28, 1994

GEORGE, Justice

We granted review in this case to resolve a conflict in decisions of the Courts of Appeal regarding whether, under Penal Code §22, evidence of voluntary intoxication is admissible in a prosecution for second-degree murder when the prosecution seeks to establish the existence of malice aforethought on an implied-malice theory, i.e., seeks to prove that defendant acted with knowledge of the danger to human life and in conscious disregard of human life. For the reasons that follow, we hold that evidence of voluntary intoxication is admissible under §22 with regard to whether the defendant harbored malice aforethought, express or implied.

We further hold that the trial court in this case correctly instructed the jury as to the proper use of evidence of voluntary intoxication in determining whether defendant was guilty of second-degree murder or, instead, of gross vehicular manslaughter while intoxicated, and did not err in refusing to provide an additional instruction, requested by defendant, concerning whether defendant was unconscious at the time of the killing. Accordingly, we affirm the judgment of the Court of Appeal upholding defendant's conviction of second-degree murder.

## I

Defendant was charged by information with murder, driving under the influence of alcohol or drugs within seven years of having suffered three previous convictions for a similar offense, driving with a blood-alcohol content of .08 percent or more within seven years of having suffered three previous convictions for a similar offense, and driving while his privilege to drive was suspended or revoked for driving under the influence of alcohol or drugs.

The evidence admitted at trial included the following: In 1989, pursuant to the sentence imposed upon his being convicted a second time for driving under the influence of alcohol, defendant attended several sessions of a program for repeat offenders and viewed a film that graphically depicted the carnage caused by intoxicated drivers, including footage of scenes of accidents caused by such drivers and interviews with relatives of persons who had been killed in this manner. On March 5, 1990, defendant suffered his third conviction for driving under the influence of alcohol.

Shortly after 1 p.m. on Saturday, November 17, 1990, defendant was driving on Van Buren Boulevard in Riverside County. Frank Diaz III, who was driving behind defendant, observed defendant's vehicle swerve in and out of the left lane and over the double yellow line dividing the road. Frank Falbo was driving in the opposite direction on Van Buren Boulevard when defendant's vehicle swerved over the double yellow line, almost colliding with Falbo's automobile, then continued straddling the double yellow line, occupying three-quarters of the oncoming lane, and collided head-on with a vehicle driven by 21-year-old Ronald Lawrence Kinsey. Kinsey was killed.

Defendant was found unconscious on the front seat of his vehicle. He smelled strongly of an alcoholic beverage. Several empty 16-ounce cans of malt liquor were on the floor of the vehicle. He was taken to a hospital for treatment of his injuries, the most serious of which was a collapsed lung. A hospital employee informed defendant he had killed someone.

At approximately 3 p.m., a sample of defendant's blood was withdrawn at the request of the police. The technician who extracted the blood heard defendant exclaim: "Take me straight to the gas chamber, I killed somebody." Analysis of the blood sample revealed a blood-alcohol content of .24 percent.

Defendant did not dispute the prosecution's evidence establishing that he was under the influence of alcohol. To the contrary, defendant sought to prove that he did not harbor implied malice aforethought because he was so intoxicated that he was unconscious at the time the accident occurred. Defense counsel elicited testimony demonstrating that, because the amount of alcohol in a person's system dissipates over time, defendant's blood-alcohol content would have been .27 percent about the time of the collision, and that individuals with blood-alcohol levels above .25 percent may become stuporous and lose consciousness. Defendant also introduced evidence indicating that an independent laboratory's analysis of the blood sample withdrawn at the request of the police, and an analysis by the hospital of a separate blood sample, revealed even higher blood-alcohol levels [of .395 percent. *People v. Whitfield*, 15 Cal.Rptr.2d 4, 17 (4th Dist. Ct. App. 1992).]

Lorena Lee testified for the defense that she drove past defendant's vehicle immediately prior to the accident and observed that defendant's head was nodding "like he was fighting sleep." Defendant also offered the testimony of a paramedic who arrived at the scene of the accident and found defendant unconscious. When defendant regained consciousness a short time later, he was incoherent, his speech was incomprehensible, and his breath smelled strongly of an alcoholic beverage. The paramedic acknowledged that defendant's apparent lack of comprehension and mumbled speech might have resulted from the accident, but he believed they were due to defendant's consumption of alcohol.

Clinical psychologist Dr. Craig Rath testified for the defense that blood-alcohol levels from .09 percent to .25 percent impair a person's memory and ability to make critical judgments and to predict the effects of one's actions. At blood-alcohol levels from .25 percent to .40 percent, a majority of individuals will become stuporous and lose consciousness, although their eyes may remain open and they may continue to function physically and even be able to operate a motor vehicle. Dr. Rath opined that a person could be capable of operating a motor vehicle even though he or she was incapable of conscious decision-making due to alcohol consumption.

On rebuttal, the prosecution introduced evidence establishing that, when questioned by police officers two days after the collision, defendant stated that during the morning of the day of the collision, he consumed the contents of two 16-ounce cans of malt liquor at his home and then drove his children to his mother's house. He purchased two more cans of malt liquor near his mother's house and consumed their contents as well. Defendant subsequently left his children with his mother and was driving home when the accident occurred. He did not remember the collision. The prosecution offered expert testimony establishing that the amount of alcohol defendant admitted having consumed was insufficient to produce a blood-alcohol level of .24 percent.

The trial court's instructions to the jury included the following. For the crime of murder "there must exist a union or joint operation of act or conduct and a certain specific intent in the mind of the perpetrator." CALJIC No. 3.31. "If the evidence shows that the defendant was intoxicated at the time of the alleged crime, you should consider the fact of intoxication, including the degree of intoxication, in determining whether defendant had such specific intent or mental state." CALJIC No. 4.21. "Every person who unlawfully kills a human being with malice aforethought is guilty of the crime of murder...." CALJIC No. 8.10. "Malice may be either express or implied. Malice is express when there is manifested an intention unlawfully to kill a human being. Malice is implied when: 1. The killing resulted from an intentional act, 2. The natural consequences of the act are dangerous to human life, and 3. The act was deliberately performed with knowledge of the danger to and with conscious disregard for human life." CALJIC No. 8.11. The trial court's instructions continued:

> The intentional act required for implied malice underlying vehicle murder is not the traffic violation which may precede

a collision, but whether the defendant was driving under the influence with a conscious disregard for human life. In order to convict defendant of second-degree murder you must examine defendant's state of mind at the time of the act. This is referred to as a subjective test. Second-degree murder based on implied malice requires that defendant acted deliberately, that defendant acted with knowledge of the danger to human life, and that defendant acted in conscious disregard for human life. If a person causes another's death by doing a dangerous act in an unlawful or criminally negligent manner, without realizing the risk involved, he is guilty of manslaughter. If, on the other hand, the person realized the risk and acted in conscious disregard of the danger to human life, malice is implied and the crime is murder.

In addition, the trial court carefully distinguished the mental state required for murder (implied malice) from the mental state required for the lesser offense of gross vehicular manslaughter (gross negligence).[2]

The trial court refused defendant's request that the jury be instructed, pursuant to CALJIC No. 8.47, that "[i]f you find that a defendant, while unconscious as a result of voluntary intoxication, killed another human being without intent to kill and without malice aforethought, the crime is involuntary manslaughter." The jury found defendant guilty as charged on all counts, fixing the degree of the murder as second degree, and the trial court sentenced defendant to prison for a term of 18 years to life.

---

[2] Gross negligence has been defined as the exercise of so slight a degree of care as to raise a presumption of conscious indifference to the consequences. On the other hand, malice may be implied when a person, knowing that his conduct endangers the life of another, nonetheless acts deliberately with conscious disregard for life. *Though these definitions bear a general similarity, they are not identical. Implied malice contemplates a subjective awareness of a higher degree of risk than does gross negligence and involves a ... wantonness which is absent in gross negligence.* [Italics mine.] A finding of gross negligence is made by applying an objective test: If a reasonable person in defendant's position would have been aware of the risk involved, then defendant is presumed to have had such an awareness. However, a finding of implied malice depends upon a determination that the defendant actually appreciated the risk involved, i.e., a subjective standard....

On appeal, defendant asserted ... that the trial court erred in refusing to instruct the jury pursuant to CALJIC No. 8.47 concerning unconsciousness caused by voluntary intoxication. The Court of Appeal affirmed the conviction, observing that, pursuant to §22, only when a specific-intent crime is charged is evidence of voluntary intoxication admissible to demonstrate that a defendant did not harbor malice aforethought, and holding that second-degree murder based upon implied malice is not a specific-intent crime. Accordingly, the Court of Appeal concluded that the trial court did not err in refusing defendant's requested jury instruction regarding unconsciousness due to voluntary intoxication. In the view of the Court of Appeal, the trial court erred *in defendant's favor* by instructing the jury that it could consider defendant's degree of intoxication in deciding whether he harbored implied malice. In so holding, the Court of Appeal disagreed with the contrary holdings in *People v. Alvarado*, 232 Cal.App.3d 501 (1991) and *People v. Ricardi*, 221 Cal.App.3d 249 (1990). We granted review to resolve this conflict.

## II

Section 22(b) provides: "Evidence of voluntary intoxication is admissible solely on the issue of whether or not the defendant actually formed a required specific intent, premeditated, deliberated, or harbored malice aforethought, when a specific-intent crime is charged." Focusing upon the final phrase of this statute—"when a specific intent crime is charged"—the Court of Appeal held that evidence of voluntary intoxication cannot establish the absence of implied malice, because second-degree murder based upon implied malice is not a specific-intent crime. We conclude the Court of Appeal misinterpreted §22.

The admissibility of evidence of voluntary intoxication to demonstrate whether a defendant charged with murder harbored malice aforethought does not depend upon whether the prosecution seeks a conviction for first- or second-degree murder, or attempts to prove that defendant harbored express or implied malice. Section 22 specifies that such evidence is admissible to establish whether a defendant "harbored malice aforethought"; the statute does not distinguish between the two types of malice aforethought—express malice and implied malice—that always have been embodied in California law. As discussed below, prior to the amendment of §22 in 1981 and 1982, it long had been established that evidence of voluntary intoxication is admissible with regard to the issue of whether a defendant harbored either express or implied malice. It is unreasonable to conclude that §22, as amended in 1981 and 1982, presently creates such a distinction simply by including the qualifying phrase "when a specific intent crime is charged."

Prior to 1981, §22 provided: "No act committed by a person while in a state of voluntary intoxication is less criminal by reason of his having been in such condition. But whenever the actual existence of any particular purpose, motive, or intent is a necessary element to constitute any particular species or degree of crime, the jury may take into consideration the fact that the accused was intoxicated at the time, in determining the purpose, motive, or intent with which he committed the act." At that time, it was well established that, under §22, evidence of voluntary intoxication was admissible with regard to whether the defendant acted with malice aforethought, on either an express- or an implied-malice theory.

In 1981, the Legislature amended §22 as part of a broader legislative enactment whose general purpose was to abolish the doctrine of "diminished capacity." A significant provision of the 1981 statute was the enactment of §28, stating: "Evidence of mental disease, mental defect, or mental disorder shall not be admitted to negate the capacity to form any mental state, including, but not limited to, purpose, intent, knowledge, or malice aforethought, with which the accused committed the act. Evidence of mental disease, mental defect, or mental disorder is admissible on the issue as to whether the criminal defendant actually formed any such mental state." The Legislature thus prohibited the admission of evidence to negate the *capacity* of the defendant to form any mental state, but retained the existing rule that evidence was admissible with regard to whether the defendant *actually formed* a specific mental state.

Pursuant to this same legislation, §22 was divided into subdivisions and amended to read as follows: "(a) No act committed by a person while in a state of voluntary intoxication is less criminal by reason of his having been in such condition. Evidence of voluntary intoxication shall not be admitted *to negate the capacity* to form any mental state, including, but not limited to, purpose, intent, knowledge, or malice aforethought, with which the accused committed the act. (b) Whenever *the actual existence* of any mental state, including but not limited to, purpose, intent, knowledge, or malice aforethought, is a necessary element to constitute any particular species or degree of crime, evidence that the accused was voluntarily intoxicated at the time of the commission of the crime is admissible on the issue as to whether the defendant actually formed any such mental state." Thus, while the Legislature, in conformity with its abolition of the concept of *diminished capacity*, rendered evidence of voluntary intoxication inadmissible to negate the defendant's *capacity* to form any mental state, including malice aforethought, it at the same time explicitly retained the existing rule that evidence of voluntary intoxication was admissible with regard to whether a defendant *actually* harbored malice aforethought. Further, the 1981 amendment made no distinction between express and implied malice, an approach consistent with the well-established rule that evidence of voluntary intoxication is admissible with regard to whether a defendant harbored either express or implied malice.

The broad references in §22(b), as amended in 1981, to "any mental state" and to "intent" raised concerns, however, that the statute could be construed, contrary to the Legislature's intent, to alter the well-settled rule that evidence of voluntary intoxication is inadmissible to negate the existence of *general* criminal intent. To eliminate the possibility that the 1981 amendment would be misconstrued to permit the admission of evidence of voluntary intoxication to negate *general* criminal intent, the Legislature, in 1982, promptly revised §22(b) to its present form, replacing the term "intent" with the phrase "a required specific intent" and adding the concluding phrase "when a specific intent crime is charged." The Legislature stated that this amendment was "declaratory of existing law," thus making clear that it was seeking simply to clarify the scope of the 1981 amendments.

There is nothing to indicate that the Legislature intended its 1982 amendment to §22 to create an unprecedented distinction between express and implied malice with regard to the admissibility of evidence of voluntary intoxication. To the contrary, an analysis by the Senate Committee on Judiciary of the proposed amendment stated, "The purpose of this bill is to make modest changes" to §22 as amended in 1981. Further, the Legislature, expressly disclaiming any intent to create a new rule, stated that the addition of the phrase "when a specific intent crime is charged" simply was "declaratory of existing law." The history of §22 thus establishes that the 1982 amendment was not intended to alter the existing rule that voluntary intoxication is admissible on whether a defendant harbored malice aforethought, either express or implied.

As we have seen, in drafting the revision of §22(b), the Legislature did not state, as it easily could have done, that evidence of voluntary intoxication is admissible solely on whether a defendant harbored express (but not implied) malice. Instead, the Legislature stated that such evidence is admissible to establish whether the defendant "harbored malice aforethought." The term "malice aforethought" includes both express and implied malice. Thus, the language of the statute clearly appears to permit the admission of evidence of voluntary intoxication on whether a defendant harbored either express or implied malice, unless a different conclusion is compelled by the concluding qualification that such evidence is admissible only "when a specific intent crime is charged."

The Attorney General proffers just such an argument, maintaining that although second-degree murder is a specific-intent crime when the prosecution relies upon a theory of express malice, second-degree murder is not a specific-intent crime when the prosecution proceeds upon a theory of implied malice. As explained below, however, the Legislature considered murder a "specific intent crime" within the meaning of the language of §22 whether the prosecution's theory is that malice is express or implied.

As this court recognized in *People v. Hood*, 1 Cal.3d 444, 456-57 (1969) (en banc), "[s]pecific and general intent have been notoriously difficult terms to define and apply...." *Hood* addressed whether defendant's voluntary intoxication could be considered in determining whether he or she committed the crime of assault. Observing that "[t]he distinction between specific- and general-intent crimes evolved as a judicial response to the problem of the intoxicated offender," this court formulated the following rule: "When the definition of a crime consists of only the description of a particular act, without reference to intent to do a further act or achieve a future consequence, we ask whether the defendant intended to do the proscribed act. This intention is deemed to be a general criminal intent. When the definition refers to defendant's intent to do some further act or achieve some additional consequence, the crime is deemed to be one of specific intent."

Having stated the general rule, however, the court in *Hood* concluded that this definition should not be applied mechanically and was insufficient to resolve the question before the court, because the crime of assault could equally well be characterized as either a specific- or a general-intent crime. The court thus concluded that "the decision whether or not to give effect to evidence of intoxication [in a prosecution for assault] must rest on other considerations." *Id.* at 458.

It would be equally futile to attempt to rely solely upon *Hood*'s general definition of a specific-intent crime in determining, in the present case, the effect of §22 where the prosecution relies exclusively upon the theory that malice was implied, rather than express.

"Murder is the unlawful killing of a human being ... with malice aforethought." Malice is express when the defendant harbored an intent unlawfully to kill. It can be argued that such intent to kill does not "refer to defendant's intent to do some *further* act or achieve some *additional* consequence," *Hood*, 1 Cal.3d at 457, beyond the act proscribed by the murder statute, i.e., the killing a human being, yet we recently reaffirmed that murder is a specific-intent crime and that, pursuant to §22, "voluntary intoxication ... may be considered in deciding whether there was malice as defined in section 188." *People v. Saille*, 54 Cal.3d 1103, 1116-17 (1991). *Saille* arose from a conviction of first-degree murder in which malice was express. But there is no reason to reach a different conclusion when, as in the present case, malice is implied.

Malice is implied "when a person does an act, the natural consequences of which are dangerous to life, which act was deliberately performed by a person who knows that his conduct endangers the life of another and who acts with conscious disregard for life." *People v. Nieto Benitez*, 4 Cal.4th 91, 104 (1992). Although it can be argued that implied malice does not constitute a specific intent as described in *Hood* because it does not involve an "intent to do some further act or achieve some additional consequence," it is quite clear that implied malice does not fit *Hood*'s description of general intent, which is "an intent merely to do a violent act." *Hood*, 1 Cal.3d at 457-58. Although implied malice may not fall literally within the *Hood* formulation of specific intent, the element of implied malice that requires that the defendant act with knowledge of the danger to, and in conscious disregard of, human life, is closely akin to *Hood*'s definition of specific intent, which requires proof that the defendant acted with a specific and particularly culpable mental state. In context, the phrase "when a specific intent crime is charged" in §22 includes murder, even where the prosecution relies exclusively upon the theory that malice is implied, rather than express.

Furthermore, this interpretation of the statutory language is confirmed by an examination of the purpose of §22(b), which specifies when evidence of voluntary intoxication is admissible with regard to whether a defendant formed a required mental state. Among the different approaches to this issue adopted in various jurisdictions, §22 exemplifies "the common law approach of permitting voluntary intoxication as a defense to specific intent offenses and barring it as a defense to general intent offenses." This distinction between specific- and general-intent crimes "is a device to permit evidence of intoxication to reduce the crime to a lower degree, but not to admit evidence of self-induced intoxication if it would result in total acquittal."[5]

Allowing a defendant charged with murder to introduce evidence of voluntary intoxication to demonstrate the absence of either express or implied malice would not result in an acquittal, but in reduction of the offense to involuntary or vehicular manslaughter, which involve the unlawful killing of a human being without malice. Thus, we conclude that §22 was not intended, in murder prosecutions, to preclude consideration of evidence of voluntary intoxication on whether a defendant harbored malice aforethought, whether the prosecution claims that malice was express or implied.

The circumstances of the present case demonstrate the logic of this conclusion. Defendant was charged with murder and was prosecuted on the theory that malice could be implied because, in light of defendant's experiences stemming from his prior convictions for driving under the influence and his resulting knowledge of the danger to others posed by such conduct, he performed an act dangerous to life and acted with conscious disregard for human life by driving while intoxicated. Defendant also was charged with the lesser offense of gross vehicular manslaughter while intoxicated, which does not require that the defendant harbor malice.

---

[5] Fletcher aptly observes: "This distinction [between specific and general intent] glides well through the sea of crimes defined by the pattern 'assault with intent to....' Yet the distinction scrapes bottom as soon as we consider more compactly defined offenses, such as murder and larceny. Though malice does not represent an unrealized goal that goes beyond the act of killing, the courts treat it as a form of specific rather than general intent. This view facilitates a compromise between the rigors of denying the relevance of intoxication and allowing it to undercut all liability; in this respect, the classification is functionally sound." Fletcher, *Rethinking Criminal Law* 849 (1978). Fletcher further notes: "The distinction between general and specific intent is frequently litigated for the simple reason that the courts tend to employ these terms as though they had a meaning beyond their function as devices for seeking a compromise verdict." *Id.* at 850.

It was undisputed that defendant drove a vehicle while having a blood-alcohol level at least three times the legal limit, that the natural consequences of this act were dangerous to human life, and that this act resulted in the death of a human being. The sole disputed issue was whether defendant knew that his conduct endangered the life of another and acted with conscious disregard for human life. If so, malice would be implied and defendant would be guilty of second-degree murder. If not, defendant would be guilty of gross vehicular manslaughter while intoxicated. The most important factor bearing upon defendant's awareness of the dangerousness of his conduct and conscious disregard of that danger was his degree of intoxication when he undertook his dangerous course of conduct. It appears obviously appropriate to permit the jury to consider defendant's degree of intoxication in determining whether he formed the mental state that distinguishes the greater offense of murder from the lesser offense of manslaughter.

The Attorney General contends it is anomalous to allow a defendant who kills another while driving under the influence to rely upon the fact of self-induced intoxication to demonstrate that he or she did not harbor malice and, therefore, is guilty only of manslaughter rather than murder. But a defendant who kills another by firing a gun may defend against a charge of murder by establishing that, due to voluntary intoxication, he or she did not harbor malice and is guilty instead of manslaughter. The laws governing prosecutions for murder must apply equally whether the defendant kills the victim by means of a firearm or an automobile.

Consider, for example, a hypothetical situation in which a defendant, with no prior history of driving under the influence, consumes alcohol at a social gathering after having arranged to be driven home by his or her spouse. The defendant's spouse unexpectedly becomes ill and the defendant, who is intoxicated, decides to drive, and causes a fatal accident. Under such circumstances, it would not be anomalous to permit the defendant to defend against a charge of murder on the ground that, due to voluntary intoxication, he or she did not appreciate the dangerousness of his or her conduct, hence did not harbor malice, and should be convicted of the lesser offense of manslaughter. For the same reason, it was proper for defendant in the present case to attempt to establish that, due to voluntary intoxication, he did not harbor malice, but the jury, as it was entitled to do, rejected this proffered defense, impliedly finding that defendant acted with knowledge, and conscious disregard, of the danger to human life in undertaking to drive while intoxicated.

It is beyond dispute that drinking drivers exact an enormous toll on society. When a defendant drives while under the influence and thereby causes the death of another, serious punishment is warranted, but such serious punishment may be imposed without altering the long-settled requirement that a defendant not be convicted of murder unless he or she actually harbored malice. The Legislature specifically has addressed the situation in which a defendant drives under the influence and thereby causes the death of another, but does not harbor malice, by enacting §191.5, which provides a maximum sentence of 10 years in prison for gross vehicular manslaughter while intoxicated.

If, in a case like the present one, voluntary intoxication actually prevented a defendant from forming implied malice, he or she is guilty of gross vehicular manslaughter rather than murder. Prohibiting the trier of fact from considering evidence of voluntary intoxication in determining whether a defendant harbored implied malice would blur this distinction between second-degree murder with implied malice and gross vehicular manslaughter while intoxicated. As we observed in *People v. Watson*, in distinguishing vehicular manslaughter from second degree murder: "A finding of gross negligence [required for the offense of vehicular manslaughter] is made by applying an *objective* test: if a *reasonable person* in defendant's position would have been aware of the risk involved, then defendant is presumed to have had such an awareness. However, a finding of implied malice depends upon a determination that the defendant *actually appreciated* the risk involved, i.e., a *subjective* standard." Watson, 30 Cal.3d at 296-97.

Allowing the trier of fact to consider the effect of the defendant's intoxication will not preclude murder convictions when warranted. The jury in the present case considered the effect of defendant's intoxication but concluded nonetheless that he acted with implied malice. The result in the present case belies the concurring and dissenting opinion's lament that, under our holding, "drunk drivers could almost never be prosecuted for murder no matter how wanton their acts."

## III

Having concluded that the trial court did not err in instructing the jury to consider defendant's degree of intoxication in determining whether he harbored malice, we turn to defendant's contention that the trial court erred in refusing his request that the jury be instructed, in accordance with CALJIC No. 8.47, that if "defendant, while unconscious as a result of voluntary intoxication, killed another human being without intent to kill and without malice aforethought, the crime is involuntary manslaughter." Although this instruction is a correct statement of law in the abstract, the trial court properly refused the instruction because, in the context of the present case, it erroneously implied that, if defendant was unconscious when the collision occurred, he could not be convicted of murder.

The circumstance that a defendant, when a fatal traffic collision occurs, is unconscious as a result of voluntary intoxication, does not preclude a finding that the defendant harbored malice, because malice may have been formed prior to that time. In *Taylor v. Superior Court*, 24 Cal.3d 890 (1979), we considered whether an intoxicated driver harbored malice sufficient to support an award of punitive damages in a personal-injury action. The complaint alleged that the defendant was an alcoholic with a history of convictions for driving under the influence, who previously had caused a serious automobile accident while driving under the influence of alcohol. Despite his alcoholism, defendant had accepted employment delivering alcoholic beverages. When the accident occurred, the defendant was on the job and consuming alcoholic beverages while driving. In holding that these allegations, if proved, were sufficient to demonstrate the malice required for an award of punitive damages, this court focused upon the defendant's decision to *begin* drinking, rather than his mental state when the collision occurred: "one who voluntarily commences, and thereafter continues, to consume alcoholic beverages to the point of intoxication, knowing from the outset that he must thereafter operate a motor vehicle demonstrates, in the words of Dean Prosser, 'such a conscious and deliberate disregard of the interests of others that his conduct may be called willful or wanton.'" *Id.* at 899.

Similarly, in *People v. Watson*, this court held there was probable cause to charge a defendant with murder, based upon evidence that he consumed alcoholic beverages at a bar, raising his blood-alcohol level to .23 percent, drove through a red traffic light, narrowly avoiding a collision, then accelerated to more than 80 miles per hour and collided with a vehicle at another intersection, killing 2 persons. Relying upon the above quoted holding in *Taylor* that one who drinks to the point of intoxication, knowing he or she thereafter must drive, exhibits a conscious disregard of the safety of others, this court observed: "Defendant [Watson] had consumed enough alcohol to raise his blood alcohol content to a level which would support a finding that he was legally intoxicated. He had driven his car to the establishment where he had been drinking, and he must have known that he would have to drive it later. It also may be presumed that defendant was aware of the hazards of driving while intoxicated." After describing the defendant's extremely dangerous driving, this court held: "In combination, these facts reasonably and readily support a conclusion that defendant acted wantonly and with a conscious disregard for human life." *Watson*, 30 Cal.3d at 300-01.

As this court recognized in *Taylor* and *Watson*, the determination whether a defendant who drives under the influence of alcohol exhibits a conscious disregard of human life does not depend exclusively upon the defendant's state of mind at the time the accident occurs. A high level of intoxication sets the stage for tragedy long before the driver turns the ignition key. In the present case, for example, it can be inferred from the presence of empty malt liquor cans in his vehicle that defendant continued to drink while he was driving. Under such circumstances, and in light of defendant's past exposure to the extreme danger posed by driving under the influence of alcohol or drugs, the jury reasonably could conclude that defendant, in undertaking this course of conduct, acted with knowledge of the dangerousness of his conduct and with conscious disregard of that danger. Because defendant knowingly embarked upon such an extremely dangerous course of conduct with conscious disregard of the danger, his malice aforethought would not be negated simply by reason of his having succeeded in rendering himself unconscious prior to the fatal collision. Accordingly, the trial court did not err in refusing defendant's proffered instruction regarding unconsciousness caused by voluntary intoxication.

Even if the trial court had erred in this regard, reversal of the resulting conviction would not be required. The jury adequately was instructed that it could consider defendant's degree of intoxication in determining whether he acted with malice. By finding defendant guilty of second-degree murder, rather than gross vehicular manslaughter while intoxicated, the jury necessarily concluded that, despite his intoxication, defendant actually appreciated the risk posed by his conduct and acted with conscious disregard of life. It is clear, therefore, that instructing the jury pursuant to CALJIC No. 8.47 would not have affected its verdict.

## Disposition

The judgment of the Court of Appeal is affirmed.

KENNARD and ARABIAN, JJ., and PANELLI, J. [by assignment], concur.

MOSK, Justice, concurring and dissenting.

Defendant, driving while intoxicated, killed another and was convicted of second-degree murder. We granted review to consider his claim that he was entitled to an instruction based on a defense of unconsciousness brought about by his voluntary intoxication, and ultimately to determine whether evidence of such intoxication is material to negate the subjective component of implied-malice murder: a conscious and antisocial disregard for human life.

The majority conclude that all murders, even those committed with implied malice aforethought, are specific-intent offenses. That is clearly incorrect. The majority properly hold that an intoxicated defendant need not be shown to have had express malice; implied malice is adequate. But then, they require the prosecution to prove the defendant had not a general but a specific intent. If a drunken driver is physically and mentally unable to develop *express* malice, how can he possibly have the cognitive ability to conceive a *specific* intent? Although this defendant does not appear to benefit from the majority opinion, its inconsistency gives a green light to all future vehicular-murder defendants to demand that the prosecution establish they had a demonstrable specific intent. As contended by the Attorney General, the foregoing virtually impossible requirement constructs a serious and unnecessary roadblock to prosecutors who seek to enforce the Legislature's command to severely punish intoxicated drivers who kill innocent victims.

The majority's legal analysis thus is flawed. It cannot be squared with the legislative intent in enacting statutes regarding murder and voluntary intoxication or with the common-law antecedents to those statutes. The effect of today's decision will be to allow the grossly intoxicated killer an unanticipated defense to murder based on unconsciousness. I doubt the Legislature ever intended such a result.

In this state, "murder is the unlawful killing of a human being, or a fetus, with malice aforethought." Such malice aforethought may be express or implied. Murder with implied malice aforethought is found when a person kills another and, *inter alia*, "the circumstances attending the killing show an abandoned and malignant heart."

As stated, the ultimate question in this case is whether evidence of voluntary intoxication is relevant to negate implied malice aforethought, specifically its subjective component of conscious and antisocial disregard for human life. Section 22 yields part of the answer. That statute provides: "(a) No act committed by a person while in a state of voluntary intoxication is less criminal by reason of his having been in such condition.... (b) Evidence of voluntary intoxication is admissible solely on the issue of whether or not the defendant actually formed a required specific intent, premeditated, deliberated, or harbored malice aforethought, when a specific intent crime is charged."

Defendant first contends that he may introduce evidence of his voluntary drunkenness to counter a charge of implied-malice murder, whether or not implied-malice murder is a specific-intent crime. Citing the well-established principle that a construction making some words redundant is to be avoided, defendant argues that §22 must permit him to introduce evidence of voluntary intoxication to negate the mental state required for implied-malice murder because "if §22 applied only to express malice murder, there would have been no reason for the drafters to include 'malice aforethought' as an enumerated mental state because express malice is identical to a specific intent to unlawfully kill."

I cannot agree. Defendant's interpretation would make wholly ineffectual the provision that "evidence of voluntary intoxication is admissible solely on the issue of whether or not the defendant actually formed a required specific intent, premeditated, deliberated, or harbored malice aforethought, when a specific intent crime is charged." §22(b). The primary goal of all statutory interpretation is to ascertain and give effect to the lawmakers' intent.

To adopt defendant's interpretation of §22 would be to render a nullity the substantial "when a specific intent crime is charged" clause, which qualifies the previous term "malice aforethought." The language of §22 is *not* ambiguous and cannot be construed to benefit defendant by reason of ambiguity—the comma immediately before the clause "when a specific intent crime is charged" unambiguously qualifies the term "malice aforethought" that preceded it, limiting it to express malice.

Should there be any doubt that the Legislature did not intend to allow voluntary intoxication to negate the mental element of all murders, temporal considerations ought to dispel it. If ever the Legislature intended to lighten the criminal culpability of those who committed implied-malice murder while intoxicated, 1981 and 1982, when the Legislature amended §22, was not the time. The laws passed in 1981 made California's drunk-driving laws among the toughest in the nation. They called for mandatory jail sentences for repeat offenders and increased fines, restricted plea bargaining and provided for treatment programs, jail sentences or restricted driving privileges for first-time offenders. After the laws went into effect in 1982, there was a dramatic drop in the number of deaths caused by drunk drivers—from 1,965 in 1981 to 1,705 in 1982. There was a further decline in 1983.

The 1981 and 1982 amendments to sections 22 and 188 were enacted to ensure that diminished capacity could not be used as a defense to crime and to replace that defense with so-called diminished actuality "when [and only when] a specific intent crime is charged" §22. Given public attitudes toward intoxication-related crime at the time §22 was amended, I believe it highly unlikely that the Legislature intended to allow evidence of voluntary intoxication to negate an element of murder with implied malice aforethought. The original version of §22 entirely barred a defendant from introducing voluntary intoxication evidence to defend against a second-degree murder charge, and I doubt the Legislature intended to liberalize the statute to create a defense of voluntary intoxication to homicides committed without specific intent.

Next, defendant asserts that second-degree murder committed with implied malice aforethought is indeed a specific-intent crime under §22. Inexplicably, the majority agree with him. I do not.... Section 22 refers to the charging of a specific-intent crime. What is usually charged in murder cases is "murder" under section 187 without amplification. However, because murder includes homicide with implied and express malice, a specific-intent crime is not necessarily involved when murder is charged.

It is beyond question that implied-malice murder is not a specific-intent crime. Although certain appellate decisions have stated otherwise, they are incorrect, as are the majority. Indeed, if a single high court in the common law world besides this new majority has ever held that implied-malice murder, as defined under a statute similar to California's, is a specific-intent offense, it has not been called to our attention. To so conclude is to ignore a long legal tradition.

"General intent" and "specific intent" are shorthand devices best and most precisely invoked to contrast offenses that, as a matter of policy, may be punished despite the actor's voluntary intoxication (general intent) with offenses that, also as a matter of policy, may not be punished in light of such intoxication if it negates the offense's mental element (specific intent). Evidence of voluntary intoxication may be introduced to negate an element of offenses requiring relatively complex cogitation—a mental function integral to many crimes that contain a "definition [that] refers to defendant's intent to do some further act or achieve some additional consequence"—because alcohol can interfere with such intent. *Hood*, 1 Cal.3d at 457-58.

In *People v. Rocha*, 3 Cal.3d 893 (1971), we rejected a contention that assault with a deadly weapon is a specific-intent crime. We explained that assault is not a specific-intent crime because voluntary intoxication so naturally lends itself to its commission. "Since alcohol is so often a factor inducing simple assaults ... it would be anomalous to permit exculpation because of intoxication." *Id.* at 898. The same is true of implied-malice murder: alcohol intoxication naturally lends itself to the crime's commission because it impairs the sound judgment or lowers the inhibitions that might stop a sober individual from committing a highly dangerous act leading to another's death. Hence implied-malice murder cannot be a specific-intent offense.

The majority rely on the statement in *Hood* that "When the definition of a crime consists of only the description of a particular act, without reference to intent to do a further act or achieve a future consequence, we ask whether the defendant intended to do the proscribed act. This intention is deemed to be a general criminal intent. When the definition refers to defendant's intent to do some further act or achieve some additional consequence, the crime is deemed to be one of specific intent." *Hood*, 1 Cal.3d at 457.

But the quoted material is only a guideline for determining on which side of the policy-based divide separating general- from specific-intent offenses a particular crime lies. The key is whether policy considerations permit the introduction of voluntary-intoxication evidence to negate an element of the crime. The majority thus interpret *Hood* backwards, relegating that case's key discussion of voluntary intoxication to a mention of "other considerations" without elaboration.

Moreover, even under the subsidiary guideline on which the majority rely, implied-malice murder cannot be said to be a specific-intent offense. Implied-malice murder does not contain the element of intent to do a further act or achieve a future consequence. There is no goal-oriented behavior, unlike in an express-malice killing. Implied-malice murder requires only that defendant intentionally do "an act with a high probability that it will result in death and do it with a base antisocial motive and with a wanton disregard for human life." *Watson*, 30 Cal.3d at 300. In other words, the only intent required is to recklessly do an act "the natural consequences of which are dangerous to [human] life"—an act "likely to kill." *People v. Washington*, 62 Cal.2d 777, 780 (1965).

Stated more generally, "implied malice is malice inferred in law from the defendant's conduct rather than by proof of an actual intention to kill. The *mens rea* encompassed by implied malice has no application in a prosecution in which a specific intent to kill is a required element of the accused offense. An instruction on implied malice in relation to the crime of attempted murder is misleading to a jury." *Keys v. State*, 104 Nev. 736 (1988) [discussing a similar Nevada statute]. Thus we have held quite recently that specific intent and implied malice are mutually exclusive. "It is well settled that both the former crime of assault with intent to commit murder ... and the crime of attempted murder require a specific intent to kill and cannot be based on mere implied malice even though implied malice would sustain a charge of murder itself." *People v. Coleman*, 48 Cal.3d 112, 138 (1989). So "where a specific intent to kill is absolutely required, reliance upon any definition of murder based upon implied malice is logically impossible, for implied malice cannot co-exist with express malice. With this fundamental concept to be reckoned with, instructions on the crime of attempt to commit murder, necessarily, when they define the underlying crime of murder, must be limited only to that kind of murder where a *specific* intent to kill or, in other words, *express* malice, is one of the elements." *People v. Lee*, 43 Cal.3d 666, 670-71 (1987). If implied-malice murder were a specific-intent crime, the jury would have to find the defendant carried out goal-oriented behavior, meaning that the defendant had the further precise purpose to kill when performing the lethal act. In that case drunk drivers could almost never be prosecuted for murder no matter how wanton their acts, for an avowed purpose to kill is virtually never present in drunk-driving homicides. The Legislature cannot have intended to grant drunk drivers such a windfall at the same time it was increasing the penalties for drunk driving. It should be plain that implied-malice murder cannot be a specific-intent offense and that the Legislature never intended for it to be....

Next, defendant contends—and probably inspired the majority—that even if implied-malice murder is not a classic specific-intent crime, the mental state required for the offense is closer to that of a specific-intent crime than to that of a general-intent crime. I disagree. To be sure, implied-malice murder requires a defendant's knowledge of the risk to life and a conscious disregard thereof. But the presence of the knowledge element in the definition of implied-malice murder does not consign that offense to the rubric of specific-intent crimes.

"First degree murder and second degree murder premised on express malice involve the specific intent to kill, whereas second degree murder premised on implied malice involves a general intent to do the act and the mental state of knowledge and conscious disregard for the risk to human life." *People v. Cleaves*, 229 Cal.App.3d 367, 380 (1991). Therefore, "second degree murder based on implied malice is a general intent crime but with the requirement of a certain mental state." *Id.* at 381. As we explained in *People v. Daniels*, 14 Cal.3d 857 (1975), the sale of a restricted dangerous drug under Health and Safety Code §11912 was a general-intent crime even though "the statutory definition of the offense focuses on the act of the sale itself to which the courts have added the element of knowledge of the character of the substance sold.... It is apparent that the offense defined in §11912 does not expressly require an intent to do a further act or achieve a future consequence." See *People v. Glover*, 233 Cal.App.3d 1476, 1479 (1991) [arson under §451 is not a specific-intent crime even though it contains the mental element of willfulness and maliciousness].

Because evidence of voluntary intoxication historically has been immaterial to defend against a charge of second-degree murder, it cannot be material to disprove the conscious and antisocial disregard for human life component of implied-malice murder, for an evidentiary fact is immaterial to prove its opposite. The law often implies malice from the manner in which the killing was done.... In such case, it is murder, though the perpetrator was drunk.... The law in such cases does not seek to ascertain the actual state of the perpetrator's mind, for the fact from which malice is implied having been proved, the law presumes its existence, *and proof in opposition to this presumption, is irrelevant and inadmissible.* Hence, a party cannot show that he was so drunk as not to be capable of entertaining a malicious feeling. The conclusion of law is against him. California law has followed that historical principle not only in §22, but also in cases such as *Watson*: evidence of voluntary intoxication followed by reckless behavior allows a trier of fact to conclude that the actor held a conscious and antisocial disregard for human life.

Defendant next asserts that §22 cannot be applied to him personally. In his view, to apply the statute retroactively to his own disadvantage would violate due process of law. I disagree. Section 22 was enacted in its present form in 1982. *People v. Hood* has explained the difference between general and specific intent offenses since 1969, and *Watson* has set forth the definition of the objective physical act and subjective mental state required for implied-malice murder since 1981. Defendant received more than he was entitled to when the court instructed the jury that it could consider defendant's voluntary intoxication for the existence *or nonexistence* of implied malice aforethought—for, as explained, evidence of voluntary intoxication is immaterial to disprove implied malice aforethought. Any decision implying or stating the contrary is erroneous....

I therefore concur with the majority that the Court of Appeal's judgment should be affirmed. But I cannot subscribe to the majority's erroneous view of the law.

Lucas, C.J., concurs.

[The separate opinion of Justice Baxter, concurring and dissenting, is omitted].

## QUESTIONS ON *WHITFIELD*

1. **Express or implied malice**.

   **a.** Malice has two modes: implied and express. Killings in either mode are murder. Express malice requires an intentional killing, whereas with implied malice, the killing is not intentional; an implied-malice killing is extremely reckless, though by no means unintentional. Justice George's opinion for the *Whitfield* majority posits that voluntary intoxication may interfere not only with forming and acting on an intention to kill, but also with appreciating and then ignoring risks that one poses to life. Is he right?

**b.** But is that really the issue? California Penal Code §22 has three iterations reviewed in the *Whitfield* opinions: 1872, 1981, and the most recent at the time of the decision, 1982. The text of the 1982 §22 addresses only specific-intent crimes. How does the majority finesse that language in reversing the Court of Appeal's ruling that evidence of voluntary intoxication should not have been admitted to negate implied malice?

**2. Guilty of unconsciousness, revisited.** Within two hours of the wreck, Whitfield's blood-alcohol level was .24 grams of alcohol per deciliter of blood. It was estimated that, due to dissipation over time, his blood-alcohol level was more like .27 if not .395 at the time of the wreck. This is a staggeringly high level of impairment, which, along with the physical signs manifested to witnesses and paramedics, suggests that Whitfield might have been unconscious at the time of the wreck.

The trial judge refused to instruct the jury on the defense of unconsciousness as outlined in CALJIC No. 8.47 (2011 Revision), which reads, in its revised but nearly identical form:

> If you find that a defendant, while unconscious as a result of voluntary intoxication, killed another human being without express or implied malice aforethought, the crime is involuntary manslaughter. The term "unconscious" means a person is not conscious of acting but performs acts or motions while in that mental state. The condition of being unconscious does not require incapacity to move or act. When a person voluntarily induces his or her own intoxication to the point of unconsciousness, he or she assumes the risk that while unconscious he or she will commit acts dangerous to human life or safety. Under those circumstances, the law implies [criminal negligence].

The California Supreme Court affirmed the trial court's ruling refusing to give the above instruction on the ground that unconsciousness at the moment of the wreck does not preclude a finding of malice based on what occurred *before* the wreck. That Whitfield had cans of malt liquor in his car indicated that he was drinking while driving, which indicates, given his expansive drunk-driving history, a conscious indifference to the lives of others with whom he may come in contact on the roads.

**a.** To what type of cases, then, would CALJIC No. 8.47 apply?

**b.** Is this interpretation by the majority on the relation between malice and unconsciousness reconcilable with *Decina*?

**c.** Even if the trial judge's refusal to instruct the jury on CALJIC No. 8.47 was error, the California Supreme Court ruled that the error could not have infected the verdict. How so?

3. **Divided opinions.** Justices Kennard, Arabian, and Panelli concur in Justice George's opinion for the majority. Justice Mosk both concurs in, and dissents from, George's opinion.

**a.** What does that mean: that Mosk agrees and disagrees at once?

**b.** When Chief Justice John Roberts took over the helm of the U.S. Supreme Court in September 2005, he sought to bring a more "collegial atmosphere" to the body and "credibility and stability" to the law by urging his new colleagues to find agreement in their opinions wherever possible. Recalling the John Marshall Court era of the early 19th century—when nearly every case handed down was unanimous—Roberts complained that the divided opinions of the modern era have been "eroding, to some extent, the capital that Marshall built up," rendering the Court "ripe for a refocus on functioning as an institution, because, if it doesn't, it's going to lose its credibility and legitimacy as an institution."

Roberts prefers unanimous or nearly unanimous decisions because they are hard to overturn, while closely divided 5-4 decisions make it harder for the public to respect the Court as an impartial institution that transcends partisan politics. Justice Scalia, for one, later reported the Roberts approach as only trivially different from his predecessor's. David A. Yalof, Joseph Mello & Patrick Schmidt, *Collegiality Among U.S. Supreme Court Justices?*, 95 Judicature 12 (2011).

An example of the vice of divided opinions is *Montana v. Egelhoff*, 116 S.Ct. 2013 (1996), referred to *supra* at the end of the introduction to Chapter 2.B. I've cribbed the following from the *Egelhoff* case syllabus in the Supreme Court Reporter:

Scalia, J., announced the judgment of the Court and delivered an opinion in which Rehnquist, C.J., Kennedy, and Thomas, JJ., joined; Ginsburg, J., filed an opinion concurring in the judgment; O'Connor, J., filed a dissenting opinion in which Stevens, Souter, and Breyer, JJ., joined; Souter, J., filed a dissenting opinion; Breyer, J., filed a dissenting opinion in which Stevens, J., joined.

Believe it or not, this sort of fracturing is *not* a rare occurrence for the high court. *See, e.g., United States v. Mendenhall*, 446 U.S. 544 (1980). What it leaves is a holding for this case only: the Montana Supreme Court's ruling is reversed. But is there a *rule* to operate in such cases as precedent after all this effort exerted toward one of maybe 65 or so cases heard on high per term?

**4. Horizontal theory applied.** In footnote 5, Justice George quotes Professor George Fletcher, who says, of the horizontal or temporal distinction between specific and general intent, that it "glides well through the sea of crimes defined by the pattern 'assault with intent to....' Yet the distinction scrapes bottom as soon as we consider more compactly defined offenses, such as murder and larceny." Fletcher makes a good point as to murder—particularly where malice is implied. But how does the distinction "scrape bottom" as to larceny, defined as a trespassory taking of property known to be that of another with the specific intent to permanently deprive?

**5. Specific or general intent?**

    a. Assault with a deadly weapon
    b. Kidnapping for the purpose of rape
    c. Battery
    d. Assault with the intent to do grave bodily injury
    e. Attempted rape
    f. Rape

## NOTES ON *WHITFIELD*

***1. Legislative overrulings.*** Notably, §22 was again amended in 1995 (since renumbered as section 29.4, effective 2013), settling that voluntary intoxication would no longer be relevant in a murder case predicated on implied malice. In other words, the California State Legislature statutorily overruled *Whitfield* (which the California Supreme Court decided in 1994), siding instead with the position set forth in Justice Mosk's separate opinion. The Court of Appeal, too, had presented a bare-bones version of what became the Mosk position. *People v. Whitfield*, 15 Cal.Rptr.2d 4, 10 (4th Dist. Ct. App. 1992) ["The fact that second degree implied malice murder includes a requirement of knowledge does not make that crime a specific intent crime."].

Principles of separation of powers give legislatures the final word in conflicts with courts unless a court (itself not overruled by a higher court) rules that the legislation violates the state or federal constitution. *See In re Estate of Laubenheimer*, 833 N.W.2d 735, 759 (Wis. 2013) (Gableman, J., dissenting) ["Though it should not be necessary, I feel compelled to note that on non-constitutional matters the legislature can overrule the courts, not vice-versa."]. If a court finds a law unconstitutional, a stubborn legislature's only recourse is to amend the constitution, which is a terrific ordeal. *See, e.g.*, David Rudenstine, Book Review, *Self-Government and the Judicial Function Cosmic Constitutional Theory*, 92 Texas Law Review 161, 163-64 & 163 n.20 (2013).

**2. Specific v. general intent.** Unlike Justice George's opinion for the majority, Justice Mosk's separate opinion in *Whitfield* confronts the distinction between general and specific intent. As Mosk notes, classification of a crime as one or the other is a judicial function: legislatures define crimes but do not classify them as specific or general intent. According to what we have been calling the "horizontal" notion of specific intent, such classification turns on whether the proscribed (complex) action contemplates a future act or consequence beyond the performance of the (basic) action. If it does, the crime is specific intent. If not, it is general intent, unless the crime is considered so trivial as to authorize strict liability.

As Justice George recounts, the distinction between general and specific intent was invented to deal with intoxicated offenders. Voluntary intoxication excuses specific-intent crimes when the evidence raises a reasonable doubt about whether, due to intoxicants, defendant did not form a criminal intention. Defendants charged with general-intent crimes, however, cannot excuse their harmful actions by citing their voluntary intoxication, which is treated as irrelevant to guilt. With assault, whose relation to homicide is that of a lesser-included offense, its classification as a general-intent crime is informed by the policy consideration that intoxication and violence go hand in hand. *People v. Hood*, 1 Cal.3d 444, 458 (1969) ["A compelling consideration is the effect of alcohol on human behavior. A significant effect of alcohol is to distort judgment and relax the controls on aggressive and anti-social impulses."].

**a. Defining assault as attempted battery.** A problematical line of cases dating back to 1951, see *People v. Carmen*, 36 Cal.2d 768 (1951), if not beyond, endeavors to establish that simple assaults (as opposed to assaults with intent to do great bodily harm, assaults with intent to rape, and so on) are *not* merely attempted batteries. See *People v. Hood*, 1 Cal.3d at 452-53 n.4 [citing cases on point back to 1857]. This, even though assault has been defined since 1850 as "an unlawful attempt, coupled with a present ability, to commit a violent injury on the person of another." Crimes and Punishments Act of 1850, ch. 99, §49, at 234; California Penal Code §240 (1872). If assaults were considered attempted batteries, the argument runs, then the crime of assault would be superfluous, subsumed by the law of attempt. *See People v. Colantuono*, 7 Cal.4th 206, 216 (1994) (en banc). *But see People v. Santana*, 133 Cal.Rptr.3d 393, 404 (4th Dist. Ct. App. 2011) [attempted battery not a crime in California]; *People v. Wright*, 100 Cal.App.4th 703, 721 n.20 (2002) [same]; *In re James M.*, 9 Cal.3d 517, 521-22 (1973) [attempted assault not a crime in California].

If "assault" did mean "attempted battery," then voluntary intoxication *would* be an excuse because all attempts are considered specific-intent crimes, see CALJIC No. 6.00, and all specific-intent crimes are subject to the excuse of voluntary intoxication. California Penal Code §29.4(b) (2013). But that is precisely the move that *Hood* precluded, given the inordinate number of assaults committed by intoxicated persons, whose criminal responsibility is hardly lessened by their rendering themselves too drunk to subdue their own passions. Closing what would otherwise be a loophole for violent drunks, reviewing courts see assaults as lacking the sort of future-looking directedness that characterizes specific-intent crimes.

So if assaults are not attempted batteries, then what are they? According to the California Supreme Court:

> The original concept of criminal assault developed at an earlier day than the doctrine of criminal attempt in general, and crystallized on a much narrower basis in the sense of a greater degree of proximity. The distinction may be thus

defined: An assault is an act done toward the commission of a battery; it must precede the battery, but it does so immediately. The next movement would, at least to all appearance, complete the battery. [A]n act constituting an attempt to commit a felony may be more remote. Assault thus lies on a definitional, not merely a factual, continuum of conduct that describes its essential relation to battery: An assault is an incipient or inchoate battery; a battery is a consummated assault. An assault is a necessary element of battery, and it is impossible to commit battery without assaulting the victim.

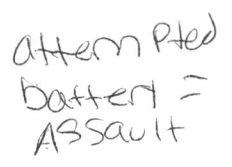

*People v. Colantuono, supra*, 7 Cal.4th at 216-17 (en banc). If that *sounds* to you like an attempt by any other name, you're in good company. *See e.g., People v. Wright, supra*, 100 Cal.App.4th at 721 n.20.

Seven years after *Colantuono*, California's high court elaborated that an assault occurs when a defendant intends to commit an act "which would be indictable [as a battery], if done, either from its own character or that of its natural and probable consequences." *People v. Williams*, 26 Cal.4th 779, 787 (2001). This odd definition, which makes it sound as though assault may be committed negligently (though the court denies this, *id.* at 788), keeps assault outside the specific-intent realm, thereby blocking the excuse of voluntary intoxication.

The standard, pattern jury instruction, intending to absorb the above rulings into its summary of assault, breaks down the crime into three elements:

> **1)** A person willfully [and unlawfully] committed an act which by its nature would probably and directly result in the application of physical force on another person;
>
> **2)** The person committing the act was aware of facts that would lead a reasonable person to realize that as a direct, natural and probable result of this act that physical force would be applied to another person; and
>
> **3)** At the time the act was committed, the person committing the act had the present ability to apply physical force to the person of another.

CALJIC No. 9.00. Needless to say, a "certain measure of understandable analytical uncertainty continues" to plague judicial attempts to pin down the *mens rea* of assault. *People v. Trujillo*, 181

Cal.App.4th 1344, 1352 (2010), quoting *Williams, supra*, 26 Cal. 4th at 787.

**b. Assault as unconsummated battery**. If assault is directed at battery, then what is battery?

> Penal Code §242 defines a battery as "any willful and unlawful use of force or violence upon the person of another." When applied to the intent with which an act is done or omitted, "willful" implies simply a purpose or willingness to commit the act, or make the omission referred to. It does not require any intent to violate law, or to injure another, or to acquire any advantage. It has long been established, both in tort and criminal law, that "the least touching" may constitute battery. In other words, *force* against the person is enough, it need not be violent or severe, it need not cause bodily harm or even pain, and it need not leave any mark. The violent injury here mentioned is not synonymous with bodily harm, but includes any wrongful act committed by means of physical force against the person of another, ... although only the feelings of such person are injured by the act. Thus, any harmful or offensive touching constitutes an unlawful use of force or violence for purposes of Penal Code §242. Even a slight touching may constitute a battery, if it is done in a rude or angry way.

*James v. State*, 229 Cal.App.4th 130, 137-38 (2014); *see People v. Rocha*, 3 Cal.3d 893, 899-900 n.12 (1971); CALJIC No. 16.140. Like assault, battery is a general-intent crime. *People v. Lara*, 44 Cal.App.4th 102, 107-08 (1996) [battery is a general-intent crime, which may be proved not by proof of negligence, but by proof that defendant acted with "conscious disregard of human life and safety"]. Also like assault, battery can *sound* like specific intent. *See People v. Wright, supra,* 100 Cal.App.4th at 721 & n.21 ["A consummated battery requires an intent to commit the battery"]; Judicial Council of California Criminal Jury Instructions (CALCRIM) No. 960 (West 2014) [to constitute a battery, the "harmful or offensive" touching must be "willful," that is, "on purpose"]; *People v. Lathus*, 35 Cal.App.3d 466, 469 (1973) ["Reckless conduct alone does not constitute a sufficient basis for assault or for battery even if the assault results in an injury"].

In a *civil* case for battery, the pattern jury instruction breaks down the tort as follows: to be found liable and therefore on the hook to compensate plaintiff in money damages, 1) defendant must touch plaintiff with the intent to harm or offend, 2) plaintiff must not have consented to the touching, and 3) plaintiff must be harmed or offended under circumstances that would offend a reasonable person. California Civil Jury Instructions (CACI) No. 1300 (West 2004). And that *sounds* like specific intent, thus supporting Professor Fletcher's claim that the real distinction between general and specific intent is not definitional. Instead, the distinction reflects a policy decision on whether to let voluntary intoxication operate as an excuse.

**3. Statutory clues as to crime classification.** Generally, the *mens rea* required for a crime indicates whether that crime is characterized as general or specific intent. In *People v. Atkins*, 104 Cal.Rptr.2d 738, 744-48 (Cal. 2001), the court ruled that arson is a general-intent crime because the statute identifies the required mental state as "willful" and "malicious." California Penal Code §451; CALJIC No. 14.80 (2014). Conversely, statutory language such as "intent" or "purpose" indicates specific-intent crimes.

How helpful this is, however, is unclear. *E.g.*, *People v. Johnson*, 67 Cal.App.4th 67, 72 (1998) ["As a general rule, a statute proscribing willful behavior is a general intent crime. A statute which includes 'willfully' language may nevertheless define a specific intent offense."].

**4. General intent and negligence.** A challenging facet of general intent is the role of negligence—ordinary or criminal. *See, e.g.*, *People v. Matthews*, 70 Cal.App.4th 164, 174-75 (1999) ["[I]f the defendant intends to place his penis in the victim's vagina, he has committed the general intent crime of rape, and does not have to have the 'specific intent' to rape"]. The meaning of such an utterance is mysterious. Nowhere is rape defined merely as penile penetration of a woman. Instead, rape requires in addition that the penetration be achieved both non-consensually and either forcibly or by placing the woman-victim in fear of imminent force. California Penal Code §261(a)(2); CALJIC No. 10.00 (2014).

Moreover, assuming that defendant actually penetrated the complainant, the only viable defense at that point is that the complainant either consented or gave defendant the impression that she was consenting. If she did not in fact consent, then defendant's belief that she did consent must be reasonable, that is, her non-consent was for him a non-negligent, unforeseeable incidental to the prospect of having mutual, reciprocal, consensual intercourse. If defendant's incorrect belief about the woman's desires must be reasonable, and if rape is a general-intent crime, then the term "general intent" to commit rape here suggests just negligently caused harm, not intentionally or recklessly caused harm.

**5. First-degree v. second-degree murder.** Prosecutors charged both Watson and Whitfield with second-degree implied-malice murder. This means that prosecutors viewed the killings in both cases as neither accidental nor intentional. Instead, prosecutors alleged that Watson and Whitfield had the general intent to kill, given insufficient proof to justify charging them with express-malice murder, which depends on the specific intent to kill. While both express- and implied-malice murder are second-degree murder, first-degree murder describes two circumstances: 1) killings that are not only expressly malicious, that is, intentional, but further, killings where the intention takes the form of premeditation and deliberation; or 2) killings that occur during the perpetration or attempted perpetration of inherently dangerous felonies such as burglary, arson, kidnapping, rape, or robbery. California Penal Code §189 (2012).

While graded murder persists in roughly one-third of American jurisdictions, the Model Penal Code's drafters eliminated graded murder; they no longer divide murder into first and second degree. The change was to debunk the "premise that there exists some dependable relation between the duration of the reflection and the gravity of the offense." *See* MPC & Commentaries §2.10.6, at 127-28 (1980) [repealed 2009]. Seeing no point in separating killers who plan ahead from killers who act on impulse, the drafters justify the change on the ground that someone with the "tortured conscience" of a "mercy killer" can deliberate and still deserve milder punishment than a hothead who kills impulsively—even spontaneously—while doing something else, such as committing a felony like arson or rape. Consequently, the Code has only one kind of murder, which covers all killings that cannot be fully or partially excused on grounds of accident, "extreme emotional disturbance," or some other excuse. *See* Daniel Yeager, J.L. Austin and the Law: Exculpation and the Explication of Responsibility 56-57 (Bucknell University Press 2006).

Despite the Code's approach, the essence of a first-degree murder, whether described as the product of "a sedate deliberate mind and formed design" or as a "willful, deliberate, premeditated" killing, is not the duration of the reflection (which is at best evidentiary), but the quality of it. A deliberate killer may suffer from a tortured conscience, but for that very reason he poses a real problem to the world because he thinks about *whether* to kill; one might say that deliberate killers are sincere, that is, they are prepared to stand by later what they do now as a manifestation of their true selves. Killers who do not deliberate may plot their killings, but can do so without confronting the pros and cons; they can do so without choosing killing over not killing. A mercy killer (who may or may not think about whether to kill) may have a tortured conscience, but he has his own reasons for killing—reasons that transcend law. Mercy killers are moral actors. But so was anti-abortion fanatic Paul Hill, who felt justified in killing a Pensacola, Florida "abortionist," who was about to "murder" un-quickened fetuses.[b] Assessing what someone like Paul Hill deserves is not, and never was, a problem that depends on how much time he took before killing.

"I act *deliberately* when I have deliberated—which means when I have stopped to ask myself, 'Shall I or shan't I?' and then decided to do X, which I did. That is to say, I weighed up, in however rudimentary a fashion, the pros and cons. And it is understood that there must be some cons." J.L. Austin, *Three Ways of Spilling Ink*, in Philosophical Papers, *supra*, at 286. It is thus quite possible, even common, that an action be done intentionally—even purposely—but not deliberately: "We walk along a cliff, and I feel a sudden impulse to push you over, and may even have devised a little ruse to achieve it: yet even then I did not act deliberately, for I did not (stop to) ask myself whether to do it or not." J.L. Austin, *A Plea for Excuses*, in Philosophical Papers, *supra*, at 195. It is not just *any* kind of prior thinking that counts as deliberation. I may deliberate over moral pros and cons or over what course of action I think is best or has most reasons recommending it. Indeed, thinking about ways and means may demonstrate forethought or premeditation, but not necessarily deliberation, which is a matter of decision (of whether to perform the action at all), not of planning (of how and when to perform the action). "That there should be slowness in moving into action or conducting it (so much relied on by lawyers) is the merest symptom" of deliberation. J.L. Austin, *Three Ways of Spilling Ink*, in Philosophical Papers, *supra*, at 286; *cf. People v.*

---

[b] *See* Tamar Lewin, *Death of a Doctor: The Moral Debate*, New York Times, July 30, 1994, at A1. Hill did not take the stand, put on any evidence, or hire a lawyer. He was convicted of capital murder and sentenced to death after a 20-minute jury deliberation. *See* Mireya Navarro, *Abortion Clinic Case Reviews a Legal Dilemma*, New York Times, Nov. 14, 1994, at A12. Hill died by lethal injection on September 3, 2003 at Florida State Prison on the authority of an execution warrant signed by Governor Jeb Bush.

*Anderson*, 70 Cal.2d 15 (1968) (en banc) [in reviewing jury verdicts finding first-degree murder, appellate courts look for evidence of 1) planning, 2) motive, and 3) a methodical manner of killing that bespeaks premeditation and deliberation].

When we talk about deliberate murder we are referring to killings done *after* deliberation, not *with* deliberation. To do something with deliberation refers to the style of performance. For example, eating one's soup *with* deliberation is a style matter (carefully savoring every drop and so on); eating one's soup *after* deliberation has to do with a process of decision preceding the execution of the action. J.L. Austin, *A Plea for Excuses*, in Philosophical Papers, *supra*, at 199-200. "Indeed, if he deliberately eats *my* soup, he is well-advised to make haste over it." J.L. Austin, *Three Ways of Spilling Ink*, in Philosophical Papers, *supra*, at 282.

**6. Whitfield paying the price**. Twenty years after killing Ronald Kinsey, Whitfield lost a belated fight to reduce a significant restitution fine to $210. *People v. Whitfield*, 2010 WL 1972952 (Cal. 4th Dist. Ct. App.) [appeal held meritless]. Whitfield remains locked up at California Health Care Facility (Stockton), 27 years into his sentence of 18 years to life, imposed in 1991.

At a recent parole hearing, Berkeley attorney Kate Brosgart represented the 59-year-old Whitfield, who showed up in a wheelchair and wearing a helmet due to his stated propensity to "fall down." Whitfield has numerous physical ailments which, according to Brosgart and parole commissioners, are believed by doctors to include brain damage. Throughout his hearing, Whitfield struggled with basic questions, halting, stumbling, and rambling in his answers. He talked about hearing voices, coping with depression, and suicidal urges. Despite Brosgart's claim that Whitfield is no longer a risk to society because he is incapable of driving a car or physical violence, commissioners denied him parole, citing his remorselessness and mental unsuitability for re-entry. "He still is not as stable as he should be," said Commissioner Michele Minor in announcing the decision, adding later that Whitfield's "mental health does lend itself to dangerousness." Sam Levin, *Trapped*, Prison Legal News, p.1 (Feb. 8, 2017).

# CHAPTER 3

## Anger and Fear as Extenuation

### A. ANGER AS PARTIAL DEFENSE: PROVOCATION/HEAT OF PASSION

*"I know what my crimes are, but my anger is stronger."* Medea

It is now familiar that murder is an unlawful killing of a human being with malice aforethought. It is equally familiar that malicious killings include not just those that are intentional, but any killing in which the killer knows that what he is doing is likely to kill someone. Some killings *seem* malicious enough, possessing the trappings of an intentional or extremely reckless killing. On further examination, however, we see a defendant not quite operating in the same frame of mind in which malicious actors operate. When a killing is by no means unintentional but is less blameworthy than it initially seems, the law recognizes the crime or partial defense of voluntary manslaughter, which is punished much less severely than murder. Voluntary manslaughter carries a base prison term of six years as opposed to the 15 years to life (or even death) that murder sentences impose on offenders. Voluntary manslaughter is an otherwise malicious killing that is performed either 1) while in the understandable throes of a heat of passion provoked by the victim; or 2) in "imperfect" self-defense, that is, under an unreasonable belief in the need to use deadly force to defend against a deadly threat, which in fact neither exists nor even apparently exists.

Although most killings are motivated by anger, the law sees anger, or at least *understandable anger*, as a mitigating factor that somehow wipes out the malice required for murder. In other words, whenever the killer's actions are explained by an uncontrollable yet understandable rage brought on by the victim, what would otherwise look like an intentional or extremely reckless killing is not considered a case of murder. The idea is that the defendant is so out of gear, so not himself, that he is entitled to be judged as less responsible for reasons that are considered as much the fault of the victim as of the defendant himself. This is not to say that the defendant is insane; he is not. But he is, due to the provocative acts of the victim, in a reduced state of responsibility that the law locates somewhere between murder and no crime.

What follows are two principal cases exploring the role of anger in the law of homicide. The first, *Greene v. Commonwealth*, 197 S.W.3d 76 (Ky. 2006), is a Kentucky case following the approach set forth in the Model Penal Code, since elaborated over the last half-century by appellate decisions rendered in the roughly two-thirds of all American jurisdictions that have adopted it in one version or another. The second, *People v. Spurlin*, 156 Cal.App.3d 119 (1984), is a California case following the approach set forth in appellate decisions interpreting the California Penal Code of 1872, which did away with the requirement under the Crimes and Punishments Act of 1850 that provocation be seriously *assaultive* to wipe out the malice associated with murder.[a] *People v. Beltran*, 56 Cal.4th 935, 946-53 (2013).

In fact, the recognition of intense anger as a partial defense to murder goes back centuries. *E.g, Manning's Case*, 83 English Reports 112 (1671) [finding husband guilty of lesser-included offense of manslaughter for killing a man "committing adultery with his wife in the very act"]; Aya Gruber, *A Provocative Defense*, 103 California Law Review 273, 303 (2014) [locating provocation principles in 15th-Century England]. While the provocation defense is arguably sexist in origin (bolstering the idea of women as property subject to "chastisement"), the defense more likely was a "response to the harshness of the extant murder liability and sentencing regime." *Ibid.*

---

[a] The California Supreme Court was empowered by article VI, section 4 of the California Constitution of 1849 to review criminal cases. By 1903, the judicial business of the state had increased to such an extent that the state supreme court was unable to keep up with the work. On November 8, 1904, article VI, section 4 of the successor state constitution (1879) was amended to create three district courts of appeal to hear appeals from the superior courts. *See Powers v. City of Richmond*, 10 Cal.4th 85, 95-98, 148 (1995) (en banc). Each new court had three justices, *In re Wells*, 174 Cal. 467, 472 (1917), who would sit in San Francisco (1st), Los Angeles (2nd), and Sacramento (3rd). *Superior Court v. County of Mendocino*, 13 Cal.4th 45, 63 n.9 (1996). Three more courts of appeal were added by the legislature in San Diego (4th), Fresno (5th), and San José (6th) in 1929, 1961, and 1981, respectively.

# SUPREME COURT OF KENTUCKY

*DENNIS R. GREENE SR., APPELLANT*

*V.*

*COMMONWEALTH OF KENTUCKY, APPELLEE*

MAY 18, 2006

SCOTT, Justice

## I. INTRODUCTION

Appellant Dennis Greene was tried and convicted by a Kenton County Jury in November 2003 for the murder of his wife, Tara Greene. He was sentenced to life in prison and now appeals to this court as a matter of right, Ky. Const. §110(2)(b), asserting that (1) the evidence was insufficient to prove he was *not* acting under an extreme emotional disturbance (EED);... (4) the trial court admitted gruesome crime scene photographs; (5) the trial court admitted portions of a "hip hop" video depicting defendant rapping about his wife's death with friends after the offense; and (6) the trial court admitted unduly prejudicial testimony about defendant's past extramarital affair. We affirm the judgment of the trial court.

## II. FACTUAL BACKGROUND

Medical testimony established Appellant killed his wife by cutting "her throat from ear to ear, so deeply that it scraped the spine." On the day of her death, he left work early to go home. Before leaving, he told a friend, "I'm going to do it. I'm going to kill her." [He told police that when he arrived home from work on the afternoon of May 4, 2003, he found their son C.G. playing in a dumpster and his wife under the influence.] Soon after the couple began to argue. During the argument she told him she had been unfaithful with four different men. After dinner, she and C.G. went to his bedroom to watch TV. While there, Appellant contends he heard his son yelp in pain. When Appellant went to the bedroom to check on C.G., Tara left the bedroom and went to the kitchen. Appellant claims C.G. then showed him a red mark on his shoulder. Appellant lit a marijuana cigarette and went to the kitchen to confront Tara. When she took from him and began smoking the cigarette, he grabbed at it, causing it to fall down her shirt. She then hit Appellant, [after which he put her] in a headlock or a chokehold for two to three minutes. At one point C.G.

came into the kitchen, but Appellant told him to go back to his room. In his own words, Appellant at this point just "snapped," reached behind him, grabbed a turkey knife out of a drawer, and "poked" his wife in the neck, that is, "cut her throat."

He then dropped her to the floor and covered her with a blanket, changed his pants and shoes, put a jacket on over his bloody shirt, and took C.G. to his mother's house in Cincinnati. Appellant then left for Chicago, where he claims he planned to kill himself. During the trip, he made several calls, most to his friends in Chicago, confessing to one of them, Matthew Kirst. Several calls were made to a former lover, Amy Baumgardener, who joined him in Chicago. Upon her arrival, Appellant was making a series of rap videotapes with his friends, several of which reflected on his thoughts and actions related to Tara's death. Appellant was arrested on May 8th at a friend's house in Chicago.

## III. ANALYSIS

### A. Extreme Emotional Distress

Appellant first argues that the evidence was insufficient to prove he was *not acting* under an extreme emotional disturbance at the time of his wife's death. In this regard we noted in *Holland v. Commonwealth*, 114 S.W.3d 792, 805 (Ky. 2003) that "once evidence was produced to prove the existence of EED, its absence became an element of the offense." Moreover, the Commonwealth has the burden of proving every element of the case beyond a reasonable doubt. Here, the essential elements are set out in Kentucky Revised Statutes 507.020 (murder) and 507.030 (manslaughter).

As for how EED fits into this statutory pattern, our prior decisions have established that a person is guilty of murder under KRS 507.020(1)(a) if he/she intentionally causes the death of another, "except ... if he acted under the influence of extreme emotional disturbance for which there was a reasonable explanation or excuse, the reasonableness of which is to be determined from the viewpoint of a person in the defendant's situation under the circumstances as the defendant believed them to be." A person is guilty of manslaughter in the first degree under KRS 507.030(1)(b) if he/she intentionally causes the death of another "under circumstances which do not constitute murder because he acts under the influence of extreme emotional disturbance, as defined in subsection (1)(a) of KRS 507.020." *Fields v. Commonwealth*, 44 S.W.3d 355, 356–57 (Ky. 2001).

Thus the same act may be murder or manslaughter in the first degree depending on a finding of EED.... Our more recent opinions have categorized EED, or more properly, the absence of it, as an element of the substantive offense, rather than as a defense. An instruction on murder need not require the jury to find that the defendant was *not acting* under the influence of extreme emotional disturbance *unless* there is something in the evidence to suggest that he *was*, thereby affording room for a reasonable doubt. *See Gall v. Commonwealth*, 607 S.W.2d 97, 109 (Ky. 1980). Conversely, when there is evidence, the instruction should be included.

Thus, where proof is presented that would support the finding of EED, and the absence of EED is then a statutory element, the burden switches to the Commonwealth to disprove it beyond a reasonable doubt. But that does not mean that it has to affirmatively introduce proof of the non-existence of EED, if such proof is already present. The Commonwealth loses if no such proof is present, but where, as here, the proof, when taken in a light most favorable to the Commonwealth, meets this burden, it is then a jury question.

Although EED is essentially a restructuring of the old common law concept of "heat of passion," the evidence needed to prove EED is different. There must be evidence that the defendant suffered "a temporary state of mind so enraged, inflamed, or disturbed as to overcome one's judgment, and to cause one to act uncontrollably from an impelling force of the extreme emotional disturbance rather than from evil or malicious purposes." *McClellan v. Commonwealth*, 715 S.W.2d 464, 468–69 (Ky. 1986). "The event which triggers the explosion of violence on the part of the criminal defendant must be sudden and uninterrupted. It is not a mental disease or illness.... Thus, it is wholly insufficient for the accused defendant to claim the defense of extreme emotional disturbance based on a gradual victimization from his or her environment, unless the additional proof of a triggering event is sufficiently shown." *Foster v. Commonwealth*, 827 S.W.2d 670, 678 (Ky. 1991). And the "extreme emotional disturbance ... must have a reasonable explanation or excuse, the reasonableness of which is to be determined from the viewpoint of a person in the defendant's situation under the circumstances as the defendant believed them to be." *Spears v. Commonwealth*, 30 S.W.3d 152, 155 (Ky. 2001).

Thus, under *Spears*, given the evidence introduced, the burden of proof in this case was on the Commonwealth, and the absence of EED was a proper element of the charge. However, viewing the evidence in a light most favorable to the Commonwealth, we conclude that "any rational trier of fact could have found the essential elements of the crime beyond a reasonable doubt." *Jackson v. Virginia*, 443 U.S. 307, 319 (1979).

It must be remembered "it is not the court but a jury that must make a factual determination of whether a particular defendant acted under the influence of extreme emotional disturbance." *McClellan*, 715 S.W.2d at 467. The courts will test the sufficiency of the evidence, and we have to view it in a light most favorable to the prosecution; however, once found sufficient, it is for the jury to find the facts, and they are not bound to view it in a light most favorable to the prosecution.

Although there certainly was evidence from which a jury could have found the presence of EED, the same evidence also supported the contrary conclusion. Thus, we cannot say the jury was wrong when, after hearing all the evidence, it returned a verdict convicting Appellant of murder. Under the evidence presented, it was clearly not unreasonable for the jury to do so. In summary, (1) if EED is made an issue by the evidence, an instruction including it as an element of the crime should be given; (2) in the same instance (being a statutory element in the case), it then becomes an element of the crime, and the burden of proof lies with the Commonwealth; (3) the courts will then test the sufficiency of the proof, if properly presented and preserved, both at trial, upon a motion for directed verdict, and "insufficiency of the evidence" on appeal; but, (4) if the evidence passes the test, the question is one for the jury, as was the case here. Therefore, we find no error....

## D. Introduction of Photographs

Appellant next charges the trial court erred by allowing the introduction of numerous photographs on matters not disputed at trial. The Commonwealth entered nearly 100 photographs into evidence, most of which were taken at the crime scene and many of which were gruesome. The general rule is that a crime-scene photograph that is otherwise admissible does not become inadmissible simply because it is gruesome and the crime is heinous. The threshold question, therefore, is whether the photographs were admissible in the first place.

Kentucky Rules of Evidence [KRE] 402 establishes that "all relevant evidence is admissible." KRE 401 states: "Relevant evidence" means evidence having any tendency to make the existence of any fact that is of consequence to the determination of the action more probable or less probable than it would be without the evidence. The photographs are relevant evidence because they prove the existence of the victim's physical injuries. Because the photographs are relevant, they are admissible unless they are properly excluded by another rule of evidence. KRE 403 states: "Although relevant, evidence may be excluded if its probative value is substantially outweighed by the danger of unfair prejudice, confusion of the issues, or misleading the jury, or by considerations of undue delay, waste of time, or needless presentation of cumulative evidence."

The question then becomes whether the photographs, although relevant, should be excluded because their prejudicial effect substantially outweighs their probative value. Photographs showing the extent of the victim's injuries are, by their very nature, prejudicial, but the photographs clearly have significant value to the jury in determining the extent of Appellant's culpability. His characterization was that he "poked her" in the neck.

Appellant argues that the cumulative effect of the photographs was so inflammatory that he was unduly prejudiced:

> The introduction of gruesome photographs, bloody clothing, and the like is almost inevitably accompanied by the risk of inflaming the minds of the jurors to the prejudice of the accused. Where necessary to prove a contested relevant fact, their probative value is usually held to outweigh any possible prejudicial effect they might have. But where the facts sought to be proved by the possibly prejudicial evidence are [conceded] by the defense, it is difficult to understand what probative value (other than as cumulative evidence) such evidence might have....

*Poe v. Commonwealth*, 301 S.W.2d 900, 902–03 (Ky. 1957). Appellant argues incorrectly, however, that because the underlying facts were essentially uncontested, the photographs provided no help to the jury on any contested, relevant fact in the case. More pointedly, he argues that the photographs serve no purpose but to inflame the jury against him. Appellant's argument fails, however, because "[t]his court knows of no rule or principle of law that requires the Commonwealth's Attorney to try his case by stipulation." *Payne v. Commonwealth*, 623 S.W.2d 867, 877 (Ky. 1981). Moreover, the photographs have significant probative value in that they would have been helpful to the jury in reaching its determination on Appellant's EED defense, as well as buttressing the testimony of the Commonwealth's other witnesses, including medical witnesses.

Even if the photographs were inflammatory, that does not automatically mean they were inadmissible. In *Adkins v. Commonwealth*, 96 S.W.3d 779, 794 (Ky. 2003), we held "[t]he rule prohibiting the exhibition of inflammatory evidence to a jury does not preclude the revelation of the true facts surrounding the commission of a crime when these facts are relevant and necessary." Because the probative value of the photographs is not substantially outweighed by their prejudicial effect, we find no abuse of discretion, and the photographs were properly admitted.

### E. Rap Video

Next, Appellant argues that the trial court violated KRE 403 and 404(b) by admitting portions of a video depicting him talking or rapping with his friends after he killed his wife. In this video, shot days after the murder, Appellant can be seen boasting of his crime in a seven-minute video montage, saying things such as: "B---- made me mad, and I had to take her life. My name is Dennis Greene and I ain't got no f---ing wife." "I knew I was gonna be givin' it to her … when I got home…." "I cut her motherf---in' neck with a sword…." "I'm sittin' in the cell starin' at four walls…." Appellant contends that showing the jury this video violated KRE 403 and 404(b) because "evidence of prior, uncharged bad acts is not admissible just because a party asserts that such evidence tends to support one of the … purposes listed in the rule." *Commonwealth v. Maddox*, 955 S.W.2d 718, 722 (Ky. 1997). We have traditionally held that evidence primarily designed to cast aspersions on the character of the defendant should not be admitted. In *Billings v. Commonwealth*, 843 S.W.2d 890, 892 (Ky. 1992), we held that "evidence of criminal conduct other than that being tried is admissible only if probative of an issue independent of character or criminal predisposition, and only if its probative value on that issue outweighs the unfair prejudice with respect to character." We also held in *Bell v. Commonwealth*, 875 S.W.2d 882, 889 (Ky. 1994) that "[i]t is a well-known fundamental rule that evidence that a defendant on trial had committed other offenses is never admissible unless it comes within certain exceptions, which are well-defined in the rule itself." For this reason, trial courts must apply the rule cautiously, with an eye towards eliminating evidence which is relevant only as proof of an accused's propensity to commit a certain type of crime.

Appellant contends that the rap video is simply character evidence introduced to prove a criminal disposition. Appellant, however, misapplies the character evidence standard. Evidence of prior arrests, convictions, or bad acts is excluded not because they are not relevant, but rather, because the probative value of the character evidence is substantially outweighed by the prejudicial effect. Here, that is not the case because (a) the video refers to Appellant's actions and emotions regarding this crime, not a previous offense, (b) the video sheds light on Appellant's EED defense by illuminating his mental state shortly after the killing, and (c) the video establishes premeditation and motive in Appellant's own words. For the foregoing reasons, we affirm the trial court's admission of the rap video montage.

### F. Evidence of a Past Affair

Lastly, Appellant argues the trial court violated KRE 404(b) by holding that if Appellant testified about his wife's assertion that she had been unfaithful, then the Commonwealth could introduce evidence of Appellant's past affair with Amy Baumgardener. With this ruling in mind, Appellant himself disclosed the affair to the jury. We note at the outset that KRE 404(b)(1) has no application to this evidence. That Rule proscribes the introduction of evidence tending to prove a particular character trait "in order to show action in conformity therewith." Evidence of immorality would not tend to prove a propensity or predisposition to commit homicide. Thus, the evidence must be tested by the general rule of relevancy, i.e., whether it has "any tendency to make the existence of any fact that is of consequence to the determination of the action more probable or less probable than it would be without the evidence." KRE 401. A "fact that is of consequence to the determination of the action" includes not only a fact tending to prove an element of the offense, but also a fact tending to disprove a defense. Relevancy is established by any showing of probativeness, however slight.

We further note that

> [a]n item of evidence, being but a single link in the chain of proof, need not prove conclusively the proposition for which it is offered. It need not even make that proposition appear more probable than not.... It is enough if the item could reasonably show that a fact is slightly more probable than it

would appear without that evidence. Even after the probative force of the evidence is spent, the proposition for which it is offered still can seem quite improbable.

*Turner v. Commonwealth*, 914 S.W.2d 343, 346 (Ky. 1996). We find that evidence of Appellant's past affair with Ms. Baumgardener is admissible because the affair speaks to his claim of EED as related to the emotional impact of his wife's disclosures about *her* affairs.

Moreover, the affair is ascribed additional relevancy because Appellant called Ms. Baumgardener several times the night of the murder, and she went to Chicago the very next day to see Appellant. A reasonable juror could find that evidence of the affair made the existence of EED less probable than it would be without the evidence. Thus, in this context, we cannot find an abuse of discretion.

### IV. CONCLUSION

For the reasons stated, we affirm.

## QUESTIONS ON *GREENE*

**1. Reasonably unreasonable?** Does Greene's defense—extreme emotional disturbance [EED] set forth in Kentucky Revised Statutes §507.020(1)(a)—set up an objective or subjective standard? What's the difference?

**2. Got mad or went mad?** The court quotes Greene's account of the killing, which he owes to his having "snapped" during a confrontation with the victim. In light of what you surmise about EED, is it helpful or hurtful to Greene's partial defense for him to "snap"?

**3. Weighing up items of evidence.**

    **a.** What is the legal rub with showing the gruesome photographs of the victim to the jury? That they were not relevant in Greene's murder trial? That they were *too* relevant? Hint: The medical examiner testified that the fatal wound went through the victim's throat all the way back to her spine.

    **b.** Which best backs up Greene's putative EED: that his wife admitted to four extramarital affairs? That she might have struck their son on the shoulder? That she stole Greene's marijuana cigarette?

**c.** After the killing, Greene called his former lover, Amy Baumgardener, who joined him in Chicago just before his capture. What was the evidentiary issue surrounding Greene's calls to, and relationship with, Ms. Baumgardener, and how was that issue resolved in the Kentucky Supreme Court?

**4. Burden of proof.** Who has the burden of proof in cases where defendant claims that a killing was manslaughter, not murder, on grounds of EED? More specifically, who has the burden of proving what to whom?

**5. Standard of review.** Applying *Jackson v. Virginia*, see *supra* Chapter 1.B, question 2 on *Flippo*, the Kentucky Supreme Court found the evidence sufficient to reject Greene's mitigating claim of EED, thereby finding the jury's conclusion that Greene committed murder as neither wrong nor unreasonable.

A reminder of the precise language of *Jackson v. Virginia* (which the *Greene* Court quotes) may be in order:

> [A] properly instructed jury may occasionally convict even when it can be said that no rational trier of fact could find guilt beyond a reasonable doubt, and the same may be said of a trial judge sitting as a jury. In a federal trial, such an occurrence has traditionally been deemed to require reversal of the conviction.

*Jackson v. Virginia*, 99 S.Ct. 2781, 2788 (1979). Eight references in all to a *rational*-juror standard appear in Justice Stewart's opinion for the 5-3 *Jackson* Court, and eight more in Justice Stevens's opinion concurring in the judgment. In opposition is this single reference—dumped into a footnote—to a *reasonable*-juror standard:

> The power of the factfinder to err upon the side of mercy, however, has never been thought to include a power to enter an unreasonable verdict of guilty.

*Id.* at 2788 n.10. Is the Kentucky Supreme Court taking liberties with the *Jackson v. Virginia* standard? Or does the word "rational" mean the same thing as the word "reasonable" as a description of the actions of jurors? And if the meanings are different, then what difference does the difference make?

**6. EED v. common law heat of passion.** The *Greene* Court remarks that "[a]lthough EED is essentially a restructuring of the old common law concept of 'heat of passion,' the evidence needed to prove EED is different."

The New York Court of Appeals states the difference this way:

> The opportunity opened for mitigation by the extreme emotional disturbance defense differs significantly from the traditional heat of passion defense. The older concept applied only to immediate actions in which "hot blood" prevented reflection. The newer concept embodies the more sophisticated psychological understanding that a significant mental trauma may not be immediately apparent, yet may diminish a person's mental capacity in ways relevant to society's determination of criminal culpability.

*People v. Fardan*, 628 N.E.2d 41, 43 (N.Y. 1993). Is that how the high court of Kentucky states the difference?

**7. A song or a confession?** Greene unsuccessfully held out his incriminating rap video as an instance of an "artistic" speech situation. He's not the first to say something meant to be art ended up misunderstood by his audience, who took it as serious speech on a literal level.

A case in point is Anthony Douglas Elonis, an active user of Facebook. In May 2010, his wife of nearly seven years left him, taking with her their two young children. Elonis then began for the first time "listening to more violent music" and posting self-styled rap lyrics inspired by the music. Eventually, he changed his Facebook name to "Tone Dougie," as whom he posted graphically violent rap lyrics, including this doozie:

> There's one way to love you but a thousand ways to kill you. I'm not going to rest until your body is a mess, soaked in blood and dying from all the little cuts. Hurry up and die, b****, so I can bust this nut all over your corpse from atop your shallow grave. I used to be a nice guy but then you became a slut. Guess it's not your fault you liked your daddy raped you. So hurry up and die, b****, so I can forgive you.

*United States v. Elonis*, 730 F.3d 321, 324-25 (3d Cir. 2013). Despite Elonis's frequent, public disclaimers that the lyrics were "fictitious," with no intentional "resemblance to real persons," neither his "estranged" wife nor his co-workers—whom Elonis had rattled if not freaked out—were buying it.

After FBI agents monitored his account, Elonis was charged and convicted in federal court of interstate communication of a threat to injure 1) his wife, 2) patrons and co-workers of the amusement park where he worked, 3) members of the Pennsylvania State Police and Berks County Sheriff's Department, 4) an FBI agent, and 5) a group of kindergarten students.

Like Greene, Elonis claimed on appeal that the violence he predicted on Facebook was artistic, not factual. But the Third Circuit found his conviction justified because he was negligent not to account for how others would (reasonably) perceive his postings. *Elonis*, 730 F.3d at 327-35. From that ruling he sought review in the U.S. Supreme Court. *Elonis v. United States*, 134 S.Ct. 2819 (2014).

Reversing Elonis's conviction, the Supreme Court found that the federal statute in question, 18 U.S.C. §875(c) (1994), could not be violated on a mere civil negligence standard. The Court took no position either on what standard the statute *did* contemplate, or on Elonis's argument that his postings were protected by the First Amendment. *Elonis v. United States*, 135 S.Ct. 2001 (2015).

On remand, the Third Circuit affirmed the conviction, finding the erroneous instruction harmless, that is, to have had no influence on the jury. *United States v. Elonis*, 841 F.3d 589, 597-601 (3d Cir. 2016). The high court recently denied Elonis's petition for certiorari from that ruling. *Elonis v. United States*, 138 S.Ct. 67 (2017).

Elonis said up front that the lyrics were fictitious. Shouldn't that be good enough to be dispositive on the issue of seriousness? After all, if the primary point of speaking is being believed, isn't believing the primary point of being spoken to?

## NOTES ON *GREENE*

***1. Rehearing.*** Three months after the Kentucky Supreme Court's ruling, that same court denied Greene's request for rehearing. Baldwin's Kentucky Rules of Civil Procedure, rule 76.32. Petitioning the same panel to reconsider its own ruling is borderline futile unless instigated by such bases as an intervening new legal principle announced by a court that applies the new rule retroactively, or the original panel misconstrued an obvious existing legal principle or undisputed fact. Sometimes the movant sees an opening, as where one judge on the original panel dissented from the published ruling and the movant is hoping to persuade just one other (susceptible?) judge on the panel to side with the movant.

Other motions for rehearing might be criticized as just a form of churning—filing the motion just because it's there, to show all concerned that the attorney is hitting it hard.

An alternative post-ruling move available to disgruntled appellate litigants is to petition all active judges on the court (there are seven in Kentucky) to rehear the case en banc, French for "in bench." *Compare* Federal Rules of Appellate Procedure, rule 35(b) (2005) [petition for en banc determination] *with* Federal Rules of Appellate Procedure, rule 40 (2011) [petition for panel rehearing].

**2. Criminal procedure: appealing criminal convictions.** The path from state trial court, to state appellate court, to state court of last resort, to the U.S. Supreme Court is referred to as that of "direct" appeal.

***a. Appeals as of right in state court.*** In the second sentence of its opinion, the Kentucky Supreme Court states that it is entertaining Greene's "appeal as of right." The Supreme Court has stuck to its position that "review by an appellate court of the final judgment in a criminal case, however grave the offense of which the accused is convicted, was not at common law, and is not now, a necessary element of due process of law." The right to appeal therefore is by legislative grace, not by federal constitutional mandate. *McKane v. Durston*, 14 S.Ct. 913, 915 (1894).

Indeed, for a century after the U.S. Supreme Court was established by the Judiciary Act of 1789 (1 Stat. 73), no appeal as of right existed in criminal cases. *Abney v. United States*, 97 S.Ct. 2034, 2038 n.3 (1977). Congress first permitted criminal appeals as of right to the Supreme Court in 1889 for "all cases of conviction of crime the punishment of which provided by law is death." Act of Feb. 6, 1889, 25 Stat. 656. The 1889 Act was followed by the Act of March 3, 1891, 26 Stat. 826, which created the circuit courts of appeals. *See United States v. Rider*, 16 S.Ct. 983 (1896). Section 5 of the 1891 Act permitted appeals from district courts (or the existing circuit courts) directly to the Supreme Court in, *inter alia*, "cases of conviction of a capital or otherwise infamous crime"; by section 6, the circuit courts of appeals would have appellate jurisdiction in all cases other than those provided for in section 5.

The Act of January 20, 1897, 29 Stat. 492, transferred from the Supreme Court to the circuit courts of appeals appellate jurisdiction in all non-capital criminal cases. This was accomplished by deleting from the just-quoted clause of section 5 of the 1891 Act the phrase "or otherwise infamous"; as a result, direct appeal to the Supreme Court was preserved only "in cases of conviction of a capital crime." Section 5 remained like that until the Judicial Code Act of March 3, 1911, 36 Stat. 1087, 1133, the upshot of which was to limit direct appeal as of right in *all* criminal cases—even capital—to the circuit courts of appeal. Supreme Court review of criminal cases would from then on be entirely discretionary, not as of right. *See Stephan v. United States*, 63 S.Ct. 1135, 1135-37 (1943).

Kentucky, like all states, makes available one non-discretionary appeal in all non-trivial criminal cases. Kentucky Constitution §115 (Baldwin 1974) ["In all cases, civil and criminal, there shall be allowed as a matter of right at least one appeal to another court, except that the Commonwealth may not appeal from a judgment of acquittal in a criminal case...."]. Once a state chooses to offer non-discretionary appeal of criminal convictions, federal constitutional principles of Due Process and Equal Protection require "access to courts." Accordingly, defendants who are convicted at trial in such states may take one appeal at state expense if they cannot afford filing fees, trial transcripts, and a lawyer to research, brief, and argue their appeal in their state intermediate appellate court. *Ross v. Moffitt*, 94 S.Ct. 2437 (1974). As noted in this book's introduction, criminal defendants, most of whom are indigent, customarily take advantage of subsidized appellate litigation without the cost-benefit analyses in which civil litigants engage.

After one appeal from a judgment of conviction or sentence, access to state courts of last resort, usually labeled "supreme," is largely discretionary, limited to cases those high courts deem worthy. I say "largely discretionary" because there are some conditions under which defendants are entitled to review of adverse trial-court rulings in their state high court with no stop along the way in their state intermediate appellate court. In Kentucky, for example, convicted defendants bypass (as Dennis Greene did) the Kentucky Court of Appeals in designated high-stakes cases: "Appeals from a judgment of the Circuit Court imposing a sentence of death or life imprisonment or imprisonment for twenty years or more shall be taken directly to the [Kentucky] Supreme Court." Kentucky Constitution §110(2)(b) (Baldwin 1976).

Arkansas, as you know, has a similar procedure applicable to appeals from death sentences. *See supra* Chapter 1.B, note 2 on *Flippo*.

**b. Appeals as of right from state court.** Whether the state high court denies a defendant's request for discretionary review or grants review and rules against the defendant on the merits, he or she may push on by seeking review in the U.S. Supreme Court. In 1988, Congress all but did away with Supreme Court appeals as of right, except in cases decided by a three-judge district court: a nearly extinct facet of federal litigation, limited by statute to challenges to the constitutionality of the apportionment of congressional districts and state legislative districts. 28 U.S.C. §§1253 & 2284(a). True appeals— cases the U.S. Supreme Court *must* hear and decide—arise rarely and appear on the Court's docket mostly on the 10-year census-and-redistricting cycle. *Easley v. Cromartie*, 121 S.Ct. 1452 (2001).

Congress occasionally includes a grant of jurisdiction in a controversial statute that is sure to be challenged on constitutional grounds. An example is the federal anti-flag burning act of 1989, which provided automatic appeal from the federal trial court directly to the Supreme Court, bypassing intermediate appeal. *United States v. Eichman*, 110 S.Ct. 2404 (1990). Today, the Supreme Court is in almost complete control of its docket, hearing and deciding cases, whether from a lower federal court or a state high court, by electing discretionary review on a petition for certiorari. 28 U.S.C. §§1254 & 1257 (1988). Thomas E. Baker, "A Primer on Supreme Court Procedures" 480 (American Bar Association 2004).

State criminal cases have no basis for review (or jurisdiction, as lawyers call it) in the U.S. Supreme Court except where defendants challenge the validity of their state conviction or sentence on *federal* grounds. This means that unless some aspect of the state conviction apparatus violates a defendant's *federal* statutory or constitutional rights, the Supreme Court will deny certiorari since it does not issue rulings on state law. An exception is civil cases involving diversity of citizenship. *Compare* 28 U.S.C. §1332(a)(1) [diversity jurisdiction] *with* 28 U.S.C. §1331 [federal-question jurisdiction].

For example, defendants whose appeals are based on the Fourth Amendment ban on unreasonable searches and seizures raise a federal claim; oppositely, those who claim, like Dennis Greene, that the court admitted irrelevant or unduly prejudicial evidence, do not. *Cf. Johnigan v. Elo*, 207 F.Supp.2d 599 (E.D. Mich. 2002) [discussing federalization of challenges to convictions based on sufficiency of the evidence under *Jackson v. Virginia*, a ruling derived from the federal Due Process clauses].

    ***c. Federal court collateral attack on state-court judgment.*** Of the roughly 7,000 certiorari petitions filed each year, the U.S. Supreme Court granted just 69 in 2017. This number reflects a progressively shrinking load. *See* Erwin Chemerinsky, *The Roberts Court at Age Three*, 54 Wayne Law Review 947, 948-52 (2008).[b] With fewer than 1% of petitioners receiving review on the merits of their federal claims in the nation's high court, state courts would have the final word in 99% of all state cases raising federal claims if certiorari were the only way to obtain federal review. Denial of relief on direct appeal is not, however, the end of the road.

    For state prisoners with federal claims, there remains the possibility of obtaining relief by way of "collateral attack" on the conviction or sentence. This cause of action, which denotes that the challenge occurs outside the direct appellate process, occurs only after 1) final judgment at trial; 2) the appeal as of right has been decided adversely to defendant; and 3) the state high court has affirmed that ruling or denied review. Collateral attacks brought in federal district courts to challenge state-court convictions and sentences, codified by the 39th or "reconstruction" Congress, are known as "writs of habeas corpus." 28 U.S.C. §2254 (1996). Habeas corpus is a remedy by which state prisoners petition the warden responsible for their incarceration to have them delivered to a federal district court for an inquiry into the lawfulness—under federal law—of their conviction or sentence.[c]

---

[b] Of the 6,475 cases filed in the Supreme Court in the 2015 Term, 4,926 (76%) were filed on the Court's *in forma pauperis* docket and 1,549 were filed on the Court's paid docket. Of the 82 cases argued, 70 were disposed of in 62 signed opinions. The Court also issued 12 *per curiam* decisions in cases that were briefed but not argued. https://www.supremecourt.gov/publicinfo/year-end/2016year-endreport.pdf at p. 11.

[c] Challenges to the conditions of confinement (brutal guards, no law library, lousy medical care) are not cognizable on federal habeas corpus, which operates only to invalidate convictions and sentences. Claims that would not, if successful, invalidate the conviction or sentence, but instead would compensate the plaintiff-prisoner for violations of federally protected rights by state officials, are remedied by 42 U.S.C. §1983 (1996), a species of tort liability, also codified by the 39th Congress.

The right of state prisoners to have a federal forum to adjudicate their federal constitutional claims is considered a perk of federal citizenship. Accordingly, it should come as no surprise that the 39th Congress created a path for *civil* defendants in state court to "remove" their case to federal court in disputes containing a "federal question." 28 U.S.C. §1441(c)(A) (1990). But because state courts are competent to rule on issues of federal constitutional law, Congress requires that state prisoners "exhaust" their state-court remedies, which means that federal-court review must await a full and fair opportunity for the state courts to correct their own errors. After exhausting their direct appellate remedies in state court without success, defendants may petition a federal district court to review their federal claims and grant relief in the form of a "writ," structured either to free the defendant-prisoners or afford them a prompt retrial.

Federal habeas petitioners were long afforded *de novo* review, that is, a fresh look in federal court unbound by state courts' conclusions on matters involving legal standards (as opposed to questions of fact, which would be reviewed more deferentially). *Wright v. West*, 112 S.Ct. 2482, 2498-2500 (1992) (Kennedy, J., concurring in the judgment). But Congress has done away with that, subbing in a standard of review that is, from petitioners' perspective, rigged in favor of affirming state-court denials of relief. According to the Antiterrorism and Effective Death Penalty Act of 1996 [AEDPA], 110 Stat. 1214, federal habeas relief shall lie only if a state court's decision involved either an unreasonable application of clearly established federal law as determined by the U.S. Supreme Court, or an unreasonable determination of the facts as presented in the state court. 28 U.S.C. §2254(d)(1). This highly deferential standard places on petitioner the burden of proving that the state court's decision was unreasonable, not just wrong. *Schriro v. Landrigan*, 127 S.Ct. 1933, 1939-40 (2007).

Congress designed AEDPA to streamline habeas, which, from the states' perspective, was burdened by abuse (manifested as successive petitions filed by the same prisoner), and a lack of finality that allowed criminal cases to drag on forever. For example, in 1941, Coney Island shopkeeper Murray Hammeroff was fatally shot with a revolver. A year later, Charles Noia and two confederates, Bonino and Caminito, were convicted of Hammeroff's murder and sentenced to life in Sing Sing Prison. Then, some 22 years after the crime, the Supreme Court, on Noia's habeas petition, ruled that due to the unreliability of a confession extracted from him by New York City police, Noia deserved a new trial. *Fay v. Noia*, 83 S. Ct. 822 (1963).

Protracted litigation of this sort was not unusual. For example, 24 years after Booker Hillery's conviction for a grisly 1962 scissors-slaying in the San Joaquin Valley, the Supreme Court granted his habeas writ, ordering a new trial, this time to be conducted without a discriminatorily selected grand jury. *Vasquez v. Hillery*, 106 S.Ct. 617 (1986). Remarkably, Hillery's retrial was held, ending in December 1986 in his re-conviction for murder. These open-ended opportunities for prisoners seeking judicial relief produced AEDPA, which established not only that at some point the curtain must close, but so too should it close in the State's favor, except where obvious blunders in the state conviction apparatus are uncovered. Hillery was denied parole in a 2003 hearing at California State Medical Facility (Vacaville) and remains incarcerated as of 2018, now age 86, at California Health Care Facility (Stockton). According to Wikipedia, Hillery is in the world's top ten among living prisoners for uninterrupted years served, and #1 in California.

**3. Making a federal case of EED.** To illustrate how state criminal defendants may remove their cases to federal court, consider *Griggs v. Meko*, 2013 WL 823323 (E.D. Ky.), denying the federal habeas petition of a Kentucky prisoner. Please note the caption, which depicts a dispute between two individuals, not a governmental entity and an accused. As a petition for federal habeas corpus, *Griggs* is civil in form, not criminal: the convicted defendant (Ivan Parker Griggs), now as civil plaintiff, is suing the warden (Joseph Meko), who runs the prison in Sandy Hook, Kentucky, where Griggs was installed before being transferred 18 miles south to West Liberty. Unlike most civil litigants, who sue for money, Griggs, as habeas petitioner, is suing for his freedom.

Griggs was charged with the murder of Mary Salyers, whom he shot on June 12, 2005 at her Lexington home. Griggs, 62 at the time with no prior record, and Salyers, 44, had a child together, Nicole, whose custody they shared since her birth in 1989. Griggs's marriage had survived his affair with Salyers, with whom he remained erotically entangled until the end. On the day of the killing, Nicole was to begin a summer visit with Griggs, who went to get her at Salyers's home, found her absent, and became angered by the inconvenience and by the presence of a man (Brian) with whom Griggs suspected Salyers was involved. After Nicole showed up at Griggs's home, Griggs returned to Salyers's home, where he shot her twice in the head.

A jury found Griggs guilty of murder; he was sentenced to 30 years. He dedicated his direct appeal as of right in the Kentucky Supreme Court to the admissibility of his confession, which he claimed was made involuntary by his having taken too many sleeping pills. After the Kentucky Supreme Court affirmed, Griggs moved the trial court for re-sentencing in a state court collateral attack per §11.42 of the Kentucky Rules of Criminal Procedure, claiming that trial counsel (Gene Lewter) was constitutionally ineffective in presenting Griggs's EED defense. The trial court denied Griggs's motion; the Kentucky Court of Appeals affirmed. Having exhausted his state-court remedies, Griggs filed a federal habeas petition reasserting his claim of ineffective assistance on Lewter's part.

To justify removal of his case to federal court, Griggs had to raise a federal claim that would invalidate his conviction or sentence. And he did: according to the Supreme Court, the Sixth Amendment guarantees not just a "right to counsel" (the letter of the law), but an "effective" one at that (the spirit of the law). *Strickland v. Washington*, 104 S.Ct. 2052, 2063-64 (1984). *Strickland* ruled that when counsel's professional judgment is both unreasonable and reasonably probable to have caused defendant an adverse ruling, reversal is proper. In ruling against Griggs on his §11.42 motion, the Kentucky courts, obeying *Strickland*'s injunction to defer to counsel's judgment even when in hindsight it looks iffy, found Lewter's performance to have been reasonable, that is, within constitutional norms. And even if it wasn't, the Kentucky courts concluded, it was the facts surrounding the killing, not attorney Lewter, that got Griggs convicted of murder instead of manslaughter (or instead of a mistrial brought about by a hung jury owing to a single juror's vote for manslaughter).

With Griggs's case exhausted in the Kentucky courts and now on federal habeas, the issue under AEDPA is not whether the federal district court would have found differently were it in the shoes of the Kentucky courts, but rather, whether the Kentucky courts unreasonably applied *Strickland*'s clearly-established-law standard to Griggs's claims.

Griggs criticized Lewter for not putting his wife Deborah (by then divorced from Griggs after 29 years) on the stand to testify to Griggs's stress from arguments with Salyers over Nicole's ADHD medication, part-time job, and visits with Griggs. Deborah also could have testified to Griggs's stress over the care of his mother, who suffered from

Alzheimer's, and to his sleeping disorder and extreme weight loss in the run-up to the killing. But as Lewter explained at the §11.42 motion, he had his reasons for not calling Deborah: first, incidents of domestic violence in their marriage would prejudice jurors, given that Griggs's slaying of Ms. Salyers was also an act of domestic violence. And second, Deborah did not want to testify: due to the marital privilege, the trial court excluded anything she might say about the night of the murder, permitting her to testify on matters that turned out to be more likely to inculpate Griggs. Plus, having reviewed Deborah's recorded conversations with police and with Griggs, because she was understandably upset about the killing, had damaging information that could come out on cross-examination, and was hesitant to testify, Lewter ruled out putting her on the stand.

Even if Deborah had testified, much of her testimony would have duplicated Griggs's taped confession that the Commonwealth played for the jury. In that tape, Griggs recounts his spats with Salyers over their daughter, and his sense that he'd been "set up": specifically, when Griggs called Salyers to say he was en route to get Nicole, she neglected to tell him Nicole was gone. As Griggs waited in the driveway, Brian came out while Salyers stood in the doorway in her robe before going back in without acknowledging Griggs or (yet) reporting that Nicole would be late. This, Griggs felt, was a plot to theatricalize the fact that Salyers had a boyfriend.

Other testimony Griggs anticipated from Deborah was unlikely to materialize in any event. For instance, while Griggs thought she would back up the stressful build-up to the killing, indicated by a sleeping disorder and precipitous 30-pound weight loss, Deborah reported at the §11.42 motion that Griggs *intended* to lose the weight and that his prescription sleep medication had been suggested by his attorney *after* the killing. Thus, the federal district court found the Kentucky courts' denial of Griggs's claim was a reasonable application of *Strickland*: counsel reasonably assessed the risks of calling Deborah to testify against her wishes.

Griggs's critique went on to record Lewter's failure to make an opening statement, an omission that all three courts reviewing the matter said made sense strategically, given Lewter's explanation at the §11.42 motion that too many clients change their tune midstream from the course set out in the opening, thus undermining the credibility of the defense team.

Griggs also perceived Lewter's closing argument as deficient for failure to argue two key points of Kentucky law on EED: first, that the reasonableness of his provocation must be judged as *he* perceived the circumstances; and second, that the EED must have a triggering event, which in turn may occur long before the killing. As to Griggs's first point, the Kentucky Court of Appeals found that during closing, Lewter stated that "the one thing that breaks his back or puts a person over the edge" must be "based upon something as perceived by the defendant. You look at it through his eyes." As to Griggs's second point, the Court of Appeals found that Lewter's closing did in fact discuss the cause of Griggs's anger prior to the time of the murder, and posited that Griggs was acting under the spell of that anger when he shot Salyers. Lewter stated that EED requires a temporary state of mind, but he also explained that the rage could continue for some time until the final act.

As to the triggering event, Lewter adequately described it as the cumulative impact of several ongoing disputes with Salyers, culminating in the events of the night of her killing. Lewter argued that the events of the day had been eating at Griggs, who, after stewing about Salyers not telling him that Nicole was not home, and about Salyers communing with Brian, confronted her to demand that she justify the scene surrounding Nicole's pick-up. Lewter went on in his closing that the killing was not planned: that it happened during a struggle. Indeed, Lewter not only litigated the EED defense well enough to get a jury instruction on manslaughter, but did so without any testimony from Griggs, whom Lewter elected not to put on.

Even had Lewter represented Griggs incompetently, Lewter did not cause Griggs's EED defense to fail. The Commonwealth demonstrated that the killing was not spur of the moment, but a mulled-over decision made hours after the triggering event. Evidence showed Griggs had been fixated on Salyers for months. According to Nicole, he had driven by Salyers's home with no good reason, as did he falsely claim to have seen Salyers having sex on the floor of her apartment with Brian. A few weeks before the killing, Nicole heard Griggs threaten to kill Salyers and Brian. Griggs's confession verified that hours after the alleged triggering event, he returned to Salyers's home armed with a knife and a gun, supporting the jury's finding that the killing resulted from considered choice, not emotional flurry.

The federal district court therefore concluded that Griggs did not meet his burden of demonstrating that the Kentucky Court of Appeals' decision interpreting *Strickland* was unreasonable.

**4. Preserving claims of trial error for appellate review.** On state habeas corpus in the Kentucky trial court, Griggs raised Lewter's constitutionally ineffective representation only after the Kentucky Supreme Court had denied Griggs's attempt to suppress his allegedly coerced confession on direct appeal.

*a. Direct appeal.* It is considered a real no-no for lawyers to raise claims on appeal not "preserved" or presented to the trial court. (This procedural requirement is alluded to at the end of section III.A of the *Greene* opinion, *supra* Chapter 3.A, and the end of the Froessel opinion in *Decina, supra* Chapter 1.A). Appellate counsel is precluded from raising an issue on appeal by 1) failing to timely raise the issue in the trial court; 2) agreeing as part of a plea bargain *not* to appeal; or 3) failing to timely notify the trial court of the intent to appeal. *See, e.g., People v. Patterson,* 2016 WL 6962526 (Cal. 4th Dist. Ct. App.).

It is trial counsel, therefore, who dictates what issues appellate counsel may pursue. Efficiency is the stated reason: the trial court should be alerted to its errors so it may correct them itself without the need to enlist new lawyers, order briefing, set oral argument, and await a ruling arrived at in the slowpoke pace of appellate litigation. To prevent a claim from being "defaulted" or "forfeited," not only must a defendant object to the action in controversy in the trial court, but the objection must also be sufficiently specific to be cognizable on appeal. *People v. Stowell,* 31 Cal.4th 1107, 1112-14 (2003).

And even when the objection *is* lodged below, some trial-court errors—as in *Elonis*—are forgiven on appeal as "harmless" or causally insignificant to the outcome, see *United States v. Elonis,* 841 F.3d 589, 597-601 (3d Cir. 2016), while other errors are deemed by the appellate court to entitle the trial court to a re-do. *See People v. Antonio (I),* 2016 WL 310104 at *3 (Cal. 4th Dist. Ct. App.) [after trial court failed to declare how multiple terms of sentence would run, appellate court remanded so trial court could start over and re-sentence defendant, even though statute clearly stated that trial court's failure to so declare results in concurrent terms].

*b. State court collateral attack on state-court judgment.* If trial counsel's incompetent failure to preserve an issue for appeal causes defendant to lose at trial, that can be sorted out later as it was in *Griggs.* Under Kentucky law, claims of constitutionally ineffective assistance of counsel are not forfeited under §11.42 and thus are cognizable on collateral attack at any time in the litigation, preserved or not. *Leonard v. Commonwealth,* 279 S.W.3d 151 (Ky. 2009).

The logic of relaxing the raise-it-or-lose-it rules for such claims is that counsel's performance cannot be resolved effectively on direct appeal, which depends entirely on the contents of the trial record. The trial record typically cannot contain the entire range of trial counsel's plausible, strategic bases for whatever course of action that the client is now calling prejudicially incompetent. For that, trial counsel must be heard from in the form of a declaration (affidavit) justifying the legal moves now in controversy. *See generally Martinez v. Ryan*, 132 S.Ct. 1309 (2012); *People v. Witcraft*, 201 Cal.App.4th 659, 664-65 (2011).

For additional detail on claims considered outside the record of trial court proceedings and therefore appropriate for state habeas/collateral review, see California Penal Code §1473.

**5. *Griggs* and other aging offenders.** When this edition went to press in 2018, Griggs was 74, having then served 11 years in medium security. The State of Kentucky says Griggs will be eligible for parole in June 2025. (http://kool.corrections.ky.gov/KOOL/Details/249950).

Consider the following concurring opinion in *United States v. Jackson*, 835 F.2d 1195, 1198-1200 (7th Cir. 1987), by Judge Richard Posner, whose take on incarcerating aging offenders (there, career bank robber Dwight Jackson) is worth presenting at length:

> I join the opinion and judgment of the court; but I think the sentence Jackson received is too harsh and I think it appropriate to point this out even though he presents no ground on which we are authorized to set aside an excessively severe sentence.
>
> Jackson is unquestionably a dangerous and hardened criminal. He has been convicted of armed robbery four times (three were bank robberies—all of the same bank!); in each robbery he was carrying a loaded gun. I do not mean to denigrate the gravity of his offenses by pointing out that he has never inflicted a physical injury; but that fact is relevant to deciding whether the sheer enormity of his conduct warrants imprisonment for the rest of his life as a matter of retributive justice. It does not. Few murderers, traitors, or rapists are punished so severely—a good example being the life sentences, with parole eligibility after 10 years, imposed on two federal prisoners for first-degree murder, each having previously murdered three people, in *United States v. Fountain*, 768 F.2d 790, 799-800 (7th Cir. 1985). The

grounds for the sentence in this case must be sought elsewhere.

One ground, the one articulated by the district judge, is the need to prevent Jackson from committing further crimes. There is little doubt that if he were released tomorrow he would commit a bank robbery, perhaps on the same day. But it is extremely unlikely that if he were released 25 or 30 years from now (he is 35 years old) he would resume his career as a bank robber. We know that criminal careers taper off with age, although with the aging of the population and the improvements in the health of the aged the fraction of crimes committed by the elderly is rising.... Crimes that involve a risk of physical injury to the criminal are especially a young man's game. In 1986 more than 62 percent of all persons arrested for robbery (any sort of robbery—I can find no breakdown by type of robbery) were below the age of 25, and only 3.4 percent were 60 years old or older.... The only age group that accounted for a smaller percentage of arrests for robbery than persons 60 to 64, or 65 and older, were children below the age of 10—and, remarkably, there were almost as many arrests in that group as there were of persons in the 65 and over group (199 versus 209)....

Bank robbery in particular, I suspect, is a young man's crime. A bank robber must be willing to confront armed guards and able to make a quick getaway. To suppose that if Jackson is fortunate enough to live on in prison into his seventies or eighties it would still be necessary to detain him lest he resume his life of crime after almost a lifetime in prison is too speculative to warrant imprisoning him until he dies of old age. The probation officer who conducted the presentence investigation of Jackson and compiled a meticulous 16-page single-spaced presentence report covering every facet of Jackson's history, personality, and criminal activity recommended a 10-year sentence. This may well be too short, but it is some indication that imprisonment for the rest of Jackson's life is too long if the only concern is with the crimes he might commit if he were ever released.

The remaining possibility is that this savage sentence is proper *pour encourager les autres*. Indeed, deterrence is the surest ground for punishment, since retributive norms are so unsettled and since incapacitation may, by removing one offender from the pool of offenders, simply make a career in crime more attractive to someone else, who is balanced on the razor's edge between criminal and legitimate activity and who now faces reduced competition in the crime "market." Thus, even if one were sure that Jackson would be as harmless as a mouse in the last 10, or 15, or 20 years of his life, his sentence might be justified if the example of it were likely to deter other people, similarly situated, from committing such crimes. This is possible, but speculative; it was not mentioned by the district judge.

We should ask how many 35 year olds would rob a bank if they knew that if they were caught it would mean 20 years in prison with no possibility of parole (the sentence I would have given Jackson if I had been the sentencing judge), compared to the number who would do so if it would mean life in prison. Probably very few would be deterred by the incremental sentence. Bank robbery is a crime of acquisition, not of passion; the only gains are financial—and are slight (in 1986 the average "take" from a bank robbery was $2,664). The net gains, when the expected cost of punishment is figured in, must be very small indeed. Clearance rates for bank robbery are very high; of all bank robberies investigated by the FBI during 1978 and 1979 (and virtually all bank robberies are reported and therefore investigated), 69 percent had been cleared by arrest by 1982.... Conviction rates are high (90 percent in federal prosecutions for bank robbery) and average punishments severe (more than 13 years for federal defendants). It's a losers' game at best. Persons who would go ahead and rob a bank in the face of my hypothetical 20-year sentence are unlikely to be deterred by tightening the punishment screws still further. A civilized society locks up such people until age makes them harmless but it does not keep them in prison until they die.

It may repay the effort to consider the pertinence of Judge Posner's point about aging offenders to the current criminal capacities of Stephen Whitfield as set forth *supra* Chapter 2.B, note 6 on *Whitfield*.

**6. *The problem of privacy revisited: parasitic speech*.** That neither Dennis Greene nor Anthony Elonis really were rappers likely contributed to their juries' rejection of their in-court claims that their controversial utterances were unserious.

In 1991, just after the Rodney King beating by LAPD officers Stacey Koon, Laurence Powell, Timothy Wind, and Theodore Briseno, rapper Ice-T and guitarist Ernie C. wrote "Cop Killer" for release the next year to debut their band, Body Count. The song, expressing a fed-up-ness with police brutality, provoked intense, negative reaction from, among others, President Bush (the elder), Vice President Quayle, and law enforcement.

Ice-T, who capitulated to pulling the song from store shelves, defended "Cop Killer" as a protest that made him no more a cop killer than David Bowie's "Space Oddity" (1969) made Bowie an astronaut. Ice-T's point was that a song is not a manifesto. It is, after all, *just* a song, or, one might say, just a *song*.

Songs *are* speech, but they are "parasitic" speech. Parasitic speech trades on, depends on, or derives its meaning from "normal" speech, but is not quite the same in that parasitic speech lacks the seriousness of normal speech. *See* J.L. Austin, How to Do Things with Words 104 (J.O. Urmson & M. Sbisa eds.) (Oxford 1975). This is not to call "Cop Killer" a joke; that would be a misreading of the use here of the word "unserious." Another example of parasitic speech is lines uttered on stage in a play. More specifically, when Iago, engineering the demise of Desdemona, enjoins Othello, "Don't do it with poison/Strangle her in her bed/The same bed she's contaminated," *Othello*, Act IV, Scene 1, no sane spectator believes that anyone is being (seriously) asked to commit murder: we do not attend *Othello* to witness, nor do we witness, a (real) jealousy-inspired murder. But neither is the depiction of Desdemona's death in any sense a joke; if it were, *Othello* would not be the engaging drama it is.

Of course, saying "it's just a song" would be a cop-out if the song really is a manifesto. But typically, the criteria of parasitic speech are not that hard to identify. For example, during a November 17, 2006 performance at the Laugh Factory in West Hollywood, Michael Richards (aka Kramer from TV's "Seinfeld"), perceiving black hecklers in the audience, responded by pacing around the stage, taunting the men for interrupting his show, and peppering his speech with profanities, the most noticeable of which were seven deployments of an unmistakable racial epithet and a reference to lynching. The comedy-club audience, captured on a videophone, was aghast.

Three days later, David Letterman gave Richards a televised chance to explain himself, though the event boomeranged when Richards's rambling discourse on American race relations prompted Letterman to interrupt, asking Richards what he would have done had the hecklers been white. Richards said this:

> I'm a performer. I push the envelope. I work in a very uncontrolled manner on stage. I do a lot of free association—it's spontaneous, I go into character. I don't know. In view of the situation and the act going the way it was going, I don't know. The rage did go all over the place. It went to everybody in the room.

This oblique claim that the rant was part of his stand-up act is Richards's attempt to fancy himself a sort of Lenny Bruce, Richard Pryor, or Sam Kinnison: edgy comics whose resort to slurs was widely criticized as in bad taste, but had at once a recognizable purpose *within the structure of their act.*

During his rant, Richards commented, "It shocks you, it shocks you," as though his role in the tiff was not a tantrum, but art: improvised comic spectacle. If Richards pushes the envelope as a professional device, then perhaps he just pushed a bit too far at the Laugh Factory that night, making it *bad* comedy (not funny or even educational in a biting way), but still comedy as opposed to the sudden surfacing of repressed racist impulses.

Richards's claim to have made his scandalous quips with a comedic intention presents the problem of privacy: he's in his body and we're in ours. How can we tell what another person's intentions are? Don't we just have to take his word for it? *Cf.* J.L. Austin, *Other Minds, in* Philosophical Papers, *supra,* at 113 ["In the complex of occurrences which induces us to say we know another man is angry, ... a peculiar place is occupied by the man's own statement as to what his feelings are. In the usual case, we accept this statement without question...."]. Despite the problem of privacy or the inaccessibility of the inner world of others (referred to by philosophers as the problem of "other minds"), Richards's calling his rant "part of the act" can't by itself make it so. Rather, his saying so is like getting married and, after a conventional, somber ceremony performed in front of witnesses and a licensed official, seeking to nullify the marriage on the ground that the ceremony was a joke. Based on what can be known in the public observable world, the Kentucky Supreme Court properly upheld the trial court's ruling admitting the video. After all, Dennis Greene is not Ice-T; he is not even Michael Richards.

As support for the idea that claiming to be engaged in artistic expression is aided by actually *being* an artist, a San Diego County Superior Court recently dismissed charges brought under California Penal Code §186.22(a) (West 2014) against rapper Tiny Doo. Prosecutors had accused Doo, né Brandon Duncan, of profiting off gang activity through his rap music, which emerged from the Lincoln Park area of San Diego where he grew up. Prosecutors operated on the premise that criminal activity by members of the Lincoln Park Bloods, alluded to in Doo's lyrics, boosted sales of "No Safety" (2014), his fourth album and first since his "What It Doo" trilogy. *See* http://www.utsandiego.com/news/2015/jan/13/rap-gang-conspiracy-charges-dropped/?#article-copy.

In January 2017, Tiny Doo sued the City of San Diego and two police detectives in a §1983 action filed in a federal district court over the damages he incurred during the seven months he spent in jail prior to dismissal of the gang charges. According to the federal court's electronic docket, argument on cross-motions for summary judgment is set for May 13, 2018.

## COURT OF APPEAL, FOURTH DISTRICT, CALIFORNIA

*THE PEOPLE, PLAINTIFF AND RESPONDENT*

*V.*

*CLYDE RICHARD SPURLIN, DEFENDANT AND APPELLANT*

MAY 21, 1984

BUTLER, Associate Justice

Clyde Richard Spurlin appeals his jury convictions of first-degree murder of his nine-year-old son Scott and second-degree murder of his wife Peggy, contending that 1) the court erred in failing to give a requested manslaughter instruction as to Scott's death, 2) the error tainted his second-degree murder conviction for Peggy's death, and 3) the evidence did not support his first-degree murder conviction for Scott's death. We affirm.

### I

Spurlin married Peggy in 1972. Scott was born in 1973 and their daughter Carrie in 1977. The first years of their marriage were uneventful. They joined a church and were viewed as a religious couple. In 1981, they embarked upon a new lifestyle, initially acting out Peggy's sexual fantasies, then moving on to involvements with others. With Spurlin's permission, Peggy dated other men and had an affair with a co-worker. She reported these events to Spurlin and with his permission quit her 9-to-5 job as an office worker and became a nude dancer at Dirty Dan's in San Diego. Her sexual escapades escalated to include lesbian episodes, mate-swapping, and possible employment as a call girl. Spurlin contracted a venereal disease from Peggy. His reluctant acquiescence in Peggy's sexual activities began to cool and they agreed she would try a new path by returning to school.

On the night of the murders, November 2, 1982, Spurlin picked up Peggy at Dirty Dan's, where they had a couple of drinks, then returned home and had some more. The children were fed, bathed and bedded. Spurlin and Peggy felt good and sat around talking. Spurlin told Peggy about three or four call girls he had patronized in earlier years during business trips. Peggy became angry, withdrew, and went upstairs to their bedroom, telling Spurlin not to bother her, and responding to his question about the marriage being over: "I don't know … all I feel like is I just want to die." Spurlin went to the kitchen, gulped some tequila and went upstairs to the bedroom. Peggy told him to leave her alone. He felt ill, nauseous, and went to the bathroom. Peggy looked in on him and returned to bed. Spurlin next remembered standing by her bed, hammer in hand, striking her with it, Peggy saying, "Don't hurt me, Rich," strangling her and knotting a tie around her neck. Death was caused by strangulation. The hammer was broken. Spurlin went downstairs to the garage, got another hammer, returned to the bedroom where Scott was sleeping and killed him with a hammer blow to the head. He also knotted a tie around Scott's neck. Entertaining thoughts of killing Carrie and himself, he walked around the house, crying, and concluded he could not kill Carrie. Packing up some clothes, he and Carrie drove to Los Angeles. Spurlin sold his car, using the money for tickets under an assumed name to Hawaii, where they stayed two days and then returned. Spurlin wrote his employer that the bodies of his wife and son were in the family home, where they were found by police on November 5, 1982. Spurlin voluntarily returned to San Diego, confessed to the crimes and related all the details to the jury.

## II

The court instructed the jury on the elements of first-degree and second-degree murder as to both killings and on voluntary manslaughter as to Peggy's killing only. The court told the jury the manslaughter instruction did not apply to Scott's killing. The court and counsel debated at length whether the voluntary manslaughter instruction should include Scott's killing. The court concluded as a matter of law the provocation to trigger the heat of passion to reduce homicide to manslaughter must emanate from a source other than an innocent victim. As Scott slept throughout the evening, the court reasoned he could not have provoked Spurlin to a heat of passion and refused the instruction.

## III

Manslaughter is the unlawful killing of a human being without malice aforethought. Penal Code §192. Voluntary manslaughter is killing as a result of "a sudden quarrel or heat of passion" sufficient to displace the element of malice. The shorthand reference to "a sudden quarrel or heat of passion" is provocation; it is the element of provocation that distinguishes voluntary manslaughter from other crimes. The amount of provocation necessary to reduce a charge from murder to voluntary manslaughter has always plagued jurists and legal commentators. Obviously, only slight provocation or passion which has had time to subside are insufficient to overcome legal malice. CALJIC No. 8.42 (1979 Revision). The fundamental inquiry is whether "the defendant's reason was, at the time of his act, ... disturbed or obscured by some passion ... to such an extent as would render ordinary men of average disposition liable to act rashly or without due deliberation and reflection, and from this passion rather than from judgment." *People v. Logan*, 175 Cal. 45, 49 (1917). Adequate provocation must be affirmatively demonstrated at trial.

At common law, the concept of adequate provocation was extremely limited. *People v. Valentine*, 28 Cal.2d 121 (1946) undertakes an historical survey of the development of the concept. The Crimes and Punishments Act of 1850, section 23, following common law principles, provided: "In cases of voluntary manslaughter there must be a serious and highly provoking injury inflicted upon the person killing, sufficient to excite an irresistible passion in a reasonable person, or an attempt by the person killed to commit a serious personal injury on the person killing." *Id.* at 138.

When Penal Code §192 was enacted by the California Legislature in 1872, no such express limitation was included in the definition of voluntary manslaughter. As *Valentine* points out, it is arguable the Legislature intended the common-law limitations to apply as the Code Commissioners' notes to section 192 state: "No words of reproach, however grievous, are sufficient provocation to reduce the offense of an intentional homicide from murder to manslaughter." *Valentine*, 28 Cal.2d at 138.

As a result, two lines of case authority developed. Commencing with *People v. Turley*, 50 Cal. 469, 471 (1875), several cases adhered strictly to the "serious and highly provoking injury" principle of common law. These courts reasoned: "Such provision was probably omitted from the code upon the ground that it was entirely unnecessary and surplusage, being simply a reiteration of a principle of law settled and established by all text-writers on the subject." *People v. Bruggy*, 93 Cal. 476, 481 (1892).

Another line of cases following *People v. Hurtado*, 63 Cal. 288, 292 (1883) held a killing to be manslaughter when committed under the influence of passion caused by *any* insult or provocation sufficient to excite an irresistible passion in a reasonable person. Thus, adequate provocation was an issue to be determined by the jury based on the facts and circumstances of the particular situation. *Valentine*, 28 Cal.2d at 139. These cases required no specific type of provocation and verbal provocation was held to be sufficient. *See People v. Berry*, 18 Cal.3d 509, 515 (1976). Adequate provocation did not necessarily mean rage or anger, but included "any violent, intense, high-wrought or enthusiastic emotion." *People v. Borchers*, 50 Cal.2d 321, 329 (1958). From this latter line of cases, there developed in California a judicially recognized crime of "nonstatutory voluntary manslaughter." *See People v. Small*, 7 Cal.App.3d 347, 355 (1970). This crime differs from the statutory definition of voluntary manslaughter in that ... malice may be rebutted by a showing of diminished mental capacity instead of the provocative conduct of the victim. *See People v. Conley*, 64 Cal.2d 310, 324-26 (1966).

On appeal, Spurlin contends the trial court erred as a matter of law in refusing to give the manslaughter instruction with reference to the killing of his son, Scott. The question presented, therefore, is whether Spurlin's crime fits into either of these judicially developed definitions of manslaughter.

## IV

At trial, the trial judge instructed the jury concerning manslaughter with regard to the facts surrounding Peggy's death. The trial court refused to give the manslaughter instruction with regard to Scott's death, however, because Spurlin's sleeping son was not the source of "adequate provocation" under §192. The court summarized its review of the applicable law as follows: "If the mental state is produced by some other source, the offense is second-degree murder, as it was at common law." Spurlin argues the trial court erred in refusing to give the manslaughter instruction; there is no requirement the victim be the source of the provocation for manslaughter to apply.

It is true §192 does not expressly state voluntary manslaughter only applies to situations involving adequate provocation *by the victim.* Counsel have cited us to no California cases dealing directly with the question of whether the provocation necessary to reduce the charge from murder to manslaughter must be caused by the victim. *People v. Saterfield*, 65 Cal.2d 752, 759-60 (1967), limited manslaughter instructions to the death of a wife killed by her husband who claimed provocation and denied the instruction as to a daughter whom the husband killed while she telephoned police. No defense was offered by the defendant on the guilt phase and there was nothing in the People's case to permit any inference of manslaughter on any theory as to the daughter's death.

However, statutory voluntary manslaughter derives from common law principles, see *People v. Graham*, 71 Cal.2d 303, 315 (1969), and several courts in other jurisdictions, interpreting common law principles, have held the deceased must be the source of the defendant's rage or passion. *See State v. Fowler*, 268 N.W.2d 220, 224 (Iowa 1978); *Tripp v. State*, 36 Md.App. 459 (1977); *State v. Russo*, 24 Del. 538 (1910); *State v. Yanz*, 74 Conn. 177 (1901); *Shufflin v. People*, 62 N.Y. 229 (1875). In each of these cases, defendants' murder convictions were upheld against their contentions they were entitled to manslaughter instructions as to their "non-provoking" victims. As a result, legal commentators have summarized common law principles regarding "adequate provocation" as follows: "the provocation must have been given by the person who was killed, except in those cases in which the wrong person was killed by accident or mistake, or deceased was present aiding and abetting the person causing the provocation." 40 *C.J.S., Homicide* §53, at 917.

In this case, the trial court correctly gave the manslaughter instruction as to Peggy's death. Her fury at Spurlin's disclosure of earlier call-girl activities can be said to have ignited his long-smoldering resentment of her sexual conduct bringing about an intense, high-wrought reaction leading to her death. However, Scott's killing lacks both elements necessary to warrant a manslaughter instruction based on provocation and heat of passion. Spurlin confessed to the police and testified before the jury that Scott's life was taken, not as a result of rage or passion or anger aroused by Scott but as part of a plan to eliminate the Spurlin family. Under common-law principles, Scott's death was not the consequence of adequate provocation or heat of passion directed at him.

### V

Spurlin's arguments are best directed not at the statutory definition of voluntary manslaughter, but rather to the judicially created category of manslaughter based on diminished capacity. Restated, Spurlin's contention is: if sufficient evidence of provocation and heat of passion required the manslaughter instruction to be given as to Peggy, then Spurlin continued to be under the whip of that provocation and subject to the demon of that unhinged mind when he killed Scott; the passion aroused by Peggy's provocative attitude carried over to Scott's killing and negated the malice necessary to prove the offense of murder.

A persuasive argument can be made the defense of diminished capacity should be enlarged to contemplate the extreme emotional disturbance resultant from a heat of passion provoked by one other than the victim as negating malice in murder and reducing the offense to manslaughter. The definition of manslaughter has not been limited by California courts to the specific non-malicious acts spelled out in §192. A finding of provocation sufficient to reduce murder to manslaughter is not the sole means by which malice can be negated and voluntary manslaughter established. As discussed above, under California law, a person who intentionally kills may be incapable of harboring malice aforethought because of a mental disease, defect or incapacitation. *People v. Conley*, 64 Cal.2d at 310, 318 (1966). "Mental incapacitation" has been liberally construed to include such things as "voluntary intoxication," *People v. Mosher*, 1 Cal.3d 379, 391 (1969), an honest but unreasonable belief the defendant is in imminent peril of loss of life or serious injury, *People v. Flannel*, 25 Cal.3d 668 (1979), and "high-wrought and enthusiastic emotion." *People v. Borchers*, 50 Cal.2d 321, 329 (1958). Logically, we see no reason why Spurlin's emotional state could not be used to negate malice in the killing of both Peggy *and Scott.*[4]

---

[4] Model Penal Code §210.3(1) (1980) states:

> Criminal homicide constitutes manslaughter when: ... (b) a homicide which would otherwise be murder is committed under the influence of extreme mental or emotional disturbance for which there is reasonable

However, in 1981, the California Legislature enacted Penal Code §28(b), which states: "As a matter of public policy there shall be no defense of diminished capacity, diminished responsibility, or irresistible impulse in a criminal action or juvenile adjudication proceeding." In June 1982, the electorate of the state adopted Proposition 8, which also purports to abolish the defense of diminished capacity in cases such as this one. Penal Code §25(a), added as a result of the ballot initiative, provides: "The defense of diminished capacity is hereby abolished. In a criminal action, as well as any juvenile court proceeding, evidence concerning an accused person's intoxication, trauma, mental illness, disease, or defect shall not be admissible to show or negate capacity to form the particular purpose, intent, motive, malice aforethought, knowledge, or other mental state required for the commission of the crime charged."

The express purpose of both statutes is to abolish the diminished capacity defense and eliminate the judicially created concept of nonstatutory voluntary manslaughter. There are differences on the interaction between §§25(a) and 28(b). One view states the statutes cover the same subject and the later enactment therefore supersedes the 1981 statute; another approach deems the statutes "complementary" and recommends that both be given effect. 1 Witkin, California Criminal Procedure §23J, at 49 (1983 Supp.). From either viewpoint, the mandate is clear—diminished capacity has been abolished as a defense to murder. *See People v. Jackson*, 152 Cal.App. 3d 961, 968 (1984).

We are therefore barred from further consideration of Spurlin's argument on appeal that he was entitled to a voluntary manslaughter instruction under the diminished capacity theory. The diminished capacity concept is no longer available to "negate" malice aforethought and, thus, reduce murder to manslaughter.

---

> explanation or excuse. The reasonableness of such explanation or excuse shall be determined from the viewpoint of a person in the actor's situation under the circumstances as he believes them to be.

The Model Penal Code [MPC] therefore rejects the legislative simplicity of §192(1) and adopts an expanded concept of diminished capacity to reduce murder to manslaughter. The elements of provocation and heat of passion are included within this broadened concept. *The MPC does not require the provocation arousing the heat of passion to emanate from the victim.* (Comments to §210.3, at 61). [Italics mine.] It is enough if the killing occurs while the defendant's capacity to form an intent to murder is diminished by an extreme mental or emotional *disturbance* deemed to have a reasonable explanation or excuse from the defendant's standpoint.

## VI

There are two answers to Spurlin's innovative argument that the heat of passion engendered by Peggy's provocation carried over to negate malice aforethought in Scott's murder.

First, we find no evidence in the record of mental defect or disease. Provocation and heat of passion are not synonymous with diminished capacity. *People v. Berry, supra*, 18 Cal.3d at 517; *People v. Conley, supra*, 64 Cal.2d at 318. Second, diminished capacity is no longer available to reduce murder to manslaughter. Penal Code §§25 and 28.

## VII

Spurlin contends his second-degree murder conviction for Peggy's death is tainted by the court's refusal to instruct the jury on manslaughter as to Scott's death. The contention is not supported by argument or by reference to the record. We do not consider it further.

Finally, Spurlin argues the evidence is insufficient to establish the elements of first-degree murder in Scott's death. The jury verdict must be upheld if supported by substantial evidence, which must be viewed in the light most favorable to the People. *People v. Johnson*, 26 Cal.3d 557, 575-79 (1980).

Substantial evidence supports the conviction. Spurlin planned Scott's murder. He decided to kill the entire family. Following Peggy's death, he went to the garage to replace the broken hammer. He selected a ball-peen hammer. He re-entered the house and returned upstairs. He stood over Scott, deliberating for a few moments. He struck a strong blow with the hammer, killing his son. He turned away to enter Carrie's bedroom. He thought upon it. He decided he could not kill her. He packed some clothes and fled, selling the car, and using an assumed name. Substantial evidence thus supports Spurlin's planning for Scott's death, his motive in killing the boy and the premeditated use of the hammer as the death weapon. *People v. Anderson*, 70 Cal.2d 15, 27 (1968).

## Disposition

Judgment affirmed.

# QUESTIONS ON *SPURLIN*

**1. To whom does the partial defense apply?**

    **a.** On the one hand, the pertinent jury instruction states that "defendant is not permitted to set up his or her own standard of conduct...." CALJIC No. 8.42 (2014). On the other hand, the same instruction states that the partial defense recognizes only "such a passion as naturally would be aroused in the mind of an ordinarily reasonable person *in the same circumstances.*" *Id.* [Italics mine.] Is it ever reasonable to kill someone who is not making an immediate deadly or near deadly threat? If not, then to whom would the partial defense of provocation apply?

    **b.** If reference to "the same circumstances" contemplates a standard that is more personal, what would someone with the exact same physical, emotional, moral, religious, ethnic, experiential, and psychological makeup as the defendant do? Under such a view, to whom would the partial defense of provocation apply?

**2. "Compromise" verdict.** In 1600's England, the law of provocation reflected the touchy, quixotic concern for "honour" that was then prevalent. Disdainful or contemptuous conduct was considered an affront to a man's reputation. To protect his honor, a man had to retaliate with a passionate and physical response that would demonstrate his Aristotelian virtues of courage and "spirit." Provided, that is, the retaliation was at least *somewhat* proportionate to the affront. Now that honor has diminished as a social good, we see "the offense of voluntary manslaughter [a]s a legal compromise." *People v. Johnson*, 280 N.E.2d 764, 766 (Ill. App. Ct. 1972). A compromise between what and what?

**3. Extreme emotional disturbance**. In footnote 4, the *Spurlin* court recites the Model Penal Code approach to manslaughter. After revisiting that footnote, take a position on whether it is correct to say that Spurlin would be acquitted of the murder of son Scott in a state that follows the Model Penal Code. Please recall that Kentucky follows the Model Penal Code. *See Greene v. Commonwealth* and *Griggs v. Meko, supra* Chapter 3.A.

**4. Domino effect.** "Spurlin contends his second-degree murder conviction for Peggy's death is tainted by the court's refusal to instruct the jury on manslaughter as to Scott's death." The Court of Appeal did not elaborate. Tainted how, exactly?

**5. Was it intentional?** The term "intentional" often appears in judicial opinions on point, see *People v. Rios*, 97 Cal.Rptr.2d 512 (Cal. 2000), and jury instructions, see CALJIC No. 8.40 (2004 Revision), to explain that provoked killings are intentional but not malicious. Is that a grammatical use of the term "intentional?" Does someone who is that out of sorts really *intend* to kill? Or do terms like "intentional" have no specific application to provoked killings, which are neither intentional nor unintentional (or, for that matter, not intentional), but rather, done "in a rage"? *See supra* Chapter 1.A, Introduction.

**6. Provocation and intoxication.** Voluntary manslaughter is a general-intent crime, which means that voluntary intoxication is no excuse. *See People v. Lee*, 20 Cal.4th 47, 60 (1999) ["The provocation must be such that an average, sober person would be so inflamed that he or she would lose reason and judgment."]; *People v. Whitfield, supra* Chapter 2.B. Legal rules aside, as a matter of logic, if defendant claims to have killed in a heat of passion, is it really irrelevant whether the passion was fueled by intoxicants? *See, e.g., Davidson v. United States*, 137 A.3d 973, 974-75 (D.C. Ct. App. 2016) [noting a century of authority declaring intoxication irrelevant to heat of passion].

**7. Misdirected heat of passion.**

   **a. Mistaking non-provokers for provokers.** Assume the following facts, based on a real event in which an urban young man was killed by a group of suburban young men who beat him with baseball bats. The attack was in retaliation for an alleged rape committed by the dead young man and a group of his friends. The putative victim was a suburban teenaged girl with whom the bat-wielding attackers were friends. The girl had falsely reported the rape after the urban youths had spit at, cursed, and threatened her, but had committed no rape, attempted rape, or any other form of sexual assault. The prosecutor has charged the bat-wielding suburban youths with second-degree murder. Defense counsel asks the court to instruct the jury on voluntary manslaughter. If the defendants get the instruction, should the jury convened in California find in their favor?

   Compare a similar case from Meath, Ireland involving the fatal shooting of a young Nigerian man whose killer shot through the peephole of the victim's flat after the killer's former girlfriend had misled the killer to think the victim had recently raped her. http://www.herald.ie/news/courts/innocent-schoolboy-was-shot-dead-after-girl-15-made-a-false-rape-claim-27900793.html.

**b. Provocation-based accidents.** Suppose that, in the heat of passion, a California resident kills his provoker. The bullet travels through the victim-provoker and also kills the victim-provoker's friend, who is standing in another room 20 feet behind the victim. What, under *Spurlin*, is the proper charge for bringing about the deaths of both the provoker and the friend?

**c. Provocation from non-specific sources.** Colin Ferguson was accused of killing 6 and wounding 19 on a Long Island Railroad commuter train in a 1994 incident. Rather than plead insanity, he argued that his acts were prompted by a condition known as "Black Rage"—a violent reaction provoked by racism. *See generally* Judd F. Sneirson, *Black Rage and the Criminal Law: A Principled Approach to a Polarized Debate*, 143 University of Pennsylvania Law Review 2251 (1995). First, how could Ferguson, if at all, have fit his case into California's heat-of-passion defense? And second, would Model Penal Code §210.3(1)(b)—followed in *Greene* and in *Griggs*—be a better fit as a way of reducing Ferguson's six murders to manslaughters?

**8. More on Double Jeopardy.** During the end of the Cowboy Era (1866-86), Robert McFarlane was an outlaw of the Merced, California river district. In 1884, he killed a man (arguably) in self-defense, then another in 1892 for which, rather than hang, he finagled a life sentence in a New Mexico prison, from which he was released due to poor health and the long reach of a sympathetic Mariposa County Sheriff. In 1901, McFarlane killed James Tucker in an argument over Tucker's ex-wife, with whom McFarlane had taken up.

For that, McFarlane was acquitted of murder, but convicted of manslaughter, eventually obtaining reversal of his conviction on an evidentiary ruling based on the trial judge's erroneous belief that a witness was the defendant's, not the prosecution's. *People v. McFarlane*, 134 Cal. 618, 619-20 (1901). By appealing, McFarlane in effect *sought* a retrial for manslaughter. Due to Double Jeopardy, McFarlane could not be convicted of murder after a prior acquittal on the same charge. Because his retrial was on an un-amended indictment for murder, jurors were instructed to return a verdict of voluntary manslaughter if they believed that McFarlane had committed murder. Finding that Double Jeopardy was *not* implicated by such an instruction, the California Supreme Court upheld the manslaughter conviction that followed. *People v. McFarlane*, 138 Cal. 481, 484-87 (1903). The ruling slowly eroded, however. *See Gomez v. Superior Court (Mendocino County)*, 328 P.2d 976, 979 (Cal. 1958) (citing *Green v. United States*, 78 S.Ct. 221 (1957) [reversal on defendant's appeal from conviction on lesser charge does *not* re-open on retrial a re-do on implied acquittal on greater charge]).

After serving six years in San Quentin for the Tucker slaying, McFarlane was killed on November 7, 1915 outside a Merced Falls saloon by shotgun blasts from his cousin, Frank Dickinson. http://www.cageweb.com/merced/bios/Merced-JRG.html. Claiming that McFarlane had shot at him first with a .22 rifle but missed, Dickinson got his charges dismissed after his preliminary hearing. Mariposa Gazette, No. 24, Nov. 13, 1915. When the justice of the peace announced his ruling not to bind the case over for trial, the Hornitos courtroom erupted with applause, the feeling being that McFarlane really had it coming. Mariposa Gazette, No. 25, Nov. 20, 1915.

*McFarlane* thus ruled that anyone who commits murder at once also commits the "lesser" offense of voluntary manslaughter, though the voluntary manslaughter is typically ignored because conviction of the greater charge—murder—is what prosecutors pursue. So does the California Supreme Court have it right—that murder *includes* voluntary manslaughter? *See Darks v. Mullin*, 327 F.3d 1001, 1008 (10th Cir. 2003) ["Oklahoma consistently has treated first degree [heat of passion] manslaughter as a lesser included offense of first degree murder"]; *People v. Rios*, 97 Cal.Rptr.2d 512, 519-20 (Cal. 2000) [Voluntary manslaughter is a lesser-included offense of murder]; *Watts v. State*, 885 N.E.2d 1228, 1232 (Ind. 2008) ["[E]ven though ... voluntary manslaughter is a lesser-included offense of murder, a conviction for murder does not mean that a defendant could also have been convicted of voluntary manslaughter. Sudden heat must be separately proved"].

**9. Standard of review.** Section VII of the court's opinion states that "Spurlin argues the evidence is insufficient to establish the elements of first-degree murder in Scott's death." His conviction was affirmed, however. Two questions here. First, when an appellate court affirms a conviction over a defendant's claim of factual insufficiency of the evidence to support the verdict, does that mean the appellate court agrees with the jury? Second, what case did the Court of Appeal cite as a California version of *Jackson v. Virginia*?

## NOTES ON *SPURLIN*

***1. Insanity compared.*** Though at the time of the killing the provoked killer is, as *Spurlin* put it, "unhinged," the defense should not be confused with a claim of insanity. Unlike a defendant who pleads insanity, a provoked killer's claim is *not* one of mental disease or defect. In addition, while insanity is a complete excuse, provocation is only a partial defense that mitigates the seriousness of the offense from one form of homicide (murder) to another (voluntary manslaughter).

Though by 1581 the insanity defense was well established within English law, the canonical event is *M'Naghten's Case*, 8 Eng. Rep. 718 (1843), involving a delusional defendant who tried to assassinate Prime Minister Robert Peel, but killed Peel's secretary by mistake. At M'Naghten's trial, the defense recited from Isaac Ray, whose theories persuaded the court that a mental illness affecting one aspect of a defendant's personality could overwhelm other healthy aspects and lead him to crime, even though he was otherwise able to distinguish between right and wrong. When the jury rendered M'Naghten not guilty, Queen Victoria summoned all 15 common-law judges to justify the ruling, 14 of whom (including Lord Chief Justice Tindall, who'd presided over the trial) recanted and re-affirmed a test that, after a long and winding road, is still good law today. *E.g.,* 18 U.S.C. §17 (1984) ["It is an affirmative defense to a prosecution under any Federal statute that, at the time of the commission of the acts constituting the offense, the defendant, as a result of a severe mental disease or defect, was unable to appreciate the nature and quality or the wrongfulness of his acts."].

The most conspicuous defendant since to have been found not guilty by reason of insanity is John Hinckley, Jr., who was tried for the March 30, 1981 attempted assassination of President Ronald Reagan. Since Hinckley's June 21, 1982 acquittal, four states have eliminated the insanity defense, while 12 others have enacted statutes permitting a verdict of "guilty but insane." The "guilty but insane" verdict lets a jury find a defendant guilty (keeping defendant in the punitive criminal-justice loop) while paradoxically acknowledging his or her need for treatment (not punishment). 1 Wharton's Criminal Evidence 2:13 (West 15th ed. 2014).

After 34 years at St. Elizabeths Hospital, a public psychiatric facility in D.C., the 61-year-old Hinckley is back home as of September

2016, to be looked after by his 91-year-old mother Jo Ann, with whom he lives in a gated community in Williamsburg. For at least a year, Hinckley is subject to various restrictions, some understandable (stay away from current or former Presidents), some peculiar (he may play guitar privately, but to contain his narcissism, may not play gigs). http://nymag.com/daily/intelligencer/2017/03/john-hinckley-is-out-of-the-mental-hospital.html.

**2. Defining "motive."** The *Spurlin* Court concludes: "Substantial evidence thus supports Spurlin's planning for Scott's death, his motive in killing the boy and the premeditated use of the hammer as the death weapon." The court's prior reference to "eliminating the family" (as in killing them) could *not*, however, be a *motive* for killing them, though eliminating them to begin an unencumbered life could be a motive. Likewise, if eliminating the family meant covering up Peggy's killing by preventing the kids from testifying, then that could count as a motive. While not all killings have motives, revenge is an apt motive for killing Peggy. Anger, however, cannot be a motive, since it has no directedness. Another way of saying this is we do things *out of* or *in* anger, but not *with the motive of* anger.

This is not our first encounter with the term "motive." Justice Richardson's opinion for the *Watson* majority observed: "malice may be implied when defendant does an act with a high probability that it will result in death and does it with *a base antisocial motive* and a wanton disregard for human life." (Emphasis mine). Chief Justice Bird's *Watson* dissent, speaking of an eyewitness to the fatal crash, found "[t]here was no evidence ... of a motive for Henke to fabricate."

What *is* a motive? And how does it relate to an intention? While motives or reasons for human action typically are mysterious, intentions are not—they are wrapped up in the actions themselves. Daniel Yeager, Review Essay, "Searches, Seizures, Confessions, and Some Thoughts on *Criminal Procedure: Regulation of Police Investigation*," 23 Florida State University Law Review 1042, 1048 (1996). A motive is a concealed purpose for an action, something in the world to be achieved or set up by the action that normally would not strike us as the upshot of the action. The normal, conventional reasons for an action are not motives.

Among those unconventional bases or reasons for actions that are purposes, a benevolent purpose in acting cannot be a motive. We say, for example, "to good purposes" or "for good purposes" (just as we say "his intentions were good" or "he did it with the best of intentions"). But we do not say "his motives were good" or "he did it with the best of motives" (except as a way of asserting that *he had no motive whatsoever*). As purposes go, motives are not just unexpected or unconventional bases or payoffs for actions, but underhanded, sinister, or deceptive ones at that. Indeed, no one would say that Robin Hood's motive was "to give to the poor." Charity was his purpose in stealing, severed from the action sure enough, but it would be eccentric to view charity as a *motive* for action.

Motives are outside the action: the motive for the generous action toward the fragile relative is to inherit under the will. The motive could be greed because greed is directed at something—here, the money that the will would make available. If the generous action is just plain generous without such directedness, then it is misleading to speak of motive, though there may be reasons for the generosity (for example, feeling good about oneself). But such reasons are not motives if they are psychological or inner, even though we tend to think of motives as inner states rather than as explanations of something to be attained in the world by a course of action. While it is common among psychologists to suggest that all actions have motives (or are motivated), in fact we use the word "motive" only infrequently in ordinary speech. We use the word only in reference to untoward actions we feel the need to assess, to make sense of.

Among those actions that do have reasons, not all reasons are necessarily directed. Considerateness or punctuality, for example, are reasons for actions, yet they are not motives; they have no aim, no directedness; they are not setting anything up.

If we say, "what was his motive?" it looks as though the action was directed at something untoward, but we are unsure what it was. When we say that Macbeth's motive in killing Duncan was ambition, we are not referring to a feeling or some internal perturbation of Macbeth; instead, the motive of ambition refers to some other actions, some other ends to be attained by the killing, whether or not the actions are known to him. Paul J. Gudel, *Beyond Causation: The Interpretation of Action and the Mixed Motives Problem in Employment Discrimination Law*, 70 Texas Law Review 17, 73 (1991). Likewise, "if a man looks pleased when praised for something trivial, or upset when mildly criticized, we can say he is vain, but we cannot say vanity is his motive for being pleased when praised." *Id.* Vanity may *explain* certain actions, but it cannot be considered a motive for them. *Id.*

Putting others on the spot by questioning their motives demands that they go on record and offer a reason for the action or deny having any reason at all. It may well be that the action had no motive, or perhaps had no reason whatsoever (as in "I just did it" or "I just felt like doing it"). We may say: "Your motive in marrying her was greed; you married her for her money." If the accused in such a pinch were to respond: "No, I married for love," that may be true, but could not be a motive since love is the conventional, ordinary reason for marriage. For this same reason, "to get property" could never be Robin Hood's (or anyone else's) motive for robbery, since that is *by definition* part of any robbery. Thus the hilarity of the non-response—"to get to the other side"—to "why did the chicken cross the road?" See Daniel Yeager, J.L. Austin and the Law: Exculpation and the Explication of Responsibility 42-50 (Bucknell 2006).

***3. A partial defense that is part justification, part excuse.*** The idea of voluntary manslaughter based on provocation or heat of passion is that someone who is provoked into killing someone who is not trying to kill anyone is operating on a different moral plane than are unprovoked intentional or extremely reckless killers. That moral plane is weakly akin to that of the self-defender, who is justified in using deadly force to defend against immediate threats of deadly or near-deadly force. Like the self-defender, the provoked killer has been wronged. If not for the unjustified deadly or near-deadly aggression by the victim, the self-defender would have no need to kill the victim. Likewise, if not for the provoker getting the killer all riled up and out of gear, the killer would not have killed. In a way, therefore, cases of self-defense and cases of provocation or heat of passion both involve victims who brought their own deaths on themselves.

But that is where the similarity ends. A self-defender is fully justified in killing. *See infra*, Chapter 3.B, Introduction ["justification" defined]. When your back is against the wall and it is kill or be killed, it is no crime to do what is necessary to defend yourself (or others). A provoked killer, however, is only partially justified in killing. Some of the killing is blamed on the victim for provoking the killer, but the rest of the blame remains with the killer for over-reacting to the provocative actions of the victim. There is nothing reasonable about losing your temper and trying to kill someone who is neither trying to kill anyone nor even appears to be trying to kill anyone. Indeed, the partial defense of provocation or heat of passion is best described as part justification (the provoker got the defendant to act rashly), part excuse (the defendant is too touchy and, as such, over-reacted to the affront), so as to split the blame for the outcome between victim and defendant. *See supra* Chapter 2.A, Introduction ["excuse" defined].

Unless defendants trace their killings to their victims' provocative acts (justification) *and* their own excessive touchiness/psychological frailty (excuse), the partial defense has little prospect of success. Another way of stating this is that the successful plea of provocation simultaneously blames both the victim (justification) and oneself (excuse) for the killing.

An example of a defendant who pleaded only the justificatory side of the partial defense is La Jolla socialite Betty Broderick, who, in 1989, killed her ex-husband and his wife in their marital bed. Betty's first jury hung 10 (murder) – 2 (manslaughter), but was unanimous at the retrial on two counts of second-degree murder, for which she is serving a 32-years-to-life sentence at California Institution for Women (Chino). Details of her plight are all over the internet. *E.g.*, http://articles.latimes.com/1991-11-15/news/mn-1451_1_firing-gun; http://www.latimes.com/la-me-broderick3jun0390-story.html; https://www.youtube.com/watch?v=g4aGpmjkD5s.

An example of a defendant who unsuccessfully pleaded only the excusing side of the partial defense is *People v. Casassa*, 404 N.E.2d 1310 (N.Y. 1980), the story of an obsessive who killed a woman he hardly knew for rejecting him. *But cf. People v. Sepe*, 111 A.D.3d 75 (N.Y. App. Div. 2013) [emphasizing it's the disturbance not the killing that needs to be reasonable under MPC, appellate court reversed murder conviction for defendant with psychiatric affliction, though victim did absolutely nothing to bring her death on herself].

**4. Leave it to the jury.** One representative position, followed in Maryland, explicitly precludes provocation claims that are based on words alone. *See State v. Girouard*, 321 Md. 532 (1991).

A second representative position, followed in California, holds that "there is no specific type of provocation required ... and ... verbal provocation may be sufficient." *People v. Wickersham*, 32 Cal.3d 307, 326 (1982) (en banc). Courts taking this second position, rather than police what sorts of provocative acts justify a manslaughter instruction, turn the matter over to jurors to sort out sufficient from insufficient sources of provocation once a defendant has proffered slight evidence of its application.

Still, some obviously negative susceptibilities of provoked defendants draw no compassion in their favor from courts. For example, in states where words alone *can* count as sufficient provocation to merit an instruction, it is in theory open to a defendant to plead, say, homophobia, to explain why a victim's homosexual advance set the defendant off to kill the advancing victim. It is not unusual, however, for trial courts, undisturbed on appeal, to refuse to instruct jurors that same-sex advances can convert what looks like a murder into a manslaughter. Instead, deadly reactions to same-sex advances are perceived by courts not as the rash actions of ordinarily reasonable persons, but as the spiteful tantrums of malicious killers who indulge their irrational urges. *E.g., Commonwealth v. Carr*, 580 A.2d 1362, 1364 (Penn. Super. Ct. 1990) [collecting cases].

In California, verbal provocations that support voluntary manslaughter instructions and convictions are narrowly construed, generally confined to repeated sexual taunts or admissions of infidelity by an unfaithful spouse. *People v. Berry*, 18 Cal.3d 509, 514-16 (1976); *People v. Borchers*, 50 Cal.2d 321, 328-29 (1958); *People v. Le*, 158 Cal.App.4th 516, 528-29 (2007). Provocation for voluntary manslaughter is *inadequate* where the act that provoked the killing was no more than insults, a technical battery, or slight touching. *People v. Gutierrez*, 45 Cal.4th 789, 826 (2009). For instance, in *People v. Manriquez*, 37 Cal.4th 547 (2005), the victim called defendant a "mother fucker" and egged him on by repeatedly asserting that if defendant had a weapon, he "should take it out and use it." *Id.* at 586. The California Supreme Court concluded that because such declarations "plainly were insufficient to cause an average person to become so inflamed as to lose reason and judgment, ... [t]he trial court properly denied defendant's request for an instruction on voluntary manslaughter." *Ibid; see also People v. Najera*, 138 Cal.App.4th 212, 225-26 (2006) [victim calling defendant "faggot" unworthy of heat-of-passion instruction].

The Model Penal Code approach to EED is self-consciously flexible. The Drafters explain:

> The critical element in the Model Penal Code formulation is the clause requiring that reasonableness be assessed "from the viewpoint of a person in the actor's situation." The word "situation" is designedly ambiguous. On the one hand, personal handicaps and some external circumstances must be taken into account. Thus, blindness, shock from traumatic injury, and extreme grief are all easily read into the term "situation...." On the other hand, idiosyncratic moral values are not part of the actor's situation. An assassin who kills a political leader because he believes it is right to do so cannot

ask that he be judged by the standard of a reasonable extremist. In between these two extremes, however, there are matters neither as clearly distinct from individual blameworthiness as blindness or handicap nor as integral a part of moral depravity as a belief in the rightness of killing. The classic illustration is the unusual sensitivity to the epithet "bastard" of a person born illegitimate. An exceptionally punctilious sense of personal honor or an abnormally fearful temperament may also serve to differentiate an individual actor from the hypothetical reasonable man, yet none of these factors is wholly irrelevant to the ultimate issue of culpability. The proper role of such factors cannot be resolved satisfactorily by abstract definition of what may constitute adequate provocation. The MPC endorses a formulation that affords sufficient flexibility to differentiate in particular cases between those special aspects of the actor's situation that should be deemed material for purpose of grading and those that should be ignored. There thus will be room for interpretation of the word "situation," and that is precisely the flexibility desired. There will be opportunity for argument about the reasonableness of explanation or excuse, and that too is a ground on which argument is required. In the end, the question is whether the actor's loss of self-control can be understood in terms that arouse sympathy in the ordinary citizen. Section 210.3 faces this issue squarely and leaves the ultimate judgment to the ordinary citizen in the function of juror assigned to resolve the specific case.

Model Penal Code & Commentaries §210.3, at 62-63 (1980).

*5. Victim at fault.* It is crucial to recognize the difference in *Spurlin* between the killing of Peggy and the killing of Scott. Because the law holds that the provoker has in a sense cheapened his own life through his own provocative acts directed at defendant, some jurisdictions insist that the provoked party see to it that the provoker and not some innocent party is the one who gets killed. However, according to *Spurlin*'s dictum (read, fluff—language non-essential to a court ruling), a defendant who kills someone other than the provoker still may assert the partial defense if that killing can be described as 1) accidental, 2) the product of a mistake, or 3) a reaction to a victim who is present and egging on the provoker.

The California Supreme Court has since rejected *Spurlin*'s dictum that a voluntary manslaughter instruction is appropriate when "deceased was present aiding and abetting the person causing the provocation." Now, "[t]he provocation which incites the defendant to homicidal conduct in the heat of passion must be caused by the victim, or be conduct reasonably believed by the defendant to have been engaged in by the victim." *People v. Verdugo*, 50 Cal.4th 263, 294 (2010); *see supra* Chapter 3.A, question 7 on *Spurlin*.

**6. Criminal procedure: burdens of proof.** It would be misleading to say either that provocation/heat of passion is or isn't an affirmative defense to murder. Whether the State must prove absence of passion/EED or defendant must prove its presence depends on how the murder statute lines up with the Due Process command that the prosecution prove up its charges beyond a reasonable doubt. *In re Winship*, 397 U.S. 358, 364 (1970).

Consider, for example, Maine's murder statute, which punishes the unlawful killing of a human being with express or implied malice. 17 Maine Revised Statutes Annotated §2651 (1964). Under Maine's manslaughter statute, provocation/heat of passion defeats malice. *Id.* at §2551. Affirming Wilbur's murder conviction, the Maine Supreme Court held that murder and manslaughter were varying degrees of the crime of felonious homicide and that the presumption of malice arising from the unlawful killing was a mere policy presumption that gave defendant the burden of proving provocation to support a manslaughter rap rather than murder. *Mullaney v. Wilbur*, 95 S.Ct. 1881, 1887-88 (1975). This, the U.S. Supreme Court ruled, violated Due Process by presuming rather than requiring proof of malice, leaving it instead to defendant to *disprove* the basic ingredient of murder. Wilbur's conviction thus could not stand. *Id.* at 1892.

Now consider New York's murder statute, which punishes intentionally causing the death of another person, subject to the affirmative defense of EED. McKinney's Consolidated Penal Laws of New York §125.25 (1975). According to the U.S. Supreme Court, EED does not defeat the intentional killing required for murder. Instead, EED *confesses* to an intentional killing but seeks to mitigate responsibility for it by raising a matter external to the element of intent: defendant's internal turmoil. Thus, the Supreme Court went on, for New York to make EED an affirmative defense that defendant must prove by a preponderance of the evidence did *not* violate Due Process. Once the prosecutor proves an intentional killing, it is on defendant to come across with proof of EED, which, if accepted, is incompatible with murder. *Patterson v. New York*, 97 S.Ct. 2319, 2324-25 (1977).

Another way of saying this is that in Maine, defendants have the "burden of production" of slight evidence of provocation or heat of passion, which, once raised, is subject to the prosecution's "burden of persuasion" to disprove the defense beyond a reasonable doubt. *Cf.* section III of *Greene v. Commonwealth, supra; People v. Barton,* 12 Cal.4th 186, 199 (1995) ["[V]oluntary manslaughter *closely resembles* an affirmative defense (placing on the defendant the burden of producing evidence of facts which, if believed by the jury, will result in the defendant's acquittal of the crime charged)."]. Because provocation denies the elements of the murder, the argument runs, the prosecution has the burden of persuading the jury of its inapplicability.

Some defenses, however—self-defense, insanity, entrapment, duress—are at times cited as examples of affirmative defenses. Affirmative defenses do not deny an element of the prosecution's case. Instead, they "confess and avoid" by copping superficially to the accusation while raising some exculpatory matter external to the elements of the crime, thus depriving uncontested facts of their ordinary legal effect. *United States v. Mersky*, 361 U.S. 431, 457-58 (1960) (Stewart, J., dissenting). In New York, defendants have both the "burden of production" and "burden of persuasion" to prove the EED partial defense by a preponderance of the evidence. *See People v. Diaz*, 62 A.D.3d 157, 160-61 (N.Y. App. Div. 2009); *cf. People v. Kohl*, 527 N.E.2d 1882, 1190 n.2 (N.Y. 1988) (Hancock, J., dissenting) [explaining distinction between burdens of production and persuasion in New York in context of affirmative defense of insanity].

For a summary of the U.S. Supreme Court's precedents allocating burdens of proof of production and persuasion between prosecution and defense, see *Dixon v. United States*, 126 S.Ct. 2437, 2449-54 (2006) (Breyer, J., dissenting).

**7. *Cooling time.*** Jurors consider not only whether defendant was provoked, but also whether the killing occurred while he or she was under the spell or influence of that provocation. If the once-provoked defendant had cooled off by the time of the killing, then the partial defense is inapplicable. Most courts see whether defendant had in fact cooled off by then as a question for the jury. *E.g., State v. Estes*, 168 So.3d 847, 857 (La. Ct. App. 2015). But *cf. Ex Parte Fraley*, 109 P. 295, 296-97 (Okla. Crim. Ct. App. 1910) ["[W]hen an unreasonable period of time has elapsed between the provocation and the killing, then the court is authorized to say as a matter of law that the cooling time was sufficient."]. Where defendants "smolder" over a provocative event for hours, even days, most courts say that it is up to the jury, not the judge, to determine whether at the time of the killing the provocation or heat of passion had persisted or subsided. See CALJIC No. 8.42 (2014); *People v. Berry*, 18 Cal.3d 509 (1976) [two weeks of provocative conduct by victim justifies heat-of-passion instruction]. *But see Commonwealth v. Keohane*, 444 Mass. 563 (2005) ["smoldering" provocation is *not* heat of passion, which must come on suddenly, not gradually].

**8. Diminished actuality**, *revisited*. In his separate opinion in *People v. Whitfield*, *supra* Chapter 2.B, Justice Mosk acknowledges the legislative abrogation of diminished capacity, which in his words was replaced by a defense of "diminished actuality." The distinction may be a precious one (as in too fine), but officially at least, there is no diminished capacity (as where defendant claims that he *cannot* form a specific intention); instead, there is only diminished actuality (as where defendant *did not* form a specific intention).

As Justice Mosk points out, the California Legislature eliminated diminished capacity as a defense in 1982, thereby abolishing as well what *Spurlin* called "nonstatutory voluntary manslaughter." Spurlin's attorney conceded that if *statutory* voluntary manslaughter requires a victim-provoker, Scott could not by any stretch be described as having provoked his father into killing him. But *non*-statutory voluntary manslaughter, the argument went on, should be available to mitigate murder to manslaughter if Spurlin was provoked at the time of the killing, but not by victim-Scott.

*Spurlin* foreclosed on such a claim, citing California Penal Code §25(a), which abrogated the diminished-capacity defense. To the extent that the defense survives, it is codified in §22 (as amended in 1995, modifying *Whitfield*), which allows voluntary intoxication to nullify criminal responsibility for specific-intent crimes. This is what Justice Mosk calls the defense of "diminished actuality." Diminished actuality is codified in §28(a), where "mental illness, defect, or disorder" not amounting to insanity may be introduced as an excuse to specific-intent crimes. Anger, however, is not a recognized mental illness, defect, or disorder within the meaning of §28(a).

Insanity claims are recognized in §25(b), under which defendant, after being convicted at the guilt phase, must demonstrate that he couldn't appreciate the nature and quality of his act or tell right from wrong. If successful, the excused defendant gets therapeutic, not punitive measures. No such claim was entered by Spurlin, who was angry, not insane (a more lasting state).

**9. Angry, just not angry enough to kill.** Anger-based partial defenses, be they provocation/heat of passion or EED, are inapplicable outside the deadly force context. *See, e.g., State v. Walsh*, 119 P.3d 645, 651 (Idaho 2005) [provocation not a defense to battery]; Aya Gruber, *Victim Wrongs: The Case for a General Criminal Defense Based on Wrongful Victim Behavior in an Era of Victims' Rights*, 76 Temple Law Review 645, 674 (2003) ["[P]rovocation applies in every jurisdiction in some formulation to murder prosecutions. It does not, however, apply universally to assaultive conduct that falls short of killing."]. An explanation for precluding use of the provocation defense in cases of *non*-deadly force is that "murder was traditionally punished by death, and society felt that the death penalty was too severe for a person who killed upon provocation. Since there was no death penalty for offenses less than murder, there was no need for the rule of provocation." James J. Gobert, *Victim Precipitation*, 77 Columbia Law Review 511, 535 (1977).

## B. FEAR AS COMPLETE JUSTIFICATION: PERFECT SELF-DEFENSE

Clyde Richard Spurlin's claim that wife Peggy provoked him was weakly plausible, but unsuccessful. Indeed, the provocations most often seen as sufficient to unhinge ordinarily reasonable persons are those that trigger self-defensive gestures to protect defendants from physical attack by their eventual victims. *See, e.g., State v. Guebara*, 696 P.2d 381, 385-86 (Kan. 1985). Much more controversial is the use of deadly force to protect one's sensibilities from *insult*. As defensive gestures go, the use of deadly force goes too far in any case adjudicated as voluntary manslaughter. That is why provocation is a *partial* defense with justificatory and excusing aspects.

*Fully* justified acts cause harm that is necessary to avoid an even greater harm. When put to a choice of evils, choosing your own life over the life of someone who is trying to kill you (or someone else) is justified as a necessary act of survival. There is no good reason to sacrifice your own life to preserve the life of someone bent on killing you. Undoubtedly, killing someone else or otherwise participating in the suffering of another is regrettable. But what is most regrettable is being in the situation in the first place—a situation in which there is no easy way out.

Consider the situation Army helicopter pilot Hugh Thompson found himself in when he happened upon heavily armed Charlie Company's massacre of 500 unarmed citizens in the village of My Lai in South Vietnam on March 16, 1968. Thompson had a choice between threatening to kill American soldiers who did not relent in the slaughter or standing by and allowing the slaughter to continue. This left Thompson with no easy way out; *any* response he might have had to the imperiled women, children, and non-combat-aged men on whose behalf he intervened would be subject to criticism. Though Thompson was eventually treated as a hero, Congressman L. Mendel Rivers's House Armed Services Committee grilled him about his rescue of the Vietnamese whom Charlie Company were about to execute. In other words, Thompson's problem was *being* in a situation with no non-problematical course of action. The best one could do in such circumstances would be to commit a justified act.

As Justice Holmes famously quipped: "Detached reflection cannot be demanded in the presence of an uplifted knife." *Brown v. United States*, 256 U.S. 335, 342 (1921). Because they tend not to make it that far in litigation, easy or obvious cases of deadly force self-defense are hard to find in reported appellate opinions. But the case in which Holmes's quip appears is such a case.

> There had been trouble between Hermis and the defendant for a long time. There was evidence that Hermis had twice assaulted the defendant with a knife and had ... threat[ened] ... the defendant that the next time, one of them would go off in a black box. On the day in question, the defendant was superintending excavation work for a post office. In view of Hermis's threats, he had taken a pistol with him and had laid it in his coat upon a dump. Hermis was driven up by a witness, in a cart to be loaded, and the defendant said that certain earth was not to be removed, whereupon Hermis came toward him, the defendant says, with a knife. The defendant retreated some twenty or twenty-five feet to where his coat was and got his pistol. Hermis was striking at him and the defendant fired four shots and killed him.

*Id.* In such circumstances, where your back is against the wall, there is no time to deliberate alternatives, be they retreat, negotiation, or nondeadly force. When you are facing an immediate threat of death or comparable enough harm, the time to act is now. Killing anyone, even an enemy, is a terrible thing. But killing is non-criminal when, after the fact, having balanced the competing interests, we conclude that the victim gave you no choice, thus providing grounds for the withdrawal of our disapproval of the action, though this is not quite the same as actually approving of it. What you did was not so much a matter of choice as it was something foisted upon you; it is not, in the end, your fault, though it is your doing. Under such an account, you may kill your attacker because he made you do it. It makes good sense that back-to-the-wall cases of deadly force let the self-defending killer off scot-free for taking a life. Better to kill than be killed, though neither outcome is optimal.

That unremarkable conclusion comes nowhere near explaining the entirety of self-defense doctrine. Most litigated cases, and most that appear in appellate reporters, are not of the back-to-the-wall variety. Litigated cases of putatively justified killings are rarely purified cases of necessity, where the self-defender kills to avoid being killed or seriously injured by the initial aggressor.

In regulating *official* (as opposed to private) use of deadly force, the U.S. Supreme Court gives police leeway to decouple deadly force from actual or even perceived necessity. Until 1985, when the Court decided *Tennessee v. Garner*, 471 U.S. 1 (1985), only conscience-shocking uses of deadly force by police would be struck down. *See, e.g., Johnson v. Glick*, 481 F.2d 1028, 1029, 1033-34 (2d Cir. 1973). Since *Garner*, states may not authorize police to "seize an unarmed, nondangerous suspect by shooting him dead." *Garner*, 471 U.S. at 11. Instead, the suspect must be believed to be armed or to have committed a violent felony, of which burglary, which only rarely involves physical violence, is *not* an example. *Id.* at 21-22. *Garner* reasoned that difficulties in apprehending suspects do not justify killing them merely due to their status as felon, a term too broad to denote dangerousness. (Indeed, perjury is a felony, but hardly dangerous when compared with, say, rape or robbery.) Plus, the use of deadly force undesirably allows police to bypass a criminal-justice system that conditions punishment on arrest, charges, and conviction, whether by trial or plea. Finally, *Garner* concluded that deadly force fails to protect police or the public, decrease the rate of crime or escape attempts, or increase the rate of live-suspect arrests. *Id.* at 19.

While *Garner* narrows the conditions under which officers may use deadly force to prevent escape, the decision still allows shooting certain fleeing felons, even in the back. Since the optimal action would be to catch the fleeing felon, talk him into turning himself in, or use nondeadly force against him, police should try or at least consider those options before resorting to shooting the suspect. Daniel Yeager, *Does Privacy Really Have a Problem in the Law of Criminal Procedure?*, 49 Rutgers Law Review 1283, 1289 (1997). Yet nothing in *Garner* specifically requires as much: With "probable cause to believe that he has committed a crime involving the infliction of ... serious physical harm, deadly force may be used if necessary to prevent escape, and if, where feasible, some warning has been given." *Garner*, 471 U.S. at 11-12.

It is not necessary to kill a *fleeing* felon as opposed to a felon who is, or appears to be, attacking police to prevent capture. An escaped felon may pose some risk to the public, but the nature and likelihood of that risk is too sketchy to call killing him immediately—with no legal process whatsoever—necessary. Accordingly, the notion that police may sometimes lawfully kill someone who is running away is incompatible with a back-to-the-wall notion of necessity. Such killings are justified not because they are necessary, but instead because, right or wrong, the law declares that in a cost-benefit sense we are better off killing the suspected felon than risking his escape or his harming those in pursuit or in the vicinity. Whether *Garner* gives police undue license to deploy deadly force as a substitute for more time-consuming, less catastrophic investigative strategies is debatable. What is not debatable is that shooting a fleeing felon—even one suspected of violence—is unnecessary in most circumstances: it would be eccentric for an officer to say "I had to shoot or he might have gotten away."

Not only does the law authorize official use of deadly force outside of purified cases of necessity, but police (or private citizens for that matter) also may use deadly force when it is unnecessary but reasonably believed to be necessary. In other words, we may justifiably kill anyone whom we mistakenly take as a deadly threat, even if they turn out to be less than deadly or even harmless. In this class of justified killings by police, easy or obvious cases are abundant. For example, police frequently shoot individuals who are wielding convincing toy guns that police mistake for real. Only after the shooting do police realize that their victims did not pose the threat they were thought to have posed. These cases are easy or obvious because someone who *holds himself out* as armed and dangerous will be treated by police *as* armed and dangerous, especially when it would be too cumbersome for police to determine otherwise. Laws aggravating the sentence for robberies committed with a gun accordingly make no distinction between using a real or a toy gun to coerce victims into parting with their property.

Our principal case on the role of fear in homicide, *People v. Goetz*, 497 N.E.2d 41 (N.Y. 1986), is central to the self-defense canon as an example of the tension between objective reasonableness and subjectivity: the tension between the inner and outer worlds in the adjudication of fear-based killings.

## COURT OF APPEALS OF NEW YORK

*THE PEOPLE OF THE STATE OF NEW YORK, APPELLANT*

*V.*

*BERNHARD GOETZ, RESPONDENT*

JULY 8, 1986

WACHTLER, Chief Judge

A Grand Jury has indicted defendant on attempted murder, assault, and other charges for having shot and wounded four youths on a New York City subway train after one or two of the youths approached him and asked for $5. The lower courts, concluding that the prosecutor's charge to the Grand Jury on the defense of justification was erroneous, have dismissed the attempted murder, assault and weapons possession charges. We now reverse and reinstate all counts of the indictment.

### I

The precise circumstances of the incident giving rise to the charges against defendant are disputed, and ultimately it will be for a trial jury to determine what occurred. We feel it necessary, however, to provide some factual background to properly frame the legal issues before us. Accordingly, we have summarized the facts as they appear from the evidence before the Grand Jury. We stress, however, that we do not purport to reach any conclusions or holding as to exactly what transpired or whether defendant is blameworthy. The credibility of witnesses and the reasonableness of defendant's conduct are to be resolved by the trial jury.

On Saturday afternoon, December 22, 1984, Troy Canty, Darryl Cabey, James Ramseur, and Barry Allen boarded an IRT express subway train in The Bronx and headed south toward lower Manhattan. The four youths rode together in the rear portion of the seventh car of the train. Two of the four, Ramseur and Cabey, had screwdrivers inside their coats, which they said were to be used to break into the coin boxes of video machines.

Defendant Bernhard Goetz boarded this subway train at 14th Street in Manhattan and sat down on a bench near the rear section of the same car occupied by the four youths. Goetz was carrying an unlicensed .38 caliber pistol loaded with five rounds of ammunition in a waistband holster. The train left the 14th Street station and headed towards Chambers Street.

Canty approached Goetz, possibly with Allen beside him, and stated "give me five dollars." Neither Canty nor any of the other youths displayed a weapon. Goetz responded by standing up, pulling out his handgun and firing four shots in rapid succession. The first shot hit Canty in the chest; the second struck Allen in the back; the third went through Ramseur's arm and into his left side; the fourth was fired at Cabey, who apparently was then standing in the corner of the car, but missed, deflecting instead off of a wall of the conductor's cab. After Goetz surveyed the scene around him, he fired another shot at Cabey, who then was sitting on the end bench of the car. The bullet entered the rear of Cabey's side and severed his spinal cord.

All but two of the other passengers fled the car when the shots were fired. The conductor, who had been in the next car, heard the shots and instructed the motorman to radio for emergency assistance. The conductor then went into the car where the shooting occurred and saw Goetz sitting on a bench, the injured youths lying on the floor or slumped against a seat, and two women who had apparently taken cover, also lying on the floor. Goetz told the conductor that the youths had tried to rob him.

While the conductor was aiding the youths, Goetz headed towards the front of the car. The train had stopped just before the Chambers Street station and Goetz went between two of the cars, jumped onto the tracks, and fled. Police and ambulance crews arrived shortly thereafter. Ramseur and Canty, initially listed in critical condition, have fully recovered. Cabey remains paralyzed, and has suffered brain damage.

On December 31, 1984, Goetz surrendered to police in Concord, New Hampshire, identifying himself as the gunman being sought for the subway shootings in New York nine days earlier. Later that day, after receiving *Miranda* warnings, he made two lengthy statements, both of which were tape recorded with his permission. In the statements, which are substantially similar, Goetz admitted that he had been illegally carrying a handgun in New York for three years. He stated that he had first bought a gun in 1981 after he had been injured in a mugging. Goetz also revealed that twice between 1981 and 1984 he had successfully warded off assailants simply by displaying the pistol.

Goetz stated that the first contact he had with the four youths came when Canty, sitting or lying on the bench across from him, asked "how are you," to which he replied "fine." Canty, followed by one of the other youths, walked over to the defendant and stood to his left, while the other two youths remained to his right, in the corner of the subway car. Canty then said "give me five dollars." Goetz stated that he knew from the smile on Canty's face that they wanted to "play with me." Although he was certain that none of the youths had a gun, he had a fear, based on prior experiences, of being "maimed."

When Canty again requested money, Goetz stood up, drew his weapon, and began firing, aiming for the center of the body of each of the four. His stated intention was to "murder them, to hurt them, to make them suffer as much as possible." Goetz recalled that the first two he shot "tried to run through the crowd [but] they had nowhere to run." Goetz then turned to his right to "go after the other two." One of these two "tried to run through the wall of the train, but ... he had nowhere to go." The other youth (Cabey) "tried pretending that he wasn't with [the others]" by standing still, holding on to one of the subway hand straps, and not looking at Goetz. Goetz nonetheless fired his fourth shot at him. He then ran back to the first two youths to make sure they had been "taken care of." Seeing that they had both been shot, he spun back to check on the latter two. Goetz noticed that the youth who had been standing still was now sitting on a bench and seemed unhurt. As Goetz told the police, "I said you seem to be all right, here's another," and he then fired the shot which severed Cabey's spinal cord. Goetz added that "if I was a little more under self-control ... I would have put the barrel against his forehead and fired."

[margin note: Why didn't you do that this time?]

He also admitted that "if I had had more [bullets], I would have shot them again, and again, and again."

## II

After waiving extradition, Goetz was brought back to New York and arraigned on a felony complaint charging him with attempted murder and criminal possession of a weapon. The matter was presented to a Grand Jury in January 1985, with the prosecutor seeking an indictment for attempted murder, assault, reckless endangerment, and criminal possession of a weapon. Neither the defendant nor any of the wounded youths testified before this Grand Jury. On January 25, 1985, the Grand Jury indicted defendant on one count of criminal possession of a weapon in the third degree (for possessing the gun used in the subway shootings), and two counts of criminal possession of a weapon in the fourth degree (for possessing two other guns in his apartment building). It dismissed, however, the attempted murder and other charges stemming from the shootings themselves.

Several weeks after the Grand Jury's action, the People, asserting that they had newly available evidence, moved for an order authorizing them to resubmit the dismissed charges to a second Grand Jury. After conducting an in-camera [read, in chambers] inquiry, the trial court granted the motion. Presentation of the case to the second Grand Jury began on March 14, 1985. Two of the four youths, Canty and Ramseur, testified. Among the other witnesses were four passengers from the seventh car of the subway who had seen some portions of the incident. Goetz again chose not to testify, though the tapes of his two statements were played for the grand jurors, as had been done with the first Grand Jury.

On March 27, 1985, the second Grand Jury filed a 10-count indictment, containing four charges of attempted murder, four charges of assault in the first degree, one charge of reckless endangerment in the first degree, and one charge of criminal possession of a weapon in the second degree. Goetz was arraigned on this indictment on March 28, 1985, and it was consolidated with the earlier three-count indictment.

On October 14, 1985, Goetz moved to dismiss the charges contained in the second indictment alleging, among other things, that the evidence before the second Grand Jury was legally insufficient to establish the offenses charged and that the prosecutor's instructions to that Grand Jury on the defense of justification were erroneous and prejudicial to the defendant so as to render its proceedings defective.

On November 25, 1985, while the motion to dismiss was pending before Criminal Term, a column appeared in the *New York Daily News* containing an interview which the columnist had conducted with Darryl Cabey the previous day in Cabey's hospital room. The columnist claimed that Cabey had told him in this interview that the other three youths had all approached Goetz with the intention of robbing him. The day after the column was published, a New York City police officer informed the prosecutor that he had been one of the first officers to enter the subway car after the shootings, and that Canty had said to him "we were going to rob [Goetz]." The prosecutor immediately disclosed this information to the court and to defense counsel, adding that this was the first time his office had been told of this alleged statement and that none of the police reports filed on the incident contained any such information. Goetz then orally expanded his motion to dismiss, asserting that resubmission of the charges voted by the second Grand Jury was required under *People v. Pelchat*, 62 N.Y.2d 97 (1984) because it appeared, from this new information, that Ramseur and Canty had committed perjury.

In an order dated January 21, 1986, the trial court dismissed all counts of the second indictment other than the reckless endangerment charge, with leave to resubmit these charges to a third Grand Jury. The court, after inspection of the Grand Jury minutes, first rejected Goetz's contention that there was legally insufficient evidence to support the charges. It held, however, that the prosecutor, in a supplemental charge elaborating upon the justification defense, had erroneously introduced an objective element into this defense by instructing the grand jurors to consider whether Goetz's conduct was that of a "reasonable man in his situation." The trial court concluded that the statutory test for whether the use of deadly force is justified to protect a person should be wholly subjective, focusing entirely on defendant's state of mind when he used such force. It concluded that dismissal was required for this error because the justification issue was at the heart of the case.

The trial court also concluded that dismissal and resubmission of the charges were required under *People v. Pelchat* because the *Daily News* column and the statement by the police officer to the prosecution indicated that the testimony of Ramseur and Canty was perjured. Because the additional evidence before the second Grand

Jury, as contrasted with that before the first Grand Jury, consisted largely of the testimony of these two youths, the court found that the integrity of the second Grand Jury was undermined by the apparently perjured testimony.

On appeal by the People, a divided Appellate Division affirmed the trial court's dismissal of the charges. The plurality opinion by Justice Kassal stated that the grand jurors should have been instructed to consider only the defendant's subjective beliefs as to the need to use deadly force. Justice Kupferman concurred in the result reached by the plurality on the ground that the prosecutor's charge did not adequately apprise the grand jurors of the need to consider Goetz's own background and learning. Neither the plurality nor the concurring opinion discussed the trial court's reliance on *Pelchat* as an alternate ground for dismissal.

Justice Asch, in a dissenting opinion in which Justice Wallach concurred, disagreed with both bases for dismissal relied upon by the trial court. On the justification question, he opined that the statute requires consideration of both the defendant's subjective beliefs and whether a reasonable person in defendant's situation would have had such beliefs. Accordingly, he found no error in the prosecutor's introduction of an objective element into the justification defense. On the *Pelchat* issue, Justice Asch distinguished the Grand Jury evidence in that case and the case at bar and concluded that the out-of-court statements attributed to Cabey and Canty did not affect the validity of the indictment. In a separate dissenting opinion, Justice Wallach stressed that the plurality's adoption of a purely subjective test effectively eliminated any reasonableness requirement contained in the statute.

On the People's appeal to this court, we agree with the dissenters that neither the prosecutor's charge to the Grand Jury on justification nor the information which came to light while the motion to dismiss was pending required dismissal of any of the charges in the second indictment.

### III

Penal Law §35 recognizes the defense of justification, which permits the use of force under certain circumstances. One such set of circumstances pertains to the use of force ... in both self-defense and defense of a third person. Penal Law §35.15(1) sets forth the general principles governing all such uses of force: "[a] person may ... use physical force upon another person when and to the extent he *reasonably believes* such to be necessary to defend himself or a third person from what he *reasonably believes* to be the use or imminent use of unlawful physical force by such other person."

Section 35.15(2) sets forth further limitations on these general principles with respect to the use of "deadly physical force": "A person may not use deadly physical force upon another person under circumstances specified in subdivision one unless (a) He *reasonably believes* that such other person is using or about to use deadly physical force ... or (b) He *reasonably believes* that such other person is committing or attempting to commit a kidnapping, forcible rape, forcible sodomy or robbery."

Thus, consistent with most justification provisions, §35.15 permits the use of deadly physical force only where requirements as to triggering conditions and the necessity of a particular response are met. As to the triggering conditions, the statute requires that the actor "reasonably believes" that another person either is using or about to use deadly physical force or is committing or attempting to commit one of certain enumerated felonies, including robbery. As to the need for the use of deadly physical force as a response, the statute requires that the actor "reasonably believes" that such force is necessary to avert the perceived threat.

Because the evidence before the second Grand Jury included statements by Goetz that he acted to protect himself from being maimed or to avert a robbery, the prosecutor correctly chose to charge the justification defense in §35.15 to the Grand Jury. The prosecutor properly instructed the grand jurors to consider whether the use of deadly physical force was justified to prevent either serious physical injury or a robbery, and, in doing so, to separately analyze the defense with respect to each of the charges. He elaborated upon the prerequisites for the use of deadly physical force essentially by reading or paraphrasing the language in Penal Law §35.15. The defense does not contend that he committed any error in this portion of the charge.

When the prosecutor had completed his charge, one of the grand jurors asked for clarification of the term "reasonably believes." The prosecutor responded by instructing the grand jurors that they were to consider the circumstances of the incident and determine "whether the defendant's conduct was that of a reasonable man in the defendant's situation." It is this response by the prosecutor—and specifically his use of "a reasonable man"—which is the basis for the dismissal of the charges by the lower courts. As expressed repeatedly in the Appellate Division's plurality opinion, because §35.15 uses the term *"he reasonably believes"*, the appropriate test, according to that court, is whether a defendant's beliefs and reactions were *"reasonable to him."* Under that reading of the statute, a jury which believed a defendant's testimony that he felt that his own actions were warranted and were reasonable would have to acquit him, regardless of what anyone else in defendant's situation might have concluded. Such an interpretation defies the ordinary meaning and significance of the term "reasonably" in a statute, and misconstrues the clear intent of the Legislature, in enacting §35.15, to retain an objective element as part of any provision authorizing the use of deadly force.

New York has long codified the right recognized at common law to use deadly force, under appropriate circumstances, in self-defense.... These provisions have never required that an actor's belief as to the intention of another person to inflict serious injury be correct in order for the use of deadly force to be justified, but they have uniformly required that the belief comport with an objective notion of reasonableness. The 1829 statute, using language which was followed almost in its entirety until the 1965 re-codification of the Penal Law, provided that the use of deadly force was justified in self-defense or in the defense of others "when there shall be a reasonable ground to apprehend a design to commit a felony, or to do some great personal injury, and there shall be imminent danger of such design being accomplished."

We have emphasized that deadly force could be justified even if the actor's beliefs as to the intentions of another turned out to be wrong, but noted there had to be a reasonable basis, viewed objectively, for the beliefs. We explicitly rejected the position that the defendant's own belief that the use of deadly force was necessary sufficed to justify such force regardless of the reasonableness of the beliefs.

In 1881, New York enacted, for the first time, a separate Penal Code. The provision in the 1881 Penal Code for the use of deadly force in self-defense or to defend a third person was virtually a reenactment of the language in the 1829 statutes, and the "reasonable ground" requirement was maintained.

The 1909 Penal Law replaced the 1881 Penal Code. Several cases from this court interpreting the 1909 provision demonstrate unmistakably that an objective element of reasonableness was a vital part of any claim of self-defense. In *People v. Lumsden*, 201 N.Y. 264, 268 (1911), we approved a charge to the jury which instructed it to consider whether the circumstances facing defendant were such "as would lead a reasonable man to believe that [an assailant] is about to kill or to do great bodily injury." We emphatically rejected the position that any belief by an actor as to the intention of another to cause severe injury was a sufficient basis for his use of deadly force, and stated specifically that a belief based upon "mere fear or fancy or remote hearsay information or a delusion pure and simple" would not satisfy the requirements of the statute. In *People v. Tomlins*, 213 N.Y. 240, 244 (1914), we set forth the governing test as being whether "the situation justified the defendant as a reasonable man in believing that he was about to be murderously attacked."

Accordingly, the Law Revision Commission, in a 1937 Report to the Legislature on the Law of Homicide in New York, summarized the self-defense statute as requiring a "reasonable belief in the imminence of danger," and stated that the standard to be followed by a jury in determining whether a belief was reasonable "is that of a man of ordinary courage in the circumstances surrounding the defendant at the time of the killing." The Report added that New York did not follow the view, adopted in a few States, that the jury is required to adopt the subjective view and judge from the standpoint of the very defendant concerned.

In 1961 the Legislature established a Commission to undertake a complete revision of the Penal Law and the Criminal Code. The impetus for the decision to update the Penal Law came in part from the drafting of the Model Penal Code [MPC] by the American Law Institute, as well as from the fact that the existing law was poorly organized and ... antiquated. Following the submission by the Commission of several reports and proposals, the Legislature approved the present Penal Law in 1965, and it became effective on September 1, 1967. The drafting of the general provisions of the new Penal Law, including the article on justification, was influenced by the MPC. While using the MPC provisions on justification as guidelines, however, the drafters of the new Penal Law did not simply adopt them verbatim.

The provisions of the MPC with respect to the use of deadly force in self-defense reflect the position that any culpability which arises from a mistaken belief in the need to use such force should be no greater than the culpability such a mistake would give rise to if it were made with respect to an element of a crime. Accordingly, under MPC §3.04(2)(b), a defendant charged with murder or attempted murder need only show that he *"believed* that the use of deadly force was necessary to protect himself against death, serious bodily injury, kidnapping or forcible sexual intercourse" to prevail on a self-defense claim. If the defendant's belief was wrong, and was recklessly, or negligently formed, however, he may be convicted of the type of homicide charge requiring only a reckless or negligent, as the case may be, criminal intent.

The drafters of the MPC recognized that the wholly subjective test set forth in §3.04 differed from the existing law in most States by its omission of any requirement of reasonableness. The drafters were also keenly aware that requiring that the actor have a "reasonable belief" rather than just a "belief" would alter the wholly subjective test. This basic distinction was recognized years earlier by the New York Law Revision Commission....

New York did not follow the MPC's equation of a mistake as to the need to use deadly force with a mistake negating an element of a crime, choosing instead to use a single statutory section providing either a complete defense or no defense at all to a defendant charged with any crime involving the use of deadly force. The drafters of the new Penal Law adopted in large part the structure and content of MPC §3.04, but, crucially, inserted the word "reasonably" before "believes."

The plurality below agreed with defendant's argument that the change in the statutory language from "reasonable ground," used prior to 1965, to "he reasonably believes" in §35.15 evinced a legislative intent to conform to the subjective standard contained in MPC §3.04. This argument, however, ignores the plain significance of the insertion of "reasonably." Had the drafters of §35.15 wanted to adopt a subjective standard, they could have simply used the language of §3.04. "Believes" by itself requires an honest or genuine belief by a defendant as to the need to use deadly force. Interpreting the statute to require only that the defendant's belief was "reasonable to *him,*" as done by the plurality below, would hardly be different from requiring only a genuine belief; in either case, the defendant's own perceptions could completely exonerate him from any criminal liability.

We cannot lightly impute to the Legislature an intent to fundamentally alter the principles of justification to allow the perpetrator of a serious crime to go free simply because that person believed his actions were reasonable and necessary to prevent some perceived harm. To completely exonerate such an individual, no matter how aberrational or bizarre his thought patterns, would allow citizens to set their own standards for the permissible use of force. It would also allow a legally competent defendant suffering from delusions to kill or perform acts of violence with impunity, contrary to fundamental principles of justice and criminal law.

We can only conclude that the Legislature retained a reasonableness requirement to avoid giving a license for such actions. The plurality's interpretation, as the dissenters below recognized, excises the impact of the word "reasonably." The change from "reasonable ground" to "reasonably believes" is better explained by the fact that the drafters of §35.15 were proposing a single section which, for the first time, would govern both the use of ordinary force and deadly force in self-defense or defense of another. Under the 1909 Penal Law and its predecessors, the use of ordinary force was governed by separate sections which, at least by their literal terms, required that the defendant was *in fact* responding to an unlawful assault, and not just that he had a reasonable ground for believing that such an assault was occurring. Following the example of the MPC, the drafters of §35.15 eliminated this sharp dichotomy between the use of ordinary force and deadly force in defense of a person. Not surprisingly then, the integrated section reflects the wording of MPC §3.04, with the addition of "reasonably" to incorporate the long-standing requirement of "reasonable ground" for the use of deadly force and apply it to the use of ordinary force as well.

The conclusion that §35.15 retains an objective element to justify the use of deadly force is buttressed by the statements of its drafters.... Nowhere in the legislative history is there any indication that "reasonably believes" was designed to change the law on the use of deadly force or establish a subjective standard. To the contrary, the legislative history equated "[he] reasonably believes" with having a reasonable ground for believing....

Statutes or rules of law requiring a person to act "reasonably" or to have a "reasonable belief" uniformly prescribe conduct meeting an objective standard measured with reference to how "a reasonable person" could have acted. In *People v. Cantor*, 36 N.Y.2d 106 (1975), we reviewed a Criminal Procedure Law authorizing a police officer to stop a person "when *he reasonably suspects* that such person is committing, has committed or is about to commit a crime." We held that this section authorized "stops" only when the police officer had "the quantum of knowledge sufficient to induce an ordinarily prudent and cautious man under the circumstances to believe criminal activity is at hand." *Id.* at 112-13.

In *People v. Collice*, 41 N.Y.2d 906 (1977), we rejected the position that §35.15 contains a wholly subjective standard. The defendant in *Collice* asserted ... that the trial court had erred in refusing to charge the justification defense. We upheld the trial court's action because we concluded that, even if the defendant had actually believed that he was threatened with the imminent use of deadly physical force, the evidence clearly indicated that "his reactions were not those of a reasonable man acting in self-defense." *Id.* at 907. Numerous decisions from other States interpreting "reasonably believes" in justification statutes enacted subsequent to the drafting of the MPC are consistent with *Collice*, as they hold that such language refers to what a reasonable person could have believed under the same circumstances. *See, e.g.*, *State v. Kelly*, 97 N.J. 178 (1984); *Weston v. State*, 682 P.2d 1119, 1121 (Alaska 1984).

The defense contends that ... *Collice* is inconsistent with our prior opinion in *People v. Miller*, 39 N.Y.2d 543 (1976). In *Miller*, we held that a defendant charged with homicide could introduce, in support of a claim of self-defense, evidence of prior acts of violence committed by the deceased of which the defendant had knowledge. The defense, as well as the plurality below, place great emphasis on the statement in *Miller* that "the crucial fact at issue is the state of mind of the defendant." *Id.* at 551. This language, however, in no way indicates that a wholly subjective test is appropriate. To begin, it is undisputed that §35.15 does contain a subjective element, namely that the defendant believed that deadly force was necessary to avert the imminent use of deadly force or the commission of certain felonies. Evidence that the defendant knew of prior acts of violence by the deceased could help establish his requisite beliefs. Moreover, such knowledge would also be relevant on the issue of reasonableness, as the jury must consider the circumstances a defendant found himself in, which would include any relevant knowledge of the nature of persons confronting him. *E.g.*, *People v. Taylor*, 177 N.Y. 237, 245 (1904)....

Goetz's reliance on *People v. Rodawald*, 177 N.Y. 408 (1904) is similarly misplaced. In *Rodawald*, decided under the 1881 Penal Code, we held that a defendant who claimed that he had acted in self-defense could introduce evidence as to the general reputation of the deceased as a violent person if this reputation was known to the defendant when he acted. We stated, as emphasized by Goetz, that such evidence, "when known to the accused, enables him to judge of the danger and aids the jury in deciding whether he acted in good faith and upon the honest belief that his life was in peril. It shows the state of his mind as to the necessity of defending himself." *Id.* at 423. Again, such language is explained by the fact that the threshold question, before the reasonableness issue is addressed, is the subjective beliefs of the defendant. Nowhere in *Rodawald* did we hold that the *only* test, as urged by Goetz, is whether the defendant honestly and in good faith believed himself to be in danger. Rather, we recognized that there was also the separate question of whether the accused had "reasonable ground" for his belief, and we upheld the trial court's refusal to charge the jury that the defendant's honest belief was sufficient to establish self-defense. *Id.* at 423, 426-27.

Goetz also argues that the introduction of an objective element will preclude a jury from considering factors such as the prior experiences of a given actor and thus, require it to make a determination of "reasonableness" without regard to the actual circumstances of a particular incident. This argument, however, falsely presupposes that an objective standard means that the background and other relevant characteristics of a particular actor must be ignored. To the contrary, we have frequently noted that a determination of reasonableness must be based on the "circumstances" facing a defendant or his "situation." *E.g., People v. Ligouri*, 284 N.Y. 309, 316 (1940). Such terms encompass more than the physical movements of the potential assailant. As just discussed, these terms include any relevant knowledge the defendant had about that person. They also necessarily bring in the physical attributes of all persons involved, including the defendant. Furthermore, the defendant's circumstances encompass any prior experiences he had which could provide a reasonable basis for a belief that another person's intentions were to injure or rob him or that the use of deadly force was necessary under the circumstances.

Accordingly, a jury should be instructed to consider this type of evidence in weighing the defendant's actions. The jury must first determine whether the defendant had the requisite beliefs under §35.15, that is, whether he believed deadly force was necessary to avert the imminent use of deadly force or the commission of one of the felonies enumerated therein. If the People do not prove beyond a reasonable doubt that he did not have such beliefs, then the jury must also consider whether these beliefs were reasonable. The jury would have to determine, in light of all the "circumstances" as explicated above, if a reasonable person could have had these beliefs.

The prosecutor's instruction to the second Grand Jury that it had to determine whether, under the circumstances, Goetz's conduct was that of a reasonable man in his situation was thus essentially an accurate charge. It is true that the prosecutor did not elaborate on the meaning of "circumstances" or "situation" and inform the grand jurors that they could consider, for example, the prior experiences Goetz related in his statement to the police. We have held, however, that a Grand Jury need not be instructed on the law with the same degree of precision as the petit jury. *People v. Valles*, 62 N.Y.2d 36, 38 (1984). This lesser standard is premised upon the different functions of the Grand Jury and the petit jury: the former determines whether sufficient evidence exists to accuse a person of a crime and thereby subject him to criminal prosecution; the latter ultimately determines the guilt or innocence of the accused, and may convict only where the People have proven his guilt beyond a reasonable doubt.

In *People v. Calbud, Inc.*, 49 N.Y.2d 389, 394-95 (1980), we stated that the prosecutor simply had to "provide the Grand Jury with enough information to enable it intelligently to decide whether a crime has been committed and to determine whether there exists legally sufficient evidence to establish the material elements of the crime." Of course, as noted above, where the evidence suggests that a complete defense such as justification may be present, the prosecutor must charge the grand jurors on that defense, providing enough information to enable them to determine whether the defense, in light of the evidence, should preclude the criminal prosecution. The prosecutor more than adequately fulfilled this obligation here. His instructions were not as complete as the court's charge on justification should be, but they sufficiently apprised the Grand Jury of the existence and requirements of that defense to allow it to intelligently decide that there is sufficient evidence tending to disprove justification and necessitating a trial. The Grand Jury has indicted Goetz. It will now be for the petit jury to decide whether the prosecutor can prove beyond a reasonable doubt that Goetz's reactions were unreasonable and therefore excessive.

## IV

The trial court's second ground for dismissal of the charges, premised upon the *Daily News* column and the police officer's statement to the prosecutor, can be rejected more summarily. The court relied upon *People v. Pelchat*, 62 N.Y.2d 97 (1980), the facts of which, however, are markedly different from those here. In *Pelchat*, the defendant was one of 21 persons arrested in a house to which police officers had seen marihuana delivered. The only evidence before the Grand Jury showing that defendant had anything to do with the marihuana was the testimony of a police officer listing defendant as one of 21 persons he had observed transporting the drug. After defendant was indicted, this same police officer told the prosecutor that he had misunderstood his question when testifying before the Grand Jury and that he had not seen defendant engage in any criminal activity. Although the prosecutor knew that there was no other evidence before the Grand Jury to establish the defendant's guilt, he did not disclose the police officer's admission, and instead, accepted a guilty plea from the defendant. We reversed the conviction and dismissed the indictment, holding that the prosecutor should not have allowed the proceedings against defendant to continue when he knew that the only evidence against him before the Grand Jury was false, and thus, knew that there was legally insufficient evidence to support the indictment.

Here, in contrast, Canty and Ramseur have not recanted any of their Grand Jury testimony or told the prosecutor that they misunderstood any questions. Instead, all that has come to light is hearsay evidence that conflicts with part of Canty's testimony. There is no statute or controlling case law requiring dismissal of an indictment merely because, months later, the prosecutor becomes aware of some information which may lead to the defendant's acquittal. There was no basis for the trial court to speculate whether Canty's and Ramseur's testimony was perjurious, and [the trial court's] conclusion that the testimony "strongly appeared" to be perjured is particularly inappropriate given the nature of the "evidence" he relied upon to reach such a conclusion and that he was not in the Grand Jury room when the two youths testified.

Moreover, unlike *Pelchat*, the testimony of Canty and Ramseur was not the only evidence before the Grand Jury establishing that the offenses submitted to that body were committed by Goetz. Goetz's own statements, together with the testimony of the passengers, clearly support the elements of the crimes charged, and provide ample basis for concluding that a trial of this matter is needed to determine whether Goetz could have reasonably believed that he was about to be robbed or seriously injured and whether it was reasonably necessary for him to shoot four youths to avert any such threat.

Accordingly, the order of the Appellate Division is reversed, and the dismissed counts of the indictment reinstated.

Judges MEYER, SIMONS, KAYE, ALEXANDER, TITONE, and HANCOCK, JR., concur.

## QUESTIONS ON *GOETZ*

**1. More on Double Jeopardy.** In *Goetz*, attempted-murder charges were submitted to two Grand Juries: the first found no probable cause; the second found probable cause, but on Goetz's motion, the trial court dismissed the charges because the jury instruction misstated New York's law of self-defense. That ruling was upheld by the intermediate appellate court, from which the People appealed to New York's high court, which held that the jury instructions on self-defense were valid. Therefore, a trial on the attempted-murder charges could follow. Why would such a trial *not* violate Double Jeopardy?

**2. Tainted testimony.** A peripheral issue in *Goetz* stems from an article the *New York Daily News* published while Goetz's motion to dismiss the indictment returned by the second grand jury was pending. What is that issue and how was it ultimately resolved?

**3. Citing a dissenting opinion from below.** Early on in his opinion for the court, Chief Judge Wachtler cites the dissenting opinions of Justices Asch and Wallach from the intermediate appellate court. This is what poker players call a "tell": a gesture that inadvertently reveals what is to follow. What, exactly, do such cites likely tell?

**4. "Your money or your life."** "Homicide is justifiable and not unlawful when committed by any person in the defense of [oneself or another] if he or she actually and reasonably believed that the individual killed intended to commit a forcible and atrocious crime and that there was imminent danger of that crime being accomplished. A person may act upon appearances whether the danger is real or merely apparent." CALJIC No. 5.13 (2014). The Model Penal Code is a bit more specific about the triggering conditions of deadly force. MPC §3.04(2)(b) [deadly force justified by reasonable fear of imminent death, serious bodily injury, kidnapping, or rape]. New York's approach is similar to the MPC, though it adds to its list robbery or attempted robbery as triggering events. New York Penal Law §35.15(2)(b). What does that say about the value of life in New York?

5. **Subjective v. objective self-defense standards.** In 1829, New York law justified deadly force when defendant had a "reasonable ground" to believe it was necessary. If wrong, the belief still would have to be reasonable for defendant's use of deadly force to be fully justified. This aspect of the law was unchanged by amendments in 1881 and 1909, after which several interpretations from New York's high court emphasized that the test was objective, that is, if reasonable only to defendant but not to others, then his or her use of deadly force is not justified. In 1937, in a report to the legislature, the Law Commission summarized New York law as requiring "reasonable belief in the imminence of danger," judged from the perspective "of a man of ordinary courage in the circumstances surrounding the defendant at the time of the killing." Inspired by preliminary drafts of the Model Penal Code, New York's revised criminal code became effective in 1967. The operative language referred no longer to a "reasonable ground" for defendant's belief in the need for deadly force, but instead to whether "he reasonably believes" in that need.

a. Goetz (with support from the courts below) claimed without success in the high court that by changing the pertinent language that way, New York's test was made subjective. How so?

b. Does the Model Penal Code recognize "imperfect" self-defense? *Murder to invol. manslaughter or negligent homicide*

c. Does New York recognize "imperfect" self-defense? *All or nothing*

d. In what way or ways, if any, is there a subjective component in New York's law of self-defense? *Yes, both Objective & Subjective*

## NOTES ON *GOETZ*

**1. Standards for charging and convicting, revisited.** At the beginning of section II of Chief Judge Wachtler's opinion for the court, he states that the first "Grand Jury indicted defendant on one count of criminal possession of a weapon" and other weapons offenses, but "dismissed ... the attempted murder ... charges stemming from the shootings themselves" that the prosecutor had filed against Goetz. As a reminder, in New York, misdemeanors are prosecuted by probable-cause determinations made by prosecutors (charged in a complaint). Felonies are prosecuted by probable-cause determinations made by a simple majority of a 23-person Grand Jury (charged in an indictment). The Grand Jury is convened for a month at a time by the prosecutor to investigate and charge crimes where there is probable cause of criminality, but not necessarily the proof beyond a reasonable doubt needed for conviction at trial. *See supra* Chapter 1.A, note 5b on *Decina*; Chapter 2.A, note 1 on *Watson*. Accordingly, the felony complaint filed by Goetz's prosecutor had to be replaced by a grand-jury indictment for the attempted-murder case to proceed to trial. Although the first grand jury found no probable cause to charge Goetz with attempted murder, the second grand jury disagreed and reinstated the charges. It is from the Appellate Division's dismissal of those charges that the People successfully appealed in the case we just read. Had the People lost their appeal, a third Grand Jury might have reconsidered the charges against Goetz.

**2. Now or never: pre-emptive strikes.** In New York as elsewhere, self-defenders resort to deadly force to repel imminent threats of serious bodily harm or death. *E.g., Lynn v. Commonwealth*, 27 Va. Ct. App. 336, 353 (1998). *Goetz* was a case where the threat did not seem particularly serious, though once the case was finally tried, jurors found otherwise. But even when the threat is serious, that doesn't necessarily mean it's *imminent*. Deadly force is supposed to be an emergency response, not retaliatory.

Consider *State v. Schroeder*, 261 N.W.2d 759 (Neb. 1978), where a state high court upheld a 19-year-old prisoner's conviction for attempted murder. Schroeder stabbed his sleeping cellmate (Riggs) at 1 a.m., *id.* at 760, then testified that 1) Riggs "had a reputation among the other prisoners for sex and violence," 2) Schroeder owed Riggs money, and 3) Riggs had threatened to make Schroeder a "punk" (a prisoner who engages in sexual acts with other prisoners) by selling the debt to another prisoner. The night of the assault, Riggs had told Schroeder "that he might walk in his sleep that night" and "collect some of [the] money" Schroeder owed him. *Ibid.*

At trial, the prosecution and the majority collapsed the time frame—"there was no specific and imminent threat of injury to the defendant" at the moment Schroeder assaulted Riggs. *Id.* at 761. Schroeder and the dissent manipulated the time frame differently. Instead of considering the situation at the moment of the assault, their perspective viewed Schroeder's predicament as extending over a longer period of time: "defendant could not be expected to remain awake all night, every night, waiting for the attack that Riggs had threatened to make." *Id.* at 762 (Clinton, J., dissenting). Schroeder saw no reasonable alternative to stabbing Riggs—his remedies were either unavailable, inadequate, or futile. Confined in a prison cell with a person who had threatened to force him to submit to sodomy, retreat was not possible. *Id.* at 761. Schroeder and his two other cellmates had already requested that Riggs be transferred to another cell, but no action had been taken. *Id.* at 760. The prosecution emphasized that Schroeder had available, adequate and effective alternatives: he could have stayed awake that night, and then requested a transfer for himself; or he could have bargained with his other cellmates to guard him from Riggs. *See* J.M. Balkin, *The Rhetoric of Responsibility*, 76 Virginia Law Review 197, 236 n.97 (1990).

Schroeder tried to extend "imminent" to "first opportunity." And while it didn't pay off for him, academics, at least, think such arguments should have more sway with courts than they do. *E.g.,* Kit Kinports, *So Much Activity, So Little Change: A Reply to the Critics of Battered Women's Self-Defense*, 23 St. Louis University Public Law Review 155 (2004); Whitley R.P. Kaufman, *Self-Defense, Imminence, and the Battered Woman*, 10 New Criminal Law Review 342 (2007).

**3. Cowardice v. ruthlessness.** "What I did was cold and ruthless," Goetz remarked in a videotaped confession played for the jury at his May 13, 1987 trial, adding, "I'm no hero. Basically I'm a coward, and I know that. Anyone—a 10-year-old—can pull a trigger." *See* Phillip Lentz, *Goetz told police he was "murderer"*, Chicago Tribune, May 14, 1987, §1, p.3. Can Goetz really be at once cowardly *and* ruthless?

In the federal-civil-rights trial of four L.A.P.D. officers for the 1991 beating of drunk-driver Rodney King, Assistant U.S. Attorney Steven Clymer gave a three-hour closing argument in which he called Officer Theodore Briseno's "stomp" on King "an act of cowardice." Indeed, just tap search terms "bombs" and "cowardice" into Google and up will come accusations that dropping bombs on nations who lack anti-aircraft artillery capable of defending such attacks is, in a word, "cowardly." *See also People v. Perez,* 2 Cal.4th 1117, 1137 n.7 (1992) [at murder trial of stalker who stabbed his married, pregnant victim dozens of times, the prosecutor argued, "If he was a stand-up guy he would have taken his medicine and been honest with the cops. But he is not. He is a coward. He is the same kind of coward that would do what he did to a woman"].

But stomping on a prone suspect or dropping bombs on cities is hardly cowardly. If, as responses to fear, a courageous act engages risk while a cowardly act dodges risk, stomping on a prone suspect or dropping bombs from outside the reach of artillery is a combination of the two responses. Like the courageous act, it is confrontational—it engages rather than dodges. Like the cowardly act, it eschews risk—stomping on a prone suspect or dropping bombs against under-equipped enemies is confrontational but without risk: the odds heavily favor the aggressor. It is this relation between action and risk-taking that characterizes ruthlessness. Accordingly, Officer Briseno's stomping of Rodney King is ruthless, not cowardly. Despite the temptation to call the rigging of odds in such encounters a mode of cowardice, cowards do no harm: at most, they let harm happen. A ruthless person is an aggressor or counter-aggressor who, unlike the coward, is characterized by action, not passivity.

Like a courageous person, Goetz was not afraid to take action. But like a coward, he would never mix it up—never take action at great risk to himself. So it makes sense for a coward prone to withdrawal rather than engagement to engage only in a risk free, ruthless way. Goetz was right about himself: he's both.

**4. Fate of parties.** On June 16, 1987, Goetz was acquitted on all but one of the 13 counts charged in the indictment, including all four attempted murders. In a judgment filed October 19, 1987, he was given six months in jail, five years probation, and a $5K fine for third degree criminal possession of a weapon, a felony. *People v. Goetz,* 137 Misc.2d 380 (Supreme Court N.Y. County 1987). The next year, on Goetz's appeal, the jail term *increased* to one year on the ground that the original sentence was illegal. *People v. Goetz,* 141 A.D.2d 446 (N.Y. App. Div. 1988), *affirmed by People v. Goetz,* 532 N.E.2d 1273 (N.Y. 1988). Goetz served eight months, at first in protective isolation at Rikers Island prison hospital before his transfer to the Brooklyn

House of Detention. Michael Freitag, *Goetz released after spending 8 months in jail*, New York Times, N.Y./Region, Sept. 21, 1989, §B10.

Goetz's most seriously injured victim, Darryl Cabey (who spent over a year hospitalized, remaining paraplegic thereafter), obtained a $43M judgment in a civil suit against him in 1996. Goetz promptly filed for bankruptcy to protect his $17K estate, which included a pet chinchilla. A defamation suit, brought by Goetz against Cabey's celebrity lawyer for opinions expressed in an autobiography, went nowhere. *Goetz v. Kunstler,* 164 Misc.2d 557 (Supreme Court N.Y. County 1995).

On November 1, 2013, Goetz, a self-employed electronics specialist who ran for mayor of New York in 2001, was arrested in Union Square Park after exchanging a personal-use amount of pot for $30 with an attractive, young, female undercover cop, who reported that the 65-year-old Goetz's plans for the two surpassed pot smoking. Soon after the 1986 *Goetz* ruling we just studied, Barry Allen got busted twice for robbery, landing in prison before being paroled in 1995. Despite a handful of arrests, Troy Canty served no time for his petty criminal forays, though he did complete a residential drug-treatment program in 1989. James Ramseur did 25 years for his role in a 1986 robbery/rape of a pregnant 18-year-old. He died by suicide in a Bronx motel room on December 22, 2011, the 27th anniversary of the subway incident.

**5. Further reading.** For a Freudian analysis of the deployment of deadly force by police, see Daniel Yeager, *Cop Killers*, 48 Criminal Law Bulletin 428 (2012).

## C. FEAR AS PARTIAL EXCUSE: IMPERFECT SELF-DEFENSE

Spurlin, Griggs, and Greene all claimed that anger led them to over-react to the wrongs done to them. None succeeded in mitigating murder to manslaughter on that basis. The other basis of voluntary manslaughter is not anger- or passion-based, but fear-based, by which defendants *try* to make out a case of self-defense to justify the deadly force they exerted against their victims. This other mode of voluntary manslaughter is *not* "perfect" self-defense, where deadly force is necessary or reasonably perceived to be necessary. Rather, it is "imperfect" self-defense, where deadly force is not only an overreaction to the perceived threat-maker, but much worse, is chalked up to a totally groundless belief in its necessity.

To begin with, both provocation and imperfect self-defense envision killings that are either intentional or extremely reckless though non-malicious. *See* CALJIC No. 8.40 (2004 Revision). Additionally, these two modes of voluntary manslaughter both inculpate (in part) *and* exculpate (also in part) defendants for overreacting to the actions of others. Finally, while imperfect self-defenders often blame their anger on the influence of alcohol or drugs, as a general-intent crime, voluntary manslaughter is excused neither in whole nor in part by voluntary intoxication.

For a peek at the workings of imperfect self-defense, consider *People v. Villanueva*, 169 Cal.App.4th 41 (2008). There, after arguing at a deli, Villanueva (defendant) and Manzano (victim) fought. After being told to leave by a third man (Vargas), Manzano threatened that he would kill Villanueva the next time they saw each other, which was four hours later. Villanueva claimed Manzano was fiddling around with the glove box of his van before accelerating toward Villanueva. In response, Villanueva shot Manzano non-fatally in the face.

Though Manzano survived, the case remains one of deadly force, given that shooting someone in the face poses a substantial risk of death. Villanueva's deadly force was necessary if Manzano really was going to run him over, or equivalent to necessary if he had good but mistaken grounds for believing Manzano was going to do so. But if the properly instructed jury believed Manzano did not pose a deadly threat, nor could he reasonably be perceived as posing such a threat, that does not mean that Villanueva is an attempted murderer. Just as imperfect self-defense reduces murder to manslaughter, CALJIC No. 5.17 (2004 Revision); *Villanueva*, 169 Cal.App.4th at 50 n.7, here such a partial excuse would mitigate attempted murder to attempted voluntary manslaughter. *See* CALJIC No. 8.41 (2004 New) [afflicted by heat of passion or an unreasonable belief in the need to defend with deadly force, a direct but ineffectual act done with specific intent to kill is attempted voluntary manslaughter]. While voluntary manslaughter is a general-intent crime, all attempts are specific-intent. CALJIC No. 6.00 (2014). Accordingly, an accusation of attempted voluntary manslaughter would open the door to voluntary intoxication as excuse. And a conviction of the same would implicitly refute any claim Villanueva made to having shot Manzano by accident. *See Villanueva*, 169 Cal.App.4th at 54 n.12 [absent specific intent to kill, there can be no attempted homicide].

*Villanueva* involves deadly force, but self-defense is regulated by the same principles when a defendant uses less than deadly force. All force, deadly or not, must be proportionate to the perceived harm threatened. *E.g., State v. Bundy*, 974 N.E.2d 139, 157 (Ohio Ct. App. 2012). Thus, except in extraordinary circumstances, it is unjustifiable to respond to a punch in the face by cracking a beer bottle over the initial aggressor's head.

Additionally, perfect and imperfect self-defense presuppose that the victim, not the defendant, was the initial aggressor. Otherwise, the defense is lost to the defendant, *e.g., People v. Quach*, 116 Cal.App.4th 294, 300-03 (2004), though not without exception:

> Where one is the first wrongdoer, but his unlawful act is not felonious, as a simple assault upon the person of another, or a mere trespass upon his property, even though forcible, and this unlawful act is met by a counter assault of a deadly character, the right of self-defense to the first wrongdoer is not lost; for, as his acts did not justify upon the part of the other the use of deadly means for their prevention, his killing by the other would be criminal, and one may always defend himself against the criminal taking of his life. But in contemplation of the weakness and passions of men, and of the provocation, which, though inadequate, was wrongfully put upon the other, it is the duty of the first wrongdoer, before he can avail himself of the plea, to have retreated to the wall, to have declined the strife, and withdrawn from the difficulty, and to have killed his adversary, under necessity, actual or apparent, only after so doing. If, however, the counter assault be so sudden and perilous that no opportunity be given to decline or to make known to his adversary his willingness to decline the strife, if he cannot retreat with safety, then, as the greater wrong of the deadly assault is upon his opponent, he would be justified in slaying forthwith in self-defense.

*People v. Hecker*, 109 Cal. 451, 464 (1895).

Defendants have tried to assert imperfect self-defense as a partial excuse to offenses other than murder, attempted murder, or attempted voluntary manslaughter. It seems to have worked in Maryland, which, having long limited the partial excuse to "criminal homicide and its shadow forms" such as attempted murder, has extended it to first-degree assault. *Christian v. State*, 951 A.2d 832, 847-48 (Md. Ct. App. 2008). In California, despite an indication that imperfect self-defense might apply as a partial defense to mayhem (simple or aggravated), *People v. McKelvy*, 194 Cal.App.3d 694, 702-03 (1987), it turns out that it does not. *People v. Sekona*, 27 Cal.App.4th 443, 448-57 (1994).

## SUPREME COURT OF CALIFORNIA

### THE PEOPLE, PLAINTIFF AND RESPONDENT
### V.
### CHARLES ELMORE, DEFENDANT AND APPELLANT

### JUNE 2, 2014

CORRIGAN, Associate Justice

A killing committed because of an unreasonable belief in the need for self-defense is voluntary manslaughter, not murder. Unreasonable self-defense, also called imperfect self-defense, obviates malice because that most culpable of mental states cannot coexist with an actual belief that the lethal act was necessary to avoid one's own death or serious injury at the victim's hand. The question here is whether unreasonable self-defense is available when belief in the need to defend oneself is entirely delusional. We conclude it is not. No state, it appears, recognizes "delusional self-defense" as a theory of manslaughter. We have noted that unreasonable self-defense involves a mistake of *fact. In re Christian S.*, 7 Cal.4th 768, 779 n.3 (1994). A purely delusional belief in the need to act in self-defense may be raised as a defense, but that defense is insanity. Under our statutory scheme, a claim of insanity is reserved for a separate phase of trial. At a trial on the question of guilt, defendant may not claim unreasonable self-defense based on insane delusion.

### I. BACKGROUND

The relevant facts are undisputed. Defendant was, by all accounts, mentally ill. He had repeatedly been institutionalized and diagnosed as psychotic. On the day of the killing, he was living in a rehabilitation center. While visiting his grandmother's house that morning, he became fidgety and anxious. At one point, he began to crawl under cars as his family and a friend tried to speak with him. He left his grandmother's home around 12:30 p.m.

Meanwhile, 53-year-old Ella Suggs was doing her weekend shopping. She wore a necklace with a charm in the shape of a turtle, which had a magnifying glass in place of the shell. She also wore reading glasses on a chain around her neck. About 1:00 p.m., Brandon Wilson looked out a restaurant window and noticed Suggs sitting at a bus stop across the street. He saw defendant walk past Suggs, stop, look in both directions, and return to confront her. Defendant did not seem to be talking to himself.

Defendant grabbed Suggs and appeared to pull on something around her neck. Suggs raised her hands defensively, stood, and tried to walk away. Defendant pushed her back to a seated position, brought his hands together over his head, and plunged them toward Suggs's chest. Then he fled, looking around as he ran. Suggs stood for a moment before falling. She had been stabbed with a paintbrush handle sharpened to a point. The weapon penetrated six or seven inches, through a lung and into her heart. Neither the turtle necklace nor the reading glasses were found at the scene or among Suggs's possessions. Within half an hour, Wilson saw defendant return and approach the bus stop. He appeared to be puzzled, and fled. After Wilson alerted a security officer, police apprehended defendant. It took four officers to subdue him. His behavior was sufficiently bizarre that he was referred for psychiatric evaluation.

Charged with murder, defendant pleaded both not guilty and not guilty by reason of insanity. At the guilt phase, forensic psychiatrists were called by both prosecution and defense. They agreed that defendant suffered from schizophrenia, but disputed whether he was actively psychotic when he stabbed Suggs. Defendant testified, and gave a confused account of the killing. On direct examination, he repeatedly said, "something went wrong out there in the street." When asked for detail he said, "Somebody was saying something violent to me, and I didn't really—it was something violent happening while I was out there." Defense counsel pursued the question of who was violent. Defendant said, "Some person out there," but could not say whether the person was a man or a woman. He claimed to have blacked out. Counsel asked, "Did you pick that paint brush off the ground?" Defendant said, "Yeah, I made an object." "What was it?" counsel asked. "I made an object after I was out on the ground dazed somewhere. After I was on the ground or whatever. However it happened." Defendant admitted using the object but refused to say how. Asked if he stabbed someone with it, he responded, "I suppose." When asked why he stabbed Suggs, defendant answered, "Person said something and did something to me, I didn't just go do it to be doing it." Defendant refused to say what had been done to him, and denied taking anything from Suggs.

The prosecutor was no more successful at eliciting a coherent version of the events. Defendant said that when he was at the bus stop, "They said something to me." He denied asking Suggs for money or being angry that she would not give him any. He admitted making the paintbrush into a weapon "after I got up. I was mad and scared." He then said he did not know if he had made it and thought he picked it up in that condition. He admitted stabbing Suggs, but claimed the act was unintentional. He denied trying to steal anything.

The prosecutor argued for first degree murder, relying on both malice aforethought and felony murder theories. The defense requested jury instructions on unreasonable self-defense, mistake of fact, and the effect of hallucination on the degree of murder. The court refused those requests, but did tell the jury to consider the evidence of defendant's mental illness in deciding whether he had acted with malice or the intent to rob Suggs.

The jury returned a first-degree murder conviction. After the guilt phase, against the advice of counsel, defendant withdrew his plea of not guilty by reason of insanity and was sentenced to 25 years to life in prison. On appeal, he challenged the court's refusal to instruct on unreasonable self-defense and hallucination. The Court of Appeal summarily rejected his argument on unreasonable self-defense, relying on *People v. Mejia–Lenares*, 135 Cal.App.4th 1437 (2006) for the rule that the doctrine does not apply when belief in the need for self-defense arises solely from defendant's delusional mental state. However, the court held that the refusal to instruct on hallucination was prejudicial error. It remanded with directions for retrial or a conviction of second degree murder, at the prosecutor's election. Because the Attorney General has not sought review, we have no occasion to consider this aspect of the Court of Appeal's judgment.

Here, defendant contends he was entitled to an instruction on unreasonable self-defense. He claims no factual basis for his belief that he had to defend himself. His argument is that unreasonable self-defense may be based solely on a defendant's delusional mental state. We granted defendant's petition for review to settle the question.

## II. DISCUSSION

A. *The Law of Homicide and Unreasonable Self-Defense*

Homicide, the killing of one human being by another, is not always criminal. In certain circumstances, a killing may be excusable or justifiable. Murder and manslaughter are the forms of criminal homicide. Murder is the unlawful killing of a human being with malice aforethought, §187(a), which may be express or implied. §188.

Express malice is "a deliberate intention unlawfully to take away the life of a fellow creature." §188. "Unlawfully" in the express malice definition means there is no justification, excuse, or mitigation for the killing recognized by the law. *People v. Saille*, 54 Cal.3d 1103 (1991).

Malice is implied when an unlawful killing results from a willful act, the natural and probable consequences of which are dangerous to human life, performed with conscious disregard for that danger. A killing with express malice formed willfully, deliberately, and with premeditation is first degree murder. Second degree murder is the unlawful killing of a human being with malice aforethought but without the additional elements, such as willfulness, premeditation, and deliberation, that would support a conviction of first degree murder. *People v. Knoller*, 41 Cal.4th 139, 151 (2007). Thus, the *mens rea* required for murder is malice, express or implied.

Manslaughter, a lesser included offense of murder, is an unlawful killing without malice. Section 192 notes three kinds of manslaughter: voluntary, involuntary, and vehicular. Only voluntary manslaughter is at issue here. Punishment is mitigated for this offense, which the law deems less blameworthy because of defendant's compromised mental state. Two factors may preclude the formation of malice and reduce murder to voluntary manslaughter: heat of passion and unreasonable self-defense.

Self-defense, when based on a *reasonable* belief that killing is necessary to avert an imminent threat of death or great bodily injury, is a complete justification, and such a killing is not a crime. §197. A killing committed when that belief is *unreasonable* is not justifiable. Nevertheless, "one who holds an honest but unreasonable belief in the necessity to defend against imminent peril to life or great bodily injury does not harbor malice and commits no greater offense than manslaughter." *People v. Flannel*, 25 Cal.3d 668, 672 (1979). We have also described this mental state as an "unreasonable but good faith belief" in the need for self-defense. *People v. Barton*, 12 Cal.4th 186,

199 (1995). Still, it is most accurately characterized as an *actual* but unreasonable belief.

A person who actually believes in the need for self-defense believes he is acting lawfully. Because express malice requires an intent to kill unlawfully, a killing in the belief that one is acting lawfully is not malicious. The statutory definition of implied malice does not contain similar language, but we have extended the imperfect self-defense rationale to any killing that would otherwise have malice, whether express or implied. A defendant who acts with the requisite actual belief in the necessity for self-defense does not act with the base motive required for implied malice. *Christian S.*, 7 Cal.4th at 780 n.4. Unreasonable self-defense is not a true defense; rather, it is a shorthand description of one form of voluntary manslaughter. Whenever there is substantial evidence that defendant killed in unreasonable self-defense, the trial court must instruct on this theory of manslaughter.

Here, defendant claims his request for an instruction on unreasonable self-defense should have been granted, even though his perception of a threat was entirely delusional. The claim fails, under both case law and statute. California cases reflect that unreasonable self-defense involves a misperception of objective circumstances, not a reaction produced by mental disturbance alone. And the statutory scheme, though it permits evidence of mental illness to show that defendant did not harbor malice, reserves the issue of legal insanity for a separate phase of trial. A belief in the need for self-defense that is purely delusional is a paradigmatic example of legal insanity.

B. *Case Law*

The difference between unreasonable self-defense and a claim that mental deficiency prevented the formation of malice was made clear in *Christian S.* There we considered whether the Legislature intended to do away with unreasonable self-defense when it abolished the defense of diminished capacity in 1981. Diminished capacity was a judicially created concept. It allowed defendants to argue that because of mental infirmity, they lacked awareness of the obligation to act within the general body of laws regulating society, and therefore were incapable of acting with malice. *Id.* at 774.

In *Christian S.*, we concluded that the Legislature did not mean to abrogate unreasonable self-defense along with diminished capacity. *Id.* at 783. In reaching that conclusion, we distinguished the two theories. Thirty years before the diminished-capacity defense was allowed, a California court approved the imperfect self-defense doctrine: If the act is committed under the influence of an uncontrollable fear of death or great bodily harm, caused by the circumstances, but without the presence of all the ingredients necessary to self-defense, the killing is manslaughter. *People v. Best*, 13 Cal.App.2d 606, 610 (1936).

We had rejected the idea that the doctrine of unreasonable belief is necessarily bound up with or limited by the concepts of either heat of passion *or diminished capacity. Flannel,* 25 Cal.3d at 677. The two doctrines relate to the concept of malice, but the similarity ends there. Unlike diminished capacity, imperfect self-defense is not rooted in any notion of mental capacity or awareness of the need to act lawfully.

Unreasonable self-defense is not premised on considerations of mental disorder. Unreasonable self-defense has long been deemed to apply when defendant's act was *caused by the circumstances,* rather than by cognitive defects alone. Unreasonable self-defense "is based on a defendant's assertion that he lacked malice because he acted under an unreasonable *mistake of fact*—that is, the need to defend himself against imminent peril of death or great bodily harm." *Christian S.,* 7 Cal.4th at 779 n.3.

*Mejia–Lenares* relied on *Christian S.* in holding that purely delusional acts are excluded from the scope of unreasonable self-defense. The Court of Appeal noted that delusional defendants tended to be treated under the rubric of diminished capacity, when that doctrine was viable, whereas cases involving factual misperceptions were analyzed in terms of unreasonable self-defense. *Mejia–Lenares* reasoned that because unreasonable self-defense is a species of mistake of fact, it cannot be founded on delusion. In our view, a mistake of fact is predicated upon a negligent perception of facts, not, as in the case of a delusion, a perception of facts not grounded in reality. A person acting under a delusion is not negligently interpreting actual facts; instead, he or she is out of touch with reality.

We agree with *Mejia–Lenares* that unreasonable self-defense, as a form of mistake of fact, has no application when defendant's actions are entirely delusional. A defendant who makes a factual mistake misperceives the objective circumstances. A delusional defendant holds a belief that is divorced from the circumstances. The line between mere misperception and delusion is drawn at the absence of an objective correlate. A person who sees a stick and thinks it is a snake is mistaken, but that misinterpretation is not delusional. One who sees a snake where there is nothing snakelike, however, is deluded. Unreasonable self-defense was never intended to encompass reactions to threats that exist only in defendant's mind.

Defendant claims this limitation is inconsistent with our decision in *People v. Wells*, 33 Cal.2d 330 (1949). It is not; delusion was not a factor in *Wells*, which unlike most cases of unreasonable self-defense, was not a homicide case, but the prosecution of a prison inmate for assault with malice under section 4500. Wells had been ejected from a disciplinary hearing for disrupting the proceedings. In the hall outside, he encountered the guard who had brought charges against him. Wells seized a heavy crockery cuspidor and threw it at the guard, severely injuring him. *Id.* at 338.

Wells testified that he had no intent to hit the guard, but only picked up the cuspidor to defend himself from another guard who struck him with a baton. The blow caused him to fall and release the cuspidor. The defense also offered testimony from prison physicians that Wells suffered from an abnormal physical and mental condition, not amounting to insanity. According to the doctors, he was in a state of tension that rendered him highly sensitive to external stimuli and abnormally fearful for his personal safety. As a result, he reacted to apparent threats more violently and unpredictably than an average person would. This court reasoned that if Wells had acted only under the influence of fear of bodily harm, in the belief, honest though unreasonable, that he was defending himself from such harm by the use of a necessary amount of force, then the essential element of malice aforethought would be lacking. *Id.* at 345; *see* §4500.

Defendant argues that Wells's attack on a prison guard was completely unprovoked, with no objective circumstances supporting the claim of unreasonable self-defense. He misreads the case. As noted in *Mejia–Lenares,* Wells held a "belief which, although skewed by mental illness, was nevertheless factually based." *Mejia–Lenares,* 135 Cal.App.4th at 1449. There was no evidence that Wells's perception of a threat was delusional. To the contrary, he claimed his actions were an attempt to defend himself from an actual baton-wielding guard. *Wells,* 33 Cal.2d at 339. The expert testimony was that Wells was abnormally sensitive to *external stimuli. Id.* at 344–45. *Wells* does not support defendant's claim that unreasonable self-defense requires no objective basis. Unreasonable self-defense entails a reaction that is caused by the circumstances. *Flannel,* 25 Cal.3d at 676. The phrase "caused by the circumstances" denotes a motivation arising from objective facts, not delusions. Our view is consistently reflected in the decisions of other state courts.

### C. *Statute*

Defendant asserts a statutory basis for his claim in section 28(a). This provision states that evidence of mental disorders is admissible on whether the accused actually formed a required specific intent, premeditated, deliberated, or harbored malice aforethought, when a specific intent crime is charged, a theory referred to as "diminished actuality." Section 28(a) bars evidence of defendant's *capacity* to form a required mental state, consistent with the abolition of the diminished capacity defense.

Defendant contends the plain language of section 28(a) permits him to introduce evidence of the mental disorder that gave rise to his belief in the need for self-defense, and precluded him from actually harboring malice. If section 28(a) is viewed in isolation, this construction is logically defensible. However, it is unsustainable when considered in light of the statutory scheme governing evidence of mental illness, and the legislative history of section 28....

Under California's statutory scheme, persons who are mentally incapacitated are deemed unable to commit a crime as a matter of law. §26. Mental incapacity under section 26 is determined by the *M'Naghten* test for legal insanity provided in section 25(b). *M'Naghten's Case*, 8 Eng. Rep. 718, 722 (1843). Under *M'Naghten*, a defendant unable either to understand the nature and quality of the criminal act, or to distinguish right from wrong when the act was committed, is legally insane. §25(b).

A claim of unreasonable self-defense based solely on delusion is quintessentially a claim of insanity under the *M'Naghten* standard of inability to distinguish right from wrong. Its rationale is that mental illness caused defendant to perceive an illusory threat, form an actual belief in the need to kill in self-defense, and act on that belief without wrongful intent. In *M'Naghten's Case* itself, the judges observed: "If under the influence of a delusion defendant supposes another man to be in the act of attempting to take away his life, and he kills that man, as he supposes, in self-defence, he would be exempt from punishment." *M'Naghten's Case,* 8 Eng. Rep. at 723. This example applies the right/wrong prong of *M'Naghten* to an insane delusion in the same manner as it is applied to other forms of insanity. The delusion results in an inability to appreciate that the act is wrong. Defendant believes he is defending himself.

Defendant attempted here to assert a claim of legal insanity at the guilt phase of his trial. That is not allowed under our statutes. Section 1026 sets out the applicable procedure when, as in this case, defendant pleads both not guilty and not guilty by reason of insanity. The trial is bifurcated, with the question of guilt tried first. Defendant is presumed innocent, but in order to reserve the issue of sanity for the second phase of trial, defendant is also conclusively presumed to have been legally sane at the time of the offense. §1026(a). Evidence of defendant's mental state may not be admitted at the guilt phase to prove insanity. §1020. If defendant is found guilty, the trial proceeds to the sanity phase, where defendant bears the burden of proof by a preponderance of the evidence. §§1026(a), 25(b). The separation of the two stages of the bifurcated trial is solely for the purpose of keeping the issues of guilt and sanity distinct; for other purposes, the trial is regarded as single and continuing. *Wells,* 33 Cal.2d at 349.

The jury should not be instructed on the presumption of sanity at the guilt phase, because the question of legal sanity is then irrelevant. The Legislature's intent in providing for bifurcation when a defendant pleads both not guilty and not guilty by reason of insanity was to *simplify* the issues before the jury, by removing entirely from the first stage of the trial any issue as to legal sanity. *Id.* at 352. Therefore, it is improper for the jury to weigh the presumption of sanity during deliberations on the question of guilt. *Ibid.* It is equally improper for the jury to consider whether defendant was legally insane under *M'Naghten.* Whether mental disease or defect prevented defendant from understanding the nature and quality of the criminal act, or appreciating its wrongfulness, are relevant only at a sanity trial.

Section 28(a) allows defendants to introduce evidence of mental disorder to show they did not actually form a mental state required for guilt of a charged crime. But the scope of the diminished actuality defense is limited by the presumption of sanity, which operates at a trial on the question of guilt to bar defendant from claiming he is not guilty *because he is legally insane.* This limitation was explored in *Wells.* Although *Wells* predated section 28, its analysis established the distinction between *actual* formation of a mental state and *capacity* to form a mental state that is now found in section 28(a).

Whenever a particular mental state, such as a specific intent, is by statute made an essential element of a crime, that specific state must be proved like any other fact. Since, however, the mental capacity to commit the crime—insofar as legal sanity is concerned—is conclusively presumed at the first section of the trial, it follows that the general rule must be deemed to be qualified to this extent: That evidence tending to show lack of mental capacity to commit the crime because of legal insanity is barred at that stage. This means that legal sanity is *not* in issue at the first stage of the trial and that the evidence must be confined to that which is pertinent to issues then being litigated. *Wells,* 33 Cal.2d at 350.

*Wells* explained that evidence challenging defendant's actual formation of a mental state is admissible, but only so long as it does not go toward a claim of legal insanity: As a general rule, on the not guilty plea, evidence tending to show that the defendant, who at this stage is conclusively presumed sane, either *did* or *did not,* in committing the overt act, possess the specific essential mental state, is admissible; but evidence tending to show legal sanity or legal insanity is not admissible. Thus, if the proffered evidence tends to show not merely that he *did* or *did not,* but rather that because of legal insanity he *could* not, entertain the essential mental state, then that evidence is inadmissible under the not guilty plea and is admissible only on the trial on the plea of not guilty by reason of insanity. Evidence which tends to show legal insanity (likewise, sanity) is not admissible at the first stage of the trial because it is not pertinent to any issue then being litigated; but competent evidence, other than proof of sanity or insanity, which tends to show that a (then presumed) legally sane defendant either did or did not in fact possess the required specific intent or motive is admissible. *Id* at 350–51; *see* §1020.

In 1981, the Legislature acted to preserve the bifurcated trial statutes and eliminate the defense of diminished capacity. At the same time the Legislature codified, in section 28(a), the distinction between capacity and actuality that was drawn in *Wells.* The following year, the voters adopted an initiative measure that again abolished the diminished capacity defense, and went further in the restoration of former law by reinstating the *M'Naghten* test for legal insanity. That standard had prevailed in California from the earliest days of our statehood until this court replaced it with an alternative formulation in *People v. Drew*, 22 Cal.3d 333, 345 (1978).

The current state of California law on the insanity defense and proof of the defendant's mental state is consistent with *Wells.* Accordingly, section 28(a) allowing evidence of diminished actuality is "qualified" by the caveat that at a trial on the question of guilt, "evidence tending to show lack of mental capacity to commit the crime because of legal insanity is barred." *Wells,* 33 Cal.2d at 350. *Wells* squarely rejected the idea that defendants have the right to present evidence of insanity at the guilt phase to persuade the jury they did not entertain a required mental state. "The force which otherwise would attach to [that] argument," said the court, "is obviated by the provisions for trial on the issue of not guilty by reason of insanity. We are satisfied that enactments providing for a bifurcated trial and a presumption of sanity at the guilt phase are a valid exercise of legislative power and that the evidence to be received at the first stage of the trial properly excludes evidence tending to show either sanity or insanity." *Id.* at 353. The United States Supreme Court has confirmed that state law does not violate due process by "restricting consideration of defense evidence of mental illness and incapacity to its bearing on a claim of insanity, thus eliminating its significance directly on the issue of the mental element of the crime charged." *Clark v. Arizona*, 548 U.S. 735, 742 (2006).

The bifurcated approach offers substantial benefits to the defense. At the guilt phase, the prosecution must prove beyond a reasonable doubt each element of the offense, including *mens rea*. Defendant can obtain an acquittal or a verdict on a lesser included offense without having to claim insanity and risk the prospect of involuntary commitment for psychiatric treatment. The defense has available the panoply of strategies open to legally sane defendants, including unreasonable self-defense based on mistake of fact. It may choose to put on no evidence, or it may introduce any relevant and admissible evidence on the question of guilt. If defendant is found not guilty, the trial is over. If there is a conviction, the trial moves to the second phase, devoted to the question of legal sanity. There defendant bears the burden of proof by a preponderance of the evidence, and may be found not guilty by reason of insanity. This process affords the defense two chances at a favorable verdict.

But the defense cannot litigate the question of legal sanity at both phases. Defendant is presumed sane at the guilt phase, and cannot introduce evidence of insanity to counter the prosecution's showing of *mens rea*. A claim of self-defense based solely on delusion is more than a claim of unreasonable self-defense; as we have shown, it is a claim of legal insanity. If section 28(a) were applied to allow defendant to make that claim at the guilt phase, the burden would shift to the prosecution to prove beyond a reasonable doubt that defendant was not insane. The statutory scheme would be turned on its head.

The evidence of a defendant's mental state at the guilt and sanity phases may be overlapping. But the extent of the overlap is limited by the rule that defendant's sanity is *irrelevant* at the guilt phase and evidence tending to prove insanity, as opposed to the absence of a particular mental element of the offense, is *inadmissible.* Defendant may employ mental state evidence in different ways at the guilt and sanity phases, but may not make the same showing twice. The diminished capacity defense allowed the duplication of evidence at the guilt and sanity phases to approach a totality. As noted above, the statutory amendments of 1981 and 1982 abolished that practice and effectively endorsed the distinctions and restrictions delineated in *Wells.* Among those restrictions is the rule that "insanity is either a complete defense or it is no defense at all." *Wells,* 33 Cal.2d at 349.

Accordingly, a claim of delusional belief in the need for self-defense is reserved for the sanity phase, where it may result in *complete exoneration* from criminal liability. *M'Naghten's Case,* 8 Eng. Rep. at 723. It may not be employed to *reduce* a defendant's degree of guilt. When the Legislature enacted section 28, it certainly did not intend to allow defendants to argue first that their mental condition made them guilty of a lesser crime, and then that the same condition made them not guilty at all by reason of insanity.

Our construction of section 28(a) has no effect on evidence of mental disorders that do not amount to legal insanity. A defendant may suffer from a diagnosable mental illness without being legally insane under *M'Naghten.* All relevant evidence of mental states short of insanity is admissible at the guilt phase under section 28(a), including evidence bearing on unreasonable self-defense. The *M'Naghten* test is a narrow one. It is only when mental illness is manifested in delusions which render the individual incapable either of knowing the nature and character of his act, or of understanding that it is wrong, that he is legally insane under the California formulation of *M'Naghten.*

Furthermore, our holding does not prevent the defense from presenting evidence of mental disease, defect, or disorder to support a claim of unreasonable self-defense based on a mistake of fact. A defendant who misjudges the external circumstances may show that mental disturbance contributed to the mistaken perception of a threat, without presenting the jury with the same question it would confront at a sanity trial. The jury must find there was an actual, unreasonable belief in the necessity of self-defense based on the circumstances, and it should be so instructed. *People v. Tewksbury*, 15 Cal.3d 953, 963 (1976). An insanity defense, on the other hand, requires no showing that defendant responded to objective circumstances. At a sanity trial, and only at a sanity trial, the defense can maintain that purely delusional perceptions caused the defendant to believe in the necessity of self-defense.

In sum, defendants who mistakenly believed that actual circumstances required their defensive act may argue they are guilty only of voluntary manslaughter, even if their reaction was distorted by mental illness. But defendants who contend they killed in self-defense because of a purely delusional perception of threat must make that claim at a sanity trial. Unreasonable self-defense and legal insanity are distinct theories, and must be adjudicated separately.

Here, defendant's claim of unreasonable self-defense was based entirely on a delusional mental state that amounted to legal insanity. The trial court properly denied his request for an instruction on unreasonable self-defense.

### III. DISPOSITION

We affirm the Court of Appeal's judgment.

CANTIL-SAKAUTE, C.J., BAXTER AND CHIN, JJ., concur.

[The separate opinion of Justice KENNARD, concurring and dissenting, joined by Justices WERDEGAR and LIU, is omitted].

## QUESTIONS ON *ELMORE*

**1. Bifurcated trials.** Much is made in *Elmore* about "bifurcated" trials. First, what is bifurcated from what? And second, to what end?

**2. Mistakes and reasonableness.** In Section II.B of *Elmore* we're told: "a mistake of fact is predicated upon a negligent perception of facts, not, as in the case of a delusion, a perception of facts not grounded in reality." What is the difference between a non-operative "delusional mistake" on the one hand and an operative, yet "unreasonable mistake" on the other? Is this distinction, if tenable, an inner-outer one, that is, a distinction that sets apart the privacy of thought from the public observable world?

3. **Diminished actuality and imperfect self-defense.** Diminished capacity is kaput, survived by diminished actuality, which plays what role, if any, in a bifurcated trial featuring a plea of imperfect self-defense?

4. **Burdens: confession and avoidance v. denial.** Who has the burden of persuasion to prove what, exactly, when a defendant's sanity is in play?

## NOTES ON *ELMORE*

*1. Remand from the state high court.* The Court of Appeal found error in the trial judge's failure to instruct on the legal effect of Elmore's hallucinations. *Cf. People v. Padilla*, 103 Cal.App.4th 675 (2002) [evidence of hallucination is not admissible to negate malice aforethought, but is admissible on whether the killer acted with deliberation and premeditation]; CALJIC No. 8.73.1 [same]. This aspect of the Court of Appeal's ruling in *Elmore* was not challenged by the Attorney General in the state high court. Consequently, back in the L.A. Superior Court (Compton) on remand, seven-plus years from the April 29, 2007 stabbing, Charles Elmore suffered a judgment of conviction on September 10, 2014, this time for second-degree murder (having been convicted in the prior trial of first-degree murder). Elmore was re-sentenced to 15 years to life, having gotten 25 years to life in the prior trial.

*2. The grammar of mistakes.* Like accidents, mistakes are operative excuses unless the legislature intended "strict liability," which it may do only if the punishment for the offense is mild or the offense is not a *malum in se* (pre-legal) wrong. *See supra* Chapter 2.B, Introduction. In other words, when accusing someone of doing something a good person would not do, the accused must be given a chance to elaborate the factual background of the act. Accusations of being a "common thief" (a pre-legal wrong) or that threaten lengthy prison sentences (a proxy for a pre-legal wrong) obligate courts to hear the accused's story about how the action misfired. Within those stories, mistakes of fact generally excuse the accused, whereas mistakes of law generally do not. Likewise, with general-intent offenses, mistakes must be reasonable to get the accused off the hook, whereas with specific-intent offenses, so-called unreasonable mistakes suffice. *See People v. Russell*, 144 Cal.App.4th 1415, 1425-27 (2006).

For example, self-defenders who unnecessarily but reasonably respond forcibly to perceived threats are mistaken about facts, which, if as perceived, would render the action noncriminal. *Commonwealth v. Scott*, 73 A.3d 599 (Pa. 2013). The same can be said of accused rapists, *People v. Mayberry*, 15 Cal.3d 143, 155 (Cal. 1975), whose mistake about consent negates the wrongfulness, but not the harmfulness, of the act. And when age is an element of a crime, as in sex with a minor, a mistake of fact—taking a minor for an adult— excuses the accused. *People v. Hernandez*, 393 P.2d 673 (Cal. 1964).

An illustration of a plea of mistake of fact is *Flippo v. State*, *supra* Chapter 1.B. Recall that father and son were hunting out of season in the woods of Lawrence County, Arkansas, where in the poor visibility of dusk, Bobby fatally shot Roy Ralph Sharp, a 225-pound man whom Bobby took for a deer from 140 yards away. Evidence suggested the fatal shot ricocheted off a low branch obscuring Sharp, whose death was hastened by the Flippos' delay in summoning help. Properly understood, Bobby's defense in his manslaughter trial was that he shot Sharp by mistake. Concluding that Bobby's aim was good, but that he aimed at and shot an improvident target, the jury convicted him for his gross negligence in hunting out of season from considerable distance when "not sure of his target."

Bobby's plea of mistake was rejected; while Sharp might have been taken for a deer, he was not shot "by mistake." For if he had been, there would be nothing to do but excuse Bobby for the killing.

While whether Sharp was man or deer was clearly an issue surrounding an historical fact, absent an authoritative pronouncement of law in force before the act in question, mistakes of *law* are entertained as excuses only if the statute is specifically designed to that end. *United States v. Barker*, 546 F.2d 940, 947 (D.C. Cir. 1976). An example of such a statute is in *Cheek v. United States*, 498 U.S. 192 (1991), where an American Airlines pilot argued he did not "willfully evade taxes" because he owed no taxes, given his baseless belief that the Internal Revenue Code did not treat wages as income. Although mistake or ignorance of law is normally no excuse, in this case Congress had built the excuse into the text of the statute by requiring not just a failure to pay tax, but a *willful* failure, which could occur only with Cheek's knowledge of his obligation to pay tax. Had Congress intended otherwise, the statute would refer merely to a failure to pay tax, not a willful failure. The Supreme Court agreed, "as incredible as such misunderstandings of and beliefs about the law might be."

The source of Cheek's beliefs? A group of lawyers, who conducted seminars denouncing the federal tax system as unconstitutional and declaring wages as non-income. The high court's solution was to order a new trial at which the trial court was barred from imposing a reasonableness requirement on Cheek's beliefs about the Internal Revenue Code.

Notably absent in *Flippo* and *Cheek* is any consideration of *why* each believed what they did: who would take a man for a deer at 140 yards, or at any distance for that matter? Where were the target's telltale antlers, tail, and spindly legs? *See supra* Chapter 1.B, question 3 on *Flippo*. And if wages aren't income, then what are they? How can a pilot earn a big salary for two decades and continue to believe his wages aren't income, even after repeatedly litigating the issue without success, once suffering Rule 11 sanctions to boot?[d] *Cheek v. Doe*, 828 F.2d 395 (7th Cir. 1987).

Mistakes involve the idea of a wrong alternative—taking one thing for another or taking one path rather than another. J.L. Austin's donkey examples are right on point here. Those examples pose that your donkey and mine graze together in a field until, having grown too weary of my donkey, I decide to do it in. In the first case, when I raise my rifle, aim, and shoot arrow-straight, the beast falls down dead. But on inspection of the victim, I'm stunned see that it is your donkey I've shot, not mine. And so I appear on your stoop to explain, but how? That I've shot your donkey by accident? Or by mistake? In the second case, just as I raise my rifle, aim, and shoot at what *really is* my donkey, the donkeys move. Again it is yours that falls down dead. When this time I show up on your stoop to make amends, what excuse do I proffer? That I've shot your donkey by accident? Or by mistake?

---

[d] On remand, after the *pro se* Cheek filed eccentric pre-trial motions, the trial court instructed jurors to acquit Cheek if he believed wages weren't income; the court also instructed jurors to judge the genuineness of a belief by its reasonableness. The Seventh Circuit upheld the subsequent re-conviction, after which Cheek was sentenced to 366 days in prison, which led American Airlines to deny him a leave of absence, instead firing him (after 20 years on the job) for his imminent unavailability to fly. Cheek lost a suit to get his job back, served six months in prison followed by three more in a Salvation Army half-way house in Chicago, and never worked for American again, a disposition evidently justified by the airline's collective-bargaining agreement with its pilots.

J.L. Austin, *A Plea for Excuses*, in Philosophical Papers, *supra*, at 185 n.1. With accidents, something befalls ("I didn't mean to shoot a donkey—any donkey"—or "that was not the donkey I was aiming at"). Daniel Yeager, *What Is an Accident?*, 51 Criminal Law Bulletin 575 (2015). With mistakes, you take the wrong one when you have both the competence and commitment to take the right one ("I meant to shoot that donkey, but thought it was mine, not yours").

Neither Cheek nor Flippo made a mistake, even though both took one thing for another. If getting things right is unlikely, guesswork, or random, then getting them wrong is not by mistake. Only if you have knowledge in the first place can your knowledge fail and count as a mistake as opposed to a wrong belief owing to something—carelessness, recklessness, fantasy, delusion—other than mistake. When you make a mistake, you mean to do exactly what you do, at least to a point. It is just that you misinterpret your situation: you take someone else's property for yours, a minor for an adult, silence for consent, a harmless prank for a deadly threat.

> [S]uppose the order is 'Right turn' and I turn left: no doubt the sergeant will insinuate that my attention was distracted, or that I cannot distinguish my right from my left—but it was not and I can, this was a simple, pure mistake. As often happens. Neither I nor the sergeant will suggest that there was any accident, or any inadvertence either.

J.L. Austin, *A Plea for Excuses*, in Philosophical Papers, *supra*, at 200 n.1, 201-02. A mistake can be made only by someone who could have gotten it right, tried to get it right, but failed—not by someone who can get it right only randomly or cares little about getting it right. For example, if you tell me "fetch my umbrella," and on seeing several in the designated area I grab an umbrella clueless as to which is yours, I am not mistaken if it turns out to be someone else's.

First, for me to fetch the wrong umbrella by mistake, I would need a basis for knowing which one is yours. If I am merely guessing, then mistake drops out as a description of what goes wrong. It would be eccentric for me to say "I made a mistake" after guessing the wrong lottery numbers. When success is only random, mistake is never the explanation of the unhappy outcome.

Second, even if I have reason to know which umbrella is yours, if I grab just any old umbrella, then you might have been mistaken to rely on me to fetch it for you by taking me for considerate and careful. But my lack of commitment to take the right one precludes my explaining that I have taken the wrong umbrella by mistake. I cannot fail at something at which I have not even tried. Incompetent or indifferent agents do not make mistakes. Instead, they fumble around, their failures predictable and their successes dumb luck. Indeed, that only a competent, committed agent may make a mistake explains why it is such a good excuse.

Although mistakes are by definition reasonable, lawyers see the matter differently, consigning *all* wrong beliefs to mistakes, calling some reasonable and the rest unreasonable. See Paul H. Robinson & Jane A. Grall, *Element Analysis in Defining Criminal Liability: The Model Penal Code and Beyond*, 35 Stanford Law Review 681, 725-32 (1983). Under such a view, unreasonable mistakes can excuse, inter alia, attempt, theft, and burglary, and can partially excuse murder. *See, e.g., People v. Braslaw*, 233 Cal.App.4th 1239, 1249-51 (2015). According to the Model Penal Code, unreasonable mistakes are at worst reckless and at best negligent. In other words, actions based on faulty, poorly formed beliefs are partially excused under the Code. The residue of the action—that which is *not* excused—is a criticism of the belief itself. As a result, a killing done in the unreasonable belief that it was necessary would not be murder, but manslaughter (if the mistake was reckless) or negligent homicide (if the mistake was negligent). MPC §3.09(2).

Significantly, Code text and commentary contain just a single example of such a situation: in a footnote borrowed from Glanville Williams, who identifies voluntary intoxication and any other "abnormal mental state" as the "only common situation in which a person makes an unreasonable mistake." MPC & Commentaries §3.09(2), at 152 n.10 (1980). This, even though intoxication is already an extant, separate excuse. MPC §2.08.

In California, which has not adopted the Model Penal Code, an unreasonable mistake of fact

> is predicated upon a negligent perception of facts, not, as in the case of a delusion, a perception of facts not grounded in reality. A person acting under a delusion is not negligently interpreting actual facts; instead, he or she is out of touch with reality. That may be insanity, but it is not a mistake as to any fact.

*Mejia-Lenares*, 135 Cal.App.4th at 1453-54 [murder conviction upheld, though no mistake instruction given at trial, for stabbing man whom defendant hallucinated was turning into devil]. As *Elmore* noted, no state recognizes delusion as a defense except within a claim of insanity. Actions based on misguided beliefs that are not correctible with more information are based on delusion or fantasy, not mistake.

Illusions can be the basis of mistakes; delusions cannot. Illusions include when a ventriloquist's dummy appears to talk, amputees feel pain in lost limbs, or a straight stick looks bent in water. It is not that something unreal is conjured up. That would be a delusion, as in "delusions of persecution or ... of grandeur." J.L. Austin, Sense and Sensibilia 23 (Oxford 1962). Because delusions "can be ... without foundation," they "are a much more serious matter—something is really wrong, ... wrong with the person who has them." *Id.* at 23-24. There is nothing wrong with someone who falls for an optical illusion. "It is quite public, anyone can see it," and we can develop procedures for testing it. *Id.* Because "[w]e are not ... quasi-infallible beings who can be taken in only where the avoidance of mistake is completely impossible," *id.* at 52, "if we are not ... to be taken in, we need to be *on our guard*; but it is no use to tell the sufferer from delusions to be on his guard. He needs to be cured." *Id.* at 24.

Even after separating the excuse of mistake from the excuse of delusion, borderline cases remain. For example, ghosts may be conjured up in the mind (delusion) or they may be just a giving-in to "shadows, or reflections, or a trick of the light" (illusion). *Id.* So too can we characterize a mirage as "conjured up by the crazed brain of the thirsty and exhausted traveler (delusion)" or as "a case of atmospheric refraction, whereby something below the horizon is made to appear above it (illusion)." *Id.* at 24-25.

If a defendant "who makes a factual mistake misperceives the objective circumstances," while a "delusional defendant holds a belief that is divorced from the circumstances," *Elmore*, 325 P.3d at 960, what, then, is objectively verifiable in the *unreasonable* mistake? If someone "who misjudges the external circumstances may show that mental disturbance"—not amounting to insanity—"contributed to the mistaken perception of a threat," *id.* at 966-67, what lies between the non-excuse of delusion and the operative excuse of "mental disturbance"? It makes only misleading sense to state that such "persons operating under a mistake of fact are reasonable people who have simply made an unreasonable mistake." *Mejia-Lenares*, 135 Cal.App.4th at 1456.

An illustration of a claim of unreasonable mistake owing to a mental affliction not amounting to insanity is *People v. Wells*, 202 P.2d

53 (Cal. 1949), discussed in *Elmore, supra.* After his boisterousness got him kicked out of his disciplinary hearing at Folsom State Prison, Wells stewed in the hall until erupting by heaving a spittoon at guards, seriously injuring the one who had initiated the hearing. *Id.* at 58-59. (As you know, Wells said he accidentally inflicted the guard's injuries during a justified attempt to defend himself from a different guard, who had unjustifiably struck him with a baton. *Ibid.*). Two days earlier, a prison doctor, "impressed" by Wells's "apparently abnormal state," had him examined by a psychiatrist, who found him in a "state of tension" where "the whole body and mind are in a state of high sensitivity to external stimuli, . . . causing [him] to react abnormally to situations. . . ." *Id.* at 62. A symptom of this state is "an abnormal fear for his personal safety and that an external stimulus apparently threatening that personal safety will cause the patient to react to it more violently and more unpredictably than the same stimulus applied to a normal person." *Ibid.*

The trial court excluded testimony about the affliction, which Wells had hoped would fully or partially excuse the aggravated assault. On appeal from his conviction, the California Supreme Court studied his dossier of in-prison scuffles, none smacking of intense psychological perturbations. Without taking a position on the psychology of a heightened state of fear accounting for an unreasonable but non-delusional over-reaction to stress, the high court concluded that the excluded evidence was just a pose by Wells that the jury would have seen right through. *Id.* at 70. At bottom, Wells was recasting his anger at the guard as a mental issue, a real no-no as defensive strategies go in California, where anger is not considered a "mental defect or disease." *See Spurlin, supra* Chapter 3.A.

Unsurprisingly, a solid example of an unreasonable mistake, or what some dub "extreme mistake," Jerome Hall, General Principles of Criminal Law 592 (2d ed. 1960), has yet to show up anywhere. Even poor examples are few. *People v. Gregory*, 124 Cal.Rptr.2d 776, 795 (5th Dist. Ct. App. 2002) [citing cases of unreasonable mistake while upholding guilty plea of schizophrenic]. Those include a home-invader "defending" himself therein by killing a random 79-year-old woman with a claw hammer in the presence of police—a self-authenticating instance of delusion, not of a reasonable person lapsing into unreasonably "making a mistake." *People v. Hardin*, 102 Cal.Rptr.2d 262 (1st Dist. Ct. App. 2000). Also held out as unreasonable mistakes are cases better understood as straight-up provocation (as where a defendant in mutual combat over the victim's wife resorts to a fatal stabbing), *Seidel v. Merkle*, 146 F.3d 750 (9th Cir. 1998), or perfect self-defense (as where years of abuse evidenced by Battered Women's Syndrome leads defendant to shoot her sleeping abuser-husband on the very evening he had threatened to kill her), *DePetris v. Kuykendall*, 239 F.3d 1057 (9th Cir. 2001). No wonder New York repudiated the unreasonable-mistake category in its version of the Model Penal Code. *People v. Goetz*, 497 N.E.2d 41, 49-50 (N.Y. 1986); *see also People v. Reese*, 815 N.W.2d 85, 98-99 & n.62 (Mich. 2012) [purporting to follow Vermont and New Jersey in repudiating imperfect self-defense].

# CHAPTER 4

# Inchoate Criminality as Partial Excuse

## A. THE *MENS REA* OF ATTEMPT

So far we have been concerned with harm-causing wrongdoing. With the possible exception of justified acts, such as those taken in self-defense, *all* harm-causing is wrongdoing. But not all wrongdoing is harm-causing. Here I'm not referring to so-called moral harms such as gambling, prostitution, or smoking pot. Instead I'm referring to inchoate, anticipatory, or non-consummated offenses, which betray what Professor Fletcher calls criminals' "subjective" (intended) or "manifest" (expressed), but not their actual, or harm-causing, criminality. *See* George Fletcher, *Constructing a Theory of Impossible Attempts*, 5 Criminal Justice Ethics 52, 66 (1986) [unlawful possession may be viewed as inchoate]; George Fletcher, *Rethinking Criminal Law* 124-32 (1978) [assault and burglary may be viewed as inchoate]. Other risk-based offenses that do wrong without harm are reckless endangerment, see MPC §211.2, or driving under the influence. *See* Texas Penal Code §49.04 (Vernon's 2011).

Our study of inchoate, anticipatory, or non-consummated offenses focuses on attempt, solicitation, conspiracy, and complicity. Each of these offenses—failing, requesting, agreeing, and helping—is best seen as a partial excuse. Specifically, putting oneself to crime is punishable, but failing to actually bring about the intended crime (or at least failing to bring it about *oneself*) operates to reduce the failed actor's responsibility for what was done, in that there is less to be responsible for.

If we begin with two people who are doing the same thing or who mean to do the same thing, to what extent is our sense of their responsibility influenced by how things turn out? If you and I both back our cars out of our driveways carelessly, what difference does it make in a responsibility-sense if a child darts behind and is fatally struck by my car but not by yours? For Judith Thomson, we are equally "bad persons." Judith Jarvis Thomson, *Morality and Bad Luck*, 20 Metaphilosophy 203, 213 (1989). She would say the same thing were we both to put ourselves to committing theft, and while we both get caught, you fail at theft by luckily picking on a victim who is broke, whereas my victim hands over to me a pile of cash just before I am arrested for having unluckily completed grand larceny. Were neither of us to be caught, then I would be the lucky one when my intentions are realized in a successful theft and yours are not. For Thomson, a difference in outcome such as this "says nothing morally interesting" about either of us. *Id.* at 212. Thomson is not alone. *E.g.*, Joel Feinberg, *Equal Punishments for Failed Attempts: Some Bad but Instructive Arguments against It*, 37 Arizona Law Review 117 (1995); Steven Sverdlik, *Crime and Moral Luck*, 25 American Philosophical Quarterly 79 (1988).

If human action which causes harm says nothing morally interesting about us that human action which avoids causing harm does not, then what *does* the difference in outcomes say about us, except maybe that morality is not all that matters? "Nothing" is the answer from the "reformist" position that has become known as "equivalency," which treats chancy outcomes that are outside our control as invariant to responsibility. Sverdlik, *supra*, at 79. Without endorsing the equivalency position, R.A. Duff does not exactly clear things up when he observes that

> [t]he equivalence theorist does not argue that the actual outcome of an action should make *no* difference to our response to the action or its agent, even if that actual outcome is to a significant degree a matter of luck; she allows that actual outcomes matter to us, and can properly affect our responses in various ways. She does argue, however, that we must distinguish our judgments of an agent's *culpability*, and the responses that directly express or depend on such judgments (blaming or morally condemning the agent, most obviously), from other kinds of response: whilst those other responses may be properly determined in part by matters of outcome-luck, judgments of culpability, and those that reflect them, should be independent of outcome-luck.

R.A. Duff, Criminal Attempts 335 (Oxford 1997). This I take to mean that "blame," an aspect of "culpability," ignores the significance of outcomes (e.g., whether the putative theft victim has or parts with any property), though these outcomes may in some unspecified way be relevant or interesting to us or somehow part of "our response to the action or its agent." Duff does not elaborate.

We punish inchoate criminality for one reason alone: its relation to crime-in-fact. Soliciting crime, conspiring to commit crime, trying but failing to commit crime, and helping crime are punishable acts *only* because of their relationship with, or tendency to lead to or bring about, "real" crime. Inchoate crimes draw their authority from the harms they threaten, but which may or may not actually occur. When someone is accused of soliciting, conspiring, trying, or helping to commit crime "*X*," the actor's criminality is evaluated in relation to a crime that did not (attempt) or need not (solicitation, conspiracy, complicity) occur. Since the other crime that gives the inchoate criminal's actions their contemptible quality is not committed at all (when the planning stages stall or misfire) or is committed by someone else, it makes sense to see the legal operation of planning, failure, and help as traceable to the partial excuses.

For example, when charged with solicitation, conspiracy, attempt, or complicity, a defendant may respond with one of three exculpatory pleas: "But I did not do '*X*' (the target offense), I did something else: I merely requested, conspired, tried, or helped to do '*X*.'" Or, "I meant to help crime '*Y*'—the principal departed from the common scheme or plan and did '*X*' all on his own." Or, finally, in response to any of these charges except that of attempt he may say, "But *I* did not do '*X*,' someone else did." These pleas would be pleas for partial excuse. Yet "few excuses get us out of it *completely*: the average excuse, in a poor situation, gets us only out of the fire into the frying pan—but still, of course, any frying pan in a fire." J.L. Austin, *A Plea for Excuses*, *supra*, at 177.

American law largely rejects equivalency. Still, American law always treats requesting, planning, trying, or helping crime as criminal, and sometimes treats them as morally identical or adjacent to actually completing the crime yourself. An equivalency regime meant to express an unwavering risk-basis of liability would ignore outcomes and punish equally the defendant who puts the razor blade that is discovered in the Halloween apple prior to its being bitten into and the defendant whose intended victim bites into the apple and suffers greatly. Accordingly, a risk-based regime would be concerned mostly with subjective or manifest (as opposed to harm-causing) criminality, and as such would tend mostly to prevent *potentially* harmful actions. This is why Joel Feinberg says that he would eliminate the crimes of murder and attempted murder in favor of his invariant-to-outcomes invention: "Wrongful Homicidal Behavior." Joel Feinberg, *Equal Punishments for Failed Attempts, supra*, at 119-22. A harm-based regime, oppositely, would be concerned mostly with harm-causing or outcome-oriented criminality, and, as such, would tend to condemn only harm-in-fact.

As an illustration of the workings of harm and risk rationales, consider California's law of attempt. Although California and the Model Penal Code have similarly phrased laws of attempt, California punishes attempts half as severely as completed offenses (which betokens a harm-orientation), whereas the Model Penal Code punishes some attempts just like it does completed offenses (which betokens a risk-orientation). When it comes to solicitation and conspiracy, both California and the Model Penal Code indicate a harm-orientation by allowing punishment only for the attempted *or* completed offense *or* its underlying request *or* agreement, but, in any event, *only* one offense of the four from which, on some facts, the prosecutor may present to jurors.

A truly harm-based regime would never punish for inchoate offenses. Indeed, a regime that punishes *any* attempts, solicitations, or conspiracies is at least *a bit* risk-based. There is no shortage of rhetoric in the Model Penal Code about manifest criminality—about the primacy of intentions that are put into action (successfully or not) rather than outcomes in assessing blame: "where failure is due to a fortuity, like a misfired gun or a recalcitrant solicited party, exculpation on that ground would involve inequality of treatment that would shock the common sense of justice. Such a situation is unthinkable in any mature system designed to serve the proper goals of penal law." MPC & Commentaries, *Introduction to Article 5*, at 294 (1980). Despite the rhetoric, when push comes to shove, the Code's equivalency position is abandoned for a compromise position on the importance of harm. While the Code purports to treat success, failure, planning, and carrying those plans out as equally blameworthy matters, it refuses to treat serious crimes that way. Thus, soliciting or conspiring to commit theft is punished identically to theft, but soliciting or conspiring to commit rape is punished less severely than rape. MPC §5.05(1). I do not see the makings of a unifying theory there.

Having set forth the rationale for inchoate criminality, we turn now to the grammar or elements of the laws of a) attempt, b) solicitation, c) conspiracy, and d) complicity. First, attempts. Attempts require substantial steps (or direct but ineffectual acts) which demonstrate the actor's intention to complete the offense. Our first case on point, *People v. Bond*, 178 Ill.App.3d 959 (1989), addresses how criminal law separates actors who try but fail to complete their criminal plan (and so are guilty of attempt) from those who 1) do not quite intend the prohibited harm that was risked; or 2) do intend the prohibited harm, but don't take it far enough (and so are not guilty of attempt). Here, *if* Bond was bent on killing, then he went about it in a way reasonably suited to that end. But was he really bent on killing?

## APPELLATE COURT OF ILLINOIS
## FOURTH DISTRICT

*THE PEOPLE OF THE STATE OF ILLINOIS, PLAINTIFF-APPELLEE*

*V.*

*JACKEY LEE BOND, DEFENDANT-APPELLANT*

JAN. 26, 1989

KNECHT, Judge

The defendant, Jackey Lee Bond, was charged by information in the circuit court of Macon County with two counts of attempted murder and two counts of unlawful use of a weapon by a felon. The circuit court dismissed the second count of attempted murder as to Ferita Sharee Hayes on defendant's motion for directed verdict at the close of the State's case. At the conclusion of the bench trial, the circuit court found defendant guilty of the first count of attempted murder as to Clara Lamb and the two counts of unlawful use of a weapon by a felon. Defendant was sentenced to one term of seven years and two terms of three years of imprisonment to be served concurrently. Defendant contends on appeal the State failed to prove him guilty of the charged offenses beyond a reasonable doubt. We disagree.

The following facts are not in dispute: On April 28, 1987, Sheila Hayes (Hayes) called defendant to tell him their daughter, Ferita Sharee Hayes (Ferita), was sick. After her call, she visited defendant at his house at 1019 North Folk Street in Decatur. Hayes requested assistance with expenses for medicine and transportation for a 1 p.m.

doctor appointment. In response, defendant gave Hayes some money for medicine and promised to attempt to arrange transportation to the doctor.

Around noon, a friend, Clara Lamb (Lamb), drove Hayes and Ferita back to defendant's house. Since there were two cars parked in front of defendant's house, Lamb parked her car across the street. Hayes got out of the car and walked up to the house. Lamb and Ferita remained in the car. Defendant's girlfriend, Celestine Cunningham (Cunningham), answered the door. When she called defendant to the door, he told Hayes that he had not been able to arrange transportation.

The remaining facts are in dispute: defendant and Hayes then walked out to Lamb's car. Defendant asked Lamb whether she could drive Hayes and Ferita to the doctor. Lamb refused as she had to go to work. Defendant questioned Lamb's friendship, and Lamb responded she did not have enough gas for the drive. Defendant offered to pay for her gas. Lamb still refused and told defendant it was not her responsibility to solve the problem of transportation. An argument ensued between defendant and Lamb. The level of violence escalated in their argument. Their initial exchange of insults progressed to the throwing of objects and culminated in the firing of a weapon.

Lamb and Hayes testified defendant walked back into his yard, picked up two bricks, and threw them at Lamb's car. In response, Lamb picked up a bottle from the floorboard of her car, got out of her car, and threw it at one of the cars parked in front of defendant's house.

Defendant disputed their testimony. Defendant testified Lamb threw a bottle at him as he approached her car. In response, he picked up a brick and threw it at her car. Lamb then got out of her car, picked up the same brick, and threw it at one of the cars parked in front of his house.

Lamb testified defendant became upset after she threw the bottle at the car. She heard him say, "I'm going to shoot that bitch." As he went into his house, she also heard him say, "I'm going in the house and get my gun." Lamb then got in her car. As she was driving away, she heard a shot. Lamb turned and saw defendant standing in his yard. He was holding a handgun aimed at her car. She heard three or four more shots. One of the shots hit the rear door on the driver's side.

Hayes also testified defendant threatened Lamb. She heard him tell Lamb "he was going to go get his gun and shoot her." Defendant went into his house and brought out a handgun. He shot once in the air. At this, Hayes yelled at Lamb and Ferita to leave. Defendant then aimed at Lamb's car and fired three times as she drove away.

Defendant again disputed the testimony of Lamb and Hayes. He testified he walked into his house without saying anything to Lamb. Once inside his house he took a handgun out of Cunningham's purse. He then went outside with the handgun to scare Lamb into leaving his house. He did not aim or fire the gun at Lamb. He fired three or four times in the air. At this, Hayes told Lamb to leave. Lamb then got into her car and drove away.

The State corroborated the testimony of Lamb and Hayes with two occurrence witnesses. The first occurrence witness was Robin Hooker (Hooker). Hooker, defendant's next-door neighbor, was at home on April 28, 1987. Shortly before 1 p.m. she heard a car followed by yelling and four or five shots. Hooker assumed the sounds came from defendant's house.

The second occurrence witness was Harry Backus (Backus). Backus, a claims agent with Norfolk & Western Railway, worked at 1735 East Condit Street in Decatur. As Backus pulled into the parking lot entrance shortly before 1 p.m. on April 28, 1987, he noticed a man holding a handgun. The man stood in a yard approximately 150 feet to the northwest of Backus. He did not notice any other persons in the yard. Backus identified the man in court as defendant. He described defendant's position as being similar to a firing range stance. He saw defendant change his position to sight and fire four times at a car as it moved north on Folk Street.

The State also corroborated the testimony of Lamb and Hayes with physical evidence. In executing the search warrant, the Decatur police found weapons and ammunition at defendant's house. Police found three discharged .45 caliber cartridge cases on the front sidewalk east of defendant's house. The cases were positioned in a semi-circle spaced approximately two feet apart. They also found one discharged .45 caliber cartridge case a few feet from the front door. Inside defendant's house, police found an empty .45 caliber cartridge clip on a nightstand in the first floor bedroom. Finally, police found a purse containing two gun cases in the basement. The first case held a loaded .45 caliber handgun. The handgun was found cocked with one live round in the chamber and one live round in the clip. The second case held a .32 caliber handgun, .45 caliber ammunition, .38 caliber ammunition, .32 caliber ammunition, and two .45 caliber clips.

Decatur police also examined Clara Lamb's car. There were two damaged areas on the driver's side rear door of the car. The damage appeared to be new. The first damaged area was a dent with small particles of mortar or concrete brick scratched into the paint. The second damaged area was a gouge coated with a lead-like substance in some places.

Defendant also corroborated his testimony with an occurrence witness, Celestine Cunningham, who acknowledged ownership of the recovered purse and its contents. Cunningham testified she was holding the handguns as collateral for a loan to a friend. She also testified she had brought the handguns to defendant's house in her purse.

With this testimony, Cunningham recanted her police statement. In her police statement, Cunningham wrote: (1) she had not brought any handguns to defendant's house; (2) she did not know how the handguns got in her purse; (3) she had seen a .45 caliber handgun, or one like it, on defendant's dining room table in the previous month; (4) she had never before seen the .32 caliber handgun; (5) she had last seen her purse in the bathroom of defendant's house; and (6) she did not know how her purse got in the basement of defendant's house. Cunningham gave two reasons for the recantation of her police statement. She testified she was told by the police in the presence of an attorney to write lies to favor the prosecution. She also testified she would not have been allowed to go to work until her statement complied with what the prosecution wanted to hear.

Defendant first argues the State failed to prove he possessed the specific intent to kill. A conviction for attempted murder requires proof of the specific intent to kill. Intent refers to the state of mind of defendant at the time of the incident. It can rarely be proved by direct evidence. Intent may be inferred from the circumstances surrounding the incident, such as the character of the assault and the use of a deadly weapon. *People v. Jackiewicz*, 517 N.E.2d 316, 318 (Ill. App. Ct. 1987); *People v. Shields*, 127 N.E.2d 440, 443 (Ill. 1955).

The witnesses for the State testified to the following version of the incident: The incident occurred at defendant's residence in daylight. He escalated the level of violence in the argument with Lamb. After their initial exchange of insults had progressed into the throwing of objects, defendant threatened Lamb. He acted immediately on his threats. Defendant went into his house and brought out a handgun. He fired once in the air, assumed a firing range stance, and changed his position to sight and fire three or four times at Lamb as she drove away. A shot hit the rear door on the driver's side of her car.

Defendant, however, testified to a different version of the incident. He denied threatening Lamb. He contended that he brought the handgun outside to frighten Lamb. He also denied shooting at Lamb. He contended that he only fired the handgun in the air.

The physical evidence corroborates the testimony of the witnesses for the State. First, the pattern and placement of the discharged cartridge cases indicate the shooter aimed and fired at a moving target. Second, the rear door on the driver's side of Lamb's car had a gouge coated with a lead-like substance in some places. This gouge indicates the impact and path of a bullet.

In the prosecution of attempted murder, the trier of fact is to resolve questions of fact about whether the State has shown the specific intent to kill. The physical evidence indicates defendant's actions exceeded any attempt to merely frighten Lamb. If he had acted with only the intent to frighten Lamb, this physical evidence would not exist. Thus, State proved that defendant possessed the specific intent to kill.

Defendant also argues the inconsistencies in the testimony of the witnesses for the State rendered the evidence insufficient to convict him of attempted murder. A conviction will be reversed in a criminal case where the material evidence is found to be so improbable or unsatisfactory as to raise serious doubt of defendant's guilt.

There were inconsistencies in the testimony of the witnesses for both the prosecution and the defense. The witnesses changed their testimony after their police interview for their court appearance. The witnesses also changed their testimony between direct examination and cross-examination. The inconsistencies in the testimony of the witnesses rest on the following points: (1) who started the argument between defendant and Lamb; (2) who was the first to throw an object; (3) what objects were thrown by Lamb; (4) where were the objects thrown; (5) the location of the parties at the time of the shooting; (6) the number and direction of the shots fired by defendant; and (7) whether any of the shots hit Lamb's car.

Exact consistency in the testimony of the witnesses for each side is not required to establish guilt beyond a reasonable doubt. The trier of fact determines the credibility of witnesses, the weight accorded to testimony, and the inferences drawn from evidence. Given this function, a reviewing court will not substitute its judgment for that of the trier of fact on conflicts in the evidence.

To a degree, the inconsistencies are a result of the very nature of the incident. The incident happened quickly. It was one charged with emotion. Hayes and Lamb were both upset at the time of their interviews with the police. This accounts for some of the inconsistencies in the testimony. The remaining inconsistencies in the testimony are resolved by the physical evidence. The police found four discharged cartridge cases in the front yard of defendant's house. One cartridge case was found a few feet from the front door. This accounts for the shot defendant fired in the air. The other cartridge cases were found east of the sidewalk. The cartridge cases were positioned in a semicircle spaced approximately two feet apart. The pattern and placement of the cartridge cases indicates defendant aimed and fired three times at a moving target.

The police also examined Lamb's car. There were two newly damaged areas on the driver's side rear door of the car. The first damaged area was a dent with small particles of mortar or concrete brick scratched into the paint. This accounts for the brick thrown by defendant. The second damaged area was a gouge coated with a lead-like substance in some places. This indicates the impact and path of a bullet.

The inconsistencies in the testimony of the witnesses are minor in nature. Such minor inconsistencies "affect only the credibility and weight to be given the testimony, and not its sufficiency." *People v. Smith*, 500 N.E.2d 605, 609 (Ill. App. Ct. 1986). The evidence here was sufficient to sustain the conviction for attempted murder.

Defendant next argues the State failed to prove he knowingly possessed the recovered weapons. The State prosecuted defendant under §24-1.1 of the Criminal Code of 1961. Section 24-1.1(a) provides in pertinent part:

> It is unlawful for a person to knowingly possess on or about his person or on his land or in his own abode or fixed place of business any weapon prohibited under §24-1 of this Act or any firearm or any firearm ammunition if the person has been convicted of a felony under the laws of this State or any other jurisdiction.

Thus, the State is required to prove defendant's knowing possession of a prohibited weapon or ammunition and his prior felony conviction.

Criminal possession of weapons or ammunition may be either actual or constructive. *People v. Nunez*, 320 N.E.2d 462, 465 (Ill. App. Ct. 1974). The resolution of the issue of criminal possession turns on the credibility of the witnesses and the weight given their testimony. These are both matters for the trier of fact. *People v. Akis*, 347 N.E.2d 733, 734-35 (Ill. 1976). Defendant admitted to firing a handgun during the incident. This admission alone is sufficient proof of possession of a prohibited weapon and ammunition. Additional proof is supplied by the eyewitness accounts of Lamb, Hayes, and Backus. Despite this admission, defendant contends he did not possess the recovered weapons and ammunition, as Cunningham brought the items into his house. There is no evidence Cunningham had more claim to possession of the recovered weapons and ammunition than defendant. Cunningham's trial testimony was not credible. She gave a totally different account about the recovered weapons and ammunition at her police interview. Given this account, the circuit court could properly conclude Cunningham's trial testimony was fabricated to protect defendant.

Defendant also argues the State failed to prove his prior felony conviction. To sustain a conviction for unlawful use of weapons, the State must prove defendant's prior felony conviction beyond a reasonable doubt. *People v. Palmer*, 472 N.E.2d 795 (Ill. 1984). Defendant mistakenly contends the State offered the certified copy of his 1983 conviction for the felony offense of unlawful possession of cannabis for the sole purpose of impeachment. If this were the case, then defendant would be entitled to reversal of the two counts of unlawful use of a weapon by a felon. A defendant cannot be found guilty of felonious unlawful use of weapons where the trier of fact considers the prior conviction only for the purpose of impeachment. *People v. Edwards*, 345 N.E.2d 496 (Ill. 1976).

The State, however, offered the certified copy of defendant's 1983 conviction for the felony offense of unlawful possession of cannabis for both impeachment and substantive purposes. At the suppression hearing, the State offered into evidence, over defendant's objection, a certified copy of defendant's prior felony conviction. The circuit court admitted the certified copy of conviction into evidence for the sole purpose of impeachment. At trial, the State again offered into evidence a certified copy of defendant's prior felony conviction. The circuit court admitted the certified copy of conviction into evidence for substantive purposes without objection by the defense.

Defendant also mistakenly contends a certified copy of conviction bearing the same name as that of defendant is insufficient proof of his prior conviction. Such a contention is no longer viable in Illinois. Identity of name in a certified copy of prior conviction gives rise to a rebuttable presumption of identity of person. Given this presumption, the State's offer of a certified copy of defendant's prior conviction in the same court as the present offense is sufficient proof under section 24-1.1.

Affirmed.

McCULLOUGH, P.J., and LUND, J., concur.

## QUESTIONS ON *BOND*

1. **Constitutional right to trial by jury**. At the opening of Judge Knecht's unanimous opinion for the court, he notes that Bond's conviction was obtained in a bench trial: a trial conducted by a judge with no jury to hear evidence and find facts. The Sixth Amendment to the United States Constitution affords criminal defendants a right to trial by jury in all serious criminal cases, which the Supreme Court has defined as cases in which punishment of more than six months of incarceration is authorized by statute. *Baldwin v. New York*, 399 U.S. 66 (1970). Serious cases can be tried before a judge if defendant knowingly, intelligently, and voluntarily waives the right to trial by jury. E.g., *State v. Gore*, 288 Conn. 770 (2008).

    Why would a defendant waive the right to trial by jury?

2. **Concurrent sentences.** Bond received concurrent sentences. In his home state of Illinois, sentences run concurrent unless the sentencing judge says otherwise. *People ex rel. Gibson v. Cannon*, 345 N.E.2d 218 (Ill. App. Ct. 1976). The same is true in California. California Penal Code §669 (2012). In the federal system, the presumption of concurrency is reversed, whereby sentences run *consecutive* unless the judge says otherwise. 18 U.S.C.A. §3584(a) (1984). What runs concurrent or consecutive to what, and what does that mean in term of a defendant's total years served?

3. **Mens rea of attempt.** All crimes of attempt require specific intent, even those that would not require specific intent in a

prosecution for the completed offense had it succeeded, not failed. For example, rape is a crime of general intent, but attempted rape is a crime of specific intent. *United States v. Daniels*, 28 M.J. 743, 747 (Air Force Ct. of Military Rev. 1989). So too are arson and kidnapping crimes of general intent, though attempted arson and attempted kidnapping are crimes of specific intent. *People v. Atkins*, 18 P.3d 660, 668 (Cal. 2001). Had Bond fatally shot Lamb instead of just shooting her car, the prosecution would not need to prove that Bond had the specific intent to kill Lamb to convict him of negligent homicide, involuntary manslaughter, voluntary manslaughter, or even second-degree implied-malice murder.

Why, then, must the prosecution prove specific intent to kill in order to convict Bond of *attempted* murder?

**4. More on "other minds" and the problem of privacy.** Bond does not admit to having tried to kill Lamb. Given his claim to having "fired three or four times in the air" in order "to frighten Lamb," he does not even admit to having intentionally shot Lamb's car.

   **a.** If the prosecution must prove that killing Lamb was Bond's intention or plan, but he denies having had such an intention or plan, is the case stalemated? In other words, how are we to know what Bond intended apart from what he tells us? *See supra* Chapter 3.A, note 6 on *Greene*; Chapter 2.A, question 5 on *Watson*.

   **b.** It is possible to shoot an occupied car without intending at once to shoot its occupants, isn't it?

   **c.** Something must take the case from one in which a car gets shot to one in which the shooter attempts to murder an occupant of the car. Which disputed facts in the case must have been resolved in favor of the prosecution to support Bond's conviction of attempted murder of Lamb?

**5. Circumstantial evidence.** Courts find it fair to assume that people intend the natural and probable consequences of their actions. For example, in *Commonwealth v. O'Searo*, 466 Pa. 224 (1976), the state high court held that the jury could have properly inferred specific intent to kill on the part of defendant (Roy O'Searo), who used a dangerous weapon (a revolver) on a vital part of another's body (victim Francis Gadola's head). In so finding, the jury rejected defendant's contention that he harbored no intent to kill the victim, but only drew his weapon out of fear when a scuffle broke out between defendant and the victim.

Do people generally intend the natural and probable consequences of their actions? If so, what does that mean for the creditor—that he did in fact intend to ruin the debtor by demanding the just debt? *See supra* Chapter 2.A, Introduction. That there is no discernible difference between actions that are not intentional (reckless) and actions that are intentional?

**6. Intentional risk v. intentional harm.** Suppose a motorist drives 100 miles per hour on the wrong side of the road on a two-lane street with a posted speed limit of 35 miles per hour. He climbs a hill steep enough to obscure whether a car is coming up the hill from the other side in the same lane. Lucky for all, no car is coming as our motorist crests the hill. Soon after, the motorist, whose driving was observed by witnesses, is arrested. If a car had been coming the other way and collided with our motorist, thus causing the death of occupants of the other car, it is safe to say our motorist could be charged with murder.

But since on the facts originally posed no one dies, could our motorist be charged with attempted murder?

**7. Doubly inchoate offenses.** As you know, some states define assault as intentionally placing another person in immediate fear of bodily injury. Those states define battery as intentionally inflicting bodily injury on another person. *E.g., Adams v. Commonwealth*, 534 S.E.2d 347, 350-51 (Va. Ct. App. 2000). Other states define assault as an attempted battery, with battery being, again, intentionally inflicting bodily injury on another person. *E.g., Goodall v. State*, 627 S.E.2d 183, 186 (Ga. Ct. App. 2006).

**a.** In those states where assault is defined as an attempted battery, could there be such a thing as attempted assault? Or is that tantamount to attempted attempt? If it is, then what's wrong with that? *See Rome v. Guillory*, 335 Fed.Appx. 425, 428 (5th Cir. 2009); *supra* Chapter 2.B, note 2a on *Whitfield*; *infra* note 7 on *Decker*.

**b.** Attempted murder is clearly a crime. So is attempted voluntary manslaughter. Attempted *involuntary* manslaughter, however, is not. *E.g., Stennet v. State*, 564 So.2d 95 (Alabama Ct. App. 1990). Why not?

# Chapter 4: Inchoate Criminality as Partial Excuse | 221

**8. The continuum from preparation to attempt.** Knowing what gestures toward crime go far enough to count as attempts is no easy task. Nor do legal formulations pointing to steps that are "direct but ineffectual" (California) or "substantial" (MPC) help much. One way of sorting this out is by choosing between a notion of attempt that emphasizes how much the actor has already done versus how much remains to be done. *E.g., State v. Daniel B.*, 137 A.3d 837, 845-48 (Conn. App. Ct. 2016) [noting and adopting MPC emphasis on steps taken, even if many remain]. Under any approach, attempts require evidence of a defendant's commitment to see the endeavor through to the end.

Below are two actual cases in which attempt convictions were entered at trial. Can you tell by intuition which of the two convictions was affirmed and which was reversed?

**a. Too late to turn back now?** In October 1967, while his wife was away on a trip, defendant-mathematician, under an assumed name, rented a second-floor office over the mezzanine of a bank in Hollywood. Below the mezzanine was the bank vault. Defendant knew the layout of the building, specifically the relation of the office he rented to the vault. He paid rent from October 23 to November 23. The landlord had 10 days before the rental period to finish repairs and painting. During this pre-rental period, defendant brought drills, acetylene gas tanks, a blow torch, a blanket, and a linoleum rug into the office. The landlord saw these items when he came in to check up on the repair work.

On Saturday, October 14, defendant drilled two groups of holes into the floor of the office above the mezzanine, but stopped drilling before the holes went through the floor. He came back to the office several times thinking he might slowly drill down, covering the holes with the linoleum rug. At some point he installed a hasp lock on a closet, and planned to, or did, put his tools in it. However, he left the closet keys on the premises. At the end of November, the landlord notified the police and turned the tools and equipment over to them. Defendant paid no more rent. It is unclear when he last entered the office, but it could have been after the landlord removed the equipment. On February 22, 1968, police arrested defendant. After receiving *Miranda* warnings, he gave the following confession:

> Saturday, the 14th, I drilled some small holes in the floor of the room. Because of tiredness, fear, and the implications of what I was doing, I stopped and went to sleep. At this point

my motives began to change. The actual commencement of my plan made me realize that even if I were to succeed, a fugitive life of living on stolen money would not give the enjoyment of the life of a mathematician, however humble a job. But I still had not given up my plan. I had made a certain investment of time, money, effort, and a certain psychological commitment to the concept. I came back several times thinking I might store the tools in the closet and slowly drill down, covering the hole with a rug of linoleum square. As time went on (after two weeks or so), my wife came back and my life as bank robber seemed more and more absurd.

**b. Searching for a victim.** Buena Park, California police found appellants Munoz, Sharrieff, and Harper in a rented car in the parking lot of the Home Savings Bank at 10:00 p.m. on September 21, 1992. Police searched them, the car, and the vicinity, finding two loaded handguns (a .44 Charter Arms Bulldog and a .357 magnum Smith and Wesson) under a bush two yards from the car. In the car was duct tape, a stun gun, and a pair of latex surgical gloves. Police found an identical pair of gloves in the pocket of Munoz's sweat pants, and six rounds of .357 magnum ammo in the pocket of the shorts he wore underneath. Some of the ammo came from the same box or lot as the ammo in the loaded .357 magnum. Appellants had $182 in cash among them and Sharrieff had an ATM card that bore the name of Kimberly Ellis.

Harper had used that ATM card just before 9:00 p.m. that night at the Buena Park Bank of America next to the Home Savings lot where the three men were parked. The ATM camera photographed Harper, who requested a $20 withdrawal from the ATM, but had not removed the cash from the drawer. This omission created a "bill trap," which causes the ATM to shut down and the company that monitors the ATM to contact service technicians to come and repair the ATM. These facts were known to Harper, who had worked for both Bank of America and one of its ATM servicers.

On the basis of this evidence, Harper, Sharrieff, and Munoz were indicted for conspiracy to rob a federally insured bank, attempted bank robbery, and a firearms offense. The prosecution theorized that Harper intentionally caused the bill trap to summon the ATM service technicians, who would have to open the ATM vault to clear the trap. At that time, the theory went, appellants planned to rob the technicians of the money in the ATM. All three appellants were convicted of all charges.

## NOTES ON *BOND*

***1. HIV and attempted murder.*** *Smallwood v. State*, 343 Md. 97 (1996) was an appeal from defendant's conviction of assault with intent to murder his rape victims. There, Maryland's high court reversed on the ground that the probability that a (knowingly) HIV-positive rapist could bring about death by AIDS in a victim is insufficient to establish an intent to kill his victims through unprotected rape. The court contrasted death by AIDS, which is *not* a probable result of engaging in a single act of unprotected HIV-intercourse, to pointing a deadly weapon at a vital part of another's body, which naturally and probably *would* cause the victim's death. The risk that Smallwood posed to the lives of his victims was too low to make the act of rape on such facts attempted murder. *Cf. Spencer v. State*, 149 A.3d 610, 630-34 (Md. Ct. App. 2016) [relying on *Smallwood*, reversing attempted-murder conviction of intoxicated driver who, while evading police in high speed chase, struck dismounted cyclist, who barely survived].

Most appellate rulings in the 90's on HIV/AIDS-based attempted-murder prosecutions disagreed with *Smallwood*. *See, e.g., State v. Hinkhouse*, 139 Or.App. 446 (1996) [upholding defendant's convictions for attempted murder on evidence of his specific intent to kill his victims indicated by his lies about his HIV-positive status, refusal to use protection, and his claim to others that if he were HIV-positive, he would spread the virus]. *Smallwood* has since made a comeback. *See, e.g., United States v. Dacus*, 66 M.J. 235, 240-41 n.1 (U.S. Armed Forces Ct. App. 2008) (Ryan, J., concurring) ["It is no doubt true that earlier cases ... throughout the country found that ... engag[ing] in sexual activity while HIV positive constituted a means likely to cause death or grievous bodily harm. There is at least a question whether traditional notions of aggravated assault comport with current scientific evidence regarding HIV and AIDS."].

***2. Actual v. constructive possession.*** The court also affirmed Bond's conviction of being a convicted felon in possession of a weapon. The idea of such a crime is that felons who possess weapons pose greater public dangers than do non-felons who possess weapons (without regard for, perhaps eccentrically, the nature of the prior felony). It makes good sense, then, that under the Illinois possession statute, one must *know* that one possesses something in order to be criminally responsible for possessing it. Possession, the *Bond* Court explained, may be actual (the meaning of which is obvious) or constructive (the meaning of which is not obvious).

The legal doctrines of "constructive possession" or "constructive knowledge" allow us to hold people responsible for having and knowing things that we cannot exactly prove they had or knew. Specifically, one who possesses items found in a car with several occupants or found on the common-area coffee table of a jointly occupied apartment may do so constructively. Does a courier who knows of a secret compartment in the car that he is loaned to make a delivery, but who intentionally avoids learning what is in that compartment, *know* that it contains drugs? The law in both instances often allows jurors to impose on the accused constructive possession or knowledge of the goods or facts at issue.

This reminds me of a talk I heard Professor Frank Michelman give while I was in law school. He was discussing the pre-constitutional doctrine of virtual or constructive representation, which assured American colonists that, although they were not entitled to vote for members of Parliament, their political interests would be voiced for them by those who *could* vote, since those voters would do what was good not just for themselves, but for the colonists (whose burden they theoretically shared) as well. Michelman enjoined his audience that, in law, whenever we hear the word "constructive" used as an adjective, we should substitute for it the word "not." In other words, "constructive possession" means "not possession." The ordinary conditions of possession, of knowledge, and in his example, of representation, had been overridden by law, presumably to achieve a socially desirable outcome.

***3. Impeachment of witnesses, revisited.*** Because Bond's conviction as felon in possession of a weapon depended on a prior, four-year-old conviction for felony possession of marijuana, that prior conviction had to be proved beyond a reasonable doubt in the new case. The prosecutor proved Bond's prior by putting into evidence a certified copy of the judgment of conviction. Bond's claim on appeal was that the prosecutor had gotten the certified copy admitted not on the issue of whether Bond in fact committed the prior offense, but rather, on a collateral issue of credibility, that is, to impeach Bond's testimony.

Evidently Bond had filed a pretrial motion to suppress evidence discovered in the execution of a search warrant. In denying the motion, the trial court had occasion to consider the prior marijuana conviction, most likely because Bond, when faced with evidence that he had at least three handguns in his house (none of which he admitted to possessing), testified to the effect that he was a law-abiding soul, thus opening the door to proof that he was not. This attempt to discredit a witness—known as "impeachment"—is not used to prove the prior, but rather, to prove the incredibility of the statement by which the witness *denies* the prior. *See also supra* Chapter 1.A, note 3 on *Decina*.

If the difference between an item of evidence being used to prove a crime as opposed to being used to discredit a witness strikes you as a fine one, then you are in good company. For example, it is not uncommon in criminal cases for defendants to challenge the admissibility of their confessions for lack of consent, that is, for not being preceded by *Miranda* warnings and a valid waiver of the rights of silence and counsel. In a pretrial hearing, a judge who finds such a blunder by police may rule that the prosecutor cannot introduce the confession at trial on the issue of guilt (on whether defendant committed the crime or crimes in question). The judge may simultaneously rule, however, that the prosecutor *can* introduce the confession at trial for impeachment, that is, to discredit a testifying defendant whose in-court claim of innocence may be called into question by his extrajudicial confession to police. The judge accomplishes this with a limiting instruction that admonishes the jury to use the confession uniquely for assessing whether defendant is lying when he denies his guilt, not for assessing whether defendant is guilty. *See supra* Chapter 1.A, note 3c on *Decina*.

Such limiting instructions understandably leave the defense camp unsatisfied with how an unMirandized confession that was ruled inadmissible ends up admissible. Nonetheless it is the law, which developed from the premise that there is no constitutional right to tell a lie in court. It is one thing to have evidence kept from the jury on the ground that it was illegally obtained by police. But it is another thing altogether to allow the defendant to *take the stand* and flat out deny the existence of the evidence. That sort of in-court lie the law will not allow. As a result, in the event they win a pretrial motion to suppress items of evidence, defense lawyers not infrequently keep their clients from taking the stand, lest the otherwise suppressed evidence re-emerge for impeachment purposes. *See Harris v. New York*, 401 U.S. 222 (1971).

In Bond's case, the appellate court ruled that the certified copy of his prior could not support his conviction as felon-in-possession if the prior had been introduced at trial only for impeachment. The court went on to rule that the prosecution had introduced Bond's certified copy of his prior for both substance (at trial) and impeachment (in a pre-trial suppression hearing). Because at trial the certified copy was introduced to prove the truth of the prior conviction (substance) and not just as an attack on the credibility of a witness who might have lied under oath (impeachment), Bond's challenge to its use failed.

**4. Jury instruction on attempt.** In 1961, Illinois became the first state to adopt the Model Penal Code, the verbatim Illinois version of which says an attempt occurs "when, with intent to commit a specific offense," the actor "does any act that constitutes a substantial step toward the commission of that offense." 720 West's Smith-Hurd Illinois Compiled Statutes Annotated 5/8-4.

California's jury instruction on the law of attempt, CALJIC No. 6.00 (2014), is similar enough, though elaborated:

> An attempt to commit a crime consists of two elements, namely, a specific intent to commit the crime, and a direct but ineffectual act done toward its commission. In determining whether this act was done, it is necessary to distinguish between mere preparation ... and the actual commencement of the doing of the criminal deed.... Mere preparation, which may consist of planning the offense or of devising, obtaining or arranging the means for its commission, is not sufficient to constitute an attempt. However, acts of a person who intends to commit a crime will constitute an attempt where those acts clearly indicate a certain, unambiguous intent to commit that specific crime. These acts must be an immediate step in the present execution of the criminal design, the progress of which would be completed unless interrupted by some circumstance not intended in the original design.

**5. Sentences for attempts v. sentences for completed offenses.** California Penal Code §664 (2011) states in pertinent part:

> Every person who attempts to commit any crime, but fails, or is prevented or intercepted in its perpetration, shall be punished ... as follows:
>
> (a) If the crime attempted is punishable by imprisonment in the state prison, the person guilty of the attempt shall be punished by imprisonment in the state prison for one-half

the term of imprisonment prescribed upon a conviction of the offense attempted. However, if the crime attempted is willful, deliberate, and premeditated murder, as defined in Section 189, the person guilty of that attempt shall be punished by imprisonment in the state prison for life with the possibility of parole. If the crime attempted is any other one in which the maximum sentence is life imprisonment or death, the person guilty of the attempt shall be punished by imprisonment in the state prison for five, seven, or nine years....

(b) If the crime attempted is punishable by imprisonment in a county jail, the person guilty of the attempt shall be punished by imprisonment in a county jail for a term not exceeding one-half the term of imprisonment prescribed upon a conviction of the offense attempted.

(c) If the offense so attempted is punishable by a fine, the offender convicted of that attempt shall be punished by a fine not exceeding one-half the largest fine which may be imposed upon a conviction of the offense attempted....

Model Penal Code §5.05(1) states:

> Except as otherwise provided in this Section, attempt, solicitation and conspiracy are crimes of the same grade and degree as the most serious offense that is attempted or solicited or is an object of the conspiracy. An attempt, solicitation or conspiracy to commit a [capital crime or a] felony of the first degree is a felony of the second degree.

**6. Concurrent sentences, revisited.** Bond had two terms of imprisonment imposed on him at the same time by the same judge: one for the attempt, the other for the weapons charge. But it is not always that way with concurrent terms. When the second judgment of sentence is ordered to run concurrent to an unexpired term from a foreign jurisdiction (read, the U.S. or another state), there is no guarantee that concurrency will work out for a defendant who is already in the physical custody of the jurisdiction rendering the second judgment. A coöperative foreign jurisdiction would allow both terms to be served at once either by accepting transfer of the prisoner or by designating the other jurisdiction's facility as the place of service. An uncoöperative foreign jurisdiction would do neither, and pick up the prisoner after the sentence is completed in the other jurisdiction (the one currently holding him) and run the terms end to end. *See People v. Antonio (I)*, 2016 WL 310104 (Cal. 4th Dist. Ct. App.); *People v. Antonio (II)*, 10 Cal.App.5th 1064 (2017).

## B. INCULPATORY MISTAKES: IMPOSSIBLE ATTEMPTS

Impossible attempts were first officially recognized as non-criminal in 1864, literalizing what then had to be a given: a person whose anti-social bent poses no appreciable risk of harm is no criminal. *Regina v. Collins*, 169 English Reports 1477 (Crown Cases Reserved 1864). Over 150 years later, scholarly output on the subject persists, marked by takes on the inner and outer worlds and an odd preoccupation with hypotheticals like "Lady Eldon." Lady Eldon smuggled English lace in from the continent, mistaking it for contraband French lace—a difficulty as unlikely to arise in the experience of lawyers as it was in 1912 when Wharton cooked it up. 1 Wharton's Criminal Law §225, n.8 (James M. Kerr ed., 11th ed. 1912). Impossible attempts are not merely a professorial hobby horse. Just tap "impossibility" into Westlaw, which will designate nearly 1500 criminal cases as on point, 900 or so more recent than 1999. Indeed, impossible attempts express a non-trivial tension between risk-taking and harm-causing within the very real world of criminal litigation.

Impossibility also merits continued study because it seemingly began to erode as a defense to a charge of attempt as soon as 15 years after its 1864 discovery. Now it is hornbook that impossible attempts *are* punishable as crimes. Specifically,

> [t]hirty-seven states have explicitly eliminated impossibility as a defense to a charge of attempt and the federal circuits that have not done likewise have so limited the range of application of the defense as to render it virtually a dead letter. As a result, one's susceptibility to punishment for attempting the impossible is today a rather uncontroversial matter of settled law.

John Hasnas, *Once More unto the Breach: The Inherent Liberalism of the Criminal Law and Liability for Attempting the Impossible*, 54 Hastings Law Journal 1, 3 (2002). Beyond the rhetoric that impossibility is no longer a defense, that it still has a place in the law of attempt was evident in the digests and law reviews long before Graham Hughes touted it 50 years ago as an area that repays close study. Graham Hughes, *One Further Footnote on Attempting the Impossible*, 42 New York University Law Review 1005, 1005 (1967). Agreement that the impossibility defense has a way of rehabilitating itself from criticism continues. What continues more precisely is a sense of a non-trivial difference between failing at larceny by picking the empty pocket of a passerby on a sidewalk and by picking the empty pocket of a mannequin in a department store. What remains up in the air is what *accounts* for that difference. Despite two absolutist positions on this—1) impossibility is a defense to a charge of attempt; and 2) impossibility is not a defense—we have a lingering sense that *some* cases should come out one way and some another. But because we have evolved no language to account for the difference, we live in a state of uneasiness about it.

Here I rehearse an argument meant to help decode the impossibility defense by meditating on what it means to make a mistake. I am certainly not the first to insist that the impossibility defense lives on. I am, however, the first to base such a claim on the grammar or criteria of mistakes, which can get us closer to the bottom of what makes attempts impossible and why it matters.

Extant impossibility cases and scholarship take mistakes as a given. But what *is* a mistake? Is the answer considered too obvious to mention? Kenneth Simons, to take just one leading authority, has written 164 law-review pages about mistakes of law and fact embedded in the impossibility defense,[a] tossing in just once that a mistake is a sort of "perception" or "empirical judgment" at odds with the world. Kenneth W. Simons, *Mistake and Impossibility, Law and Fact, and Culpability: A Speculative Essay*, 81 Journal of Criminal Law & Criminology 447, 469 (1990). He does not elaborate.

Nor do others engaged in like projects. Within the stock hypotheticals of impossible attempts, a man shoots a tree stump or a corpse, each having been mistaken for a live person, or he administers to a live person an innocuous substance he has mistaken for poison. These stick-figure sketches pose whether attempted murder has occurred. But because it is *stipulated* that each action owes to mistake,

---

[a] Kenneth W. Simons, *Ignorance and Mistake of Criminal Law, Noncriminal Law, and Fact*, 9 Ohio State Journal of Criminal Law 487 (2012); Kenneth W. Simons, *Mistake of Fact or Mistake of Criminal Law? Explaining and Defending the Distinction*, 3 Criminal Law & Philosophy 213 (2009); Kenneth W. Simons, *Mistake and Impossibility, Law and Fact, and Culpability: A Speculative Essay*, 81 Journal of Criminal Law & Criminology 447 (1990).

we are told so little about what happened that of course the question is hard to answer. Any chance of making sense of the hypotheticals is stymied by an absence both of facts and of any concern for what can *count as* a mistake. My contribution here to the considerable work of others is to locate the impossibility defense within an actual context of human action and concern, which is the only way we can become clear for ourselves what *is* a mistake and what is not. We will find that the situations in which the law deploys the notion of mistake are not always situations in which we would find the use of that term natural or responsive to our human need to locate mistakes in the world.

While so far here in our course our interest in mistakes has been in their capacity for excusing harm-causing action, mistakes also have point in converting harmless action into punishable instances of criminal attempt. Criminal attempts are punishable even though the intended crime is unconsummated. Although the intended crime fails because in one way or another the attempter gets caught before he can pull the crime off, the attempter remains partially on the hook, though less than if he had succeeded. Failure, accordingly, is a partial excuse, which (for the most part) mitigates punishment below that meted out for the successful offense. Attempts are said to be impossible when a criminal's efforts fail due to factors *apart from getting caught*. That is, an attempt is impossible when the means selected for its execution are so shabby that we could have predicted the failure of the criminal effort even before the plan was put into action. *See* Steven Shavell, *Deterrence and the Punishment of Attempts*, 19 Journal of Legal Studies 435, 451 (1990).

For example, murder is *not* impossible when the accused intentionally shoots a victim who survives through the intervention of life-saving surgery. Nor is theft impossible when a victim fights off the accused, who obtains no property. Although a thief cannot pick an empty pocket, if the thief does not know the pocket is empty, does that mean he has not attempted theft? No, the would-be thief is still punishable for attempted theft. *See Commonwealth v. McDonald*, 5 Cush. 365 (Mass. 1850). Next time, the argument runs, he may figure out who has money and who does not. Thus, for deterrence purposes he should this time be only partially excused for having fallen short. Richard A. Posner, *An Economic Theory of the Criminal Law*, 85 Columbia Law Review 1193, 1217-18 (1985). The case of the failed pickpocket therefore is not a case of impossibility.

But what if someone intends to commit rape or murder, but fails because his would-be rape or murder victim is already dead? Or his would-be murder victim is alive but sleeping in another room when the "murderer" shoots through a window, striking a pillow, which is taken for the victim? And what about someone who intends to take a deer out of season, but the deer turns out to be a stuffed decoy?

The answer to each question posed above is embedded first in an answer to a prior question: is defendant trying to commit what really is a crime? George Fletcher, Rethinking Criminal Law §3.3., at 178 (1978). If it is, then his failure—which manifests nothing redeeming about him—is something for which he deserves only partial credit: bad intention, lucky result. If he *meant* to rape or shoot a dead person (not a live one), shoot a pillow (not an enemy), or take a stuffed deer (not a real one) out of season, then he is not attempting anything. He *is* violating or shooting a corpse, shooting a pillow, or taking a stuffed deer, actions whose criminality, if any, has nothing to do with rape, murder, or preservation of deer from overzealous hunters.

Even if defendant owns up to having tried to commit what really is a crime, there must—because of the limits of what it means to fail due to a mistake—be some instances where he should get off scot-free. Those limits explain how the term "impossibility" insinuated itself into the law of attempt: blame has no place when the prohibited harm never had a chance to occur. As such, an impossible plan (if plan there be) lacks the proximity to success that justifies a conviction of attempt. Success is impossible when these would-be thieves, rapists, murderers, and scofflaw hunters go about things in such an unlikely way as to make their failure the inevitable upshot of delusion or fantasy, not mistake. They give us doubt about whether they intended to commit a crime or take the requisite "substantial" or "direct but ineffectual" step toward its completion. Though they well may need some sort of reprogramming or warehousing, because they are too disconnected from reality to have "made a mistake," they are not to be dealt with in the same way we deal with fully responsible agents who barely fall short of the harms they threaten.

For example, what are the conditions under which someone could think a decoy deer is a real deer? A convincing decoy deer in the woods staged there by the game warden should lead to the conviction of someone who shoots at it of attempting to take a deer out of season:

> The State's evidence shows that conservation agents, about two weeks before the alleged offense, had procured the hide

of a 2½ year old doe which had been killed by an automobile in Pulaski County. They had taken it to a taxidermist, who soaked it to soften it, stuffed it with excelsior and boards, inserted rods in the legs so it would stand upright and used the doe's skull in the head part of the hide so it would hold its former shape. For eyes, which had not been preserved, two small circular pieces of scotchlight reflector tape of a 'white to amber color', had been placed over the eyeless sockets.

*State v. Guffey*, 262 S.W.2d 152, 153 (Mo. Ct. App. 1953). The Missouri statute which conservation agents sought to enforce criminalized unauthorized pursuit, taking, killing, possession, or disposing of all wildlife, not just deer. *Id.* at 152-53, *quoting* Vernon's Annotated Missouri Statutes §252.040. In fact, the defendants were in search of a *wolf* they saw run across a road they took en route to a frog-hunting expedition. They consequently were attempting to take a wolf out of season by shooting at a decoy deer that they took—on these facts justifiably—for a wolf. But move the decoy deer to the end of a grocery-store aisle or any other place where deer are quite unlikely to appear, or lower the quality of the decoy so that it looks fake from any distance, and a conviction of attempt becomes manifestly absurd.

The deer was not in a grocery-store aisle, but staged in a place and manner where anyone might be taken in and mistake it for live, off-limits wildlife. This makes it all the more remarkable that Guffey's conviction of attempt was reversed. To the appellate court, Guffey's project was not an illegal attempt to take protected wildlife, but a perfectly legal taking of an unprotected stuffed deer by way of a shotgun blast. Because by his own account Guffey took the stuffed decoy for alive, it is hard to locate the appellate court's ruling within any notion of attempt, impossible or otherwise.

As for shooting a pillow, we would need thorough knowledge of the episode: did the enemy really resemble a pillow? In the actual case where Newton Mitchell's conviction of attempted murder of John O. Warren was upheld by Missouri's high court, Mitchell, who had known Warren at least 20 years, had at one time boarded at Warren's house where the attempt occurred, thus educating himself on the layout. Moreover, when he shot twice through the window at the downstairs bed (one shot striking the pillow, the other the dresser), Mitchell was unaware that Warren, who had seen Mitchell and another man skulking around his grounds, had taken the precaution of retiring to the upstairs where his wife and children slept. Plus, Mitchell had a well-publicized motive for the attack: he fancied Warren's wife, whom he had pledged, apparently without encouragement, to extricate from her marriage by any means necessary. *State v. Mitchell*, 71 S.W. 175, 177-78 (Mo. 1902). And there is nothing "impossible" about *that* attempt.

J.L. Austin once put to students in a seminar at Harvard: "if a man hacks away with an axe at a pile of logs under the bedclothes, thinking it to be a man in his bed, isn't this attempted murder, despite the fact that the courts hold that it is not?" George Pitcher, *Austin: A Personal Memoir*, in Essays on J.L. Austin 20 (Oxford 1973). But *cf.* James Fitzjames Stephen, Digest of the Criminal Law 53 (7th ed. 1926) ["If *A*, mistaking a log of wood for *B*, and intending to murder *B*, strikes the log of wood with an axe, *A* has not attempted to murder *B*."]. Austin's question was rhetorical. After all, elsewhere he criticized a judge whose instructions to the jury made the defendant, by comparison, stand out as an "evident master of the Queen's English." As for the judge,

> he probably manages to convey his meaning somehow or other. Judges seem to acquire a knack of conveying meaning, and even carrying conviction, through the use of a pithy Anglo-Saxon which sometimes has literally no meaning at all. Wishing to distinguish the case of shooting at a post in the belief that it was an enemy, as not an 'attempt,' from the case of picking an empty pocket in the belief that money was in it, which is an 'attempt', the judge explains that in shooting at the post *'the man is never on the thing at all.'*

J.L. Austin, *A Plea for Excuses*, in Philosophical Papers, *supra*, at 197 n.1 [italics mine]; *cf. Commonwealth v. Kennedy*, 48 N.E. 770, 770 (Mass. 1897) (Holmes, J.) [referring to "the classic instance of shooting at a post supposed to be a man" as no attempt]. Austin is right: the expression may be meaningless at the literal level, but the judge does manage to get his point across somehow. What would make the man take a post for an enemy, anyway? Without good grounds for taking the one for the other, the man "is never on the thing at all," the "thing" being the successful shooting of an enemy, a risk so remote that the man is never "on" it. His means (shooting at a post) are so poorly selected for the desired ends (shooting a man) that success is too unlikely from the get-go to treat the project as a serious attempt. There is something wrong with *him*, not with what he saw; he is not mistaken (missing a bit of information), but delusional (at odds with reality). Before we could consider this shooting an attempted murder, we would need to know more about the incident, more than the stick-figure sketch that Austin—a lover of facts—gave us. Only then could we be in a position to say that the man had a basis for taking the post for an enemy; only then could we be in a position to say that in shooting at the post "by mistake" did he attempt to kill a man.

Another way of saying this is that we *can* imagine situations in which shooting a post would be an attempt, just as we can imagine situations in which shooting a stuffed deer (in, say, the grocery store) would not be an "attempt to take a deer." For example, shooting a bare post sticking in the ground from three feet is not an attempt to commit murder, though it may conceivably be an attempt to commit murder to shoot a very realistic scarecrow from 50 yards. What we need is a process for distinguishing the one from the other.

And what would be the conditions under which one could take a dead person for a live one? Narrow indeed, such as when the would-be killer, without checking for signs of life, shoots a man in the head with a .32 a few minutes after the man had died from shots to the chest by another person with a .38. See *People v. Dlugash*, infra.

But how, exactly, could someone sexually penetrate a dead person, taken for alive? Consider in this vein *United States v. Thomas*, 13 USCMA 278 (1962), where McClellan (a Navy airman, age 19) began dancing at a bar with a young woman he had just met when she promptly collapsed on the dance floor, dead from "acute interstitial myocarditis," a heart disease. *Id.* at 280. With help from Thomas (a Navy airman, age 20) and Abruzzese (a Navy airman, age 18), McClellan loaded the woman in his car, where he recommended they violate her because she "was just drunk" and "would never know the difference." After all three men took their exploitive turn in the car, McClellan and Thomas dropped off Abruzzese at the USO before taking the woman to a gas station, where an attendant called police, who arrived soon after and declared her dead. Because evidence indicated she had died on the dance floor, rape was precluded. Convictions of attempted rape, however, were upheld on the ground that defendants took the deceased for alive when they penetrated her. *Id.* at 280-81, 292.

In two opinions taking up 22 pages in the Court Martial Reports, the only allusion to what led defendants to think the deceased was alive is the coroner's remark that *rigor mortis* had not set in before the multiple penetrations. *Id.* at 280. That offhand remark, however, is a weak basis for concluding that defendants made a mistake about life and death. Can the line between the two states be that fine? The whole thing seems fishy, too fantastic to count as a mistake. As "sordid and revolting a picture" of human action as it is, *id.*, *Thomas* does not bespeak an attempt, not without more than the scant factual development the court provides.

Violating a corpse is a perversion quite apart from anything like real rape. In fact, someone who violates a corpse very likely does so *because* the person is dead ("and I will kill thee, and love thee after"). Othello 5.2.18-19 (David Bevington ed.) (New York: Bantam 1988). Such an action should provoke negative reaction sure enough, but not the same as to someone who has put himself to commit rape and failed due to, say, resistance on the would-be survivor's part. *E.g., State v. Martinez*, 230 P. 379, 383 (N.M. 1924); *cf. Waters v. State*, 234 A.2d 147, 153-54 (Md. Spec. Ct. App. 1967) [upholding attempted-rape conviction of 80-year-old who doubted his capacity to achieve erection].

One *could* conceivably take a barely dead person for a barely live person on facts like those of *Doyle v. State*, 921 P.2d 901 (Nev. 1996), where three men had intercourse with a profoundly intoxicated 20-year-old woman, who then threatened to accuse them of rape before being kidnapped to an area outside Las Vegas and murdered. Either just before or just after she expired from being choked, beaten, and smashed in the face with a brick, a four-inch twig was inserted in her rectum. To conspiracy, kidnapping, and murder charges was consequently added sexual assault, Doyle's conviction of which was reversed for lack of proof as to whether penetration with the foreign object occurred before death. *Id.* at 905-07, 912-15. Although Nevada is among those states that condition rape convictions on live victims, the state high court noted in dictum that felony murder may be predicated on attempted rape, which may lie when a would-be rapist justifiably takes a barely dead victim for alive. Nevada Revised Statutes Annotated §200.030(1)(b). *But see Nay v. State*, 167 P.3d 430, 435 (Nev. 2007) ["Robbery does not support felony murder where the evidence shows that the accused kills a person and only later forms the intent to rob...."].

This distinction—between earnest and stillborn gestures, between failures owing to mistake (attempts) and delusion (non-attempts)—is what the Model Penal Code trades on when holding that attempt law should not punish persons who demonstrate insufficient "dangerousness." For the Code drafters, "[t]he innocuous character of the particular conduct becomes relevant only if the futile endeavor itself indicates a harmless personality, so that immunizing the conduct from liability would not result in exposing society to a dangerous person." The Code cites "black magic" (aka voodoo) as a means that indicates non-dangerousness, at once acknowledging that "it is by no means clear that those who make unreasonable mistakes will not be *potentially* dangerous." MPC & Commentaries §5.01, at 316 n.88 (1985) [italics added]. Indeed, anyone out of touch enough to take just any old pillow for a person may in fact be dangerous. *Cf.* Joshua Dressler, Understanding Criminal Law §27.07, at 401 (7th ed. 2015). Dangerous or not, no progress can be made by declaring, as many do, the "black magic" scenario a mistake. *See, e.g.,* Peter Westen, *Impossibility Attempts: A Speculative Thesis*, 5 Ohio State Journal of Criminal Law 523, 535-36 (2008).

Black magic has nonetheless become a stock example of the staying power of the impossibility defense, despite the universally held official position that impossibility is no longer a defense to a charge of attempt. Larry Alexander, *Inculpatory and Exculpatory Mistakes and the Fact/Law Distinction: An Essay in Memory of Myke Bayles*, 12 Law & Philosophy 33, 48 n.40 (1993). As a clear and high example of a stillborn attempt, these cases of "incantations" are deployed by courts and commentators to demonstrate "some validity to decisions that distinguish the tree stump from the empty pocket case." Jerome Hall, *Criminal Attempt—A Study of Foundations of Criminal Liability,* 49 Yale Law Journal 789, 836 (1940).

Accordingly, exertions that are "inapt" or "doomed" ex ante— where failure is an "intrinsic" or "inherent" feature of an "unreasonable" criminal design that is too unlikely in a causation-sense to amount to much—are feeble gestures, not criminal attempts. Ken Levy, *It's Not Too Difficult: A Plea to Resurrect the Impossibility Defense*, 45 New Mexico Law Review 225, 265-74 (2014). The method by which this exemption from the law of attempt is explicated, however, devolves too often into whacky, admittedly "ridiculous" hypotheticals, Kevin Cole, *The Voodoo We Do: Harm, Impossibility, and the Reductionist Impulse,* 1994 Journal of Contemporary Legal Issues 31, 53-54, which, while entertaining to a point, cut us off from our principal job of decoding what was done: from the factual background of the incident or *why* of it all.

Why hypotheticals are substituted for the abundant real-life criminal cases on hand is opaque. The stick-figure nature of the hypotheticals boils things down sure enough, but the upshot of this activity does more harm than good by impeding assessments of whether a mistake has been made. Take, for example, Clarissa, a cheated-on spouse who, after enduring "the final straw, ... stirs what she believes to be a spoonful of the arsenic she had purchased for this eventuality into his coffee," only to realize "that she mistakenly added sugar to his coffee, just as she does every morning." As an act of repentance, Clarissa then turns herself in, apparently as attempted murderer. Hasnas, *Once More unto the Breach, supra,* at 2.

On that lean backstory, frankly, it is hard to have any reaction at all to Clarissa. We are to take it as given that she "mistakenly" took sugar for poison. But how? Any amateur student of the mind would conclude that Clarissa did not want her husband dead (not, at least, by her own hand). Imagine the trembling hands, racing mind, and complex of emotions leading up to the contemplated act. If genuinely committed to doing him in, what went wrong? Did someone switch the sugar and arsenic containers? Did Clarissa have two identical containers side by side with no distinguishing markings and guess which was the deadly one? What kind of murderer does *that*? No mistake occurs where no precautions are taken. That she would turn herself in manifests a justifiably guilty conscience, but at the level of action she "was never on the thing at all." J.L. Austin, *A Plea for Excuses*, in Philosophical Papers, *supra,* at 197 n.1.

John Hasnas finds this bare-bones hypothetical "apparently derived from" *State v. Clarissa,* 11 Ala. 57, 60-61 (1847), which he characterizes as a "classically illustrative ... case in which a slave attempted to poison her master with an innocuous substance." Hasnas, *Once More unto the Breach, supra,* at 2 n.1. George Fletcher concurs with that characterization. See George P. Fletcher, *The Metamorphosis of Larceny*, 89 Harvard Law Review 469, 522 (1976). In the real case, the real Clarissa dropped two ounces of Jamestown (aka Jimson) weed in the coffee of two "free white persons," one her "overseer" Nelson Parsons, who consequently found himself "so near dying," but not dead. Due to an inartfully pled indictment and an inadmissible confession that Parsons coerced from Clarissa, her capital conviction of "'attempt to poison' a white person" was reversed. *Clarissa,* 11 Ala. at 59-62.

But this much is clear: Jamestown weed is no innocuous substance, understood both then and now as deadly if administered in more than medicinal doses. See *Pitts v. State,* 43 Miss. 472, 483 (1870) [calling Jamestown weed "narcotic poison"]; Dan J. Tennenhouse, 3 Attorneys Medical Deskbook 4th §36:6 (Oct. 2016) [Jamestown weed causes "agitation, death, hallucinations, hypertension, seizures, tachycardia"]. Clarissa might have made a mistake pure and simple in the dosage, or maybe Parsons had a stocky constitution, but her efforts were far from doomed ex ante, quite apart from whether Parsons had it coming to him. In this respect does Clarissa's actual litigation get us much closer than the "classic" hypothetical version to discovery or agreement about both the basis of her mistake (if mistake there be) and what to do about it.

Nothing is more central to the understanding of untoward human action than the operation of mistakes. And nothing is more conventional than the notion that mistakes may be unreasonable, even "extreme." Indeed, Richard Singer wrote about "unreasonable mistakes" for 84 pages in the *Boston College Law Review*, tracing their operation in law back to Blackstone, yet without pausing to consider whether all wrong beliefs, whatever their foundation, can constitute mistakes. Richard Singer, *The Resurgence of Mens Rea: II – Honest but Reasonable Mistakes of Fact in Self Defense,* 28 Boston College Law Review 459 (1987). If I have succeeded at all here, then I have made a case for the idea that they cannot. Because mistakes are tied to the public observable world and not to the inner world of privacy and psychology, they are by definition reasonable. A mistake occurs when someone *able* to take the right one *tries* to take the right one, but takes the wrong one anyway. When that occurs, terms like negligence and recklessness have no specific application to what was done. Mistakes may either exculpate or inculpate when competently pled. Delusions, oppositely, may have some place in the law, but they bear no relation to the meaning and operation of mistakes.

Our principal case, *People v. Dlugash*, 41 N.Y.2d 725 (1977), a ruling from New York's high court, addresses criminal responsibility for shooting a man in the head immediately after his having died from shots to the thorax fired just a few minutes before by another person. Consider both whether Dlugash's attempt to murder Geller is properly characterized as "impossible," and the significance of such a label.

# COURT OF APPEALS OF NEW YORK

*THE PEOPLE OF THE STATE OF NEW YORK, APPELLANT*
*V.*
*MELVIN DLUGASH, RESPONDENT*

MAY 12, 1977

JASEN, Justice

    The criminal law is of ancient origin, but criminal liability for attempt to commit a crime is comparatively recent. At the root of the concept of attempt liability are the very aims and purposes of penal law. The ultimate issue is whether an individual's intentions and actions, though failing to achieve a manifest and malevolent criminal purpose, constitute a danger to organized society of sufficient magnitude to warrant the imposition of criminal sanctions. Difficulties in theoretical analysis and debate over very pragmatic questions of blameworthiness appear dramatically in reference to situations where the criminal attempt failed to achieve its purpose solely because the factual or legal context in which the individual acted was not as the actor supposed them to be. Phrased somewhat differently, the concern centers on whether an individual should be liable for an attempt to commit a crime when, unknown to him, it was impossible to successfully complete the crime attempted.

    For years, serious studies have been made on the subject to resolve the continuing controversy when, if at all, the impossibility of successfully completing the criminal act should preclude liability for even making the futile attempt. The 1967 revision of the Penal Law approached the <u>impossibility defense</u> to the inchoate crime of attempt in a novel fashion. The statute provides that, if a person engages in conduct which would otherwise constitute an attempt to commit a crime, "it is no defense to a prosecution for such attempt that the crime charged to have been attempted was, under the attendant circumstances, factually or legally impossible of commission, if such crime could have been committed had the attendant circumstances been as such person believed them to be." Penal Law §110.10. This appeal presents to us, for the first time, a case involving the application of the modern statute. We hold that, under the proof presented by the People at trial, defendant Melvin Dlugash may be held for attempted murder, though the target of the attempt may have already been slain, by the hand of another, when Dlugash made his felonious attempt.

On December 22, 1973, Michael Geller, 25 years old, was found shot to death in the bedroom of his Brooklyn apartment. The body, which had been riddled by bullets, was found lying face-up on the floor. An autopsy revealed that the victim had been shot in the face and head no less than seven times. Powder burns on the face indicated that the shots had been fired from within one foot. Four small caliber bullets were recovered from the victim's skull. The victim had also been critically wounded in the chest. One heavy caliber bullet passed through the left lung, penetrated the heart chamber, pierced the left ventricle of the heart upon entrance and again upon exit, and lodged in the victim's torso. A second bullet entered the left lung and passed through to the chest, but without reaching the heart area. Although the second bullet was damaged beyond identification, the bullet tracks indicated that these wounds were also inflicted by a bullet of heavy caliber. A tenth bullet, of unknown caliber, passed through the thumb of the victim's left hand. The autopsy report listed the cause of death as "multiple bullet wounds of head and chest with brain injury and massive bilateral hemothorax with penetration of the heart." Subsequent ballistics examination established that the four bullets recovered from the victim's head were .25 caliber bullets and that the heart-piercing bullet was of .38 caliber.

Detective Joseph Carrasquillo of the New York City Police Department was assigned to investigate the homicide. On December 27, 1973, five days after the discovery of the body, Detective Carrasquillo and a fellow officer went to defendant's residence in an effort to locate him. The officers arrived at approximately 6:00 P.M. Defendant answered the door and, when informed that the officers were investigating the death of Michael Geller, a friend of his, defendant invited the officers into the house. Detective Carrasquillo informed defendant that the officers desired any information defendant might have regarding the death of Geller and, since defendant was regarded as a suspect, administered the standard pre-interrogation warnings. Defendant told officers that he and another friend, Joe Bush, had just returned from a four- or five-day trip "upstate someplace" and learned of Geller's death only upon his return.

Since Bush was also a suspect in the case and defendant admitted knowing Bush, defendant agreed to accompany the officers to the station house for the purposes of identifying photographs of Bush and of lending assistance to the investigation. Upon arrival at the police station, Detective Carrasquillo and defendant occupied an interview room. Carrasquillo advised defendant that he had witnesses and information to the effect that as late as 7:00 P.M. on the day before the body was found, defendant had been observed carrying a .25 caliber pistol. Once again, Carrasquillo administered the standard pre-interrogation statement of rights. Defendant then proceeded to relate his version of the events which culminated in the death of Geller. Defendant stated that, on the night of December 21, 1973, he, Bush and Geller had been out drinking. Bush had been staying at Geller's apartment and, during the course of the evening, Geller several times demanded that Bush pay $100 towards the rent on the apartment.

According to defendant, Bush rejected these demands, telling Geller that "you better shut up or you're going to get a bullet." All three returned to Geller's apartment at approximately midnight, took seats in the bedroom, and continued to drink until sometime between 3:00 and 3:30 in the morning. When Geller again pressed his demand for rent money, Bush drew his .38 caliber pistol, aimed it at Geller, and fired three times. Geller fell to the floor. After the passage of a few minutes, perhaps two, perhaps as much as five, defendant walked over to the fallen Geller, drew his .25 caliber pistol, and fired approximately five shots in the victim's head and face. Defendant contended that, by the time he fired the shots, "it looked like Mike Geller was already dead." After the shots were fired, defendant and Bush walked to the apartment of a female acquaintance. Bush removed his shirt, wrapped the two guns and a knife in it, and left the apartment, telling Dlugash that he intended to dispose of the weapons. Bush returned 10 or 15 minutes later and stated that he had thrown the weapons down a sewer two or three blocks away.

After Carrasquillo had taken the bulk of the statement, he asked defendant why he would do such a thing. According to Carrasquillo, defendant said, "gee, I really don't know." Carrasquillo repeated the question 10 minutes later, but received the same response. After a while, Carrasquillo asked the question for a third time and defendant replied, "well, gee, I guess it must have been because I was afraid of Joe Bush."

At approximately 9:00 P.M., defendant repeated the substance of his statement to an Assistant District Attorney. Defendant added that the time he shot at Geller, Geller was not moving and his eyes were closed. While he did not check for a pulse, defendant stated that Geller had not been doing anything to him at the time he shot because "Mike was dead."

Defendant was indicted by the Grand Jury of Kings County on a single count of murder in that, acting in concert with another person actually present, he intentionally caused the death of Michael Geller. At the trial, there were four principal prosecution witnesses: Detective Carrasquillo, the Assistant District Attorney who took the second admission, and two physicians from the office of the New York City Chief Medical Examiner. For proof of defendant's culpability, the prosecution relied upon defendant's own admissions as related by the detective and the prosecutor. From the physicians, the prosecution sought to establish that Geller was still alive at the time defendant shot at him. Both physicians testified that each of the two chest wounds, for which defendant alleged Bush to be responsible, would have caused death without prompt medical attention. However, the victim would have remained alive until such time as his chest cavity became fully filled with blood. Depending on the circumstances, it might take 5 to 10 minutes for the chest cavity to fill. Neither prosecution witness could state, with medical certainty, that the victim was still alive when, perhaps five minutes after the initial chest wounds were inflicted, defendant fired at the victim's head.

The defense produced but a single witness, the former Chief Medical Examiner of New York City. This expert stated that, in his view, Geller might have died of the chest wounds "very rapidly" since, in addition to the bleeding, a large bullet going through a lung and the heart would have other adverse medical effects. "Those wounds can be almost immediately or rapidly fatal or they may be delayed in there, in the time it would take for death to occur. But I would say that wounds like that which are described here as having gone through the lungs and the heart would be fatal wounds and in most cases they're rapidly fatal."

The trial court declined to charge the jury, as requested by the prosecution, that defendant could be guilty of murder on the theory that he had aided and abetted the killing of Geller by Bush. Instead, the court submitted only two theories to the jury: that defendant had either intentionally murdered Geller or had attempted to murder Geller.

The jury found defendant guilty of murder. Defendant then moved to set the verdict aside. He submitted an affidavit in which he contended that he "was absolutely, unequivocally and positively certain that Michael Geller was dead before [he] shot him." Further, defendant averred that he was in fear for his life when he shot Geller. "This fear stemmed from the fact that Joseph Bush, the admitted killer of Geller, was holding a gun on me and telling me, in no uncertain terms, that if I didn't shoot the dead body I, too, would be killed." This motion was denied.[1]

On appeal, the Appellate Division reversed the judgment of conviction on the law and dismissed the indictment. The court ruled that "the People failed to prove beyond a reasonable doubt that Geller had been alive at the time he was shot by defendant; defendant's conviction of murder thus cannot stand." *People v. Dlugash*, 51 A.D.2d 974, 975 (N.Y. 1976). Further, the court held that the judgment could not be modified to reflect a conviction for attempted murder because "the uncontradicted evidence is that defendant, at the time he fired the five shots into the body of the decedent, believed him to be dead, and ... there is not a scintilla of evidence to contradict his assertion in that regard." *Id.* at 975.

Preliminarily, we state our agreement with the Appellate Division that the evidence did not establish, beyond a reasonable doubt, that Geller was alive at the time defendant fired into his body. To sustain a homicide conviction, it must be established, beyond a reasonable doubt, that defendant caused the death of another person. The People were required to establish that the shots fired by Dlugash were a sufficiently direct cause of Geller's death. While defendant admitted firing five shots at the victim approximately two to five minutes after Bush had fired three times, all three medical expert witnesses testified that they could not, with any degree of medical certainty, state whether the victim had been alive at the time the latter shots were fired by defendant. Thus, the People failed to prove

---

[1] Joe Bush pleaded guilty to first-degree manslaughter. When he entered his plea, Bush detailed his version of the homicide. He said Dlugash was a drug dealer who claimed that Geller owed him a large sum of money from drug purchases. Bush was in the kitchen alone when Geller entered and threatened him with a shotgun. Bush pulled out his .38 caliber pistol and fired five times at Geller. Geller slumped to the floor. Dlugash then entered, drew his .25 caliber pistol and fired five shots into the deceased's face. Bush, however, never testified at Dlugash's trial.

beyond a reasonable doubt that the victim had been alive at the time he was shot by defendant. Whatever else it may be, it is not murder to shoot a dead body. Man dies but once.

Before analyzing the attempt issue, there is a further point to be made. A person may be criminally liable for the criminal conduct of another person when, "acting with the mental culpability required for the commission thereof, he solicits, requests, commands, importunes, or intentionally aids such person to engage in such conduct." Penal Law §20.00. We believe that the evidence in the record supports a reasonable inference that Dlugash intentionally aided Bush in killing Geller and destroying telltale evidence. However, the trial court refused to permit the jury to consider this theory and the question of accessorial liability is, therefore, out of the case. The court dismissed the murder count insofar as it reflected accessorial liability, an action which may be taken only by a trial order of dismissal. We have held that the People may not appeal trial orders of dismissal "where retrial of the defendant, or indeed any supplemental fact finding, might result from appellate reversal of the order sought to be appealed." *People v. Brown*, 40 N.Y.2d 381, 393 (1976). Thus, in this case, we are without authority to direct a new trial. The judgment must stand or fall on the present record. Since the record fails to support a conviction for intentional murder, if the evidence also fails to support a conviction for attempted murder as a matter of law, defendant is free of all liability.

The procedural context of this matter, a non-appealable but erroneous dismissal of the issue of accessorial conduct, contributes to the unique nature of the attempt issue presented here. Where two or more persons have combined to murder, proof of the relationship between perpetrators is sufficient to hold all for the same degree of homicide, notwithstanding the absence of proof as to which specific act of which individual was the immediate cause of the victim's death. On the other hand, it is quite unlikely and improbable that two persons, unknown and unconnected to each other, would attempt to kill the same third person at the same time and place. Thus, it is rare for criminal liability for homicide to turn on which of several attempts actually succeeded. In the case of coconspirators, it is not necessary to do so and the case of truly independent actors is unlikely. However, procedural developments make this case the unlikely one and we must now decide whether, under the evidence presented, defendant may be held for attempted murder, though someone else perhaps succeeded in killing the victim.

The concept that there could be criminal liability for an attempt, even if ultimately unsuccessful, to commit a crime is comparatively recent. The modern concept of attempt has been said to date from *Rex v. Scofield*, decided in 1784. In that case, Lord Mansfield stated that "the intent may make an act, innocent in itself, criminal; nor is the completion of an act, criminal in itself, necessary to constitute criminality. Is it no offence to set fire to a train of gunpowder with intent to burn a house, because by accident, or the interposition of another, the mischief is prevented?" The Revised Penal Law now provides that a person is guilty of an attempt to commit a crime when, with intent to commit a crime, he engages in conduct which tends to effect the commission of such crime. Penal Law §110.10.

The most intriguing attempt cases are those where the attempt to commit a crime was unsuccessful due to mistakes of fact or law on the part of the would-be criminal. A general rule developed in most American jurisdictions that legal impossibility is a good defense but factual impossibility is not. Thus, for example, it was held that defendants who shot at a stuffed deer did not attempt to take a deer out of season, even though they believed the dummy to be a live animal. The court stated that there was no criminal attempt because it was no crime to "take" a stuffed deer, and it is no crime to attempt to do that which is legal. *State v. Guffey*, 262 S.W.2d 152 (Mo. Ct. App. 1952); *see State v. Taylor*, 345 Mo. 325 (1939) [no attempted bribe of juror where person bribed not a juror]. These cases are illustrative of legal impossibility....

On the other hand, factual impossibility was no defense. For example, a man was held liable for attempted murder when he shot into the room in which his target usually slept and, fortuitously, the target was sleeping elsewhere in the house that night. *State v. Mitchell*, 71 S.W. 175 (Mo. 1902). Although one bullet struck the target's customary pillow, attainment of the criminal objective was factually impossible. *State v. Moretti*, 52 N.J. 182 (1968) presents a similar instance of factual impossibility. Defendant agreed to perform an abortion, then a criminal act, upon a female undercover police investigator who was not, in fact, pregnant. The court sustained the conviction, ruling that "when the consequences sought by a defendant are forbidden by the law as criminal, it is no defense that defendant could not succeed in reaching his goal because of circumstances unknown to him." *Id.* at 190. On the same view, it was held that men who had sexual intercourse with a woman, with the belief that she was alive and did not consent to the intercourse, could be charged for attempted rape when the woman had, in fact, died from an unrelated ailment prior to the acts of intercourse. *United States v. Thomas*, 13 USCMA 278 (1962).

The New York cases can be parsed out along similar lines. One of the leading cases on legal impossibility is *People v. Jaffe*, 185 N.Y. 497 (1906), in which we held that there was no liability for the attempted receipt of stolen property when the property received by defendant in the belief that it was stolen was, in fact, under the control of the true owner. Similarly, in *People v. Teal*, 196 N.Y. 372 (1909), a conviction for attempted subornation of perjury was overturned on the theory that the testimony attempted to be suborned was irrelevant to the merits of the case. Since it was not subornation of perjury to solicit false, but irrelevant, testimony, "the person through whose procuration the testimony is given cannot be guilty of subornation of perjury and, by the same rule, an unsuccessful attempt to do that which is not a crime when effectuated, cannot be held to be an attempt to commit the crime specified." *Id.* at 377. Factual impossibility, however, was no defense. Thus, a man could be held for attempted grand larceny when he picked an empty pocket. *People v. Moran*, 123 N.Y. 254 (1890); *see also People v. Bauer*, 32 A.D.2d 463, 468 (N.Y. 1969).

As can be seen from even this abbreviated discussion, the distinction between "factual" and "legal" impossibility was a nice one indeed and the courts tended to place a greater value on legal form than on any substantive danger defendant's actions posed for society. The approach of the Model Penal Code was to eliminate the defense of impossibility in virtually all situations. Under the code provision, to constitute an attempt, it is still necessary that the result intended or desired by the actor constitute a crime. However, the code suggested a fundamental change to shift the locus of analysis to the actor's mental frame of reference and away from undue dependence upon external considerations. The basic premise of the code provision is that what was in the actor's own mind should be the standard for determining his dangerousness to society and, hence, his liability for attempted criminal conduct.

In the belief that neither of the two branches of the traditional impossibility arguments detracts from the offender's moral culpability, the Legislature substantially carried the code's treatment of impossibility into the 1967 revision of the Penal Law. Thus, a person is guilty of an attempt when, with intent to commit a crime, he engages in conduct which tends to effect the commission of such crime. It is no defense that, under the attendant circumstances, the crime was factually or legally impossible of commission, if such crime could have been committed had the attendant circumstances been as such person believed them to be. Thus, if defendant believed the victim to be alive at the time of the shooting, it is no defense to the charge of attempted murder that the victim may have been dead.

Turning to the facts of the case before us, we believe that there is sufficient evidence in the record from which the jury could conclude that defendant believed Geller to be alive at the time defendant fired shots into Geller's head. Defendant admitted firing five shots at a most vital part of the victim's anatomy from virtually point blank range. Although defendant contended that the victim had already been grievously wounded by another, from defendant's admitted actions, the jury could conclude that defendant's purpose and intention was to administer the *coup de grace*. The jury never learned of defendant's subsequent allegation that Bush had a gun on him and directed defendant to fire at Geller on the pain of his own life. Defendant did not testify and this statement of duress was made only in a post-verdict affidavit, which obviously was never placed before the jury. In his admissions that were related to the jury, defendant never made such a claim. Nor did he offer any explanation for his conduct, except for an offhand aside made casually to Detective Carrasquillo. Any remaining doubt as to the question of duress is dispelled by defendant's earlier statement that he and Joe Bush had peacefully spent a few days together on vacation in the country. Moreover, defendant admitted to freely assisting Bush in disposing of the weapons after the murder and, once the weapons were out of the picture, defendant made no effort at all to flee from Bush. Indeed, not only did defendant not come forward with his story immediately, but when the police arrived at his house, he related a false version designed to conceal his and Bush's complicity in the murder. All of these facts indicate a consciousness of guilt which defendant would not have had if he had truly believed that Geller was dead when he shot him.

Defendant argues that the jury was bound to accept, at face value, the indications in his admissions that he believed Geller dead.

Certainly, it is true that defendant was entitled to have the entirety of the admissions, both the inculpatory and the exculpatory portions, placed in evidence before the trier of facts. However, the jury was not required to automatically credit the exculpatory portions of the admissions.

The general rule is, of course, that the credibility of witnesses is a question of fact and the jury may choose to believe some, but not all, of a witness's testimony. The general rule applies with equal force to proof of admissions. Thus, it has been stated that "where that part of the declaration which discharges the party making it is itself highly improbable or is discredited by other evidence, the [jury] may believe one part of the admission and reject the other." *People ex rel. Perkins v. Moss*, 187 N.Y. 410, 428 (1907). In *People v. Miller*, 247 A.D. 489, 493 (N.Y. 1936), relied upon by defendant, Justice Lewis ... concluded that the damaging aspects of an admission should not be accepted and the exculpatory portion rejected "unless the latter is disputed by other evidence in the case, or is so improbable as to be unworthy of belief."

In this case, there is ample other evidence to contradict defendant's assertion that he believed Geller dead. There were five bullet wounds inflicted with stunning accuracy in a vital part of the victim's anatomy. The medical testimony indicated that Geller might have been alive at the time defendant fired at him. Defendant voluntarily left the jurisdiction immediately after the crime with his co-perpetrator. Defendant did not report the crime to the police when left on his own by Bush. Instead, he attempted to conceal his and Bush's involvement with the homicide. In addition, the other portions of defendant's admissions make his contended belief that Geller was dead extremely improbable. Defendant, without a word of instruction from Bush, voluntarily got up from his seat after the passage of just a few minutes and fired five times point blank into the victim's face, snuffing out any remaining chance of life that Geller possessed. Certainly, this alone indicates a callous indifference to the taking of a human life. His admissions are barren of any claim of duress,[2] and reflect, instead, an unstinting co-operation in efforts to dispose of vital incriminating evidence. Indeed, defendant maintained a false version of the occurrence until police informed him that they had evidence

---

[2] Notwithstanding the Appellate Division's implication to the contrary, the record indicates that defendant told the Assistant District Attorney that Bush, after shooting Geller, kept his gun aimed at Geller, and not at Dlugash. As defendant stated, "this was after Joe had his .38 on him, I started shooting on him."

that he lately possessed a gun of the same caliber as one of the weapons involved in the shooting. From all of this, the jury was warranted in concluding that defendant acted in the belief that Geller was yet alive when shot by defendant.

The jury convicted defendant of murder. Necessarily, they found that defendant intended to kill a live human being. Subsumed within this finding is the conclusion that defendant acted in the belief that Geller was alive. Thus, there is no need for additional fact-findings by a jury. Although it was not established beyond a reasonable doubt that Geller was, in fact, alive, such is no defense to attempted murder since a murder would have been committed "had the attendant circumstances been as [defendant] believed them to be." Penal Law §110.10. The jury necessarily found that defendant believed Geller to be alive when defendant shot at him.

The Appellate Division erred in not modifying the judgment to reflect a conviction for the lesser-included offense of attempted murder. An attempt to commit a murder is a lesser-included offense of murder and the Appellate Division has the authority, where the trial evidence is not legally sufficient to establish the offense of which defendant was convicted, to modify the judgment to one of conviction for a lesser-included offense which is legally established by the evidence. Thus, the Appellate Division, by dismissing the indictment, failed to take the appropriate corrective action. Further, questions of law were erroneously determined in favor of the appellant at the Appellate Division. While we affirm the order of the Appellate Division to the extent that the order reflects that the judgment of conviction for murder cannot stand, a modification of the order and a remittal for further proceedings is necessary.

## Disposition

Accordingly, the order of the Appellate Division should be modified and the case remitted to the Appellate Division for its review of the facts and for further proceedings with respect to the sentence in the event that the facts are found favorably to the People. As so modified, the order of the Appellate Division should be affirmed.

Chief Judge BREITEL and Judges GABRIELLI, JONES, WACHTLER, FUCHSBERG and COOKE, concur.

## QUESTIONS ON *DLUGASH*

**1. Aiding and abetting Bush.** The prosecutor asked the trial court to submit three bases of liability to the jury: 1) Dlugash murdered Geller; 2) Dlugash attempted murder of Geller; and 3) Dlugash aided and abetted (helped) Bush's murder of Geller. The trial court refused to instruct the jury on aiding and abetting and dismissed that charge altogether. Due to the constitutional ban on Double Jeopardy, that dismissal precluded a retrial on such a theory, given that the dismissal counts as an acquittal. But New York's high court made no secret of its view that in so doing the trial court had erred, though the error was irreversible. According to the high court, "the record would support a reasonable inference that Dlugash intentionally aided Bush in killing Geller and destroying telltale evidence."

This states two different contributions by Dlugash. Intentionally aiding the killing is distinct from covering it up. While aiding the killing makes possible a conviction of murder on the aider's part, covering up the killing makes possible only an after-the-fact form of accessorial liability, a much less serious offense. *See infra* Chapter 4.D, note 4a on *Zielesch* [citing federal accessory-after-the-fact statute].

   **a.** Did the trial court really err in refusing to give the aiding and abetting instruction? How, exactly, would Dlugash have helped Bush kill Geller? By killing Geller himself (that is, by firing fatal shots to his skull)? By shooting Geller after Bush had already killed him? *See infra* Chapter 4.E, question 5 on *McCoy*.

   **b.** If the Court of Appeals can modify the judgment of conviction from murder to attempted murder, why not modify the judgment of conviction from murder on a theory of principal liability (Dlugash is the one who killed Geller) to a judgment of conviction based on a theory of accessorial liability (Bush is the one who killed Geller, but Dlugash helped him)?

**2. Belated claim of duress.** In a post-verdict affidavit, Dlugash claimed that Bush made him shoot Geller. This was apart from what the court called an "aside" to Detective Carrasquillo, the only mention of a claim of duress on Dlugash's part. *Cf.* MPC §2.09(1) ["It is an affirmative defense that the actor engaged in the conduct charged to constitute an offense because he was coerced to do so by the use of, or a threat to use, unlawful force against his person or the person of another, that a person of reasonable firmness in his situation would have been unable to resist."].

   a. Had this claim of duress been before the jury, to what elements of Dlugash's liability is it relevant?

   b. Had this claim of duress been before the jury, who would have the burden of production? And who would have the burden of persuasion? *See* McKinney's Consolidated Laws of New York Annotated §40.00; *supra* Chapter 3.A, note 6 on *Spurlin*.

**3. Dead, alive, or a liminal space between?**

   a. Two physicians from the coroner's office testified for the prosecution. What were their findings? Were they consistent with the findings of Dlugash's witness, the retired coroner?

   b. What did the Appellate Division to whom Dlugash originally appealed conclude about the relation between the findings of those witnesses and the sustainability of Dlugash's murder conviction?

   c. What did the Appellate Division to whom Dlugash originally appealed conclude about the possibility that the proof supported a conviction of attempted murder on Dlugash's part?

**4. Fate of putative principal murderer.** Bush did not testify, but we do know his story, which is set forth in footnote 1. First, of what was he convicted? And second, is his story consistent with Dlugash's?

**5. Legal v. factual impossibility.** The court cites a "general rule developed in most American jurisdictions that legal impossibility is a good defense but factual impossibility is not." That much is true. An act is legally impossible and thus not even an attempt if what defendant is trying to do is not a crime. As examples of legal impossibility, the court cites *State v. Guffey*, *State v. Taylor*, and *People v. Jaffe*. An act is factually impossible and thus an attempt if what defendant is trying (but fails) to do is a crime. As examples of factual impossibility, the court cites *State v. Mitchell*, *United States v. Thomas*, and *People v. Moran*. Looking at the thin facts of these six cases as presented, are you persuaded that *Guffey*, *Taylor*, and *Jaffe* really are cases of legal as opposed to factual impossibility? Hint: they're not. *See supra* Chapter 4.B, Introduction.

**6. Post-crime acts: more on "other minds."** Do Dlugash's trip upstate with Bush after the murder, his assistance in hiding the weapons, and subsequent lie to police about his and Bush's role in Geller's death indicate beyond a reasonable doubt that he believed Geller to be alive when he shot Geller in the head between four and seven times with his .25 caliber pistol?

## NOTES ON *DLUGASH*

*1. Mitigation provision.* The state high court insists that revised New York Penal Code §110.10 (1967), borrowing from Model Penal Code §5.01, "eliminate[d] the defense of impossibility in virtually all situations," focusing instead "on what was in the actor's own mind." But the Model Penal Code did not really eliminate impossibility as a defense. Consider MPC §5.05(2):

> If the particular conduct charged to constitute a criminal attempt, solicitation, or conspiracy is so inherently unlikely to result or culminate in the commission of a crime that neither such conduct nor the actor presents a public danger warranting the grading of such offense under this Section, the Court shall exercise its power ... to enter judgment and impose sentence for a crime of lower grade or degree or, in extreme cases, may dismiss the prosecution.

*2. Issues of law v. issues of fact.* The *Dlugash* court makes the difference between legal and factual impossibility sound obvious. But it's not. Moreover, the court seemed relieved that the difference no longer matters. But it does. *See* MPC §5.05(2) above.

An example of a pure issue of law would be whether police must receive an express waiver of an arrestee's right to counsel before interrogation. An example of a pure issue of fact would be whether the arrestee was denied food, water, and contact with the outside world. Many issues, however, are neither uniquely legal nor uniquely factual. They are instead what the U.S. Supreme Court calls "mixed questions of law and fact." An example would be whether a suspect's waiver was "voluntary" in a constitutional sense. *Miller v. Fenton*, 106 S.Ct. 445, 449-51 (1985). Analysis of the voluntariness of the waiver combines historical facts (defendant's education, age, mental afflictions, length of the detention, whether police gave *Miranda* warnings or made threats or promises) with legal conclusions (the confession was voluntary v. involuntary, i.e., coerced v. spontaneous). *See Lambert v. Blodgett,* 393 F.3d 943, 976-77 & n.23 (9th Cir. 2004).

The *Dlugash* Court's attempt to classify *Jaffe* and *Guffey* (to name just two) as cases involving legal mistakes, and *Mitchell* and *Thomas* (to name just two) as cases involving factual mistakes comes off to some as incomprehensible. A question much more important than "what kind of mistake: legal, factual, or mixed?" is this: has defendant attempted a crime? For that I recommend the following approach: 1) Did defendant *succeed* in committing a crime? If he did, then no issue of attempt, impossible or otherwise, arises. 2) If defendant did *not* succeed in committing a crime, then is what he was *trying* to do illegal? If it is not, then no issue of attempt arises. 3) If what he was trying to do *is* illegal, then *why* did he fail? 4) Did he fail due to a *mistake*? If so, then he has attempted the target crime. 5) Did he fail instead due to a *delusion or fantasy*? If so, then he has, due to "impossibility," committed no crime, not even an attempt.

## C. SOLICITATION AND ITS RELATION TO ATTEMPT

There are two bases for saying that it may be proper to treat some cases as less than, or other than, attempts: 1) the actor could not have had the intention to commit a crime; or 2) the actor did not take a substantial step toward the completed offense. In our next case, *People v. Superior Court (Decker),* 41 Cal.4th 1 (2007), there is no question that defendant intended that a crime occur: audio- and video-recordings memorialized discussions of his plan to have his sister killed. The issue thus is not what defendant intended, but how far the plan went toward the intended offense: did it go beyond mere preparation and become an attempt? Or did the execution of the plan stop short of an attempt and count as mere preparation? In addition, please consider that while mere preparation is insufficient to count as an attempt, it *can* count as other crimes—solicitation and conspiracy—the elements and scope of which we take up now.

Soliciting someone to commit a crime is a crime in itself because it tends to excite the solicited party first into agreement, and then, much more significantly, into action. Solicitation is criminal even though the social harm in the request is nothing like the social harm in acting on the request. Nor is asking or agreeing with someone else to commit a crime quite like trying (and failing) to commit a crime, let alone like actually pulling the crime off.

The crime of solicitation occurs whenever, with the specific intent that the crime or crimes occur, at least one person asks at least one other person to commit a crime. *The Florida Bar v. Marable*, 645 So.2d 438, 442-43 (Fla. 1994). As a specific-intent crime, solicitation is subject to the excuse of voluntary intoxication. *People v. Bottger*, 142 Cal.App.3d 974, 978-79 (1983). The crime is completed when the request is made and received by the solicited party, whether or not the solicited party acts on the request. *Ibid.* But *cf.* MPC §5.02(2) [unreceived request still counts as solicitation]. Proof that a solicitation has occurred requires either two witnesses or at least the corroboration of a single witness's testimony. CALJIC No. 6.35 (2014).

All jurisdictions allow for the soliciting party to avoid responsibility for both the solicitation and its target offense(s) once the request is made, though there is some variation as to what the soliciting party must do to nullify responsibility for both the request and what comes of it. Hornbook bases for dodging a conviction for solicitation and its upshots are: 1) the soliciting party must prevent the solicited party from completing the target offense; 2) the soliciting party must renounce the request to the solicited party prior to the solicited party's commission of the offense (whether or not that succeeds in preventing the target offense from occurring); or 3) the soliciting party must alert law enforcement to the solicitation prior to the solicited party's commission of the offense (whether or not that succeeds in preventing the target offense from occurring). See generally Code of Alabama §13A-4-1 (1977). But *cf.* MPC §5.02(3) [renunciation is legally inoperative if crime occurs anyway]. Absent such an attempt by the soliciting party to repudiate the request, if the solicited party agrees to the request, acts on the request, and completes the offense as requested, then the soliciting party has committed solicitation, conspiracy, and the completed offense, though in no jurisdiction may he be punished for all three.

In *Decker*, the solicitation did not culminate in either a conspiracy or in the completion of the target offense. Instead, the soliciting party's plan was stymied early on by the intervention of law enforcement. In your reading of *Decker*, before taking a position on whether Decker's solicitation somehow evolved into an attempt, consider carefully the relation between the three inchoate offenses: attempt, solicitation, and conspiracy.

# SUPREME COURT OF CALIFORNIA

## THE PEOPLE, PETITIONER
## V.
## THE SUPERIOR COURT OF LOS ANGELES COUNTY, RESPONDENT
## RONALD DECKER, REAL PARTY IN INTEREST

### MAY 21, 2007

BAXTER, Justice

Defendant and real party in interest Ronald Decker has been charged with the attempted willful, deliberate, and premeditated murder of his sister, Donna Decker, and her friend, Hermine Riley Bafiera. Penal Code §664(a). According to the evidence offered at the preliminary hearing, Decker did not want to kill these women himself—as he explained, "he would be the prime suspect" and "would probably make a mistake somehow or another"—so he sought the services of a hired assassin.

Decker located such a person (or thought he did). He furnished the hired assassin with a description of his sister, her home, her car, and her workplace, as well as specific information concerning her daily habits. He also advised the assassin to kill Hermine if necessary to avoid leaving a witness behind. Decker and the hired assassin agreed on the means to commit the murder, the method of payment, and the price. The parties also agreed that Decker would pay $5,000 in cash as a down payment. Before Decker handed over the money, the assassin asked whether Decker was sure he wanted to go through with the murders. Decker replied, "I am absolutely, positively, 100 percent sure, that I want to go through with it. I've never been so sure of anything in my entire life." All of these conversations were recorded and videotaped because, unknown to Decker, he was talking with an undercover police detective posing as a hired assassin.

Decker does not dispute that the foregoing evidence was sufficient to hold him to answer to the charge of solicitation of the murder of Donna and Hermine, but argues that this evidence was insufficient to support a charge of their attempted murder. The magistrate and the trial court, believing themselves bound by *People v. Adami*, 36 Cal.App.3d 452 (1973), reluctantly agreed with Decker and dismissed the attempted-murder charges. The Court of Appeal disagreed with *Adami* and issued a writ of mandate directing the trial court to reinstate the dismissed counts. We granted review to address the conflict and now affirm.

## I. BACKGROUND

Ronald Decker was charged by felony complaint with the attempted willful, deliberate, and premeditated murder of his sister, Donna Decker, and her friend, Hermine Riley Bafiera; the solicitation of Detective Wayne Holston to commit these murders; and the solicitation of Russell Wafer to murder Donna Decker. The undisputed evidence presented at the preliminary hearing revealed the following: On August 20, 2003, Ronald Decker placed a telephone call to Russell Wafer, a gunsmith in Temple City (Los Angeles County). Decker said he was looking for someone to do some "work" for him and arranged to meet privately with Wafer the following week. During that meeting, Decker explained that he had been in contact with *Soldier of Fortune* magazine, had done some research, and came up with Wafer's name as a possible "contractor" for a local "job"—"basically it was that he wanted someone taken care of." Decker added that he could not kill the victim himself because he would be a prime suspect. Wafer advised that while he could not handle the job, his friend "John" from Detroit might be interested. After Decker offered to pay the killer $35,000 and an additional $3,000 to Wafer as a finder's fee, Wafer said he would try to contact John. He instructed Decker to call him back the following week.

In reality, however, Wafer did not know a "John" in Detroit who would be interested in a contract murder. Wafer instead called the Los Angeles County Sheriff's Department, spoke to Detective Wayne Holston, and agreed to assist in a sting operation. When Decker called Wafer on September 2, Wafer claimed he had been in contact with "John," who was coming to town shortly. Wafer asked Decker for his phone number and promised to arrange a meeting with "John." Based on the physical description Wafer had provided and on the phone number Decker had supplied, Holston located a photograph of Decker. Wafer immediately recognized Decker as the man he had met the previous week. At Holston's request, Wafer arranged a meeting with Decker for the evening of September 5 at a golf course parking lot in Arcadia. Holston accompanied Wafer to the meeting and was introduced as "John" from Detroit. Holston was wearing a "wire," and the encounter was both videotaped and recorded.

After Wafer left the two men alone, Decker explained that a "lady" owed him a lot of money and that the only way for him to get it back was "to take her out." Decker subsequently identified the target as his sister, Donna Decker, and provided descriptions of her person, mode of dress, residence, office, car, and daily habits. Decker offered Holston $25,000 to perform the execution, with a $10,000 bonus if it was a "nice, neat, clean job." Decker reiterated that he could not do it himself, as "he would be the prime suspect," and might "slip up" somewhere. When Decker proposed that Holston kill Donna in an automobile accident, Holston warned him that she might survive such an accident. Decker agreed that this may not be the best method, since he wanted her "totally expired," and said he appreciated Holston's advice: "I want a professional—someone that's gonna do the job, and do it right—and do it right." When Holston then proposed killing Donna during a staged robbery or carjacking, Decker said that would be "great" and urged Holston to "shoot her in the heart and head both, just to make sure." Decker added that Donna spent a lot of time with her friend and coworker, Hermine Riley Bafiera, and that Holston might need to "take out" Hermine as well to avoid having a witness. Decker did not care for Hermine, either.

When Holston said he could complete the job within a week, Decker replied, "Marvelous.... The sooner the better." Holston also asked for some money up front, and Decker said he could supply him with $5,000 in cash as a down payment in a couple of days "so you can start right away." The down payment was also designed to prove Decker's sincerity, since "once this goes into effect—she's gonna be killed." Decker could barely contain his eagerness: "Well that's what I want. I don't want go to the hospital then come home. I want absolutely positively expired. Totally expired."

Decker and Holston met again at the golf course on September 7. This meeting was also videotaped and recorded. Decker gave Holston $5,000 in cash, wrapped in two plastic bundles. He reiterated that Holston, after Donna had been murdered, should use a pay phone to leave him a voicemail message—Holston was to say that "the paint job has been completed"—and that Holston would get the rest of the money about a month later. Decker also reiterated that "if Hermine is in the car, with her, you cannot, I understand if I were in your business, I would never leave a witness. You have to take her out too. Whoever's with her you gotta take the other person out too. But don't charge me double."

Holston told Decker that he had already performed some intelligence work, that he was "convinced" he would see the victim the next day, and that he could get this "job" done quickly—eliciting another "marvelous" from Decker—and explained that "once I leave here, it's done. So, you sure you want to go through with it?" Decker replied, "I am absolutely, positively, 100 percent sure, that I want to go through with it. I've never been so sure of anything in my entire life.... Do it very fast ... as fast as you can." At the end of the conversation, Decker seemed "very pleased" and thanked Holston and Wafer. A short time after Holston and Wafer drove off, Decker was arrested.

## II. DISCUSSION

The superior court's dismissal of the attempted murder charges, which was based on undisputed facts, constitutes a legal conclusion subject to independent review on appeal. *People v. Watson*, 30 Cal.3d 290, 300 (1981). The question for us is whether "it appears from the preliminary examination that a public offense has been committed, and there is sufficient cause to believe the defendant guilty thereof. 'Sufficient cause' ... means such a state of facts as would lead a man of ordinary caution or prudence to believe and conscientiously entertain a strong suspicion of the guilt of the accused...." *Williams v. Superior Court*, 71 Cal.2d 1144, 1147 (1969). "Evidence which will justify prosecution under the above test need not be sufficient to support a conviction." *Id.*

Attempted murder requires the specific intent to kill and the commission of a direct but ineffectual act toward accomplishing the intended killing. The uncontradicted evidence that Decker harbored the specific intent to kill his sister (and, if necessary, her friend Hermine) was overwhelming. Decker expressed to both Wafer and Holston his desire to have Donna killed. He researched how to find a hired assassin. He spent months accumulating cash in small denominations to provide the hired assassin with a down payment and had also worked out a method by which to pay the balance. He knew the layout of his sister's condominium and how one might enter it surreptitiously. He had tested the level of surveillance in the vicinity of her home and determined it was "not really that sharp." He chronicled his sister's daily routine at both her home and her office. He offered Holston recommendations on how his sister should be killed and what materials would be necessary. And, at both meetings with Holston, he insisted that Hermine, if she were present, be killed as well, to prevent her from being a witness.

The controversy in this case is whether there was also a direct but ineffectual act toward accomplishing the intended killings. For an attempt, the overt act must go beyond mere preparation and show that the killer is putting his or her plan into action; it need not be the last proximate or ultimate step toward commission of the crime, nor need it satisfy any element of the crime. However, as we have explained, between preparation for the attempt and the attempt itself, there is a wide difference. The preparation consists in devising or arranging the means or measures necessary for the commission of the offense; the attempt is the direct movement toward the commission after the preparations are made. It is sufficient if it is the first or some subsequent act directed towards that end after the preparations are made. As simple as it is to state the terminology for the law of attempt, it is not always clear in practice how to apply it. Much ink has been spilt in an attempt to arrive at a satisfactory standard for telling where preparation ends and attempt begins. None of the various tests used by the courts can possibly distinguish all preparations from all attempts. Although a definitive test has proved elusive, whenever the design of a person to commit crime is clearly shown, slight acts in furtherance of the design will constitute an attempt. Viewing the entirety of Decker's conduct in light of his clearly expressed intent, we find sufficient evidence under the slight-acts rule to hold him to answer to the charges of attempted murder.

Decker's plan was to get rid of his sister so that he could recover money that she owed him. He was concerned, however, that he would be considered an obvious suspect in her murder, so he sought out someone else to carry out his plan. To that end, he conducted research into the underworld of professional killers, budgeted to pay for those services, evaluated how and where the murder should be done, tested the level of security around his sister's condominium, and considered the possibility that there might be a witness and what should be done in that event. Once he met Detective Holston, whom he believed was a professional assassin, they agreed Holston would kill Donna and (if necessary) her friend Hermine, agreed on a price, and agreed it would be done within the week. Decker provided Holston with all of the necessary information concerning his sister, her home and office, habits, and demeanor. He also gave Holston the agreed-on down payment of $5,000 cash. Before he did, Holston warned him, "I want you to know, once I leave here, it's done. So, you sure you want to go through with it?" Decker replied, "I am absolutely, positively, 100 percent sure, that I want to go through with it. I've never been so sure of anything in my entire life."

At the time Decker handed Holston the down payment on the murder, Decker's intention was clear. It was equally clear that he was actually putting his plan into action. Decker had secured an agreement with Holston to murder Donna (and, if necessary, her friend Hermine); had provided Holston with all the information necessary to commit the crimes; had given Holston the $5,000 down payment; and had understood that "it's done" once Holston left with the money. These facts would lead a reasonable person to believe a crime is about to be consummated absent an intervening force—and thus that the attempt is underway. Indeed, as Justice Epstein noted below, "there was nothing more for Decker to do to bring about the murder of his sister." Although Decker did not himself point a gun at his sister, he did aim at her an armed professional who had agreed to commit the murder.[1]

As contrary authority, Decker relies on *Adami*, which affirmed the dismissal of an attempted murder charge on similar facts, and relies also on the small number of out-of-state ... opinions that have followed *Adami*. In *Adami*, the defendant sought to have his wife killed because she had stolen money from him. He agreed on a price with an undercover police agent posing as an assassin and supplied the agent with a photograph of the victim, a description of the victim and her residence and vehicles, and other pertinent information. The defendant gave the police agent a $500 down payment and announced he was not going to change his mind. *Adami* declared that these acts consisted solely of solicitation or mere preparation and concluded, in accordance with the weight of authority, that solicitation alone is not an attempt.

First, *Adami* makes no mention of the slight-acts rule, which has long been the rule for attempted crimes in California. Indeed, *Adami's* progeny make no attempt to reconcile their analysis with the slight-acts rule and instead explicitly reject it. Our adoption of the slight-acts rule in *People v. Anderson*, 1 Cal.2d 687, 690 (1934), was supported by a citation to *Stokes v. State*, 92 Miss. 415 (1908), one of the leading U.S. cases on attempts and which (like the present case) involved a defendant who hired another to perform a murder. The cases on

---

[1] Decker does not argue here that the attempted murder charges must be dismissed because, notwithstanding Decker's own conduct, Detective Holston never intended to commit the murders.

which Decker relies thus conflict not only with California law but also with the fairly general agreement that slight acts are enough when the intent to murder is clear. Indeed, where (as here) the crime involves concerted action—and hence a greater likelihood that the criminal objective will be accomplished—there is a *greater* urgency for intervention by the state at an *earlier* stage in the course of that conduct. Had Decker struck an agreement with and paid earnest money to a real hired killer, he could have been prosecuted for conspiracy to commit murder, which is punishable to the same extent as the completed crime of first-degree murder. Because of the fortuity that Decker's hired killer was actually an undercover detective, Decker faces the much less serious charge of attempted murder. Neither Decker nor the dissent offers any reason for us to create an exception to the slight-acts rule for attempted murder, especially in *Stokes*'s classic formulation where the attempt involves concerted action with others, merely to further reduce Decker's maximum potential punishment.

Second, *Adami* misconceived the issue under these circumstances to be "whether the solicitation itself was sufficient to establish probable cause to believe that defendant attempted the murder." *Adami*, 36 Cal.App.3d at 455. Decker similarly expends considerable effort to convince us that "solicitation of another to commit a crime is an attempt to commit that crime if, but only if, it takes the form of urging the other to join with the solicitor in perpetrating that offense, not at some future time or distant place, but here and now, and the crime is such that it cannot be committed by one without the cooperation and submission of another." But a solicitation requires only that a person invite another to commit or join in an enumerated crime (including murder) with the intent that the crime be committed. Penal Code §653f. The solicitation is complete once the request is made and is punishable "irrespective of the reaction of the person solicited." *In re Ryan N.*, 92 Cal.App.4th 1359, 1377 (2001). In this case, the solicitation was complete early in Decker's first conversation with Holston, when he asked Holston to kill Donna. But the People do not contend that this request was sufficient to prosecute Decker for attempted murder. They argue instead that the solicitation, in combination with Decker's subsequent conduct, revealed his plan to have Holston murder Donna (and, if necessary, her friend Hermine) and that Decker put this plan into operation no later than the point at which he completed the agreement with Holston, finalized the details surrounding the murders, and paid Holston $5,000 in earnest money.

The issue, then, is not whether "solicitation alone" is sufficient to establish an attempt, but whether a solicitation to commit murder, combined with a completed agreement to hire a professional killer and the making of a down payment under that agreement, can establish probable cause to believe Decker attempted to murder these victims. A substantial number of our sister states have held that it can. *E.g., State v. Mandel*, 78 Ariz. 226 (1954); *United States v. Church*, 32 M.J. 70, 73 (USCMA 1991). Additional jurisdictions have held that a solicitation to murder, in combination with a completed agreement to hire a professional killer and further conduct implementing the agreement, can similarly constitute an attempted murder. *E.g., Braham v. State*, 571 P.2d 631, 638 (Alaska 1977) [completed agreement, plus a visit by the hired killer to the victim to "foster a relationship of trust and confidence"]; *State v. Group*, 98 Ohio St.3d 248, 262 (2002) ["Group did more than merely solicit the firebombing of Mrs. Lozier's house. He took all action within his power, considering his incarceration, to ensure that the crime would be committed"]. We find these authorities persuasive.

Third, *Adami* mistakenly assumes that there can be no overlap between the evidence that would prove solicitation to murder and that which would prove attempted murder. Indeed, Decker asserts that these are "mutually exclusive crimes." But it could not be plainer, as Chief Justice Holmes put it, that while "preparation is not an attempt," nonetheless "*some* preparations may amount to an attempt." *Commonwealth v. Peaslee*, 177 Mass. 267 (1901). Conduct that qualifies as mere preparation and conduct that qualifies as a direct but ineffectual act toward commission of the crime exist on a continuum, "since all acts leading up to the ultimate consummation of a crime are by their very nature preparatory." *State v. Sunzar*, 331 N.J. Super. 248 (1999). The difference between them is a question of degree. There is thus no error in resting a finding of attempted murder in part on evidence that *also* tends to establish solicitation to commit murder and vice versa. *State v. Kilgus*, 519 A.2d 231, 236 (N.H. 1986) ["whether the defendant's actions constituted solicitation was not important so long as his actions also constituted an attempt"]. After all, even under Decker's analysis, evidence of a solicitation to commit murder can support a finding of attempted murder if the defendant then "provides the hit man the instrument or other means to procure the death." See *Adami*, 36 Cal.App.3d at 457. Decker offers no principled basis for a different result when the hit man already has a weapon and the defendant instead begins payment under the contract to kill.

Fourth, we reject the contention, endorsed by Decker and by *Adami*'s progeny, that there is no persuasive reason why a solicitation to commit murder should be treated differently merely because part of the agreed-upon fee has passed hands. As the People point out, a down payment on a contract to murder serves the same purpose as a down payment on any other type of contract. It evidences the solicitor's seriousness of purpose and makes the object of the contract closer to fruition. *State v. Molasky*, 765 S.W.2d 597, 602 (Mo. 1989); *cf. Johnson v. Sheriff, Clark County*, 91 Nev. 161 (1975) [no down payment was offered to the would-be killer]. It blinks reality to equate the threat posed by an individual who has merely invited another, perhaps unsuccessfully, to commit murder with the threat posed by an individual who has already reached an agreement with a hired killer to commit murder, finalized the plans, and made the down payment under the contract to kill. But for Holston's status as an undercover detective, it is likely that Decker's conduct would have resulted in the murder of these victims. Where, as here, the defendant's intent is unmistakable, the courts should not destroy the practical and common-sense administration of the law with subtleties as to what constitutes preparation and what constitutes an act done toward the commission of a crime.

The purpose of requiring an overt act is that until such act occurs, one is uncertain whether the intended design will be carried out. When, by reason of the defendant's conduct, the situation is "without any equivocality," and it appears the design will be carried out if not interrupted, the defendant's conduct satisfies the test for an overt act. Here, the record supported at least a strong suspicion that Decker's intent to have his sister (and, if necessary, her friend) murdered was unambiguous and that he had commenced the commission of the crime by doing all that he needed to do to accomplish the murders.

In finding the record sufficient to hold Decker to answer to the charges of attempted murder here, we do not decide whether an agreement to kill followed by a down payment is *always* sufficient to support a charge of attempted murder. Whether acts done in contemplation of the commission of a crime are merely preparatory or whether they are instead sufficiently close to the consummation of the crime is a question of degree and depends upon the facts and circumstances of a particular case. A different situation may exist, for example, when the assassin has been hired and paid but the victims have not yet been identified. In this case, however, Decker had effectively done all that he needed to do to ensure that Donna and her friend be executed. Accordingly, he should have been held to answer to the charges of attempted murder. We disapprove of *Adami* to the extent it is inconsistent with this opinion.

### DISPOSITION

The judgment of the Court of Appeal is affirmed.

GEORGE, C.J., KENNARD, CHIN, MORENO and CORRIGAN, JJ., concur.

WERDEGAR, Justice, dissenting.

My colleagues hold that defendant's conduct in soliciting the murder of his sister, reaching an agreement with a hired assassin to do the killing, and making a down payment under the agreement establishes probable cause to believe defendant himself attempted the murder. I respectfully dissent. "An attempt to commit a crime consists of two elements: a specific intent to commit the crime, and a direct but ineffectual act done toward its commission." Penal Code §21a. Defendant's conduct in this case does not include "a direct but ineffectual act" done toward the murder's commission. Accordingly, he cannot be guilty of attempted murder.

As we have long recognized, the required act for an attempt under California law must be directed towards immediate consummation of the crime attempted. As the majority details, defendant's conduct included numerous *indirect* acts toward accomplishing the murder of his sister: he sought the services of a hired assassin; he located a person (actually an undercover police detective) he thought would act as such; he furnished the supposed assassin with a description of his sister, her home, car, and workplace, as well as information concerning her daily habits; he discussed how the murder would be done and how and when he would pay for the work, agreeing to furnish $5,000 in cash as a down payment; and, finally, just before he was arrested, he stated he was "absolutely, positively, 100 percent sure, that I want to go through with it" and urged the supposed assassin to do it "as fast as you can."

I agree with the majority that as evidence defendant harbored the specific intent to kill his sister, these facts are overwhelming. None of them, however, constitutes a *direct* but ineffectual act done toward the murder's commission. As the majority states, defendant "did not himself point a gun at his sister"; neither did he otherwise directly menace her. Instead, he relied on the person he thought had agreed to commit the murder to do the actual deed.[1] The direct object of defendant's preparatory acts was the person he sought to engage as his agent—not the ultimate, intended victim of the scheme.

We previously have stated that for attempt, it must be "clear from a suspect's acts what *he* intends to do...." *People v. Dillon*, 34 Cal.3d 441, 455 (1983). In this case, what defendant intended to do was have his sister killed *by someone else*. Defendant's own conduct did not include even "slight" acts toward actual commission of the murder. That he hired another, supplied him with information, and paid him a down payment only highlights his intention not to perform the act himself.

The California cases the majority purports to rely on generally involve single actors, i.e., defendants who acted directly on their victims.[2] These cases simply confirm that for attempt a defendant must have committed a direct act toward commission of the crime. Defendant here committed no direct act toward commission of the

---

[1] Although the majority asserts defendant "did aim at [his sister] an armed professional who had agreed to commit the murder," the armed professional referred to (the detective) only *pretended* to agree so that in fact there was no agreement, though defendant thought there was. This absence of actual agreement presumably is why the case was not prosecuted as a conspiracy. See *People v. Jurado*, 38 Cal.4th 72, 120 (2006) ["A conviction of conspiracy requires proof that the defendant and another person had the specific intent to agree or conspire to commit an offense, as well as the specific intent to commit the elements of that offense, together with proof of the commission of an overt act by one or more of the parties to such agreement in furtherance of the conspiracy"].

[2] *See, e.g., People v. Memro*, 38 Cal.3d 658, 699 (1985) [ushering a boy into a room and standing close by during a strobe display were direct acts sufficient for the attempted commission of a lewd or lascivious act on a minor]; *Dillon*, 34 Cal.3d at 456 [arriving on land armed and disguised, and dividing into groups to encircle a field, were direct acts sufficient for the attempted robbery of a marijuana farm]; *People v. Anderson*, 1 Cal.2d 687, 690 (1934) [approaching a ticket office and pulling out a gun were direct acts sufficient for the attempted armed robbery of a theater]; *People v. Morales*, 5 Cal.App.4th 917, 926-27 (1992) [threatening twice to "get" the victim, going home, loading a gun, driving to the victim's neighborhood, and hiding in a position with a clear shot were direct acts sufficient for attempted murder].

murder, since his scheme interposed a third party between himself and his intended victim, and the third party never acted. The majority goes astray in applying to this solicitation-of-murder case, where action by another person was required to effectuate (or attempt) the intended killing, principles applicable when an offense is intended and attempted by a single individual.

Although defendant's conduct went beyond the minimum required for solicitation, for purposes of attempt law his arrangements constitute mere preparation. Reprehensible as they were, his acts "did not amount to any more than the mere arrangement of the proposed measures for the accomplishment" of the crime. *Adami*, 36 Cal.App.3d at 457-58. This is because, as a logical matter, they did no more than "leave the intended assailant only in the condition to commence the first direct act toward consummation of the defendant's design." *Id.* at 458. To do all one can to motivate and encourage another to accomplish a killing—even to make a down payment on a contract to kill—while blameworthy and punishable, is neither logically nor legally equivalent to attempting the killing oneself. The majority's supportive reasoning likewise conflates the two separate elements of attempt, specific intent and direct act: "Viewing the entirety of defendant's conduct *in light of his clearly expressed intent*, we find sufficient evidence under the slight-acts rule to hold him to answer to the charges of attempted murder." As a court, we are not authorized to ignore the statutory requirements.

The majority's criticisms of *Adami* are unpersuasive. The majority faults *Adami* for not mentioning the slight-acts rule, but since the *Adami* court concluded no "appreciable fragment of the crime charged was accomplished," *id.* at p. 457, the rule had no application. Nor, contrary to the majority's account, did *Adami* assume that evidence of solicitation cannot also be evidence of attempt. *Adami* simply held that hiring a murderer, planning the murder, and making a down payment logically constitute "solicitation or mere preparation," not attempted murder.

Confronted with statutory language and judicial precedent contrary to its conclusion, the majority relies on out-of-state cases. Several of these interpret attempt statutes distinguishable from our own. Others involve more than a completed agreement with a hired killer, including a direct act *toward the victim*.[5] The remaining cases

---

[5] *See, e.g., State v. Mandel*, 278 P.2d 413, 415–16 (Ariz. 1954) [defendant planned to entice victim to murder scene and drove assassin in her car to view victim's home

are in my view mistaken for the same reason the majority is mistaken: they implicitly allow that a defendant may be guilty of attempt when no direct act toward the commission of the crime has been done. Courts in some other jurisdictions have, as the majority fails to acknowledge, maintained the distinction between preparation and attempt in cases similar to this.

Had the supposed assassin hired to kill defendant's sister actually attempted to kill her, defendant would be punishable as a principal in the offense, either as aider and abettor or as co-conspirator. But here, neither defendant nor the supposed assassin took a direct act toward commission of the offense. Defendant's conduct was confined to encouraging and enabling his intended agent to kill (or attempt to kill), but the detective with whom he dealt took no such action. There was no attempt.

For the foregoing reasons, I dissent.

## QUESTIONS ON *DECKER*

**1. Procedural posture.**

**a.** The caption lists Decker as the "real party in interest" after naming the superior court as defendant. Are the People suing the court? Prosecuting Decker? Both?

**b.** Was Decker convicted of any crime? If not, then what is the procedural posture of the case? Can a criminal defendant get to the California Supreme Court without ever having been tried at all?

**2. Double-counting crimes**. The complaint charged Decker with soliciting Russell Wafer and Wayne Holston to commit murder. Does this mean that if Holston had declared himself unsuited to the job, but recommended a third (and then a fourth) hit-man, and Decker approached the third (and then the fourth) man as well, he would have committed three (or four) acts of solicitation? Why not just one?

For examples of cases where prosecutors succeeded in piling on

---

and arroyo where body was to be disposed of]; *State v. Kilgus*, 519 A.2d 231, 235–36 (N.H. 1986) [defendant said he was "going to have to get involved" and made arrangements for the victim to be alone]; *State v. Burd*, 419 S.E.2d 676, 680 (W. Va. 1991) [defendant offered to drive the assassin to show him the victim's house and provided a fake suicide note to leave at the crime scene and money for a gun].

counts from a single transaction or occurrence, see *People v. Fichtner*, 118 N.Y.S.2d 392 (App. Div. 1952) [extortionist commits two counts of extortion by receiving down payment and one installment from victim], and *Graham v. United States*, 187 F.2d 87 (D.C. Cir. 1950) [unscrupulous attorney commits two counts of fraud by receiving two payments from client-victim to satisfy one fraudulent demand for $2K in unearned fees].

**3. Standard of review.** The California Supreme Court cites *People v. Watson*, *supra* Chapter 2.A, as controlling precedent for determining the standard of review to be applied to the issues raised in Decker's appeal. Is the standard as articulated in *Decker* faithful to the standard the court applied in *Watson*? On this, see *infra* note 2 on *Decker*.

**4. How far did Decker go on the attempt continuum?**

   **a.** There are two elements in any attempt, both of which must be proved by the prosecution beyond a reasonable doubt: 1) specific intent to complete the crime; and 2) a substantial step toward the completed offense or, what is the same, a direct but ineffectual act to that end. There is ample evidence that Decker intended that his sister be killed, though nowhere does the case state how this would have achieved his stated purpose of recouping the money she owed him. (Did the siblings jointly hold property? Did his sister name him beneficiary to her life insurance policy?) In order for his acts manifesting that intention to count as "substantial" or "direct but ineffectual," they must surpass "mere preparation." To cross that line, the *Decker* Court notes, the attempter need not take "the last proximate or ultimate step toward commission of the crime or crimes." For the court, determining what counts as an attempt occurs on a continuum. That is, California, like the Model Penal Code, focuses not on how much remains to be done before the target offense is completed, but on how much already has been done. See *supra* Chapter 4.A, question 8 on *Bond*; see also *State v. Disanto*, 688 N.W.2d 201, 217-18 (S.D. 2004). ["[I]t is universally recognized that the acts of solicitation and attempt are a continuum between planning and perpetration of the offense."].

   If "slight acts" are enough to count as an attempt, then how are "slight acts" distinguished from "mere preparation"? By requiring that those acts be "unequivocal" or "unambiguous"? What does *that* add?

**b.** The majority clarifies that the issue is not whether solicitation alone is an attempt. Apart from asking "John" (Detective Holston) to kill his sister and, if present, her friend, too, what additional gestures did Decker make that put the request beyond mere preparation and into the realm of attempt?

**c.** The Supreme Court emphasizes that by the time Holston received $5,000 for the job, Decker's plan was in action. Quoting the Court of Appeal below, the Supreme Court insisted that "'there was nothing more for Decker to do to bring about the murder of his sister.'" While Decker aimed no gun at her, "he did aim at her an armed professional" in the person of Holston. At this point the Supreme Court drops a footnote (n.1) pointing out that Decker is *not* arguing that the fact that Holston never lifted a finger toward killing Decker's sister somehow blocks Decker from being properly charged with attempted murder.

But Decker *is* arguing that, isn't he?

**5. Feigned principal really feigns it up.** Neither Wafer nor Holston took any steps toward killing Decker's sister or her friend. If either solicited party actually did attempt murder, then convicting Decker of attempt as well would follow on a theory of aiding and abetting the perpetrator in the act. But suppose Holston went to Decker's sister's home and, while Decker waited in the car, pretended to try to kill her in a charade, after which Holston produced doctored photos of her bullet-riddled "corpse" for Decker, whose response is a first-class fit of fake grief. Suppose as well that Decker, pleased with the results, promptly paid over to Holston the $20,000 balance of the $25,000 debt, plus the additional $10,000 bonus as promised for a job exceptionally well done.

Would dissenting Justice Werdegar and the authorities on which she relies take a different position on those facts as to whether Decker had attempted murder?

## NOTES ON *DECKER*

**1. What is at stake: punishment costs.** In seeking to reverse the trial court's dismissal of the attempted-murder charges against Decker, the prosecution resisted the prospect of a trial charging him only with solicitation of murder. As the majority points out, "had

Decker struck an agreement with and paid earnest money to a real hired killer, he could have been prosecuted for conspiracy to commit murder, which is punishable to the same extent as the completed crime of first degree murder." But no conspiracy charge fit the case because no actual agreement had been reached between Decker and either Wafer or Holston, just the appearance of such an agreement.

The punishment for solicitation is less than that of the completed offense. California Penal Code §653f (2012) states in pertinent part:

> (a) Every person who, with the intent that the crime be committed, solicits another to offer, accept, or join in the offer or acceptance of a bribe, or to commit or join in the commission of carjacking, robbery, burglary, grand theft, receiving stolen property, extortion, perjury, subornation of perjury, forgery, kidnapping, arson or assault with a deadly weapon or instrument or by means of force likely to produce great bodily injury, or, by the use of force or a threat of force, to prevent or dissuade any person who is or may become a witness from attending upon, or testifying at, any trial, proceeding, or inquiry authorized by law, shall be punished by imprisonment in a county jail for not more than one year or ... by a fine of not more than ten thousand dollars ($10,000), or the amount which could have been assessed for commission of the offense itself, whichever is greater, or by both the fine and imprisonment.
>
> (b) Every person who, with the intent that the crime be committed, solicits another to commit or join in the commission of murder shall be punished by imprisonment in the state prison for three, six, or nine years.
>
> (c) Every person who, with the intent that the crime be committed, solicits another to commit rape by force or violence, sodomy by force or violence, oral copulation by force or violence, or any violation of [other enumerated sex offenses], shall be punished by imprisonment in the state prison for two, three, or four years....

Refer now in our materials to *supra* Chapter 4.A, note 5 on *Bond*, where the punishments for attempt are set forth in an excerpt from California Penal Code §664. Although California generally gives a 50% discount in punishment for failing to complete the target offense, attempted premeditated murder (§664(a)), just like conspiracy to commit murder (§182(a)(1)), is punishable by a life sentence.

Compare that with §653f, which sets the base term for solicitation of murder at six years. It may now be clearer what is staked in the *Decker* litigation: the difference between six years and life imprisonment.

***2. Standard of review.*** In question 3 above on *Decker*, I asked what standard of review the California Supreme Court applied to Decker's claims on appeal. The California Supreme Court identified the standard as arising out of *People v. Watson*, also a case, you recall, where the prosecution sought reinstatement of charges dismissed on defendant's pre-trial motion. The *Decker* Court stated the standard of review of the trial court's dismissal of attempted-murder charges as follows:

> The superior court's dismissal of the attempted murder charges, which was based on undisputed facts, constitutes a legal conclusion subject to independent review on appeal. *People v. Watson*, 30 Cal.3d at 300. The question for us is whether it appears from the preliminary examination that a public offense has been committed, and there is sufficient cause to believe the defendant guilty thereof. 'Sufficient cause' ... means such a state of facts as would lead a man of ordinary caution or prudence to believe and conscientiously entertain a strong suspicion of the guilt of the accused.... Evidence which will justify prosecution under the above test need not be sufficient to support a conviction.

This standard is reconcilable with the normal deference that appellate courts give trial-court rulings (reversible only if plainly erroneous) only by careful attention to the function in the above passage of the term "undisputed facts."

Please recall Chief Justice Bird's dissent in *Watson*, where she accused the majority of "ignor[ing] facts and apply[ing] an improper legal standard to reverse the magistrate's refusal to hold [Watson] to answer and the superior court's grant of [his] motion to dismiss the charge of murder...." To Bird, the majority could reach the result it did only by repudiating the testimony of witness Paul Henke, who must have contributed to the magistrate's finding of no probable cause of malice on Watson's part.

Bird's principal point about the appellate standard of review of a magistrate's ruling on whether a prosecutor's charges are supported by probable cause is worth quoting at length:

The majority claim that they are only reviewing undisputed facts.... But material facts—whether [Watson] drove down Cypress Avenue at 55 or 60 as opposed to 70 or 80 miles per hour, and whether he had a green light as he started into the intersection where the accident occurred—were disputed. The majority acknowledge Henke's testimony. However, in making the crucial determination as to whether there was probable cause to hold [Watson] to answer, they conveniently ignore Henke's testimony.... The only way that they can ignore this testimony, which is in [Watson's] favor, is to first decide that Henke was not a credible witness. This is not an undisputed fact. It is a conclusion impermissibly drawn by the majority.

If the magistrate had held [Watson] to answer, the court could draw all legitimate inferences from the evidence which favored that action.... Deference is given to a magistrate's finding of probable cause. The magistrate weighs the evidence, resolves any factual conflicts, and determines the credibility of the witnesses.... The superior or appellate court may not substitute its judgment for that of the magistrate as it relates to conflicts in or the weight of the evidence.

This rule is in accord with the general rule of appellate review that evidence adduced in the trial court is viewed on appeal in the light most favorable to the judgment entered below....

Here, the magistrate failed to find probable cause. Therefore, there is no legal or factual basis for this court to defer to the validity of the [charges]. No deference can be given under these circumstances without directly interfering with the magistrate's power to weigh the evidence and decide disputed factual issues. Yet, that is what the majority have done.

When a superior or appellate court reviews a magistrate's determination that probable cause did not exist, the court should resolve all conflicts and draw all reasonable inferences in favor of the judgment below.

In this case any inferences drawn should be in favor of the magistrate's determination of lack of probable cause. These would include the facts that [Watson] had a green light on Cypress and that he was driving at 55 to 60 miles per hour.

> These inferences are reasonable. There was no evidence of fabrication or of a motive for Henke to fabricate. He did not know [Watson]. He had a reasonable explanation for waiting more than a day to give a statement to the police. The officers at the scene of the accident had told him to keep away.

After reading the above two passages from *Decker* and *Watson*, it should be clearer how appellate courts (the masters of *law*) need not defer to the judgments of trial courts (the masters of *facts*) when facts, witness credibility, or weight of evidence are *not* in dispute. In *Decker*, the facts really were undisputed: Decker's plot to kill his sister was recorded. Thus the Court of Appeal had nothing *to* defer to below; instead, it was free to independently assess whether, with the facts as given, there was probable cause that Decker attempted murder of his sister despite Holston's role as feigned principal. The Court of Appeal therefore permissibly substituted its own judgment for the trial court's on whether the undisputed facts support the legal conclusion that Decker should be tried for attempted murder.

Compare this with *Watson*, where, as Chief Justice Bird noted, the Supreme Court was not just exercising its independent judgment about whether undisputed facts about the fatal car crash constituted malice on Watson's part. Instead, she insisted (with good grounds, too), that reinstating the charges of second-degree murder against Watson could be justified only by rejecting Henke's testimony, which the magistrate and trial judge did not do in dismissing Watson's charges of second-degree murder. Since Henke's testimony conflicted with evidence more favorable to the prosecution, appellate review of such conflict must defer to the trial judge's ruling below—overruling the trial judge's ruling only if plainly erroneous. Thus Chief Justice Bird's quarrel with the majority's ruling arose out of her impression that the majority erred by independently reviewing facts (which it may not do), rather than independently reviewing only legal conclusions (which it may do).

### 3. *Criminal procedure.*

*a. **More on preliminary hearings.*** At the outset of Justice Baxter's majority opinion, he mentions "the evidence offered at the preliminary hearing." "Prelims," as they are called, are held promptly after felony charges are filed against a defendant. *E.g.*, West's Kansas Statutes Annotated §22-2902. Their stated purpose is to have a judge evaluate whether there is probable cause to bind the case over for trial. *See supra* Chapter 2.A, note 1 on *Watson*. Though arrest warrants authorize police to bring suspects into custody, judicial authorization to *arrest* suspects is separate from judicial authorization to *charge* them. The only time one judicial action will authorize both charges and arrest is when a Grand Jury (which is said to be a judicial body, though no judge is present) issues an indictment. If the judge at the prelim finds probable cause to support the charges, then the case is bound over for trial. If the judge finds that the charges are not supported by probable cause, then the charges are dismissed, but without prejudice. That is, since jeopardy does not attach until trial, the prosecution can send the police out to beef up the case against the suspect without running afoul of the ban on Double Jeopardy.

The unstated purpose of prelims is to allow the defendant a sneak-peek at the prosecution's case against him, from the theory of the case to the strength of the evidence, including the credibility of the State's witnesses, be they an arresting police officer or a civilian whose testimony is crucial to the charges. By discovering key ingredients of the prosecution's case, the defendant can use the prelim (referred to cynically as a "fishing expedition") to help prepare his defense and to make a more informed decision about whether to test the case at trial rather than settle it through plea bargain. *See McKeldin v. State*, 516 S.W.2d 82, 85-86 (Tenn. 1974).

**b. Division of labor between judges and magistrates.** Please note that the California Supreme Court refers to the fact that the magistrate and the trial court agreed that there was no probable cause that Decker had attempted murder. The trial court of course is the trial judge, who in this case granted Decker's motion to dismiss the attempted-murder charges. Magistrates are judicial officers who do much of the fact-finding that bogs down trial courts. Among the functions that magistrates perform in criminal courts are: 1) ruling on applications by police for search and arrest warrants; 2) promptly reviewing arrests that took place without a warrant to see if there was probable cause to support what police did; 3) ruling (as in *Decker*) whether charges against defendant are supported by probable cause; 4) determining the conditions of defendant's enlargement on bail; 5) accepting pleas in and trying petty criminal cases; and 6) whatever other functions are conferred on magistrates by statute. These functions may require official approval of the trial court before becoming the law of the case. For the process of the appointment and tenure of federal magistrates, see 28 U.S.C.A. §631 (2010).

***c. Probable cause, quantified.*** Probable cause is a criminal-law standard that justifies all arrests and charges (and most searches and seizures). It requires roughly a 50% probability that defendant did what police or prosecutors suspect him of doing. (Some estimate the requisite probability may be lower than that). This standard is more demanding of police and prosecutors than the criminal-law standard of reasonable suspicion—roughly a 25% probability—which since 1968 justifies some police searches and seizures that are quite limited in scope. *See, e.g., Lindsey ex rel. Lindsey v. Caddo Parish School Bd.*, 954 So.2d 272, 274 n.1 (La. Ct. App. 2007); *cf.* William J. Stuntz, *Privacy's Problem in the Law of Criminal Procedure*, 93 Michigan Law Review 1016, 1023-24 & n.29 (1995) ["extrapolating" reasonable suspicion as "a one in four chance" as opposed to probable cause, which is "a significantly tougher standard"].

Proof at trial of guilt beyond a reasonable doubt is the highest standard of proof in law. It is by all accounts much more demanding than probable cause, yet short of 100% certainty. *See In re As. H.*, 851 A.2d 456, 461 (D.C. Ct. App. 2004) [noting study where nine judges on one federal court estimated beyond a reasonable doubt as 76%, 80%, 85%, 85%, 85%, 85%, 90%, 90%, 95%].

***d. Writ of mandate.*** The Court of Appeal issued a writ of mandate ordering the trial court to reinstate the attempted-murder charges against Decker. The writ of mandate is a procedure that allows appellate courts to intervene prior to a final judgment in the case to correct erroneous trial-court action where there is no right of appeal. A trial court's pre-trial ruling dismissing charges against a defendant is not a final judgment because such a ruling does not constitute a judgment of acquittal or conviction. Prosecution or defense appeals are generally precluded prior to a final judgment, though not without exception. *See supra* Chapter 4.C, question 1 on *Decker*; Chapter 2.A, note 2 on *Watson*.

**4. More on doing one's own dirty work.** The *Decker* majority correctly states that criminal associations *tend* to succeed more than solo ventures do. Whether this statement is true poses a complex empirical question; but absent evidence that too many cooks spoil the broth, there is nothing wrong with treating criminal associations *as though* they create excessive risks of harm-causing criminality.

Sound social policy discourages criminal associations, giving credit where credit is due: not merely to the ringleader, but to the ring as well. But we go too far when we conclude that soliciting or conspiring is identical to their target crimes. The request is too mediated by the will of the requested party to be treated as though the contemplated harm has taken or must take place. This is not to say that the target of the plot would be indifferent to the plot so long as it is never carried out. For example, parents who discover a razor blade in their child's apple *feel* harmed, though much less so than if the parents were less vigilant.

**5. Soliciting party's intentions.** If I ask you to try to score a basket against LeBron James, it would be eccentric for me to say (provided I have not placed such constraints on your will, or knowingly so exploited your *ex ante* lack of autonomy that it ceases to be your spontaneous act), "*I have tried to score against LeBron James.*" I have encouraged *you* to try to score against him. Whether an attempt takes place is at this point up to you, regardless of where the idea originates. Yet *Decker* holds otherwise. The central point of Justice Werdegar's dissent in *Decker* is that the placement of Holston between Decker and his sister makes whether an attempt occurs dependent on Holston's actions, no longer on Decker's intentions.

The same criticism of solicitations as attempts is just as easily directed at re-descriptions of conspiracies as attempts. *See* Phillip Johnson, *The Unnecessary Crime of Conspiracy*, 61 California Law Review 1137 (1973) [arguing conspiracies are attempts]. Conspiracies may demonstrate their members' bad intentions, but by agreeing to kill someone tomorrow or next month, the parties have no more attempted or tried to commit murder than those who engage to marry attempt to marry, or those who register for a Bar-Examination prep-course attempt to take the Bar Exam merely by registering. To be sure, the Model Penal Code's flexible definition of attempt *can* convert some preparatory behavior into an attempt (e.g., searching for a victim, reconnoitering, or possessing materials to be used in crime). MPC §5.01(2)(a)-(f). But even the Code rules out acts of solicitation as attempts except in specialized cases where, for example, the recruited agent is a child or insane. MPC §5.01(2)(g).

**6. Failure as excuse.** It is hard to imagine a blame regime in which the distinction between intentions and outcomes, between manifest and harm-causing criminality, would *not* be acknowledged. For example, who would judge the base urges of Jimmy Carter, who famously admitted to lust in his heart, as comparable to those of Bill

Clinton, who infamously gratified his lusts? *See* Robert Scheer, *Jimmy (Carter), We Hardly Know Y'all*, Playboy, November 1976, at 86. Like solicitation and conspiracy, attempt is an inchoate offense. Inchoate offenders do not bring about the harm they've set themselves to. That they don't is what it means to *be* an inchoate offender. Take an instance in which you and I both take aim and fire loaded guns at the President, whom each of us intends to kill to express our opposition to executive action taken abroad. I fail, whether it is a nearby bird, bad aim, or a miraculous surgeon that accounts for the failure. You succeed in the killing, whether it is due to meticulous planning, good aim, or a lucky shot. When both of us are apprehended and our accounts of our actions are evaluated, it is plausible to say we have in a sense both done the same thing: we have both shot at the President. If that is a satisfactory description of our actions, then clearly I have a ready excuse that you do not: I failed, I missed, I blundered, I was lucky—I killed no one. Luck matters, in and out of court.

**7. More on doubly inchoate offenses.** Suppose Decker's solicitations ended up unreceived by his intended recipients when lost in the mail, intercepted by a prison warden, or, if received, then for some reason not comprehended (illiterate, not a native speaker). According to the Model Penal Code, a solicitation has still occurred. MPC §5.02(2). Elsewhere, the approach is that solicitations must be received, but *attempted* solicitations need not, and are crimes in their own right, despite their doubly inchoate nature. *E.g., People v. Boyce*, 27 N.E.3d 77 (Ill. 2015); *People v. Saephanh*, 80 Cal.App.4th 451, 460-61 (2000); *supra* Chapter 4.C, Introduction; Chapter 4.A, question 7 on *Bond*.

## D. CONSPIRACY

*[handwritten note: Not every solicitation leads to a conspiracy]*

In asking someone to commit a crime, the act of solicitation is more an attempted conspiracy than an attempt to commit the solicited crime. Decker tried to enter a conspiracy with Wafer and Holston, but he failed. Neither Wafer nor Holston actually agreed to commit the murder of Decker's sister: there was only the pretense of an agreement directed at apprehending Decker before any harm could come to his sister. Solicitations are criminal because they tend to lead to conspiracies. Conspiracies, in turn, are criminal because they tend to lead to the commission of the target offense, or at least come dangerously close, as with attempts.

Like both solicitation and attempt, conspiracy is a specific-intent crime. *E.g., Palmer v. People*, 964 P.2d 524, 527 (Colo. 1998) (en banc). As a reminder, a key consequence of labeling a crime "specific intent" is that voluntary intoxication is an excuse if proof of it raises a reasonable doubt as to whether a defendant had the specific intent to commit the crime. An agreement is insufficient to constitute the crime of conspiracy until some overt act in furtherance of the agreement occurs. An overt act need not constitute an attempt, an element of the offense, or even an illegal act: instead, an overt act could take the form of a small gesture that converts words into action, even preliminary action, such as looking up the target victim's address in a directory. CALJIC No. 6.10 (2014).

The question in conspiracy law is whether two or more parties have agreed to commit a crime. While the law has never recognized agreements—be their ends legal or illegal—entered by coercion, nor does the law require that conspirators formally agree in writing or otherwise. While the conspiratorial agreement can be informal, CALJIC No. 6.12 (2014), often alleged conspirators behave in a merely "consciously parallel" manner to other alleged conspirators without having quite agreed that each would do so. *See Theatre Enterprises, Inc. v. Paramount Film Distrib. Corp.*, 346 U.S. 537, 540-41 (1954).

To prove a conspiracy based on consciously parallel behavior, plaintiffs must show: 1) defendants' behavior was parallel; 2) defendants were conscious of each other's conduct and that this awareness was an element in their decision-making processes; and 3) certain "plus" factors. Moreover, to show that parallel behavior is not the result of independent conduct, plaintiffs must show that defendants 1) acted against their *solo* interests, 2) have a motive to conspire, and 3) have left behind evidence implying a traditional criminal conspiracy. *E.g., In re Chocolate Confectionary Antitrust Litigation*, 999 F.Supp.2d 777 (M.D. Penn. 2014). Lastly, a range of circumstantial evidence can be plus factors: have defendants held meetings together? Engaged in parallel behavior that would be irrational *without* an agreement? Were there invitations to take common action? *City of Moundridge v. Exxon Mobil Corp.*, 429 F.Supp.2d 117, 130-31 (D.D.C. 2006).

For example, imagine that several airlines, in setting their purchase prices for a round-trip ticket from Los Angeles to Chicago, exchange information before setting their prices. After studying the information in a detailed electronic dialogue, all airlines involved in the exchange of price information set their prices identically, down to the penny (say, $524.64). Congress has outlawed conspiracies to fix prices on the ground that such conspiracies are anti-competitive. 15 U.S.C.A. §1 (2004). In the actual airlines case, the exchange of information led to increases in prices and elimination of discounts; consequently, consumers paid out over one billion dollars in increased travel costs. *See United States v. Airline Tariff Pub. Co.*, 1994 WL 502091 (D.D.C.). Did the participating airlines on these facts fix the price of an L.A.-Chicago ticket? Is the answer any clearer if instead we suppose that one airline wrote to the others, literally inviting them to fix prices? Suppose as well that the anticipated collusive advantages to the recipients are set forth in the sender's invitation, as are the anticipated disadvantages to the recipients should they *not* fix prices. Without communicating to each other or to the sender of the letter, each recipient-airline follows the proposed pricing scheme as set forth in the letter. Have the airlines on those facts conspired to fix prices? The answer is not at all easy.

Nor is it easy to find an agreement in many alleged criminal conspiracies to murder, kidnap, and steal. The actions of the putative conspirators are coördinated, but where is the communication? Where is the manifestation of the intent to go along? The conscious parallelism "plus"? That proof of agreements may be circumstantial makes things a bit easier for the prosecution, but association with criminals does not come close to demonstrating that one has conspired with them to commit crimes. CALJIC No. 6.13 (2014).

Like both attempt and solicitation, if a conspiracy is found, conspirators may conceivably dodge conviction any time after formation by thwarting or otherwise "voluntarily" renouncing the criminal objective. *See, e.g., Sanchez v. State*, 23 S.W.3d 30, 37 (Tex. Crim. App. 2000).

In our principal case on point, *People v. Zielesch*, 179 Cal.App.4th 731 (2009), the issue is not so much whether there was a conspiracy in the first instance. It is by this point in the case a given that there was, though the evidence for such a conclusion is far from overwhelming. The issue is to what extent conspirators are responsible for the acts of their co-conspirators, when those acts were *not* part of the common conspiratorial scheme or design.

## COURT OF APPEAL, THIRD DISTRICT, CALIFORNIA

### THE PEOPLE, PLAINTIFF AND RESPONDENT
### V.
### GREGORY FRED ZIELESCH, DEFENDANT AND APPELLANT

### NOV. 23, 2009, AS MODIFIED DEC. 3, 2009

SCOTLAND, Presiding Justice

The tragic loss of life in this case illustrates the danger that faces law enforcement officers every day, even during what on the surface appear to be routine encounters. Defendant Gregory Fred Zielesch bailed Brendt Volarvich out of jail and asked that, in return, Volarvich kill Doug Shamberger, who had been sleeping with defendant's wife. Volarvich agreed but needed a "piece" to carry out the hit. Defendant provided Volarvich with a .357 magnum revolver and $400 to purchase some methamphetamine. The next day, while driving back to defendant's house, Volarvich was stopped by California Highway Patrol Officer Andrew Stevens for a traffic violation. High on methamphetamine and afraid of being sent back to jail, Volarvich shot and killed Officer Stevens with defendant's gun when the officer walked up to the driver's window and greeted Volarvich with a friendly, "How are you doing today?"

Defendant was convicted of the first-degree murder of Officer Stevens, conspiracy to murder Doug Shamberger, and other offenses and enhancements not relevant to the issues raised on appeal. He was sentenced to state prison for an indeterminate term of 50 years to life (two consecutive terms of 25 to life), plus a consecutive determinate term of seven years. He appeals.

We reject defendant's contentions that his murder conviction must be reversed because the shooting of Officer Stevens was not in furtherance of the conspiracy to kill Shamberger and "was both unforeseen and unforeseeable." As we will explain, when defendant bargained for the assassin's services and armed him with a gun and money to buy methamphetamine, defendant knew that the assassin had an unstable personality, with the "mentality" to kill someone other than the intended victim of the assassination. Defendant also knew that the assassin had just been released from jail, was on searchable probation, and would not want to be returned to custody if law enforcement found the assassin in possession of methamphetamine and defendant's gun. From these facts, jurors reasonably could conclude the cold-blooded murder of Officer Stevens was a natural and probable consequence of the conspiracy to kill Shamberger because a reasonable person, knowing what defendant knew, would recognize that if the unstable, methamphetamine using, armed assassin were detained by a law enforcement officer before the assassination was completed, he would likely kill the officer to avoid arrest and complete his mission. Consequently, we shall affirm the judgment.

## FACTS

On the afternoon of November 17, 2005, Officer Stevens stopped Volarvich on a road outside of Woodland, California. Stevens approached the vehicle, lowered his head towards the driver's side window, and greeted Volarvich with a friendly, "How are you doing today?" Volarvich responded, "Pretty good," then shot Stevens in the face with a Taurus .357 magnum revolver. Death was instantaneous. Stevens collapsed on the side of the road, and Volarvich drove away.

The events that culminated in the murder of Officer Stevens began three days earlier at a motel in Woodland, where Volarvich and his girlfriend, Rebecca Pina, were staying. After a night of using methamphetamine, they failed to check out of the motel at the scheduled time on November 14. Woodland police officers, summoned to evict the holdover tenants, discovered marijuana on Pina and brass knuckles and methamphetamine on Volarvich. The officers arrested Volarvich.

Pina, who had been involved in an intimate relationship with defendant, drove Volarvich's car to defendant's house and asked for help with bail for Volarvich. Defendant reluctantly agreed and ultimately arranged a deal with a local bail bondsman whereby defendant would co-sign for the full amount of the $10,000 bond and pay $300 of the $1,000 bond premium, and Volarvich would pay the remaining $700 after he was released from jail.

When Volarvich was released from jail on November 16, defendant and Pina took Volarvich to defendant's house, where they "got high" on methamphetamine with Lindsey Montgomery, one of Pina's friends. That afternoon, Volarvich and Pina gave defendant a ride to the Yolo County courthouse, where defendant attended a custody hearing regarding defendant's children with his estranged wife, Michelle. Michelle was living with Doug Shamberger, whom defendant "hated" and considered an "asshole." Defendant suspected that both Michelle and Shamberger had burglarized his house; and Shamberger had threatened defendant several times because Michelle paid periodic visits to defendant. In response to these threats, defendant bought a .357 magnum to protect himself from Shamberger.

On the way back to defendant's house following the custody hearing, defendant told Volarvich that he could "take care of" Shamberger as payment for defendant having bailed Volarvich out of jail. When Volarvich remarked that he "needed a piece," defendant replied he "had that taken care of." Volarvich asked: "Do you want Michelle done?" Defendant said no. Upon arriving at the house, the threesome again got high, and defendant gave Volarvich the .357 magnum and $400 to pick up some more methamphetamine in Roseville.

At this point, Volarvich and Pina got into a heated argument. Volarvich called Montgomery, arranged to go to her house, and left defendant's house alone. He then picked up Montgomery and drove to a hotel in Rocklin.[1] En route, Volarvich told Montgomery that defendant had given him a gun because defendant "wanted Shamberger taken out." After checking into a hotel room, Volarvich pulled defendant's gun out of a black bag to show Montgomery and started playing with the revolving chamber. Later that night, Volarvich and Montgomery went to Wal-Mart, where Volarvich bought a laser sight. Back at the hotel room, Volarvich unsuccessfully attempted to attach the laser sight to the gun with electrical tape. He then tried to Super Glue the laser sight to the gun; this attempt also failed. Because Volarvich was afraid of sleeping past check-out time and being sent back to jail, he and Montgomery stayed up all night.

After leaving the hotel the morning of November 17, Volarvich and Montgomery went to a friend's house and smoked methamphetamine. They then drove back to Montgomery's house in Woodland. As Volarvich drove across the I-5 causeway, he pulled out the gun and started playing with the revolving chamber, spinning the chamber and loading it with bullets. Afraid she would get in trouble because Volarvich was playing with a gun while they drove down the causeway, Montgomery told him to put the gun down. Volarvich

---

[1] Volarvich and Montgomery were not old enough to rent the hotel room. Thus, Volarvich called an older friend, Ryan Nicholson, and arranged for Nicholson's girlfriend, Erin Owen, to rent the room in exchange for gas money.

complied, placing it on the driver's side floorboard. They smoked more methamphetamine when they arrived at Montgomery's house.

Meanwhile, Pina was still at defendant's house. Furious that Volarvich had not returned with the methamphetamine he was supposed to buy the night before, defendant hit Pina in the head to rouse her from sleep and yelled that, because of her, Volarvich did not come back and that defendant "was out $400 plus the money for the bail bondsman." Unable to connect with Volarvich through his cell phone, Pina called Montgomery, told her that defendant had hit her because Volarvich had not returned, and asked if she had heard from him. Montgomery told Pina that she would "try to get ahold of him." At Montgomery's request, Volarvich called Pina and told her that he was on his way to pick her up.

When Volarvich left Montgomery's house, he was "upset" that defendant had hit Pina. Volarvich brought the gun with him because "he was worried that it was going to be a setup" and he did not want to go back to jail. According to Montgomery, Volarvich believed that either defendant or the bail bondsman was setting him up because he had taken defendant's $400 without returning with the methamphetamine and had not met with the bail bondsman the day before to sign the bond paperwork.

Apparently on his way to defendant's house to pick up Pina, Volarvich used defendant's .357 magnum revolver to shoot and kill Officer Stevens after Volarvich was pulled over by Stevens. After the shooting, Volarvich called Montgomery, said that he "fucked up," asked if she could hear sirens, but hung up the phone before explaining further. When Volarvich called Montgomery back, he asked her to pick him up on El Dorado Drive. She agreed, borrowed a friend's car, and found Volarvich standing behind his car holding the license plate. Volarvich and Montgomery then switched cars and drove a short distance to Delta Drive, where they left Volarvich's car and returned to Montgomery's house. On the way to the house, Montgomery noticed that the black bag which had contained the gun was missing. When she asked Volarvich what had happened to it, he explained that he "had to get rid of the gun" and buried it near County Road 96 and County Road 24, which is where the gun was found the next day. Montgomery also overheard Volarvich on the phone telling his mother that he had "shot the cop" but "didn't know if he was serious or not" and thought that "he was just tweaking." Volarvich then called two friends to drive him from Woodland to Roseville, telling them along the way that he "had shot a cop" because "he didn't want to go to jail."

When defendant told Pina an officer had been shot, she turned on the television and saw the news broadcast about the killing. She asked whether he had given Volarvich his gun. Defendant replied that Volarvich's "mentality was there." Meanwhile, Montgomery received a call from Volarvich telling her to buy window decals to disguise his car. Acceding to Volarvich's request, Montgomery bought decals and window tinting from Wal-Mart, returned to Delta Drive to retrieve the car, and re-attached the license plate that Volarvich had apparently removed. After receiving another call from Volarvich informing her where to meet him, Montgomery drove Volarvich's car back to the hotel in Rocklin.[2] There, Volarvich confessed to Montgomery, explaining that when he was pulled over by Officer Stevens, "he just turned and shot him." According to Volarvich, he was "scared" because he "didn't want to go to jail" and believed that being pulled over was part of a set-up orchestrated by the bail bondsman.

Volarvich and Montgomery were arrested at the hotel during the early morning hours of November 18, the same day that defendant was arrested after his house was searched and officers discovered a rifle, methamphetamine, and drug paraphernalia. During questioning, defendant confirmed the antagonistic relationship between himself and Shamberger, and admitted that he had purchased the .357 magnum in order to protect himself from Shamberger. But he denied asking Volarvich to kill Shamberger and denied giving Volarvich the gun that killed Officer Stevens. According to his version of events, defendant merely showed Volarvich the gun the night before the shooting and discovered that it was missing the next morning.

## DISCUSSION

### I

Defendant asserts that his murder conviction must be reversed because the shooting of Officer Stevens was not in furtherance of the conspiracy to kill Shamberger and "was both unforeseen and unforeseeable." Defendant is mistaken.

---

[2] Volarvich again rented the hotel room through Nicholson and Owen, and told them he "killed an officer" and that he "fucked up" and "blasted him in the face." He also told Nicholson that the reason he shot Officer Stevens was that he "didn't want to go back to jail."

[Handwritten margin note: "But... not universally accepted"]

The law has been settled for more than a century that each member of a conspiracy is criminally responsible for the acts of fellow conspirators committed in furtherance of, and which follow as a natural and probable consequence of, the conspiracy, even though such acts were not intended by the conspirators as a part of their common unlawful design. *People v. Kauffman*, 152 Cal. 331, 334 (1907); *Pinkerton v. United States*, 328 U.S. 640, 647-48 (1946).

Recognizing that criminal agency poses a greater threat to society than that posed by an independent criminal actor, the law "seeks to deter criminal combination by recognizing the act of one as the act of all." *People v. Luparello*, 187 Cal.App.3d 410, 437 (1986); *People v. Zacarias*, 157 Cal.App.4th 652, 658 (2007) ["conspiracy to commit a target offense makes it more likely that additional crimes related to the target offense will be committed"]. "In combining to plan a crime, each conspirator risks liability for conspiracy as well as the substantive offense; in planning poorly, each risks additional liability for the unanticipated, yet reasonably foreseeable consequences of the conspiratorial acts, liability which is avoidable by disavowing or abandoning the conspiracy." *Luparello*, 187 Cal.App.4th at 438.

The question whether an unplanned crime is a natural and probable consequence of a conspiracy to commit the intended crime is not whether the aider and abettor *actually* foresaw the additional crime, but whether, judged objectively, the unplanned crime was *reasonably* foreseeable. To be reasonably foreseeable the consequence need not have been a strong probability; a possible consequence which might reasonably have been contemplated is enough. Whether the unplanned act was a "reasonably foreseeable consequence" of the conspiracy must be evaluated under all the factual circumstances of the individual case and is a factual issue to be resolved by the jury, whose determination is conclusive if supported by substantial evidence.

The trial court properly instructed the jury:

> A member of a conspiracy is criminally responsible for any act of any member of the conspiracy if that act is done to further the conspiracy and that act is a natural and probable consequence of the common plan or design of the conspiracy. This rule applies even if the act was not intended as part of the original plan. Under this rule, a defendant who is a member of the conspiracy does not need to be present at the

time of the act. A natural and probable consequence is one that a reasonable person would know is likely to happen if nothing unusual intervenes. In deciding whether a consequence is natural and probable, consider all of the circumstances established by the evidence. A member of a conspiracy is not criminally responsible for the act of another member if that act does not further the common plan or is not a natural and probable consequence of the common plan. To prove that defendant Gregory Fred Zielesch is guilty of the murder of Officer Stevens, the People must prove that: One, defendant Gregory Fred Zielesch conspired with defendant Brendt Volarvich to commit the murder of Doug Shamberger; Two, Brendt Volarvich, as a member of the conspiracy to murder Doug Shamberger, committed the murder of Andrew Stevens in order to further the conspiracy to murder Doug Shamberger; and Three, the murder of Andrew Stevens was a natural and probable consequence of the common plan or design of the crime that both defendants Zielesch and Volarvich conspired to commit.

CALCRIM No. 417. After requesting clarification on the meaning of certain language in the instruction ("in order to further the conspiracy" and "likely to happen if nothing unusual intervenes"), the jurors informed the trial court that they had reached verdicts on all counts except the murder charge alleged against defendant.

The trial court then allowed the parties to present supplemental closing arguments focusing solely on whether the murder of Officer Stevens was committed in furtherance of, and followed as a probable and natural consequence of, the conspiracy. The People argued the murder furthered the goals of the conspiracy because, in order to successfully murder Shamberger, one of the goals of the conspiracy had to be to avoid detection; and the murder was a natural and probable consequence of the conspiracy because "a reasonable person would foresee that there would be police intervention" at some point during the execution of the plot to kill Shamberger, and defendant, with actual knowledge of Volarvich's "volatile and unstable" nature, gave him the gun to carry out the murder. Defendant's attorney argued no conspiracy existed between defendant and Volarvich; being pulled over by an officer on a country road in Woodland constituted an "extremely unusual" event, the intervention of which rendered Officer Stevens's death not a natural and probable consequence of the alleged conspiracy; and Volarvich killed Officer Stevens because "he did not want to go to jail," not because of a conspiracy to kill Shamberger. After further deliberation, the jury found defendant guilty of both the conspiracy and murder charges, implicitly finding the murder of Officer Stevens was committed in furtherance of, and followed as a natural and probable consequence of, the conspiracy.

As he did in the trial court, defendant claims the murder of Officer Stevens "was both unforeseen and unforeseeable." We conclude the jury's contrary finding is supported by substantial evidence. The object of the conspiracy between defendant and Volarvich was to end the life of defendant's nemesis with the .357 magnum revolver supplied by defendant for that purpose. Defendant knew Volarvich had a proclivity for using methamphetamine, having used the drug with Volarvich the night before he gave him the gun to carry out the hit, and having given Volarvich $400 to purchase more methamphetamine. Defendant admitted knowing Volarvich had an unstable personality; after receiving news of Officer Stevens's murder, defendant told Pina that Volarvich's "mentality was there." Defendant also had reason to know that Volarvich, who was on searchable probation, would be taken into custody if a law enforcement officer detained him and found the gun. From these facts, the jury could find that a natural and probable consequence, i.e., a reasonably foreseeable "possible consequence" of the defendant's conspiracy with assassin Volarvich to murder Shamberger was that, if Volarvich were detained by a law enforcement officer before completing the job, Volarvich would kill the officer to avoid arrest and complete his mission to assassinate Shamberger.

Indeed, given defendant's knowledge of Volarvich's unstable mental state, use of methamphetamine, and desire not to return to jail, we conclude the prospect that defendant's arming Volarvich with defendant's .357 magnum revolver to assassinate Shamberger would lead to the shooting of a law enforcement officer is just as foreseeable as was the murder that the California Supreme Court recently held to be the natural and probable consequence of a "failed assault" by gang members who had been disrespected by a rival gang member. *People v. Medina*, 46 Cal.4th 913, 923-25 (2009).

Defendant's argument that the murder of Officer Stevens with defendant's gun was not "in furtherance of the charged conspiracy" does not benefit him for two reasons. First, a natural and probable consequence of a conspiracy need not be an act in furtherance of the conspiracy; it simply must be a reasonably foreseeable consequence of the intended crime aided and abetted. Second, although Volarvich was not on his way to carry out the assassination of Shamberger when Volarvich was pulled over by Officer Stevens, and although there is evidence that Volarvich was upset with defendant for hitting Pina, the jury was not required to conclude that the conspiracy to murder Shamberger had reached an end. Volarvich still "owed" defendant for bailing him out of jail and for the $400 given to him the previous day to purchase methamphetamine, and Volarvich still possessed the gun given to him by defendant to assassinate Shamberger. Thus, the jury could reasonably have concluded that the conspiracy to murder Shamberger persisted despite Volarvich's anger at defendant, and that the hit would be carried out whenever the opportunity presented itself. The jury could also have concluded, quite reasonably, that a simultaneous goal of the conspiracy to assassinate Shamberger was to avoid detection and forcibly resist arrest. In fact, when Volarvich was pulled over by Officer Stevens, he correctly concluded that, unless he took drastic action with the gun given to him by defendant, Volarvich was going back to jail. Thus, the jury could reasonably have found that, because Volarvich would not have been able to complete his assignment from a jail cell, avoiding arrest at any cost furthered the murderous goal of the conspiracy by giving Volarvich more time to find the target.

Defendant points out "there appear to be no cases like this one," and posits the reason for the dearth of appellate decisions dealing with this factual scenario is "this case is far outside the scope of *Kauffman* and *Pinkerton*." We are not persuaded. While it may be possible to imagine scenarios in which the conduct of an assassin is so outrageous and unpredictable that it falls outside the scope of a conspiracy to commit murder, one who bargains for an assassin's services, and then arms the assassin with a gun, takes the assassin as he finds him. If the hired killer is an unstable methamphetamine user who, before the assassination is completed, finds it necessary to kill a law enforcement officer to avoid being sent back to jail, the conspirator who hired and armed the assassin is guilty not only of conspiracy to murder the intended target, but also the murder of the peace officer. It would be a rare case indeed where a murder is an unforeseeable result of a conspiracy to commit murder.

Affirmed.

[Parts II-IV, VI, and VII were not certified for publication. Part V, redacted here, finds harmless the wearing by trial spectators of badges embossed with a photograph of Officer Stevens.]

## QUESTIONS ON *ZIELESCH*

**1. Evidence of conspiracy to kill Shamberger.** Defendant (Zielesch) killed no one. His involvement with the killer (Volarvich) arose out of Zielesch's involvement with Volarvich's girlfriend (Pina), "who had been involved in an intimate relationship with defendant." Feeling he had done Pina a favor that benefitted Volarvich, Zielesch asked for a favor in return from Volarvich: kill Shamberger, with whom Zielesch's estranged wife was living. Just before killing a state trooper, Volarvich had been communing with one of Pina's friends (Montgomery), whose company he had left just before the shooting. Zielesch never copped to hiring Volarvich to kill Shamberger or to lending Volarvich his gun, which Zielesch claims Volarvich took from him without permission. Pina corroborated Volarvich's claim that Zielesch hired him to kill Shamberger. Is that proof beyond a reasonable doubt of a conspiracy between Zielesch and Volarvich?

**2. Determinate v. indeterminate sentencing.** Zielesch "was sentenced to state prison for an indeterminate term of 50 years to life (two consecutive terms of 25 years to life), plus a consecutive determinate term of seven years." In 1976, California replaced its system of indeterminate sentencing with a system of determinate sentencing. *See* California Penal Code §1170; California Rules of Court, rule 4.420 [sentencing court to consider aggravating and mitigating factors before selecting a statutorily fixed base/middle term, low term, or high term for imprisonable offenses]. The United States did the same in 1987, a move from which it has retreated. *United States v. Booker*, 125 S.Ct. 738 (2005) [to avoid unconstitutionally impinging on juries, federal sentencing guidelines are held *advisory*, not mandatory].

Indeterminate sentencing schemes featured "the exercise of vast judicial discretion within broad legislative ranges." *People v. Lockridge*, 870 N.W.2d 502, 515-16 n.19 (Mich. 2015). For example, a California statute (struck down in 1972) provided for a prison term of one year to life for persons convicted of indecent exposure with a prior. *In re Lynch*, 503 P.2d 921 (Cal. 1972) (en banc). If discretion was the virtue of indeterminate sentencing, then it was also its vice, characterized by 1) great variation among sentences imposed by different judges upon similarly situated offenders; and 2) uncertainty as to the time offenders would spend in prison. *State v. De La Cruz*, 393 S.E.2d 184, 186 (S.C. 1990). Indeed, it was junior bureaucrats in the executive branch—wardens and parole boards—that were deciding the ultimate term of service once prisoners were handed over by sentencing judges. See *Apprendi v. New Jersey*, 120 S.Ct. 2348, 2394 (2000) (O'Connor, J., dissenting).

If California eliminated indeterminate sentencing in 1976, and Zielesch was sentenced in 2008, then how could he receive an *indeterminate* sentence of 50 years to life?

**3. On the hook for the acts of others.** The Court of Appeal began its discussion of the law on point by stating:

> The law has been settled for more than a century that each member of a conspiracy is criminally responsible for the acts of fellow conspirators committed in furtherance of, and which follow as a natural and probable consequence of, the conspiracy, even though such acts were not intended by the conspirators as a part of their common unlawful design.

It is not a universally accepted principle, however. The Model Penal Code holds conspirators liable only for the offenses to which they agree. Any excess crimes performed by other members of the conspiracy are theirs alone. See Model Penal Code and Commentaries §2.06(3), cmt. 6(b), at 312 (1985) ["[L]iability of an accomplice ought not to be extended beyond the purposes that he shares"].

When one member of a conspiracy ignores the plan and improvises, committing crimes without the approval of other members, why would those nonparticipating members be responsible for the excess crimes? Is it just a sort of additional punishment for entering the conspiracy—so it's *their* fault that another secretly decided to depart from the common scheme or design?

**4. The grammar of "natural and probable."** After quoting the doctrine that holds conspirators liable for the "natural and probable" upshots of their conspiracy, the court quotes *People v. Luparello* for the proposition that each conspirator "risks additional liability for the unanticipated, yet reasonably foreseeable consequences of the conspiratorial acts" unless the conspirator has disavowed or abandoned the conspiracy.

**a.** Consider CALJIC No. 6.11 (2014) (characterized in *Zielesch* as CALCRIM No. 417), which states:

> In determining whether a consequence is 'natural and probable' you must apply an objective test based not on what the defendant actually intended but on what a person of reasonable and ordinary prudence would have expected would be likely to occur. The issue is to be decided in light of all of the circumstances surrounding the incident. A 'natural consequence' is one which is within the normal range of outcomes that may be reasonably expected to occur if nothing unusual has intervened. 'Probable' means likely to happen.

These formulations—"natural and probable" on the one hand and "reasonably foreseeable" on the other hand—are different, aren't they? Which demands of the prosecution a higher standard of proof? How does each term line up with "more likely than not"?

**b.** That "'probable' means likely to happen" was not lost on Judge Weiner, who wrote separately in *Luparello* to complain of the court's interchangeable use of the distinct terms "foreseeable" and "probable." *People v. Luparello*, 187 Cal.App.3d 410, 452 n.2 (1986) (Weiner, J., concurring).

Luparello was a married, Santa Ana chiropractor desperate to find his former mistress and patient Terri, whom he knew had reconciled with her husband. Dr. Luparello recruited four guys (one named Spooky) whom he paid piddly amounts of money to find Terri, even if that required "thumping" an acquaintance of hers (Mark Martin), whom Luparello suspected would know where she was. Instead of interrogating Martin as instructed, one of Luparello's recruits, who had armed themselves with a rifle, nunchakus, and a sword, lay in wait in the driveway and murdered Martin when he came outside on the pretense of repairing their car, from or near which six shots were fired.

Luparello was found to have conspired to commit assault. He was convicted of that conspiracy and of the first-degree murder of Martin, given that lying in wait is a species of premeditation and deliberation. Ruling that Luparello's instructions to his recruits constituted a conspiracy to assault Martin, the Court of Appeal ruled that Martin's murder was a natural and probable upshot of the conspiracy. *Was* it?

**5. The path from Shamberger to Stevens.** The court's theory of why Stevens's murder was natural and probable goes like this: First, the plan to kill Shamberger implicitly included a plan not to get caught; second, killing someone is always likely to provoke police intervention; and finally, recruiting an "unstable" drug-using probationer who is subject to suspicionless searches by police makes violent, escape-driven action in the event of police intervention likely.

**a.** Is this a stretch? Or is there a sufficient link-up between the conspiracy to murder Shamberger to call the murder of Stevens a natural and probable consequence?

**b.** Zielesch argued that Volarvich's murder of Officer Stevens as an upshot of the conspiracy to kill Shamberger was "unforeseen and unforeseeable." What does this mean? That from Zielesch's perspective, Volarvich's murder of Stevens was a *not-intentional* upshot of the conspiracy to kill Shamberger? An *unintentional* upshot of the conspiracy to kill Shamberger? If unintentional, is Zielesch arguing that he took sufficient precaution to prevent Stevens's murder (making Zielesch non-negligent)? Or would Zielesch be off the hook for Stevens's murder so long as it was accidental from his perspective, regardless of whether Zielesch took sufficient precaution to control Volarvich? *Cf. supra* Chapter 2.A, Introduction.

## NOTES ON *ZIELESCH*

*1. Sentencing for conspiracy.* Unlike the inchoate crimes of solicitation and attempt, the sentence in California for a conspiracy is equivalent to the sentence for the target offense of the conspiracy. California Penal Code §182 (West 2011) states, in pertinent part:

> (a) If two or more persons conspire:
> (1) To commit any crime....
>
> They are punishable as follows:
>
> When they conspire to commit any other felony, they shall be punishable in the same manner and to the same extent as is provided for the punishment of that felony. If the felony is one for which different punishments are prescribed for

> different degrees, the jury or court which finds the defendant guilty thereof shall determine the degree of the felony the defendant conspired to commit. If the degree is not so determined, the punishment for conspiracy to commit the felony shall be that prescribed for the lesser degree, except in the case of conspiracy to commit murder, in which case the punishment shall be that prescribed for murder in the first degree.
>
> If the felony is conspiracy to commit two or more felonies which have different punishments and the commission of those felonies constitute but one offense of conspiracy, the penalty shall be that prescribed for the felony which has the greater maximum term....

An exception is conspiracy to commit murder, which is not punishable by death unless defendant maliciously contributed to the actual, not just planned, death of another. See *Kennedy v. Louisiana*, 554 U.S. 407 (2008).

**2. Unpublished opinions.** The Court of Appeal affirmed Zielesch's conviction in an opinion with seven-parts, only two of which are published. Not only are attorneys barred by court rule from citing such a case in court documents, but the opinion is not even accessible for public consumption or study. California Rules of Court, rule 8.1115(a). Commentators cite four purposes for selectively publishing opinions: 1) conservation of judicial resources (lawyers and courts can spend less time wading through duplicative or unimportant decisions); 2) increased court productivity (dedicating in *all* cases the significant time needed to write a full decision exceeds courts' capacity); 3) reduction of costs (courts and lawyers need not buy costly case reporters full of unimportant decisions); and 4) greater emphasis on published opinions (published decisions are necessary only where the court establishes a new rule of law; expands, alters, or modifies an existing rule; addresses a legal issue of continuing public interest; criticizes existing law; or resolves a conflict of authority).

**3. State high court implicitly invalidates conviction.** In *People v. Chiu*, 325 P.2d 972, 974 (Cal. 2014), the California Supreme Court ruled that "an aider and abettor may not be convicted of first degree premeditated murder under the natural and probable consequences doctrine." Second-degree murder, yes; first-degree, no longer. Now extended to conspiracy cases, *People v. Rivera*, 234

Cal.App.4th 1350 (2015), *Chiu* implicitly invalidates the convictions of Luparello and Zielesch. Nor do these over-rulings come too late, at least for Zielesch, who is still in custody. *Chiu* was recently held to apply retroactively, even to final judgments. That means that even though Zielesch's direct appeal is exhausted, he may still rely on *Chiu* on state habeas corpus. *In re Lopez*, 246 Cal.App.4th 350, 356-60 (2016).

### 4. Fate of parties.

*a. Lindsey Montgomery.* Montgomery pleaded no contest to being an accessory after the fact in Volarvich's murder of Stevens. She was sentenced to five years' probation and eight months at a drug rehabilitation clinic. As a reminder (this came up in *Dlugash* as well), accessories *after* the fact make no contribution to the commission of the crime; instead, their crime consists of concealing the crime, just as Montgomery did here. *Cf.* 18 U.S.C. §3 (1948) [accessories punished at 50% of the offense of which they sought to hinder investigation].

*b. Brendt Volarvich.* Footnote 1 of *Zielesch* records that Brendt Volarvich was too young in 2005 to rent a hotel room. Volarvich, now 32, is on death row at San Quentin. Of additional interest may be that his father, former Los Altos Police Officer Dennis Volarvich, was elevated after 11 years' service to investigator for the Santa Clara County D.A., where he got fired for taking up with a witness/suspect: the widow of a murder victim whose death he was investigating. From there, Dennis worked in private security before taking up bank robbery, shooting himself fatally in the head on December 10, 1997 after a brief police chase from the Bank of America (Fremont) he had just robbed. Brendt was 12 at the time.

*c. Gregory Zielesch.* Unlike Volarvich, Zielesch was no kid: 47 at the time of Officer Stevens's murder, 60 at the time of this writing, 10 years into his 57-year sentence at Donovan Correctional Facility (San Diego). After the state high court denied review of the ruling we read, Zielesch authored his own habeas petition in federal court based in part on ineffective assistance of counsel, who failed to compel the testimony of witnesses (including Volarvich), and to put Zielesch himself on the stand. If given the chance, Zielesch would have testified that 1) consideration for bailing out Volarvich was that Pina would make a sex tape with Zielesch, not that Volarvich would kill Shamberger; and 2) Pina, who had conspired to rob or kill Zielesch for his having struck her, stole Zielesch's .357 at Volarvich's request. *Zielesch v. Lewis*, 2012 WL 4050092 (E.D. Ca.).

Zielesch's habeas petition also challenged a range of evidentiary rulings, including the trial court's refusal to immunize the testimony of Shamberger, whom Zielesch wanted to put on for two purposes: 1) to show that any rift between Shamberger and Zielesch had been ironed out, thus undermining the prosecution's theory that Zielesch would want Shamberger dead; and 2) to show that Pina had given several different accounts of the entire episode, insisting throughout that Shamberger back up her story only to prevent her from going to jail. Shamberger said he would refuse to testify if the prosecutor made good on his threat to reveal through cross-examination some of Shamberger's criminal escapades. In Zielesch's view, his constitutional right to put on a defense and compel witnesses to testify on his behalf was blocked by the trial judge's refusal to override the prosecutor's refusal to immunize Shamberger's testimony. Had Shamberger testified, it is conceivable that the jury would have found no conspiracy to kill Shamberger. Without a conspiracy to commit crime 'A' (murder Shamberger), there can be no liability on Zielesch's part for crime 'B' (murder Stevens) as a natural and probable consequence of the conspiracy to commit crime 'A.'

Zielesch's federal habeas petition was denied. Relevant or not, his trial counsel has since suffered a series of disciplinary actions in unrelated matters, including suspensions from the practicing Bar.

# E. COMPLICITY (helping)

## 1. POSITIVE ASSOCIATION WITH THE VENTURE

The inchoate nature of the crime, or partial excuse, of attempt is undisputed: punishing attempts regulates risk-taking, not harm-causing. The dispute in attempt law arises over whether criminal law should regulate risk-taking and harm-causing with equal punishments. Unlike attempt, solicitation, or conspiracy, the crime, or partial excuse, of complicity is conventionally seen as a way of regulating harm, not risk. For this reason, it is worth paying close attention to whether complicity is, as it now is viewed, an instance where unwavering equivalency makes sense.

Complicity rests on the premise that someone whom the law interchangeably calls an "accessory," "accomplice," "aider and abettor," "secondary party," or "helper" in his principal's offense is derivatively, not vicariously, liable for that offense. The difference between derivative and vicarious liability is that derivative liability is based partly on the defendant's own actions, not merely on his relationship with someone else. Derivative liability, and therefore punishment, is shared equally between principals and helpers. Proof of the helper's derivative liability is heavily mediated by the actions and intentions of the principal. If the principal commits a crime, then equal credit goes to the helper as well, provided that the crime which occurs is one the helper knew about and intended to facilitate when he provided his help.

But in what way is it *as though* helpers who do not coerce or manipulate their principals commit their principals' offenses? The helper has merely helped. But helping, say, burglary, is not committing burglary; help can be withheld, or it would not be helping. Nor does helping burglary count as *trying* to commit burglary, any more than "argue" means "try to convince," or "warn" means "try to alarm" or "alert." Because helping crime is distinct from committing the crime that is being helped, complicity mischaracterizes a helper as a principal.

The law nevertheless treats a helper as a principal so long as the helper intentionally contributes to the principal's offense. "Contribute" in this sense is akin to "cause," but not in its ordinary or strong sense that would be familiar to any first-year student of torts. That familiar sense requires that a condition be a *sine qua non* or at least a substantial factor in the occurrence in question. Indeed, cause in the law of complicity does not mean cause at all, although some characterize it as such. *See, e.g.*, K.J.M. Smith, A Modern Treatise on Complicity 55-93 (Oxford 1991). At a minimum, a helper must render "actual" aid that "mattered," "contributed," "made a difference," or "presumably caused" the principal's actions. Only when the helper's actions could not have been successful in any case is there no liability. And it takes such an extended use of cause or contribution to support the conclusion that lending a man a smock to keep a battery victim's blood from staining the batterer's suit made enough difference to the batterer to justify our treating the smock-lender as a batterer; or, that an angry judge's interception of a telegram might have mattered in a murder because, had the victim received the telegram, he might have anticipated the gunman behind him when three gunmen stood before him and the wire had read, "Four men on horseback with guns following. Look out." *State ex rel. Attorney General v. Tally*, 15 So. 722, 734 (Alabama 1894). Even a door opened for a burglar *might* make a difference to burglary through the window.

While these are exceptional examples, even essential cases of complicity, such as where a helper lends his principal a crowbar for a burglary or drives him to the site of the crime, are not cases where the helper has caused the offense, even if the principal has no crowbar or cannot drive a car. So long as the principal might have acted anyway, even if by other means, then why say "caused" or even the less objectionable "made a difference" if we mean "helped" or in some cases, "tried to help"? "Cause" for purposes of complicity is said to cover *any* influence on "an event's exact occurrence, including time, place, extent and type of harm, and so on." K.J.M. Smith, *A Modern Treatise on Complicity*, supra, at 84. Such an extravagant notion of cause furnishes the law with a way of passing through the mysterious workings of the principal, a wild card whose will otherwise poses "a barrier through which the causal inquiry cannot penetrate." H.L.A. Hart & Antony Honoré, Causation in the Law 69 (1959). So we say it is *as though* the helper committed the offense because it is *as though* he caused the principal to commit it.

Certainly one can perform an action by getting others to perform it. We say "Louis XIV built Versailles" even though the actual construction was done by others. In fact, we can think of cases where the principal is not a principal at all, but is simply a tool, instrument, or means of someone else, such as where the helper recruits a lunatic or a child to do the deed. *See, e.g.,* Model Penal Code §5.01(2)(g). But those cases involve such coercion or manipulation of susceptible parties that the agent's act is fishy enough to be called "not responsible" or "not spontaneous." In such cases the crime can be entirely attributable to the string-puller. *See, e.g.,* MPC §2.06(2)(a). Thus, I find it unimaginable, although the law does not, that my providing a gun for a lunatic—I being *unaware* of his incapacity—to use to assault someone makes the assault mine and not his. For my agent's act to be mine, I must *see* his act as such; one does not "use" someone else inadvertently. Apart from the exceptional circumstances in which the principal performs the action through an innocent agent, in evaluating the responsibility of the helper—who has positively associated himself with the principal's doings—what difference does it make whether the helper makes a difference?

The resilience of causal accounts of complicity may be due to the nature of derivative liability. For the helper's liability to flow backward from the principal's offense, the helper must have had something to do with the offense and not merely with the offender. Complicity requires that the helper be connected to his principal—since helpers must know the principal's plan and encourage or assist him—*and* to the offense, since the helper must intend to facilitate and then cause or make a difference in the principal's offense. The helper's relation to the principal reflects an endangerment- or risk-basis of liability, and the helper's relation to the crime reflects an outcome- or harm-basis of liability.

Hornbook complicity is as concerned with harm as with crime. Under the popularized "broad" view of complicity, most defenses that exculpate the principal are characterized as excuses that benefit only or remain personal to the principal. *See, e.g.*, MPC §5.01(3). This view would hold liable as accessory a sober helper who naïvely assisted a drunk burglar's entry and theft even if the principal burglar is acquitted on grounds that he was too drunk to form the intention to steal. This is a heavy tax laid on the helper, but it does leave intact the basic assumption that a helper's liability is mediated and unmediated at once. It is mediated in that the helper must help what he knows *his principal means to do*. It is unmediated in that, if their jointly intended harm occurs, however forgivably on the principal's part (usually because he is clumsy, mistaken, intoxicated, provoked, or exempt from prosecution in his role as *agent provocateur*), then it is *as though* the helper committed a crime that, well, is not a crime at all. So viewed, liability is derivative not so much of criminality, but of harmful results, even those harmful results that are brought about by excused or unconvictable principals. Thus, it is as much the helper's association with harm as with other criminals at which the law of complicity strikes.

This state of affairs may express our belief that someone who helps an excused wrongdoer is just the sort of person with whom the criminal law should concern itself. This is true enough, but only because the helper has intentionally put himself to another's criminal purpose, which may or may not succeed. Judge Learned Hand put it best in a 1938 counterfeiting case when he explained that complicity demands that the helper "associate himself with the venture, that he participate in it as in something that he wishes to bring about, that he seek by his action to make it succeed." *United States v. Peoni*, 100 F.2d 401, 402 (2d Cir. 1938). The absence of references to causal contributions or other attempts to measure the helper's input or aid indicates that Judge Hand saw complicity as a matter of the manifest intentions of the helper as opposed to the helper's influence on the principal or whether the principal can be convicted of a crime.

Complicity therefore presupposes that the principal has caused some legally prohibited harm, whether or not the principal has a full or partial defense that allows him to avoid liability. Helping cannot exist in a vacuum. If the principal does nothing legally prohibited, then there is no wrong for which the helper can be held derivatively liable. The grammar of helping not only requires that the principal do something, but it also demands that the helper do something. Thus, the U.S. Supreme Court held long ago that a would-be helper who does not encourage or conspire with his principal, but goes along secretly ready to help if necessary (but never says so and help turns out to be unnecessary), has helped nothing. *Hicks v. United States*, 150 U.S. 442 (1893). But fixating on the helper's relation to the principal's crimes or harms depends on a flimsy sense of "cause," even when it is toned down to "making a difference." Our instincts are correct about the propriety of punishing the helper, but not because we are satisfied that without the helper the crime could not have occurred: the harm may have nothing that can be demonstrated, or even nothing at all, to do with the helper. The helper is an excessive risk-taker who deserves punishment whether his aid or encouragement informs or merely glances off of his principal. Because it is fair to assume that criminal associations *tend* to succeed more than solo ventures do, we need to give credit not just to the ringleader, but to the ring as well. But we go too far when we conclude that, because helpers tend to add something to their principals' doings, helping is just like doing.

[margin note: helper needs to add something like aid or encouragement]

Here, I am not talking about cases of "joint principality," where two parties divide the elements of an offense; for example, two parties rob when one commits the assault and the other the larceny. Since both the force or threat of force and the taking of property are elementally necessary to *any* robbery, neither party is *helping* robbery; both are *committing* it.

Nor am I talking about the application of principles of complicity to dangerous games like drag racing or Russian roulette. Take a drag race where an unlucky racer drives off the road or over the centerline, killing himself or another; or a game of Russian roulette, where an unlucky player spins the chamber to what he knows could be a live round, pulls the trigger, and kills himself. In those cases, courts sometimes dub the lucky, surviving participant as culpable killer of the unlucky opponent, even though the survivor doesn't run the opponent off the road or shoot him in the head. The theory? The lucky survivor *helps* the unlucky player kill himself. But one cannot help drag racing or Russian roulette simply *by participating*. Certainly a buyer does not help a seller in the act of selling the goods by paying for the goods any more than a betrothed couple help each other get married by marrying each other, or someone helps someone else kiss simply by kissing them. However angry we may be at lucky survivors of dangerous games, multi-party game cases do not instantiate helping by one whose participation is elementally necessary to the crime itself. Manslaughter—the charge typically made against lucky survivors of dangerous games—has two elements: 1) conscious excessive risk-taking and 2) causing death. If the excessive risk for which the killer is being criticized was drag racing, then it is not an element that can be helped *by drag racing*. Manslaughter is not, elementally, a two-or-more-party offense; nor is it divided into one (you steer, I accelerate) as obscene phone-calling could be were one person to dial and the other to talk obscenely. To use someone's elementally necessary participation as a means of describing their role as that of helping an unlucky dangerous-game player's actions ignores the distinction between helping and doing: help can be withheld, or it would not be helping at all.

Oppositely, where the help of one party is necessary only as an empirical or synthetic matter—that is, where a helper does not fulfill a statutory definition of a crime or one of its elements, but his actions *happen to be* necessary for the crime to succeed *on these facts*—then he is helping and not doing, regardless of how he characterizes his own actions. For example, although a getaway driver may be necessary for a successful robbery, getaway drivers are not elementally necessary to robbery. Consequently, getaway drivers are helpers, not do-ers or joint principals, regardless of how they characterize their actions. Though American law treats helpers and do-ers identically, getaway drivers and their analogues should have an excuse, albeit partial: they didn't really *do* it (or really didn't do *it*). They were *merely* helping.

That the law treats helpers and their principals identically in a punishment sense is explained by problems that arose over and over in holding helpers accountable. Because the principal's conviction was historically a necessary condition of the helper's conviction, *any* basis of the principal's acquittal precluded the helper's conviction. Thus, if the principal escaped, died, or came up with his own defense that worked at trial or even on appeal, the helper would be automatically immune from prosecution or entitled to an annulment of his conviction. To get around this snag in bringing helpers to book, courts began to subversively interpret the term "principal." Helpers were long recognized as "accessories before the fact" who helped, but were not present at the scene of the crime. By fiction they became "constructive" principals who, though absent, were *deemed* present and operating at the scene of the crime. This way, if everyone involved in the offense could be called "principal," an escaped, dead, or exonerated principal would have no effect on the prosecution of other members of the criminal enterprise (other "principals"), even those whose roles were comparatively minor. Parliament and Congress ratified this judicial charade over a century ago by eliminating the legal significance of the terminology that had plagued the prosecution of helpers: the legal fate of the principal would no longer influence that of the helper. Also cast aside was any notion that the roles that defendants played in an offense should influence the punishment that they deserved: *all* members of the criminal enterprise would be punished equally, regardless of what they did. Despite the law's intention to treat principals and helpers identically regardless of their role, it does not always work out that way. In some cases, the principal does the dirty work and gets off scot-free due to a "personal" defense while the helper pays full price for someone else's actions.

The current state of complicity expresses our indignation at behind-the-scenes masterminds in gambling, counterfeiting, drug manufacturing, prostitution, and other far-flung enterprises that rely on hierarchy and division of labor. What this indignation expresses is only that *we* think that "game," "counterfeit," "manufacture drugs," and "sell sex" describe actors and actions that the law does not. To answer who the real perpetrator is in these cases would require thorough knowledge of the enterprise, of who really has a stake in the outcome, of who, if anyone, exercises "hegemony over the act." Also must we ask whether, for instance, an underling's running a printing press is what we mean by "counterfeiting" as opposed to merely "helping counterfeiting." Making these hard calls is part of judging, informing them is part of lawyering, and being subject to them is part of being a criminal defendant who has treaded into areas of questionable legality.

Perhaps this argument I have been making here is just a reminiscence on the days of indeterminate sentencing, which gave judges significant leeway in selecting the punishment for participants based on the importance of the role that each played in the offense. Such an approach is now anathema in America, but examples of careful role-sorting-out can be found elsewhere. For example, Leo Katz summarizes a case that reached the German Reichsgericht in 1940 in which two sisters conspired to conceal their pregnancies from their tyrannical father, who threatened to put them both out of the house if they got pregnant. The dominant sister took her pregnancy to term; her submissive sister miscarried. After the still-pregnant, dominant sister somehow disguised her condition from their father, she secretly gave birth. Katz further recounts:

> The new mother implored her sister, who was just bathing the baby, to kill it lest their father toss them out on the street. After refusing for some time, the sister finally gave in and drowned the baby. Both were charged with murder. The court, nevertheless, found only the mother guilty of murder and convicted her sister merely as an accessory even though it was she who had actually carried out the killing.

Leo Katz, Bad Acts and Guilty Minds 258 (Chicago 1987). The court got to the bottom of this lopsided sibling relation by relying on the "hegemony" over the act exercised by the new mother/dominant sister. Cf. George Fletcher, Rethinking Criminal Law §§8.6.2-8.7.4, at 654-73 (1978). That is, the new mother's "illegitimate" power over her sister characterized their relation and thus in the court's eyes explained that while the ostensible perpetrator was the submissive sister (after all, she drowned her newborn niece), a more thorough knowledge of their relation and of the episode supported a conviction of murder for the new mother. The submissive sister, meanwhile, was convicted of the less-serious offense of accessory to murder, thereby flipping the conventional application of the terms "perpetrator" and "accessory." A judge later explained: "If someone can be perpetrator without raising a finger in the actual execution, I don't see why someone can't be accessory, who executes the offensive act. If perpetration is to be defined exclusively in terms of whose will was controlling, I can see no principled difference between the two cases." Leo Katz, Bad Acts and Guilty Minds, *supra*, at 258, *quoting* Fritz Hartung, *Der Badewannenunfall*, 430-31 Juristenzeitung (1954).

If we know who the *real* principal is (the one running the printing press that makes the counterfeit bills? Or the one who set up the scheme?), then his helpers are punishable for one reason: with an intention to associate themselves with a criminal venture, they increase the risk of crime by bolstering or enlightening someone with encouragement, information, or materials. It is not as though they've done nothing; they *have* done something we should "stigmatize," "censor," or "disgrace." But given its essentially inchoate basis, complicity, like all inchoate criminality, should be viewed as a form of partial excuse ("I *merely* helped," "I didn't do it—*he* did," "I was there, but....") in order to acknowledge the law's responsibility for making careful distinctions about who is answerable for what.

One response to this argument against the equivalency position is that since 'tis not in mortals to command success, our inability to *control* the outcomes of what we put ourselves to makes those outcomes irrelevant in a responsibility-sense. Peter Heath, *Trying and Attempting*, Proceedings of the Aristotelian Society, Supplementary Volume XLV (1971). This is why Professor Ross says that all one promises in promising to do so-and-so is to do one's best to fulfill the promise, but not actually to fulfill it, because "we are under no obligation to effect changes, only to set ourselves to do so." Sir William David Ross, *Foundations of Ethics*, The Gifford Lectures delivered in the Univ. of Aberdeen 1935-6, at 108 (Oxford 1960). Such a way of responding to the fact that much of what we do in the world depends on the world, not just on us, has led to our eliminating crucial distinctions between requesting, agreeing, trying, helping, and doing. Eliminating these distinctions caves in to a view of responsibility which suggests that the results of our actions are something *other* than the things that we do. If such a view is the one we accept, if manifested intentions are all that matter and results do not, then "it becomes gradually clear that actions are events and people things. Eventually nothing remains which can be ascribed to the responsible self and we are left with nothing but a portion of the larger sequence of events, which can be deplored or celebrated, but not blamed or praised." Thomas Nagel, *Moral Luck*, *in* Mortal Questions 37 (Cambridge 1979). Thus, including complicity among the partial excuses preserves a realm for the responsible self where not only do results matter, but so too does the difference between the results of *my* actions and someone else's: where we acknowledge that "a man's relation to his own acts is quite different from his relation to the acts of other people." Peter Winch, *Trying*, in Ethics in Action 140 (D.Z. Phillips ed.) (London: Routledge and Kegan Paul 1972).

In our first principal case on complicity, *United States v. Fountain*, 768 F.2d 790 (7th Cir. 1985), consider just what sort of stance a helper must have toward the crime that the helper is assisting. Is rendering some sort of aid with indifference to the outcome enough to implicate the helper in the principal's offense? Or is something more needed? Must, as Judge Hand would put it, the helper actually *seek* by his action to make the crime succeed?

### U.S. COURT OF APPEALS FOR THE SEVENTH CIRCUIT

UNITED STATES OF AMERICA, PLAINTIFF-APPELLEE

V.

CLAYTON FOUNTAIN, THOMAS E. SILVERSTEIN, AND RANDY K. GOMETZ, DEFENDANTS-APPELLANTS

JULY 8, 1985

POSNER, Judge

This case involves the consolidated appeals in two closely related cases of murder of prison guards in the Control Unit of the federal penitentiary at Marion, Illinois—the maximum-security cell block in the nation's maximum-security federal prison—by past masters of prison murder, Clayton Fountain and Thomas Silverstein.

Shortly before these crimes, Fountain and Silverstein, both of whom were already serving life sentences for murder, had together murdered an inmate in the Control Unit of Marion, and had again been sentenced to life imprisonment. *See United States v. Silverstein*, 732 F.2d 1338 (7th Cir. 1984). After that, Silverstein killed another inmate, pleaded guilty to that murder, and received his third life sentence. At this point Fountain and Silverstein had each killed three people. The prison authorities belatedly took additional security measures. Three guards would escort Fountain and Silverstein (separately), handcuffed, every time they left their cells to go to or from the recreation room, the law library, or the shower. (Prisoners in Marion's Control Unit are confined, one to a cell, for all but 60-90 minutes a day, and are fed in their cells). But the guards would not be armed; nowadays guards do not carry weapons in the presence of prisoners, who might seize the weapons.

The two murders took place on the same October day in 1983. In the morning, Silverstein, while being escorted from the shower to his cell, stopped next to Randy Gometz's cell; and while two of the escorting officers were for some reason at a distance from him, reached his handcuffed hands into the cell. The third officer, who was closer to him, heard the click of the handcuffs being released and saw Gometz raise his shirt to reveal a home-made knife ("shank"), which had been fashioned from the iron leg of a bed, protruding from his waistband. Silverstein drew the knife and attacked one of the guards, Clutts, stabbing him 29 times and killing him. While pacing the corridor after the killing, Silverstein explained that "this is no cop thing. This is a personal thing between me and Clutts. The man disrespected me and I had to get him for it." Having gotten this off his chest he returned to his cell.

Fountain was less discriminating. While being escorted that evening back to his cell from the recreation room, he stopped alongside the cell of another inmate (who was not prosecuted for his part in the events that followed) and reached his handcuffed hands into the cell, and when he brought them out he was out of the handcuffs and holding a shank. He attacked all three guards, killing one (Hoffman) with multiple stab wounds (some inflicted after the guard had already fallen), injuring another gravely (Ditterline, who survived but is permanently disabled), and inflicting lesser though still serious injuries on the third (Powles). After the wounded guards had been dragged to safety by other guards, Fountain threw up his arms in the boxer's gesture of victory, and laughing, walked back to his cell.

A jury convicted Fountain of first-degree murder and lesser offenses unnecessary to go into here. The judge sentenced him to 50-150 years in prison, and ordered him to make restitution of $92,000 to Hoffman's estate, $98,000 to Ditterline, and $300,000 to the Department of Labor. The money for the Department was to reimburse it for disability, medical, and funeral payments that it had made or would make to Ditterline, Powles, and Hoffman's estate. The money for Ditterline was to compensate for past and future lost earnings not compensated for by the Department of Labor and for unreimbursed medical expenses.

Silverstein and Gometz were tried together (also before a jury, and before the same judge who presided at Fountain's trial) for the murder of Clutts, and both received the same 50-150 year sentences as Fountain and were ordered to pay restitution to Clutts's estate and to the Department of Labor of $68,000 and $2,000 respectively. Fountain and Silverstein are now confined in different federal prisons, in what were described at argument as "personalized" cells.

Gometz argues that the evidence was insufficient to convict him of aiding and abetting Silverstein in murdering Clutts. This argument requires consideration of the mental element in "aiding and abetting." Under the older cases, it was enough that the aider and abettor knew the principal's purpose. After the Supreme Court adopted Judge Learned Hand's test—that the aider and abettor "in some sort associate himself with the venture, that he participate in it as in something that he wishes to bring about, that he seek by his action to make it succeed"—it came to be generally accepted that the aider and abettor must share the principal's purpose in order to be guilty of violating 18 U.S.C. §2, the federal aider and abettor statute. But there is support for relaxing this requirement when the crime is particularly grave. For example, one who sells a gun to another knowing that he is buying it to commit a murder would hardly escape conviction as an accessory to the murder, though he received full price for the gun. This conclusion makes so compelling an appeal to common sense that even Gometz's opening brief in his appeal stated, "Defendant Gometz has no quarrel with this rule of law."

In *People v. Lauria*, 251 Cal.App.2d 471 (1967) (not a federal case but illustrative of the general point), the court, en route to holding that knowledge of the principal's purpose would not suffice for aiding and abetting of just any crime, said it would suffice for "the seller of gasoline who knew the buyer was using his product to make Molotov cocktails for terroristic use." Compare the following hypothetical cases. In the first, a shopkeeper sells dresses to a woman whom he knows to be a prostitute. The shopkeeper would not be guilty of aiding and abetting prostitution unless the prosecution could establish the elements of Judge Hand's test. Little would be gained by imposing criminal liability in such a case. Prostitution, anyway a minor crime, would be but trivially deterred, since the prostitute could easily get her clothes from a shopkeeper ignorant of her occupation. In the second case, a man buys a gun from a gun dealer after telling the dealer that he wants it in order to kill his mother-in-law, and he does kill her. The dealer would be guilty of aiding and abetting the murder. This liability would help to deter—and perhaps not trivially given public regulation of the sale of guns—a most serious crime. In a federal prosecution, aiding and abetting murder is established by proof beyond a reasonable doubt that the supplier of the murder weapon knew the purpose for which it would be used. This interpretation of the federal aider and abettor statute is consistent with though not compelled by precedent.

Gometz argued that there was insufficient evidence that he knew why Silverstein wanted a knife. But the circumstances made clear that the drawing of the knife from Gometz's waistband was prearranged. There must have been discussions between Silverstein and Gometz. Gometz must have known through those discussions or others that Silverstein had already killed three people in prison—two in Marion—and while this fact could not be used to convict Silverstein of a fourth murder, it could ground an inference that Gometz knew that Silverstein wanted the knife in order to kill someone. If Silverstein had wanted to conceal it on his person to take it back to his cell and keep it there for purposes of intimidation, escape, or self-defense (or carry it around concealed for any of these purposes), he would not have asked Gometz to release him from his handcuffs (as the jury could have found he had done), for that ensured that the guards would search him. Since the cuffs were off before Silverstein drew the shank from Gometz's waistband, a reasonable jury could find beyond a reasonable doubt that Gometz knew that Silverstein, given his history of prison murders, could have only one motive in drawing the shank and that was to make a deadly assault.

Accordingly, Gometz's conviction is affirmed.

## QUESTIONS ON *FOUNTAIN*

**1. Helping versus doing.** An aider and abettor is anyone who intentionally helps the crime without actually committing an element of the crime itself. Anyone who actually commits an element of the crime is principal, not aider and abettor. Thus, there can be multiple principals in a case. For example, robbery is defined as a larceny committed by assault. That is, the thief intentionally uses force or a threat of force to acquire property known to be that of another with the specific intent to permanently deprive the victim of that property. With that in mind, suppose one party holds the victim at gunpoint while the other empties the cash register in a store stickup. Who is principal robber? Who is aider and abettor?

2. **Knowingly helping v. intentionally helping.** Judge Posner writes in *Fountain* that his interpretation of aiding and abetting (of complicity, of accomplice liability) "is consistent with though not compelled by precedent." In support of his interpretation of federal law, Posner cites a California conspiracy case, *People v. Lauria*, 251 Cal.App.2d 471 (1967). Louis Lauria ran a telephone answering service that was relied on by as many as 10 prostitutes. Lauria knew he had prostitute-customers, but that is not, without more, proof of a conspiracy: conspirators must *agree* to break the law, that is, share a specific intent, not just an awareness, that one or more of their members will commit the target offense(s). *Lauria* deduced from precedents the following rule for addressing when "knowledge alone" can satisfy the intent element in the law of conspiracy:

> [T]he intent of a supplier who knows of the criminal use to which his supplies are put to participate in the criminal activity connected with the use of his supplies may be established by (1) direct evidence that he intends to participate, or (2) through an inference that he intends to participate based on, (a) his special interest in the activity, or (b) the aggravated nature of the crime itself.

*Id.* at 482. Applying that standard, the Court of Appeal affirmed for lack of proof the trial court's ruling dismissing the information charging Lauria with conspiracy to commit prostitution. In light of the rule quoted above, what in your estimation should count as a supplier's "special interest in the activity"? That wasn't Posner's interest in *Lauria*. What *was*?

3. **Elements of complicity.** California does not allow for the conviction of an accomplice who lends a hand knowing of the principal's criminal purpose, but is indifferent to whether the principal achieves that criminal purpose. The three elements of complicity require that the accomplice/helper: 1) know the principal/perpetrator's criminal purpose; 2) intend to further that

purpose; and 3) aid or encourage that purpose. CALJIC No. 3.01 (Spring 2009 Revision).

**a. Indifferent actions.** Is it possible to know what crime a perpetrator intends, aid the effort (as in, by driving the perpetrator to the situs of the crime), but somehow *not* intend to further the perpetrator's plan? *See, e.g., State v. Gladstone*, 474 P.2d 274 (Wash. 1970) (en banc) [although defendant, who was out of stock, directed pot customer to another seller who ended up making the sale, with no conspiracy with (or kickback expected or received from) the other seller, defendant helped the sale indifferently, *not* as accomplice].

**b. Indifferent words.** Is it possible to know what crime a perpetrator intends, encourage the effort (as in, calling out "you can do it!" or "don't chicken out!"), but somehow *not* intend to further the perpetrator's plan? *See, e.g. Michael R. v. Jeffrey B.*, 158 Cal.App.3d 1059 (1984) [civil case finding triable issue as to whether saying "go for it" to tortfeasor who then blinded plaintiff with a marble shot from a wrist-rocket counts as criminal solicitation].

## NOTES ON *FOUNTAIN*

***1. More on the indifferent helper.*** In *People v. Beeman*, 35 Cal.3d 547 (1984), the California Supreme Court clarified that accomplice liability is a specific-intent crime. There, principals Burk and Gray pleaded guilty to robbery after successfully moving the trial court to try them separately. Beeman was involved in the planning of the robbery of Beeman's sister-in-law, Marjorie. He admitted to bragging, at least to Burk, about Marjorie's valuable jewels; Gray added that Beeman described to him the cars driven by Marjorie's family. Though Burk and Gray admitted that Beeman wanted nothing to do with the actual robbery, both indicated that Beeman (6'5" tall, 310 pounds) was more worried about being recognized than about dispossessing his sister-in-law of her jewels. Burk and Gray testified that Beeman had detailed the layout of Marjorie's house just before the robbery, and Burk testified that Beeman had discussed how Burk would pose as a poll-taker to gain entry. Burk and Gray added that Beeman ended up mad at them for stealing more from Marjorie than was originally discussed. Burk claimed that Beeman consequently demanded an increase from 20% to 33% as his cut of any post-robbery sale of the loot.

Beeman admitted to, in effect, clothing the robbers, whom he knew had bought a gun and handcuffs for the job. So too did he admit to describing for them Marjorie's jewels, the floor-plan of the house, and the family cars; but he insisted he did so in idle conversation, not as part of a scheme. While Beeman also admitted to telling the others that he would in no way interfere with their plan, he never took seriously the idea that they would actually go through with it. Once the robbery occurred, Beeman claimed, he recovered the jewels for Marjorie and only pretended to be interested in fencing them.

Certainly Beeman knew what was going on. But the upshot of the California Supreme Court's ruling reversing Beeman's conviction is that he was not accomplice to the robbery if his stance toward the principal robbers' plan was one of indifference.

### 2. Criminal procedure.

**a. Burden of proof.** Consider *People v. Acero*, 161 Cal.App.3d 217 (1984) (decided less than a year after *Beeman*), where Acero and Copeland were party crashers who had outworn their welcome at Randy Vasquez's graduation celebration. Police learned from seven witnesses that Acero, Copeland, and two others returned to the dwindling party around 4:30 a.m., 2-1/2 hours after being kicked out. Acero wielded a BB-gun to facilitate the near-fatal stabbing of Steven Queen, either by Copeland or someone else, but Acero ended up falling into a hot tub as the scuffle petered out.

Two errors doomed the trial court's instructions culminating in Acero's conviction of attempted murder (and Copeland's acquittal): 1) attempted murder can be committed with implied malice; and 2) an accomplice to a crime is someone who knowingly aids, promotes, encourages, or instigates the principal's unlawful purposes. Accurate instructions would have reflected that both the principal (who inflicted Queen's injuries) and the helper (who kept onlookers at bay with a gun) must have the specific intent that the principal commit murder if both are to be attempted murderers.

To cope with difficulties in decoding what the helper intended his principal to do, courts instruct jurors that the helper may be *presumed* to intend the natural and probable consequences of his acts. Another way of saying this is that courts instruct jurors that helpers' intentions to promote their principals' offenses may be *inferred* from the helpers' knowledge that what they are doing is helping their principals' criminal purpose. Please note that here I say a helper's intention *may* be inferred, not *must*.

Acero cites *Connecticut v. Johnson*, 460 U.S. 73 (1983) for the proposition that a *conclusive* presumption that we intend the natural and probable consequences of our actions violates a defendant's Due Process right to place on the prosecution the burden to prove its case beyond a reasonable doubt. *Cf. supra* Chapter 3.A, note 6 on *Spurlin*. Johnson kidnapped, robbed, raped, and attempted murder of a woman driver who had asked him and his three (later four) confederates for directions. He was convicted of all four offenses based on the trial court's charge to the jury that harm, when natural and probable, is conclusively presumed to be intentionally brought about. The U.S. Supreme Court upheld the Connecticut Supreme Court's ruling reversing the attempted-murder and robbery convictions and affirming the kidnapping and rape convictions. Because rape is not a crime of intention, its proof was not contaminated by the conclusive presumption. As for the kidnapping, the trial court had rescued the conclusive presumption by noting that the proof of intention to kidnap is a matter of permissive, not mandatory, inference.

*Acero* involved that distinction between a permissive and mandatory (or conclusive) inference (or presumption) of intent. But by erroneously omitting from the instructions that Acero needed specific intent that Copeland or someone else murder Queen for Acero to be an accomplice to attempted murder, the trial court did not impose a *presumption* of intent, conclusive or permissive. Instead, it *eliminated* the issue of intent altogether. And that violates Due Process.

**b. Harmless error.** "A defendant is entitled to a fair trial but not a perfect one." *Lutwak v. United States*, 344 U.S. 604, 619 (1953). It is not unusual for appellate defense counsel to find something wrong with the conduct of the trial (whether in or out of the judge's control): allowing in evidence that should have been excluded; juror misconduct; improper comment by the prosecutor; or trial counsel's failure to request an instruction on a pertinent defense or lesser offense. But not all errors justify reversal. Rather, only those errors that infect the verdict justify reversal. *See supra* Chapter 3.A, question 7 [discussing harmless trial error in *Elonis*]; note 4a on *Greene* [same].

The *Acero* majority listed two standards for assessing whether an error at trial infected the verdict. First, if the error is of non-constitutional magnitude, the appellate court asks whether there is a *reasonable probability* that the guilty verdict was caused by the error. *People v. Watson*, 299 P.2d 243 (Cal. 1956). Second, if the error is of constitutional magnitude, the appellate court asks whether the prosecution has demonstrated *beyond a reasonable doubt* that the guilty verdict was not caused by the error. *Chapman v. California*, 386 U.S. 18 (1967). The *Chapman* standard makes it more difficult than the *Watson* standard for appellate courts to find the error harmless. Some errors, however, referred to by the Supreme Court as "structural," require automatic reversal, thus bypassing harmless-error review of any kind. See *United States v. Gonzalez-Lopez*, 548 U.S. 140, 148-51 (2006) [listing examples of structural errors].

Although *Acero* points out that in *Johnson* the Supreme Court divided 4-4 on whether an instructional error eliminating the intent element could in any case be harmless, the Pennsylvania Supreme Court, by a 5-4 margin, has read *Johnson* as precluding harmless-error analysis. *Commonwealth v. Kelly*, 724 A.2d 909, 914 & n.6 (Pa. 1999). But cf. *People v. Flood*, 957 P.2d 869, 891 (Cal. 1998) ["[I]nstructional error that improperly describes or omits an element of an offense, or that raises an improper presumption or directs a finding or a partial verdict upon a particular element, generally is not a structural defect in the trial mechanism that defies harmless error review and automatically requires reversal under the federal Constitution."].

**3. "Bad hombres."** Redacted from *Fountain* is this:

> At both trials the judge ordered defendants and their inmate witnesses to be shackled at the ankles while in court. Curtains at counsel tables shielded the shackles from the jury's view, but apparently the shackles were visible when witnesses were en route to or from the witness stand; and Fountain and Silverstein each testified in his own trial. Although disfavored for obvious reasons, the shackling of inmate witnesses in a jury trial is permissible *in extremis*. The prudence of requiring shackles in this case was shown by Fountain's and Silverstein's extraordinary history of violence in the face of maximum security precautions, the fact that most of the witnesses were murderers, and above all the fact that defendants are wholly beyond the deterrent reach of the law. If they were not shackled, there would be a grave danger of their attacking people in the courtroom or trying to escape. Silverstein's long disciplinary record includes one

escape, while Gometz's includes three episodes of planning and attempting escape. The prejudice of shackling was mitigated by jurors' awareness that the entire *dramatis personae* in the two cases were prison inmates—most of them murderers—and guards. The shackles could not have come as much of a surprise. The judge did not abuse his discretion in requiring them.

*Fountain, supra,* 768 F.2d at 794. Clayton Fountain, an infamous racist who murdered his Marine Corps staff sergeant in the Philippines, was as a result installed at Ft. Leavenworth, where he was too much for military guards, who got him transferred to Marion. There, as you know, he murdered three prisoners before stabbing Hoffman, Ditterline, and Powles. That got him moved to a customized, Hannibal Lecter cage at the federal medical facility in Springfield, Missouri, where Fountain found, in order, love (a pen-pal), God, and death by heart attack in 2004 at 48. The Clutts murder consigned Thomas Silverstein (now 66), former leader of the Aryan Brotherhood, to live out his years in solitary at the Florence, Colorado supermax federal facility for incorrigibles, conceived by the Bureau of Prisons as a reaction to the Marion incident. Because lifer Randy Gometz (now 62) had never transcended bank robbery and attempted murder of a prisoner until he supplied Silverstein with a shank, he was recently downgraded from Florence to a medium-security federal facility in Atlanta and then upgraded again to Tucson. His recent habeas suit was dismissed. *Gometz v. United States*, 2015 WL 3814652 (S.D. Ill.).

## 2. DEPARTURES FROM THE COMMON SCHEME

Gometz, like Acero and Beeman, could not seriously contend that his principal's crime came as a surprise. Instead, all three of these accomplice-defendants claimed not to have *intended* to help their principals' crimes along. Contrariwise, recall Zielesch, who claimed that Volarvich's murder of Officer Stevens was an improvised move by a freelancing principal who, rather than pursue the alleged common scheme of murdering Shamberger, murdered a highway-patrol officer in order to conceal his possession of methamphetamine. Yet according to the Court of Appeal, Zielesch's responsibility for Stevens's death arose out of the conspiracy to kill Shamberger, which made Volarvich's killing of Stevens a natural and probable incidental or upshot of the target offense.

Not all cases of accomplice liability involve conspiracies, however. Our next principal case, *People v. Prettyman*, 14 Cal.4th 248 (1996), reveals that the rules for addressing an accomplice's liability for a freelancing principal's excessive crimes that surpass the common scheme or design are the same as the rules that govern a co-conspirator's liability for a freelancing co-conspirator's excessive crimes that surpass the common conspiratorial scheme or design.

## SUPREME COURT OF CALIFORNIA
### THE PEOPLE, PLAINTIFF AND RESPONDENT
### V.
### RICHARD D. PRETTYMAN ET AL., DEFENDANTS AND APPELLANTS

### DEC. 9, 1996

KENNARD, Justice

Under California law, a person who aids and abets a confederate in the commission of a criminal act is liable not only for that crime (the target crime), but also for any other offense (nontarget crime) committed by the confederate as a natural and probable consequence of the crime originally aided and abetted. To convict a defendant of a nontarget crime as an accomplice under the "natural and probable consequences" doctrine, the jury must find that, with knowledge of the perpetrator's unlawful purpose, and with the intent of committing, encouraging, or facilitating the commission of the target crime, the defendant aided, promoted, encouraged, or instigated the commission of the target crime. The jury must also find that the defendant's confederate committed an offense other than the target crime, and that the nontarget offense perpetrated by the confederate was a natural and probable consequence of the target crime that the defendant assisted or encouraged.

In this case, defendant Debra Jane Bray was charged with murder; the prosecution's theory at trial was that she was guilty as an accomplice. The trial court instructed the jury that it could find Bray guilty of murder if it determined either that she had aided and abetted the murder or that the murder was a natural and probable consequence of any uncharged offense(s) that Bray had aided and abetted. The court did not, however, identify or describe any such uncharged target offense. At issue here is whether, absent a request by counsel, the court should have so instructed the jury.

We conclude that when the prosecutor relies on the "natural and probable consequences" doctrine, the trial court must identify and describe the target crimes that the defendant might have assisted or encouraged. An instruction *identifying* target crimes will assist the jury in determining whether the crime charged was a natural and probable consequence of some other criminal act. And an instruction *describing* the target crimes will eliminate the risk that the jury will engage in uninformed speculation with regard to what types of conduct are criminal.

## I. Facts

Codefendant Richard D. Prettyman and defendant Debra Jane Bray were charged with the murder of Gaylord "Vance" Van Camp, and with conspiring to murder Van Camp. A jury convicted both of first-degree murder, but acquitted them of conspiracy. The Court of Appeal affirmed codefendant Prettyman's murder conviction. *People v. Prettyman*, 24 Cal.App.4th 211 (1994). The following evidence was presented at their trial.

Defendant Bray and codefendant Prettyman held themselves out as husband and wife. They, as well as victim Van Camp, were among the homeless living in the Pacific Beach area of San Diego. Van Camp was beaten to death with a steel pipe on the morning of July 20, 1992, while asleep in the courtyard of the Pacific Beach Presbyterian Church. The prosecution contended that Prettyman beat Van Camp to death with the pipe, and that Bray, described by the prosecutor as an "argumentative drunk," encouraged Prettyman to kill Van Camp in order to obtain Bray's wallet, which Bray had given to Van Camp for safekeeping the previous evening.

On the evening preceding the murder, defendant Bray and Van Camp had dinner at the church. Codefendant Prettyman was not present during the dinner, but he attended the religious service that followed. After the service, Bray, who was intoxicated, argued with Prettyman. According to prosecution witness Dennis Charette, a homeless man who observed the argument, Bray demanded that Prettyman return to her certain identification papers that she needed to collect a benefit check. When the argument became heated, Van Camp asked the church's preschool director, Stephanie Hansen, to intervene. At trial, Hansen mentioned that it was "pretty common" for the "street people" she knew to argue and to threaten one another, and that she had heard Bray arguing with Prettyman on other occasions.

After talking to Bray and Prettyman, Hansen asked Van Camp to take Prettyman away from the church until the latter had calmed down. The two men left. Before they went, Bray handed her wallet to Van Camp. According to Charette, Bray told Van Camp to hold the wallet for safekeeping, to prevent Prettyman from stealing it.

Prettyman and Van Camp returned to the church courtyard. Prettyman lay down next to Bray, while Van Camp found a sleeping spot a short distance away. When Charette got up at 2 a.m. to urinate, he noticed that Bray and Prettyman were gone, but that Van Camp was still asleep in the courtyard. At 3:00 or 4:00 a.m., Edward Eash, a homeless man sleeping in a car near the church courtyard, was awakened by the sound of loud voices. Looking out a car window, he saw Bray and codefendant Prettyman. Bray repeatedly said: "We are going to get that fucker Vance. He has no idea who he is messing with. He ain't getting away with this shit." Prettyman nodded his head and said, "Yep. Okay." Between 4:00 and 5:30 a.m., Charette was awakened by the sound of thumping noises in the church courtyard. He heard codefendant Prettyman say, "Take that." Sitting up, Charette saw Prettyman leave the courtyard with a three-to-four-foot pipe. Charette heard Van Camp make "gagging" noises.

Immediately after Prettyman's departure, Bray came "flying up" to Charette. She told him to leave and not to look at Van Camp. Charette obeyed. He later met Bray and Prettyman in front of the church. Prettyman then went back into the church courtyard. He returned within a few minutes, and reported that Van Camp had choked on his own blood. Prettyman then said, "teach him to steal a wallet and to threaten us," adding that Van Camp had "deserved it." Both Bray and Prettyman told Charette not to tell anyone what had happened.

Shortly after 6:00 a.m., codefendant Prettyman told Robert Walker, another homeless man, that he had killed Van Camp with a metal pipe and then had started looking for Bray's wallet. He told Walker that he eventually found the wallet under Van Camp's head. At 6:30 a.m., preschool director Hansen arrived at the church. She saw a figure lying in the church courtyard and heard a moaning sound, but she did not investigate, assuming that the person was waking up. At 7:20 a.m., the custodian told her there was a dead body in the courtyard, and she called the police. When police arrived, they saw Van Camp's body lying in the courtyard, a bloody jacket next to his head. Papers, items of clothing, and Van Camp's backpack were strewn on the steps to the church sanctuary. The police retrieved a three-foot long piece of galvanized steel pipe from the ivy on church grounds.

Dr. Harry James Bonnell, Chief Deputy Medical Examiner for San Diego County, testified that Van Camp's death was caused by three blows to the head from a blunt instrument, and that the blows could have been inflicted by the steel pipe that the police had found on the church grounds. The pipe had no bloodstains or fingerprints. Dr. Bonnell stated that if some garment had covered Van Camp's head when the fatal blows were struck, this might explain the absence of bloodstains on the pipe. According to prosecution witness Dennis Charette, Van Camp customarily covered his head with his coat before going to sleep in the church courtyard.

Both defendant Bray and codefendant Prettyman attempted to show that someone other than Prettyman had killed Van Camp. The chief defense witness was Charles Dunner, a homeless man. Between 12:00 and 1:30 on the night of the killing, Dunner was "dumpster diving" in an alley across the street from the Pacific Beach Presbyterian Church. As he left the alley, he saw a car with two occupants. A Hispanic man with a beard and slick hair got out of the car and ran into the church courtyard, carrying a bat or club. After looking around, the man repeatedly hit someone or something with the club. Dunner could not see what the man was hitting because his view was partially obstructed by a planter box. The man then returned to the car, got in, threw the club in the back seat, and the car took off. The defense also called Summer Boyd, a licensed vocational nurse. She testified that she attended a meeting at the Pacific Beach Presbyterian Church on the morning that Van Camp was killed, arriving about 7:10. During the meeting, at 7:17 a.m., she heard some men shouting, "Let's get out of here, they are coming." She then saw two Hispanic men and one White male with long scraggly light-brown hair run down the alley next to the church.

The defense also presented expert testimony. David Fortman, a defense investigator who had taught courses in forensics, blood spatter evidence, and criminology, testified that, based on blood spatters photographed at the scene, significant quantities of blood must have been transferred to the murder weapon when it was used to strike the fatal blows to Van Camp's head. Because the steel pipe found by police bore no bloodstains and was dirty (indicating that it had not been washed), Fortman concluded that the pipe was not the murder weapon.

In an effort to impeach prosecution witnesses Charette and Eash, the defense presented evidence that Charette was "extremely intoxicated" on the night Van Camp was killed and that Eash, who had testified he was sober on the night of the murder, was a convicted felon, had a drinking problem, and once had given a written report to his probation officer falsely stating that he had not been arrested for alcohol-related offenses during the month preceding the report.

The trial court gave the jury the standard instructions defining aiding and abetting: CALJIC No. 3.00 (5th ed. 1988) [principals defined], CALJIC No. 3.01 [aiding and abetting defined], and CALJIC No. 3.03 [termination of liability of one who aids and abets]. Also included was this instruction:

> One who aids and abets is not only guilty of the particular crime aided and abetted, but is also liable for the *natural and probable consequences* of the commission of such crime. You must determine whether the defendant is guilty of the crime originally contemplated, and, if so, whether any other crime charged was a natural and probable consequence of such *originally contemplated* crime.

This instruction was substantially similar to the original 1988 version of CALJIC No. 3.02. The trial court did not give the 1992 revision of CALJIC No. 3.02, which would have specified the possible criminal acts that Bray might have "originally contemplated," nor did the trial court give an instruction describing the elements of any such crimes. Although the record is unclear, the instruction on the "natural and probable consequences" rule was apparently given by the trial court on its own initiative.

The jury convicted both defendant Bray and her confederate, co-defendant Prettyman, of first-degree murder, but acquitted them of conspiracy to commit murder. The trial court sentenced Bray to a term of 25 years to life in prison. She appealed. Prettyman also appealed, but on different grounds.

The Court of Appeal affirmed Bray's conviction. It held that the trial court had properly instructed the jury on aiding and abetting, rejecting Bray's contention that the trial court had erred in neither identifying nor describing any target or predicate crime that she might have "originally contemplated" within the meaning of CALJIC No. 3.02. The court, however, noted the disagreement in the Courts of Appeal regarding the need to so instruct the jury: *People v. Mouton*, 15 Cal.App.4th 1313 (1993) held that a trial court must name and define any target or predicate offense that the accomplice might originally have assisted or encouraged. In contrast, *People v. Solis*, 20 Cal.App.4th 264 (1993), expressly disagreeing with *Mouton*, held that such instructions are generally unnecessary. To resolve this conflict, we granted defendant Bray's petition for review.

### II. General Principles of Aiding and Abetting Liability

Under California law, a person who aids and abets the commission of a crime is a "principal" in the crime, and thus shares the guilt of the actual perpetrator. Accomplice liability is "derivative," that is, it results from an act by the perpetrator to which the accomplice contributed. When an accomplice chooses to become a part of the criminal activity of another, she says in essence, "your acts are my acts," and forfeits her personal identity. We euphemistically may impute the actions of the perpetrator to the accomplice by "agency" doctrine; in reality, we demand that she who chooses to aid in a crime forfeits her right to be treated as an individual.

In *People v. Beeman*, 35 Cal.3d 547 (1984), we discussed the mental state necessary for liability as an aider and abettor. To prove that a defendant is an accomplice, we said, "the prosecution must show that the defendant acted with knowledge of the criminal purpose of the perpetrator *and* with an intent or purpose either of committing, or of encouraging or facilitating commission of, the offense." *Id.* at 560. When the offense charged is a specific intent crime, the accomplice must "share the specific intent of the perpetrator"; this occurs when the accomplice "knows the full extent of the perpetrator's criminal purpose and gives aid or encouragement with the intent or purpose of facilitating the perpetrator's commission of the crime." *Id.* Thus, we held, an aider and abettor is a person who, "acting with (1) knowledge of the unlawful purpose of the perpetrator; and (2) the intent or purpose of committing, encouraging, or facilitating the commission of the offense, (3) by act or advice aids, promotes, encourages or instigates, the commission of the crime." *Id.* at 561.

It sometimes happens that an accomplice assists or encourages a confederate to commit one crime, and the confederate commits another, more serious crime (the nontarget offense). Whether the accomplice may be held responsible for that nontarget offense turns not only upon a consideration of the general principles of accomplice liability set forth in *Beeman*, but also upon a consideration of the "natural and probable consequences" doctrine, which is at issue in this case and will be discussed below.

### III. The "Natural and Probable Consequences" Doctrine

At common law, a person encouraging or facilitating the commission of a crime was criminally liable not only for that crime, but for any other offense that was a natural and probable consequence of the crime aided and abetted. Although the "natural and probable consequences" doctrine has been subjected to criticism, it is an established rule of American jurisprudence. It is based on the recognition that "aiders and abettors should be responsible for the criminal harms they have naturally, probably and foreseeably put in motion." *People v. Luparello*, 187 Cal.App.3d 410, 439 (1986). The first California decision to embrace this doctrine was *People v. Kauffman*, 152 Cal. 331 (1907).

In *Kauffman*, the defendant and five friends planned to break into a safe at a cemetery. Armed with guns, a bottle of nitroglycerin (to blow open the safe), and burglary tools, they went to the cemetery, where they found an armed guard by the safe. They turned back. On their way home, an encounter with a police officer led to a gunfight in which the officer was killed. The defendant, who had been carrying the nitroglycerin, was unarmed and did not participate in the shooting, but was charged with and convicted of the officer's murder. *Id.* at 332-34. On appeal, the defendant argued that the evidence was insufficient to support his conviction.

In affirming the defendant's conviction in *Kauffman*, this court said:

> The general rule is well settled that where several parties conspire or combine together to commit any unlawful act, each is criminally responsible for the acts of his associates or confederates committed in furtherance of any prosecution of the common design for which they combine.... Each is responsible for everything done by his confederates, which follows incidentally in the execution of the common design as one of its probable and natural consequences, even though it was not intended as a part of the original design or common plan. Nevertheless the act must be the ordinary and probable

> effect of the wrongful act specifically agreed on, so that the connection between them may be reasonably apparent, and not a fresh and independent product of the mind of one of the confederates outside of, or foreign to, the common design.

*Id.* at 334. We then concluded in *Kauffman* that, based on the evidence presented, the jury could reasonably find that the plan in which the defendant had conspired included not only breaking into the safe at the cemetery, but also protecting all members of the group from arrest or detection while going to and returning from the scene of the proposed burglary, and that the policeman's death was a natural and probable consequence of this unlawful enterprise. *Id.* at 335-37.

*Kauffman* involved the liability of conspirators for substantive crimes in the course of a conspiracy, not the liability of aiders and abettors, as does this case. But later decisions have applied the "natural and probable consequences" doctrine to aiders and abettors. In *People v. Croy*, 41 Cal.3d 1 (1985), we set forth the principles of the "natural and probable consequences" doctrine as applied to aiders and abettors:

> An aider and abettor is guilty not only of the offense he intended to facilitate or encourage, but also of any reasonably foreseeable offense committed by the person he aids and abets.... It follows that a defendant whose liability is predicated on his status as an aider and abettor need not have intended to encourage or facilitate the particular offense ultimately committed by the perpetrator. His knowledge that an act which is criminal was intended, and his action taken with the intent that the act be encouraged or facilitated, are sufficient to impose liability on him for any reasonably foreseeable offense committed as a consequence by the perpetrator. It is the intent to encourage and bring about conduct that is criminal, not the specific intent that is an element of the target offense, which ... must be found by the jury.

*Id.* at 12 n.5. Thus, under *Croy*, a defendant may be held criminally responsible as an accomplice not only for the crime he or she intended to aid and abet (the target crime), but also for any other crime that is the natural and probable consequence of the target crime.

As we pointed out earlier, under general principles of aiding and abetting, "an aider and abettor must act with knowledge of the criminal purpose of the perpetrator *and* with an intent or purpose either of committing, or of encouraging or facilitating commission of, the offense." Beeman, 35 Cal.3d at 560. Therefore, when a particular aiding-and-abetting case triggers application of the "natural and probable consequences" doctrine, the *Beeman* test applies, and the trier of fact must find that the defendant, acting with (1) knowledge of the unlawful purpose of the perpetrator; and (2) the intent or purpose of committing, encouraging, or facilitating the commission of a predicate or target offense; (3) by act or advice aided, promoted, encouraged or instigated the commission of the target crime. But the trier of fact must also find that (4) the defendant's confederate committed an offense *other than* the target crime;[4] and (5) the offense committed by the confederate was a natural and probable consequence of the target crime that the defendant aided and abetted.

Until recently, decisions involving the "natural and probable consequences" doctrine in aiding and abetting cases were limited to consideration of whether the evidence was sufficient to support the defendant's conviction. These decisions most commonly involved situations in which a defendant assisted or encouraged a confederate to commit an assault with a deadly weapon or with potentially deadly force, and the confederate not only assaulted but also murdered the victim. In those instances, the courts generally had no difficulty in upholding a murder conviction, reasoning that the jury could reasonably conclude that the killing of the victim death was a natural and probable consequence of the assault that the defendant aided and abetted. *People v. Martinez*, 239 Cal.App.2d 161 (1966) [attempted murder of rival gang member was natural and probable consequence of defendant's suggestion that members of his gang beat up rival gang members]. *But see People v. Butts*, 236 Cal.App.2d 817, 836-37 (1965) [killing of victim held not to be a natural and probable consequence of an assault when the defendant did not know that his confederate would use a deadly weapon]. Other cases applied the "natural and probable consequences" doctrine where a defendant assisted in the commission of an armed robbery, during which a confederate assaulted or tried to kill one of the robbery victims. In those cases,

---

[4] In this case we do not decide whether a defendant may be convicted under the "natural and probable consequences" doctrine when the target criminal act was not committed.

courts upheld jury verdicts convicting the defendant of assault and/or attempted murder on the ground that the jury could reasonably conclude that the crime was a natural and probable consequence of the robbery aided by the defendant. *People v. Rogers*, 172 Cal.App.3d 502 (1985).

More recently, appellate courts have had to deal with questions regarding the adequacy of jury instructions with respect to the "natural and probable consequences" doctrine. This case concerns one such question: whether the trial court should have identified and described the predicate or target offense(s) assisted and encouraged by the defendant.

### IV. Instructions on "Natural and Probable Consequences"

In instructing a jury in a criminal case on the applicable law, California trial judges are guided in general by the standard jury instructions contained in California Jury Instructions, Criminal (CALJIC). These are prepared by the Committee on Standard Jury Instructions, Criminal, of the Superior Court of Los Angeles County. Although not mandated by statute, their use is recommended by the Judicial Council of California.

The pattern instructions on accomplice liability in CALJIC's first, second, and third editions (published in 1946, 1958, and 1970, respectively) made no reference to the "natural and probable consequences" doctrine.[5] The rule was first mentioned in a 1976 supplement to the third edition of CALJIC, which suggested, at the end of a pattern instruction defining the "principals" of a crime, this optional instruction: "One who aids and abets is not only guilty of the particular crime that to his knowledge his confederates are contemplating committing, but he is also liable for the natural and reasonable or probable consequences of any act that he knowingly aided or encouraged." CALJIC No. 3.00 (3d ed. 1976 rev.). This sentence was retained in the fourth edition of CALJIC, which was published in 1979. Then, in 1988, in apparent response to a statement by the Court of Appeal in *People v. Hammond*, 181 Cal.App.3d 463, 469 (1986), which criticized the instruction as inadequate, the Committee on Standard Jury Instructions, Criminal drafted a separate new

---

[5] Early editions of CALJIC did, however, cite the "natural and probable consequences" rule as a principle of conspiracy law. CALJIC No. 932 (1st ed. 1946); CALJIC No. 932 (2d ed. 1958); CALJIC No. 6.11 (3d ed. 1970).

instruction to explain the "natural and probable consequences" doctrine. CALJIC No. 3.02 (5th ed. 1988).

The 1988 version of CALJIC No. 3.02 made no mention of *identifying* for the jury any target or predicate unlawful act that had been aided and abetted by the defendant and that led, as a natural and probable consequence, to the confederate's commission of the crime with which the defendant was charged. In 1992, however, CALJIC No. 3.02 was revised to include this information. And an accompanying "use note" stated: "This instruction must be accompanied by ... instructions defining all crimes encompassed in this instruction." CALJIC No. 3.02 (5th ed. 1992 Supp. at 19).

At issue here is whether, when a trial court instructs a jury on the "natural and probable consequences" doctrine, the identification and description of potential target offenses are "general principles of law that are commonly or closely and openly connected to the facts before the court and that are necessary for the jury's understanding of the case," *People v. Montoya,* 7 Cal.4th 1027, 1047 (1994), thus triggering the trial court's duty to so instruct the jury on the court's own initiative. This issue first arose in *People v. Mouton*, 15 Cal.App.4th 1313 (1993), where a man fought with his girlfriend. Hearing that the girlfriend's relatives had armed themselves and were looking for him, the man asked the defendant and one Albert Reed to bring their guns to the apartment complex where the altercation had occurred. When the latter two came to the apartment building with guns, one of the residents told them to leave. An argument ensued. Reed then fired three shots at the resident, missing him but killing a bystander.

Mouton was charged, as an aider and abettor, with murdering the bystander. At trial, the prosecution conceded that the defendant and Reed had not planned to kill the bystander; the prosecution argued, however, that the defendant was nevertheless guilty of the murder as an aider and abettor, because the killing of the bystander was a natural and probable consequence of target crimes whose commission the defendant had intentionally aided and abetted. Among those crimes, the prosecutor contended, were carrying a concealed firearm, brandishing a deadly weapon, assault with a deadly weapon, and shooting at an occupied dwelling. The trial court instructed the jury that the defendant could be held responsible for any crime that was the natural and probable consequence of the unlawful act(s) the defendant had aided and abetted. But, as in this case, the trial court neither identified nor described the target crimes that, under the prosecutor's theory, the defendant facilitated or encouraged and that could have led to the killing. The jury convicted the defendant of second-degree murder.

The Court of Appeal in *Mouton* reversed defendant's murder conviction. It held that the trial court should, on its own initiative, have identified and defined the target offenses that the defendant might originally have aided and abetted, in view of the trial court's general duty "to instruct the jury on all general legal principles raised by the evidence and necessary for the jury's understanding of the case." *Mouton*, 15 Cal.App.4th at 1319. As a result, the court said, the jury "was left to determine defendant's guilt of the charged murder without guidance concerning the identity or definition of the originally contemplated (or target) offenses ...." *Id.*

Six months later, the Court of Appeal in *People v. Solis*, 20 Cal.App.4th 264 (1993), disagreed with *Mouton*. In *Solis*, the defendant, a juvenile gang member, was challenged to a fight by members of another gang. He retreated but returned later that evening, driving a car containing two passengers, one of whom fired at members of the rival gang, killing one of them. The defendant was charged with murder. As in this case and in *Mouton*, the trial court in *Solis* instructed the jury on the "natural and probable consequences" doctrine, but neither specified nor described the elements of any target or predicate offense that the defendant might have aided or encouraged. The jury convicted defendant of second-degree murder.

In affirming the murder conviction, the court in *Solis* stated: "The finder of fact need identify the nature of the predicate offense only in a generalized manner, reaching a conclusion that some 'criminal' or 'nefarious' conduct was intended by the defendant." *Id.* at 273. Therefore, the court concluded, "it is not necessary to provide instructions as to the possible predicate crimes, which ... are uncharged and irrelevant to the offense ultimately committed and charged." *Id.* The *Solis* court acknowledged that "if there is a dispute as to whether the predicate planned acts are criminal, a determination as to the nature of those acts and instruction on the criminal definitional nature of such will be required." *Id.* at 274 n.8. But in the court's view such cases are uncommon, and in the "ordinary case" such an instruction is unnecessary. *Id.*

## V. Duty of Trial Court to Identify and Describe the Elements of Potential Target Crimes

In this case, defendant Bray, relying on *Mouton*, contends that the trial court should, on its own initiative, have instructed the jury with the 1992 revision to CALJIC No. 3.02, specifying for the jury the target or predicate crime(s) that, under the evidence, Bray might have aided and abetted and that could have led, as a natural and probable consequence, to the murder of Van Camp by codefendant Prettyman. Again relying on *Mouton*, Bray argues that in addition to CALJIC No. 3.02, the court should have given an instruction describing or defining the elements of the target crimes. The Attorney General, relying on *Solis*, contends the contrary. We agree with Bray.

Although the issue is one of first impression in this court, instructive here is our decision in *People v. Failla*, 64 Cal.2d 560 (1966). In *Failla*, the defendant was charged with burglary. The trial court instructed the jury in the language of the statute prohibiting burglary (§459), which provides that one who enters a building with the intent to commit theft "or any felony" is guilty of burglary. But the court did not tell the jury what target act(s) that the defendant might have intended to commit after entering the building would constitute felonies. We reversed the defendant's burglary conviction, concluding that the trial court committed prejudicial error by failing to give, on its own initiative, an instruction "defining 'felony' and advising the jury which acts the defendant, upon entry, may have intended to commit would amount to felonies." *Failla*, 64 Cal.2d at 564. We explained:

> Where the evidence permits an inference that the defendant at the time of entry intended to commit one or more felonies and also an inference that his intent was merely to commit one or more misdemeanors or acts not punishable as crimes, the court must define 'felony' and must instruct the jury which acts, among those which the jury could infer the defendant intended to commit, amount to felonies. Failure to do so is error, for it allows the triers of fact to indulge in unguided speculation as to what kinds of criminal conduct are serious enough to warrant punishment as felonies and incorporation into the burglary statute.

Id.

As in *Failla*, the central issue here is whether the trial court must identify and describe uncharged target offenses for the jury. As in

*Failla*, we conclude that such an instruction is necessary and should be given whenever uncharged target offenses form a part of the prosecution's theory of criminal liability and substantial evidence supports the theory. When these conditions are satisfied, an instruction identifying and describing potential target offenses is necessary to minimize the risk that the jury, generally unversed in the intricacies of criminal law, will "indulge in unguided speculation," *id.* at 564, when it applies the law to the evidence adduced at trial.

In an aiding and abetting case involving application of the "natural and probable consequences" doctrine, identification of the target crime will facilitate the jury's task of determining whether the charged crime allegedly committed by the aider and abettor's confederate was indeed a natural and probable consequence of any uncharged target crime that, the prosecution contends, the defendant knowingly and intentionally aided and abetted. The facts of this case illustrate this point. If, for example, the jury had concluded that defendant Bray had encouraged codefendant Prettyman to commit an assault on Van Camp but that Bray had no reason to believe that Prettyman would use a deadly weapon such as a steel pipe to commit the assault, then the jury could not properly find that the murder of Van Camp was a natural and probable consequence of the assault encouraged by Bray. *People v. Butts*, 236 Cal.App.2d 817, 836 (1965). If, on the other hand, the jury had concluded that Bray encouraged Prettyman to assault Van Camp with the steel pipe, or by means of force likely to produce great bodily injury, then it could appropriately find that Prettyman's murder of Van Camp was a natural and probable consequence of that assault. Therefore, instructions identifying and describing the crime of assault with a deadly weapon or by means of force likely to produce great bodily injury (§245) as the appropriate target crime would have assisted the jury in determining whether Bray was guilty of Van Camp's murder under the "natural and probable consequences" doctrine.

To apply the "natural and probable consequences" doctrine to aiders and abettors is not an easy task. The jury must decide whether the defendant (1) with knowledge of the confederate's unlawful purpose, and (2) the intent of committing, encouraging, or facilitating the commission of any target crime(s), (3) aided, promoted, encouraged, or instigated the commission of the target crime(s); whether (4) the defendant's confederate committed an offense *other than* the target crime(s); and whether (5) the offense committed by the confederate was a natural and probable consequence of the target crime(s) that the defendant encouraged or facilitated. Instructions describing each step in this process ensure proper application by the jury of the "natural and probable consequences" doctrine.

As pointed out by the court in *Solis*, to convict a defendant of a crime under this doctrine, the jury need not unanimously agree on the particular target crime the defendant aided and abetted. *See also People v. Pride*, 3 Cal.4th 195, 249-50 (1992) [jury may convict defendant of first-degree murder despite lack of unanimity as to whether killing was premeditated murder or felony murder]; *Failla*, 64 Cal.2d at 569 [in burglary prosecution, jury need not agree on which felony defendant intended to commit upon entering building]. In many cases in which the doctrine is applicable, the defendant is not charged with the target crime, but with another crime that was allegedly committed by the defendant's confederate. Still, at trial each juror must be convinced, beyond a reasonable doubt, that the defendant aided and abetted the commission of a *criminal act*, and that the offense actually committed was a natural and probable consequence of that act. Contrary to *Solis*, a conviction may not be based on the jury's generalized belief that the defendant intended to assist and/or encourage unspecified "nefarious" conduct. To ensure that the jury will not rely on such generalized beliefs as a basis for conviction, the trial court should identify and describe the target or predicate crime that the defendant may have aided and abetted.

In *Failla*, we held that when a defendant is charged with burglary, the trial court must, *on its own initiative*, give instructions to the jury identifying and defining the target offense(s) that the defendant allegedly intended to commit on entering the building. Similarly, when the prosecution relies on the "natural and probable consequences" doctrine to hold a defendant liable as aider and abettor, the trial court must, *on its own initiative*, identify and describe for the jury any target offense allegedly aided and abetted by defendant. As we explained in *Failla*, such instructions are "necessary to the jury's understanding of the charge and are closely and openly connected with the facts of the case before the court." *Id.* at 565.

The workload of our trial courts is increased whenever we impose on trial judges an obligation to provide a jury instruction sua sponte. We also recognize that the trial court cannot be required to anticipate every possible theory that may fit the facts of the case before it and instruct the jury accordingly. But the sua sponte duty to instruct that is imposed here is quite limited. It arises only when the prosecution has elected to *rely* on the "natural and probable consequences" theory of accomplice liability and the trial court has determined that the evidence will support instructions on that theory. The trial court, moreover, need not identify *all* potential target offenses supported by the evidence, but only those that the prosecution wishes the jury to consider....

The trial court should grant a prosecutor's request that the jury be instructed on the "natural and probable consequences" rule only when (1) the record contains substantial evidence that the defendant intended to encourage or assist a confederate in committing a target offense, and (2) the jury could reasonably find that the crime actually committed by the defendant's confederate was a natural and probable consequence of the specifically contemplated target offense. If this test is not satisfied, the instruction should not be given, even if specifically requested.

*Solis* ruled that an aider and abettor can "become liable for the commission of a very serious crime" committed by the aider and abettor's confederate even though the target offense contemplated by his aiding and abetting may have been trivial. Rarely, if ever, is that true. Murder, for instance, is *not* the natural and probable consequence of "trivial" activities. To trigger application of the "natural and probable consequences" doctrine, there must be a close connection between the target crime aided and abetted and the offense actually committed.

In this case, the record does not show that the prosecutor sought to have the jury instructed on the "natural and probable consequences" doctrine as a basis for convicting defendant Bray of the murder of Van Camp committed by codefendant Prettyman, and the prosecutor made no mention of the doctrine in his closing argument to the jury. Because the prosecutor did not rely on this doctrine, the trial court was under no duty to instruct the jury on it, for it was not one of the "general principles of law that are commonly or closely and openly connected to the facts before the court and that are necessary for the jury's understanding of the case." *Montoya*, 7 Cal.4th at 1047.

Alternatively, the court could have asked the prosecutor if he wanted the jury instructed on the rule, and if so, what target crimes the prosecutor believed appropriate. Had the prosecutor so elected, for example, the evidence in this case would have supported an instruction on the "natural and probable consequences" rule that identified assault with a deadly weapon or by means of force likely to produce great bodily injury (§245) as a target crime.

But once the trial court, without a request, chose to instruct the jury on the "natural and probable consequences" rule, it had a duty to issue instructions identifying and describing each potential target offense supported by the evidence. By failing to do so, the trial court erred....

[Sections VI & VII are omitted].

### Conclusion

The judgment of the Court of Appeal is affirmed [because the instructional error was harmless. The separate opinions of Justices MOSK, BAXTER, and BROWN are omitted].

## QUESTIONS ON *PRETTYMAN*

**1. People v. whom?** The caption of the case in *People v. Prettyman et al.* Who is the real party in interest?

**2. Complicity without conspiracy.** When introducing the facts for the court, Justice Kennard states that "[a] jury convicted both [Richard Prettyman and Debra Jane Bray] of first-degree murder, but acquitted them of conspiracy." In light of CALJIC No. 3.01's three elements of complicity (1. helper's knowledge of principal's purpose; 2. helper's intent to further that purpose; and 3. helper's aid or encouragement of that purpose), can you explain how one might be an accomplice in an offense *without* having at once conspired as well? In other words, can complicity and conspiracy exist without one another?

**3. Alibi: justification, excuse, or neither?** After an argument between Bray and Prettyman (who held themselves out as married), victim Vance Van Camp left a church dinner with Prettyman, apparently to separate Prettyman from Bray, who gave Van Camp her wallet to keep it safe from Prettyman as the two men departed together. When all three reunited that night in the church courtyard, a witness first overheard Bray and Prettyman discussing retaliating against Van Camp, and second, the sounds and aftermath of Prettyman's fatal attack on Van Camp with a three-foot steel pipe.

Prettyman in effect confessed to that witness and thereafter to another witness, though the pipe that police recovered was not bloodstained. Bray and Prettyman denied killing Van Camp. What was their defense? Does that defense, if believed, constitute an excuse?

**4. Revised jury instruction.** Shortly before Van Camp's murder in July 1992, CALJIC No. 3.02 (1988) was revised.

**a.** What is the principal difference between the 1988 and 1992 versions?

**b.** The Court of Appeal found no error on the trial court's part for failure to charge the jury on the amended version of §3.02. What authority was there for such a ruling?

**5. Excess crimes committed to avoid apprehension.** The California Supreme Court relies on one of its old precedents, *People v. Kauffman*, 152 Cal. 331, 334 (1907), which stated that the "natural and probable consequences" rule requires a "reasonably apparent" connection between the target crime and the excess crime, "not a fresh and independent product of the mind of one of the confederates outside of, or foreign to, the common design." *Kauffman* ruled that a common design to break into a safe at a San Mateo cemetery included "protecting all members of the group from arrest or detection while going to and returning from the scene...." *Id.* at 335. The *Kauffman* conspirators called off the plan when they saw an armed guard at the scene, after which one conspirator (Woods) fatally shot a police officer (Robinson), who had intercepted them on foot on their way home. The high court held every member of the six-man conspiracy to burgle the cemetery—including Kauffman, who was unarmed and apparently had his hands in the air when police appeared—liable for their cohort Woods's murder of Officer Robinson.

If such a conclusion follows, is it fair to say that crimes directed at avoiding apprehension are *always* natural and probable consequences of any nontrivial crime? *Cf. People v. Zielesch*, supra Chapter 4.D.

**6. Relation of CALJIC No. 3.01 to No. 3.02.** By now the three elements of complicity as set forth in CALJIC No. 3.01 (Spring 2009 Revision) are familiar. They are also the first three of the five elements of the "natural and probable consequences" rule under CALJIC No. 3.02 (Fall 2012 Revision).

**a.** What are the last two elements?

**b.** In footnote 4 of *Prettyman*, Justice Kennard states that "[i]n this case we need not address ... whether a defendant may be convicted under the 'natural and probable consequences' doctrine when the target criminal act was not committed." If the court had addressed the issue, what should it have ruled?

**7. History of CALJIC No. 3.02.** Where and when did the "natural and probable consequences" rule first appear in CALJIC?

*[handwritten: 1976]*

**8. Setting forth the CALJIC No. 3.01 offense with particularity.** A judge is obligated sua sponte "to instruct the jury on all general legal principles raised by the evidence and necessary for the jury's understanding of the case." *People v. Mouton*, 15 Cal.App.4th at 1319.

**a.** According to *Prettyman*, how precise must those instructions be in describing the predicate or target offense(s) under No. 3.01 before the jury may assess the relation between the predicate or target offense(s) and the excess offense(s) under No. 3.02? Please include in your answer the example of burglary as the predicate or target offense.

**b.** What, exactly, was the prosecution's theory (factually and legally) of Bray's liability at trial? *[handwritten: Conspired to kill Van Camp or put him up to assault and encouraged him]*

**9. Unanimity requirement.** Must a jury be unanimous as to which predicate or target offense(s) the helper intended to facilitate in order for the blame for the principal's excess offense(s) to be shared by the helper? *[handwritten: Not needed]*

**10. Did Bray *murder* Van Camp?** The prosecution's case against Bray consisted of the statement of a convicted felon who sleeps in his car and drinks to excess, Edward Eash, who heard her say, "[w]e are going to get that fucker Vance." After being denied parole at an October 3, 2014 hearing, Bray apparently was paroled after April 2015 (when the first edition of this text went to press). She had at that point served 22 years of her 25-to-life sentence at California Institution for Women (Corona). For *what*?

# NOTES ON *PRETTYMAN*

**1. Asymmetrical elements of murder.** Citing cases from the 1930s, 40s, 50s, 60s, and 70s, the *Prettyman* Court observed that the "natural and probable consequences" rule was at first limited to cases like *Prettyman* itself and *Luparello*, where the predicate or target offense was assault and the excess offense was murder. The vague intention to "get" Van Camp was interpreted as a plan to seriously assault him, just as in *Luparello*, the vague intention to get information from Martin by "thumping" him was interpreted as a plan to seriously assault him. Because under CALJIC No. 3.01 the specific intent required for complicity extends only to the predicate or target offense(s), there is no need in either *Prettyman* or *Luparello* for Bray or Luparello to have harbored malice toward Van Camp and Martin, respectively. This is a heavy tax laid on co-conspirators (under CALJIC No. 6.11) or accomplices (under CALJIC No. 3.02): the principal murderer who does the deed cannot be convicted of murder without malice, though an assistant, who kills no one, can.

The California Supreme Court recently clarified that, even though the target offense from which Prettyman departed in murdering Van Camp was assault with a deadly weapon (§245), simple assault (§240) is not necessarily precluded as a qualifying target offense when the excess offense sought to be blamed on both accomplice and principal is murder. *People v. Gonzalez & Soliz*, 52 Cal.4th 254, 297-300 (2011). Yet the court *has* recently precluded CALJIC No. 3.02 as a basis of first- as opposed to second-degree murder. *Supra* Chapter 4.D, note 3 on *Zielesch*, citing *People v. Chiu*, 325 P.2d 972, 974 (Cal. 2014).

**2. Convictions of multiple inchoate and substantive offenses.**

*a.* In California, if a solicitation culminates in a conspiracy, the solicitor has committed and may be convicted of both offenses, but punishment may be imposed for only one. California Penal Code §654(a). Prosecutors who allege conspiracies obtain evidentiary advantages by which otherwise inadmissible hearsay evidence may be admitted to prove such a charge. Federal Rules of Evidence, rule 801(d)(2)(E) (2014). There is no such advantage for alleging mere solicitations. If a solicitation or conspiracy is put into action and culminates in the target offense being attempted or completed, then the soliciting party may be convicted of all inchoate and completed offenses that are proved up at trial. *People v. Travis*, 171 Cal.App.2d

842, 844 (1959). The solicited conspirator may be convicted of the same (minus, of course solicitation). I emphasize: *Convicted*, yes; *punished*, no. See generally People v. Mesa, 277 P.3d 743, 745 (Cal. 2012) ["Since 1962 we have interpreted section 654 to allow multiple convictions arising out of a single act or omission, but to bar multiple punishment for those convictions."].

***b.*** The Model Penal Code rejects the doctrine of natural and probable consequences. *See* MPC §2.06(3). On the facts presented in note 2a above, the MPC allows *prosecution* for multiple offenses arising out of the same conduct, but entry of a *judgment* of conviction against the soliciting party only for the solicitation *or* the conspiracy *or* the attempt *or* the completed offense. The solicited co-conspirator may be convicted of the conspiracy *or* the attempt *or* the completed offense. *See* MPC §§1.07(1)(b), 5.05(3).

### 3. TRANSFERABILITY OF DEFENSES FROM PRINCIPAL TO ACCOMPLICE

*Prettyman*'s interpretation of CALJIC No. 3.02 addressed the helper's liability for acts of the principal that go beyond the common scheme or design. Our next principal case, *People v. McCoy*, 25 Cal.4th 1111 (2001), considers the helper's liability for acts of the principal that lead to *acquittal* of the principal on the charged offense. This is the reverse of the sort of problem that *Prettyman* posed in that here, too, in a manner of speaking, the principal departs from the common scheme or design. But instead of taking things too far as in *Prettyman*, here the principal doesn't take them far enough by, to the principal's benefit, coming up with a viable defense, partial or complete.

For example, imagine an employee who, in order to ensnare a thief, agrees to the thief's suggestion that they steal barrels of meat from the employee's workplace to satisfy a debt that the employee owes the thief. The plan of the employee and the thief, secretly authorized by the employer, is that the shipping clerk would load three barrels of meat into the vehicle of the thief, who will have driven up to the loading dock posing as a legitimate customer. Unbeknownst to the thief, however, was the employer's plan that once the meat was loaded into the thief's car, security would accost the thief and turn him over to police for prosecution as accomplice to larceny.

Everything went as planned, but no larceny occurred since the meat was acquired permissively. If complicity is a form of derivative liability where the helper's guilt depends on the principal's guilt, then there can be no complicity in larceny on the part of the accomplice-thief here, given that there is no principal thief who has unlawfully dispossessed the rightful possessor of their meat with the intent to steal. Accordingly, the plan fails and the accomplice-thief is off the hook for larceny. See *Topolewski v. State*, 130 Wis. 244 (1906) [reversing putative accomplice-thief's larceny conviction]; *cf. Topolewski v. Plankington Packing Co.*, 143 Wis. 52 (1910) [dismissing putative accomplice-thief's claim against trap-setting employer for malicious prosecution, while ordering a new trial on his claim of false imprisonment against same].

Courts do not see the matter as so clear-cut, however. In *McCoy*, the would-be principal is *not* an undercover agent. Instead, he is an imperfect self-defender. Is self-defense "personal" to the principal actor? Or should that defense transfer to the putative accomplice on the ground that the accomplice's liability is derivative of the principal's? In its most boiled-down form, therefore, the question is: can the accomplice be guilty of a crime when the principal is not?

## SUPREME COURT OF CALIFORNIA

*THE PEOPLE, PLAINTIFF AND RESPONDENT*
*V.*
*EJAAN DUPREE MCCOY ET AL., DEFENDANTS AND APPELLANTS*

JUNE 25, 2001

CHIN, Justice

We granted review to decide whether an aider and abettor may be guilty of greater homicide-related offenses than those the actual perpetrator committed. Because defenses or extenuating circumstances may exist that are personal to the actual perpetrator and do not apply to the aider and abettor, the answer, sometimes, is yes. We reverse the judgment of the Court of Appeal, which concluded otherwise.

### I. History

Codefendants Ejaan Dupree McCoy and Derrick Lakey were tried together and convicted of crimes arising out of a drive-by shooting in

Stockton in 1995. McCoy drove the car and Lakey was in the front passenger seat, with others in the back. The car approached four people standing on a street corner. McCoy leaned out of the window and shouted something. A flurry of shots was fired from the car toward the group. Witnesses saw both McCoy and Lakey shooting handguns. Two of the group were shot, one fatally. The other two escaped injury. Someone from outside the car returned fire, wounding Lakey. The evidence showed that McCoy fired the fatal bullets.

At trial, McCoy but not Lakey testified. McCoy admitted shooting but claimed he did so because he believed he would be shot himself. He said that earlier that day, he had driven by that same intersection, and someone fired shots in his direction. He decided to seek out a friend who might be able to help him determine who had fired at him. McCoy brought his gun for protection and picked up Lakey, who also had a gun. Across the street from his friend's house, McCoy saw three men standing near a tree. Thinking that one of them might be his friend, McCoy drove slowly toward the group, stopped, and called out to get their attention. McCoy then saw that the man was not his friend and that he held a "dark something" that appeared to be a gun. Believing that the man was going to shoot him, McCoy grabbed his own gun and fired until the gun was empty. Lakey also fired his gun out the car window.

A jury found McCoy and Lakey guilty of various crimes, including first-degree murder and two counts of attempted murder. The Court of Appeal unanimously reversed McCoy's murder and attempted murder convictions, finding that the trial court prejudicially misinstructed the jury on McCoy's theory of unreasonable self-defense, a theory that, if the jury had accepted it, would have reduced the crimes to voluntary manslaughter and attempted voluntary manslaughter.

The Court of Appeal also reversed Lakey's murder and attempted murder convictions "for two independent reasons: (1) under California law, a defendant who is tried as an aider and abettor cannot be convicted of an offense greater than that of which the actual perpetrator is convicted, where the aider and abettor and the perpetrator are tried in the same trial upon the same evidence, and (2) on this record, we cannot conclude with reasonable certainty that any participant acted with malice in connection with the murder and attempted murder counts, so we cannot say that the crimes of murder or attempted murder have been committed." Justice Hull dissented as to Lakey and would have affirmed his conviction.

We granted the Attorney General's petition for review limited to whether the Court of Appeal correctly reversed Lakey's murder and attempted murder convictions.

## II. Discussion

If a person kills or attempts to kill in the unreasonable but good faith belief in having to act in self-defense, the belief negates what would otherwise be malice, and that person is guilty of voluntary manslaughter or attempted voluntary manslaughter, not murder or attempted murder. McCoy's testimony provided evidence that he acted in unreasonable self-defense, so the trial court instructed on that theory. The Court of Appeal reversed McCoy's murder and attempted murder convictions because it concluded the court's instructions on unreasonable self-defense were prejudicially erroneous. We did not grant review on that issue, so we accept the Court of Appeal's conclusion as to McCoy. Thus, it is possible that on retrial McCoy will be found guilty of manslaughter and attempted voluntary manslaughter rather than murder and attempted murder.

The question before us is whether reversal of McCoy's convictions also requires reversal of Lakey's. The Court of Appeal divided on the question. The majority found that McCoy, whose gun fired the fatal bullets, was guilty as the direct perpetrator and Lakey as an aider and abettor. It interpreted certain cases to mean that an aider and abettor may not be guilty of a greater offense than the direct perpetrator and concluded therefore that if McCoy was guilty of crimes less than murder or attempted murder, then Lakey also could only be guilty of those lesser crimes. Accordingly, it concluded that reversal of McCoy's convictions compelled reversal of Lakey's convictions. Justice Hull disagreed. He argued that "neither law nor logic requires that an aider and abettor be afforded the benefit of a mitigating factor applicable only to the actual perpetrator to reduce a homicide from murder to manslaughter."

Resolution of this question requires a close examination of the nature of aiding and abetting liability. "All persons concerned in the commission of a crime, ... whether they directly commit the act constituting the offense, or aid and abet in its commission, ... are principals in any crime so committed." Pen. Code §31; *People v. Prettyman*, 14 Cal.4th 248, 259-60 (1996). Thus, a person who aids and abets a crime is guilty of that crime even if someone else committed some or all of the criminal acts. Because aiders and abettors may be criminally liable for acts not their own, cases have described their liability as "vicarious." *E.g., People v. Croy*, 41 Cal.3d 1, 12, n.5 (1985). This description is accurate as far as it goes. But, as we explain, the aider and abettor's guilt for the intended crime is not entirely vicarious. Rather, that guilt is based on a combination of the direct perpetrator's acts and the aider and abettor's *own* acts and *own* mental state.

It is important to bear in mind that an aider and abettor's liability for criminal conduct is of two kinds. First, an aider and abettor with the necessary mental state is guilty of the intended crime. Second, under the "natural and probable consequences" doctrine, an aider and abettor is guilty not only of the intended crime, but also "for any other offense that was a 'natural and probable consequence' of the crime aided and abetted." *Prettyman*, 14 Cal.4th at 260. Thus, for example, if a person aids and abets only an intended assault, but a murder results, that person may be guilty of that murder, even if unintended, if it is a natural and probable consequence of the intended assault. In this case, however, the trial court did not instruct the jury on the "natural and probable consequences" doctrine. It instructed only on an aider and abettor's guilt of the intended crimes. Accordingly, only an aider and abettor's guilt of the intended crime is relevant here. Nothing we say in this opinion necessarily applies to an aider and abettor's guilt of an unintended crime under the "natural and probable consequences" doctrine.

Except for strict liability offenses, every crime has two components: (1) an act or omission, sometimes called the actus reus; and (2) a necessary mental state, sometimes called the *mens rea*. Pen. Code §20. This principle applies to aiding and abetting liability as well as direct liability. An aider and abettor must do something *and* have a certain mental state.

We have described the mental state required of an aider and abettor as different from the mental state necessary for conviction as the actual perpetrator. The difference, however, does not mean that the mental state of an aider and abettor is less culpable than that of the actual perpetrator. On the contrary, outside of the "natural and probable consequences" doctrine, an aider and abettor's mental state must be at least that required of the direct perpetrator. To prove that a defendant is an accomplice, the prosecution must show that the defendant acted with knowledge of the criminal purpose of the perpetrator *and* with an intent or purpose either of committing, or of encouraging or facilitating commission of, the offense. When the offense charged is a specific intent crime, the accomplice must share the specific intent of the perpetrator; this occurs when the accomplice knows the full extent of the perpetrator's criminal purpose and gives aid or encouragement with the intent or purpose of facilitating the perpetrator's commission of the crime. *Prettyman*, 14 Cal.4th at 259. This means that when the charged offense and the intended offense—murder or attempted murder—are the same, i.e., when guilt does not depend on the "natural and probable consequences" doctrine, the aider and abettor must know and share the murderous intent of the actual perpetrator.

Aider and abettor liability is thus vicarious only in the sense that the aider and abettor is liable for another's actions as well as that person's own actions. When a person chooses to become a part of the criminal activity of another, she says in essence, "your acts are my acts." But that person's *own* acts are also her acts for which she is also liable. Moreover, that person's mental state is her own; she is liable for her *mens rea*, not the other person's. As stated by Professor Dressler,

> many commentators have concluded that there is no conceptual obstacle to convicting a secondary party of a more serious offense than is proved against the primary party. As they reason, once it is proved that the principal has caused an *actus reus*, the liability of each of the secondary parties should be assessed according to his own *mens rea*. That is, although joint participants in a crime are tied to a single and common *actus reus*, the individual *mentes reae* or levels of guilt of the joint participants are permitted to float free and are not tied to each other in any way. If their *mentes reae* are different, their independent levels of guilt ... will necessarily be different as well.

Joshua Dressler, Understanding Criminal Law §30.06[C], at 450 (2d ed. 1995). In that same passage, Professor Dressler explained how this concept operates with homicide:

> An accomplice may be convicted of first-degree murder, even though the primary party is convicted of second-degree murder or of voluntary manslaughter. This outcome follows, for example, if the secondary party, premeditatedly, soberly and calmly, assists in a homicide, while the primary party kills unpremeditatedly, drunkenly, or in provocation. Likewise, it is possible for a primary party negligently to kill

another (and, thus, be guilty of involuntary manslaughter), while the secondary party is guilty of murder, because he encouraged the primary actor's negligent conduct, with the intent that it result in the victim's death.

The statement that an aider and abettor may not be guilty of a greater offense than the direct perpetrator, although sometimes true in individual cases, is not universally correct. Aider and abettor liability is premised on the combined acts of all the principals, but on the aider and abettor's own *mens rea*. If the *mens rea* of the aider and abettor is more culpable than the actual perpetrator's, the aider and abettor may be guilty of a more serious crime than the actual perpetrator.

Moreover, the dividing line between the actual perpetrator and the aider and abettor is often blurred. It is often an oversimplification to describe one person as the actual perpetrator and the other as the aider and abettor. When two or more persons commit a crime together, both may act in part as the actual perpetrator *and* in part as the aider and abettor of the other, who also acts in part as an actual perpetrator. Although Lakey was liable for McCoy's actions, he was an actor too. He was in the car and shooting his own gun, although it so happened that McCoy fired the fatal shots. Moreover, Lakey's guilt for *attempted* murder might be based entirely on his own actions in shooting at the attempted murder victims. In another shooting case, one person might lure the victim into a trap while another fires the gun; in a stabbing case, one person might restrain the victim while the other does the stabbing. In either case, both participants would be direct perpetrators as well as aiders and abettors of the other. The aider and abettor doctrine merely makes aiders and abettors liable for their accomplices' actions as well as their own. It obviates the necessity to decide who was the aider and abettor and who the direct perpetrator or to what extent each played which role.

The majority below relied on *People v. Williams*, 75 Cal.App.3d 731 (1977), which, although also stating generally that "an aider or abettor cannot be guilty of a greater offense than the principal offender," *id.* at 737, supports our conclusion here. In *Williams*, the appellant struggled with the victim over her own weapon, which was never fired. She appealed to her sister to shoot the victim, which the sister did, killing him. The sister was acquitted, but the appellant was convicted of murder. *Id.* at 733. The appellant argued on appeal that her conviction was inconsistent with the acquittal of the actual shooter. The court disagreed. It found the jury "justified in finding that the appellant, with malice, caused the victim's death by using her sister as an innocent agent to accomplish the intended death of the victim.... Through her entreaty, she was the effective cause of the discharge of the firearm in her sister's hand. The fact that the sister was acquitted is of no comfort to appellant, because each acted under different circumstances." *Id.* at 733-34.

*Williams* essentially found the appellant had used an innocent agent, and was liable for that agent's action even though the agent was herself entirely innocent. We see no reason the outcome should be different if the actual killer was not entirely innocent but instead guilty of a lesser crime than the indirect actor. The same principles should apply whenever a person aids, or perhaps induces, another to kill, whether that other person is entirely innocent, as in *Williams*, or less culpable, as possibly here, or, potentially, more culpable. In any of these circumstances, each person's guilt would be based on the combined actus reus of the participants, but also solely on that person's own *mens rea*. Each person's level of guilt would "float free." Dressler, Understanding Criminal Law, §30.06[C], at 450.

As another example, assume someone, let us call him Iago, falsely tells another person, whom we will call Othello, that Othello's wife, Desdemona, was having an affair, hoping that Othello would kill her in a fit of jealousy. Othello does so without Iago's further involvement. In that case, depending on the exact circumstances of the killing, Othello might be guilty of manslaughter, rather than murder, on a heat of passion theory. Othello's guilt of manslaughter, however, should not limit Iago's guilt if his own culpability were greater. Iago should be liable for his own acts as well Othello's, which he induced and encouraged. But Iago's criminal liability, as Othello's, would be based on his own personal *mens rea*. If, as our hypothetical suggests, Iago acted with malice, he would be guilty of murder even if Othello, who did the actual killing, was *not*.

We thus conclude that when a person, with the mental state necessary for an aider and abettor, helps or induces another to kill, that person's guilt is determined by the combined acts of all the participants as well as that person's own *mens rea*. If that person's *mens rea* is more culpable than another's, that person's guilt may be greater even if the other might be deemed the actual perpetrator.[3]

---

[3] Because we cannot anticipate all possible non-homicide crimes or circumstances, we express no view on whether these principles apply outside the homicide context.

As applied here, Lakey and McCoy were to some extent both actual perpetrators and aiders and abettors. Both fired their handguns, although McCoy's gun inflicted the fatal wounds. Once the jury found, as it clearly did, that Lakey acted with the necessary mental state of an aider and abettor, it could find him liable for both his and McCoy's acts, without having to distinguish between them. But Lakey's guilt was also based on his own mental state, not McCoy's. McCoy's unreasonable self-defense theory was personal to him. A jury could reasonably have found that Lakey did not act under unreasonable self-defense even if McCoy did. Thus, his conviction of murder and attempted murder can stand, notwithstanding that on retrial McCoy might be convicted of a lesser crime or even acquitted.

As an independent basis for reversing Lakey's convictions, the majority below also concluded that, because the jury may have erroneously found McCoy acted with malice, it did not necessarily find that *any* participant acted with malice. This conclusion also reflects a misunderstanding about the mental state needed for an aider and abettor (again, aside from the "natural and probable consequences" doctrine not relevant here). The trial court instructed the jury both regarding direct perpetrator liability and aiding and abetting liability. It also instructed on the malice requirement of murder. To the extent the jury based its verdict as to Lakey on his personal acts, it necessarily found malice. To the extent it based it on McCoy's acts—finding that Lakey aided and abetted those acts—it necessarily found that Lakey knew of McCoy's unlawful purpose and intended to ... encourage or facilitate that purpose. The only unlawful purpose charged here was an unlawful killing. Absent some circumstance negating malice one cannot knowingly and intentionally help another commit an unlawful killing without acting with malice. Whether McCoy killed in unreasonable self-defense, thus negating what would be malice as to him, McCoy's unreasonable self-defense would not negate the implicit jury finding that Lakey knowingly and intentionally helped McCoy commit the crime, which constitutes malice.[4]

---

[4] In the Court of Appeal, Lakey also argued that the instructional error prejudiced him even without reference to McCoy. The court did not consider the question in light of its reversing the judgment on other grounds. It should do so on remand.

## III. Conclusion

We reverse the judgment of the Court of Appeal and remand the matter for further proceedings consistent with our opinion.

GEORGE, C.J., KENNARD, BAXTER, WERDEGAR, and BROWN, JJ., concurred.

# QUESTIONS ON *McCOY*

**1. People v. whom?** The case is captioned *People v. McCoy* et al. Who is the real party in interest?

**2. Additional facts.** As reported in the Court of Appeal below, *People v. McCoy*, 93 Cal.Rptr.2d 827, 830-32 (3d Dist. Ct. App. 2000):

> The victim, Calvin Willis, was standing on the sidewalk near the intersection of Flint Avenue and Georgia Street in the Conway Homes area of Stockton on the evening of September 4, 1995; with him were his sister Tashambe Willis and his cousins Tubiya McCormick and Simon McCormick. Tubiya McCormick held a can of beer in one hand. Soon after the four met and began talking, a dark car drove up. Defendant McCoy was driving the car and defendant Lakey was in the front passenger seat. Some witnesses testified that Matthew McGee and Patrick Hall were in the back seat. When he saw the car drive up, Simon McCormick became nervous, and moved behind a tree. As McCoy leaned out of the window and shouted "What's up now nigger," a flurry of shots were fired from the car toward the group. Witnesses saw McCoy and Lakey shooting handguns. Tubiya McCormick was shot in the chest, but survived. At trial, Tubiya McCormick testified that he turned toward the car after he heard someone say "What's up nigger," and was immediately shot. Calvin Willis was fatally shot in the back of the head as he tried to run away. Tashambe Willis and Simon McCormick were not shot. During the melee, one or more persons outside McCoy's car began returning fire, and bullet casings were found afterward near the tree where Calvin Willis and his family had been standing. Defendant Lakey was shot and survived. Police questioning Lakey at the hospital found him evasive about the circumstances of his injury, although he

eventually stated he had been shot while walking alone in a different part of Stockton.

Defendants McCoy and Lakey, together with Matthew McGee, were charged and tried together. The prosecution's theory of the case was that the Willis shooting was an intended retaliation in an ongoing feud between two Stockton gangs referred to as the "Southside Mob" ... and the "Conway Homes Gangsters." In the prosecution's view, the victims were not gang members, but innocent bystanders. [Both McCoy and Lakey were convicted of, *inter alia*, first-degree murder of Calvin Willis and attempted murder of Tubiya McCormick and Simon McCormick; both were acquitted of attempted murder of Tashambe Willis].... McCoy was sentenced to [an] ... aggregate term [of] 50 years and 4 months to life.... Lakey was sentenced to [an] ... aggregate term [of] 46 years and 4 months to life.

Much of the above narrative cannot be found in the California Supreme Court's opinion. Do any of these additional facts help resolve Lakey's and McCoy's responsibility for the crimes of which they were convicted?

**3. Defenses personal to the principal.** Relying on credible authorities (Professors Dressler, Perkins and Boyce, LaFave and Scott), the state high court disagreed with the conclusions of the court below. If a premeditated killing is partially excused by the principal's voluntary intoxication, reasoned the court, that partial excuse should not benefit the sober accomplice; so too, the court continued, if the malice of an otherwise murderous act is negated by the principal's heat of passion brought on by provocative acts of the victim, that partial excuse should not benefit the accomplice, who is unprovoked (or, in the *Othello* example, is the one who actually provoked the principal toward the victim).

**a.** If in both scenarios above the excuse is partial, then of what crime would each defendant in the above scenarios be guilty?

**b.** The above scenarios work well enough to make the California Supreme Court's point that the excuses in these instances should remain personal to the principal: the accomplice would have to raise his own defenses to avoid liability for the harm done by the principal. But does this third example relied on by the court work as well? "It is possible for a primary party negligently to kill another (and, thus, be guilty of involuntary manslaughter), while the secondary party is guilty of murder, because he encouraged the primary actor's negligent conduct, with the intent that it result in the victim's death."

What sort of example must Dressler have had in mind here? On this, consider *State v. McVay et al.*, 132 A. 436 (R.I. 1926), where George Kelley was charged as accessory before the fact to involuntary manslaughter. Particularly, Kelley "procured" the ship's captain and engineer (both of whom were convicted as principals) to fire up a steam-boiler so worn and corroded that it exploded, killing three. Rhode Island's high court saw no legal reason why Kelley, who knew the boiler was rickety, could not be held responsible for encouraging the captain and engineer to act grossly negligently.

**c.** The *McCoy* Court argues that its position accords with *People v. Williams*, 75 Cal.App.3d 731 (1977), which is explained by the involvement of an "innocent agent." Who was "innocent" in *Williams*? Who was not? And what bearing does it have on *McCoy*?

**4. Division of labor.** The California Supreme Court notes that the line between principal and accomplice "is often blurred." It then presents cases in which actors may be both principal and accomplice to each other (and later indicates that *McCoy* is such a case). Are the examples clear? Are they cases of joint principality?

**5. Helping *how*—by *doing*?** This, according to the state high court: "Although Lakey was liable for McCoy's actions, he was an actor too. He was in the car and shooting his own gun, although it so happened that McCoy fired the fatal shots. Moreover, Lakey's guilt for *attempted* murder might be based entirely on his own actions in shooting at the attempted murder victims."

**a.** So how does that work, exactly? By shooting at (but missing) the group huddled around the tree, Lakey attempted murder as principal and by the very same act murdered Calvin Willis as accomplice? So in trying to shoot someone himself, Lakey also helped McCoy shoot (that same) someone?

**b.** Of what other principal case of ours does this peculiarity remind you? [Dlugash]

## NOTES ON *McCOY*

***1. Derivative liability.*** *Prettyman* canvassed how an accomplice's participation in an assault can lead to his responsibility for his principal's murderous acts, though the murderer exceeded the common scheme or design that the accomplice sought to further. That is because the liability of the accomplice is derivative of the acts of the principal. The Court of Appeal in *McCoy* reasoned that if the principal has a defense that reduces his own liability for the harm done, so too should the notion of derivative liability benefit the accomplice. Thus, there was no principled way in the view of the Court of Appeal to hold Lakey (as accomplice) liable for murder if McCoy (as principal) committed only voluntary manslaughter. But the high court disagreed.

***2. Misconstruing imperfect self-defense.*** The California Supreme Court mentioned in a footnote that it was not reviewing the Court of Appeal's ruling that the trial judge's instructions on unreasonable self-defense were prejudicially erroneous. The trial judge had erroneously instructed that for self-defense to be imperfect, defendant must reasonably but mistakenly believe in the need for deadly force. This mis-statement on the judge's part came at the end of his otherwise correct recitation of CALJIC No. 5.17 (2014), until he improvised: "An 'imminent' peril or danger is one that is apparent, present, immediate and must be instantly dealt with or must so appear at the time to the slayer *as a reasonable person.*" *McCoy*, 93 Cal.Rptr.2d at 835. That, of course, states the complete justification of perfect self-defense. Imperfect self-defense, properly understood, partially excuses erroneous beliefs that are *unreasonable.*

***3. Issue preclusion: different juries/different verdicts.*** That McCoy might have committed only voluntary manslaughter did not implicitly invalidate Lakey's conviction. Lakey's conviction was predicated on his own malice, which is an element of murder for an accomplice under CALJIC No. 3.01 (on which the case relied), though not under CALJIC No. 3.02 (which was never in play in the case). Please recognize that McCoy and Lakey were jointly tried. Even under the account of the Court of Appeal, a prior acquittal or manslaughter conviction of the *perpetrator* is not inconsistent with a later murder conviction of the *accomplice* because the evidence presented in the separate proceedings might have been different. In other words, despite acquittal of the principal in the first proceeding, a subsequent jury may logically conclude in the accomplice's trial that the principal *did* in fact commit a murder and the accomplice willingly participated. Double Jeopardy is not implicated because the acquitted principal is not risking conviction in the subsequent trial of the accomplice, who is being tried for the first time. As explained by the U.S. Supreme Court in a bribery case, differing results in separate trials do "no more than manifest the simple, if discomforting, reality that 'different juries may reach different results.... That is one of the consequences we accept under our jury system.' While symmetry of results may be intellectually satisfying, it is not required." *Standefer v. United States*, 447 U.S. 10, 25 (1980).

**4. More on defenses personal to the principal.** There are at least three approaches to the accomplice's liability when the principal is fully or partially acquitted for the harms he has brought about: 1) Liability is derivative: this approach was argued unsuccessfully by McCoy in the California Supreme Court, though it succeeded in the Court of Appeal; 2) Defenses are personal, not derivative: this approach, also known as "grafting," was endorsed by the California Supreme Court in *McCoy*. The harmful act of the principal is "grafted" on to the *mens rea* for the offense held by the accomplice, who aids or encourages the harm which is not a crime as to the principal (or not *that* crime as to the principal) for reasons that are personal to the principal and do not therefore benefit the accomplice; and 3) The accomplice has *attempted* the target crime: this is the approach of Model Penal Code §5.01(3), which states that because the principal's defense or partial defense precludes the completed offense, the accomplice has tried and failed to participate in that completed offense.

Applied to the theft-of-meat scenario (*Topolewski*) presented *supra* in my introduction to *McCoy*, MPC §5.01(3) would find that attempted larceny on the part of the would-be accomplice and no crime on the part of the undercover agent/employee. *See, e.g.*, *United States v. Partida*, 385 F.3d 546, 554-56 (5th Cir. 2004) [accomplice attempted to aid drug dealing although principal had no intent to deal drugs, just to catch accomplice].

**5. Fate of parties.** Derrick Lakey's blood found in McCoy's car was identified by DNA evidence, which while old hat by now, was in 1996 a first for any San Joaquin County Superior Court. On remand from the state high court, Lakey's convictions were affirmed in *People v.*

*McCoy*, 2002 WL 864283 (Cal. 3d Dist. Ct. App.). The trial court's misleading instruction on imperfect self-defense did not prejudice Lakey, the Court of Appeal reasoned in its unpublished opinion, because the evidence that Lakey was afraid when he opened fire was, in a word, "insubstantial." *Id.* at *9-10. Just 18 at the time of the shooting, Lakey is in his 23rd year at California State Prison (Solano), where he has been busy challenging his conviction and sentence in direct and collateral attacks that are summarized in *Lakey v. Hickman*, 633 F.3d 782 (9th Cir. 2011).

As for McCoy's remand, the Court of Appeal gave the trial court an election to either: 1) reverse McCoy's murder and attempted-murder convictions and retry him, this time with a proper instruction on imperfect self-defense; or 2) not retry McCoy on those counts and enter judgments of conviction on voluntary manslaughter and attempted voluntary manslaughter. When no retrial followed, the trial court gave McCoy the high term on the partially excused killing (11 years), and 1/3 of the three-year midterm on each of the two attempts. (For an explanation of why 1/3, see California Penal Code §1170.1). But because McCoy's counts for inflicting great bodily injury, personal use of a firearm, and being a felon in possession stayed intact, his vacated 50.3-year sentence was still an impressive 32.3 years—all terms again structured on the re-do to run consecutive. From that action in the trial court, McCoy's sentence was upheld on appeal. *People v. McCoy,* 2005 WL 737711 (Cal. 3d Dist. Ct. App.). At 44, McCoy remains locked up, also at Solano, where he is now parole eligible, while Lakey—who killed no one—will become eligible not before 2020.

# CHAPTER 5

# Felony Murder

## A. THE CRITERIA OF FELONY MURDER

California Penal Code §189 (West 2012) states:

> All murder which is perpetrated by means of a destructive device or explosive, a weapon of mass destruction, knowing use of ammunition designed primarily to penetrate metal or armor, poison, lying in wait, torture, or by any other kind of willful, deliberate, and premeditated killing, or which is committed in the perpetration of, or attempt to perpetrate, arson, rape, carjacking, robbery, burglary, mayhem, kidnapping, train wrecking, or any act punishable under Section 206 [torture], 286 [sodomy with a minor], 288 [lewd and lascivious acts on a child under 14], 288a [oral copulation with a minor], or 289 [forcible sexual penetration of a minor], or any murder which is perpetrated by means of discharging a firearm from a motor vehicle, intentionally at another person outside of the vehicle with the intent to inflict death, is murder of the first degree. All other kinds of murders are of the second degree.

Based on the above phrasing, three primary challenges to the felony-murder rule have persisted, which I take up in turn.

### 1. MALICE OR NO MALICE?

One challenge emphasizes that because the statute refers to "[a]ll *murder* which is ... committed in the perpetration of, or attempt to perpetrate, arson, rape ... robbery, burglary, mayhem, kidnapping ....", the felony-murder rule is a grading device, not a basis for establishing a no-malice mode of murder. In other words, because the statute refers to *murder,* not merely to *killings,* the legislature must have intended to take run-of-the-mill, implied-malice murders that occur during enumerated felonies and elevate them from second degree to first degree. Under such an approach, the point is to inflict additional punishment on the accused for having committed the murder during the felony. See *People v. Aaron*, 409 Mich. 672, 718-21 (1980). In no uncertain terms, however, the California Supreme Court declined to give the statute such a reading in *People v. Dillon*, 34 Cal.3d 441, 462-72 (1983). Nor has the state high court presumed the presence of malice in the underlying inherently dangerous felony, though it admits to having repeatedly so read the statute. *Id.* at 473 & n.20. In fact, the high court continues to do so, *People v. Elmore*, 325 P.3d 951, 958 n.6 (Cal. 2014), even while acknowledging, not overruling, *Dillon*. See *People v. Friend*, 211 P.3d 520, 573-74 (Cal. 2000).

The California Supreme Court reads section 189 as saying that all killings (intentional, not intentional, unintentional) committed during the perpetration or attempted perpetration of enumerated felonies *are* murder, with no need to otherwise show, presume, or even reference the malice that is normally key to any murder case. Nonetheless, non-malicious bit players in such killings are precluded by operation of the Eighth Amendment ban on disproportionate sentences from being sentenced to death. See *Tison v. Arizona*, 481 U.S. 137, 158 (1987); *Enmund v. Florida*, 458 U.S. 782, 800-02 (1982).

## 2. INHERENTLY DANGEROUS FELONIES

As the pertinent statute (§189) puts it, a murder (read, killing) committed during the perpetration or attempted perpetration of enumerated felonies "is murder of the first degree." The statute goes on to say that "[a]ll other kinds of murders are of the second degree." It makes good sense that some offenses are inherently dangerous enough to trigger the rule, but not quite as inherently dangerous as the offenses that the legislature has already enumerated in §189. But §189 enumerates only the offenses that trigger first-degree felony murder and makes no mention of the offenses that trigger second-degree felony murder: litigants don't learn that an offense qualifies for second degree until they come to court. Accordingly, second-degree felony murder has been criticized on two related bases. First, as a judicial usurpation of a legislative prerogative. See *People v. Patterson*, 49 Cal.3d 615, 641-42 (1989) (Panelli, J., dissenting). Second, as an ex-post-facto law that, in cases of first impression, suspends the determination of which crimes qualify for second-degree felony murder until after the crime is committed, thus offending principles of notice (aka legality) embedded in the Due Process Clause. See *People v. Romero*, 2002 WL 533216 (Cal. 3d Dist. Ct. App.). Still, felony murder has always had a way of rehabilitating itself from criticism. See *People v. Sarun Chun*, 45 Cal.4th 1172, 1182-88 (2009) [identifying an historical statutory basis for the "venerable" crime].

Assuming a legitimate statutory basis of both first- and second-degree felony murder, another difficulty for felony murder arises out of this requirement that the crimes that trigger the rule must be inherently dangerous enough to justify the shortcut in proof needed for a murder conviction. Some crimes are too unlikely to result in death to justify the rule. Larceny, for example, unlike robbery, involves no aggression against another person; the probability that larceny or attempted larceny will lead to the death of another person is negligible. With that in mind, the California Supreme Court has overturned numerous convictions obtained by prosecutors who persuaded trial judges to give second-degree-murder instructions based on a theory of felony murder where the underlying felony was not dangerous enough to trigger the felony-murder rule. See, e.g., *People v. Howard*, 34 Cal.4th 1129, 1136 (2007) [listing examples of traffic violations too easily done safely to count as inherently dangerous for purposes of felony murder].

[margin note: Crime evaluated in the abstract]

For example, in *People v. Williams*, 63 Cal.2d 452 (1965), defendants argued with their drug dealer and stabbed him to death, assertedly in self-defense. The California Supreme Court reversed their convictions for second-degree murder due to the trial court's improper instruction to the jury that defendants were guilty if the jury found the killing to have occurred in the perpetration of the felony of conspiracy to possess Methedrine without a prescription. In reversing, the state high court explained that, in evaluating the inherent dangerousness of a particular felony, they "look to the elements of the felony in the abstract, not the particular 'facts' of the case." *Id.* at 458 n.5. Because *possession* of almost anything is neutral and not necessarily life-threatening, the conspiracy in *Williams* was deemed insufficiently dangerous to human life to trigger the felony-murder rule. *Id.* at 458. A murder conviction of Williams would depend therefore on proof of malice.

A small list makes up the crimes that elementally ("in the abstract") are inherently dangerous to life, but are not already enumerated in §189: burning an automobile, administering uncut heroin or methyl alcohol, and felony child abuse for the purpose of punishment constitute the small reach of second-degree felony murder. Again, one reason there are so few crimes that courts have identified as inherently dangerous enough is that the most dangerous felonies (arson, kidnapping, rape, robbery, etc.) have already been identified and enumerated as first-degree felony murder in §189.

### 3. A NON-ASSAULTIVE ELEMENT: MERGER

Another reason so few crimes count for purposes of second-degree felony murder is that some of the most inherently dangerous crimes are in a sense *too* dangerous, in that they are merely assaultive crimes with no statutory element apart from intentional, highly dangerous, unjustified aggressions against others. Every qualifying crime of felony murder is not only inherently dangerous, but also has in its elements what courts call an independent or collateral *non-assaultive purpose*. As counterintuitive as it may seem, it is that non-assaultive purpose that prevents the felony from "merging" into the killing. To say that a felony merges into a killing is to preclude application of the felony-murder rule to that crime, thus relegating the prosecution to proof of malice to obtain a murder conviction.

For example, robbery has two elements: 1) assault (intentionally placing the victim in immediate apprehension of serious bodily injury); and 2) larceny (a trespassory taking of property known to be that of another with the specific intent to permanently deprive). Without the intention to abscond with another's property, all that would be left of robbery is an assault, which, even if inherently dangerous, could not by itself support the felony-murder rule. While the assaultive part of robbery is what makes it much more dangerous than, say, larceny, it is the intention to take property that prevents the assault from merging (or disappearing) into the killing. *See, e.g.*, *People v. Burton*, 6 Cal.3d 375, 384-88 (1971) (en banc).

If any assault that led to death were to count as felony murder, then the law of felony murder would wipe out the function of malice in murder prosecutions (far beyond the extent to which felony murder already achieves such a result). In this vein, to explain why assault with a deadly weapon merged with defendant's killing of his wife, the California Supreme Court reasoned that to allow use of felony murder in such a case would constitute a "bootstrapping" by which every deadly assault would be elevated to murder without proof of malice. *See People v. Ireland*, 70 Cal.2d 522, 539 (1969) (en banc). Nearly all killings are assaultive. Some assaults that bring about death are malicious; some are not. Indeed, some assaults produce outright accidental deaths. The only assaults that can trigger the felony-murder rule are not *merely* assaultive. Instead, the felony-murder rule applies when the assault is elementally paired with a non-assaultive element. The thinking here is that offenders' appetite for assault may be unfazed by the felony-murder rule, but their appetite for stealing and other non-assaultive aspects of the underlying felonies may be deterred by their knowing a murder conviction could be obtained against them if that collateral purpose leads to their killing someone, even accidentally. *People v. Robertson*, 34 Cal.4th 156, 170-72 (2004).

An example of the limitation that merger places on felony murder is *People v. Sarun Chun*, 45 Cal.4th 1172 (2009). Chun was a member of the (Stockton) Tiny Rascals street gang, three of whom shot from inside their car into the car where victim Bounthavy Onethavong rode behind the driver, Sophal Ouch. In the passenger's seat was Judy Onesavanh, whose absent brother George—of the rival Asian Boyz street gang—might have been the intended target. Chun admitted to police to having been in the car during the shooting and to firing a .38, which was found to be one of two guns that discharged lethal shots to the victim's head. The trial court improvidently issued an instruction on second-degree felony murder based on the crime of maliciously shooting at an occupied vehicle—which had no non-assaultive purpose. California Penal Code §246 (1988). That Chun fired his gun to frighten or intimidate the occupants of the other car could not count as a collateral purpose to assault, since the intent to frighten is elementally part and parcel of any assault.

In a footnote, the California Supreme Court confined its ruling to the merger doctrine within the meaning of second-degree felony murder. *Sarun Chun*, *supra*, 45 Cal.4th at 1189 n.6. The court was not about to revisit the enumerated offenses of §189 and invalidate any as a basis of first-degree felony murder if no non-assaultive element was discernible. The court's lack of interest in examining the §189 offenses for their non-assaultive elements became explicit three months later in *People v. Farley*, 46 Cal.4th 1053 (2009). Farley burgled the offices of his former employer, Electromagnetic Systems Laboratory in Sunnyvale, where he fatally shot six employees (after killing one in the parking lot) and wounded four others, including Laura Black, a woman he had been stalking for four years. Burglary is defined as entering a building with the specific intent to commit a felony or theft therein. California Penal Code §459 (West 1991). The felony Farley contemplated at the time of the entry was to assault Black with one of the deadly weapons he brought into the building.

Forty years earlier, the California Supreme Court had invalidated the first-degree felony-murder conviction of Rufus Wilson, who had committed a burglary with the intent to assault his estranged wife with a shotgun. Wilson had been married for nine years before his wife left him and filed for divorce. A year later, Wilson killed her and a man named Washington, with whom Wilson found her. The question was whether a burglary where the contemplated crime that made the entry a burglary was merely assaultive would merge with the killing, thereby precluding first-degree felony murder, even though burglary is enumerated in §189. Had Wilson intended, for example, to commit larceny or robbery therein, the felony and the killing would not have merged. But as it was, if not for the intent to commit assault with a deadly weapon therein, Wilson's *entry* into his wife's apartment would not have been felonious. Ruling that burglary merges whenever the contemplated offense at the time of the entry has no non-assaultive purpose, the California Supreme Court reversed Wilson's first-degree felony-murder conviction for killing his wife. His conviction for the second-degree, malice-based murder of Washington was undisturbed. *People v. Wilson*, 1 Cal.3d 431 (1969).

Faced with *Wilson* as precedent, the California Supreme Court first focused its attention in *Farley* on the difference between 1) burglary where the entry leads to the killing of the intended assault victim, and 2) burglary where the victim was not the intended assault victim at the time of the entry. This distinction had arisen in *People v. Gutierrez*, 28 Cal.4th 1083 (2002), where defendant forced his way into the home of his estranged wife, whom defendant's accomplice restrained in the living room while defendant forced his way into the bathroom, killing his wife's boyfriend. The jury was instructed on first-degree felony murder based upon burglary committed by defendant with the intent to commit assault with a deadly weapon upon his wife. The court upheld defendant's first-degree felony-murder conviction, noting that assaulting *the boyfriend* was not alleged as a target offense of the burglary, thus precluding merger.

In *Farley*, the court did not just follow *Gutierrez* and hold that the intent to assault one person would not cause a burglary to merge as to the assault/killing of others. Instead, the court overruled *Wilson* altogether. Because the legislature enumerated burglary as a triggering offense for felony murder over 150 years ago, limiting felony murder to only non-merging burglaries is a move that the legislature could have made before or after 1969 when the merger doctrine came into being in *Ireland* and *Wilson*. But the legislature did not. Accordingly, while pre-*Farley* the merger doctrine applied to second-degree felony murder and to first-degree felony murders based on burglaries where the contemplated offense at the time of the entry had no non-assaultive purpose, *Farley* established that the merger doctrine would apply only to second-degree felony murder.

It is consequently now assumed by courts that the offenses enumerated in §189 are inherently dangerous in the abstract, and have a non-assaultive purpose, also in the abstract. *See Sarun Chun*, 45 Cal.4th at 1200. And for the most part, assuming so works no real mischief. For example, kidnapping includes the taking of the victim to another location, an element distinct from the kidnapper's assault of the victim. *See People v. Escobar*, 48 Cal.App.4th 999, 1010-14 (1996). So too does robbery include the taking of property (however insignificant the relocation may be), an element distinct from the robber's assault of the victim. *See People v. Burton*, 6 Cal.3d 375, 384-88 (1971) (en banc). As for arson, because the offense elementally entails torching an inhabited building, it is an aggression both against its occupants and the property itself: that arson is designed to achieve the collateral purpose of destroying property, not just inhabitants, qualifies it for felony murder. *See People v. Billa*, 125 Cal.Rptr.2d 842, 850 (3d Dist. Ct. App. 2002). Rape, too, is assumed to have a non-assaultive purpose: the sexual gratification of the attacker is the objective (or an objective) of the forcible penetration of the victim. If rape were considered merely assaultive and not at all sexual, the felony would merge into the homicide, precluding felony murder, thus requiring that the prosecution prove malice to support a conviction of murder should the rapist kill his victim. *See People v. Rupp*, 41 Cal.2d 371, 382 (1953) (en banc).

Though innocuous after *Farley*, the assumption that all offenses enumerated in §189 possess both assaultive and non-assaultive aspects may be a little misleading, quite apart from the context of assault-based burglaries. Consider, for example, another offense enumerated in §189—simple mayhem—which occurs when a person "maliciously deprives a human being of a member of his body, or disables, disfigures, or renders it useless, or cuts or disables the tongue, or puts out an eye, or slits the nose, ear, or lip...." California Penal Code §203 (West 1989). The intended upshot of disfigurement is said to be the collateral purpose, see *People v. Gonzalez*, 51 Cal.4th 894, 942-43 (2011), but it is hard to see that as outside the assault any more than intending to frighten or even kill the victim is collateral to (a non-assaultive purpose of) assault with a deadly weapon. See *People v. Robertson*, 34 Cal.4th 156, 183 (2004) (Kennard, J., dissenting) ["An intent to scare a person by shooting at the person is *not independent* of the homicide because it is, in essence, nothing more than the intent required for an assault...."].

## B. PRINCIPAL AND ACCOMPLICE LIABILITY IN FELONY MURDER

The notion that malice is an element of murder is hardly new. Nor is it at all new that killings committed by felons in the perpetration or attempted perpetration of inherently dangerous felonies make proof of malice unnecessary. *E.g., People v. Olsen*, 80 Cal. 122 (1889). As I emphasize above (*supra* Chapter 5.A), felony murders dispense with proof of malice not because malice is *presumed* from the offender's manifested intention to commit the inherently dangerous felony, but because malice is not an element of felony murder at all. *People v. Dillon*, 34 Cal.3d 441, 475 (1983). *But cf. People v. Friend*, 211 P.3d 520, 573-74 (Cal. 2000). The felonies that uniformly trigger the operation of this rule are burglary, arson, rape, robbery, and kidnapping. Whether other crimes (as in, say, escape from prison) trigger the rule depends on the jurisdiction. See *infra* Chapter 5.B, note 1 on *Stamp*.

Although there are different formulations of the rule, "all states have endorsed ... felony murder in some form," *Stevens, v. Epps*, 2008 WL 4283528 at *15 (S.D. Miss.), the main differences arising out of 1) whether it matters who does the killing (an aggressing felon as opposed to a defending police officer, victim, or witness), 2) who gets killed (again, a felon as opposed to an innocent), or 3) whether malice is an element. See, e.g., Model Penal Code & Commentaries §210.2(1)(b), cmt. 6, at 29-30 [killings during perpetration or attempted perpetration of enumerated felonies raise rebuttable presumption of malice].

Our introductory, principal case to the law of felony murder, *People v. Stamp*, 2 Cal.App.3d 203 (1969), reveals the sometimes tenuous connection between the defendant's course of conduct and the victim's death, which can in extreme cases bear little relation to murder at all. In reading *Stamp*, please consider whether: 1) Stamp, Koory, or Lehman killed Honeyman; 2) the killing (if killing there be) was done with malice as you have come to understand the term; and if it wasn't, 3) an absence of malice nonetheless allows for a murder conviction.

## COURT OF APPEAL, SECOND DISTRICT, CALIFORNIA

*THE PEOPLE OF THE STATE OF CALIFORNIA, PLAINTIFF AND RESPONDENT*

*V.*

*JONATHAN EARL STAMP, MICHAEL JOHN KOORY, BILLY DEAN LEHMAN, DEFENDANTS AND APPELLANTS*

DEC. 1, 1969

COBEY, Associate Justice

These are appeals by Jonathan Earl Stamp, Michael John Koory, and Billy Dean Lehman following jury verdicts of guilty of robbery and murder, both in the first degree. Each man was given a life sentence on the murder charge together with the time prescribed by law on the robbery count. Defendants appeal their conviction of the murder of Carl Honeyman who, suffering from a heart disease, died between 15 and 20 minutes after Koory and Stamp held up his business, the General Amusement Company, on October 26, 1965, at 10:45 a.m. Lehman, the driver of the getaway car, was apprehended a few minutes after the robbery; several weeks later Stamp was arrested in Ohio and Koory in Nebraska. [The prosecution's case depended in part on post-arrest, extrajudicial confessions from Koory and Stamp].

Broadly stated, the grounds of this appeal are: (1) insufficiency of the evidence on the cause of Honeyman's death; (2) inapplicability of the felony-murder rule to this case; [and] (3) errors in the choice of instructions given and refused.... On this appeal appellants primarily rely upon their position that the felony-murder doctrine should not have been applied in this case due to the unforeseeability of Honeyman's death.

## FACTS

Defendants Koory and Stamp, armed with a gun and a blackjack, entered the rear of the building housing the offices of General Amusement Company, ordered the employees they found there to go to the front of the premises, where the two secretaries were working. Stamp, the one with the gun, then went into the office of Carl Honeyman, the owner and manager. Thereupon Honeyman, looking very frightened and pale, emerged from the office in a "kind of hurry." He was apparently propelled by Stamp who had hold of him by an elbow.

The robbery victims were required to lie down on the floor while the robbers took the money and fled out the back door. As the robbers, who had been on the premises 10 to 15 minutes, were leaving, they told the victims to remain on the floor for five minutes so that no one would "get hurt."

Honeyman, who had been lying next to the counter, had to use it to steady himself in getting up off the floor. Still pale, he was short of breath, sucking air, and pounding and rubbing his chest. As he walked down the hall, in an unsteady manner, still breathing hard and rubbing his chest, he said he was having trouble "keeping the pounding down inside" and that his heart was "pumping too fast for him." A few minutes later, although still looking very upset, shaking, wiping his forehead and rubbing his chest, he was able to walk in a steady manner into an employee's office. When the police arrived, almost immediately thereafter, he told them he was not feeling very well and that he had a pain in his chest. About two minutes later, which was 15 to 20 minutes after the robbery had occurred, he collapsed on the floor. At 11:25 he was pronounced dead on arrival at the hospital. The coroner's report listed the immediate cause of death as heart attack.

The employees noted that during the hours before the robbery Honeyman had appeared to be in normal health and good spirits. The victim was an obese, 60-year-old man, with a history of heart disease, who was under a great deal of pressure due to the intensely competitive nature of his business. Additionally, he did not take good care of his heart.

Three doctors, including the autopsy surgeon, Honeyman's

physician, and a professor of cardiology from UCLA, testified that although Honeyman had an advanced case of atherosclerosis, a progressive and ultimately fatal disease, there must have been some immediate upset to his system which precipitated the attack. It was their conclusion in response to a hypothetical question that, but for the robbery, there would have been no fatal seizure at that time. The fright induced by the robbery was too much of a shock to Honeyman's system. There was opposing expert testimony to the effect that it could not be said with reasonable medical certainty that fright could ever be fatal.

### SUFFICIENCY OF THE EVIDENCE OF CAUSATION

Appellants' contention that the evidence was insufficient to prove that the robbery factually caused Honeyman's death is without merit. The test on review is whether there is substantial evidence to uphold the judgment of the trial court, and in so deciding, this court must assume in the case of a jury trial the existence of every fact in favor of the verdict which the jury could reasonably have deduced from the evidence. *People v. Redmond*, 71 Cal.2d 745 (1969) (en banc). A review of the facts as outlined above shows that there was substantial evidence of the robbery itself, that appellants were the robbers, and that but for the robbery, the victim would not have experienced the fright which brought on the fatal heart attack.

### APPLICATION OF THE FELONY MURDER RULE

Appellants' contention that the felony-murder rule is inapplicable to the facts of this case is also without merit. Under the felony-murder rule of §189 of the Penal Code, a killing committed in either the perpetration of or an attempt to perpetrate robbery is murder of the first degree. This is true whether the killing is willful, deliberate and premeditated, or merely accidental or unintentional, and whether or not the killing is planned as a part of the commission of the robbery. *People v. Lookadoo*, 66 Cal.2d 307, 314 (1967). *People v. Washington*, 62 Cal.2d 777 (1965) merely limits the rule to situations where the killing was committed by the felon or his accomplice acting in furtherance of their common design. *People v. Gilbert*, 63 Cal.2d 690, 705 (1965).

The doctrine presumes malice aforethought on the basis of the commission of a felony inherently dangerous to human life. *Washington*, 62 Cal.2d at 780. This is a rule of substantive law in California and not merely an evidentiary shortcut to finding malice as it withdraws from the jury the requirement that they find either express or implied malice. Under this rule no intentional act is necessary other than the attempt to or the actual commission of the robbery itself. When a robber enters a place with a deadly weapon with the intent to commit robbery, malice is shown by the nature of the crime.

There is no requirement that the killing occur "while committing" or "while engaged in" the felony, or that the killing be "a part of" the felony, other than that the few acts be a part of one continuous transaction. *People v. Chavez*, 37 Cal.2d 656, 670 (1951). Thus the homicide need not have been committed "to perpetrate" the felony. There need be no technical inquiry as to whether there has been a completion or abandonment of or desistence from the robbery before the homicide itself was completed. *Id.* at 669-70.

The doctrine is not limited to those deaths which are foreseeable. See 1 Witkin, California Crimes §§78-79, at 79-80 (1963); *Chavez*, 37 Cal.2d at 669-70. Rather, a felon is held strictly liable for *all* killings he or his accomplices commit in the course of the felony. *People v. Talbot*, 64 Cal.2d 691, 704 (1966). As long as the homicide is the direct causal result of the robbery, the felony-murder rule applies whether or not the death was a natural or probable consequence of the robbery. So long as a victim's predisposing physical condition, regardless of its cause, is not the *only* substantial factor bringing about his death, that condition, and the robber's ignorance of it, in no way destroys the robber's criminal responsibility for the death. So long as life is shortened as a result of the felonious act, it does not matter that the victim might have died soon anyway. *People v. Phillips*, 64 Cal.2d 574, 579 (1966). In this respect, the robber takes his victim as he finds him.

## CLAIMED ERRORS IN INSTRUCTIONS

Appellants claim five errors in the jury instructions given and refused. They argue that: (1) the trial court erred in refusing to give appellants' proffered instruction as to proximate cause; (2) the jury should have been instructed on the court's own motion that there must be a finding of specific intent to commit the robbery before the felony-murder rule can be applied; (3) the jury should not have been instructed on the felony-murder rule; (4) the jury should have been instructed on the matter of foreseeability; and (5) the felony-murder rule applies only when the killing was committed *in order to* perpetrate a felony, and not when the killing occurs merely *in* the perpetration of a felony. In accordance with our discussion of the felony-murder doctrine, we find the claimed instruction errors numbered (3), (4), and (5) to be without merit.

Appellants contend that the trial court erred in refusing their proffered instruction on proximate cause, which reads: "Where defendant's criminal act is not the proximate cause of the death and the sole proximate cause was the negligent or reckless conduct of the victim, a conviction is unwarranted." They assert that article VI, section 13 of the California Constitution guarantees the right of a defendant to have the jury determine every material issue presented by the evidence. Refusal of the trial court to give the instruction was arguably justified. The evidence before the jury was not such that the jury could have reasonably assumed that Honeyman's negligence or recklessness was the sole cause of his death. But the instructions given on the issue of the proximate causation of Honeyman's death were much more complete and accurate than appellants' quoted instruction.[4] Any error in this respect was harmless.

As to the second objection, since the jury was fully instructed both as to what constitutes robbery and as to what constitutes felony murder,[5] the court was not required to instruct them on its own

---

[4] If the victim's death was by natural causes and not a proximate result of defendant's unlawful activity, defendant is not guilty of murder, which requires an unlawful act that proximately caused the death of another human. The proximate cause of death is that which, in a sequence unbroken by any intervening cause, produces the death, and without which the result would not have occurred. It is the efficient cause—the one that sets in operation the factors that accomplish the death. A person who proximately causes another's death has committed unlawful homicide even if the unlawful act was not the only cause of the death, and the person killed had been already enfeebled by disease, injury, physical condition or other cause, and it is probable a person in sound physical condition would not have died as a result of the act, and it is probable the act only hastened the death of the deceased person, who would have died soon thereafter anyhow from another cause or causes.

[5] Robbery is the felonious taking of personal property of any value in the possession of another, from his person or immediate presence, and against his will, accomplished by means of force or fear. Robbery perpetrated by someone armed with a dangerous weapon is robbery in the first degree. All other kinds of robbery are of the second degree. If someone is killed by any one of several persons jointly engaged at the time of such killing in the perpetration of, or attempt to perpetrate, the crime of robbery, and if the killing is done in furtherance of a common design and agreement to commit such crime or is an ordinary and probable effect of the pursuit of that design and agreement, all such persons so jointly engaged are guilty of murder of the first degree, whether such killing be intentional, unintentional, or accidental.

motion that in order to apply the felony-murder rule, appellants must have had the specific intent to commit the robbery. This is so because the jury could not have found them guilty of murder under the felony-murder doctrine without first having found them guilty of robbery. Moreover, failure to instruct the jury that in order to apply the felony-murder doctrine appellants must have had the specific intent to commit the robbery does not constitute prejudicial error where, as here, the evidence permits of no other interpretation than that appellants had the specific intent to steal. See *People v. Ford*, 60 Cal.2d 772, 792-93 (1964).

[The portion of the opinion addressing defendants' unsuccessful challenge to the introduction into evidence of their extrajudicial confessions to police is omitted. The Court of Appeal did not reach the merits of that challenge because trial counsel, by not raising it below, rendered it forfeited/unreviewable on appeal. See *supra* Chapter 3.A, note 4a on *Greene*].

The judgment is affirmed.

SCHWEITZER and ALLPORT, JJ., concur.

## QUESTIONS ON *STAMP*

1. **Whose side are you on, anyway?** Stamp, armed with a gun, led Honeyman from his office in the General Amusement Company by the elbow and ordered him to the floor. About 15-20 minutes after Stamp and Koory left the scene of the robbery, Honeyman had a fatal heart attack. Three witnesses for the prosecution were physicians who testified that Honeyman was suffering from "atherosclerosis, a progressive and ultimately fatal disease." How, then, are they *prosecution* witnesses?

2. **New York version of *Stamp*.** In the wee hours of October 17, 1989, Eddie Matos and two accomplices broke into a McDonald's on Seventh Avenue and 40th Street in Manhattan by shattering the glass door with a sledgehammer. Once inside, the three burglars rounded up employees at gunpoint. A maintenance worker, however, escaped and returned to the restaurant with three police officers, who then saw Matos run to the back of the restaurant and climb a ladder that led to the roof. Police Officer Dwyer hurriedly climbed up the ladder

right behind Matos. Ten seconds later, Sergeant Flanagan climbed the ladder to the roof, from where he saw Dwyer lying on his back 25 feet down an airshaft. It took emergency services personnel about 45 minutes to extricate Dwyer, who was later pronounced dead at Bellevue Hospital.

What result under *Stamp*? *People v. Matos*, 634 N.E.2d 157 (N.Y. 1994); *cf.* http://www.nydailynews.com/news/national/pa-dies-15-foot-fall-chasing-armed-teens-article-1.2289884.

[handwritten: murder]

**3. State law version of *Jackson v. Virginia*.** What is the California case cited by the court that sets out the standard for defense appeals claiming factual insufficiency of the evidence? [handwritten: People v. Redmond]

**4. Absence of malice.** All killings in the perpetration or attempted perpetration of enumerated felonies are first-degree murder on the part of both the principal killer and all principals and accomplices in the felony or its attempt, whether the killing is premeditated or deliberate on the one hand or even accidental on the other. To be sure, *Stamp* said that felony murder "presumes malice aforethought on the basis of the commission of a felony inherently dangerous to human life." But as this chapter has so far emphasized, the state high court (sort of) clarified some 14 years later that malice is *not* an element of felony murder, presumed or otherwise. *See People v. Dillon*, 34 Cal.3d 441, 473-76 (1983). Either way—whether malice is a non-element or a presumed element—the felony-murder rule deems accidental killings (like Honeyman's) murders in the context of certain felonious activity. What would be the objective(s) of such a rule? [handwritten: Deter the lesser felony]

**5. Perpetration problems.** At the very earliest, Honeyman died about 15 minutes after Stamp and Koory left Honeyman's business to escape in accomplice Lehman's car. Citing *People v. Chavez*, 37 Cal.2d 656, 669-70 (1951), the Court of Appeal notes that the law requires that the killing be "in ... the perpetration" of the underlying crime or its attempt, but need not be committed "to perpetrate" the crime. [handwritten: killing cause by perpetration]

a. What is the difference between these two formulations?

b. In what sense did Honeyman's death occur *during* the robbery? [handwritten: Robbery caused the inflammation of the already present heart problems]

**6. Felony murder and causation.** The Court of Appeal stated: "So long as life is shortened as a result of the felonious act, it does not matter that the victim might have died soon anyway.... In this respect, the robber takes his victim as he finds him."

**a.** What does the first sentence mean? Suppose defendant #1 pushes victim off the top floor of a 100-story skyscraper. As victim is falling to a certain death, defendant #2 shoots victim in the head as he plummets just outside defendant #2's office window in the same building. The bullet wound from defendant #2's shot instantly causes victim's death. Does the first sentence in the above quote mean that defendant #2, not defendant #1, has killed the victim?

**b.** What does the second sentence mean? That it is always foreseeable that a robbery victim may have a bad heart? Or that it makes no difference to guilt whether such a condition is foreseeable?

**7. Inherently dangerous felony + killing = murder.** Here, though it may go too far to say that Stamp, Koory, and Lehman "killed" Honeyman, it would not (or did not) go too far for the Court of Appeal to rule that the robbers did cause his death. What result if in the course of the robbery Stamp had fatally shot Koory? Does it matter if such a killing was intentional, not intentional, or unintentional? On this, see *infra* Chapter 5.B, note 3 on *Stamp*.

## NOTES ON *STAMP*

**1. Which felonies trigger the felony-murder rule?** Section 189 lists arson, rape, carjacking, robbery, burglary, mayhem, kidnapping, train wrecking, torture, sodomy with a minor, lewd and lascivious acts on a child under 14, oral copulation with a minor, forcible sexual penetration of a minor, or any murder which is perpetrated by means of discharging a firearm from a motor vehicle, intentionally at another person outside of the vehicle with the intent to inflict death. *See supra* Chapter 5.A, Introduction [detailing §189]. Model Penal Code §210.2(1)(b) lists arson, rape, robbery, burglary, kidnapping, and escape. Which offenses trigger the felony-murder rule is idiosyncratic state to state. *See* Model Penal Code and Commentaries §210.2(1)(b), cmt. 6, at 32 n.78; *see also* 18 U.S.C.A. §1111(a) (2003) [Congress adds to the usual list of felonies three with uniquely federal angles: treason, espionage, and sabotage].

**2. Specific intent to commit underlying felony.** In Stamp's second objection to the jury instructions given at trial, he faults the trial court for not instructing, *sua sponte*, that an element of felony murder is the specific intent to commit the underlying felony, which is either attempted or completed. In some cases, such an oversight on the court's part could constitute reversible error. But not here. To the Court of Appeal, no jury could have found that armed robbers comporting themselves as these three did could possibly have *lacked* specific intent to steal. So the error was ruled harmless. See also supra Chapter 4.E.1, note 2b on *Fountain* [discussing harmless error].

A case in which such an oversight could be reversible error is *People v. Sears*, 62 Cal.2d 737 (1965), where a theory of the prosecution's case was that defendant committed felony murder of his wife's daughter from a previous marriage during the perpetration of mayhem. Simple (as opposed to aggravated) mayhem occurs when a person "maliciously deprives a human being of a member of his body, or disables, disfigures, or renders it useless, or cuts or disables the tongue, or puts out an eye, or slits the nose, ear, or lip...." California Penal Code §203 (West 1989); *supra* Chapter 5.A.3. The aggravating adverb, fault term, or mental state in the California mayhem statute quoted above—"maliciously"—can be satisfied without proof of specific intent to bring about the prohibited harm. *Sears*, 62 Cal.2d at 744-45. That much we know from our study of the difference between, for example, first-degree premeditated-and-deliberate murder and second-degree implied-malice murder. Thus, for the prosecution to get a conviction of mayhem, defendant need only perform the harmful action by consciously ignoring the excessive risk of the ultimate injury (disfigurement, etc.) as listed in the statute. However, for the prosecution to get a conviction of felony murder *based on* mayhem, specific intent to commit mayhem becomes an element of the felony murder, even though mayhem ordinarily is a general-intent crime. (The same is true when the prosecution seeks a conviction of felony murder based on rape, arson, or kidnapping, each of which is otherwise a general-intent crime).

Remember that voluntary intoxication is not a defense to general-intent crimes, but it is a defense to specific-intent crimes. Consequently, voluntary intoxication, if believed by the jury to have prevented the formation of specific intent, would negate a defendant's responsibility for felony murder regardless of which underlying, triggering felony the prosecution relies on. Also remember that mistakes must be reasonable to defeat liability for general-intent crimes, but need be only actual (if unreasonable) to defeat liability for specific-intent crimes.

### 3. Emphasis on who does the killing, not on who gets killed.

**a. All for one and one for all.** Consider *People v. Cabaltero*, 31 Cal.App.2d 52 (1939), which established the still-intact notion that under California's felony-murder rule, all members of the felonious enterprise are treated identically. That's the law regardless of who among them does the killing and regardless of who gets killed, provided that the killing is done by a member of that felonious enterprise during the perpetration or attempted perpetration of an inherently dangerous felony (enumerated in note 1 on *Stamp* above):

> The robbery occurred on a farm near Campbell, in Santa Clara county. It was one of several farms operated in that county by Nishida, a Japanese, upon which he employed many Filipino laborers, among them being Fred and Marcella Avelino. Being so employed, the Avelinos knew that it was Nishida's custom to pay the wages of his men in cash about the noon hour on a certain day of the week, in a building on that farm; and the Avelinos entered into a conspiracy with Dasalla, Flores, Velasco, Cabaltero and Ancheta (all being Filipinos and residents of San Francisco), to rob Nishida at that time and place; and the robbery was carried out as planned.
>
> Fred Avelino was off the premises during the robbery, but all of the others were present and actively participated therein, and all except Marcella Avelino were armed. Cabaltero waited nearby with an automobile to provide means of escape; Marcella Avelino entered the farm building with other Filipino laborers ostensibly to receive his wages, but in fact to start an altercation with Nishida, so that during the confusion the robbery could be perpetrated. Velasco and Ancheta stood guard at the outer door, while Dasalla and Flores entered the building, and with drawn pistols held up Nishida, forcibly taking from him approximately $1,200. After seizing the money Dasalla and Flores started for the outer door, but before reaching it two shots were fired from the outside, and as Dasalla made his exit through the door he shot and fatally wounded Ancheta. As a witness in his own behalf he denied having done so, but Nishida testified positively that he saw him fire the shot, and then saw Dasalla, Flores and Velasco assist Ancheta, who had fallen, to the waiting automobile in which they made their escape.

From the scene of the robbery they drove to a ranch just north of Gilroy, where they left the wounded Ancheta. Later that afternoon Cabaltero and Flores were arrested on the highway near the ranch, but Dasalla and Velasco succeeded in making their way back to San Francisco. During the night Ancheta was removed to the county hospital, and about two weeks later he died from the effects of the gunshot wounds. Shortly after Ancheta's death Dasalla and Velasco were arrested in San Francisco. Part of the evidence introduced by the prosecution against Velasco consisted of a confession made by him to an officer shortly after his arrest, wherein he related the circumstances attending the shooting of Ancheta. In this regard he stated, so the officer testified, that while the robbery was being perpetrated, an automobile drove up in which were two Filipinos; that Ancheta commanded them to stay in the car, but they jumped out and started to run, whereupon Ancheta fired two shots at them; that immediately following the firing of the shots Dasalla emerged through the door of the building and exclaiming to Ancheta, "Damn you, what did you shoot for," fired a shot at Ancheta; that Ancheta fell wounded, and that they, Velasco, Dasalla and Flores picked him up and assisted him to the waiting automobile in which they fled.

The murder charge was based on section 189 of the Penal Code, and all of the essential elements thereof were pleaded in the charge. Said section declares that "All murder which is … committed in the perpetration or attempt to perpetrate arson, rape, robbery, burglary, or mayhem, is murder of the first degree"; and it is well settled that one who kills another under such circumstances is guilty of murder of the first degree by force of the statute, altogether regardless of any question of intent. The killing may be willful, deliberate and premeditated, or it may be absolutely accidental; in either case the slayer is equally guilty since the statute applies to all homicide so committed, not merely to such as might be planned as a part of the execution of the felony intended; and it is proper so to instruct the jury....

Furthermore, it is well established that if a homicide is committed by one of several confederates while engaged in perpetrating the crime of robbery in furtherance of a common purpose, the person or persons engaged with him in the perpetration of the robbery but who did not actually do the killing, are as accountable to the law as though their own hands had intentionally fired the fatal shot or given the fatal blow, and such killing is murder of the first degree. The jury has no option but to return a verdict of murder of the first degree whether the killing was intentionally or accidentally done, and it is proper so to instruct the jury....

It is contended that the statements so made by Velasco show that Dasalla shot Ancheta deliberately and with the intention of killing him or doing him great bodily harm; that consequently Dasalla alone is accountable for the killing; and in furtherance of such theory an instruction was proposed by them which the court refused to give, to the effect that if the jury found that Ancheta was a coconspirator and was shot intentionally by his confederate, each of the coconspirators other than the one who fired the shot should be acquitted, despite the fact that the shooting occurred while all were participating in the robbery. In other words, they seek to invoke the benefit of the doctrine that if one member of a conspiracy departs from the original design as agreed upon by all members, and does an act which was not only not contemplated by those who entered into the common purpose but was not in furtherance thereof, and not the natural and probable consequence of anything connected therewith, the person guilty of such act if it was itself unlawful is alone responsible therefore....

Such doctrine is not available, however, to coconspirators in cases such as this, where the killing is done during the perpetration of a robbery in which they were participating. The law is also well settled that where two or more persons enter into a conspiracy to commit a robbery or burglary and one of the conspirators commits a murder in the perpetration of the crime, all of said conspirators are equally guilty with said coconspirator of murder of the first degree, and it is no defense that those who did not actually participate in the killing did not intend that life should be taken in the perpetration of the robbery, or had forbidden their associate to kill, or regretted that it had been done. Nor is it of the slightest consequence that the conspirators may not have intended to bring about their victim's death. The killing, having occurred in the perpetration of robbery, was murder of the first degree. Here the killing was done while the conspirators were attempting to flee from the scene of the robbery with the fruits thereof in their possession. Therefore the homicide was committed in the perpetration of the robbery.

**b. All for one (aftermath).** Dasalla, Cabaltero, Marcella Avelino, Flores, and Velasco were convicted of first-degree murder and robbery; Fred Avelino, only of robbery. *Cabaltero*, 31 Cal.App.2d at 54-55. None appealed their robbery conviction. The five murderers were given life sentences: Dasalla, Cabaltero, Avelino, and Flores to serve theirs at San Quentin; Velasco to serve his at Folsom. There is some authority to suggest that all five were paroled within 10 years of their sentencing date, none serving fewer than seven. *Paroles Are Granted to Filipinos*, San Jose Evening News, Mar. 27, 1944, at 5; *Murderer Will Ask Parole*, San Jose Evening News, Mar. 4, 1944, at 2 [indicating a scheduled parole hearing at Folsom for Velasco].

### 4. Who is principal, who is accomplice?

**a. In Cabaltero.** Dasalla is principal murderer: the one who killed Ancheta. Dasalla and Flores are principal robbers of Nishida: the ones who performed the forcible taking of property from Nishida's person. If the unarmed Marcella Avelino's "altercation" with Nishida was assaultive, then he, too, would be principal robber. Otherwise, Velasco, Cabaltero, and the Avelinos are accomplices to the robbery, including Fred Avelino, who was not present at the scene, but had conspired to rob. Just as the law makes no distinction between principals and accomplices for the robbery—both are punished as principals—so too does the law make no distinction between the principal killer and the other robbers, be they principal robbers (like Flores) or accomplices to robbery (like Velasco and Cabaltero). Accordingly, in addition to Dasalla (who actually shot Ancheta), Flores, Velasco, Cabaltero, and Marcella Avelino all were convicted and sentenced as principal murderers. There remains continued support for the *absent* accomplice Fred Avelino's acquittal of murder charges. See *People v. Billa*, 125 Cal.Rptr.2d 842 (3d Dist. Ct. App. 2002). Still, "not all states have foreclosed felony murder convictions when an accused is not present." See *United States v. Wilson*, 2015 WL 3536715 at *3 (U.S. Air Force Ct. Crim. App.)

**b. In Stamp.** Stamp and Koory robbed Honeyman and other employees of Honeyman's General Amusement Company. Both Stamp and Koory acted as principal robbers in that both committed both the assaultive and larcenous elements of robbery, though each robber need satisfy only one of the two elements of the offense to be principal as opposed to accomplice to the offense. Whether a robbery or other triggering offense is completed or attempted, or whether a defendant's participation in the completed or attempted robbery or other triggering offense is as principal or accomplice, all will be first-degree murderers when a member of their number kills—even accidentally—in the perpetration or attempted perpetration of the underlying offense enumerated in §189.

**c. In another (Cavitt).** To link up a non-killer with the killing requires proof of the non-killer's role, either as principal or accomplice, in the underlying, enumerated felony. That underlying felony must have a logical relation to the killing. While *Stamp* ruled that the killing need not be committed *to* perpetrate the felony or even *while* engaged in the performance of the elements of the felony, neither may the underlying felony and the killing be utterly disconnected. Instead, to establish felony murder on the part of a non-killer, the prosecution must demonstrate "both a causal relationship and a temporal relationship between the underlying felony and the act resulting in death." *People v. Cavitt*, 33 Cal.4th 187, 193 (2004).

In *Cavitt*, James Freddie Cavitt (17) conspired with his girlfriend Mianta McKnight (17) and Robert Williams (16) to burgle the home of Mianta's stepmom (Betty McKnight, 58) for purposes of theft. During the burglary, which staged Mianta as a co-victim, Betty died by asphyxiation, either from the duct tape Cavitt used to subdue her, or soon after by the hand of Mianta, who hated her. Although it was Cavitt's theory that a private grievance motivating Mianta to kill Betty decoupled the burglary from the killing enough to absolve him and Williams of felony murder, the California Supreme Court disagreed. As long as the felony and the killing were part of a continuous transaction not yet terminated by all felons having escaped to a place of temporary safe harbor, it doesn't really matter why Betty got killed, or by whom, as long as the joint engagement of the felons led one of them to do the fatal deed. *Id.* at 206-10; *cf. People v. Wilkins*, 56 Cal.4th 333, 342-48 (2013) [clarifying that even if Cavitt and Williams had fled and reached safe harbor by the time of Betty's death, Mianta had not fled, thus keeping the burglary-robbery alive and all three participants on the hook for felony murder].

After all three were found unfit for prosecution as juveniles, they were tried separately in adult court. Cavitt and Williams were found guilty of first-degree murder of Betty (whether the killing was intentional, unintentional, or not intentional) based on the triggering felonies burglary and robbery. Their consolidated direct appeals were unavailing through the state high court, after which Williams abandoned his fight while Cavitt's dragged on. Betty McKnight was murdered on December 1, 1995. The U.S. Supreme Court denied Cavitt's certiorari petition on federal habeas corpus on March 10, 2014. *Cavitt v. Cullen*, 134 S.Ct. 1522 (2014). He was paroled in September 2016.

Because Mianta lived in the suburban San Francisco home with her father and Betty, possessing in property terms "an unconditional right of entry," she could not be convicted of burglary, which criminalizes unlawful entries into the premises *of another* with the specific intent to commit a felony or theft therein. California Penal Code §459 (1991). In other words, one cannot be guilty of burglarizing one's own home. See *People v. Gauze*, 15 Cal.3d 709 (1975) (en banc).

Mianta's 1999 trial ended in her conviction of second-degree murder, a reduced charge she took in exchange for her cooperation. Her appeal that followed was based on a claim that police took her in-custody confession without first obtaining a waiver of her rights to silence and counsel. See *People v. McKnight*, 2002 WL 59612 (Cal. 1st Dist. Ct. App.); http://www.sfgate.com/bayarea/article/Woman-Is-Convicted-In-Stepmothers-Death-2898180.php. In 2013, at age 34, Mianta was paroled from Chowchilla women's prison. See http://www.smdailyjournal.com/articles/lnews/2013-08-02/woman-convicted-in-stepmoms-death-granted-Parole/1772847.html.

While her status as occupant with a possessory right in the home prevented Mianta from being *principal* burglar, there is no reason why her felony murder (which, recall, was based on her role in the robbery of Betty) could not be predicated on her role as *accomplice* to the burglary by principals Cavitt and Williams, their guilt in no way nullified by Mianta's consent to enter. *See, e.g., People v. Maciel*, 2011 WL 5120839. (Cal. 3d Dist. Ct. App.).

Addressing this issue in a case in which defendant Spriggs, let's loosely call him "tenant," entered his apartment with several non-tenants to assault a co-tenant (Morgan), the District of Columbia Court of Appeals explained in *Spriggs v. United States*, 52 A.3d 878, 883-84 (D.C. Cir. 2012):

Although Mr. Morgan's apartment may have been Spriggs's dwelling, two people other than Spriggs entered the home and attacked Mr. Morgan. Even if Spriggs could not be convicted of burglarizing his own home acting alone, we perceive no logical reason why a person cannot aid and abet an offense for which he could not be convicted if committed by him personally. In the era in which a husband could not legally rape his wife, there was universal acceptance of the rule that a husband can be charged with the crime of rape or assault to commit rape on his wife where he acted as a procurer or accomplice in arranging or permitting such a sexual attack to be perpetrated upon his wife by a third person. [W]e hold that a person may, as a matter of law, be convicted of aiding and abetting in the burglary of the home where he dwells where the crime intended to be committed in the home infringes upon the peaceful use and occupancy of a co-dweller of that home.

**d. And another (Dominguez).** An example of confusion at trial as to who did what, both in terms of the underlying offense and the killing, is *People v. Dominguez*, 39 Cal.4th 1141 (2006). Irma Perez was last seen alive on August 23, 1997, when police saw her outside a Hollister bar at 2:00 a.m. getting into a cab with Dominguez, Martinez, and Salcedo, headed to a labor camp in San Benito where Dominguez and Martinez picked apples.

Four days later, a tractor unearthed Ms. Perez's body in a walnut orchard. Marks in the soil suggested her corpse had been dragged from near the road to where it was found, about 10 rows (250 feet) into the orchard. Near a corner of the orchard, 25 feet from the road and 10-12 feet below it, officers found a pair of shoes and a shallowly buried pair of jeans together with underwear and a sock. About 25 yards separated the clothes from the nearest drag marks.

Ms. Perez died from strangulation and blunt force injury. She experienced choking, beating, and bruising of the vaginal walls indicative of very forceful sexual penetration. DNA tests proved semen from two donors, the more recent being Dominguez. The more remote donor was the father of Ms. Perez's children, who had had consensual sex with her on the morning before she disappeared.

Dominguez and Martinez were charged in July 1999 with murder, kidnapping for rape, rape, rape in concert, and mayhem. By the start of trial in January 2001, Martinez had died of cancer. Dominguez testified that after the cab ride to the camp, he walked with Ms. Perez, expressing his desire to have sex. She at first demurred, but, as Dominguez recounted, eventually had sex with him at the side of the road, undressing herself and acting of her own free will, never indicating otherwise. Martinez arrived soon after, angry with Dominguez for diverting Perez's attentions after Martinez had enjoyed a flirtation with her at the bar. Rather than walk Ms. Perez home, Dominguez claimed to have returned to the camp, leaving her with Martinez.

Instructions on murder, kidnapping for rape, and rape were submitted to the jury, which returned guilty verdicts on all three counts. The court sentenced Dominguez to 25 years to life on the murder and stayed the sentences on the other counts under Penal Code §654(a). *See supra* Chapter 2.A, note 2b on *Watson* & Chapter 4.E, note 2a on *Prettyman* [explaining §654]. On appeal, Dominguez challenged his conviction on all three counts.

**1) Murder.** The trial court refused to instruct the jury as requested by the defense to establish how Dominguez could be felony murderer of Ms. Perez if Martinez was the one who killed her.[a] Under felony murder, all principals and accomplices in the felony (here, rape) are liable for the felony and any sufficiently related killing that any of them commits in the joint engagement of that felonious purpose, regardless of who plays what role (principal or accomplice) in the felony *or* the killing. Dominguez's jury received one instruction that presupposed Dominguez as killer of Ms. Perez. A second instruction charged that if Martinez was the killer, the jury was to hold Dominguez jointly responsible, though the charge made no reference to the elements of complicity under CALJIC No. 3.01 to tie Dominguez to the killing through the rape.

Knowing that Ms. Perez was last seen with Dominguez and Martinez, and was brutally beaten and forcibly penetrated, the jury found that Dominguez, who admittedly had sexual relations with her,

---

[a] The omitted instruction, CALJIC No. 8.27 (2005 Revision), states:

> If a human being is killed by any one of several persons engaged in the commission or attempted commission of [fill in §189 felony here], all persons, who either commit the act constituting that crime, or who with knowledge of the unlawful purpose of the perpetrator of the crime and with the intent or purpose of committing, encouraging, or facilitating the commission of the offense, aid, promote, encourage, or instigate by act or advice its commission, are guilty of murder of the first degree, whether the killing is intentional, unintentional, or accidental.

committed rape. If Martinez killed Perez, he did not necessarily do so as a result of, or while jointly engaged in, Dominguez's rape of Perez, or while Dominguez was assisting *him* thereafter in an attempted rape. Jurors could have believed (as a question they put to the court implied) that Martinez killed Perez during a subsequent assault in which Dominguez played no role. Nor need that assault have been sexual in nature; Martinez might have killed her in a jealous rage. In any of these scenarios the jury might have found that the killing was independent of any felony committed *by* Dominguez.

The state high court nonetheless concluded that the jury was justified in finding a continuous transaction linking the rape and the killing in light of evidence that two people dragged Ms. Perez from where her clothing was found to where her body was found. Whoever actually killed her did it in the same spot where Dominguez had committed rape. Even if the trial court should have instructed the jury on CALJIC No. 8.27, the error was harmless in the eyes of the California Supreme Court: Either Dominguez killed Perez himself, or Martinez killed her within the context of Dominguez's rape. Either way, Perez's killing was sufficiently related to Dominguez's act of rape to hold Dominguez responsible as felony murderer per *Cavitt*.

**2) Rape.** Dominguez argued on appeal that the trial court erred by failing to instruct the jury on the defense described in *People v. Mayberry*, 15 Cal.3d 143, 155 (1975). An accused rapist is excused under *Mayberry* if he acted under a "reasonable and bona fide belief that the [complainant] voluntarily consented to accompany him and to engage in sexual intercourse." The *Mayberry* defense is embodied in CALJIC No. 10.65, which Dominguez argued the trial court should have read to the jury on its own motion. While the trial court has a *sua sponte* duty to instruct on defenses supported by substantial evidence, Dominguez put on no such evidence.

Rape requires an act of sexual intercourse with another against that person's will by means of force, violence, duress, menace, or fear of immediate and unlawful bodily injury. California Penal Code §261(a)(2) (West 2013). *Mayberry* instructions are required only when there is substantial evidence of 1) equivocal conduct, 2) that would have led defendant to reasonably believe consent existed, 3) where it did not. Another way of saying this is a *Mayberry* instruction entitles a defendant to consideration of his mistake as to the victim's consent only when the victim seems to have consented, but in fact did not.

If the jury believed Dominguez's account, they would have concluded not that Perez *seemed* to have consented but did not, but rather, that she *did* consent. No *Mayberry* instruction was therefore required since Dominguez made no claim that he was misled, that is, mistaken, about Perez's desires. Instead, he claimed that she acted on those desires. In closing argument, defense counsel declared that Dominguez "had voluntary sex with this lady." If Perez really did disrobe willingly and partake with no equivocation, then there was no need for a *Mayberry* instruction because there was no mismatch between appearance and reality. As indicated by his conviction of rape, the jury did not believe Dominguez; nor could they have concluded, even if instructed, that Perez's conduct was sufficiently "enigmatical," "equivocal," or "ambiguous" to lead him reasonably to mistake her gestures for consent. That she went to the labor camp with him is not a sign of desire to have intercourse. In affirming his conviction, the state high court took the position that the *Mayberry* instruction would not help the jury rule whether Ms. Perez's lack of consent was reasonably taken for consent; either she did consent or, if not, there was no good basis for Dominguez to believe that she had.

**3) Kidnapping for rape.** Although the jury instructions identified rape as the triggering offense for Dominguez's felony murder of Ms. Perez, her kidnap was an alternative basis for upholding Dominguez's conviction of felony murder, regardless of who (Dominguez or Martinez) killed her. *See Dominguez*, 39 Cal.4th at 1162 ["[B]ecause the facts overwhelmingly demonstrate defendant directly and actively participated in Perez's rape and kidnapping, the trial court's failure to instruct the jury with CALJIC No. 8.27 or its equivalent was harmless under any standard."].

It was Dominguez's thesis that the facts were insufficient to establish the asportation, or movement, needed to convict him of kidnapping for rape. The prosecution's thesis was that Dominguez, with or without help from Martinez, forced Ms. Perez down a 10-12 foot embankment into a walnut orchard, where he (or they) raped and murdered her before dragging her body 250 feet farther into the orchard. The rape occurred where her shoes and jeans were found in the orchard 25 feet from the road.

Penal Code §207(a), first enacted in 1872, now known as "simple kidnapping" (carrying a five-year sentence), is the taking of a person by force or fear and "carrying" him or her "into another country, state, or county, or into another part of the same county." Due to a spate of kidnappings for ransom, the California Legislature came to recognize "aggravated kidnapping," a much more serious crime that includes the specific intent to commit robbery, extortion, or ransom as the final cause of the kidnapping. Aggravated kidnapping did away with the asportation requirement of simple kidnapping, instead criminalizing coercive movements of the victim of as little as a few feet.

California Penal Code §209(b)(1) (West 2006) states: "Any person who kidnaps or carries away any individual to commit robbery, rape, spousal rape, oral copulation, [or] sodomy ... shall be punished by imprisonment in the state prison for life with the possibility of parole." It was an earlier but functionally identical statute under which Dominguez, whose crimes occurred in 1997, was prosecuted. Some effort is still made to stay true to the notion that kidnappers somehow carry their victims away a nontrivial distance. That effort is codified in §209(b)(2): "This subdivision shall only apply if the movement of the victim is beyond that merely incidental to the commission of, and increases the risk of harm to the victim over and above that necessarily present in, the intended underlying offense." At the time of Dominguez's crimes, that statute, though not yet enacted, was already expressed in case law. *See People v. Daniels & Simmons*, 71 Cal.2d 1119 (1969).

*Dominguez* fretted over whether Martinez's moving Perez some 25 feet from a road down an embankment to a walnut orchard was "incidental" to the rape. *Daniels & Simmons*, relying on the Model Penal Code, had reasoned that because §207 defines kidnapping as forcible movement of the victim "into another part of the same county, ... a court would be justified in reading into this phrase some requirement of substantial displacement." *Daniels & Simmons*, 71 Cal.2d at 1138 n.11. The significance of the movement is tied to the extent to which the movement surpasses what is necessary to commit the target crime at which the kidnapping is aimed. So, when a rape victim was moved across a motel hallway, into and across a room, and into the room's bathroom, kidnapping occurred since the movement was not "natural," "related," or merely "incidental" to rape. *People v. Salazar*, 33 Cal.App.4th 341, 346-49 (1995).

The California Supreme Court found substantial evidence to support the jury's verdict that Dominguez committed aggravated kidnapping:

> Defendant forced the victim in the middle of the night from the side of the road to a spot in an orchard 25 feet away and 10 to 12 feet below the level of the road. Though the distance is not great, an aerial photograph of the scene confirms the victim was moved to a location where it was unlikely any passing driver would see her. Not only was the place to which she was moved substantially below the road—one witness testified it was a down a "fairly steep" hill—it was within an orchard where the trees would obscure defendant's crime from any onlookers. The movement thus changed the victim's environment from a relatively open area alongside the road to a place significantly more secluded, substantially decreasing the possibility of detection, escape, or rescue. This case is thus unlike the brief and trivial movements of the robbery victims around a room, as in *Daniels*, or of a robbery victim from the teller area of a bank to a back room where the vault was located, movements found to be merely incidental to commission of the offense. Here, defendant's movement of the victim down an embankment and into an orchard cannot be said to have been merely incidental to the rape.

*Dominguez*, 39 Cal.4th at 1153-54. The attack on Ms. Perez occurred in 1997. Dominguez, age 44 in 2018, is serving his 25-years-life sentence at California Correctional Institution (Tehachapi), where his legal battle seems to have ended, now that the U.S. Supreme Court has declined to review his federal habeas petition. *Dominguez v. Felker*, 562 U.S. 1241 (2011). Dominguez's contention on federal habeas was that he kidnapped and raped Ms. Perez, whom Martinez fatally strangled, completely independent from the kidnapping/rape in which Martinez played no role. In a short opinion, the Ninth Circuit offered this recitation of California law:

> Even assuming that one or more members of Dominguez's jury was uncertain as to whether Dominguez, Martinez, or both strangled the victim, Dominguez's conviction for felony murder was not an unreasonable application of clearly established Supreme Court precedent. Dominguez contends that his due process rights were violated by the trial court's failure to instruct the jury on certain elements of California's felony murder rule. Any instructional error, however, was harmless. Even if the jury determined that Dominguez

[handwritten annotation: "misleading quote"]

kidnapped and brutally raped his victim and then stood idly by as Martinez killed her, as a matter of California law this satisfies the "logical connection" element of the state's felony murder rule. *Cavitt,* 33 Cal.4th at 196, 203. Similarly, even if the jury did not find that Martinez intended to aid and abet Dominguez in the underlying rape, California's felony murder rule did not so require. *Dominguez,* 39 Cal.4th at 1162, citing *Cavitt, supra.* Because we are bound by state courts' interpretations of their own laws, we are unpersuaded by Dominguez's claim of instructional error.

*Dominguez v. Felker,* 400 Fed.Appx. 153, 155-56 (9th Cir. 2010). This I take to be an inaccurate statement of law *unless* Martinez was accomplice to the kidnapping or rape. Otherwise the killing would just float free, cut off from any legal link between the two men. In this regard, *Cavitt,* relied on by the California Supreme Court and the Ninth Circuit in *Dominguez,* is inapposite. There was no doubt that all three—Cavitt, Williams, and McKnight—were principal or accomplice in the burglary/robbery of Betty, whose killing was temporally and causally related to the underlying offense(s), regardless of which of the participants smothered her. Without establishing Martinez not just as killer but also as Dominguez's accomplice in the kidnapping or rape, Dominguez's felony-murder conviction is legally unsupportable.

## C. PROVOCATIVE-ACT MURDER: A TRACT ON CAUSATION

By upholding the convictions of Stamp, Koory, and to an even greater extent, Lehman (as getaway driver), *Stamp* deployed a jarringly extended notion of causal responsibility by calling all three "murderers" of Honeyman, who died from fright. But at least *Stamp* was true to the all-for-one principle enunciated in *Cabaltero,* which ruled that killings by felons are shared by (nearly) all members of the felonious enterprise. But what is the fate of a felon when the killing is committed by someone *outside* the crime, say, a self-defending victim, a police officer, or an intervening bystander? We could say that in such cases the felony is a but-for cause of the killing, but that may go so far as to surpass the limits of proximate causation.

Cases like these are treated in a variety of ways: from 1) letting the felon off the hook for the killing; to 2) holding all felons responsible for the killing, even one committed by an outsider (regardless of the likelihood that death would occur in such a manner); to 3) a middle position relying on a version of malice that requires that the felon undertake action knowing it to be dangerous to life, whether that danger is posed by a) the felon himself, b) a confederate, or c) the potential deadly reaction of someone outside the felony altogether. This third or middle position, sometimes referred to as "provocative act murder," is designed to resolve cases that can be complex tracts on causation.

In our next principal case, *People v. Cervantes*, 26 Cal.4th 860 (2001), the victim is not only killed by someone *outside* an underlying triggering felony, but by someone who is neither a back-to-the-wall victim nor a police officer doing his or her job. Instead, the killer is a bystander with no realistic claim to have been forced by the felon into defending against a serious, potentially deadly, aggression. Specifically, the killing is a deliberate act of revenge against an innocent person, whose death is blamed on a surviving felon, whose "provocative" actions motivated the killer to use deadly force.

Whose fault, exactly, is such a response?

## SUPREME COURT OF CALIFORNIA

THE PEOPLE, PLAINTIFF AND RESPONDENT

V.

ISRAEL CERVANTES, DEFENDANT AND APPELLANT

AUG. 27, 2001

BAXTER, Justice

This case presents a question concerning proof of proximate cause in a provocative act murder case. We granted review to decide whether defendant, a member of a street gang, who perpetrated a nonfatal shooting that quickly precipitated a revenge killing by members of an opposing street gang, is guilty of murder on the facts before us. We conclude that he is not.

## Facts and Procedural History

Shortly after midnight on October 30, 1994, defendant and fellow Highland Street gang members went to a birthday party in Santa Ana thrown by the Alley Boys gang for one of their members. Joseph Perez, the prosecution's gang expert, testified the Highland Street and Alley Boys gangs were not enemies at the time. Over 100 people were in attendance at the party, many of them gang members.

Outside of the house, defendant approached a woman he knew named Grace. She was heavily intoxicated and declined defendant's invitation to go to another party with him, which prompted him to call her a "ho," leading to an exchange of crude insults. Juan Cisneros, a member of the Alley Boys, approached and told defendant not to "disrespect" his "homegirl." Richard Linares, also an Alley Boy, tried to defuse the situation, but Cisneros drew a gun and threatened to "cap [defendant's] ass." After someone slipped a gun into defendant's pocket and warned him in Spanish to "be careful," defendant brandished the gun, prompting Linares to intervene again, pushing or touching defendant on the shoulder to try to separate him from Cisneros. In response, defendant stated "nobody touches me" and shot Linares through the arm and chest.

A crowd of some 50 people was watching these events unfold. Someone yelled, "Why did you shoot my home boy?" or "your home boy shot your own homeboy," to which someone responded "Highland Street is the one that shot." A melee erupted, and gang challenges were exchanged. Somewhere between several seconds and a minute or two later, a group of Alley Boys spotted Hector Cabrera entering his car and driving away. Recognizing him as a member of the Highland Street gang, they fired a volley of shots, killing him. A variety of shell casings recovered from the street evidenced that at least five different shooters had participated in the murder of Cabrera.

Perez testified that although the Highland Street and Alley Boys gangs were not enemies at the time of the shootings, both gangs would be expected to be armed. The Alley Boys would consider the shooting of Linares to be an act of "major disrespect" to their gang on defendant's part. They would be expected to respond quickly with equal or greater force against defendant or Highland Street members. Therefore, Perez opined, Cabrera's death was a reasonably foreseeable result of defendant's actions.

Defendant testified he did not intend to shoot Linares, but was simply trying to protect himself from Cisneros, who drew his weapon first. He was surprised when his gun went off, because he did not feel it fire or see any flash. He testified, "I don't know if I shot Linares or somebody else shot him, but what I do know is that if I had attempted to murder anybody, I would have shot him while he was on the floor." In the confusion following the shooting of Linares, defendant heard someone say, "Your home boy shot your own home boy," and then he heard someone say "Highland's the one that shot." Realizing he was in danger, defendant ran from the party and sped off with several others. He heard shots being fired as they drove away. He was stopped by police and arrested a short distance away.

Defendant was charged with the murder of Cabrera, attempted murder of Linares, plus drug and weapons offenses. The relevant instructions informed the jury that murder is unlawful homicide with malice aforethought, that malice could be implied from the deliberate doing of a dangerous act with indifference to human life, and that the doing of a provocative act that resulted in death could be such an act.[6]

The jury was further instructed that liability for homicide requires a causal connection between an unlawful act and death, namely, that the direct, natural and probable consequences of the act be death.... A direct, natural and probable consequence must be reasonably foreseeable, measured objectively under a reasonable person test.[8] The jury convicted defendant of all charges. He appeals only his conviction of the murder of Cabrera, fixed at second degree.

---

[6] A homicide committed during the commission of a crime by a person who is not a perpetrator of such crime, in response to an intentional provocative act by a perpetrator of the crime other than the deceased, is an unlawful killing by the surviving perpetrator of the crime. An intentional provocative act is defined as follows: 1) The act was intentional; 2) The natural consequences of the act were dangerous to human life; and 3) The act was deliberately performed with knowledge of the danger to, and with conscious disregard for human life.

In order to prove such crime, each of the following elements must be proved: 1) The crime of assault with a firearm or attempted voluntary manslaughter or attempted murder was committed; 2) During the commission of the crime the defendant committed an intentional provocative act; 3) Another person not a perpetrator of the crime of assault with a firearm or attempted voluntary manslaughter or attempted murder, in response to the provocative act, killed another person; and 4) The defendant's commission of the intentional provocative act was a cause of the death of Hector Cabrera.

If you find that the crime of murder was committed, you must find it to be of the second degree. CALJIC No. 8.12.

[8] The jury was told: A direct, natural and probable consequence is reasonably

## Discussion

Provocative act murder was the sole theory under which defendant was tried and convicted of the murder of Hector Cabrera. At the close of evidence, defendant sought judgment of acquittal on the murder charge for want of "sufficient evidence of a provocative act to permit the jury to find the defendant liable for the death of Hector Cabrera." The trial court denied the motion.[9]

In affirming the conviction, the Court of Appeal commented:

> We have considerable difficulty with an argument conceding this was a 'pure, deliberate revenge killing,' yet tries to distance itself from the concept of provocative act. We see no reason the provocative act doctrine should not apply. Granted, a couple of minutes may have elapsed between the time Linares and Cabrera were shot. However, during this relatively brief interval, the potential for violence escalated rapidly as gang members drew weapons and issued threats. And as soon as the Alley Boys spotted their target (Cabrera), they wasted no time exacting their deadly revenge. Because Cervantes set in motion a fast-moving chain of events which led directly to Cabrera's death, it is immaterial the killing occurred a few minutes after the provocative act.

Now on appeal from the Court of Appeal, the question before us is whether sufficient evidence supports defendant's conviction of murder based on provocative act murder. Viewing the evidence in the light most favorable to the guilty verdict, we ask whether any rational trier of fact could have found the essential elements of the crime beyond a reasonable doubt. *See People v. Staten*, 24 Cal.4th 434, 460

---

foreseeable. The defendant need not intend that the ultimate crime be committed, nor need he even personally foresee that it may be committed. It is enough that objectively it is reasonably foreseeable that the ultimate crime may occur. With respect to the foreseeability of the ultimate result, the issue does not turn on the defendant's subjective state of mind but on whether, under all the circumstances presented, a reasonable person in the defendant's position would have or should have known that the ultimate result was a reasonably foreseeable consequence of the intended crime.

[9] Defendant also sought to have the jury instructed that in order to convict him of provocative act murder it had to find the Alley Boys' response to his provocative act was "reasonable." The trial court denied the request to modify the standard provocative act murder instruction. CALJIC No. 8.12.

(2000). The element at issue here is proximate cause in a provocative act murder case.

In homicide cases, a "cause of the death is an act or omission that sets in motion a chain of events that produces as a direct, natural and probable consequence of the act or omission the death of the decedent and without which the death would not occur." CALJIC No. 3.40. In general, "proximate cause is clearly established where the act is directly connected with the resulting injury, with no intervening force operating." 1 Witkin & Epstein, California Criminal Law §36, at 242 (3d ed. 2000). In this case there was an intervening force in operation—at least five persons at the party, presumably all members of the Alley Boys, shot and killed Highland Street gang member Hector Cabrera in a hail of bullets shortly after the melee erupted. But that does not end our inquiry, because the "defendant may also be criminally liable for a result directly caused by his or her act, even though there is another contributing cause." *Id.* at §37, at 243; CALJIC No. 3.41.

Beginning with *People v. Washington*, 62 Cal.2d 777 (1965) and *People v. Gilbert*, 63 Cal.2d 690 (1965), we have found implied malice murder when criminal defendants neither kill nor intend to kill, but cause a third party to kill in response to their life-threatening provocative acts. The provocative act murder doctrine was originally conceived as a form of implied malice murder, derived as an offshoot of the felony murder rule. *See Washington*, 62 Cal.2d at 782 ["Defendants who initiate gun battles may also be found guilty of murder if their victims resist and kill. Under such circumstances, the defendant for a base, antisocial motive and with wanton disregard for human life, does an act that involves a high degree of probability that it will result in death, and it is unnecessary to imply malice by invoking the felony murder doctrine."].[10]

Provocative act murder has typically been invoked when the perpetrator of the underlying crime instigates a gun battle, either by firing first or by otherwise engaging in severe, life-threatening, and usually gun-wielding conduct, and the police, or a victim of the

---

[10] The provocative act murder doctrine does not itself define a crime, as that is a legislative function. Instead, it is a descriptive category or shorthand formula denoting certain circumstances under which a defendant comes within the statutory definition of murder when his or her unlawful conduct provokes another into committing the fatal act.

underlying crime, responds with privileged lethal force by shooting back and killing the perpetrator's accomplice or an innocent bystander. *See, e.g., Washington, supra* [robbery victim kills accomplice]; *Gilbert, supra* [police officer kills accomplice].[11] In both *Gilbert* and *Washington*, defendants' provocative acts consisted of starting a gun battle during a robbery, causing a victim or a police officer to shoot and kill another. In *Washington* we were concerned mainly with distinguishing the doctrine from felony murder. It was in *Gilbert* that we first developed the provocative act theory of murder more fully. One of defendant's accomplices started a gun battle and a police officer mortally wounded another accomplice in response. After deciding the jury had been improperly instructed in matters not relevant here, we articulated "principles that may be invoked to convict a defendant of murder for a killing committed by another." *Gilbert*, 63 Cal.2d at 704.

We first explained there must be proof of malice aforethought; in *Gilbert*, implied malice:

> When the defendant or his accomplice, with a conscious disregard for life, intentionally commits an act that is likely to cause death, and his victim or a police officer kills in reasonable response to such act, the defendant is guilty of

---

[11] *See also People v. Caldwell*, 36 Cal.3d 210 (1984) [police officer kills accomplice]; *Taylor v. Superior Court*, 3 Cal.3d 578 (1970) [robbery victim kills accomplice], *overruled on other grounds in People v. Antick*, 15 Cal.3d 79, 92 n.12 (1975); *People v. Garcia*, 69 Cal.App.4th 1324 (1999) [home invasion robbery victim kills accomplice].

In *Pizano v. Superior Court*, 21 Cal.3d 128 (1978), we held that the provocative act murder doctrine could be applied where the "shield" victim of a residential robbery was shot and killed *by a neighbor* who was trying to prevent the robbers from escaping. We explained that "the principles announced in *Gilbert* and its progeny are not limited to cases in which the person actually committing the homicide is either a victim of the felony or a police officer." *Id.* at 136. Several recent cases have invoked the doctrine when the provoked shooter who responds with deadly force to the defendant's felonious and life-threatening provocative conduct is himself engaged in criminal conduct. *See, e.g., In re Aurelio R.*, 167 Cal.App.3d 52 (1985) [A minor and his fellow gang members drove into rival gang territory armed and intent upon exacting revenge for an earlier attack on one of their own. In the ensuing gun battle, one of the minor's accomplices was killed by a rival gang member]; *People v. Gardner*, 37 Cal.App.4th 473 (1995) [defendant, a drug dealer, shot at the victim, also a drug dealer, who in the course of fleeing defendant's shots was fatally gunned down by yet a third armed drug dealer who believed defendant's shots were being fired at him].

> murder. In such a case, the killing is attributable, not merely to the commission of a felony, but to the intentional act of the defendant or his accomplice committed with conscious disregard for life.

*Id.* We then discussed causation: "The victim's self-defensive killing or the police officer's killing in the performance of his duty cannot be considered an independent intervening cause for which the defendant is not liable, for it is a reasonable response to the dilemma thrust upon the victim or the policeman by the intentional act of the defendant or his accomplice." *Id.* at 705.

In short, *Gilbert* described provocative act murder in terms of proximate cause and malice, implicitly reaffirming that no criminal liability attaches to an initial remote actor for an unlawful killing that results from an independent intervening (superseding) cause. In contrast, when the death results from a dependent intervening cause, the chain of causation remains unbroken and the initial actor is liable for the homicide.

This basic principle of proximate cause was articulated over a century ago in our decision in *People v. Lewis*, 124 Cal. 551 (1899), where defendant shot the victim in the intestines, sending him toward a painful and inevitable death he hastened by slitting his own throat. We held Lewis was properly convicted of manslaughter because the victim's response, though suicidal, was natural and understandable; hence it was not an independent intervening cause of death. Even "if the deceased did die from the effect of the knife wound alone, no doubt the defendant would be responsible if the jury could have found from the evidence that the knife wound was caused by the wound inflicted by the defendant in the natural course of events." *Id.* at 555. By contrast, "[s]uppose one assaults and wounds another intending to take life, but the wound, though painful, is not even dangerous, and the wounded man knows that it is not mortal, and yet takes his own life to escape pain, would it not be suicide only?" The answer would be yes, and there would be no homicide liability, if "the wound induced the suicide, but the wound was not, in the usual course of things, the cause of the suicide" (*id.*)—in other words, if death would not have inevitably followed and instead occurred through the independent intervening cause of the victim's own will to die.

The principle was revisited in *People v. Fowler*, 178 Cal. 657 (1918). Fowler bludgeoned Duree with a club and left him lying in the road, where a motorist drove over him. We explained it did not matter whether the immediate instrument of death was Fowler's club or the motorist's car, because so long as the driver did not purposely drive over Duree, Fowler's acts proximately caused Duree's death. Therefore, Fowler's liability varied in accordance with his *mens rea* in committing the act that proximately caused Duree's death; he could be guilty of murder, manslaughter, or no crime at all. *Id.* at 669.

More recently, in *People v. Roberts*, 2 Cal.4th 271 (1992) (en banc), we reiterated that "[t]he criminal law thus is clear that for liability to be found, the cause of the harm not only must be direct, but also not so remote as to fail to constitute the natural and probable consequence of the defendant's act." *Id.* at 319. Commentators and drafters have made this conclusion explicit. *See* MPC §2.03(2)(b) [when purpose or knowledge of a result is an element of an offense, the actor is not liable for an unintended or uncontemplated result unless "the actual result involves the same kind of injury or harm as that designed or contemplated and is not too remote or accidental in its occurrence to have a bearing on the actor's liability or on the gravity of his offense."].

In *Roberts*, a state prison inmate walked down a corridor as his fellow inmates, including the defendant, lounged against the walls on both sides. He was attacked and emerged with 11 stab wounds that shortly caused his death. The dying inmate, in an "unconscious state brought on by hypovolemic shock," grabbed a knife from the floor and pursued one of his assailants up a flight of stairs to the second floor where he reflexively plunged the knife into the chest of a prison guard, killing him. *Id.* at 316. The defendant was charged with the murder of both the inmate and the correctional officer. Although ultimately reversing for instructional error, we found the evidence sufficient for the jury to find the defendant's acts were a proximate cause of the officer's death.

We placed reliance in *Roberts* on several out-of-state authorities. In an early Illinois case, *Belk v. People*, 125 Ill. 584 (1888), defendants were alleged to have negligently allowed their team of horses to break loose on a narrow country lane. The team collided with a wagon in plain sight just ahead, causing that wagon's team of horses to panic and run away, throwing the victim, a passenger, to her death. The Illinois court reversed the resulting manslaughter convictions on other grounds, but reasoned that "'[b]etween the acts of omission or commission of the defendants, by which it is alleged the collision occurred, and the injury of the deceased, there was not an interposition of a human will acting independently or any extraordinary natural phenomena, to break the causal connection.'" *Roberts*, 2 Cal.4th at 318, quoting *Belk*, 17 N.E. at 745.

We also cited *Madison v. State*, 234 Ind. 517 (1955), in which the court found implied malice and affirmed a conviction of second degree murder when the defendant threw a hand grenade at one Couch who, presumably impulsively and not as an act of will, kicked it to another who was killed. The fact that Couch kicked the grenade did not break the line of causation. *Roberts*, 2 Cal.4th at 319.

And we recalled *Wright v. State*, 363 So.2d 617 (Fla. 1st D.C.A. 1978), where defendant was convicted of manslaughter for firing from his car into his intended victim's car. The intended victim had "'rapidly accelerated his car while ducking bullets'" and fatally ran over a pedestrian. *Roberts*, 2 Cal.4th at 319, *quoting Wright*, 363 So.2d at 618. We found the significance of the facts and holding in *Wright* to be as follows: "Shots that cause a driver to accelerate impulsively and run over a nearby pedestrian suffice to confer liability; but if the driver, still upset, had proceeded for several miles before killing a pedestrian, at some point the required causal nexus would have become too attenuated for the shooter to be liable even for manslaughter, much less for first degree murder." *Roberts*, 2 Cal.4th at 321.

In sum, an independent intervening cause will absolve a defendant of criminal liability. However, to be independent the intervening cause must be unforeseeable—an extraordinary and abnormal occurrence, which rises to the level of an exonerating, superseding cause. On the other hand, a dependent intervening cause will not relieve the defendant of criminal liability. A defendant may be criminally liable for a result directly caused by his act even if there is another contributing cause. If an intervening cause is a normal and reasonably foreseeable result of defendant's original act, the intervening act is dependent and not a superseding cause, and will not relieve defendant of liability. The consequence need not have been a strong probability; a possible consequence which might reasonably have been contemplated is enough. The precise consequence need not have been foreseen; it is enough that the defendant should have foreseen the possibility of some harm of the kind which might result from his act. One commentator explained the acts of a second party to be a remote, independent intervening (superseding) cause in these terms: "The free, deliberate, and informed intervention of a second person, who intends to exploit the situation created by the first, but is not acting in concert with him, relieves the first actor of criminal responsibility." Hart & Honoré, Causation in the Law 326 (2d ed. 1985).

In *Roberts*, we explained that "there is no bright line demarcating a legally sufficient proximate cause from one that is too remote. Ordinarily the question will be for the jury, though in some instances undisputed evidence may reveal a cause so remote that a court may properly decide that no rational trier of fact could find the needed nexus." *Roberts*, 2 Cal.4th at 320 n.11. The matters of policy which determine just where the limitations of juridical recognition shall be placed upon the broad field of actual cause, are grounded partly upon notions of fairness and justice.

Turning to the facts at hand, we agree with defendant that the evidence introduced below is insufficient to support his conviction of provocative act murder, for it fails to establish proximate cause. The facts are distinct from classic provocative act murder in a number of respects. Defendant was not the initial aggressor in the incident that gave rise to the provocative act.[12] There was no direct evidence that Cabrera's unidentified murderers were even present at the scene of the provocative act, i.e., in a position to actually witness defendant shoot Linares. Ballistics evidence supported the inference that Cabrera was murdered by several individuals. Although there was some evidence that Cisneros and prosecution witness Francisco Guluarte were among the shooters, they were not prosecuted for Cabrera's murder, nor did the prosecution seek to use their possible complicity in the murder to establish its case-in-chief against defendant for provocative act murder.

Defendant was not present where Cabrera was fatally gunned down; the only evidence introduced on point suggests he was already running away from the party or speeding off in his car when the

---

[12] Cisneros confronted defendant for "disrespecting" his "homegirl," and pulled out his gun with which he threatened defendant. The People do not contend that defendant's act of talking to Grace, a woman he knew who was associated with the Alley Boys, or even his calling her a "ho" when she rebuffed him, was itself a provocative act that would foreseeably give rise to threats of violence from the Alley Boys, much less escalate into a retaliatory murder. The prosecution's own gang expert testified that the Highland Street and Alley Boys gangs were not enemies; that both gangs attended the party, and conversed instead of immediately shooting when the situation escalated to pushing and shoving and the display of guns, reflected the participants were not enemies.

victim was murdered. But the critical fact that distinguishes this from other provocative act murder cases is that here the actual murderers were not responding to defendant's provocative act by shooting back at him or an accomplice, in the course of which someone was killed.[15] They were not in the shoes of the police officers in *Gilbert* or *Caldwell* who shot back and killed an accomplice as an objectively "reasonable response to the dilemma thrust upon them" by the defendant's malicious and life-endangering provocative acts. *Gilbert*, 63 Cal.2d at 705. Nor were they acting without volition as was the inmate in *Roberts* who, having been rendered unconscious from stab wounds inflicted by defendant Roberts, "reflexively" responded by stabbing a prison guard to death, *Roberts*, 2 Cal.4th at 321, or as was the intermediary in *Madison v. State*, 234 Ind. 517 (1955), who instinctively kicked away a live hand grenade thrown at him by defendant Madison, resulting in the death of another.

Although cases like *Fowler*, *Roberts* and *Madison* are intervening-act causation homicide cases in that the victims' deaths came at the hands of an intermediary, it would be a misnomer to label them provocative act murder cases. Neither the unidentified driver who ran over the victim left in the roadway in *Fowler*, the inmate who unconsciously and reflexively stabbed the prison guard in *Roberts*, nor the intermediary who instinctively kicked the hand grenade away from himself in *Madison* were "provoked" into taking their deadly actions in the sense that the police officers in *Gilbert* and *Caldwell* were provoked into shooting back during the robberies involved in those cases. Because provocative act murder was derived from felony murder (usually robberies) and was conceived as a caveat to the felony murder rule, confusion can be avoided if use of the term "provocative act murder" is reserved for that category of cases where,

---

[15] In *Washington* and *Gilbert* we first applied principles of implied-malice murder and intervening-act causation to situations in which criminal defendants neither killed nor intended to kill, but instead caused a third party to kill *in response* to their life-threatening provocative acts. The traditional provocative act factual pattern is but a subset of those homicide cases in which death results through the acts of an intermediary. In all homicide cases in which the conduct of an intermediary is the actual cause of death, the defendant's liability will depend on whether it can be demonstrated that his own conduct *proximately* caused the victim's death—i.e., whether it can be shown that the intermediary's conduct was merely a dependent intervening cause of death, and not an independent superseding cause. If proximate causation is established, the defendant's level of culpability for the homicide in turn will vary in accordance with his *mens rea*.

during commission of a crime, the intermediary (a police officer or crime victim) is provoked by the defendant's conduct into shooting back, resulting in someone's death.

In classic provocative act murder, *malice is implied* from the provocative act, and the resulting crime is second-degree murder. But whether or not a defendant's unlawful conduct is literally "provocative," when it proximately causes an intermediary to kill through a dependent intervening act, the defendant's liability for the homicide will be fixed in accordance with his mens rea. If the defendant proximately causes a homicide through the acts of an intermediary and does so with malice and premeditation, his crime will be murder in the first degree, *Gilbert, supra*, at 705, irrespective of whether his conduct, in a literal sense, provoked the intermediary into killing. If the defendant proximately causes a homicide through the acts of an intermediary and does so without malice, his crime will be manslaughter, once again, irrespective of whether the conduct, in a literal sense, provoked the intermediary into taking deadly action.

To the contrary, the acts of the actual murderers here were themselves criminal, felonious, and perpetrated with malice aforethought. The fatal shots were fired, not at the defendant or an accomplice, but instead at a third party (Cabrera) who was not a party to the initial provocative act. It can further be said that the murderers of Cabrera intended to exploit the situation created by defendant, but were not acting in concert with him, a circumstance normally held to relieve the first actor of criminal responsibility. In short, nobody forced the Alley Boys' murderous response in this case, if indeed it was a direct response to defendant's act of shooting Linares. The willful and malicious murder of Cabrera by others was an independent intervening act on which defendant's liability for the murder could not be based.

That the murder occurred a very short time after defendant shot Linares, and the opinion of prosecution gang expert Perez that Cabrera's murder was a foreseeable consequence of defendant's shooting of Linares in the context of a street gang's code of honor mentality, was the only evidence on which the jury was asked to find that Cabrera's murder was "a direct, natural, and probable consequence" of defendant's act of shooting Linares. Given that the murder of Cabrera by other parties was itself felonious, intentional, perpetrated with malice aforethought, and directed at a victim who was not involved in the original altercation between defendant and

Linares, the evidence is insufficient to establish the requisite proximate cause to hold defendant liable for murder.

### Conclusion

The judgment of the Court Appeal affirming defendant's conviction of murder is reversed, and the matter remanded for proceedings consistent with the views expressed herein.

GEORGE, C.J., KENNARD, CHIN, WERDEGAR, and BROWN, JJ., concurred.

## QUESTIONS ON *CERVANTES*

**1. Scapegoating in the courts below.** Cervantes was in the Highland Street gang and attended a birthday party thrown by the Alley Boys gang in Santa Ana. When Cervantes argued with a woman named Grace outside the house, Cisneros—an Alley Boy and friend to Grace—took up on her behalf. Linares, also an Alley Boy, was non-fatally shot by Cervantes in the arm and chest while trying to mediate between Cisneros and Cervantes, both of whom were armed. Very shortly thereafter, at least five different Alley Boys shot at Highland Street's Hector Cabrera, killing him as he entered his car to flee.

Cervantes claimed his shooting Linares was accidental. After drawing the weapon that someone slipped him during the scuffle as a self-protective gesture, he had no recollection of pulling the trigger. Thus, when he fled thereafter, he was motivated by fear, not guilt. Cervantes disputed any causal connection between his shooting Linares on the one hand and the Alley Boys shooting Cabrera on the other. Nonetheless, Cervantes was charged with and convicted of, *inter alia*, attempted murder of Linares and second-degree implied-malice murder of Cabrera. He appealed only his murder conviction to the Court of Appeal, which affirmed. In the California Supreme Court, he renewed his challenge to his murder conviction, which, he successfully claimed, lacked sufficient evidence of a causal connection between his actions and the death of Cabrera to justify a conviction of implied-malice murder on his part.

Although five Alley Boys performed a "pure, deliberate revenge killing" of Cabrera anywhere from a few seconds to a couple of minutes after Cervantes had shot Linares, in the view of the jury and the Court of Appeal, the malicious acts of Cervantes somehow killed

Cabrera. But if such a causal account of the killing is plausible, then why not also blame Cabrera's death 1) on Cisneros, who pulled a gun on Cervantes, who was arguing with Grace? 2) on Cervantes's provocative act of insulting Grace? 3) on Grace herself, for doing whatever she did to provoke Cervantes into insulting her? See *Cervantes*, 26 Cal.4th at 872 n.12.

Which two of the three questions I've just posed above must be rhetorical, that is, asked only for effect? *What* effect?

**2. Judicially created crime?** In footnote 10, the California Supreme Court states that "provocative act murder" is not a crime, given that only a legislature can invent a crime, not a court. Though the legislature has invented no such crime as "provocative act murder," it is mentioned in the very first line of the court's section entitled "Discussion" and numerous (by my count, 14) times elsewhere in the opinion. Is "provocative act murder" a crime or not? For that matter, is implied-malice murder a crime? How about express-malice murder?

**3. Doctrinal limits of provocative act murder.** Footnote 11 is divided into two paragraphs. The first paragraph features cases of a type different from two of the four cases featured in the second paragraph.

a. With which cases from footnote 11 does *Cervantes* fit best?

b. With which cases from footnote 11 does the following, an excerpt from a recent state high court ruling, fit best?

> This record contains ample evidence to support a conclusion that Perla committed a provocative act that caused Canas to kill Morales. The evening before the killing, Perla plotted with Ricardo and other members of the family to "kick Canas's ass." That night, Perla went with Morales and Jorge to meet Canas, anticipating a violent confrontation. Morales brought a BB gun and shot it out the car window several times while waiting for Canas, [who] did not appear. The next morning, Perla roused Jorge and then Morales for another attack on Canas. It was Perla's idea to ambush Canas at the corner where he routinely picked up his young daughter. [Perla] then drove to the corner with a loaded rifle in her car, and tried to induce [Ricardo's mother] to leave the scene before their target arrived. While Morales attacked Canas and stabbed him, Perla stayed near the car containing the rifle she had brought.

When Canas appeared to get the upper hand in the fight, Morales ran to Perla. Perla got the rifle from her car, cocked it, and turned toward Canas. Having made clear to Morales what she intended him to do, she handed him the rifle. A struggle ensued during which Canas was shot three times. He then managed to seize the gun and [fatally] shoot his attacker. By bringing a loaded rifle to the scene, preparing it for firing, then handing it to her accomplice, Perla dramatically escalated the level of violence in the encounter. Introducing a loaded firearm into the fight went beyond the acts necessary to "kick Canas's ass." In producing the rifle, turning it toward Canas, and putting it in the hands of Morales, who had just stabbed Canas in the face, Perla performed acts fraught with grave and inherent danger to human life.

**4. Reasonableness of what?** The California Supreme Court credits its own ruling in *People v. Gilbert*, 63 Cal.2d 690 (1965) with wedging "provocative act murder" into the law of murder. There the state high court found a sufficient causal connection between Gilbert initiating a gun battle during a robbery and a police officer's on-the-scene use of deadly force against one of Gilbert's accomplices (Weaver). *Cervantes* quotes with approval *Gilbert*'s remark that robbers can be held responsible for an innocent's use of deadly force as "'a reasonable response to the dilemma thrust upon the victim or the policeman by the intentional act of the defendant or his accomplice.'" *Cervantes*, 26 Cal.4th at 868 (quoting *Gilbert*, 63 Cal.2d at 704).

Relying on CALJIC No. 3.40, the *Cervantes* trial court instructed that the Alley Boys' deadly response to the malicious acts of Cervantes had to be "a consequence which is reasonably foreseeable." *Id.* at 865 n.8. Yet the *Cervantes* Court noted without comment that the trial court rejected Cervantes's request that the jury be instructed to read into the causal element of murder that the Alley Boys' deadly response to the shooting of Linares be "reasonable." *Id.* at 866 n.9. Is "reasonable" as used in footnote 9 referring to the same notion of "reasonable" as is used in footnote 8? Put slightly differently, did the trial court err in rejecting Cervantes's requested instruction?

## NOTES ON *CERVANTES*

***1. Inheriting the malice of co-felons.*** Compare *Cervantes* with *People v. Caldwell*, 36 Cal.3d 210 (1984) (en banc), where the

California Supreme Court upheld the "provocative act murder" convictions of a principal robber and an accomplice/getaway driver who drove in the early evening with his lights off for 5-10 miles at high speeds while being chased by L.A. County Sheriff's Deputies. The two culprits and a third man had just robbed $24 from a Church's Fried Chicken store. When a police cruiser eventually rammed the suspects' car head-on, a shotgun discharged without incident and flew out the window of the front-seat passenger (Washington). The driver (Caldwell) took cover behind his door while the victim/rear passenger (Belvin) pointed a gun at deputies, prompting them to open fire, a shot—"probably" from Deputy Lopez—killing Belvin.

Caldwell and Washington appealed their murder convictions on the ground that it was Belvin's malice alone—for aiming a gun at the deputies—that prompted them to open fire. While Washington was malicious as well for wielding a shotgun during the getaway, he and Caldwell contended that because Washington was disarmed before police opened fire, his malice made no causal contribution to Belvin's death. Caldwell denied any malice on his own part: all he had done was refuse to turn himself in. Although Deputy McSweeney thought Caldwell had a gun, only Belvin's handgun and Washington's shotgun were recovered. Still, the California Supreme Court ruled that either Caldwell or Washington demonstrated sufficient malice that causally contributed to Belvin's death, thus upholding their murder convictions.

Crucial to the convictions of Caldwell and Washington for murdering Belvin is that at least one surviving felon was malicious and causally contributed to his death. In other words, if Belvin was the only malicious actor of the three, and his malice alone caused the deputies to open fire and kill only him, then neither Caldwell nor Washington would be responsible for Belvin's death. The reason would be that a felon had to have murdered Belvin before other felons could share the blame. If Belvin was the sole malicious actor who caused Deputy Lopez to kill him, then he did not commit murder, which requires the killing of *another person, not himself.* If Belvin killed himself, then there was no legally cognizable murder for him to share with Caldwell and Washington. See *People v. Antick*, 15 Cal.3d 79, 92 n.12 (1975). *If*, in addition to Belvin, Washington too had been deemed malicious (which he was) and Caldwell had been deemed non-malicious (which he was not), still Caldwell would be on the hook for Belvin's murder, committed by Washington "through" Lopez.

The theory? Application of CALJIC Nos. 3.01 and 3.02. The 3.01 crime is robbery, to which Caldwell, who never entered the store, was accomplice to Washington and Belvin, both of whom were principal robbers. On such an account, the 3.02 crime was the "provocative act murder" of Belvin by Washington, again, "through" Deputy Lopez, who was just doing his job. That natural and probable consequence of the robbery would be shared by all surviving members of the robbery, provided that there was at least one malicious felon whose malice caused a death other than his own. Reviewing the conduct of both Caldwell and Washington, the California Supreme Court found them both to be malicious and causally relevant to Deputy Lopez's fatal shooting of Belvin, even though finding only one to have been so would have sufficed to hold the other responsible.

**2. Jury instruction on provocative act murder.** In footnote 6, the California Supreme Court quotes the trial court's instruction on provocative act murder: CALJIC No. 8.12 (1998). The more generalized instruction in California's book of pattern jury instructions was, as always, tailored by the trial court to fit the specific facts of the case. Thus, it is worth clarifying that CALJIC No. 8.12 (Spring 2013 Revision) applies now as it did then to other inherently dangerous underlying crimes apart from "assault with a firearm or attempted voluntary manslaughter or attempted murder." It is just that those were the crimes that, according to the prosecution, provoked the Alley Boys into going after Cabrera. Because the trial court knew that no one apart from Cervantes could be said to have riled up the Alley Boys into killing Cabrera, the instruction went on to state that, for Cervantes to have committed murder as understood by CALJIC No. 8.12, he must *himself* have committed an act that provoked someone into killing Cabrera. That is, Cervantes must have been malicious in his own right.

**3. Fate of parties.** Cervantes got his murder conviction reversed, but was resentenced to a whopping 60 years, based on attempted murder of Linares (25 years), possession of meth (25 years), and firearms offenses (10 years), a sentence puffed up by, of all things, his juvenile record. *People v. Cervantes*, 2003 WL 1611397 (Cal. 4th Dist. Ct. App.). On federal habeas corpus, constitutional challenges to his sentence based on due process, trial by jury, and cruel and unusual punishment went nowhere. See *Cervantes v. Hall*, 185 Fed.Appx. 690 (9th Cir. 2006). Cervantes is locked up at Folsom, parole-eligible in 2029. As for Linares, he barely survived being shot in the chest by Cervantes, only to be murdered in his Santa Ana driveway the next year at 23. See articles.latimes.com/1995-12-20/local/me-16170_1_gang-member.

4. **Proximate cause as a means of limiting responsibility.** The *Cervantes* Court relied on CALJIC Nos. 3.40-.41, which establish California's principles of proximate cause, which, in turn, recognize that there can be more than one cause of a harm so long as each variable makes a direct, foreseeable contribution to the harm, without which the harm would not have occurred. Proximate cause is a narrower alternative to but-for cause, which the law deems too broad for application in either civil or criminal contexts. Under but-for cause, we ask only: if we take away defendant's act, would the victim's harm have occurred anyway? If the answer is "no," then defendant is a but-for cause of the victim's harm. If the answer is "yes," then defendant is not a but-for cause of the victim's harm. Because many but-for causes are legally insignificant, but-for cause is a necessary but not sufficient basis of causal responsibility in law.

For example, suppose a defendant is accused of causing a friend's death after recommending that the friend take up cigarette smoking, hang-gliding, or psychoactive drugs. If the deceased already was a smoker, hang-glider, or drug-user at the time of the recommendation, then the recommending friend would not be a but-for cause of the death owing to those activities. As such, the recommending friend would have no causal responsibility for the ensuing activity-related death. But if the recommending friend actually *introduces* the activity to the deceased (who was not engaged in or even in the process of taking up the activity), then the friend is a but-for cause of the ensuing activity-related death. Yet, in such a case, the recommending friend would be off the hook because the death resulted from the independent choice of the deceased, whose *own* risk-taking did him or her in. It is that very sort of scenario that proximate cause serves to cut off from legal responsibility for an outcome: where defendant is a but-for cause of harm, but there's good reason to let defendant off the hook anyway. The good reason? When allocating responsibility between victim and defendant who both contributed to victim's demise, fairness must be informed by foreseeability. In other words, proximate cause is a legal device designed mainly to limit the responsibility of defendants who are *merely* but-for causes of the harms in question.

*Cervantes* reviewed proximate causation in criminal cases from an 1888 Illinois ruling through its own rulings both older (à la *Gilbert*: 1965) and newer (à la *Roberts*: 1992). What the state high court found to pervade those rulings was a longstanding though blurry line between "intervening" variables that do not break the causal chain of events begun by defendant and "superseding" variables that do break the causal chain of events begun by defendant. An intervening variable that does not break the causal chain keeps defendant on the hook as a proximate cause of the victim's harms; a superseding variable that does break the causal chain lets defendant off the hook on the ground that defendant was not a proximate cause of the victim's harms.

Thus, for example, initial non-mortal wounds inflicted by defendants could be superseded by the suicidal acts of their victims if such a response from their victims seems to us a wild overreaction: too remote from the initial injury inflicted by defendant to be fairly blamed on defendant. *See, e.g., People v. Lewis*, 124 Cal. 551 (1899). Whether the suicidal act breaks the causal chain (supersedes defendant's responsibility) or merely continues it (intervenes but does not supersede) is at times clear enough. For example, if a defendant batters a victim whose injuries require medical care that turns out to be negligently rendered, defendant remains on the hook as the proximate cause of the harms compounded by the medical staff (who also are on the hook for their own harm-causing actions). But suppose now that after the same battery a member of the medical staff intentionally compounds the victim's harms due to a personal grievance the staff member holds against the victim. In such a case defendant would be responsible only for the initial harm, not the harm intentionally aggravated by the retaliatory staff member.

In other cases, however, whether the subsequent occurrence supersedes defendant's contribution or merely intervenes is by no means clear; instead, it is a matter of what lawyers are fond of calling "policy." *Cervantes* is such a case, where the but-for connection between his actions and Cabrera's death is manifest, but whether to hold him responsible is a more complicated matter, informed by issues of fairness, foreseeability, and risk-allocation—again, what lawyers call policy issues.

**5. Proximate cause as a means of expanding responsibility.** In *Sindell v. Abbott Laboratories*, 26 Cal.3d 588 (1980), civil plaintiff Judith Sindell sued 11 drug companies on behalf of herself and other similarly situated women. The complaint alleged that between 1941 and 1971, defendants marketed and manufactured diethylstilbesterol (DES), a synthetic compound of the female hormone estrogen. The drug was administered to plaintiff's mother and the mothers of the class she represents, for the purpose of preventing miscarriage. In 1947, the Food and Drug Administration (FDA) authorized the marketing of DES as a miscarriage preventative, but only on an experimental basis, with a requirement that the drug contain a warning label to that effect.

DES may cause cancerous vaginal and cervical growths in the daughters exposed to it before birth, because their mothers took the drug during pregnancy. The form of cancer from which these daughters suffered is known as adenocarcinoma, and it manifests after a minimum latent period of 10-12 years. It is a fast-spreading and deadly disease, and radical surgery is required to prevent it from spreading. DES also causes adenosis, precancerous vaginal and cervical growths which may spread to other areas of the body. The treatment for adenosis is cauterization, surgery, or cryosurgery. Women who suffer from this condition must be monitored by biopsy or colposcopic examination twice a year, a painful and expensive procedure. Thousands of women whose mothers received DES during pregnancy were unaware of its effects.

In 1971, the FDA ordered defendants to cease marketing and promoting DES for the purpose of preventing miscarriages, and to warn physicians and the public that the drug should not be used by pregnant women because of the danger to their unborn children. During the period in which defendants marketed DES, they knew or should have known that it was a carcinogenic substance, that there was a grave danger after varying periods of latency it would cause cancerous and precancerous growths in the daughters of the mothers who took it, and that it was ineffective to prevent miscarriage. Nevertheless, defendants continued to advertise and market the drug as a miscarriage preventative. They failed to test DES for efficacy and safety; the tests performed by others, upon which they relied, indicated that it was not safe or effective. In violation of the authorization of the FDA, defendants marketed DES on an unlimited basis rather than as an experimental drug, and they failed to warn of its potential danger.

Because of defendants' advertised assurances that DES was safe and effective to prevent miscarriage, plaintiff was exposed to the drug prior to her birth. She became aware of the danger from such exposure within one year of the time she filed her complaint. As a result of the DES ingested by her mother, plaintiff developed a malignant bladder tumor which was removed by surgery. She suffered from adenosis and needed constant monitoring by biopsy or colposcopy to insure early warning of further malignancy.

Each of plaintiff's several causes of action alleged that defendants were jointly liable because they acted in concert, on the basis of express and implied agreements, and in reliance upon and ratification and exploitation of each other's testing and marketing methods. Plaintiff sought compensatory damages of $1 million and punitive damages of $10 million for herself. For the members of her class, she sought equitable relief in the form of an order that defendants warn physicians and others of the danger of DES and the necessity of performing certain tests to determine the presence of disease caused by the drug, and that they establish free clinics in California to perform such tests. Defendants demurred to the complaint. While the complaint did not expressly allege that plaintiff could not identify the manufacturer of the precise drug ingested by her mother, she stated in her points and authorities in opposition to the demurrers filed by some of the defendants that she was unable to make the identification, and the trial court sustained the demurrers of these defendants on the ground that plaintiff could not identify which defendant had manufactured the drug responsible for her injuries. Thereupon, the court dismissed the action. The appeal involved only five of ten defendants named in the complaint: Abbott Laboratories, Eli Lilly and Company, E.R. Squibb and Sons, The Upjohn Company, and Rexall Drug Company. The action was dismissed or the appeal abandoned on various grounds as to other defendants named in the complaint; e.g., one defendant demonstrated it had not manufactured DES during the period plaintiff's mother took the drug.

This case was one of a number filed throughout the country seeking to hold drug manufacturers liable for injuries allegedly resulting from DES prescribed to the plaintiffs' mothers since 1947. The estimated number of women who took the drug during pregnancy range from 1.5 million to 3 million. Hundreds, perhaps thousands, of the daughters of these women suffered from adenocarcinoma, and the incidence of vaginal adenosis among them was 30 to 90 percent. Most of the cases resulted in judgments in favor of the drug-company defendants because of the failure of the plaintiffs to identify the manufacturer of the DES prescribed to their mothers.

*Summers v. Tice*, 33 Cal.2d 80 (1948) best exemplifies the rule on which plaintiffs relied. In *Summers*, plaintiff was injured when two hunters negligently shot in his direction. It could not be determined which of them had fired the shot which actually caused the injury to the plaintiff's eye, but both defendants were nevertheless held jointly and severally liable for the whole of the damages. The California Supreme Court unanimously reasoned that both were wrongdoers, both were negligent toward the plaintiff, and it would be unfair to require plaintiff to isolate the defendant responsible, because if the one pointed out were to escape liability, the other might also, and the plaintiff-victim would be without a remedy. In these circumstances, the burden of proof shifted to the defendants, "each to absolve himself if he can." *Id.* at 86. *Summers* stated that under these or similar circumstances, defendants are ordinarily in a far better position to offer evidence to determine whether he or another defendant caused the injury. *Summers* relied upon *Ybarra v. Spangard*, 25 Cal.2d 486 (1944), a case in which the plaintiff was injured while he was unconscious during the course of surgery. He sought damages against several doctors and a nurse who attended him while he was unconscious. The court held that it would be unreasonable to require him to identify the particular defendant who had performed the alleged negligent act because he was unconscious at the time of the injury and the defendants exercised control over the instrumentalities which caused the harm. Therefore, an inference of negligence arose that defendants were required to meet by explaining their conduct.

In *Sindell*, central to the court's reinstatement of the action against the manufacturers was that advances in science and technology create fungible goods which may harm consumers and which cannot be traced to any specific producer. The response of the courts can be either to adhere rigidly to prior doctrine, denying recovery to those injured by such products, or to fashion remedies to meet these changing needs. *Sindell* acknowledged that some adaptation of the rules of causation and liability was appropriate in these recurring circumstances. In the court's view, the most persuasive reason for reinstating plaintiff's cause of action was advanced in *Summers*: between an innocent plaintiff and negligent defendants, the latter should bear the cost of the injury. Here, as in *Summers*, plaintiff was not at fault in failing to provide evidence of causation, and although the absence of such evidence is not attributable to the defendants either, their conduct in marketing a drug whose effects are delayed for many years played a significant role in creating the unavailability of proof.

From a broader policy standpoint, defendants were better able to bear the cost of injury resulting from the manufacture of a defective product. The cost of an injury and the loss of time or health may be an overwhelming misfortune to the person injured, and a needless one, for the risk of injury can be insured by the manufacturer and distributed among the public as a cost of doing business. The manufacturer is in the best position to discover and guard against defects in its products and to warn of harmful effects; thus, holding it liable for defects and failure to warn of harmful effects provides an incentive to product safety. These considerations are particularly significant where medication is involved, for consumers are helpless to protect themselves from serious, sometimes permanent, sometimes fatal, injuries caused by deleterious drugs.

Where, as here, all defendants produced a drug from an identical formula and the manufacturer of the DES which caused plaintiff's injuries cannot be identified through no fault of plaintiff, a modification of the rule of *Summers* is warranted because an undiluted *Summers* rationale could not function to fairly shift the burden of proof of causation to defendants. In *Summers*, one of the defendant-hunters undoubtedly injured the plaintiff. Here, however, if the chance that any particular manufacturer supplied the injury-causing product were measured by the number of producers of DES, there is a possibility that none of the five defendants in the case produced the offending substance and that the responsible manufacturer, not named in the action, would escape liability.

*Sindell* consequently approached the issue of causation from a different perspective, holding it reasonable to measure the likelihood that any of the defendants supplied the product which allegedly injured plaintiff by the percentage which the DES sold by each of them bore to the entire production of the drug sold by all for the purpose of preventing miscarriages. Plaintiff asserted in her briefs that Eli Lilly and Company and five or six other companies produced 90 percent of the DES marketed. If this was established to be fact at trial, then there was a corresponding likelihood that this handful of producers manufactured the DES which caused plaintiff's injuries, and only a 10 percent likelihood that the offending producer would escape liability.

The court explained the connection between percentage of market share and liability as follows: If *X* Manufacturer sold one-fifth of all the DES prescribed for pregnancy and identification could be made in all cases, *X* would be the sole defendant in approximately one-fifth of all cases and liable for all the damages in those cases. Under alternative liability, *X* would be joined in all cases in which identification could not be made, but liable for only one-fifth of the total damages in these cases. *X* would pay the same amount either way. Although the correlation is not, in practice, perfect, it is close enough so that defendants' objections on the ground of fairness lose their value.

If plaintiff joined in the action the manufacturers of a substantial share of the DES which her mother might have taken, the injustice of shifting the burden of proof to defendants to demonstrate that they could not have made the substance which injured plaintiff is diminished. While 75 to 80 percent of the market was suggested by commentators as the requirement, *Sindell* held only that a "substantial" percentage was required. The presence in the action of a substantial share of the appropriate market also provided a ready means to apportion damages among the defendants. Each defendant would be held liable for the proportion of the judgment represented by its share of that market unless it demonstrated that it could not have made the product which caused plaintiff's injuries. In *Sindell*, one DES manufacturer was dismissed from the action upon filing a declaration that it had not manufactured DES until after plaintiff was born. Once plaintiff met her burden of joining the required defendants, they in turn could cross-complain against other DES manufacturers, not joined in the action, which they could allege might have supplied the injury-causing product.

Under this approach, each manufacturer's liability would approximate its responsibility for the injuries caused by its own products. Some minor discrepancy in the correlation between market share and liability is inevitable; therefore, a defendant may be held liable for a somewhat different percentage of the damage than its share of the appropriate market would justify. It is probably impossible, with the passage of time, to determine market share with mathematical exactitude. But the difficulty of apportioning damages among the defendant-producers, in exact relation to their market share, does not seriously militate against the rule. As the court said in *Summers* with regard to the liability of independent tortfeasors, where a correct division of liability cannot be made, "the trier of fact may make it the best it can." *Summers*, 33 Cal.2d at 88.

*Sindell* was not unmindful of the practical problems involved in defining the market and determining market share, but saw these as largely matters of proof which cannot be determined at the pleading stage of proceedings. Defendants urged that it would be unfair and contrary to public policy to hold them liable for plaintiff's injuries in the absence of proof that one of them supplied the drug responsible for the damage. Most of their arguments, however, were based upon the assumption that one manufacturer would be held responsible for the products of another or for those of all other manufacturers if plaintiff ultimately prevailed. But under the rule *Sindell* adopted, each manufacturer's liability for an injury would be approximately equivalent to the damages caused by the DES it manufactured.

**6. *Cervantes* + *Sindell* = flexible proximate cause.** Ultimately, plaintiff Sindell could recover from defendants without a shred of proof that any of them caused her injuries. That owes to the court's manipulation of the doctrine of proximate cause not to limit responsibility despite but-for causation, but rather to expand responsibility despite the absence of but-for causation. In this way, proximate cause is best seen not as a doctrine of the mechanics of how injuries are produced, but as a tool meant to establish or deny responsibility for those injuries. It can be used to limit responsibility (as in *Cervantes*) or to expand responsibility (as in *Sindell*). As a legal tool, proximate causation is flexible enough to achieve results at odds with causal realities by manipulating those realities to achieve what courts take to be socially desirable outcomes. In the end, the party in the best or most deserving position to accept responsibility is held responsible, even if that requires the deployment of a notion of cause that stretches or shrinks the term all out of shape.

That *Sindell* is a civil case in no way undermines this observation. For like-minded criminal cases that use proximate cause to expand responsibility (at least to a point), see *Commonwealth v. Atencio*, 345 Mass. 627, 630 (1963); *Jacobs v. State*, 184 So.2d 711, 716 (Fla. 1st D.C.A. 1966); *People v. Abbot & Moon*, 84 A.D.2d 11 (N.Y. 1981); *People v. Russell*, 693 N.E.2d 193 (N.Y. 1998).

**7. Possession and causation.** I recently represented a juvenile (Hector H.) whose friend stole a 1990 Toyota Camry, then picked up my client before crashing the car in a ditch. After six juveniles jumped out and fled, a witness identified Hector as a back-seat passenger. The D.A. rejected the recommendation of Oceanside police that Hector be charged with auto theft, instead filing an allegation of knowing receipt of stolen property. Hector knew the car was stolen when he hopped in (the ignition was dangling at the driver's knee). But he neither encouraged nor assisted in any way the taking or driving. Instead, he copped to "constructive possession" of the car, an element of receiving stolen property. See supra Chapter 4.A, note 2 on *Bond*. The prosecutor asked the juvenile court to order Hector to pay the victim of the theft $8,000 for damage to the wrecked Camry. Trial counsel, contrariwise, insisted Hector hadn't caused even 8 cents in damage, all of which was brought on by the driver and whoever else had a role in the taking or operation of the car. Without discussion of anything but bluebook value, the juvenile court ordered Hector to pay $1,690 in restitution to the car's owner.

Affirming in an unpublished opinion that might mystify anyone with even a casual command of causation, the Court of Appeal said only this: "Although there is insufficient proof to establish that Hector stole the vehicle or drove it, he admittedly received the vehicle and thereby enjoyed the benefits of its use, relinquishing it only after it was damaged to the extent of being unusable. In addition, Hector's presence in the vehicle made the crash more likely to occur." *In re Hector H.*, 2017 WL 2644678 at *9 (Cal. 4th Dist. Ct. App.). As to *how* Hector's presence increased the likelihood of a crash, the court did not say.

Like *respondeat superior* (whereby employers are held responsible for a wide range of actions of their employees), proximate cause is normally an effective legal device for preventing scapegoating. Not for Hector, however.

# CHAPTER 6

## Tying It All Together: The Case of Theft

## A. OVERVIEW

After nearly a term devoted to the legal rules that regulate the killing of human beings, we are about to apply the concepts underlying those rules to the law of theft, which criminalizes unconsented-to appropriations of others' property though various means. The purpose of closing our course by changing our focus from homicide to theft is twofold: first, to verify our command over connections between the special (arson, assault, battery, burglary, kidnapping, manslaughter, mayhem, murder, rape, robbery) and general (justifications, excuses, *mens rea*, group criminality, attempt) parts of criminal law. It will soon be evident that the same notions that inculpate and exculpate defendants in homicide cases have point elsewhere in law, both inside and outside the law of theft. Second, this final chapter is an *hommage* to Bar exams throughout the U.S., where year in and year out the intricacies of theft law pervade the multistate questions. A detailed analysis of theft here will make the licensing process much more manageable than the largely autodidact method of a Bar-prep crash course, a non-optimal approach to a subject so technical as this.

Breaking theft down into two main categories—forcible and non-forcible—may help. Allegations or convictions of forcible theft—robbery—have occupied much of our readings: Judge Posner criticized the lengthy sentence of Dwight Jackson, who'd been convicted of robbing the same bank three times; Decker solicited an undercover agent to kill his sister Donna in a feigned robbery; Beeman, Burk, and Gray robbed Beeman's sister-in-law; Mianta McKnight, Cavitt, and Williams robbed Betty McKnight (killing her in the process); Stamp, Koory, and Lehman robbed Honeyman (giving him a heart attack in the process); Caldwell, Washington, and Belvin robbed a Church's Fried Chicken (getting Belvin killed by a sheriff's deputy in the process); Cabaltero and others robbed Nishida (getting Ancheta killed by Dasalla in the process); and Goetz feared four youths were bent on robbing him (before opening fire on them).

In robbery, the thief uses physical force or the threat of physical force to overcome the will of the victim, who involuntarily parts with his or her property. See California Penal Code §211 (1872). Despite an extended reliance on a notion of consent that makes only misleading sense, extortion, too, is a forcible form of theft by which the thief frightens the victim into parting with his or her property. California Penal Code §518 (1939). The primary differences between robbery and extortion are 1) robbery can occur only in a face-to-face encounter whereas extortion can occur either face-to-face or remotely, as where the thief threatens the victim by telephone, letter, or electronic mail; and 2) robbery regulates threats only against the body (as in "your money or your life") and property (as in "give me your wallet or I'll burn your house down"), whereas extortion also protects the victim's reputation (as in "give me $10,000 or I will accuse you of a crime, tell the newspaper about your extramarital affair, or disseminate embarrassing facts about you"). See generally *People v. Umana*, 138 Cal.App.4th 625 (2006); Wayne R. LaFave, Criminal Law §20.4(a), at 1064-65 (West, 5th ed. 2010) [statutory extortion, aka blackmail, invented to compensate for narrowness of threats prohibited by robbery]. Unfortunately, the similarities between robbery and extortion dwarf their differences. See *State v. Coffin*, 504 N.W.2d 893, 896-97 (Iowa 1993) [because robbery contains no elements that extortion does not, extortion is *not* a lesser-included offense of robbery].

Both robbery and extortion involve coercion. *People v. Krist*, 97 Mich.App. 669, 672-73 (1980). Accordingly, their punishments are significant: depending on the presence of aggravating circumstances, robbery sentences run from two years on the low end to nine years on the high end. See California Penal Code §213 (1994). Any extortion that is not at once a robbery carries a base term of three years. See California Penal Code §520 (2011).

Likewise, telling one form of *non*-forcible theft from another can be a tedious undertaking. Non-forcible thefts can potentially dispossess victims of their entire wealth—just ask the ripped-off clients of Bernard Madoff (or, if you can remember back that far, Ivan Boesky, or much further, Charles Ponzi). But because such thefts involve no coercion, they are punished less severely than forcible thefts. Depending on the value of the property—which separates petty from grand thefts, see California Penal Code §487(a) (2014) [drawing line for most purposes at $950]—non-forcible thefts are punished with incarcerative sentences that range from six months if petty, California Penal Code §490 (1976), to a year if grand (three if a firearm is taken). California Penal Code §489 (2014). There are four forms of non-forcible theft: larceny, embezzlement, larceny by trick, and fraud (aka theft by false pretenses). *See* CALJIC No. 14.00 (2014). All theft crimes require specific intent to steal or what lawyers call *animus furandi*.

## B. LARCENY

Although larceny is a non-forcible form of theft, it nonetheless criminalizes acquisitions of property by trespass, that is, property acquired from the rightful possessor or victim non-permissively. Accordingly, a larcenist is not entrusted with the victim's property; nor does a larcenist trick the victim into parting with possession or title to the property. Instead, a larcenist takes the property from the actual or "constructive" possession of the victim, although without a struggle. Picture, for example, either a pick-pocket on the one hand who gets away with a wallet, or a thief on the other hand who removes a purse, laptop, television, or other property when the victim is distracted or absent. Those are both instances of larceny. If the victim were to resist, however, as where a purse-snatcher grapples with the owner for the purse, the crime would be robbery, not larceny.

Nor is the acquisition larcenous if the acquirer comes into possession permissively, that is, without trespass. In this vein, numerous cases feature defendants who are set up by authorities or others who leave property to be "stolen" for the purpose of apprehending the acquirer, who "steals" the very property these *agents provocateurs* meant for him to acquire. Depending on how far the trap-setters go to manifest an intention to part with their property, *see Topolewski, supra* Chapter 4.E.3, courts are free in such cases to call the ultimate acquisition *attempted* larceny because an essential element of larceny—trespass—is missing, despite the acquirer's *animus furandi*. *Free* to call it an attempt, yes; *prone* to, no. And while this is the position of the Model Penal Code, see MPC §5.01(3), I could find no supporting case law on point and, for that matter, precious little against. *E.g., People v. Rollino*, 233 N.Y.S.2d 580 (Supreme Court 1962).

The black-letter law of larceny is set forth in CALJIC No. 14.02, which states:

> Every person who steals, takes, carries, leads, or drives away the personal property of another with the specific intent to deprive the owner permanently of his or her property is guilty of the crime of theft by larceny. To constitute a 'carrying away,' the property need not be actually removed from the place or premises where it was kept, nor need it be retained by the perpetrator. In order to prove this crime, each of the following elements must be proved: 1. A person took personal property of some value belonging to another; 2. When the person took the property he or she had the specific intent to deprive the alleged victim permanently of his or her property; and 3. The person carried the property away by obtaining physical possession and control for some period of time and by some movement of the property.

The reference in the above-quoted instruction to "'carrying away'" is a proxy for the technical term "asportation," without which the thief cannot be said to have "taken" the property. Yet, note how trivial, as phrased, the carrying away may be to still constitute a taking and thus to fulfill larceny's element of trespass.

## C. EMBEZZLEMENT

[Can form animus furandi after proper acquisition]

An embezzler comes into possession of the victim's property without *animus furandi*. The victim entrusts the property to the embezzler, who *at first* intends to safe-keep or manage the property as promised. Indeed, if the acquirer did not at first intend to safe-keep or manage the property as promised, then there would be by definition no entrustment, just the appearance of one. At some point after taking possession, an embezzler develops the intent to permanently deprive the victim of the property and absconds with it. Embezzlement is the only form of theft in which the initial acquisition is lawful, that is, the property is acquired without *animus furandi* on the acquirer's part. Another way of putting this is to say that the embezzler acquires the victim's property permissively.

The black-letter law of embezzlement is set forth in CALJIC No. 14.07, which states:

> Every person to whom property has been entrusted who fraudulently appropriates that property to his or her own use or purpose, is guilty of the crime of theft by embezzlement. In order to prove this crime, each of the following elements must be proved: 1. A relation of trust and confidence existed between two persons; 2. Pursuant to that relationship one of those persons accepted property entrusted to him or her by the other person; and 3. With the specific intent to deprive the other person of his or her property, the person appropriated or converted it to his or her own use or purpose.

Not every permissive acquirer of property who thereafter absconds with it with *animus furandi* is an embezzler. The first element of the above instruction requires a "relation of trust and confidence" between the thief and the victim (or the victim's agent). CALJIC No. 14.08. That limits the class of acquirers who are capable of embezzlement to what the law calls "fiduciaries," a stand-in for "relation[s] of trust and confidence."

A fiduciary is paid to exercise sound judgment for the beneficiary (aka principal, grantor) whom the fiduciary serves. Fiduciaries who exploit their superior expertise to their own advantage at their beneficiaries' expense tortiously violate their duty to avoid "self-dealing," a cardinal sin for professionals. Attorneys, physicians, stock brokers, bankers, accountants, and sports or theatrical agents, to name a few, are fiduciaries of their clients and patients, just as professional partnerships make partners fiduciaries of the partnership, that is, of one another.

Most employment relations, however, are *not* fiduciary. A store clerk, for example—even one who handles money—is not the fiduciary of either the store or the customer. Store clerks have a job to do; but the relationships they are obligated to cultivate and tend are not about creating and maintaining confidences, fully disclosing the employee's own interests, and constantly weighing up the employee's obligations to the store and to customers in areas of discretionary decision-making. Instead, the clerk's relation to both the store and the customer is seen as a simple, arm's length, economic transaction not informed by *special* duties of loyalty, secrecy, and sound judgment. Conceivably, some upper store management would have fiduciary duties to the store, to stockholders if any, to other managers, and to non-management, though not at all likely to shoppers. *See generally*, Daniel Yeager, *Fiduciary-isms, A Study of Academic Influence on the Expansion of the Law*, 65 Drake Law Review 179, 201-02 (2017).

Whether the putative embezzler is a fiduciary of the victim is a threshold question in the law of embezzlement. Some permissive acquirers who promise to safe-keep or manage property do so as "bailee," not as fiduciary. Bailees enter "bailments" by agreeing to receive property from "bailors." A bailment is a contract, express or implied, whereby the bailee/acquirer is to safe-keep personal property to be returned on demand intact to the bailor/prior rightful possessor. *See Morgan Stanley & Co. Inc. v. JP Morgan Chase Bank, N.A.*, 645 F.Supp.2d 248, 256 (S.D.N.Y 2009). Bailees, which include, to name just a few, kennels, car washes, and hotels with whom guests bail jewels, are not regulated by the law of embezzlement. *But cf.* Wisconsin Statutes Annotated §943.20 (West 2012) [criminally punishing *all* absconding bailees, not just embezzling fiduciaries, who, after promising to safe-keep property, change their minds and run off with it]. If the putative embezzler is a fiduciary who comes into possession permissively, then embezzlement occurs once the fiduciary manifests the specific intent to permanently deprive the victim of the entrusted property. If the fiduciary never intended to re-unite the victim with the property, then no embezzlement occurs because the victim will have been *tricked* out of possession, thus precluding the element of entrustment from occurring.

If the fiduciary intends all along—from start to finish—to re-unite the victim with the entrusted property, then there is no *animus furandi* and thus no embezzlement. But the fiduciary/acquirer cannot put the victim's property at great risk and still claim an intention to return it. *See People v. Davis*, 19 Cal.4th 301, 307 n.4 (1998). For example, a fiduciary who dips into the company till to play the ponies with the intention of returning the original sum after placing winning bets at the track has committed embezzlement of the appropriated sum, even if he wins and returns the original sum. *See United States v. Hamilton*, 499 F.3d 734, 736 (7th Cir. 2007) ["If you embezzle from your employer, you are not excused just because you had an honest intention of replacing the money, maybe with interest—you embezzled to gamble and were honestly convinced that you were on a lucky streak and would win enough to cover the defalcation comfortably."]. As a pertinent jury instruction puts it, "specific intent

... is satisfied by either an intent to deprive an owner permanently of his or her property, or to deprive an owner temporarily, but for an unreasonable time, so as to deprive him or her of a major portion of its value or enjoyment." CALJIC No. 14.03 (2014).

Finally, it is important to note that one cannot embezzle what one already owns. Therefore, any property that has been lawfully gifted or sold to the acquirer cannot be the subject of embezzlement on the part of the acquirer. *See People v. Holder*, 53 Cal.App. 45, 48 (1921). For the longest time, courts ruled that partners who abscond with partnership assets abscond necessarily with their *own* assets, thus cannot be convicted of embezzlement, which requires that the subject property be that of *another*. *State v. Reddick*, 48 N.W. 846 (S.D. 1891). But that view has been rendered obsolete. Both in and out of South Dakota, the majority position developed since *Reddick* views partnership assets as subject to the law of embezzlement. *State v. Gard*, 742 N.W.2d 257 (S.D. 2007) [overruling *Reddick*].

For a summary of theft law's approaches to a spouse's right to appropriate marital property against the will of the other spouse (as in cleaning out jointly held bank accounts), see Robert D. Feder, *Valuation Strategies in Divorce* §8.42 (5th ed. Supp. 2017).

## D. LARCENY BY TRICK

Sometimes the thief appears to have acquired the victim's property permissively, but in actuality has tricked the victim into parting with possession. The idea in such cases is that, had the acquirer revealed his true intentions to abscond with the property, the victim never would have parted with the property in the first place. No entrustment takes place when the victim is tricked out of possession, just the appearance of entrustment. In such cases, the acquisition, if preceded by the specific intent to steal, is deemed larceny by trick.

The black-letter law of larceny by trick is set forth in CALJIC No. 14.05, which states:

> Every person who, with the specific intent to deprive permanently another person of his or her property, obtains possession of personal property of another by either (1) a false promise without intent to perform, or (2) fraud, artifice, trick, or device, is guilty of the crime of theft by trick and device. In order to prove this crime, each of the following

elements must be proved: 1. A person obtained possession of personal property of some value belonging to the alleged victim; 2. That person obtained possession by making a false promise which he or she had no intention of performing, or by means of other fraud, artifice, trick, or device; 3. In surrendering possession of the property, the alleged victim did not intend to transfer the ownership; and 4. The person who obtained possession did so with the specific intent to deprive the alleged victim permanently of his or her property.

In a typical case, the thief intentionally misleads the victim into thinking that the thief is merely borrowing or renting the property. It is on that basis that the victim parts with the property. But in fact, there is no entrustment or bailment due to the deceit; fiduciaries and bailees alike acquire by definition without *animus furandi*. Plausible cases of larceny by trick rarely feature claims by the acquirer that the victim gifted or sold the acquirer the property (claims which, if believed, would prevent conviction of that offense). Instead, the acquirer defends against a charge of larceny by trick by claiming to have lacked *animus furandi* at the time of the acquisition.

The most well-known example of larceny by trick is *King v. Pear*, 168 English Reports 208 (Crown Cases Reserved 1779). Pear rented a horse from Finch, stating that he would ride the horse to Surrey. In fact, he rode to Smithfield and sold the horse. It turned out that Pear had also lied about his place of residence. Together, these two facts indicated a lie on Pear's part when he told Finch he would return the rental horse that evening.

Prior to *Pear*, larceny had been defined as the taking from another without consent, but in *Pear* the owner had seemingly given consent to the original transfer of possession. *Pear* thus expanded the law of larceny to cover cases where the thief induces the victim to consent to the acquisition by deception or trick. In such a case, the deception or trick is a substitute for the thief's trespass as an unlawful/non-permissive means of coming into possession of the victim's property. *See People v. Edwards*, 72 Cal.App. 102, 112-13 (1925) [victim conned out of $900 paid in three installments to family "friend," who pocketed money she'd given him to help her husband and brother-in-law fight case against them in an unrelated grand larceny]. If proof persuades the court that the intent to steal was either absent throughout, or formed only after the acquisition, then larceny by trick has not occurred.

## E. FRAUD (FALSE PRETENSES)

If proof establishes not only that the thief tricked the victim out of possession of the property, but also tricked the victim out of title/ownership, then the crime is fraud (aka theft by false pretenses), not larceny by trick. "Although the crimes of larceny by trick ... and obtaining property by false pretenses are much alike, they are aimed at different criminal acquisitive techniques. Larceny by trick ... is the appropriation of property, the possession of which was fraudulently acquired; obtaining property by false pretenses is the fraudulent or deceitful acquisition of both title and possession." *People v. Curtin*, 22 Cal.App.4th 528, 531 (1994), quoting *People v. Ashley*, 42 Cal.2d 246, 258 (1954). "[I]t was difficult at times," however, "to determine whether a defendant had acquired title to the property, or merely possession, a distinction separating theft by false pretenses from larceny by trick." *People v. Williams*, 57 Cal.4th 776, 785 (2013). And difficult it still is.

Possession is by definition temporary and places severe limits on the possessor's rights: the owner at some point will reclaim the property. *Permanent* leases of property are rare if extant. *E.g., Pechenik v. Baltimore & Ohio Railroad Co.*, 205 S.E.2d 813, 815 (W. Va. 1974) ["West Virginia disfavors perpetual leases"]. Title, on the other hand, is permanent and places few limits on the owner's rights as to how to dispose of the property. A titleholder/owner, unlike a mere possessor, can sell or gift the property, even if the property is encumbered. For example, someone who borrows money from a bank to buy a car owns an encumbered title interest in the car; he or she may sell the collateralized car subject to satisfaction of the outstanding loan, the surplus from the transaction benefitting the borrower-seller if any is left over after repayment of the lender-bank. Another way of saying this is that the borrower can sell the car despite the debt secured by the car, but the unpaid balance of the loan must be paid to the lender before the borrower can realize any profit from selling the encumbered car. A borrower who obtains a car loan with no intention of repayment has tricked the lender out of title to the loan, not just possession, and the crime is fraud (false pretenses). *See, e.g., Whitmore v. State*, 298 N.W. 194 (Wis. 1941).

Fraud (false pretenses) can occur when the owner of property conveys it to an acquirer in exchange for the counter-performance of the acquirer (payment in a sale transaction, or directing the payment in the acquirer's sound discretion into an investment), but the acquirer/trickster/wrongdoer has no intention of keeping his word. For example, in *People v. Jones*, 36 Cal.2d 373 (1950), Jones committed fraud (false pretenses) when he induced two investors to part with title and possession to sums in exchange for partnership interests in his insulation business, which was in pretty bad shape. Jones had materially misrepresented the health of the business and his plans for the invested sums, as a result obtaining not just the money, but significant discretion over its disposal, which diverted profoundly from his stated plan. *Cf. In re North American Coin & Currency*, 767 F.2d 1573 (9th Cir. 1985) [debtor's failure to disclose dire financial situation that put debtor on brink of insolvency is not necessarily an intent to defraud if debtor actually believed company could be saved].

There is substantial authority, however, for the proposition that the owner does *not* relinquish title to the subject property and the crime committed is larceny by trick if defendant fraudulently obtains property for a discrete, specific, agreed-to purpose. For example, in *People v. Traster*, 111 Cal.App.4th 1377 (2003), $132,296 given to defendant (a computer consultant) to purchase Microsoft licenses conveyed to defendant possession of, not title to, the money. Title would vest in defendant only once he had performed the agreed-to purchase of the licenses, which he neither did nor ever intended to do. So too, a lawyer who received $2,000 from a client on the lawyer's hollow claim to need the funds to bribe police in the client's misdemeanor matter fraudulently acquired possession not title, which would vest only when the lawyer fulfilled his stated purpose. *Graham v. United States*, 187 F.2d 87 (D.C. Cir. 1950).

The black-letter law of fraud (false pretenses) is set forth in CALJIC No. 14.10 (2014), which states:

> Every person who knowingly and designedly by any false or fraudulent representation or pretense, defrauds another person of money, labor, real or personal property, is guilty of the crime of theft by false pretense. In order to prove this crime, each of the following elements must be proved: 1. A person made or caused to be made to the alleged victim by word or conduct, either (1) a promise without intent to perform it, or (2) a false pretense or representation of an existing or past fact known to the person to be false or made recklessly and without information which would justify a reasonable belief in its truth; 2. The person made the pretense, representation or promise with the specific intent

> to defraud; 3. The pretense, representation or promise was believed and relied upon by the alleged victim and was material in inducing him or her to part with his or her money or property even though the false pretense, representation or promise was not the sole cause; and 4. The theft was accomplished in that the alleged victim parted with his or her money or property intending to transfer ownership thereof.

Like larceny and larceny by trick but unlike embezzlement, fraud (false pretenses) is an illegal means of acquiring, not disposing of, property. Because it is the deceptive obtaining of title to property that is punished, "it is not necessary that the evidence show ... that the person against whom the offense is directed suffer a financial loss or permanently be deprived of his or her money or property...." CALJIC No. 14.12 (2014). Thus, an attorney, who with no intent to perform, induces a client to pass title to a retainer fee that the attorney deposits in a personal (not client) account for the attorney's own benefit (not the client's), the payment is gotten by fraud (false pretenses) even if the money remains in the account and the client ends up getting it all back. *But cf. Sonnesyn v. Akin*, 104 N.W. 1026, 1028 (N.D. 1905) ["It is a well-settled maxim that fraud without injury is not actionable."].

Defendants in theft cases where fraud is alleged sometimes obtain title to their victims' goods, services, or money and never perform in return. But that, without more, does not mean defendants acquired their victims' goods, services, or money with the specific intent to withhold performance on their own end. Many, indeed most, defaulting debtors do not *cheat* their creditors. Instead, they receive goods, services, or money intending to perform their own end of the deal, but circumstances change or do not improve when they expect them to and the debtors become unable to perform. Because alleging an instance of cheat as opposed to viewing the matter as non-fraudulent commercial default is easily done, CALJIC No. 14.14 states that

> defendant cannot be convicted of theft by false pretense unless: 1. The false pretense, or some note or memorandum thereof, is in a writing subscribed by the defendant or is in his or her handwriting; or 2. An oral false pretense is accompanied by a false token or writing; or 3. The false pretense is proved by the testimony of two witnesses or that of one witness and corroborating circumstances.

A false token, in turn, "is any tangible object or a document that is not genuine, is not what it appears or purports to be, and is intended to be used and is used to deceive the person to whom it is presented." CALJIC No. 14.15 (2014).

Because the property subject to *larceny* had to be moveable, crops and real estate were exempt. Crops are now included within the property subject to larceny (or robbery for that matter), though real estate and intangible property such as services are not. *People v. Dillon*, 34 Cal.3d 441, 456-62 (1983) [marijuana plants illegal to possess may be the subject of actionable theft]. Because embezzlement, larceny by trick, and fraud (false pretenses) have no asportation element, real estate and intangible property such as services *are* subject to those species of theft law. *E.g.*, Model Penal Code §223.7. Indeed, some contemporary theft laws protect "anything of value, including money, real estate, tangible or intangible personal property, ... anything severed from land, library material, contract rights, choses-in-action, interests in or claims to wealth, credit, admission or transportation tickets, captured or domestic animals, food and drink, electric or other power." Tennessee Code Annotated §39–11–106(a)(28) (West 2014).

Right or wrong, "property" contemplates a not-unlimited range of valued human activity. For example, Professor Robin West argues that an intentionally deceptive Casanova who induces women to part with their "giving and receiving selves" and engage in sexual exchanges predicated on the stated feelings and intentions not actually held by the Casanova, commits the crime of fraud. *Compare* Robin West, *Legitimizing the Illegitimate: A Comment on "Beyond Rape,"* 93 Columbia Law Review 1442 (1993) *with* Donald A. Dripps, *Beyond Rape: An Essay on the Difference between the Presence of Force and the Absence of Consent*, 92 Columbia Law Review 1780 (1992).

In California, larceny, embezzlement, larceny by trick, and fraud (false pretenses) have been consolidated into the single crime of theft, but their elements have not been changed. California Penal Code §484 (2001). The purpose of the consolidation was to remove the technicalities that plagued the pleading and proof of these crimes at common law. Frequently one offense would be pleaded, but another would be proved. *See, e.g., Commonwealth v. Ryan*, 30 N.E. 364, 365 (Mass. 1892) ["The distinction may be arbitrary, but, as it does not affect the defendant otherwise than by giving him an opportunity, whichever offense he was convicted of, to contend that he should have been convicted of the other...."]. To avoid that technical pleading-versus-proof pitfall whereby defendant would argue on appeal for reversal on the ground that he committed *a* crime but not *this* crime, complaints, informations, and indictments can now charge defendants with the generalized crime of "theft," simply alleging an "unlawful taking."

Juries consequently need no longer be *as* concerned with the technical differences between modes of theft, and can return a general verdict—of theft—if they find that an unlawful taking has been proved. Again, however, the elements of the several types of theft included within §484 have not been changed; a conviction of theft can be sustained only if the evidence meets the elements of one of the four consolidated offenses. *People v. North*, 131 Cal.App.3d 112, 118 (1982) [judgment of conviction "must be affirmed if there is sufficient evidence to support a theft conviction on *any* theory"]. Although all criminal verdicts must be unanimous, a jury need not agree "upon which category of theft was committed, so long as there is sufficient evidence of at least one of the types of theft" on which jurors were instructed. *People v. Ramirez*, 109 Cal.App.3d 529, 540 (1980).

As a reminder, punishment for all four non-forcible theft offenses is identical. California Penal Code §489 (2014) [grand theft: unless subject property is a firearm, one year maximum and $5,000 fine], California Penal Code §490 (1976) [petty theft: six months maximum and $1,000 fine], or, under §490.1 (1991), a wrist-slap if the property is worth under $50.

## SUPREME COURT OF CALIFORNIA

*THE PEOPLE, PLAINTIFF AND RESPONDENT*
*V.*
*KENNETH D. DAVIS, DEFENDANT AND APPELLANT*
NOV. 5, 1998

Mosk, Justice

We granted review to determine what crime is committed in the following circumstances: the defendant enters a store and picks up an item of merchandise displayed for sale, intending to claim that he owns it and to "return" it for cash or credit; he carries the item to a sales counter and asks the clerk for a "refund"; without the defendant's knowledge his conduct has been observed by a store security agent, who instructs the clerk to give him credit for the item; the clerk gives the defendant a credit voucher, and the agent detains him as he leaves the counter with the voucher; he is charged with theft of the item. In the case at bar the Court of Appeal held the defendant is guilty of theft by trespassory larceny. We agree, and therefore affirm the judgment of the Court of Appeal.

## Facts

Defendant entered a Mervyn's department store carrying a Mervyn's shopping bag. As he entered he was placed under camera surveillance by store security agent Carol German. While German both watched and filmed, defendant went to the men's department and took a shirt displayed for sale from its hanger; he then carried the shirt through the shoe department and into the women's department on the other side of the store. There he placed the shirt on a sales counter and told cashier Heather Smith that he had "bought it for his father" but it didn't fit and he wanted to "return" it. Smith asked him if he had the receipt, but he said he did not because "it was a gift." Smith informed him that if the value of a returned item is more than $20 and there is no receipt, the store policy is not to make a cash refund but to issue a Mervyn's credit voucher. At that point Smith was interrupted by a telephone call from German; German asked her if defendant was trying to "return" the shirt, and directed her to issue a credit voucher. Smith prepared the voucher and asked defendant to sign it; he did so, but used a false name. German detained him as he walked away from the counter with the voucher. Upon being questioned in the store security office, defendant gave a second false name and three different dates of birth; he also told German that he needed money to buy football cleats, asked her if they could "work something out," and offered to pay for the shirt.

Count 1 of the information charged defendant with petty theft with a prior theft-related conviction, a felony-misdemeanor, alleging that defendant did "steal, take and carry away the personal property" of Mervyn's in violation of Penal Code §484(a). In a motion for judgment of acquittal filed after the People presented their case, defendant argued that on the facts shown he could be convicted of no more than an *attempt* to commit petty theft, and therefore sought dismissal of the petty theft charge. The court denied the motion.

The only theories of theft submitted to the jury in the instructions were theft by larceny and theft by trick and device. The jury found defendant guilty of petty theft as charged in the information. Defendant waived further jury trial, and the court found the allegation of a prior conviction to be true. The court denied defendant's motion to treat the petty theft as a misdemeanor and sentenced him to state prison.

The Court of Appeal deemed defendant's primary contention to be that the evidence was insufficient to support his conviction of petty theft on either theory submitted to the jury. The court held defendant could properly have been convicted of theft by larceny; the court therefore declined to reach the alternate theory of theft by trick and device, and affirmed the judgment. We granted review.

I

When the formerly distinct offenses of larceny, embezzlement, and obtaining property by false pretenses were consolidated in 1927 into the single crime of "theft" defined by §484, most of the procedural distinctions between those offenses were abolished. But their substantive distinctions were not: "The elements of the several types of theft included within §484 have not been changed, however, and a judgment of conviction of theft, based on a general verdict of guilty, can be sustained only if the evidence discloses the elements of one of the consolidated offenses." *People v. Ashley*, 42 Cal.2d 246, 258 (1954).

The elements of theft by larceny are well settled: the offense is committed by every person who (1) takes possession (2) of personal property (3) owned or possessed by another, (4) by means of trespass and (5) with intent to steal the property, and (6) carries the property away. *See, e.g., People v. Edwards*, 72 Cal.App. 102, 112-16 (1925); CALJIC No. 14.02; Perkins & Boyce, Criminal Law 292-335 (3d ed. 1982). The act of taking personal property from the possession of another is always a trespass unless the owner consents to the taking freely and unconditionally or the taker has a legal right to take the property.[3] Perkins, at 303-04. The intent to steal or *animus furandi* is the intent, without a good faith claim of right, to permanently deprive the owner of possession. *Id.* at 326-27. And if the taking has begun, the slightest movement of the property constitutes a carrying away or

---

[3] Consent procured by fraud is invalid and the resulting offense is larceny by trick and device. *Edwards*, 72 Cal. App. at 113; CALJIC No. 14.05.

asportation. *Id.* at 323-25. Applying these rules to the instant facts, we have no doubt that defendant (1) took possession (2) of personal property (the shirt) (3) owned by Mervyn's and (4) moved it sufficiently to satisfy the asportation requirement. Defendant does not contend otherwise.

Defendant does contend, however, that the elements of trespass and intent to steal are lacking. He predicates his argument on a distinction he draws by dividing his course of conduct into two distinct "acts." According to defendant, his first "act" was to take the shirt from the display rack and carry it to Smith's cash register. He contends that act lacked the element of intent to steal because he had no intent to permanently deprive Mervyn's *of the shirt*; he intended to have the shirt in his possession only long enough to exchange it for a "refund." His second "act," also according to defendant, was to misrepresent to Smith that he had bought the shirt at Mervyn's and to accept the credit voucher she issued. He contends that act lacked the element of trespass because the store, acting through its agent German, *consented* to the issuance of the voucher with full knowledge of how he came into possession of the shirt.

Defendant's argument misses the mark on two grounds: it focuses on the wrong issue of consent, and it views that issue in artificial isolation from the intertwined issue of intent to steal. To begin with, the question is not whether Mervyn's consented to Smith's issuance of the voucher after defendant asked to "return" the shirt; rather, the question is whether Mervyn's consented to defendant's taking the shirt in the first instance. As the Court of Appeal correctly reasoned, a self-service store like Mervyn's impliedly consents to a customer's picking up and handling an item displayed for sale and carrying it from the display area to a sales counter with the intent of purchasing it; the store manifestly does not consent, however, to a customer's removing an item from a shelf or hanger if the customer's intent in taking possession of the item is to steal it.

Although we have found no California case addressing the precise question, a recent decision of the Ohio Court of Appeals is relevant. In *State v. Higgs*, 1990 WL 1351 (Ohio Ct. App.), defendant entered a Sears store and was observed on camera by store security agents as he removed a paper bag from his pocket, took a toy airplane from the merchandise display, and put it in the bag. He then carried the bag to a cashier and told her that the airplane had been a gift to his son but he was "returning" it because his son was too young for the toy. A security agent telephoned the cashier and instructed her to proceed with the transaction; the cashier gave the defendant a cash refund, and the security agents detained him. He was convicted of theft by larceny.

On appeal, defendant contended that although the indictment charged theft of the toy airplane, the evidence showed the crime was, instead, theft of the cash refund by means of false pretenses; that the store, acting through its agents, consented to the refund and thereby vitiated an element of the crime; and that in any event the store also consented to customers' carrying merchandise around the store without first paying for it.

Rejecting those claims and affirming the conviction, the appellate court reasoned:

> The fact that a retail store permits customers to carry merchandise from one area of the store to another does not imply consent to conceal the merchandise in a bag and return the same for a cash refund. This act, not the act of taking the refund, constituted the criminal offense for which appellant was charged.... The fact that Sears consented to permitting a refund for the toy airplane was not relevant to the disposition of this case. The item unlawfully taken was the airplane, not the money. The record reveals neither Sears nor its authorized agents consented to the taking of that airplane.

*Id.* at p. *3. In these circumstances the issue of consent—and therefore trespass—depends on the issue of intent to steal. We turn to that issue.

The general rule is that the intent to steal required for conviction of larceny is an intent to deprive the owner *permanently* of possession of the property. For example, we have said it would not be larceny for a youth to take and hide another's bicycle to "get even" for being teased, if he intends to return it the following day. But the general rule is not inflexible: the word "permanently," as used here is not to be taken literally. Our research discloses three relevant categories of cases holding that the requisite intent to steal may be found even though defendant's primary purpose in taking the property is not to deprive the owner permanently of possession: i.e., (1) when defendant intends to "sell" the property back to its owner, (2) when defendant intends to claim a reward for "finding" the property, and (3) when, as here, defendant intends to return the property to its owner for a "refund." There is thus ample authority for the *result* reached in the case at bar; the difficulty is in finding a rationale for so holding that is consistent with basic principles of larceny. The cases in these three categories offer a variety of such rationales, some more relevant or more persuasive than others.

## A. The "Sale" Cases

The classic case of the first category is *Regina v. Hall*, 169 Eng. Rep. 291 (1848). Defendant, an employee of one Atkin who made candles from tallow, took tallow owned by Atkin and put it on Atkin's own scales, claiming it belonged to a butcher who was offering to sell it to Atkin. The jurors were instructed that if they found defendant took Atkin's property with the intent to sell it back to him as if it belonged to another and appropriate the proceeds, he was guilty of larceny. The jury so found, and the conviction was upheld on appeal.

Defendant contended that his assertion of temporary ownership of the property for a particular purpose was not enough to constitute the required intent to permanently deprive. The justices expressed two rationales for holding to the contrary. First, one justice stressed that the deprivation would in fact have been permanent unless the owner had agreed to the condition imposed by defendant, i.e., to "buy" the property. Baron Parke reasoned, "The intention was that the goods should never revert to the owner as his own property except by sale. They were therefore severed from the owner completely unless he chose to buy back what was in truth his own property." *Hall*, 169 Eng. Rep. at 291.

The second rationale was that defendant's claim of the right to sell the property was an assertion of a *right of ownership* and therefore evidence of an intent to permanently deprive. Chief Justice Denman reasoned, "The only question attempted to be raised here is as to the *animus furandi*, the intent to deprive the owner of his property. What better proof can there be of such intent, than the assertion of such a right of ownership by the prisoner as to entitle him to sell it." *Id.* at 292; *accord*, *Regina v. Manning*, 169 Eng. Rep. 619 (1852) [defendant took bags owned by a potato-bag dealer, presented them to the dealer as new bags, and demanded payment for them; held, larceny].

The latter rationale—that an intent to permanently deprive is shown by the assertion of a right of ownership in the property—was again invoked when *Hall* was distinguished from a case in which a pieceworker sought to increase his pay by adding goods produced by other workers to those produced by him. In that case Justice Erle explained, "The distinction between the two is sufficiently clear. The test is, whether the person who takes the property assumes to exercise dominion over it as owner. In *Hall*, the offer to sell the property to the owner was one of the strongest acts of dominion." *Regina v. Poole*, 7 Cox Crim. Cas. 373, 374 (1857).

Perkins offers yet another rationale for the rule that a defendant who takes property for the purpose of "selling" it back to its owner has the requisite intent to permanently deprive. By so doing the defendant creates a *substantial risk of permanent loss*, because if the owner does not buy back his property the defendant will have a powerful incentive to keep it in order to conceal the theft. As Perkins explains, "there is also a very considerable risk that the owner will not get back the property at all. If, for example, he should decide that his supply was ample and decline to pay the price, the trespasser would take away the property in order to conceal his own wrongdoing." Perkins, at 329. We find this rationale persuasive.

### B. The "Reward" Cases

The cases in the second category hold that a defendant who takes property for the purpose of claiming a reward for "finding" it has the requisite intent to permanently deprive. Again the courts invoke differing rationales for this holding. One line of these cases is exemplified by *Commonwealth v. Mason*, 105 Mass. 163 (1870). The defendant took possession of a horse that had strayed onto his property, with the intent to conceal it until the owner offered a reward and then to return it and claim the reward, or until the owner was induced to sell it to him for less than its worth. The court affirmed a conviction of larceny on the theory that the requisite felonious intent was shown because the defendant intended to deprive the owner of "a portion of the value of the property." *Id.* at 168. The court did not explain this theory further, but later cases suggested that the "portion of the value" in question was the right to claim a reward—ordinarily less than the property's full value—for its return.

Thus in *Slaughter v. State*, 38 S.E. 854 (Ga. 1901), the defendants were private detectives who induced an employee to steal merchandise from a store, then returned the merchandise to the store owner as "evidence" of the thefts and persuaded him to pay them a reward if they could catch the thief. The court affirmed a conviction of larceny, reasoning that "It is not necessary to constitute larceny, that the property should be itself permanently appropriated. It is sufficient if the property be taken and carried away with the intent to appropriate any pecuniary right or interest therein, as where it is taken with the expectation of claiming a reward for its return." *Id.* at 855.

Another line of cases in this category also noted the taker's intent to appropriate "part of the value" of the property, but went on to emphasize a different rationale, i.e., that the taker had made the return of the property *contingent* on the offer of a satisfactory reward, and if the contingency did not materialize the taker would keep the property. A leading case of this type is *Berry v. State*, 31 Ohio St. 219 (1877). The defendants took two horses from a stable without their owner's consent, with the intent to conceal them until the owner offered a reward, and then to return them and claim the reward. The court affirmed a conviction of larceny, rejecting the defendants' contention that their intent was to deprive the owner only temporarily of his property. As its principal reason, the court stressed that the defendants' intent to return the horses was *contingent* on the offer of a reward:

> In this case there was an utter absence of intention to restore the property *unless* money was paid for its restoration. There was no evidence tending to show a purpose to return the property *unless* a reward was offered. A return, at all events, was not designed. It is true, that all parties concerned in the taking contemplated and expected that the owner would offer such reward; but the purpose to return was founded wholly on the contingency that a reward would be offered, and *unless the contingency happened the conversion was complete.*

*Id.* at 227. The same rationale has been invoked when defendant sought not a reward but a ransom. Thus in *State v. Hauptmann*, 115 N.J.L. 412 (1935), defendant kidnapped the infant son of Charles Lindbergh. The child was wearing a sleeping suit when he was abducted. In preliminary negotiations with Condon, Lindbergh's representative, defendant agreed to send Condon the sleeping suit as evidence that Condon was dealing with "the right party"; the negotiations continued, defendant sent the sleeping suit to Condon, and Condon thereupon accepted defendant's ransom terms. The child was later found dead. Defendant was convicted of murder and of larceny of the sleeping suit.

On appeal to the New Jersey high court, defendant contended that there was no larceny because his intent was not to keep the sleeping suit permanently but to return it in order to advance the ransom negotiations. The court's rationale for rejecting the claim was the same as that of the "reward" cases discussed above: "the intent to return should be unconditional; and, where there is an element of coercion or of reward, as a condition of return, larceny is inferable." *Id.* at 427. The court acknowledged that the sleeping suit

> was surrendered without payment; but, on the other hand, it was an initial and probably essential step in the intended extortion of money, and it seems preposterous to suppose that it would ever have been surrendered except as a result of the first conversation between Condon and the holder of the suit, and as a guaranty that there was no mistake as to the 'right party.' It was well within the province of the jury to infer that, if Condon had refused to go on with the preliminaries, *the sleeping suit would never have been delivered*. In that situation, the larceny was established.

*Id.* The only relevant California cases we have found are two that fall into the reward/ransom category. They contribute little, however, to the rationales articulated in the prior cases.

Thus in *People v. Stay*, 19 Cal.App.3d 166 (1971), the defendant made a business of taking shopping carts from streets and sidewalks near supermarkets where they had been left by store customers, and then offering to return the carts if the stores paid him a "finder's fee" of 10 times the going rate charged by legitimate cart retrieval services; when a store refused to pay—as most did—the defendant removed all indicia of ownership from the carts and sold them to smaller stores. Convicted of grand theft, the defendant argued on appeal that the evidence showed no intent to deprive the stores permanently of the carts because his purpose was to take them only in order to collect the "reasonable charge" to which a "finder" is entitled by statute for saving and preserving "lost" property. Civil Code §2080. Affirming the conviction, the Court of Appeal held that (1) the carts were not "lost" within the meaning of the finder's statute, and (2) the evidence supported the trial court's finding that the defendant "intended to permanently deprive the owners of these carts if they didn't pay his expenses, plus a reward." *Stay*, 19 Cal.App.3d at 175.

The case is not helpful, however, because the Court of Appeal does not state a rationale to support its holding on the intent issue.

Instead, it simply reiterates the facts, and concludes broadly that "His intent to permanently deprive the markets of their property is reflected in defendant's high-handed method of operation and obvious lack of good faith in acting under the finder's statute." *Id.* at 176. Yet one of the facts emphasized by the Court of Appeal—that the defendant "well knew the markets would not pay" the exorbitant finder's fee he demanded—made a sham of the defendant's claim that he took the carts only to collect the fee.

The second California case is *In re Albert A.*, 47 Cal.App.4th 1004 (1996). The minor defendant took the bicycle of a minor named Ali by threat of force, saying he intended to keep it until his own bicycle, which had allegedly been stolen by a relative of Ali's, was returned to him. The juvenile court believed that was in fact the defendant's motive, but also believed he intended to keep Ali's bicycle "for as long as it would take" to recover his own bicycle. *Id.* at 1007. For this reason the court found the defendant intended to permanently deprive Ali of the bicycle; the court concluded that the defendant had therefore committed robbery, and ruled that a prior order of wardship would continue in effect.

Affirming the order, the Court of Appeal agreed that the defendant had the requisite intent to permanently deprive. The court's theory appears to have been an extension of the "contingency rationale" of the prior cases. The court reasoned not just that the return of the property was contingent on a future event—the recovery of the defendant's own bicycle—but that the contingency was so "remote" and unlikely to occur; the court analogized it to "winning the lottery"—that it could be disregarded as a matter of law: The intent to return property under these circumstances is tantamount to an intent to permanently deprive the victim of his or her property because the intent to return the property is too tenuous and illusory to have any legal effect. Whatever its theoretical validity, this seems an exaggerated view of the facts of the case.

Finally, Perkins again proposes the rationale of a substantial risk of permanent loss. He reasons that a taking with intent to hold for reward creates such a risk because "the intent will result in a permanent loss to the owner if he fails to offer or give a reward for the return of the property." Perkins, at 330. Indeed, even the offer or payment of a reward may not eliminate the risk because the defendant still has an incentive to keep the property rather than expose himself to detection by returning it.

## C. The "Refund" Cases

The third category comprises a substantial number of recent cases from our sister states affirming larceny convictions on facts identical or closely similar to those of the case at bar: in each, the defendant took an item of merchandise from a store display, carried it to a sales counter, claimed to own it, and asked for a "refund" of cash or credit. Although the cases are thus factually on point, the reasoning of their opinions is, ironically, of less assistance than the "sale" or "reward" cases in our search for a satisfactory rationale on the issue of the intent to permanently deprive. This is so for three reasons.

First, many of the opinions in the "refund" cases offer no rationale at all on the issue of intent. Instead, in each case the defendant contends the evidence is insufficient to support the conviction of larceny, and the appellate court simply reviews the facts and concludes otherwise without further analysis. Second, in other cases in this category the opinion either states or implies that the defendant was charged with theft of the *cash* obtained as a refund, rather than theft of the property taken from the display counter. We are concerned with the latter: as noted at the outset, defendant in the case at bar was charged with theft of "personal property" of Mervyn's, i.e., the shirt. Third, the remaining opinions in this category are statute-specific, i.e., each turns on the wording of the larceny statute in force in that particular jurisdiction. The California statute making larceny a crime is declaratory of the common law and is therefore to be construed by application of common law principles. By contrast, the cases now under discussion arise in jurisdictions that have modernized their larceny statutes by adopting, or enacting variations on, the provisions of the Model Penal Code governing theft. MPC §§223.0-223.9. Accordingly, to the extent these opinions provide any legal analysis at all, they do so in terms of the wording of their governing statutes rather than the common law.

For example, in *State v. Martin*, 1996 WL 761215 (Ohio Ct. App.), defendant took four shirts from a display in a department store, carried them to a sales counter and asked for a refund, saying they had been gifts to her sons; the clerk gave defendant a receipt for a refund; and a store security agent who had observed defendant's course of conduct detained her before she left the store. Defendant was convicted of violating an Ohio statute declaring guilty of theft whoever shall knowingly "obtain or exercise control over" the property of another, without consent and "with purpose to deprive" the owner of the property. Ohio Rev. Code Ann. §2913.02(A). On appeal, the reviewing court held defendant's conduct came within the terms of the statute: the court reasoned that "By claiming she had ownership of the shirts, defendant exercised control over the shirts in a manner which was contrary to the store's ownership. In effect, there was a verbal concealment and exertion of control by defendant." *Martin*, 1996 WL 761215 at p. *4.

Turning to the issue of the defendant's intent to "deprive," the court stressed that the Ohio statutory definition of that term included the act of withholding property "with purpose to restore it only upon payment of a reward or other consideration." Ohio Rev. Code Ann. §2913.01(C)(1). The court reasoned, "Under the foregoing definition, if the defendant takes the property of another and does not intend to give it back until consideration is paid, the defendant has 'deprived' the victim, first of the property, and second of the consideration." *Martin*, 1996 WL 761215 at p. *4. Weaving these two themes together, the court concluded: "By telling the sales associate that the shirts had been given to her sons as gifts, defendant exercised verbal control and concealment, thus, exerting control over the shirts for the purpose of obtaining consideration from the store." *Id*.

We have set forth the Ohio court's reasoning in order to show how closely it follows the wording of the local statute—and, by the same token, how far it has moved away from the common law of larceny. The same is true, moreover, of the other cases in this category: their reasoning is often more conclusory than that of the Ohio case just discussed, but the statutes on which they rely are equally remote from the common law, and hence from the question before us.

## II

Several of the rationales articulated in the "sale" and "reward" cases, however, are also applicable to the "refund" cases. On close analysis, moreover, the relevant rationales may be reduced to a single line of reasoning that rests on both a principled and a practical basis. First, as a matter of principle, a claim of the right to "return" an item taken from a store display is no less an assertion of a *right of ownership* than the claim of a right to "sell" stolen property back to its owner. And an intent to return such an item to the store only if the store pays a satisfactory "refund" is no less *conditional* than an intent to return stolen property to its owner only if the owner pays a satisfactory "reward." Just as in the latter case, it can be said in the former that the purpose to return was founded wholly on the contingency that a refund would be offered, and unless the contingency happened the conversion was complete. It follows that a defendant who takes an item from a store display with the intent to claim its ownership and restore it only on condition that the store pay him a "refund" must be deemed to intend to permanently deprive the store of the item within the meaning of the law of larceny.

Second, as a practical matter, the risk that such a taking will be permanent is not a mere theoretical possibility; rather, by taking an item from a store display with the intent to demand a refund a defendant creates a substantial risk of permanent loss. This is so because if defendant's attempt to obtain a refund for the item fails for any reason, he has a powerful incentive to keep the item in order to avoid drawing attention to the theft. A person who has taken an item from a store display and has claimed the right to "return" it at a sales counter, but has been rebuffed because, for example, he has no receipt, will not be inclined to run the risk of confirming the suspicions of the sales clerk or store security personnel by *putting the item back* in the display. Instead, just as in the case of a failed attempt to "sell" property back to its owner, the trespasser would take away the property in order to conceal his own wrongdoing.

This, too, is not a mere theoretical possibility: our research discloses cases in which a defendant, rebuffed in an attempt to "return" an item taken from a display in the same store, simply took the item with him when he left the store. The most recent example is the California case of *People v. McLemore*, 27 Cal.App.4th 601 (1994). There defendant entered a store empty-handed but subsequently asked a sales clerk to "exchange" a dress he was then carrying; the clerk became suspicious when she noticed that the dress still bore an electronic sensor and a complete sales tag (such tags were normally torn in half when items were purchased). The clerk called the manager, who asked for a receipt. Defendant became angry and demanded the dress back, insisting it was his. The manager handed him the dress, and defendant left the store with it.

Similarly, in *Ray v. State*, 1992 WL 117452 (Tex. Ct. App.), defendant took shoes from a store display and asked for a refund at the checkout counter. After the clerk twice asked for a receipt and he twice failed to produce one, defendant became angry and the clerk called the manager. When the manager reiterated the demand for a receipt, defendant asked for a bag, the clerk put the shoes in it, and defendant left the store with the shoes....

In *Grady v. State*, 466 S.W.2d 770, 771 (Tex. Crim. App. 1971), defendant took an electric saw from a store display and asked a clerk for a refund. When she was unable to produce a receipt, the clerk told her to go to the customer-service counter. Instead, defendant went in the opposite direction and left the store with the saw. *See also People v. Dungy*, 122 Ill.App.3d 314 (1984) [defendant took a purse from a mannequin on the fifth floor of a department store and asked for a refund; when she was unable to obtain a refund she left the counter and took a "down" escalator, still carrying the purse].

### III

Applying the foregoing reasoning to the facts of the case at bar, we conclude that defendant's intent to claim ownership of the shirt and to return it to Mervyn's only on condition that the store pay him a "refund" constitutes an intent to permanently deprive Mervyn's of the shirt within the meaning of the law of larceny, and hence an intent to "feloniously steal" that property within the meaning of §484(a). Because Mervyn's cannot be deemed to have consented to defendant's taking possession of the shirt with the intent to steal it, defendant's conduct also constituted a trespassory taking within the meaning of the law of larceny. It follows that the evidence supports the final two elements of the offense of theft by larceny, and the Court of Appeal was correct to affirm the judgment of conviction. This determination makes it unnecessary to address defendant's contention that he cannot be convicted of larceny by trick and device or obtaining property by false pretenses.... For the foregoing reasons the judgment of the Court of Appeal is affirmed.

GEORGE, C.J., KENNARD, BAXTER, WERDEGAR, CHIN, and BROWN, JJ., concur.

## QUESTIONS ON *DAVIS*

**1. More facts.** Mervyn's store investigator, Aaron Rossiter, testified that on August 27, 1995, he saw Davis, a black male, drive into a mall parking lot near the Mervyn's store where Rossiter worked. Davis exited a white Honda Civic while his female companion remained in the vehicle. (Record Transcript pp. 121-22.) Rossiter became suspicious because the female remained in the car and Davis walked into the store "pretty fast with a Mervyn's bag in his hand." (RT 123.) Before Davis could enter the store, Rossiter entered and went to the store's viewing booth where he could watch Davis enter. Once inside, Rossiter phoned another security officer/loss prevention agent, Carol German, to alert her to Davis's presence so she could train the video surveillance camera on him. (RT 122-23.) Agent German testified that she set up the store's video camera to film Davis's every move from the moment he entered the store until German left the security office/surveillance room to arrest Davis. (RT 76, 88.)

German observed Davis carrying a Mervyn's bag with a shoebox inside as he entered the store. (RT 64.) After Davis was detained, German ascertained the shoebox did contain women's shoes. (RT 64, 89.) Davis walked through the store to the men's department, looked at some merchandise, left the department, went to the fine jewelry area, then turned the corner and proceeded back to the men's department. German observed Davis approach a "Fila active wear" display, look at some of the merchandise, then remove a Fila baseball style shirt off its hanger and fold it up. He carried the shirt in his hand, walked out of the men's department to the shoe department and then into the women's department where he approached the service desk.

Most of the rest of the story you know. Redacted from the California Supreme Court's version of the facts is Davis's testimony that he went to Mervyn's because his girlfriend, Raynika Brown, gave him shoes to return so she could purchase football cleats for him from another store as a gift. He had a game the following day. (RT 140-41.) He was playing for Pasadena City College and this was the sixth game. (RT 141.) Brown drove Davis to Mervyn's in her car and waited there while he went in. (RT 142.) Davis testified he picked up the shirt because he was going to buy it, but changed his mind. He took the shirt to a counter and told the clerk he did not want it, that it would have been a good gift for his father. The phone rang and when the clerk returned to the counter, she handed Davis a voucher and told him to sign it. Davis was confused and signed the voucher without reading it, just scribbling in any name. Brown testified consistently with Davis's testimony.

Do any of the above facts redacted from the California Supreme Court's opinion make a difference to whether Davis committed or attempted theft?

**2. Waiver of jury trial *after* conviction?** The *Davis* Court notes that the jury found Davis guilty of petty theft with a prior. That is a crime that ups the punishment cost to a one-year jailable term for petty thieves who, in a nutshell, have already been convicted of a theft-related offense (be it forcible or not), for which they did prison time. See California Penal Code §666(a) (2014) The state high court goes on to say that Davis "waived further jury trial." But he had just *been* tried by a jury. What would a further jury trial address? See supra Chapter 4.A, note 3 on *Bond*.

3. **Elemental analysis.**

   a. **Breaking down larceny.** The *Davis* Court set forth the six elements of larceny. Which of those elements did Davis contest on appeal? [*handwritten: Trespassing & animus furandi*]

   b. **"Conditional intent".** Did Davis really steal the *shirt*? How? By walking around with it? It is one thing to take someone else's property and sell it to someone other than the victim. But to sell it back to the victim—is that really the same?

   (1) Or is it manifest that Davis would have absconded with the shirt if Smith had refused him the voucher? If rebuffed by Smith, Davis then left the shirt on the counter, would he at that point have committed any crime at all?

   (2) Or is Davis's theft of the shirt predicated on the idea that holding himself out as owner of the shirt (who has the right to return it) is the act of a larcenist?

   c. **Mervyn's as *agent provocateur*.**

   (1) Did security agent Carol German consent to Davis's acquisition of the voucher? Did clerk Heather Smith?

   (2) If German and Smith had mismatched intentions, would that render Davis's project "impossible"?

   (3) What interest did German/Smith pass to Davis: possession? Or possession and title?

   (4) Suppose Rossiter had not noticed Davis and Brown pull into the parking lot, German had not observed Davis at all, German had not told Smith to accept the shirt in exchange for the voucher, and Smith naïvely issued Davis the voucher anyway. Then what?

[*handwritten: Only permissible passing of possession on voucher like Topolewski*]

# Chapter 6: The Case of Theft | 433

**4. Variance: when charges differ from proof.**

    **a.** At the close of the prosecution's case, Davis sought to dismiss the petty-theft charge on the ground that the prosecution's proof, which made out only a case of attempted theft at most, varied from the charge. He is right, though, isn't he—that on these facts he could only attempt, not commit, theft? What property of Mervyn's did Davis attempt to steal?

    **b.** The *Davis* Court ruled it was "unnecessary to address defendant's contention that he cannot be convicted of larceny by trick ... or obtaining property by false pretenses." Why?

**5. When was the *animus furandi* formed?** Suppose Davis took the shirt from the rack intending to go to the dressing room to conceal it under his own clothing, sneak out of the store, and present the shirt to his dad as a gift. What crime would that be?

**6. Testing theft knowledge.**

    **a.** Suppose a man enters a diner for lunch without a penny to his name. Knowing he is flat broke, his plan is to sneak out undetected at some opportune time after eating, either before or after receiving the bill. After his meal he is arrested in the parking lot by police, to whom he admits having entered the diner with no intention to pay. What crime has he committed? *[handwritten: in CA ↓ Fraud]*

    **b.** Suppose now the man can afford a meal, but he forgot his wallet at home. He realizes this only after getting the bill after eating his meal. He panics and quickly sneaks out of the diner, hoping no one will notice. Again, he is arrested in the parking lot and admits to having left the diner with no intention of repaying his debt. What crime has he committed? *[handwritten: No crime]*

    **c.** Suppose now the same facts as in (b) above, except this time, once he realizes that his wallet is not on his person, he goes out to his car to see if by chance he had left it there. When he is then arrested in the parking lot, he admits to having left the restaurant without paying, but truthfully denies having done so with no intention of repaying his debt. What crime has he committed? *[handwritten: No crime]*

    **d.** Would it matter in any of the above scenarios (a)-(c) whether our non-paying diner was heavily intoxicated? *[handwritten: Yes]*

## Criminal Law: Trials, Appeals, Theories

**e.** Now for a real case. On July 4, 2009, defendant Demetrius Lamont Williams entered a Walmart in Palmdale, California. Using either a MasterCard or a Visa re-encoded with a third party's credit card information, he bought a $200 Walmart gift card from a recently hired cashier, who was filling in for a cashier on a break. Williams then tried to buy three more gift cards from the same cashier. At that point, the regular cashier came back and, after learning of the previous transaction, told Williams of Walmart's policy prohibiting the use of credit cards for purchases of gift cards. Williams was permitted to keep the $200 gift card he had initially bought.

He then went to a different cash register and again presented a re-encoded payment card and got another $200 gift card. The transaction was observed by a Walmart security guard who, accompanied by another guard, asked Williams for the receipt and payment card used. Williams complied. When told that the payment card's last four digits did not match those on the receipt, he produced two other re-encoded payment cards, but their numbers did not match those on the receipt either.

Williams began walking toward the exit, followed by the two security guards. When told to stop, he produced yet another re-encoded payment card, but this card's last four digits also did not match those on the receipt. As he continued walking toward the exit, he pushed one of the guards, dropped some receipts, and started running away. After a brief struggle inside the store, the guards wrestled Williams to the ground and handcuffed him. Recovered from his possession were four payment cards issued by MasterCard and Visa and several gift cards from Walmart and elsewhere.

Williams was charged with 10 counts: four counts of robbery, one count of burglary, one count of fraudulent use of an access card, one count of grand theft, and three counts of forgery. The information also alleged Williams had one prior serious or violent felony conviction (robbery) within the meaning of the "Three Strikes" law. On the grand theft count, the court instructed the jury on fraud/false pretenses. The jury found Williams guilty as charged, and the trial court sentenced him to a total prison term of 23 years eight months.

The Court of Appeal reversed defendant's forgery convictions for insufficient evidence and modified the judgment to stay imposition of the burglary sentence under §654(a), which, as a reminder, prohibits punishment for more than one crime arising from a single indivisible course of conduct. In all other respects, the Court of Appeal affirmed the trial court's judgment, including defendant's robbery convictions. As he did in the Court of Appeal, Williams argued in the state high court that his robbery convictions were invalid because robbery requires theft by larceny, whereas the theft he committed was by false pretenses.

Williams prevailed in *People v. Williams*, 57 Cal.4th 776 (2013). Can you explain why? Your path toward an answer may stall out unless informed by the idea of a so-called *Estes* robbery, a peculiarity that makes robbery a "continuing" offense from the larcenous acquisition to safe harbor. *See People v. Estes*, 147 Cal.App.3d 23 (1983).

[Handwritten margin note: Security guard had Constructive Possession]

## NOTES ON *DAVIS*

**1. Gap-filling in retail theft.** Suppose Davis really did come to Mervyn's to buy his Dad a shirt as a gift. He and his Dad are the same size, so Davis takes the shirt from the rack, says he wants to try it on, and does so in a dressing room he is shown to by the sales clerk. Although he intends to buy or at least seriously consider buying the shirt, he experiences "sticker shock" when he sees the price tag, which is twice what he thought it would be. Hastily, he puts his own shirt on over the Mervyn's shirt and absconds with it before being accosted by security as he reaches the store exit. *Cf.* question 6(b) above.

On these facts, he has committed no crime. First, he has committed no larceny (CALJIC No. 14.02) because he acquired the shirt innocently/permissively according to the terms that retailers allow their customers to enjoy. Second, he has committed no embezzlement, which, according to CALJIC No. 14.07, requires a "relation of trust and confidence" between the acquirer and the theft victim. In no sense is Davis the fiduciary of Mervyn's. They may "trust" him with their merchandise in a very limited sense, but theirs is not a "relation of trust and confidence"—far from it. Third, he has committed no larceny by trick (CALJIC No. 14.05) because he did not dupe the store (as courts were fond of saying, "with trick or artifice") into allowing him to try on the shirt—his intentions were good when he took the shirt to try it on. And last, he has committed no fraud (false pretenses) (CALJIC No. 14.10) because, again, he did not trick the store into allowing him to try on the shirt; thus, the question of whether he obtained possession as opposed to possession and title never arises.

The *Davis* Court observed that one solution to the sticky business of identifying the precise crime that Davis committed has been solved in some jurisdictions by specialized theft statutes designed to deal with shoplifting. Those statutes do away with the element of trespass, which had inhibited proof of larceny since the initial acquisition in store settings is either consensual or, if by trick, the trick is difficult to prove. Moreover, regarding initially consensual acquisitions, these newer statutes do away with the requirement that the thief/shopper be a fiduciary of the victim/store, which had inhibited charges of embezzlement. Some states, for example, have generalized misappropriation statutes or statutes criminalizing what some call "larceny by bailee"; those statutes criminalize all bailments that are converted with *animus furandi*. *E.g.*, Wisconsin Statutes Annotated §943.20(1)(c) (West 2012).

As a reminder, "bailment" means that the bailee (acquirer) actually accepts (not feigns to accept) the agreed-to terms of possession set by the bailor (prior possessor). The absconding bailee then has a change of heart and decides (only then) to steal the property of which he had lawful possession (not title). By regulating *all* bailments, not just those between parties who stand in relations of trust and confidence, those newer statutes avoid the impediments that the limited store-shopper relation had posed for embezzlement laws. Indeed, some such statutes even tinker with the notion of *animus furandi* itself.

For example, interpreting New York's larceny statute, Penal Law §155.05, New York's high court ruled:

> In view of the modern definition of the crime of larceny, and its purpose of protecting individual property rights, a taking of property in the self-service store context can be established by evidence that a customer exercised control over merchandise wholly inconsistent with the store's continued rights. Quite simply, a customer who crosses the line between the limited right he or she has to deal with merchandise and the store owner's rights may be subject to prosecution for larceny. Such a rule should foster the legitimate interests and continued operation of self-service shops, a convenience which most members of the society enjoy.

*People v. Olivo*, 52 N.Y.2d 309, 321 (1981). Under *Olivo*, exercising control over property inconsistent with the owner's rights is stealing (reasoning not unlike that taken in *Davis*). The *Olivo* approach closed up gaps between the four forms of non-forcible theft. Olivo had concealed goods from a department store hardware aisle in his clothing and headed for the exit. Another defendant whose case was joined with his had removed the price tag from a jacket before putting it on and bypassing several cash registers. A third man whose case was jointly heard put a book from a store shelf in his briefcase and looked around furtively. Upholding the convictions of all three men, the New York high court's reading of the larceny statute overcame any inherent ambiguity of such in-store gestures, which were, if nothing else, "inconsistent" with what store owners want from their customers.

**2. Shoplifting.** The previous note refers to "specialized theft statutes designed to deal with shoplifting." While in New York "shoplifting" characterizes any unlawful acquisition or disposition of store property, the term is deployed quite narrowly in California, where it is considered a petty commercial burglary. Specifically, "shoplifting is defined as entering a commercial establishment with intent to commit larceny while that establishment is open during regular business hours, where the value of the property that is taken or intended to be taken does not exceed nine hundred fifty dollars ($950). Any other entry into a commercial establishment with intent to commit larceny is burglary." California Penal Code §459.5 (2014).

**3. O.J. Simpson as robber.** Simpson's drama began with Rodney King's March 3, 1991 videotaped beating by four LAPD officers. While the video made clear their guilt of excessive force and assault with a deadly weapon, a Ventura County jury acquitted all four officers on April 29, 1992. The conduct of the LAPD both in King's case and Simpson's (Detective Mark Fuhrman came off as racist) led jurors to look the other way when sitting in judgment of accused murderer Simpson. *See supra* Chapter 1.A, note 4 on *Decina*.

On September 13, 2007, as the battle over his assets dragged on, an intoxicated Simpson planned with six cronies to recover items of personal property that he suspected his agent, Mike Gilbert, had stolen from him. In that plan, Simpson and five others lured two memorabilia dealers (Fromong and Beardsley) to the Vegas Palace Station hotel room of the group's sixth member (Riccio). After the first to enter (Stewart) shoved Fromong into a chair, another (Alexander) revealed a gun in his waist, while a third (McClinton) waived a gun around as two others (Cashmore and Ehrlich) stuffed goods (some Simpson's) in pillowcases. Riccio, an auctioneer with a long criminal history, went on to sell his tape-recordings of the event to tabloids and testify with immunity against the other six. Alexander, McClinton, Cashmore, and Ehrlich exchanged guilty pleas for probation.

On October 3, 2008, Simpson and Stewart were convicted by a jury, who bloated the caper into a misdemeanor and 11 manifestly overlapping felonies: one count each of conspiracy to commit kidnapping, conspiracy to commit robbery, and burglary while in possession of a deadly weapon, plus two counts each of first-degree kidnapping with use of a deadly weapon, robbery with use of a deadly weapon, assault with a deadly weapon, and coercion with use of a deadly weapon.

On December 5, 2008, after dismissing the coercion counts as redundant to the kidnapping, Judge Jackie Glass gave both Simpson and Stewart 33 years. Stewart served 27 months before winning an appeal for having been prejudiced by being jointly tried with a known murderer. Rather than face re-trial, Stewart agreed to nine months' house arrest.

Simpson thereafter argued that because his lead attorney Yale Galanter was of the mind that forcible retrieval of one's own property cannot be robbery, talk of a plea never came up. In other jurisdictions, including his home state of Florida, Galanter would be correct, but not in Nevada. Simpson also argued that on learning that even the two gun-wielders in the heist got off with probation, he pressed his lawyers for like treatment. According to prosecutor David Roger, no pre-trial offer was made because Galanter had told him that Simpson insisted on probation, a deal-killer for Roger. During trial, Simpson's local counsel, Gabriel Grasso, fielded an offer of two-to-five years on a single count of robbery. Galanter was not in chambers to hear the offer, but did recall a break in the hallway when Simpson said he would accept no more than a year. Roger also recalls making Galanter a mid-trial offer of 30 months, but it was tied to an identical offer being accepted by Stewart, who turned it down.

Simpson's seven years of post-conviction challenges to what above I called "manifestly overlapping felonies" went nowhere, whether couched in the constitutional ban on double jeopardy or Nevada's (now defunct) ban on redundant punishments. Nevada courts managed to deem the luring of Fromong and Beardsley to Riccio's hotel room two counts of kidnapping, aggravated by use of a gun which, however, played no role in the luring. To cut off the assaults from the robberies and kidnappings to prevent their being "the same offense" in double-jeopardy terms, the Nevada high court characterized holding the victims at gunpoint *after* the pillowcases were full as a *separate* armed assault. While in another case a federal court sitting in Nevada found such a move to be an unlawful sort of double-counting, the Nevada Supreme Court found Galanter's failure to cite the federal case insufficient to count as constitutionally ineffective assistance of counsel because the case was merely persuasive, not controlling.

To be sure, leaving Simpson's long sentence intact was facilitated by the deferential standards of review that pervade criminal law in and out of Nevada. But it certainly was not dictated by them: Nevada law gave Judge Glass discretion to structure the sentences to all run concurrent. But she didn't.

To impose and let stand the 33-year term took a conviction apparatus bent on sticking it to Simpson. Indeed, it was game-on from the opening argument, when D.A. Chris Owens reminded jurors of Simpson's adverse tort judgment, which Owens said made Simpson desperate enough to rob back his property in Nevada to avoid the California post-judgment remedies on which Fred Goldman was relying. This, too, from Judge Glass at Simpson's sentencing:

> And when I first started this trial and I talked to the jury when we had the whole panel in, I stated to the group that if this was—if they were here because they wanted to punish Mr. Simpson for what happened previously, then this was not the case for them. And I meant that. As the judge in this case, I'm not here to sentence Mr. Simpson for what has happened in his life previously in the criminal justice system.

Glass later swore that pronouncing Simpson's judgment on October 3, 2008—the 13th anniversary of his infamous acquittal—was, after a three-week trial, pure coincidence.

Courts have acknowledged the public perception that Simpson got away with murder. That Judge Glass threw the book at Simpson as a tit-for-tat gesture is not a secret, dug up only by the likes of *NPR* and *Huffington Post* (though dig it up they did). Even Howard Stern saw the retaliatory nature of this second Simpson punishment. Within two years of Simpson's sentencing hearing, Judge Glass, a former T.V. news reporter, had theatricalized the memorabilia heist to the point that she left the bench to star in a short-lived reality show, *Swift Justice*, where she replaced Nancy Grace.

Most importantly, Glass was sure Simpson's 33-year sentence was lawful. Yet consider, for a moment, the argument that what matters most in justifying a death sentence is whether the defendant committed a death-eligible offense, not whether *other* death-eligible defendants received death sentences themselves. But how other death-eligible defendants were treated is *precisely* the point. One cannot "negate the negation" (cancel out crime through punishment) here and there, now and then, not without subordinating equality.

Simpson's eligibility for 33 years does not, without more, justify the sentence except in the most superficial sense. That he can be said to have earned such a sentence by somehow committing eleven felonies in one transaction can pass for argument only when considered in light of the treatment of other similarly situated offenders. How many offenders who stole personal property by like methods would be punished for *eleven* felonies? Simpson, who had *no* priors, served the statutorily required nine-year minimum of the 33 before being paroled from Lovelock Correctional Center on October 1, 2017 at age 70. For what it's worth, I have a client who pistol-whipped three drug dealers in their apartment, took their cash, and got sentenced to eight years, despite a considerable criminal history. The lesson of O.J. Simpson, Part II? If humans are ends in themselves, the avoidance of even the appearance of scapegoating is a worthy goal, despite the temptation to believe in the come-uppance as a worthy objective.

# TABLE OF CASES

Aaron, People v., 409 Mich. 672 (1980), 350
Abbot & Moon, People v., 84 A.D.2d 11 (N.Y. 1981), 403
Abney v. United States, 97 S.Ct. 2034 (1977), 68, 122
Acero, People v., 161 Cal.App.3d 217 (1984), 310-13
Adami, People v., 36 Cal.App.3d 452 (1973), 255, 260-64, 266
Adams v. Commonwealth, 534 S.E.2d 347 (Va. Ct. App. 2000), 220
Adkins v. Commonwealth, 96 S.W.3d 779 (Ky. 2003), 116
Airline Tariff Pub. Co., United States v., 1994 WL 502091 (D.D.C.), 279
Akis, People v., 347 N.E.2d 733 (Ill. 1976), 217
Albert A., In re, 47 Cal.App.4th 1004 (1996), 426
Albright, People v., 173 Cal.App.3d 883 (1985), 72
Alejandro B., In re, 186 Cal.Rptr.3d 763 (5th Dist. Ct. App. 2015), 70
Alvarado, People v., 232 Cal.App.3d 501 (1991), 81
Alvarez, United States v., 132 S.Ct. 2537 (2012), 19
Anderson, People v., 70 Cal.2d 15 (1968), 107-08, 144
Anderson, People v., 1 Cal.2d 687 (1934), 260, 265 n.2
Angelo, People v., 246 N.Y. 451 (1927), 7, 14
Antick, People v., 15 Cal.3d 79 (1975), 384 n.11, 394
Antonio (II), People v., 10 Cal.App.5th 1064 (2017), 227-28
Antonio (I), People v., 2016 WL 310104 (Cal. 4th Dist. Ct. App.), 131, 227-28

Apfelbaum, United States v., 100 S.Ct. 948 (1980), 19
Apprendi v. New Jersey, 120 S.Ct. 2348 (2000), 290
Ashley, People v., 42 Cal.2d 246 (1954), 413, 419
As. H., In re, 851 A.2d 456 (D.C. Ct. App. 2004), 275
Atencio, Commonwealth v., 189 N.E. 2d 627 (Mass. 1963), 403
Atkins, People v., 104 Cal.Rptr. 2d 738 (Cal. 2001), 105
Atkins, People v., 18 P.3d 660 (Cal. 2001), 219
Aurelio R., In re, 167 Cal.App.3d 52 (1985), 384 n.11

Baldwin v. New York, 399 U.S. 66 (1970), 218
Barker v. United States, 546 F.2d 940 (D.C. Cir. 1976), 200
Barton, People v., 12 Cal.4th 186 (1995), 157, 189-90
Bauer, People v., 32 A.D.2d 463 (N.Y. 1969), 246
Beeman, People v., 35 Cal.3d 547 (1984), 309-10, 319-22
Belk v. People, 125 Ill. 584 (1888), 386
Bell v. Commonwealth, 875 S.W.2d 882 (Ky. 1994), 116
Beltran, People v., 56 Cal.4th 935 (2013), 110
Berry, People v., 18 Cal.3d 509 (1976), 140, 144, 154, 158
Berry v. State, 31 Ohio St. 219 (1877), 424
Best, People v., 13 Cal.App.2d 606 (1936), 191
Beverley's Case, 76 English Reports 1118 (King's Bench 1603), 75-76

Billa, People v., 125 Cal.Rptr.2d 842 (3d Dist. Ct. App. 2002), 355, 369
Billings v. Commonwealth, 843 S.W.2d 890 (Ky. 1992), 116
Billingslea v. State, 780 S.W.2d 271 (Tex. Crim. App. 1989) (en banc), 44
Blockburger, United States v., 52 S.Ct. 180 (1932), 68
Blueford v. Arkansas, 132 S.Ct. 2044 (2012), 46
**Bond, People v., 178 Ill.App.3d 959 (1989), 211-19, 223-27**
Booker, United States v., 125 S.Ct. 738 (2005), 289
Borchers, People v., 50 Cal.2d 321 (1958), 140, 142, 154
Bottger, People v., 142 Cal.App.3d 974 (1983), 254
Bowens v. Superior Court, 1 Cal.4th 36 (1991) (en banc), 67
Boyce, People v., 27 N.E.3d 77 (Ill. 2015), 277
Braham v. State, 571 P.2d 631 (Alaska 1977), 262
Braslaw, People v., 233 Cal.App.4th 1239 (2015), 203
Brown v. State, 955 S.W.2d 276 (Tex. Crim. App. 1997), 23-24
Brown, People v., 40 N.Y.2d 381 (1976), 244
Brown v. United States, 256 U.S. 335 (1921), 160
Bruggy, People v., 93 Cal. 476 (1892), 140
Buffington, People v., 304 N.Y.S.2d. 746 (Supreme Court Monroe County 1969), 18
Bundy, State v., 974 N.E. 2d 139 (Ohio Ct. App. 2012), 185
Burd, State v., 419 S.E.2d 676 (W. Va. 1991), 266 n.5
Burton, People v., 6 Cal.3d 375 (1971) (en banc), 352, 355
Butts, People v., 236 Cal.App.2d 817 (1965), 322, 327

Cabaltero, People v., 31 Cal.App.2d 52 (1939), 366-69, 378

Calbud Inc., People v., 49 N.Y.2d 389 (1980), 176
Caldwell, People v., 36 Cal.3d 210 (1984) (en banc), 384 n.11, 389, 393-95
Cannon, People ex rel. Gibson v., 345 N.E.2d 218 (Ill. App. Ct. 1976), 218
Cantor, People v., 36 N.Y.2d 106 (1975), 173-74
Carmen, People v., 36 Cal.2d 768 (1951), 102
Carr, Commonwealth v., 580 A.2d 1362 (Penn. Super. Ct. 1990), 154
Casassa, People v., 404 N.E.2d 1310 (N.Y. 1980), 153
Superior Court (Caudie), People v., 221 Cal.App.3d 1190 (1990), 70
Cavitt v. Cullen, 134 S.Ct. 1522 (2014), 371
Cavitt, People v., 33 Cal.4th 187 (2004), 370-71, 374, 378
Cervantes v. Hall, 185 Fed.Appx. 690 (9th Cir. 2006), 395
Cervantes, People v., 2003 WL 1611397 (Cal. 4th Dist. Ct. App.), 395
***Cervantes, People v., 26 Cal.4th 860 (2001), 379-97, 403***
Chapman v. California, 386 U.S. 18 (1967), 312
Chavez, People v., 37 Cal.2d 656 (1951), 360, 363
Cheek v. United States, 498 U.S. 192 (1991), 200-01
Cheek v. Doe, 828 F.2d 395 (7th Cir. 1987), 201
Chiu, People v., 325 P.2d 972 (Cal. 2014), 293-94, 333
Chocolate Confectionary Antitrust Litigation, In re, 999 F.Supp.2d 777 (M.D. Penn. 2014), 278
Christian S., In re, 7 Cal.4th 768 (1994), 186, 190-91
Christian v. State, 951 A.2d 832 (Md. Ct. App. 2008), 186
Church, United States v., 32 M.J. 70 (USCMA 1991), 262

City of Moundridge v. Exxon Mobil Corp., 429 F.Supp.2d 117 (D.D.C. 2006), 278

Clarissa, State v., 11 Ala. 57 (1847), 237

Clark v. Arizona, 548 U.S. 735 (2006), 196

Cleaves, People v., 229 Cal.App.3d 367 (1991), 96

Coffin, State v., 504 N.W.2d 893 (Iowa 1993), 406

Cogdon, King v., Victoria (1950) (unreported), 24

Cohen v. Beneficial Industrial Loan Corp., 69 S.Ct. 1221 (1949), 67

Colantuono, People v., 7 Cal.4th 206 (1994) (en banc), 102-03

Coleman, People v., 48 Cal.3d 112 (1989), 95

Collice, People v., 41 N.Y.2d 906 (1977), 174

Collins, Regina v., 169 English Reports 1477 (Crown Cases Reserved 1864), 228

Conley, People v., 64 Cal.2d 310 (1966), 140, 142, 144

Contreras, People v., 26 Cal.App.4th 944 (1994), 71-72

Cooper, People v., 307 N.Y. 253 (1954), 11

Croy, People v., 41 Cal.3d 1 (1985), 321, 338

Curtin, People v., 22 Cal.App.4th 528 (1994), 413

Dacus, United States v., 66 M.J. 235 (U.S. Armed Forces Ct. App. 2008), 223

Daniel B., State v., 137 A.3d 837 (Conn. App. Ct. 2016), 221

Daniels, United States v., 28 M.J. 743 (Air Force Ct. of Military Rev. 1989), 219

Daniels, People v., 14 Cal.3d 857 (1975), 96

Daniels & Simmons, People v., 71 Cal. 2d 1119 (1969), 376

Darks v. Mullin, 327 F.3d 1001 (10th Cir. 2003), 148

Davidson v. United States, 137 A.3d 973 (D.C. Ct. App. 2016), 146

***Davis, People v., 19 Cal.4th 301 (1998), 410, 417-37***

***Decina, People v., 2 N.Y.2d 133 (1956), 2-23, 38, 43, 47-52, 65-66, 99***

Decina, People v., 1 A.D.2d 592 (N.Y. App. Div. 1956), 16, 19

***Superior Court (Decker), People v., 41 Cal.4th 1 (2007), 253-77***

De La Cruz, State v., 393 S.E.2d 184 (S.C. 1990), 290

Denaro v. Prudential Ins. Co., 154 A.D. 840 (N.Y. 1913), 10

DePetris v. Kuykendall, 239 F.3d 1057 (9th Cir. 2001), 206

Diaz, People v., 62 A.D.3d 157 (N.Y. App. Div. 2009), 157

DiBella, United States v., 82 S.Ct. 654 (1962), 68

Dillon, People v., 34 Cal.3d 441 (1983), 265 & n.1, 350, 356, 363, 416

Disanto, State v., 688 N.W.2d 201 (S.D. 2004), 268

Dixon, United States v., 548 U.S. 1 (2006), 157

***Dlugash, People v., 41 N.Y.2d 725 (1977), 234, 238-53, 294***

Dlugash, People v., 51 A.D.2d 974 (N.Y. 1976), 243

Dominguez v. Felker, 562 U.S. 1241 (2011), 377

Dominguez v. Felker, 400 F. App'x 153 (9th Cir. 2010), 377-78

Dominguez, People v., 39 Cal.4th 1141 (2006), 372-78

Downs v. State, 962 So.2d 1255 (Miss. 2007), 69

Doyle, State v., 921 P.2d 901 (Nev. 1996), 235

Drew, People v., 22 Cal.3d 333 (1978), 195

Dungy, People v., 122 Ill.App.3d 314 (1984), 430

Easley v. Cromartie, 121 S.Ct. 1452 (2001), 124

Edwards, People v., 345 N.E.2d 496 (Ill. 1976), 217
Edwards, People v., 72 Cal.App. 102 (1925), 412, 419 & n.3
Eichman, United States, v., 496 U.S. 310 (1990), 124
***Elmore, People v., 325 P.3d 951 (Cal. 2014), 186-99, 350***
Elonis, United States v., 138 S.Ct. 67 (2017), 121
Elonis, United States v., 841, F.3d 589 (3d Cir. 2016), 121, 131
Elonis, United States v., 135 S.Ct. 2001 (2015), 121
Elonis v. United States, 134 S.Ct. 2819 (2014), 121
Elonis, United States v., 730 F.3d 321 (3d Cir. 2013), 120-21
Enmund v. Florida, 458 U.S. 782 (1982), 350
Escobar, People v., 48 Cal.App.4th 999 (1996), 355
Estes, State v., 168 So.3d 847 (La. Ct. App. 2015), 157
Estes, People v., 147 Cal.App.3d 23 (1983), 435
Exxon Shipping Co. v. Baker, 554 U.S. 471 (2008), 21

Failla, People v., 64 Cal.2d 560 (1966), 326-28
Farley, People v., 46 Cal.4th 1053 (2009), 353-55
Fardan, People v., 628 N.E.2d 41 (N.Y. 1993), 120
Fay v. Noia, 83 S.Ct. 822 (1963), 127
Fichtner, People v., 118 N.Y.S.2d 392 (App. Div. 1952), 267-68
Fields v. Commonwealth, 44 S.W.3d 355 (Ky. 2001), 112
Flannel, People v., 25 Cal.3d 668 (1979), 142, 189, 191-92
***Flippo v. State, 258 Ark. 233 (1975), 34-44, 47, 51-52, 200-02***
Flood, People v., 957 P.2d 869 (Cal. 1998), 312
Florida Bar v. Marable, 645 So.2d 438 (Fla. 1994), 254

FMC Corp., United States v., 84 S.Ct. 4 (1963), 67
Ford, People v., 60 Cal.2d 772 (1964), 362
Foster v. Commonwealth, 827 S.W.2d 670 (Ky. 1991), 113
***Fountain, United States v., 768 F.2d 790 (7th Cir. 1985), 132, 304-08, 312-13***
Fowler, State v., 268 N.W.2d 220 (Iowa 1978), 141
Fowler, People v., 178 Cal. 657 (1918), 385-86, 389
Fraley, Ex Parte, 109 P. 295 (Okla. Crim. Ct. App. 1910), 157
Friend, People v., 211 P.3d 520 (Cal. 2000), 350, 356
Fuller, People v., 86 Cal.App.3d 618 (1978), 61

Gall v. Commonwealth, 607 S.W.2d 97 (Ky. 1980), 113
Garcia, People v., 69 Cal.App.4th 1324 (1999), 384 n.11
Gard, State v., 742 N.W.2d 257 (S.D. 2007), 411
Gardner, People v., 37 Cal.App.4th 473 (1995), 384 n.11
Garner, Tennessee v., 471 U.S. 1 (1985), 161-62
Gauze, People v., 15 Cal.3d 709 (1975) (en banc), 371
Gilbert, People v., 63 Cal.2d 690 (1965), 359, 383-85, 384 n.11, 389 & n.15, 390, 393, 397
Girouard, State v., 321 Md. 532 (1991), 153
Gladstone, State v., 474 P.2d 274 (Wash. 1970) (en banc), 309
Glover, People v., 233 Cal.App.3d 1476 (1991), 96
Goetz v. Kunstler, 164 Misc.2d 557 (Supreme Court N.Y. County 1995), 183
Goetz, People v., 141 A.D.2d 446 (N.Y. App. Div. 1988), 182
Goetz, People v., 532 N.E.2d 1273 (N.Y. 1988), 46, 182

Goetz, People v., 137 Misc.2d 380 (Supreme Court N.Y. County 1987), 182

**Goetz, People v., 497 N.E.2d 41 (N.Y. 1986), 163-83, 206**

Gometz v. United States, 2015 WL 3814652 (S.D. Ill.), 313

Gomez v. Perez, 93 S.Ct. 872 (1973), 45

Gomez v. Superior Court (Mendocino County), 328 P.2d 976 (Cal. 1958), 148

Gonzalez, People v., 51 Cal.4th 894 (2011), 356

Gonzalez & Soliz, People v., 52 Cal.4th 254 (2011), 333

Gonzalez-Lopez, United States v., 548 U.S. 140 (2006), 312

Goodall v. State, 627 S.E.2d 183 (Ga. Ct. App. 2006), 220

Gore, State v., 288 Conn. 770 (2008), 218

Grady v. State, 466 S.W.2d 770 (Tex. Crim. App. 1971), 430

Graham, People v., 71 Cal.2d 303 (1969), 141

Graham v. United States, 187 F.2d 87 (D.C. Cir. 1950), 268, 414

Green v. United States, 78 S.Ct. 221 (1957), 148

Green, State v., 38 Wash.2d 240 (1951), 36, 40

**Greene v. Commonwealth, 197 S.W.3d 76 (Ky. 2006), 110-24, 134, 136, 147, 157**

Gregory, People v., 124 Cal.Rptr.2d 776 (5th Dist. Ct. App. 2002), 205

Griffin v. California, 85 S.Ct. 1229 (1965), 19

Griggs v. Meko, 2013 WL 823323 (E.D. Ky.), 127-31

Group, State v., 98 Ohio St.3d 248 (2002), 262

Guebara, State v., 696 P.2d 381 (Kan. 1985), 159

Guffey, State v., 262 S.W.2d 152 (Mo. Ct. App. 1953), 231-32, 245, 251, 253

Gutierrez, People v., 45 Cal.4th 789 (2009), 154

Gutierrez, People v., 28 Cal.4th 1083 (2002), 354

Hall, Regina v., 169 Eng. Rep. 291 (1848), 422-23

Hamilton, United States v., 499 F.3d 734 (7th Cir. 2007), 410

Hammond, People v., 181 Cal.App.3d 463 (1986), 323-24

Hardin, People v., 102 Cal.Rptr.2d 262 (1st Dist. Ct. App. 2000), 205

Harris v. New York, 401 U.S. 222 (1971), 20, 225

Hauptmann, State v., 115 N.J.L. 412 (1935), 424-25

Hecker, People v., 109 Cal. 451 (1895), 185

Hector H., In re, 2017 WL 2644678 (Cal. 4th Dist. Ct. App.), 403-04

Hernandez, People v., 393 P.2d 673 (Cal. 1964), 200

Hicks v. United States, 150 U.S. 442 (1893), 299

Higgs, People v., 1990 WL 1351 (Ohio Ct.App.), 420

Hinkhouse, State v., 139 Or.App. 446 (1996), 223

Hobbs v. Hullman, 183 A.D. 743 (N.Y. 1918), 10

Holder, People v., 53 Cal.App. 45 (1921), 411

Holland v. Commonwealth, 114 S.W.3d 792 (Ky. 2003), 112

Holloway, People v., 164 Cal.App.4th 269 (2008), 26

Hood, People v., 1 Cal.3d 444 (1969) (en banc), 84-85, 94-95, 97, 102

Howard, People v., 34 Cal.4th 1129 (2007), 351

Hoyle v. State, 268 S.W.3d 313 (Ark. 2007), 43

Hurtado, People v., 63 Cal. 288 (1883), 140

Ireland, People v., 70 Cal.2d 522 (1969) (en banc), 352-53, 355

Jackiewicz, People v., 517 N.E.2d 316 (Ill. App. Ct. 1987), 214
Jackson, United States v., 835 F.2d 1195 (7th Cir. 1987), 132-34
Jackson, People v., 152 Cal.App.3d 961 (1984), 143
Jackson v. Virginia, 443 U.S. 307 (1979), xv, 39, 72, 114, 119, 125, 148
Jacobs v. State, 184 So.2d 711 (Fla. 1st D.C.A. 1966), 403
Jaffe, People v., 185 N.Y. 497 (1906), 246, 251, 253
James M., In re, 9 Cal.3d 517 (1973), 102
James v. State, 229 Cal.App.4th 130 (2014), 104
Johnigan v. Elo, 207 F.Supp.2d 599 (E.D. Mich. 2002), 125
Johnson v. Commonwealth, 308 Ky. 709 (1948), 37
Johnson v. Glick, 481 F.2d 1028 (2d Cir. 1973), 161
Johnson v. Sheriff, Clark County, 91 Nev. 161 (1975), 263
Johnson, Connecticut v., 460 U.S. 73 (1983), 311-12
Johnson, People v., 67 Cal.App.4th 67 (1998), 105
Johnson, People v., 174 Ill.App.3d 812 (1988), 42
Johnson, People v., 26 Cal.3d 557 (1980), 144
Johnson, People v., 280 N.E.2d 764 (Ill. App. Ct. 1972), 145
Jones v. United States, 308 F.2d 307 (D.C. Cir. 1962), 37-38, 44
Jones, People v., 36 Cal.2d 373 (1950), 414
Joyce, State v., 139 Vt. 638 (1981), 29
Jurado, People v., 38 Cal.4th 72 (2006), 265 n.1

Kansas v. Ventris, 129 S.Ct. 1841 (2009), 20
Kauffman, People v., 152 Cal. 331 (1907), 285, 288, 320-21, 331
Kelly, Commonwealth v., 724 A.2d 909 (Pa. 1999), 312
Kelly, State v., 97 N.J. 178 (1984), 174
Kennedy v. Louisiana, 554 U.S. 407 (2008), 293
Kennedy, Commonwealth v., 48 N.E. 770 (Mass. 1897), 233
Keohane, Commonwealth v., 444 Mass. 563 (2005), 158
Ketchum v. Ward, 422 F.Supp. 934 (W.D.N.Y. (1976), 18
Keys v. State, 104 Nev. 736 (1988), 95
Kilgus, State v., 519 A.2d 231 (N.H. 1986), 262, 265-67 n.2
Kleppe, State v., 800 N.W.2d 311 (N.D. 2011), 73
Knoller, People v., 41 Cal.4th 139 (2007), 189
Koerner, People v., 154 N.Y. 355 (1897), 9
Kohl, People v., 527 N.E.2d 1882 (N.Y. 1988), 157
Krist, People v., 97 Mich.App. 669 (1980), 406

Lambert v. Blodgett, 393 F.3d 943 (9th Cir. 2004), 252-53
Lara, People v., 44 Cal.App.4th 102 (1996), 104
Lathus, People v., 35 Cal.App.3d 466 (1973), 104
Estate of Laubenheimer, In re, 833 N.W.2d 735 (Wis. 2013), 101
Lauria, People v., 251 Cal.App.2d 471 (1967), 306-08
Le, People v., 158 Cal.App.4th 516 (2007), 154
Lee, People v., 20 Cal.4th 47 (1999), 146
Lee, People v., 43 Cal.3d 666 (1987), 95
Leonard, Commonwealth v., 279 S.W.3d 151 (Ky. 2009), 131
Lewis, People v., 124 Cal. 551 (1899), 385, 397
Ligouri, People v., 284 N.Y. 309 (1940), 175
Linda R.S. v. Richard D., 93 S.Ct. 1146 (1973), 45

Lindsey ex rel. Lindsey v. Caddo Parish School Bd., 954 So. 2d 272 (La. Ct. App. 2007), 275
Liotard, United States v., 817 F.2d 1074 (3d Cir. 1987), 68
Lockridge, People v., 870 N.W.2d 502 (Mich. 2015), 289
Logan, People v., 175 Cal. 45 (1917), 139
Lookadoo, People v., 66 Cal.2d 307 (1967), 359
Lopez, In re, 246 Cal.App.4th 350 (2016), 294
Lukenbill, People v., 234 Cal.App.3d Supp. 1 (1991), 66
Lumsden, People v., 201 N.Y. 264 (1911), 171
Luparello, People v., 187 Cal.App.3d 410 (1986), 285, 290-91, 320, 333
Lutwak v. United States, 344 U.S. 604 (1953), 311
Lynch, In re, 503 P.2d 921 (Cal. 1972) (en banc), 289-90
Lynn, Commonwealth v., 27 Va.Ct.App. 336 (1998), 180

Maciel, People v., 2011 WL 5120839 (Cal. 3d Dist. Ct. App.), 371
Maddox, Commonwealth v., 955 S.W.2d 718 (Ky. 1997), 116
Madison v. State, 234 Ind. 517 (1955), 387, 389
Maloney, State v., 490 A.2d 772 (N.H. 1985), 46
Mandel, State v., 78 Ariz. 226 (1954), 262, 266 n.5
Manning's Case, 83 English Reports 112 (1671), 110
Manning, Regina v., 169 Eng. Rep. 619 (1852), 422
Manriquez, People v., 37 Cal.4th 547 (2005), 154
Manson et al., People v. Charles, 132 Cal.Rptr. 265 (2d Dist. Ct. App. 1976), 66
Marbury v. Brooks, 20 U.S. 556 (1822), 30
Martin, State v., 1996 WL 761215 (Ohio Ct. App.), 427-28

Martinez, People v., 239 Cal.App.2d 161 (1966), 322
Martinez v. Ryan, 132 S.Ct. 1309 (2012), 132
Martinez, State v., 230 P. 379 (N.M. 1924), 235
Mason, Commonwealth v., 105 Mass. 163 (1870), 423
Matos, People v., 634 N.E.2d 157 (N.Y. 1994), 362-63
Matthews, People v., 70 Cal.App.4th 164 (1999), 105
Mayberry, People v., 15 Cal.3d 143 (1975), 200, 374-75
McClellan v. Commonwealth, 715 S.W. 2d 464 (Ky. 1986), 113-14
McConnell, People v., 373 N.Y.S.2d 971 (Sup. Ct. 1975), 67
McCoy, People v. 2005 WL 737711 (Cal. 3d Dist. Ct. App.), 348
McCoy, People v., 2002 WL 864283 (Cal. 3d Dist. Ct. App.), 347-48
**McCoy, People v., 25 Cal.4th 1111 (2001), 334-48**
McCoy, People v., 93 Cal.Rptr.2d 827 (3d Dist. Ct. App. 2000), 343-44
McDonald, Commonwealth v., 5 Cush. 365 (Mass. 1850), 230
McDonough, In re, 930 N.E.2d 1279 (Mass. 2010), 45
McFarlane, People v., 138 Cal. 481 (1903), 147-48
McFarlane, People v., 134 Cal. 618 (1901), 147-48
McKane v. Durston, 153 U.S. 684 (1894), 122
McKeldin v. State, 516 S.W.2d (Tenn. 1974), 274
McKelvy, People v., 194 Cal.App.3d 694 (1987), 186
McKnight, People v., 2002 WL 59612 (Cal. 1st Ct. App.), 371
McLemore, People v., 27 Cal.App.4th 601 (1994), 429
McVay et al., State v., 132 A. 436 (R.I. 1926), 345
Medellin v. Superior Court, 166 Cal.App.3d 290 (1985), 66

Medina, People v., 46 Cal.4th 913 (2009), 287
Mejia-Lenares, People v., 135 Cal.App.4th 1437 (2006), 188, 191-92, 203-04
Memro, People v., 38 Cal.3d 658 (1985), 265 n.2
Mendenhall, United States v., 446 U.S. 544 (1980), 100
Superior Court v. County of Mendocino, 13 Cal.4th 45 (1996), 110 n.a
Mersky, United States v., 361 U.S. 431 (1960), 157
Mesa, People v., 277 P.3d 743 (Cal. 2012), 334
Michael R. v. Jeffrey B., 158 Cal.App.3d 1059 (1984), 309
Millar v. Berg, 316 S.W.2d 499 (Mo. 1958), 46
Miller v. Fenton, 106 S.Ct. 445 (1985), 252
Miller, People v., 39 N.Y.2d 543 (1976), 174
Miller, People v., 247 A.D. 489 (N.Y. 1936), 248
Miranda v. Arizona, 384 U.S. 436 (1966), 20, 165, 221, 225, 252
Missouri v. Seibert, 124 S.Ct. 2601 (2004), 20
Mitchell v. Forsyth, 105 S.Ct. 2806 (1985), 67
Mitchell, State v., 71 S.W. 175 (Mo. 1902), 232-33, 245, 251, 253
M'Naghten's Case, 8 Eng. Rep. 718 (1843), 149, 193-95, 197
Molasky, State v., 765 S.W.2d 597 (Mo. 1989), 263
Montana v. Egelhoff, 518 U.S. 37 (1996), 76, 99
Montoya, People v., 7 Cal.4th 1027 (1994), 324, 329
Moore, People v., 187 Cal.App.4th 937 (2010), 72
Morales, People v., 5 Cal.App.4th 917 (1992), 265 n.2
Moran, People v., 123 N.Y. 254 (1890), 246, 251
Moretti, State v., 52 N.J. 182 (1968), 245
Morgan Stanley v. JP Morgan Chase Bank, 645 F.Supp.2d 248 (S.D.N.Y 2009), 410
Mosher, People v., 1 Cal.3d 379 (1969), 142
Moss, People ex rel. Perkins v., 187 N.Y. 410 (1907), 248
Mouton, People v., 15 Cal.App.4th 1313 (1993), 319, 324-26, 332
Mullaney v. Wilbur, 95 S.Ct. 1881 (1975), 156-57

Najera, People v., 138 Cal.App.4th 212 (2006), 154
Nay, State v., 167 P.3d 430 (Nev. 2007), 235
Newberg, State v., 278 P. 568 (Or. 1929), 40
Newland, People v., 15 Cal.2d 678 (1940), 39
Newton, People v., 87 Cal.Rptr. 394 (1st Dist. Ct. App. 1970), 26
Nieto Benitez, People v., 4 Cal.4th 91 (1992), 85
Nixon v. Fitzgerald, 102 S.Ct. 2690 (1982), 68
North American Coin & Currency, In re, 767 F.2d 1573 (9th Cir. 1985), 414
North Carolina v. Pearce, 89 S.Ct. 2072 (1969), 68
North, People v., 131 Cal.App.3d 112 (1982), 417
Nunez, People v., 320 N.E.2d 462 (Ill. App. Ct. 1974), 217

Oliver, People v., 258 Cal.Rptr. 138 (1st Ct. App. 1989), 40-41
Olivo, People v., 52 N.Y.2d 309 (1981), 436
Olsen, People v., 80 Cal. 122 (1889), 356
Oregon v. Kennedy, 102 S.Ct. 2083 (1982), 46
O'Searo, Commonwealth v., 466 Pa. 224 (1976), 219-20

Overton, New Jersey v., 815 A.2d 517 (N.J. App. Div. 2003), 27

Padilla, People v., 103 Cal.App.4th 675 (2002), 199
Palmer, People v., 964 P.2d 524 (Colo. 1998) (en banc), 278
Palmer, People v., 472 N.E.2d 795 (Ill. 1984), 217
Partida, United States v., 385 F.3d 546 (5th Cir. 2004), 347
Patterson, People v., 2016 WL 6962526 (Cal. 4th Dist. Ct. App), 131
Patterson, People v., 49 Cal.3d 615 (1989), 350
Patterson v. New York, 97 S.Ct. 2319 (1977), 156-57
Payne v. Commonwealth, 623 S.W.2d 867 (Ky. 1981), 115
Pear, King v., 168 Eng. Rep. 208 (Crown Cases Reserved 1779), 412
Peaslee, Commonwealth v., 177 Mass. 267 (1901), 262
Pechenik v. Baltimore & Ohio Railroad Co., 205 S.E.2d 813 (W. Va. 1974), 413
Peck v. Dunn, 574 P.2d 367 (Utah 1978), 73
Pelchat, People v., 62 N.Y.2d 97 (1984), 167-68, 177
Peoni, United States v., 100 F.2d 401 (2d Cir. 1938), 298-99
Percival v. People, 2014 WL 3936333 (Virgin Islands 2014), 30
Perez, People v., 2 Cal.4th 1117 (1992), 182
Phillips, People v., 64 Cal.2d 574 (1966), 58, 360
Pinkerton v. United States, 328 U.S. 640 (1946), 285, 288
Pitts, State v., 43 Miss. 472 (1870), 237
Pizano v. Superior Court, 21 Cal.3d 128 (1978), 384 n.11
Poe v. Commonwealth, 301 S.W.2d 900 (Ky. 1957), 115
Poole, Regina v., 7 Cox Crim. Cas. 373 (1857), 423

Powers v. City of Richmond, 10 Cal.4th 85 (1995) (en banc), 110 n.a
**Prettyman, People v., 14 Cal.4th 248 (1996), 314-34, 337-39, 346**
Prettyman, People v., 24 Cal.App.4th 211 (1994), 315
Pride, People v., 3 Cal.4th 195 (1992), 328

Quach, People v., 116 Cal.App.4th 294 (2004), 185

Ramirez, People v., 109 Cal.App.3d 529 (1980), 417
Ray v. State, 1992 WL 117452 (Tex. Ct. App.), 429-30
Reddick, State v., 48 N.W. 846 (S.D. 1891), 411
Redmond, People v., 71 Cal.2d 745 (1969) (en banc), 359
Reese, People v., 815 N.W.2d 85 (Mich. 2012), 206
Ricardi, People v., 221 Cal.App.3d 249 (1990), 81
Rider, United States v., 16 S.Ct. 983 (1896), 122
Rios, People v., 97 Cal.Rptr.2d 512 (Cal. 2000), 146-48
Rivera, People v., 234 Cal.App.4th 1350 (2015), 293-94
Roberts, People v., 2 Cal.4th 271 (1992) (en banc), 386-89, 397
Roberts v. United States, 445 U.S. 552 (1980), 33
Robertson, People v., 34 Cal.4th 156 (2004), 353, 356
Rocha, People v., 3 Cal.3d 893 (1971), 94, 104
Rodawald, People v., 177 N.Y. 408 (1904), 174-75
Rogers, People v., 172 Cal.App.3d 502 (1985), 323
Rollino, People v., 233 N.Y.S.2d 580 (Sup. Ct. 1962), 407-08
Rollins v. State, 302 S.W.3d 617 (Ark. Ct. App. 2009), 43
Rome v. Guillory, 335 Fed.Appx. 425 (5th Cir. 2009), 220

Romero, People v., 2002 WL 533216 (Cal. 3d Ct. App.), 350-51
Ross v. Moffitt, 417 U.S. 600 (1974), 123
Rufo v. Simpson, 86 Cal.App.4th 573 (2001), 21
Rupp, People v., 41 Cal.2d 371 (1953) (en banc), 355
Russell, People v., 144 Cal.App.4th 1415 (2006), 199-200
Russell, People v., 693 N.E.2d 193 (N.Y. 1998), 403
Russo, State v., 24 Del. 538 (1910), 141
Ryan N., In re, 92 Cal.App.4th 1359 (2001), 261
Ryan, Commonwealth v., 30 N.E. 364 (Mass. 1892), 416

Saephanh, People v., 80 Cal.App.4th 451 (2000), 277
Saille, People v., 54 Cal.3d 1103 (1991), 85, 189
Salazar, People v., 33 Cal.App.4th 341 (1995), 376
Sanchez, People v., 24 Cal.4th 983 (2001), 69-70
Sanchez, State v., 23 S.W.3d 30 (Tex. Crim. App. 2000), 279
Santana, People v., 133 Cal.Rptr.3d 393 (4th Dist. Ct. App. 2011), 102
Sarun Chun, People v., 45 Cal.4th 1172 (2009), 351, 353, 355
Saterfield, People v., 65 Cal.2d 752 (1967), 141
Schriro v. Landrigan, 127 S.Ct. 1933 (2007), 126
Schroeder, State v., 261 N.W.2d 759 (Neb. 1978), 180-81
Schuyler, People v., 106 N.Y. 298 (1887), 9
Scofield, Rex v., Cald. 397 (1784), 245
Scott, Commonwealth v., 73 A.3d 599 (Pa. 2013), 200
Sears, People v., 62 Cal.2d 737 (1965), 365
Seidel v. Merkle, 146 F.3d 750 (9th Cir. 1998), 205-06

Sekona, People v., 27 Cal.App.4th 443 (1994), 186
Sepe, People v., 111 A.D.3d 75 (N.Y. App. Div. 2013), 153
Shields, People v., 127 N.E.2d 440 (Ill. 1955), 214
Shufflin, People v., 62 N.Y. 229 (1875), 141
Silverstein, United States v., 732 F.2d 1338 (7th Cir. 1984), 304
Sindell v. Abbott Laboratories, 26 Cal.3d 588 (1980), 397-404
Slaughter v. State, 38 S.E. 854 (Ga. 1901), 423-24
Small, People v., 7 Cal.App.3d 347 (1970), 140
Smallwood v. State, 343 Md. 97 (1996), 223
Smith, People v., 500 N.E.2d 605 (Ill. App. Ct. 1986), 216
Solis, People v., 20 Cal.App.4th 264 (1993), 319, 325-29
Solomon, In re, 465 F.3d 114 (3d Cir. 2006), 68
Sonnesyn v. Akin, 104 N.W. 1026 (N.D. 1905), 415
Sparer v. Travelers Ins. Co., 173 N.Y.S. 673 (App. Div. 1919), 10
Spears v. Commonwealth, 30 S.W.3d 152 (Ky. 2001), 113-14
Spencer v. State, 149 A.3d 610 (Md. Ct. App. 2016), 223
Spriggs v. United States, 52 A.3d 878 (D.C. Cir. 2012), 371-72
**Spurlin, People v., 156 Cal.App.3d 119 (1984), 110, 137-50, 155-59, 205**
Stack v. Boyle, 72 S.Ct. 1 (1952), 68
**Stamp, People v., 2 Cal.App.3d 203 (1969), 357-66, 370, 378**
Standefer v. United States, 447 U.S. 10 (1980), 347
Staten, People v., 24 Cal.4th 434 (2000), 382-83
Stay, People v., 19 Cal.App.3d 166 (1971), 425
Stephan, United States v., 63 S.Ct. 1135 (1943), 123

Stennet v. State, 564 So.2d 95 (Ala. Ct. App. 1990), 220
Stevens v. Epps, 2008 WL 4183528 (S.D. Miss.), 356
Stokes v. State, 92 Miss. 415 (1908), 260
Stowell, People v., 31 Cal.4th 1107 (2003), 131
Strickland v. Washington, 104 S.Ct. 2052 (1984), 128
Summers v. Tice, 33 Cal.2d 80 (1948), 400-01, 403
Sunzar, State v., 331 N.J.Super. 248 (1999), 262
Superior Court (1973 Grand Jury), People v., 13 Cal.3d 430 (1975), 66

Talbot, People v., 64 Cal.2d 691 (1966), 360
Tally, State ex rel. Attorney General v., 15 So. 722 (Alabama 1894), 296-97
Taylor v. Superior Court, 24 Cal.3d 890 (1979), 58, 63, 89-90
Taylor v. Superior Court, 3 Cal.3d 578 (1970), 384 n.11
Taylor, State v., 345 Mo. 325 (1939), 245, 251
Taylor, People v., 177 N.Y. 237 (1904), 174
Teal, People v., 196 N.Y. 372 (1909), 246
Tewksbury, People v., 15 Cal.3d 953 (1976), 197-98
Theatre Enterprises. v. Paramount Film Distrib., 346 U.S. 537 (1954), 278
Thomas, United States v., 13 USCMA 278 (1962), 234-35, 246, 251, 253
Tison v. Arizona, 481 U.S. 137 (1987), 350
Tomlins, People v., 213 N.Y. 240 (1914), 171
Topolewski v. Plankington Packing Co., 143 Wis. 52 (1910), 335, 347, 407
Topolewski v. State, 130 Wis. 244 (1906), 335, 347, 407
Traster, People v., 111 Cal.App.4th 1377 (2003), 414
Travis, People v., 171 Cal.App.2d 842 (1959), 333-34
Tripp, State v., 36 Md.App. 459 (1977), 141
Trujillo, People v., 181 Cal.App.4th 1344 (2010), 103-04
Turley, People v., 50 Cal. 469 (1875), 140
Turner v. Commonwealth, 914 S.W.2d 343 (Ky. 1996), 118

Umana, People v., 138 Cal.App.4th 625 (2006), 406

Valentine, People v., 28 Cal.2d 121 (1946), 139-40
Valles, People v., 62 N.Y.2d 36 (1984), 176
Vargas, People v., 174 Cal.Rptr.3d 277 (Cal. 2014), 70
Vasquez v. Hillery, 106 S.Ct. 617 (1986), 127
Velez, People v., 175 Cal.App.3d 785 (1985), 27
Verdugo, People v., 50 Cal.4th 263 (2010), 156
Villanueva, People v., 169 Cal.App.4th 41 (2008), 184-85

Wakefield v. Department of State Police, 994 N.E.2d 722 (Ill. App. Ct. 2013), 42
Walsh, State v., 119 P.3d 645 (Idaho 2005), 159
Warren v. District of Columbia, 444 A.2d 1 (D.C. 1981), 31
Washington, People v., 62 Cal.2d 777 (1965), 95, 359, 383-84, 389 n.15
Waters, State v., 234 A.2d 147 (Md. Spec. Ct. App. 1967), 235
Watson v. People v., 198 Cal.Rptr. 26 (3d Dist. Ct. App. 1983), 72
**Watson, People v., 637 P.2d 279 (Cal. 1981), 52-72, 88-90, 95, 97, 106, 150, 258, 268, 271-73**
Watson, People v., 108 Cal.App.3d 677 (1980), 67
Watson, People v., 299 P.2d 243 (Cal. 1956), 311-12

Watts v. State, 885 N.E.2d 1228 (Ind. 2008), 148
Wells, People v., 33 Cal.2d 330 (1949), 192, 194-97
Wells, People v., 202 P.2d 53 (Cal. 1949), 204-05
Wells, In re, 174 Cal. 467 (1917), 110 n.a
Weston v. State, 682 P.2d 1119 (Alaska 1984), 174
Whitfield, People v., 2010 WL 1972952 (Cal. 4th Dist. Ct. App.), 108
**Whitfield, People v., 7 Cal.4th 437 (1994) (en banc), 76-102, 106, 108, 134, 146, 158**
Whitfield, People v., 15 Cal.Rptr.2d 4 (4th Dist. Ct. App. 1992), 101
Whitmore v. State, 298 N.W. 194 (Wis. 1941), 413
Wickersham, People v., 32 Cal.3d 307 (1982) (en banc), 153
Wilkins, People v., 56 Cal.4th 333 (2013), 370
Williams v. State, 257 Ark. 8 (1974), 34
Williams v. State of California, 34 Cal.3d 18 (1983), 31
Williams v. Superior Court, 71 Cal.2d 1144 (1969), 258
Williams, People v., 57 Cal.4th 776 (2013), 413, 434-35
Williams, People v., 26 Cal.4th 779 (2001), 103-04

Williams, People v., 75 Cal.App.3d 731 (1977), 340-41, 345
Williams, People v., 63 Cal.2d 452 (1965), 351
Williamson, In re, 43 Cal.2d 651 (1954), 54-56
Wilson, People v., 1 Cal.3d 431 (1969), 354-55
Wilson, United States v., 2015 WL 3536715 (U.S. Air Force Ct. Crim. App.), 369
Winship, In re, 397 U.S. 358 (1970), 156
Witcraft, People v., 201 Cal.App.4th 659 (2011), 132
Wright v. State, 363 So.2d 617 (Fla. 1st D.C.A. 1978), 387
Wright v. West, 112 S.Ct. 2482 (1992), 126
Wright, People v., 100 Cal.App.4th 703 (2002), 102-04

Yanz, State v., 74 Conn. 177 (1901), 141
Ybarra v. Spangard, 25 Cal.2d 486 (1944), 400

Zacarias, People v., 157 Cal.App.4th 652 (2007), 285
**Zielesch, People v., 179 Cal.App.4th 731 (2009), 279-89, 291**
Zielesch v. Lewis, 2012 WL 4050092 (ED. Ca.), 294-95

# TABLE OF STATUTES

**ALABAMA**
Code §13A-4-1, 254
**ARKANSAS**
Act 1975, No. 928, §3 (Ark. Crim. Code §41-101, et seq. (1976), 43
Ark. Stat. Ann. §41-121 (Repealed 1964), 37, 39
Ark Stat. Ann. §41-2209 (Repealed 1964), 36, 38
Ark. Rules of Appellate Procedure (Criminal) 10 (2001), 43
**CALIFORNIA**
CIVIL CODE
  §2080, 425
HEALTH & SAFETY CODE
  §3110, 44
  §3125, 44
  §3354, 44
  §11912, 96
PENAL CODE
  §21a, 264
  §22, *passim*
  §22(b), 81, 83-85, 92
  §25, 144
  §25(a), 143, 158
  §25(b), 158, 193-94
  §26, 27, 193
  §28, 82, 144, 193-94, 197
  §28(a), 158, 193-97
  §28(b), 143
  §29.4, 100
  §29.4(b), 102

§31, 337
§182, 292-93
§182(a)(1), 270
§186.22(a), 136
§187, 54-56, 93
§187(a), 54, 189
§188, 54, 85, 93, 189
§189, 54, 71, 106, 227, 349-55, 359, 364, 367, 370
§190(a), 71
§191.5, 71, 88
§192, *passim*
§192(c)(2), 52
§192(3)(a), 54, 56-57
§193, 56
§193(b), 71
§197, 189
§203, 356, 365
§206, 349
§207, 376
§207(a), 375
§209(b)(1), 376
§209(b)(2), 376
§211, 406
§213, 406
§240, 102, 333
§242, 104
§245, 327, 330, 333
§246, 353
§261(a)(2), 105, 374
§286, 349, 364

# Table of Statutes

**CALIFORNIA, cont.**
   §288, 349, 364
   §288a, 349, 364
   §289, 349, 364
   §451, 96, 105
   §459, 326, 354, 371
   §459.5, 437
   §484, 416-17, 419
   §484(a), 418, 430
   §487(a), 407
   §489, 407, 417
   §490, 407, 417
   §490.1, 417
   §518, 406
   §520, 406
   §653f, 261, 270-71
   §654, 334
   §654(a), 70, 333, 373, 434
   §664, 226, 270
   §664(a), 255, 270
   §666(a), 432
   §669, 218
   §737, 66
   §738, 66
   §740, 66
   §859b, 66
   §871, 66
   §872, 66
   §995, 53, 59
   §1020, 194-95
   §1026, 194
   §1026(a), 194
   §1170, 289
   §1170.1, 348
   §1473, 132
   California Penal Code of 1872, xxv, xviii, 110
   Crimes and Punishments Act of 1850, 102, 110, 139

VEHICLE CODE
   §500, 56
   §§20001-20004, 44

**COLORADO**
   Revised Stat. Ann. §18-1.3-102, 42

**FLORIDA**
   Stat. Ann. §794.027, 29 n.b

**HAWAII**
   Revised Stat. §663-1.6, 29 n.b

**ILLINOIS**
   Stat. Ann. §5/5-6-1, 42
   Stat. Ann. §5/8-4, 226
   Crim. Code of 1961 §24-1.1, 216, 218

**INTERNAL REVENUE CODE**
   §7203, 44

**KANSAS**
   Stat. Ann. §22-2902, 273

**KENTUCKY**
   Revised Stat. §507.020, 112
   Revised Stat. §507.020(1)(a), 112, 118
   Revised Stat. §507.030, 112
   Revised Stat. §507.030 (1)(b), 112
   Rules of Civil Procedure 76.32, 121
   Criminal Procedure Rule 11.42, 128-29, 131
   Rules of Evidence 401, 114, 117
   Rules of Evidence 402, 114
   Rules of Evidence 403, 115-16
   Rules of Evidence 404(b), 116-17
   Rules of Evidence 404(b)(1), 117

**MAINE**
   Revised Stat. Ann. § 2651, 156

**MASSACHUSETTS**
   Gen. Laws Ann. ch. 268, §40, 29 n.b

**MODEL PENAL CODE**
   §1.07(1)(b), 334
   §2.01, 27

**MODEL PENAL CODE, cont.**
§2.01(3), 43
§2.02, 71, 75
§2.03(2)(b), 386
§2.06(2)(a), 297
§2.06(3), 290, 334
§2.08, 203
§2.09(1), 250
§2.10.2, 71
§2.10.2(1), 71
§2.10.6, 106
§3.04, 172-73
§3.04(2)(b), 172, 179
§3.09(2), 203
§5.01, 236, 252
§5.01(2)(a)-(f), 276
§5.01(2)(g), 276, 297
§5.01(3), 298, 347, 407
§5.05, 222, 298
§5.05(1), 210, 227
§5.05(2), 252
§5.05(3), 334
§210.2(1)(b), 356, 364
§210.3, 143 n.4, 155
§210.3(1), 142 n.4
§210.3(1)(a), 71
§210.3(1)(b), 147
§210.4, 48, 51
§210.4(1), 71
§211.2, 207
§223.0-.9, 427
§223.7, 416
Introduction to Article 5, 210

**MINNESOTA**
Stat. Ann. §604A.01, 29 n.a

**MISSOURI**
Stat. Ann. §252.040, 232

**NEVADA**
Rev. Stat. Ann. §200.030(1)(b), 235

**NEW YORK**
CIVIL PRACTICE ACT
§352, 8-11
§353, 10
PENAL LAW
§20.00, 244
§35.15, 169-70, 172-75
§35.15(1), 168
§35.15(2), 169, 179
§40.00, 251
§60.35, 19
§110.10, 239, 245, 249, 252
§125.25, 156
§155.05, 436
§1052, 13
§1053-a, 7-8, 12-14, 16-17, 38

**OHIO**
Rev. Code Ann. §2901.21(D)(2), 27
Rev. Code Ann. §2913.01(C)(1), 428
Rev. Code Ann. §2913.02(A), 427-28
Rev. Code Ann. §2921.22, 29 n.b

**PENNSYLVANIA**
Criminal Code of 1794, xxv, 71
18 PA Stat. and Consolidated Stats §2502 (1978), 71

**RHODE ISLAND**
General Laws of R.I., 1956, §11-56-1 (1984), 29 n.b

**SOUTH DAKOTA**
Codified Laws §22-11-12, 29 n.b

**TENNESSEE**
Code Ann. §39–11–106(a)(28), 416
Code Ann. §39-15-101, 44

**TEXAS**
Penal Code §49.04, 207

**UNITED STATES CODE**
Act of Jan. 20, 1897, 29 Stat. 492, 123
Act of Feb. 6, 1889, 25 Stat. 656, 122

## Table of Statutes

**UNITED STATES CODE, cont.**

Act of Mar. 3, 1891, 26 Stat. 826, 122-23

  Antiterrorism and Effective Death Penalty Act of 1996, 110 Stat. 1214, 126

Crimes Act of 1790, xxv

Judicial Code Act of Mar. 3, 1911, 36 Stat. 1087, 123

15 U.S.C. §1, 279

18 U.S.C. §2, 306

18 U.S.C. §3, 294

18 U.S.C. §4, 30

18 U.S.C. §17, 149

18 U.S.C. §704, 19

18 U.S.C. §875(c), 121

18 U.S.C. §1111(a), 364

18 U.S.C. §3584(a), 218

28 U.S.C. §631, 274

28 U.S.C. §1253, 124

28 U.S.C. §1254, 124

28 U.S.C. §1257, 124

28 U.S.C. §1291, 67

28 U.S.C. §1331, 124

28 U.S.C. §1332(a)(1), 124

28 U.S.C. §1441(c)(A), 126

28 U.S.C. §2254, 125

28 U.S.C. §2254(d)(1), 126

28 U.S.C. §2284(a), 124

42 U.S.C. §1983, 125 n.c

50 U.S.C. app. §462, 44

**VERMONT**

  Vermont Stat. Ann. tit. 12, §519, 29 n.a

**WASHINGTON**

  Rev. Code Ann. §9.69.100, 29 n.b

**WISCONSIN**

  Stat. Ann. §940.34, 29 n.a

  Stat. Ann. §943.20, 410

  Stat. Ann. §943.20(1)(c), 436

# TABLE OF SECONDARY AUTHORITIES

**RULES**

California Rules of Court, rule 4.420, 289

California Rules of Court, rule 8.1115(a), 293

Federal Rules of Appellate Procedure, rule 35, 122

Federal Rules of Appellate Procedure, rule 40, 122

Federal Rules of Evidence, rule 801(d)(1)(A), 19

Federal Rules of Evidence, rule 801(d)(2)(E), 333

**CONSTITUTIONS**

Arkansas Constitution, Amendment 58 (1978), 43

California Constitution, Art. VI, §4, 110 n.a

California Constitution, Art. VI, §13, 361

California Constitution Art. 1, §14.1, 67

Kentucky Constitution §110(2)(b), 111, 124

Kentucky Constitution §115, 123

U.S. Constitution amends. I, IV, V, VI, VIII, XIV, 19, 20, 30, 68, 97, 121, 124, 128, 156, 196, 218, 311, 350, 395

**TREATISES**

40 *C.J.S.*, Homicide §53, 141

Dressler, Joshua, Understanding Criminal Law § 27.07 (7th ed. 2015), 236

Dressler, Joshua, Understanding Criminal Law § 30.03[C] (2d ed. 1995), 339-41

Duff, R.A, Criminal Attempts (Oxford 1997), 208

Feder, Robert D., *Valuation Strategies in Divorce* §8.42 (5th ed. Supp. 2017), 411

Fletcher, George, Rethinking Criminal Law (1978), 86 n.5, 207, 231, 302

Hall, Jerome, General Principles of Criminal Law 592 (2d ed. 1960), 205

Hart, H.L.A. & Antony Honoré, Causation in the Law (1959), 297

Hart & Honoré, Causation in the Law 326 (2d ed. 1985), 387-88

**TREATISES, cont.**

Keeton, W., Page et al., Prosser and Keeton on the Law of Torts (5th ed. 1984 & Supp. 1988), 44

LaFave, Wayne R., Criminal Law §20.4(a) (West, 5th ed. 2010), 406

LaFave, Wayne R. & Austin W. Scott, Jr., Criminal Law (1972), 37, 44

Perkins on Criminal Law (2d ed. 1969), 37

Perkins & Boyce, Criminal Law (3d ed. 1982), 419, 423, 426

Smith, K.J.M., A Modern Treatise on Complicity (Oxford 1991), 296-97

Stephen, James Fitzjames, Digest of Criminal Law 53 (7th ed. 1926), 233

1 Wharton's Criminal Evidence 2:13 (West 15th ed. 2014), 149

1 Wharton's Criminal Law 225, n.8 (James M. Kerr ed., 11th ed. 1912), 228

Witkin, California Crimes §§78-79, at 79-80 (1963), 360

Witkin, California Criminal Procedure §23J (1983. Supp.), 143

Witkin & Epstein, California Criminal Law § 36, at 242 (3d ed. 2000), 383

**RESTATEMENTS**

Restatement (Second) of Torts (2d ed. 1965), 44

**BOOKS & SCHOLARLY ARTICLES**

Alexander, Larry, *Inculpatory and Exculpatory Mistakes and the Fact/Law Distinction: An Essay in Memory of Myke Bayles,* 12 Law & Philosophy 33 (1993), 236

Austin, J.L., *A Plea for Excuses, in* Philosophical Papers (J.O. Urmson & G.J. Warnock eds.) (3d ed. Oxford 1979), 107-08, 202, 209, 233, 237

Austin, J.L., *Other Minds, in* Philosophical Papers (J.O. Urmson & G.J. Warnock eds.) (3d ed. Oxford 1979), 136

Austin, J.L., *Three Ways of Spilling Ink*, in Philosophical Papers 272 (J.O. Urmson & G.J. Warnock eds.) (3d ed. Oxford 1979), 49, 107-08

Austin, J.L., How to Do Things with Words 104 (J.O. Urmson & M. Sbisa eds.) (Oxford 1975), 135

Austin, J.L., Sense and Sensibilia (G. Warnock ed.) (Oxford 1962), 204

Baker, Thomas E., A Primer on Supreme Court Procedures 480 (ABA 2004), 124

Balkin, J.M., *The Rhetoric of Responsibility,* 76 Virginia Law Review 197 (1990), 181

Bibas, Stephanos, *Regulating the Plea-Bargaining Market: From Caveat Emptor to Consumer Protection*, 99 California Law Review 1117 (2011), xxii

## BOOKS & SCHOLARLY ARTICLES, cont.

Chemerinsky, Erwin, *The Roberts Court at Age Three*, 54 Wayne Law Review 947 (2008), 125

Candeub, Adam, *Consciousness and Culpability*, 54 Alabama Law Review 113 (2002), 25

Cole, Kevin, *The Voodoo We Do: Harm, Impossibility, and the Reductionist Impulse*, Journal of Contemporary Legal Issues 31 (1994), 236

Dershowitz, Alan, Reversal of Fortune: Inside the von Bülow Case 204 (Random House, 1986), 19

Dershowitz, Alan, The Best Defense 95 (Vintage Books, 1982), 19

Dripps, Donald A., *Beyond Rape: An Essay on the Difference between the Presence of Force and the Absence of Consent*, 92 Columbia Law Review 1780 (1992), 416

Eichelberger, Eunice A., *Annotation, Automatism or Unconsciousness as a Defense to a Criminal Charge*, 27 A.L.R. 4th 1067 (1984), 25

Feinberg, Joel, *Equal Punishments for Failed Attempts: Some Bad but Instructive Arguments against It*, 37 Arizona Law Review 117 (1995), 208, 210

Fletcher, George, *Constructing a Theory of Impossible Attempts*, 5 Crim. Just. Ethics 52, 66 (1986), 207

Fletcher, George, *The Metamorphosis of Larceny*, 89 Harvard Law Review 469 (1976), 237

Gobert, James J., *Victim Precipitation*, 77 Columbia Law Review 511 (1977), 159

Gruber, Aya, *A Provocative Defense*, 103 California Law Review 273 (2014), 110

Gruber, Aya, *Victim Wrongs: The Case for a General Criminal Defense Based on Wrongful Victim Behavior in an Era of Victims' Rights*, 76 Temple Law Review 645 (2003), 159

Gudel, Paul. J., *Beyond Causation: The Interpretation of Action and the Mixed Motives Problem in Employment Discrimination Law*, 70 Texas Law Review 17 (1991), 151

Hall, Jerome, *Criminal Attempt- A Study of Foundations for Criminal Liability*, 49 Yale Journal 789 (1940), 236

Hart, H.L.A., Punishment and Responsibility (Oxford 1968), 17

Hartung, Fritz, *Der Badewannenunfall*, 430-31 Juristenzeitung (1954), 303

Hasnas, John, *Once More unto the Breach: The Inherent Liberalism of the Criminal Law and Liability for Attempting the Impossible*, 54 Hastings La Journal 1 (2002), 228, 237

Heath, Peter, *Trying and Attempting*, Proceedings of the Aristotelian Society, Supplementary Volume XLV (1971), 303

Hughes, Graham, *One Further Footnote on Attempting the Impossible*, 42 New York University Law Review 1005 (1967), 229

**BOOKS & SCHOLARLY ARTICLES, cont.**

Johnson, Phillip, *The Unnecessary Crime of Conspiracy*, 61 California Law Review 1137 (1973), 276

Katz, Leo, Bad Acts and Guilty Minds (Chicago 1987), 302-03

Kaufman, Whitley R.P., *Self-Defense, Imminence, and the Battered Woman*, 10 New Criminal Law Review 342 (2007), 181

Kinports, Kit, *So Much Activity, So Little Change: A Reply to Critics of Battered Women's Self-Defense*, 23 St. Louis University Public Law Review 155 (2004), 181

Leavens, Arthur, *A Causation Approach to Criminal Omissions*, 76 California Law Review 547 (1988), 44

Levy, Ken, *It's Not Too Difficult: A Plea to Resurrect the Impossibility Defense*, 45 New Mexico Law Review 225 (2014), 236

Levy, Ken, *Killing, Letting Die, and the Case for Mildly Punishing Bad Samaritanism*, 44 Georgia Law Review 607 (2010), 33-34

Morris, Norval, *Somnambulistic Homicide, Ghosts, Spiders, and North Koreans*, 5 Res Judicate 29 (1951), 24

Nagel, Thomas, *Moral Luck, in* Mortal Questions 37 (Cambridge 1979), 303

Pitcher, George, *Austin: A Personal Memoir, in* Essays on J.L. Austin 20 (Oxford 1973), 233

Posner, Richard A., *An Economic Theory of Criminal Law*, 85 Columbia Law Review 1193 (1985), 230

Robinson, Paul H., *Criminal Liability for Omissions: A Brief Summary and Critique of the Law in the United States*, 29 New York Law School Law Review 101 (1984), 44

Robinson, Paul H. & Jane A. Grall, *Element Analysis in Defining Criminal Liability: The Model Penal Code and Beyond*, 35 Stanford Law Review 681 (1983), 203

Ross, Sir William David, *Foundations of Ethics*, The Gifford Lectures delivered in the Univ. of Aberdeen 1935-6, at 108 (Oxford 1960), 303

Roth, William, *General v. Specific Intent: A Time for Terminological Understanding in California*, 7 Pepperdine Law Review 67 (1979), 74

Rudenstine, David, *Self-Government and the Judicial Function Cosmic Constitutional Theory* (Book Review), 92 Texas Law Review 161 (2013), 101

Shavell, Steven, *Deterrence and the Punishment of Attempts*, 19 Journal of Legal Studies 451 (1990), 230

Simons, Kenneth W., *Ignorance and Mistake of Criminal Law, Noncriminal Law, and Fact*, 9 Ohio State Journal of Criminal Law 487 (2012), 229 n.a

Simons, Kenneth W., *Mistake of Fact or Mistake of Criminal Law? Explaining and Defending the Distinction*, 3 Criminal Law & Philosophy 213 (2009), 229 n.a

## BOOKS & SCHOLARLY ARTICLES, cont.

Simons, Kenneth W., *Mistake and Impossibility, Law and Fact, and Culpability: A Speculative Essay*, 81 Journal of Criminal Law & Criminology 447 (1990), 229 & n.a

Sneirson, Judd F., *Black Rage and the Criminal Law: A Principled Approach to a Polarized Debate*, 143 University of Pennsylvania Law Review 2251 (1995), 147

Stuntz, William J., *Privacy's Problem in the Law of Criminal Procedure*, 93 Michigan Law Review 1016 (1995), 275

Sverdlik, Steven, *Crime and Moral Luck*, 25 American Philosophical Quarterly 79 (1988), 208

Tennenhouse, Dan J., 3 Attorneys Medical Deskbook 4th §36:6 (Oct. 2016), 237-38

Thomson, Judith Jarvis, *Morality and Bad Luck*, 20 Metaphilosophy 203 (1989), 208

West, Robin, *Legitimizing the Illegitimate: A Comment on "Beyond Rape,"* 93 Columbia Law Review 1442 (1993), 416

Westen, Peter, *Impossibility Attempts: A Speculative Thesis*, 5 Ohio State Journal of Criminal Law 523 (2008), 236

Winch, Peter, *Trying*, *in* Ethics in Action 140 (D.Z. Phillips ed.) (Routledge & Kegan Paul 1972), 304

Yalof, David A., Joseph Mello & Patrick Schmidt, *Collegiality Among U.S. Supreme Court Justices?*, 95 Judicature 12 (2011), 99

Yeager, Daniel B., *Fiduciary-isms, A Study of Academic Influence on the Expansion of the Law*, 65 Drake Law Review 179 (2017), 410

Yeager, Daniel B., *What Is an Accident?*, 51 Criminal Law Bulletin 575 (2015), 24, 202

Yeager, Daniel B., *Cop Killers*, 48 Criminal Law Bulletin 428 (2012), 183

Yeager, Daniel B., J.L. Austin and the Law: Exculpation and the Explication of Responsibility (Bucknell University Press 2006), 106, 152

Yeager, Daniel B., *Does Privacy Really Have a Problem in the Law of Criminal Procedure?*, 49 Rutgers Law 1283 (1997), 162

Yeager, Daniel, Review Essay, "Searches, Seizures, Confessions, and Some Thoughts on *Criminal Procedure: Regulation of Police Investigation*," 23 Florida State University Law Review 1042 (1996), 150

Yeager, Daniel B., *A Radical Community of Aid: A Rejoinder to Opponents of Affirmative Duties to Help Strangers*, 71 Washington University Law Quarterly 1 (1993), 30

# INDEX

access to courts, 122-24
accessorial liability, 30, 241-45, 250, 295-398
accessories after the fact, 29-30, 37, 250, 294
accessories before the fact, 241-45, 250, 252, 295-397
accident, *passim*
accomplice liability, 241-45, 250, 295-398
accomplices, 241-45, 250, 295-398
action, 1-2, 14-27
acute interstitial myocarditis, 234
affidavit, 66, 132, 243, 247, 250
affirmative defense, 149, 156-57, 199, 250
agent, 409
*agent provocateur*, 255-77, 298, 334-35, 407, 432
aging offenders, 132-34
aiding and abetting, 241-45, 250, 295-398
AIDS/HIV, 223
alibi, 25, 330-31
Allen, Barry, 164, 183
anger, 109-59
*animus furandi*, 407-12, 419, 422, 433, 436
Anthony, Casey, 20
anticipatory offenses, 207-348
appeals as of right, xxiii-xxiv, 22-24, 43, 122-25, 128
arrest of judgment, 23
arrest warrant, 274
arson, 75, 96, 105-06, 219, 270, 349-56, 364-67, 405
Asian Boyz, 353
asportation, 375-77, 408, 416, 419-420
assault, *passim*
assault as attempted battery, 102-04

assault as unconsummated battery, 104-05
assault with a deadly weapon, 27, 69, 94, 100, 270, 322, 324, 327, 330, 333, 352, 354, 356, 437-38
ATM robbery, 222
attempt (elements), 226, 268, 347
attempt (sentence), 226-27, 251, 270-71, 333-34
attempted arson, 219
attempted assault, 102, 220
attempted attempt, 220
attempted battery, 102, 220
attempted burglary, 61, 221-22
attempt continuum, 103, 221, 262, 268
attempted involuntary manslaughter, 220
attempted kidnapping, 219
attempted larceny, 246, 347, 351, 407
attempted murder, 95, 163-86, 211-28, 232-33, 239-51, 310-11, 336-48, 395
attempted rape, 100, 146, 219, 234-35, 246, 374
attempted robbery, 179, 222, 265 n.2, 370
attempted voluntary manslaughter, 184-86, 336-37, 348, 381 n.6, 395
attorney-client privilege, 10-11
Austin, J.L., 49, 107-08, 135-36, 201-02, 204, 209, 233-34, 237
automatism, 17, 24-25
Azcanazy, Iris, 21-22
Azcanazy, Jacob, 21-22

Bad Samaritan Laws, 28-32, 45
bail (enlargement on), 68, 274, 280-84, 288, 294
bailee, 410, 412, 436
bailment, 410, 412, 436

## Index

bailor, 410, 436
bank robbery, 132-34, 294, 313
bankruptcy, 21, 30, 183
bar exam, xii, 276, 405
basic actions, 101
battered woman syndrome, 181, 206
battery, 100, 102-05, 154, 159, 220, 397, 405
Baumgardener, Amy, 112, 117-19
Beeman, Marjorie, 309-10
Belli, Melvin, 19
bench trial, 211, 218
bifurcated trials, 194-99
Black, Laura, 353
black magic/voodoo, 236
black rage, 147
blood-alcohol content (level), 53, 58, 62, 77-79, 87, 89-90, 98
Body Count, 134-35
Boesky, Ivan, 406
Bowie, David, 135
bribe (bribery), 245, 270, 347, 414
Briseno, Theodore, 134, 181-82
Broderick, Betty, 153
Brosgart, Kate, 108
Brown, Nicole, 21
Brown, Raynika, 431-32
Bruce, Lenny, 136
burden(s) of proof, 8, 22, 59, 112-14, 119, 126, 156-57, 180, 194-96, 251, 310-11, 400-02
burglary, 31, 74, 106, 161, 203, 207, 270, 296-97, 320-21, 326, 328, 332, 349, 354-56, 364, 367-68, 370-72, 378, 405, 434
Bush, Jeb, 107 n.b
Bush, Joe, 239-52
Bush, President (the elder), 135
but-for cause, 378, 396-97, 403
bystander(s), 27-29, 32-33, 324, 344, 378-79, 384

Cabey, Darryl, 164-68, 183
cannabis, 27, 111, 118, 207, 217, 224, 265 n.2, 281, 309, 416
Canty, Troy, 164-68, 177, 183
capital cases, 25, 107 n.b, 122-24, 237, 350
carjacking, 257, 270, 349, 364

Carter, Jimmy, 276-77
case captions, 18, 24, 127, 267, 330, 343
Cash Jr., David, 33-34
Cavitt, James Freddie, 370-71, 378, 405
certified copy of judgment, 217-18, 224-26
character evidence, 116-17
charging instruments, 22, 66-67, 180
chastisement, 110
Cheek, John, 200-02
child abuse, 27, 352
child support, 45
Church's Fried Chicken, 394, 406
circumstantial evidence, 65, 219-20, 278-79
civil cases, xxiii-iv, 21-22, 104
civil-rights offenses, 75
Clarissa, 237-38
Clinton, Bill, 276-77
Clymer, Steven, 181-82
coercion (coerced), 2, 15, 131, 163, 237, 250-51, 253, 278, 297, 376, 406-07, 425
Cogdon, Patti, 24
collateral attacks on judgments, 18, 125, 128, 131-32, 294, 348
common scheme or design, 277-334
complicity without conspiracy, 330
compensation, 21-22, 51, 104, 125 n.c, 305-06, 399
complaint, 22, 66, 166, 180, 267, 417
complex actions, 101
complicity, 207, 209, 242-45, 247, 250, 295-348, 373-74
complicity (elements), 308-09, 319-20, 322, 327, 330-32, 338-39
complicity (sentence), 333-34
compulsory process, 67
conclusive presumptions, 62, 310-12
concurrent causes, 356-404
concurrent sentences, 72, 131, 211, 218, 227-28, 439
conditional intent, 424-26, 432
confess and avoid, 149, 156-57, 199, 250

confessions, xxii, 20, 120, 126-31, 181, 199, 221-22, 225, 237, 252-53, 357, 362, 367, 371
confrontation clause, 67
conscious parallelism, 277-79
consecutive sentences, 218, 280, 289-90, 348
consolidation of theft offenses, 416-17, 419
conspiracy, 74-75, 207, 209-10, 222, 227, 235, 252, 261, 265 n.1, 270, 277-95, 308, 321, 323 n.5, 330-31, 333-34, 366-68
conspiracy as attempt, 253-54, 276-77
conspiracy (elements), 278, 292
conspiracy (sentence), 261, 270, 292-93, 333-34
constructive possession, 217, 223-24, 404, 407
constructive principals, 301
contract killing, xxii, 256-58, 264
cooling time, 157-58
Congress, xxv, 19, 33, 67, 122-26, 200, 279, 301
Cornejo, Carlos, 40-41
counterfeiting, xxv, 298, 301-03
courage, 171, 179, 182
cowardice, 181-82
cowboy era, 147
crime scene photographs, 111, 114-16, 118
criminal possession of a weapon, 166, 180, 182, 216-17, 223-24
criminal procedure, 22-23, 43, 66-70, 122-27, 156-57, 173-74, 178, 273-75, 310-12
cross-appeal, 22-23
cruel and unusual punishment, 395

dangerousness, 87, 90, 108, 161, 235-36, 246, 252, 299-300, 350-52
damages, xxiii-xxiv, 21-22, 28, 89, 104, 137, 399-403
deadly force, 109, 152, 159-85, 346, 379, 384 n.11, 393
debtor-creditor, 49-51, 220, 415
defense appeals, 22-23, 275, 363

defenses personal to the principal, 298, 301, 334-48
defenses transferable to the accomplice, 296-299, 334-48
delusion, 171-173, 186-198, 202-05, 228-38, 253
delusional self-defense, 186
demurrer, 7-8, 11, 14, 22-23, 65, 399
*de novo* review, 65, 126, 271-73
departures from the common scheme, 290-92, 313-34
derivative liability, 295-304, 319, 334-35, 346-47
Dershowitz, Alan, 19
Desdemona, 135, 341
determinate sentencing, 280, 289-90
Dickinson, Frank, 148
dicta/dictum, 61, 155-56, 235
diminished actuality, 93, 158, 193-99
diminished capacity, *passim*
directed verdict, 46, 114, 211
discretionary appeals, 122-25
DNA evidence, 347, 372
domestic violence, 129
double-counting crimes, 267-68, 439
doubly inchoate offenses, 102, 220, 254, 277
Double Jeopardy, xvii, xxiv 46, 68-72, 147-48, 178, 243-45, 250, 273-74, 346-47, 438-39
drag racing, 299-300
Duff, R.A., 208-09
Duncan, Brandon ("Tiny Doo"), 136-37
Dunlap, Terry, 35-36
due process, xxiv, 14, 97, 122-25, 156, 196, 311, 351, 377, 395
duress, 2, 15, 75, 157, 247-51, 374
duty to aid/rescue, 27-45

Eighth Amendment, 350, 395-96
Elonis, Anthony, 120-21, 131, 134, 311
Electromagnetic Systems Lab, 353
embezzlement, 75, 407-11, 415-16, 419, 435-36
entrapment, 157
epilepsy, 6, 9, 13, 16-17
equal protection, xxiv, 45, 123

equivalency, 207-11, 295, 303
Ernie C., 134-35
escape from prison, 356, 364
espionage, 364
exculpatory mistakes, 198-206, 365, 374-75
excuses, 207-11, 276-77, 298, 330-31, 344
exhaustion of remedies, 125-28
ex post facto, 350-51
expungement, 42
extortion, 75, 268, 270, 376, 406, 425
extreme emotional disturbance (EED), 106, 109-20, 127-30, 142-43, 145-46, 154-55

factual insufficiency, 39-40, 72, 114, 119, 125, 148, 359, 363
fact v. law, 7, 65, 248, 252-53, 268, 271-73
fake guns, 162-63
Falatar, Scott, 24-25
false pretenses, 407, 413-17, 419, 421, 433-35
false token, 415-16
fantasy, 199-206, 228-38, 253
FBI, 121, 134
fear, 32, 155, 159-206, 406
Federal Constitution, xxiv, 13, 19, 30, 45-46, 67-68, 101, 122-28, 131, 201, 218, 224-25, 250-52, 289, 295, 311-12, 395, 438-39
Federal Criminal Code, xxiii, xxv
Federal Sentencing Guidelines, 289-90
feigned principal, 253-77, 297-98, 334-35
Feinberg, Joel, 208-10
felon in possession, 217, 223-25, 348
felony, *passim*
felony murder, 75, 188, 235, 328, 349-404
Ferguson, Colin, 147
fiduciary, 409-12, 435-36
Fifth Amendment (*Miranda* warning), 20, 29-30, 165, 220-21, 224-26, 252-53, 295
filing fees, 123
final judgment, 67, 122-25, 275

first aggressor, 161, 184-85, 388
First Amendment, 19, 120-21, 134-37
first-degree murder, *passim*
Fletcher, George, 86 n.5, 100, 105, 207, 231, 237, 302
forcible theft, 405-07
forfeiture of claims, 131-32
forgery, 270, 434
Fourth Amendment, 68, 124-25
fraud, 75, 268, 407-16, 419 n.3, 434-35
Frey, John, 25-26
Fuhrman, Mark, 437

Galanter, Yale, 438-39
general intent, 73-108, 146, 184, 199, 219, 365
Gilbert, Mike, 437
Glass, J. Jackie, 438-40
Goldman, Fred, 21, 439
Goldman, Ronald, 21
Good Samaritan laws, 28
Grace, Nancy, 440
grafting, 298-99, 347
grand jury, 11, 22, 66-67, 127, 163-69, 176-78, 180, 242, 274
Grasso, Gabriel, 438
Griffin, Eddie Dean, 19-20
Griggs, Ivan, 127-32, 183
Griggs, Nicole, 127-30
group criminality, 253-404

habeas corpus, 18, 125-32, 294-95, 371, 377, 395
hallucination, 188, 199, 203, 238
Hammeroff, Murray, 126
Hand, J. Learned, 298-99, 304, 306
Hannibal Lecter, 313
happenings, 1-2, 14-17, 24
harmless error, 99, 131, 311-12, 330, 360-61, 365, 374-75, 377-78
Heanes, Herbert, 25-26
heat of passion, 109-59, 185, 189, 191, 341, 344
hegemony, 301-02
helper (indifferent helper), 295-304, 308-11, 330, 334-35
helping v. doing, 295-304
Hermis, 160-61

Hill, Paul, 107
Hillery, Booker, 127
Hinckley, Jr., John, 149-50
Hodson, Essie Mae, 19-20
Homeland Security, Dept. of, xxv
homophobia, 154
homosexual advance, 154
*Huffington Post*, 439
Hughes, Graham, 228-29
humble mathematician, 221-22

Iago, 135, 341
Ice-T, 134-36
ignorance of law, 199-201
illusion, 204
imminence (in self-defense), 180-81, 346
immunity from prosecution/suit, 68, 295, 301, 438
impeachment of witnesses, 19-20, 217, 224-26, 318
imperfect self-defense, 109, 179, 183-206, 346, 348
impossible attempts, 228-53
impossibility, 228-53
in-camera hearing, 166
inchoate criminality, 103, 207-348
incidental(s), 49-52, 75, 105, 313, 376-77
inculpatory mistakes, 228-53
indeterminate sentencing, 280, 289-90, 302
indictment, 22, 66-67, 166-68, 177-78, 180, 274, 417
ineffective assistance of counsel, 128-32, 294-95, 439
information(s), 66, 72, 77, 211, 417
inherently dangerous felonies, 106, 350-52
innocent agency, 297-98, 302-03, 340-42, 345, 385, 389 n.15, 392-93
insanity, 25, 110, 147-50, 157-59, 186-98, 203-04, 276
intangible property, 416
intentional, *passim*
interlocutory appeals, 64, 67-70
intoxication, 8, 16, 25-26, 52, 58, 71-105, 142-43, 146, 158, 184, 203, 254, 278, 344, 365

involuntary action, 1-3, 14-27, 252-53
involuntary intoxication, 26
involuntary manslaughter, *passim*
involuntary manslaughter (elements), 71
involuntary manslaughter (sentence), 71
involuntary movement, 1-3, 14-27
irresistible impulse, 139-40, 143
Internal Revenue Code, 200-01
issue preclusion, 346-47
Iverson, Sherrice, 33

Jackson, Dwight, 132-34, 405
Jamestown/Jimson Weed, 237-38
joint principality, 299-301, 307-08, 339-40, 345
judicially created crimes, 140-41, 143, 350-52, 392
judgment notwithstanding the verdict (JNOV), 46
judgment of acquittal, 123, 275, 382, 418
judgment of conviction, 11, 42, 123, 199, 224, 243, 249-50, 334, 417, 419, 430
jurisdiction, 121-32
jury instructions, xxv-vi, 226
jury nullification, 46
jury trial (right to), 218, 312, 395, 419, 431-32
justifications, 152-53, 159-83, 189, 330-31

kidnapping, 75, 106, 169, 172, 179, 219, 235, 270, 311, 349, 352, 355-56, 364-65, 372-78, 405, 437-40
kidnapping for rape, 100, 372-78
King, Rodney, 134, 181-82, 437
Kinnison, Sam, 136
Kinsey, Ronald, 78, 108
knowingly, 16, 23, 29, 37, 59, 71, 90, 216, 223, 308, 310, 323, 327, 342, 414
Koon, Stacey, 134

Lady Eldon, 228
Lamb, Clara, 211-19

larceny, 69, 74-75, 86, 100, 208, 229, 299, 307-08, 334-35, 351-52, 407-37
larceny by bailee, 436
larceny by trick, 411-37
larceny (elements), 407-408, 419
Laugh Factory, 135
law v. fact, 7, 65, 248, 252-53, 268, 271-73
legislative history, 43, 54, 56, 66, 92-94, 100-01, 139-40, 170-76, 179, 193
lesser-included offense, 69-70, 101, 110, 147-48, 189, 196-97, 249, 311, 341-42, 406
Letterman, David, 135
Lewter, Gene, 128-31
Lindbergh, Charles, 424-25
luck, 203, 208, 231, 277, 299-300
Luparello, Thomas, 291-94, 333

*Macbeth*, 151
Madoff, Bernard, 406-07
magistrate, 53, 57, 59-61, 65, 67, 255, 271-74
malice, *passim*
*malum in se*, 199
mandatory presumptions, 310-12
manifest criminality, 210
Manzano, Evelio, 184-85
marital privilege, 129
Marshall, C.J. John, 30, 99
Marshall, J. Thurgood, 33
*Mayberry* instruction, 200, 374-75
mayhem, 186, 349, 355, 364-67, 372, 405
McFarlane, Robert, 147-48
McKnight, Mianta, 370-71, 378, 405
Medea, 109
Meko, Joseph, 127
mens rea, 73-76, 95, 103, 105, 189, 196, 207-11, 218, 338-42, 347, 386, 389 n.15, 390
mental disease, 82, 113, 142-43, 149, 158, 194, 197
mercy killers, 106-07
mere preparation, 221, 226, 253, 259-62, 266-69
merger (felony murder), 352-56

Mervyn's, 418, 420, 427, 430-35
methamphetamine, 280-84, 287-88, 313
methedrine, 351
Michelman, Frank, 224
Microsoft, 414
Minor, Michele, 108
misdemeanor, 22, 66, 180, 326, 414, 419
misdirected heat of passion, 140-42, 146-47, 155-56
misprision of felony, 29-30
mistake of fact, 141, 155-56, 180-82, 186, 188, 191, 196-206, 228-38, 253, 274-75
mistake of law, 199-206, 228-38
mistrial, 46, 68, 128
Mitchell, Newton, 232-33
motive, 82, 107-08, 117, 143-44, 150-52, 190, 195, 278, 307
murder, *passim*
My Lai massacre, 160

natural and probable consequences, 103, 189, 219-20, 281, 285-87, 290-93, 295, 310-11, 314-15, 318, 320-29, 331-34, 338-39, 342, 360, 368, 381 & n.8, 383, 386, 390, 395
necessity, xii, 12, 46, 161-62, 169, 175, 184-85, 189-90, 197-98, 340, 399
negligence (civil, criminal, culpable, gross), *passim*
Newton, Huey, 25-26
Noia, Charles, 126-27
non-assaultive purposes, 352-56
nonaction, xi-xii, 1, 2, 14, 15, 17, 23, 27, 31
nondangerous, 161
nondeadly force, 161-62
nonforcible theft, 405-07
nonforcible theft (sentence), 407, 417
nonstatutory voluntary manslaughter, 140, 143, 158
nontarget offense, 314, 320
not intentional, 50-52, 64, 73, 75, 97, 146, 220, 350, 364, 371
*NPR*, 439

objective, 48, 51, 55, 64, 80 n.2, 88, 97, 118, 163, 167, 168, 170, 171, 173, 175, 179, 190, 191-93, 198, 204, 245, 261, 291, 255
occurrences, 1-2, 14-17, 24
omissions, xi-xiii, 13, 27-28, 34, 39, 41, 43-44
O'Searo, Roy, 219-20
*Othello*, 135, 235, 341, 344
other minds, 65, 136, 219, 251-52
overt act, 195, 259, 263, 265 n.1, 278
Owens, Chris, 439

parasitic speech, 120-21, 134-35
Parliament, 224, 301
parole, 25, 108, 127, 132, 134, 183, 227, 290, 332, 348, 369, 371, 376, 395, 440
Pasadena City College, 431
Parsons, Nelson, 237
partial defense, *passim*
partial excuse, 106, 152, 183-86, 203, 205-09, 230, 295, 303, 344
partial justification, 26, 152
partnerships, 409, 411, 414
perjury, xv, 167, 246, 270
permissive acquirer, 408-10
permissive presumptions, 311
perpetration by means, 297-98, 302-03, 340-42, 345, 385, 389 n.15, 392-93
petty offenses, 42, 183, 274, 407, 417-19, 431-33, 437
physician-patient privilege, xv, 8-10, 19
pick-pockets, 230, 407
piracy, xxv
plain error, 40, 44
plea bargaining, xxii-xxiii, 93, 131, 274
poison, 13, 16, 135, 229, 236-38
Ponzi, Charles, 406-07
Posner, Judge Richard, 132, 134, 230, 304, 308, 405
post-trial motion, xvii, 46, 68
Powell, Laurence, 134
pre-emptive strike, 180-81
pre-legal wrongs, 199

preliminary hearing, xvii, 53, 59, 61, 66-67, 148, 255-56, 258, 271, 273-74
premeditated and deliberate murder, xiii, 47, 54, 74-75, 81, 106-08, 189, 199, 256, 291, 293, 359, 363, 365, 367
pre-trial [...], xvii, 15, 65, 67-69, 201, 217, 224-26, 271, 275
price-fixing, 279
prior convictions, 86, 217-18, 224, 226, 419
privacy, 33, 65, 134-36, 198, 219, 238
probable cause, xv, xvii, 22, 53, 57-58, 60-61, 65-69, 89, 162, 178, 180, 261-62, 264, 271-75, 285
probation, 42, 133, 182, 280, 287, 292, 294, 318, 438
probative value of evidence, 63, 115-18
prosecution appeals, xxiv, 68-69
prosecutorial discretion, 45
prostitution, 207, 301, 306, 308
provocation, 25, 54, 75, 109-10, 130, 139-42, 143 n.4, 144-47, 149, 152-59, 184-85, 205, 339
provocative-act murder, 378-81, 381 n.6, 382 & n.9, 383 & n.10, 384 & n.11, 385, 388 & n.12, 389 & n.15, 390, 392-95
proximate cause, 360-61, 361 n. 4, 379, 383, 385-86, 388, 391, 396-98, 403
Pryor, Richard, 136
punishment, xi, xvii, xxiv, 13-14, 22, 34, 45, 51, 68, 70, 73, 88, 106, 122, 133-34, 149, 161, 189, 193, 199, 210, 218, 228, 230, 261, 269-70, 290, 292-93, 295-96, 299, 301-02, 326, 333-34, 350, 352, 395, 406, 417, 434
punitive damages, 21, 89, 399

Quayle, Vice President, 135

Ramseur, James, 164-67, 177, 183
rape, xi-xii, xxii, 29, 31-32, 75, 100, 102, 105-06, 146, 169, 179, 183, 200, 210, 219, 223, 230-31, 234-35,

246, 270, 311, 349, 352, 355-56, 364-65, 367, 372-78, 405
real party in interest, 255, 267, 330, 343
reasonable doubt, *passim*
reasonable suspicion, 275
reasonably foreseeable consequences, 285, 287, 290, 380-81, 381 n.8, 387, 393
reckless endangerment, 166-67, 207
reckless(ness), *passim*
rehearing(s), 121-22
removal jurisdiction, xvii, 126-28
renunciation of inchoate crimes, 254, 279
*respondeat superior*, 404
responsibility, *passim*
restitution, 108, 305-06, 404
retrial, 26, 46, 69, 126-27, 147-48, 153, 188, 244, 250, 337, 342, 348,
Richards, Michael (Kramer), 135-36
right to counsel, 67, 128, 252
risk v. harm, 18, 209-11, 220, 228, 295
Rivers, Mendel, 160
robbery, xii, xxv, 2, 15, 31, 69, 75, 106, 132-34, 152, 169, 179, 183, 222, 235, 257, 265 n.2, 270, 294, 299-300, 307, 309-11, 313, 322-23, 349, 351-52, 354, 356-61, 361 n.5, 362-71, 376-78, 384 & n.11, 393, 395, 405-07, 416, 426, 434-35, 437-40
robbery (elements), 69, 307, 352, 355, 361 n.5, 406
robbery (sentence), 406
Robin Hood, 151
Roger, David, 438
Ross, William David, 303
Rufo, Sharon, 21
Russian roulette, 299-300
ruthlessness, 181-82

sabotage, 364
Salyers, Mary, 127-30
scapegoating, 391, 404, 440
Schroeder, Mark, 180-81
search warrant, 68, 213, 224, 274

second-degree murder (elements), 55, 58-59, 61, 64, 75, 80-81, 84, 88, 93, 106, 140, 350, 355, 390
second-degree murder (sentence), 70-71
Seinfeld, 135
self-defense, *passim*
self-defense (elements), 168-69, 171, 189-91, 346
sentencing, xvii, 42-43, 70-71, 76, 110, 289-90, 292, 302, 369
separation of powers, 101
Sharp, Roy Ralph, 35-52, 200
shock-induced frenzy, 25
shoplifting, 42, 435-37
Simons, Kenneth, 229
Simpson, O.J., 21, 437-40
Singer, Richard, 238
Sing Sing Prison, 126
sisters case, 302-03
Sixth Amendment, 128, 218
sleepwalking, 17, 24
slight acts, 259, 261, 268
smoldering provocation, 158
sodomy, 169, 181, 270, 349, 364, 376
solicitation, 75, 207, 209, 211, 227, 252-56, 260-63, 266-67, 277-78, 292, 295, 309, 333-34
solicitation as attempt, 210-11, 253, 261-62, 266, 268-69, 276-78
solicitation (elements), 254, 261
solicitation (sentence), 254, 270-71
special relationships, 27-31, 44
specific intent, 56, 73-108, 158, 185, 193-95, 214-15, 218-19, 223, 226, 254, 258, 264-65, 265 n.1, 266, 268, 278, 308-11, 319, 321, 333, 339, 352-53, 360-62, 265-66, 371, 376, 407-12, 415
Spurlin, Peggy, 137-46, 150, 155, 159
Spurlin, Scott, 137-46, 150, 155
standard of review, 39, 65, 119, 126, 148, 268, 271-73
state constitutions, 43, 67, 101, 110 n.a, 123-24, 361
statutory voluntary manslaughter, 141, 158
Stern, Howard, 439

Stevens, Officer, 281, 283-88, 292, 294-95, 313,
strict liability, 73, 101, 199, 338
Strohmeyer, Jeremy, 33-34
structural error, 312
subjective, 51, 55-57, 64, 80, 88, 91-92, 97, 118, 167-68, 171-77, 179, 207, 381 n.8
subjective criminality, 73, 209
subpoena, 66
substantial steps, 211, 226, 253, 268
Suggs, Ella, 187-88
suspended judgment, 42
suspended sentence, xvii, 34, 41-42

target offense, 209, 254, 268, 270, 277, 285, 292, 308, 315, 318-19, 321-34, 354
tax evasion, 200-01
theft, xii, xxii-xxiii, 74-75, 203, 208, 210, 230, 270, 298, 326, 353-54, 370-71, 405-09, 411, 413-19, 421, 423, 425, 427, 429-36
Thirty-Ninth Congress, 125-26, 126 n.c
Thompson, Hugh, 160
Thomson, Judith, 207-08
three strikes law, 434
Tiny Rascals, 353
title (v. possession), 407, 413-15, 432, 435-36
torts, 21, 30, 48, 51, 104-05, 125 n.c, 296, 309, 403-04, 409, 439
torture, 349, 364
toy guns, 162-63
treason, xxv, 364
trial by jury, xvii, 218, 395
trial courts, *passim*
trial transcripts, xviii, xxiv, 123
Tucker, James, 147-48

unanimity requirement, 46, 328, 332, 417
unconsciousness, 2, 8, 16-17, 24-27, 81, 90-91, 98-99
undercover, 183, 245, 255, 260-61, 263-64, 335, 347, 405
unduly prejudicial evidence, 115, 125
unintentional, *passim*

unpublished opinions, 293, 348, 404
unreasonable mistakes, 191, 198, 200, 203-06, 236, 238
unreasonable self-defense, 109, 118-19, 145, 176, 185-86, 188-93, 196-206, 336-37, 342, 346

variance in pleading v. proof, 416-17, 433
Vegas Palace Station hotel, 437
vehicular homicide, 52, 54, 56-59, 71
vicarious liability, 296, 338-39
Villanueva, Roberto, 184-85
voluntary, 1-3, 12, 14-15, 56-57, 252-53, 375
voluntary assumption of care, 28, 40-41, 44
voluntary intoxication, *passim*
voluntary manslaughter, *passim*
voluntary manslaughter (elements), 109, 139, 141, 148
voodoo/black magic, 236

waiver 20, 225, 252, 371, 431-32
Walmart, 434
West, Robin, 416
Wilson, Rufus, 354
Wind, Timothy, 134
words alone, 153
writ of habeas corpus, 125-32, 294-95, 313, 371, 377, 395
writ of mandate, 255-56, 275